Concurrent Programming

INTERNATIONAL COMPUTER SCIENCE SERIES

Consulting Editors   A D McGettrick   University of Strathclyde
                        J van Leeuwen   University of Utrecht

OTHER TITLES IN THE SERIES

Programming in Ada (2nd Edn.) *J G P Barnes*

Software Engineering (2nd Edn.) *I Sommerville*

A Structured Approach to FORTRAN 77 Programming *T M R Ellis*

The UNIX System *S R Bourne*

Handbook of Algorithms and Data Structures *G H Gonnet*

Microcomputers in Engineering and Science *J F Craine and G R Martin*

UNIX for Super-Users *E Foxley*

Software Specification Techniques *N Gehani and A D McGettrick* (eds.)

Data Communications for Programmers *M Purser*

Local Area Network Design *A Hopper, S Temple and R C Williamson*

Prolog Programming for Artificial Intelligence *I Bratko*

Modula-2: Discipline & Design *A H J Sale*

Introduction to Expert Systems *P Jackson*

Prolog *F Giannesini, H Kanoui, R Pasero and M van Caneghem*

Programming Language Translation: A Practical Approach *P D Terry*

System Simulation: Programming Styles and Languages *W Kreutzer*

Data Abstraction in Programming Languages *J M Bishop*

The UNIX System V Environment *S R Bourne*

The Craft of Software Engineering *A Macro and J Buxton*

An Introduction to Programming with Modula-2 *P D Terry*

UNIX™ is a registered trademark of AT&T in the USA and other countries

AT&T

Concurrent Programming

Narain Gehani
AT&T Bell Laboratories

Andrew D. McGettrick
University of Strathclyde

ADDISON-WESLEY
PUBLISHING
COMPANY

Wokingham, England · Reading, Massachusetts · Menlo Park, California
New York · Don Mills, Ontario · Amsterdam · Bonn
Sydney · Singapore · Tokyo · Madrid · San Juan

Cover graphic by kind permission of Dicomed
Typeset by Times Graphics, Singapore
Printed in Great Britain by T. J. Press (Padstow), Cornwall

First printed 1988.

British Library Cataloguing in Publication Data
Gehani, Narain
   Concurrent programming.
   1. Parallel processing (Electronic
   computers) 2. Operating systems (Computers)
   I. Title   II. McGettrick, Andrew D.
   005.4'2   QA76.6

   ISBN 0-201-17435-9

Library of Congress Cataloguing in Publication Data
Concurrent programming.

   1. Parallel programming (Computer science)
I. Gehani, Narain, 1947–   II. McGettrick,
Andrew D., 1944–
QA76.6.C643   1988   005.4'2   87–26907
ISBN 0-201-17435-9

Preface

1   Introduction

Concurrent (parallel) programming[1] has become important in recent years because multiprocessors,[2] particularly networks of microcomputers, are rapidly becoming attractive alternatives to traditional maxi-computers.

The reasons for the importance of concurrent programming include:

- Notational convenience and conceptual elegance in writing systems in which many events occur concurrently, for example, in operating systems, real-time systems and database systems.
- Preserving the structure of concurrent algorithms.
- Speeding up program execution on genuine multiprocessing hardware such as a network of microcomputers.
- Speeding up program execution even on uniprocessors; concurrent programming allows lengthy input/output operations and the CPU operation to proceed in parallel.

One argument against concurrent programming is that it introduces yet another dimension of complexity to the already difficult task of

---

[1] Distributed programming is a special case of concurrent programming that refers to writing programs for multiprocessors.

[2] To be precise, a multicomputer is a computer architecture consisting of several processors, each with its own local memory but no shared memory, that communicate with each other by sending messages. A multiprocessor is a computer architecture consisting of several processors that share common memory but which do not have any local memory. Many parallel computers fall in between these two categories: they have both local memory and shared memory. Consequently, the term 'multiprocessor' will be used to refer to all computer architectures with multiple processors.

writing correct sequential programs. Instead of using multiprocessing hardware, it is argued that faster processors should be used to speed up sequential program execution. Unfortunately, hardware technology puts a limit on the processor speed and the faster computers – the so-called supercomputers – are quite expensive.

Let us take a look at the rate of improvement in hardware performance over the last 40 years or so. Roughly speaking, computer execution speed has gone up by a factor of two every year. This rate of improvement cannot continue indefinitely, at least on a cost effective basis for the end user. Multiprocessors, or a network of computers, offer an alternative and cost effective way of speeding up program execution. Even now, a multiprocessor is cheaper than a uniprocessor mainframe or a supercomputer with equivalent processing power. The 'catch' is that to use multiprocessors, concurrent programs have to be written.

One advantage of concurrent programming not covered in this book is 'fault tolerance'. Unlike sequential programs, appropriately written concurrent programs running on multiprocessors can be fault tolerant with respect to hardware failure. Failure of a single processor need not cause failure of the whole program; the system could continue to operate, in a possibly degraded mode, until the failed hardware is rectified.

2   About the book

How does one write concurrent programs? Numerous programming languages now provide concurrent programming facilities, for example, Concurrent Pascal, Modula-2, *MOD, Concurrent C, Concurrent Euclid, Mesa and the Ada language. Unlike sequential programming languages, no consensus has yet emerged on the 'right facilities' for concurrent programming.

There are many interesting questions about the design of concurrent programming languages that need to be answered; for example,

(1) Why are the facilities provided by the different languages different?

(2) What are the advantages and disadvantages of the concurrent programming models they are based on?

(3) What is the experience of the people using these facilities?

(4) What applications are these languages best suited for?

(5) What sort of problems arise from writing concurrent programs?

(6) Are there tools for detecting concurrent programming errors?

(7) Are the languages suitable for harnessing the processing power of multiprocessors? What if the number of processors runs into the thousands and even hundreds of thousands?

(8)   Are concurrent programming facilities dependent on the presence of shared memory for efficient implementation?

We believe that this book, which is a collection of recent papers on concurrent programming, is a step towards answering such questions. The book is organized into five sections dealing with the following topics:

(1)   A survey of concurrent programming.

(2)   Concurrent programming languages.

(3)   Concurrent programming models.

(4)   Assessment of concurrent programming languages.

(5)   Concurrent programming issues (e.g., deadlock).

Each section begins with an introduction to tie the papers together and to provide continuity between the sections.

3   Audience

This book will be appropriate as one of two or three text books used in a course on concurrent programming, programming languages, advanced programming and operating systems

It will also be suitable as a reference book for computer scientists and professionals interested in finding out more about concurrent programming.

Narain Gehani
Murray Hill, NJ

Andrew McGettrick
Glasgow, Scotland

October 1987

Acknowledgments

We are indebted to the authors and publishers for giving us their permission to reprint their papers. The individual credits are listed below:

- Andrews, G.R. and Schneider, F.B. Concepts and Notations for Concurrent Programming. Copyright © 1983 ACM. Reprinted with permission from *Computing Surveys*, **15** (1), 3–43.

- Brinch Hansen, P. The Programming Language Concurrent Pascal. Copyright © 1975 IEEE. Reprinted with permission from *IEEE Transactions on Software Engineering*, **SE-1** (2), 199–207.

- Cook, R.P. *MOD – A Language for Distributed Programming. Copyright © 1980 IEEE. Reprinted with permission from *IEEE Transactions on Software Engineering*, **SE-6** (6), 563–571.

- Gehani, N.H. and Roome, W.D. Concurrent C. Copyright © 1986 John Wiley and Sons, Ltd. Reprinted with permission from *Software: Practice and Experience*, **16** (9), 821–844.

- Roubine, O. and Heliard, J.-C. Parallel Processing in Ada. Copyright © 1980 Cambridge University Press. Reprinted with permission from *On the Construction of Programs*, edited by R.M. McKeag and A.M. Macnaghten, pp 193–212.

- Ackerman, W.B. Data Flow Languages. Copyright © 1982 IEEE. Reprinted with permission from *Computer*, **15** (2), 15–25.

- Andrews, G.R. Synchronizing Resources. Copyright ©1981 ACM. Reprinted with permission from *ACM Transactions on Programming Languages and Systems*, **3** (4), 405–430.

- Brinch Hansen, P. Distributed Processes: A Concurrent Programming Concept. Copyright © 1978 ACM. Reprinted with permission from *Communications of the ACM*, **21** (11), 934–941.

- Gehani, N.H. Broadcasting Sequential Processes (BSP). Copyright © 1984 IEEE. Reprinted with permission from *IEEE Transactions on Software Engineering*, **SE-10** (4), 343–351.

- Hoare, C.A.R. Monitors: An Operating System Structuring Concept. Copyright © 1974 ACM. Reprinted with permission from *Communications of the ACM*, **17** (10), 549–557.

- Hoare, C.A.R. Communicating Sequential Processes. Copyright © 1978 ACM. Reprinted with permission from *Communications of the ACM*, **21** (8), 666–677.

- Liskov, B. and Scheifler, R. Guardians and Actions: Linguistic Support for Robust, Distributed Programs. Copyright © 1983 ACM. Reprinted with permission from *ACM Transactions on Programming Languages and Systems*, **5** (3), 381–404.

- Wetherell, C. Design Considerations for Array Processing Languages. Copyright © 1980 John Wiley and Sons, Ltd. Reprinted with permission from *Software: Practice and Experience*, **10**, 265–271.

- Coleman, D., Gallimore, R.M., Hughes, J.W. and Powell, M.S. An Assessment of Concurrent Pascal. Copyright © 1979 John Wiley and Sons, Ltd. Reprinted with permission from *Software: Practice and Experience*, **9**, 827–837.

- Gehani, N.H. and Cargill, T.A. Concurrent Programming in the Ada Language: The Polling Bias. Copyright © 1984 John Wiley and Sons, Ltd. Reprinted with permission from *Software: Practice and Experience*, **14** (5), 413–427.

- Kieburtz, R.B. and Silberschatz, A. Comments on 'Communicating Sequential Processes'. Copyright © 1979 ACM. Reprinted with permission from *ACM Transactions on Programming Languages and Systems*, **1** (2), 218–225.

- Lampson, B.W. and Redell, D.D. Experience with Processes and Monitors in Mesa. Copyright © 1980 ACM. Reprinted with permission from *Communications of the ACM*, **23** (2), 105–117.

- Stotts, P. David. A Comparative Survey of Concurrent Programming Languages. Copyright © 1982 P.D. Stotts. Reprinted with permission from *SIGPLAN Notices*, **17** (10), 76–87.

- Roberts, E.S., Evans, A., Jr., Morgan, C.R. and Clarke, E.M. Task Management in Ada – A Critical Evaluation for Real-Time Multiprocessors. Copyright © 1981 John Wiley and Sons, Ltd. Reprinted with permission from *Software: Practice and Experience*, **11**, 1019–1051.

- Wegner, P. and Smolka, S.A. Processes, Tasks and Monitors: A Comparative Study of Concurrent Programming Primitives. Copyright © 1983 IEEE. Reprinted with permission from *IEEE Transactions on Software Engineering*, **SE-9** (4), 446–462.

- Wirth, N. Schemes for Multiprogramming and Their Implementation in Modula-2. Copyright © 1984 Niklaus Wirth. Reprinted with permission from an ETH technical report.

- Liskov, B., Herlihy, M. and Gilbert, L. Limitations of Synchronous Communication with Static Process Structure in Languages for Distributed Computing. Copyright © 1986 ACM. Reprinted with permission from *Proceedings of the 13th ACM Symposium on Principles of Programming Languages*, St. Petersburg, Florida, January 1986.

- Bristow, G., Drey, C., Edwards, B. and Riddle, W. Anomaly Detection in Concurrent Programs. Copyright © 1979 IEEE. Reprinted with permission from *Proceedings of the Fourth International Conference on Software Engineering*, Munich, West Germany, September 17–19, 1979, pp 265–273.

- Taylor, R.N. A General-Purpose Algorithm for Analyzing Concurrent Programs. Copyright © 1983 ACM. Reprinted with permission from *Communications of the ACM*, **26** (5), 362–376.

Contents

PART ONE
Survey of Concurrent Programming

In a field such as concurrent programming that has not as yet matured, terminology is not standardized and there is no general agreement on the best models and best facilities for writing concurrent programs. Concurrent programming models can be classified into two broad categories: shared memory and message passing. To an extent the appropriateness of a model is likely to be affected by the underlying hardware, for example, a message passing model is the likely choice in the absence of shared memory. There is no consensus, however, as to what sort of facilities should be used to control access to shared memory, or to send and receive messages.

Greg Andrews and Fred Schneider begin this book with an excellent and comprehensive survey of concurrent programming. They lead up to the current state of the art by giving an historical perspective of concurrent programming models, notations and languages.

Concepts and Notations for Concurrent Programming

Gregory R. Andrews
University of Arizona

Fred B. Schneider
Cornell University

Much has been learned in the last decade about concurrent programming. This paper identifies the major concepts of concurrent programming and describes some of the more important language notations for writing concurrent programs. The roles of processes, communication, and synchronization are discussed. Language notations for expressing concurrent execution and for specifying process interaction are surveyed. Synchronization primitives based on shared variables and on message passing are described. Finally, three general classes of concurrent programming languages are identified and compared.

Categories and subject descriptors: D.1.3 [**Programming Techniques**]: Concurrent Programming; D.3.3 [**Programming Languages**]: Language Constructs – *concurrent programming structures, coroutines*; D.4.1 [**Operating Systems**: Process Management; D.4.7 [**Operating Systems**]: Organization and Design.

General terms: algorithms, languages.

Introduction

The complexion of concurrent programming has changed substantially in the past ten years. First, theoretical advances have prompted the

This work was supported in part by NSF Grants MCS 80-01688 and MCS 82-02869 at Arizona and MCS 81-03605 at Cornell.

definition of new programming notations that express concurrent computations simply, make synchronization requirements explicit, and facilitate formal correctness proofs. Second, the availability of inexpensive processors has made possible the construction of distributed systems and multiprocessors that were previously economically infeasible. Because of these two developments, concurrent programming no longer is the sole province of those who design and implement operating systems; it has become important to programmers of all kinds of applications, including database management systems, large-scale parallel scientific computations, and real-time, embedded control systems. In fact, the discipline has matured to the point that there are now undergraduate-level text books devoted solely to the topic [Holt *et al.*, 1978; Ben-Ari, 1982]. In light of this growing range of applicability, it seems appropriate to survey the state of the art.

This paper describes the concepts central to the design and construction of concurrent programs and explores notations for describing concurrent computations. Although this description requires detailed discussions of some concurrent programming languages, we restrict attention to those whose designs we believe to be influential or conceptually innovative. Not all the languages we discuss enjoy widespread use. Many are experimental efforts that focus on understanding the interactions of a given collection of constructs. Some have not even been implemented; others have been, but with little concern for efficiency, access control, data types, and other important (though nonconcurrency) issues.

We proceed as follows. In Section 1 we discuss the three issues that underlie all concurrent programming notations: how to express concurrent execution, how processes communicate, and how processes synchronize. These issues are treated in detail in the remainder of the paper. In Section 2 we take a closer look at various ways to specify concurrent execution: coroutines, **fork** and **cobegin** statements, and **process** declarations. In Section 3 we discuss synchronization primitives that are used when communication uses shared variables. Two general types of synchronization are considered – exclusion and condition synchronization – and a variety of ways to implement them are described: busy-waiting, semaphores, conditional critical regions, monitors, and path expressions. In Section 4 we discuss message-passing primitives. We describe methods for specifying channels of communication and for synchronization, and higher level constructs for performing remote procedure calls and atomic transactions. In Section 5 we identify and compare three general classes of concurrent programming languages. Finally, in Section 6, we summarize the major topics and identify directions in which the field is headed.

1 Concurrent programs: Processes and process interaction

513 556 7402

1.1 Processes

A *sequential program* specifies sequential execution of a list of statements; its execution is called a *process*. A *concurrent program* specifies two or more sequential programs that may be executed concurrently as *parallel processes*. For example, an airline reservation system that involves processing transactions from many terminals has a natural specification as a concurrent program in which each terminal is controlled by its own sequential process. Even when processes are not executed simultaneously, it is often easier to structure a system as a collection of cooperating sequential processes rather than as a single sequential program. A simple batch operating system can be viewed as three processes: a *reader* process, an *executer* process, and a *printer* process. The *reader* process reads cards from a card reader and places card images in an input buffer. The *executer* process reads card images from the input buffer, performs the specified computation (perhaps generating line images), and stores the results in an output buffer. The *printer* process retrieves line images from the output buffer and writes them to a printer.

A concurrent program can be executed either by allowing processes to share one or more processors or by running each process on its own processor. The first approach is referred to as *multiprogramming; it is* supported by an operating system kernel [Dijkstra, 1968a] that multiplexes the processes on the processor(s). The second approach is referred to as *multiprocessing* if the processors share a common memory (as in a multiprocessor [Jones and Schwarz, 1980]), or as *distributed processing* if the processors are connected by a communications network.[1] Hybrid approaches also exist – for example, processors in a distributed system are often multiprogrammed.

The rate at which processes are executed depends on which approach is used. When each process is executed on its own processor, each is executed at a fixed, but perhaps unknown, rate; when processes share a processor, it is as if each is executed on a variable-speed processor. Because we would like to be able to understand a concurrent program in terms of its component sequential processes and their interaction, without regard for how they are executed, we make no assumption about execution rates of concurrently executing processes, except that they all are positive. This is called the *finite progress*

---

[1] A concurrent program that is executed in this way is often called a *distributed program*.

assumption. The correctness of a program for which only finite progress is assumed is thus independent of whether that program is executed on multiple processors or on a single multiprogrammed processor.

1.2 Process interaction

In order to cooperate, concurrently executing processes must communicate and synchronize. Communication allows execution of one process to influence execution of another. Interprocess communication is based on the use of shared variables (variables that can be referenced by more than one process) or on message passing.

Synchronization is often necessary when processes communicate. Processes are executed with unpredictable speeds. Yet, to communicate, one process must perform some action that the other detects – an action such as setting the value of a variable or sending a message. This only works if the events 'perform an action' and 'detect an action' are constrained to happen in that order. Thus one can view synchronization as a set of constraints on the ordering of events. The programmer employs a *synchronization mechanism* to delay execution of a process in order to satisfy such constraints.

To make the concept of synchronization a bit more concrete, consider the batch operating system described above. A shared buffer is used for communication between the *reader* process and the *executer* process. These processes must be synchronized so that, for example, the *executer* process never attempts to read a card image from the input if the buffer is empty.

This view of synchronization follows from taking an *operational approach* to program semantics. An execution of a concurrent program can be viewed as a sequence of *atomic actions*, each resulting from the execution of an indivisible operation.[2] This sequence will comprise some interleaving of the sequences of atomic actions generated by the individual component processes. Rarely do all execution interleavings result in acceptable program behavior, as is illustrated in the following. Suppose initially that $x = 0$, that process $P1$ increments x by 1, and that process $P2$ increments x by 2:

$$P1: x := x + 1 \qquad P2: x := x + 2$$

It would seem reasonable to expect the final value of x, after $P1$ and $P2$ have executed concurrently, to be 3. Unfortunately, this will not always

---

[2] We assume that a single memory reference is indivisible; if two processes attempt to reference the same memory cell at the same time, the result is as if the references were made serially. This is a reasonable assumption in light of the way memory is constructed. See Lamport [1980b] for a discussion of some of the implications of relaxing this assumption.

be the case, because assignment statements are not generally implemented as indivisible operations. For example, the above assignments might be implemented as a sequence of three indivisible operations:

(i) load a register with the value of x;

(ii) add 1 or 2 to it; and

(iii) store the result in x.

Thus, in the program above, the final value of x might be 1, 2, or 3. This anomalous behavior can be avoided by preventing interleaved execution of the two assignment statements – that is, by controlling the ordering of the events corresponding to the atomic actions. (If ordering were thus controlled, each assignment statement would be an indivisible operation.) In other words, execution of $P1$ and $P2$ must be synchronized by enforcing restrictions on possible interleavings.

The *axiomatic approach* [Floyd, 1967; Hoare, 1969; Dijkstra, 1976] provides a second framework in which to view the role of synchronization.[3] In this approach, the semantics of statements are defined by axioms and inference rules. This results in a formal logical system, called a 'programming logic.' Theorems in the logic have the form:

$$\{P\}\; S\; \{Q\}$$

and specify a relation between statements (S) and two predicates, a *precondition P* and a *postcondition Q*. The axioms and inference rules are chosen so that theorems have the interpretation that if execution of S is started in any state that satisfies the precondition, and if execution terminates, then the postcondition will be true of the resulting state. This allows statements to be viewed as relations between predicates.

A *proof outline*[4] provides one way to present a program and its proof. It consists of the program text interleaved with assertions so that for each statement S, the triple (formed from:

(1)   the assertion that textually precedes S in the proof outline;

(2)   the statement S; and

(3)   the assertion that textually follows S in the proof outline)

is a theorem in the programming logic. Thus the appearance of an assertion R in the proof outline signifies that R is true of the program state when control reaches that point.

When concurrent execution is possible, the proof of a sequential

---

[3] We include brief discussions of axiomatic semantics here and elsewhere in the paper because of its importance in helping to explain concepts. However, a full discussion of the semantics of concurrent computation is beyond the scope of this paper.

[4] This sometimes is called an asserted program.

process is valid only if concurrent execution of other processes cannot invalidate assertions that appear in the proof [Ashcroft, 1975; Keller, 1976; Owicki and Gries, 1976a, 1976b; Lamport, 1977, 1980a; Lamport and Schneider, 1982]. One way to establish this is to assume that the code between any two assertions in a proof outline is executed atomically[5] and then to prove a series of theorems showing that no statement in one process invalidates any assertion in the proof of another. These additional theorems constitute a proof of *noninterference*. To illustrate this, consider the following excerpt from a proof outline of two concurrent processes $P1$ and $P2$:

$$P1: \qquad ... \qquad P2: \qquad ...$$
$$\{x > 0\} \qquad\qquad \{x < 0\}$$
$$S1 : x := 16 \qquad\qquad S2 : x := -2$$
$$\{x = 16\} \qquad\qquad ...$$
$$...$$

In order to prove that execution of $P2$ does not interfere with the proof of $P1$, part of what we must show is that execution of $S2$ does not invalidate assertions $\{x > 0\}$ and $\{x = 16\}$ in the proof of $P1$. This is done by proving:

$$\{x < 0 \ \textbf{and} \ \ x > 0\} \qquad x := -2 \qquad \{x > 0\}$$

and:

$$\{x < 0 \ \textbf{and} \ \ x > 0\} \qquad x := -2 \qquad \{x = 16\}$$

Both of these are theorems because the precondition of each, $\{x < 0$ **and** $x > 0\}$, is false. What we have shown is that execution of $S2$ is not possible when either the precondition or postcondition of $S1$ holds (and thus $S1$ and $S2$ are mutually exclusive). Hence, $S2$ cannot invalidate either of these assertions.

Synchronization mechanisms control interference in two ways. First, they can delay execution of a process until a given condition (assertion) is true. By so doing, they ensure that the precondition of the subsequent statement is guaranteed to be true (provided that the assertion is not interfered with). Second, a synchronization mechanism can be used to ensure that a block of statements is an indivisible operation. This eliminates the possibility of statements in other processes interfering with assertions appearing within the proof of that block of statements.

Both views of programs, operational and axiomatic are useful. The operational approach – viewing synchronization as an ordering of events – is well suited to explaining how synchronization mechanisms work. For

---

[5] This should be construed as specifying what assertions must be included in the proof rather than as a restriction on how statements are actually executed.

that reason, the operational approach is used rather extensively in this survey. It also constitutes the philosophical basis for a family of synchronization mechanisms called *path expressions* [Campbell and Habermann, 1974], which are described in Section 3.5.

Unfortunately, the operational approach does not really help one understand the behavior of a concurrent program or argue convincingly about its correctness. Although it has borne fruit for simple concurrent programs – such as transactions processed concurrently in a database system [Bernstein and Goodman, 1981] – the operational approach has only limited utility when applied to more complex concurrent programs [Akkoyunlu *et al.*, 1978; Bernstein and Schneider, 1978]. This limitation exists because the number of interleavings that must be considered grows exponentially with the size of the component sequential processes. Human minds are not good at such extensive case analysis. The axiomatic approach usually does not have this difficulty. It is perhaps the most promising technique for understanding concurrent programs. Some familiarity with formal logic is required for its use, however, and this has slowed its acceptance.

To summarize, there are three main issues underlying the design of a notation for expressing a concurrent computation:

(i) how to indicate concurrent execution;
(ii) which mode of interprocess communication to use;
(iii) which synchronization mechanism to use.

Also, synchronization mechanisms can be viewed either as constraining the ordering of events or as controlling interference. We consider all these topics in depth in the remainder of the paper.

2   Specifying concurrent execution

Various notations have been proposed for specifying concurrent execution. Early proposals, such as the **fork** statement, are marred by a failure to separate process definition from process synchronization. Later proposals separate these distinct concepts and characteristically possess syntactic restrictions that impose some structure on a concurrent program. This structure allows easy identification of those program segments that can be executed concurrently. Consequently, such proposals are well suited for use with the axiomatic approach, because the structure of the program itself clarifies the proof obligations for establishing noninterference.

Below, we describe some representative constructs for expressing concurrent execution. Each can be used to specify computations having a *static* (fixed) number of processes, or can be used in combination with process-creation mechanisms to specify computations having a *dynamic* (variable) number of processes.

2.1 Coroutines

Coroutines are like subroutines, but allow transfer of control in a symmetric rather than strictly hierarchical way [Conway, 1963a]. Control is transferred between coroutines by means of the **resume** statement. Execution of **resume** is like execution of procedure **call**: it transfers control to the named routine, saving enough state information for control to return later to the instruction following the **resume**. (When a routine is first resumed, control is transferred to the beginning of that routine.) However, control is returned to the original routine by executing another **resume** rather than by executing a procedure **return**. Moreover, any other coroutine can potentially transfer control back to the original routine. (For example, coroutine $C1$ could **resume** $C2$, which could **resume** $C3$, which could **resume** $C1$.) Thus **resume** serves as the only way to transfer control between coroutines, and one coroutine can transfer control to any other coroutine that it chooses.

A use of coroutines appears in Figure 1. Note that **resume** is used to transfer control between coroutines A and B, a **call** is used to initiate the coroutine computation, and **return** is used to transfer control back to the caller P. The arrows in Figure 1 indicate the transfers of control.

Each coroutine can be viewed as implementing a process. Execution of **resume** causes process synchronization. When used with care, coroutines are an acceptable way to organize concurrent programs that share a single processor. In fact, multiprogramming can also be implemented using coroutines. Coroutines are not adequate for true parallel processing, however, because their semantics allow for execution of only one routine at a time. In essence, coroutines are concurrent processes in which process switching has been completely specified, rather than left to the discretion of the implementation.

Statements to implement coroutines have been included in discrete event simulation languages such as SIMULA I [Nygaard and Dahl, 1978] and its successors; the string-processing language SL5 [Hanson and Griswold, 1978]; and systems implementation languages including BLISS [Wulf *et al.*, 1971] and most recently Modula-2 [Wirth, 1982].

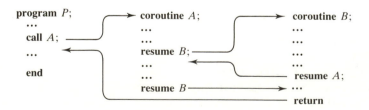

Figure 1   A use of coroutines.

2.2   The fork and join statements

The **fork** statement [Dennis and Van Horn, 1966; Conway, 1963b], like a **call** or **resume**, specifies that a designated routine should start executing. However, the invoking routine and the invoked routine proceed concurrently. To synchronize with completion of the invoked routine, the invoking routine can execute a **join** statement. Executing **join** delays the invoking routine until the designated invoked routine has terminated. (The latter routine is often designated by a value returned from execution of a prior **fork**.) A use of **fork** and **join** follows:

```
program P1;      program P2;
   ...              ...
   fork P2;         ...
   ...              ...
   join P2;         end
   ...
```

Execution of $P2$ is initiated when the **fork** in $P1$ is executed; $P1$ and $P2$ then execute concurrently until either $P1$ executes the **join** statement or $P2$ terminates. After $P1$ reaches the **join** and $P2$ terminates, $P1$ executes the statements following the **join**.

Because **fork** and **join** can appear in conditionals and loops, a detailed understanding of program execution is necessary to understand which routines will be executed concurrently. Nevertheless, when used in a disciplined manner, the statements are practical and powerful. For example, **fork** provides a direct mechanism for dynamic process creation, including multiple activations of the same program text. The UNIX[6] operating system [Ritchie and Thompson, 1974] makes extensive use of variants of **fork** and **join**. Similar statements have also been included in PL/I and Mesa [Mitchell et al., 1979].

2.3   The cobegin statement

The **cobegin** statement[7] is a structured way of denoting concurrent execution of a set of statements. Execution of:

```
cobegin S₁ ‖ S₂ ‖ ... ‖ Sₙ coend
```

causes concurrent execution of $S_1, S_2, ..., S_n$. Each of the S_i's may be any statement, including a **cobegin** or a block with local declarations. Execution of a **cobegin** statement terminates only when execution of all the S_i's have terminated.

---

[6] UNIX is a trademark of Bell Laboratories.
[7] This was first called **parbegin** by Dijkstra [1968b].

Although **cobegin** is not as powerful as **fork/join**,[8] it is sufficient for specifying most concurrent computations. Furthermore, the syntax of the **cobegin** statement makes explicit which routines are executed concurrently, and provides a single-entry, single-exit control structure. This allows the state transformation implemented by a **cobegin** to be understood by itself, and then to be used to understand the program in which it appears.

Variants of **cobegin** have been included in ALGOL68 [van Wijngaarden *et al.*, 1975], Communicating Sequential Processes [Hoare, 1978], Edison [Brinch Hansen, 1981], and Argus [Liskov and Scheifler, 1982].

2.4 Process declarations

Large programs are often structured as a collection of sequential routines, which are executed concurrently. Although such routines could be declared as procedures and activated by means of **cobegin** or **fork**, the structure of a concurrent program is much clearer if the declaration of a routine states whether it will be executed concurrently. The *process declaration* provides such a facility.

Use of process declarations to structure a concurrent program is illustrated in Figure 2, which outlines the batch operating system described earlier. We shall use this notation for process declarations in the remainder of this paper to denote collections of routines that are executed concurrently.

In some concurrent programming languages (e.g., Distributed Processes [Brinch Hansen, 1978] and SR [Andrews, 1981]), a collection of process declarations is equivalent to a single **cobegin**, where each of the declared processes is a component of the **cobegin**. This means there is exactly one instance of each declared process. Alternatively, some languages provide an explicit mechanism – **fork** or something similar – for activating instances of process declarations. This explicit activation mechanism can only be used during program initialization in some languages (e.g., Concurrent PASCAL [Brinch Hansen, 1975] and Modula [Wirth, 1977a]). This leads to a fixed number of processes but allows multiple instances of each declared process to be created. By contrast, in

---

[8] Execution of a concurrent program can be represented by a *process flow graph*: an acyclic, directed graph having one node for each process and an arc from one node to another if the second cannot execute until the first has terminated [Shaw, 1974]. Without introducing extra processes or idle time, **cobegin** and sequencing can only represent series-parallel (properly nested) process flow graphs. Using **fork** and **join**, the computation represented by any process flow graph can be specified directly. Furthermore, **fork** can be used to create an arbitrary number of concurrent processes, whereas **cobegin** as defined in any existing language, can be used only to activate a fixed number of processes.

```
program OPSYS;
  var input_buffer : array [0..N − 1] of cardimage;
      output_buffer : array [0..N − 1] of lineimage;

  process reader;
    var card : cardimage;
    loop
      read card from cardreader;
      deposit card in input_buffer
      end
    end;

  process executer;
    var card : cardimage;
        line : lineimage;
    loop
      fetch card from input_buffer;
      process card and generate line;
      deposit line in output_buffer
      end
    end;

  process printer;
    var line : lineimage;
    loop
      fetch line from output_buffer;
      print line on lineprinter
      end
    end

end
```

Figure 2   Outline of batch operating system.

other languages (e.g., PLITS [Feldman, 1979] and Ada [U.S. Department of Defense, 1981]) processes can be created at any time during execution, which makes possible computations having a variable number of processes.

3   Synchronization primitives based on shared variables

When shared variables are used for inter-process communication, two types of synchronization are useful: mutual exclusion and condition synchronization. *Mutual exclusion* ensures that a sequence of statements is treated as an indivisible operation. Consider, for example, a complex data structure manipulated by means of operations implemented as sequences of statements. If processes concurrently perform operations on the same shared data object, then unintended results might occur. (This was illustrated earlier where the statement $x := x + 1$ had to be executed indivisibly for a meaningful computation to result.) A sequence of statements that must appear to be executed as an indivisible operation is called a *critical section*. The term 'mutual exclusion' refers to mutually exclusive execution of critical sections. Notice that the effects of execution interleavings are visible only if two computations access shared variables. If such is the case, one computation can see intermediate results produced by incomplete execution of the other. If two routines have no variables in common, then their execution need not be mutually exclusive.

Another situation in which it is necessary to coordinate execution of concurrent processes occurs when a shared data object is in a state inappropriate for executing a particular operation. Any process attempting such an operation should be delayed until the state of the data object (i.e., the values of the variables that comprise the object) changes as a result of other processes executing operations. We shall call this type of synchronization *condition synchronization*.[9] Examples of condition synchronization appear in the simple batch operating system discussed above. A process attempting to execute a 'deposit' operation on a buffer (the buffer being a shared data object) should be delayed if the buffer has no space. Similarly, a process attempting to 'fetch' from a buffer should be delayed if there is nothing in the buffer to remove.

Below, we survey various mechanisms for implementing these two types of synchronization.

3.1 Busy-waiting

One way to implement synchronization is to have processes set and test shared variables. This approach works reasonably well for implementing condition synchronization, but not for implementing mutual exclusion, as will be seen. To signal a condition, a process sets the value of a shared variable; to wait for that condition, a process repeatedly tests the variable until it is found to have a desired value. Because a process waiting for a condition must repeatedly test the shared variable, this technique to delay a process is called *busy-waiting* and the process is said to be *spinning*. Variables that are used in this way are sometimes called *spin locks*.

To implement mutual exclusion using busy-waiting, statements that signal and wait for conditions are combined into carefully constructed protocols. Below, we present Peterson's solution to the two-process mutual exclusion problem [Peterson, 1981]. (This solution is simpler than the solution proposed by Dekker [Shaw, 1974].) The solution

---

[9] Unfortunately, there is no commonly agreed upon term for this.

involves an *entry protocol*, which a process executes before entering its critical section, and an *exit protocol*, which a process executes after finishing its critical section:

```
process P1;
  loop
     Entry Protocol;
     Critical Section;
     Exit Protocol;
     Noncritical Section
     end
  end

process P2;
  loop
     Entry Protocol;
     Critical Section;
     Exit Protocol;
     Noncritical Section
     end
  end
```

Three shared variables are used as follows to realize the desired synchronization. Boolean variable *enteri* ($i = 1$ or 2) is true when process Pi is executing its entry protocol or its critical section. Variable *turn* records the name of the next process to be granted entry into its own critical section; *turn* is used when both processes execute their respective entry protocols at about the same time. The solution is:

```
program Mutex_Example:
  var enter1, enter2 : Boolean initial (false, false);
      turn : integer initial ("P1");    { or "P2" }

  process P1;
    loop
       Entry_Protocol:
          enter1 := true;    { announce intent to enter }
          turn := "P2";    { set priority to other process }
          while enter2 and turn = "P2"
             do skip; { wait if other process is in and it is his turn }
       Critical Section;
       Exit_Protocol:
          enter1 := false;    { renounce intent to enter }
       Noncritical Section
       end
    end;
```

```
process P2;
  loop
    Entry_Protocol:
      enter2 := true;  { announce intent to enter }
      turn := "P1";    { set priority to other process }
      while enter1 and turn = "P1"
        do skip; { wait if other process is in and it is his turn }
    Critical Section;
    Exit_Protocol:
      enter2 := false;  { renounce intent to enter }
    Noncritical Section
    end
  end
end
```

In addition to implementing mutual exclusion, this solution has two other desirable properties. First, it is *deadlock free*. *Deadlock* is a state of affairs in which two or more processes are waiting for events that will never occur. Above, deadlock could occur if each process could spin forever in its entry protocol; using *turn* precludes deadlock. The second desirable property is *fairness*:[10] if a process is trying to enter its critical section, it will eventually be able to do so, provided that the other process exits its critical section. Fairness is a desirable property for a synchronization mechanism because its presence ensures that the finite progress assumption is not invalidated by delays due to synchronization. In general, a synchronization mechanism is *fair* if no process is delayed forever, waiting for a condition that occurs infinitely often; it is *bounded fair* if there exists an upper bound on how long a process will be delayed waiting for a condition that occurs infinitely often. The above protocol is bounded fair, since a process waiting to enter its critical section is delayed for at most one execution of the other process' critical section; the variable *turn* ensures this. Peterson [1981] gives operational proofs of mutual exclusion, deadlock freedom, and fairness; Dijkstra [1981a] gives axiomatic ones.

Synchronization protocols that use only busy-waiting are difficult to design, understand, and prove correct. First, although instructions that make two memory references part of a single indivisible operation (e.g., the TS (test-and-set) instruction on the IBM 360/370 processors) help, such instructions do not significantly simplify the task of designing synchronization protocols. Second, busy-waiting wastes processor cycles. A processor executing a spinning process could usually be employed more productively by running other processes until the awaited condition occurs. Last, the busy-waiting approach to synchronization burdens the programmer with deciding both what synchronization is required

---

[10] A more complete discussion of fairness appears in Lehmann *et al.* [1981].

and how to provide it. In reading a program that uses busy-waiting, it may not be clear to the reader which program variables are used for implementing synchronization and which are used for, say, interprocess communication.

3.2   Semaphores

Dijkstra was one of the first to appreciate the difficulties of using low-level mechanisms for process synchronization, and this prompted his development of semaphores [Dijkstra, 1968a, 1968b]. A *semaphore* is a nonnegative integer-valued variable on which two operations are defined: **P** and **V**. Given a semaphore s, **P**(s) delays until $s > 0$ and then executes $s := s - 1$; the test and decrement are executed as an indivisible operation. **V**(s) executes $s := s + 1$ as an indivisible operation.[11] Most semaphore implementations are assumed to exhibit fairness: no process delayed while executing **P**(s) will remain delayed forever if **V**(s) operations are performed infinitely often. The need for fairness arises when a number of processes are simultaneously delayed, all attempting to execute a **P** operation on the same semaphore. Clearly, the implementation must choose which one will be allowed to proceed when a **V** is ultimately performed. A simple way to ensure fairness is to awaken processes in the order in which they were delayed.

Semaphores are a very general tool for solving synchronization problems. To implement a solution to the mutual exclusion problem, each critical section is preceded by a **P** operation and followed by a **V** operation on the same semaphore. All mutually exclusive critical sections use the same semaphore, which is initialized to one. Because such a semaphore only takes on the values zero and one, it is often called a *binary* semaphore.

To implement condition synchronization, shared variables are used to represent the condition, and a semaphore associated with the condition is used to accomplish the synchronization. After a process has made the condition true, it signals that it has done so by executing a **V** operation; a process delays until a condition is true by executing a **P** operation. A semaphore that can take any nonnegative value is called a *general* or *counting* semaphore. General semaphores are often used for condition synchronization when controlling resource allocation. Such a semaphore has as its initial value the initial number of units of the

---

[11] P is the first letter of the Dutch word 'passeren,' which means 'to pass'; V is the first letter of 'vrygeven,' the Dutch word for 'to release' [Dijkstra, 1981b]. Reflecting on the definitions of **P** and **V**, Dijkstra and his group observed the **P** might better stand for 'prolagen' formed from the Dutch words 'proberen' (meaning 'to try') and 'verlagen' (meaning 'to decrease') and V for the Dutch word 'verhogen' meaning 'to increase.' Some authors use **wait** for **P** and **signal** for **V**.

resource; a **P** is used to delay a process until a free resource unit is available; **V** is executed when a unit of the resource is returned. Binary semaphores are sufficient for some types of condition synchronization, notably those in which a resource has only one unit.

A few examples will illustrate uses of semaphores. We show a solution to the two-process mutual exclusion problem in terms of semaphores in the following:

```
program Mutex_Example;

    var mutex : semaphore initial (1);

    process P1;
      loop
        P(mutex);          { Entry Protocol }
        Critical Section;
        V(mutex);          { Exit Protocol }
        Noncritical Section
        end
      end;

    process P2;
      loop
        P(mutex);          { Entry Protocol }
        Critical Section;
        V(mutex);          { Exit Protocol }
        Noncritical Section
        end
      end

    end.
```

Notice how simple and symmetric the entry and exit protocols are in this solution to the mutual exclusion problem. In particular, this use of **P** and **V** ensures both mutual exclusion and absence of deadlock. Also, if the semaphore implementation is fair and both processes always exit their critical sections, each process eventually gets to enter its critical section.

Semaphores can also be used to solve *selective mutual exclusion* problems. In the latter, shared variables are partitioned into disjoint sets. A semaphore is associated with each set and used in the same way as *mutex* above to control access to the variables in that set. Critical sections that reference variables in the same set execute with mutual exclusion, but critical sections that reference variables in different sets execute concurrently. However, if two or more processes require simultaneous access to variables in two or more sets, the programmer must take care or deadlock could result. Suppose that two processes, *P*1 and *P*2, each require simultaneous access to sets of shared variables *A* and *B*. Then, *P*1 and *P*2 will deadlock if, for example, *P*1 acquires access to set *A*, *P*2 acquires access to set *B*, and then both processes try to acquire access to the set that they do not yet have. Deadlock is avoided here (and in general) if processes first try to acquire access to the same set (e.g., *A*), and then try to acquire access to the other (e.g., *B*).

Figure 3 shows how semaphores can be used for selective mutual exclusion and condition synchronization in an implementation of our

```
program OPSYS;

  var in_mutex, out_mutex : semaphore initial (1,1);
      num_cards, num_lines : semaphore initial (0,0);
      free_cards, free_lines : semaphore initial (N,N);
      input_buffer : array [0..N − 1] of cardimage;
      output_buffer : array [0..N − 1] of lineimage;

process reader;
  var card : cardimage;
  loop
    read card from cardreader;
    P( free_cards); P(in_mutex);
      deposit card in input_buffer;
    V(in_mutex); V(num_cards)
    end
  end;

process executer;
  var card : cardimage;
      line : lineimage;
  loop
    P(num_cards); P(in_mutex);
      fetch card from input_buffer;
    V(in_mutex); V( free_cards);
    process card and generate line;
    P( free_lines); P(out_mutex);
      deposit line in output_buffer;
    V(out_mutex); V(num_lines)
    end
  end;

process printer;
  var line : lineimage;
  loop
    P(num_lines); P(out_mutex);
      fetch line from output_buffer;
    V(out_mutex); V( free_lines);
    print line on lineprinter
    end
  end
end.
```

Figure 3   Batch operating system with semaphores.

simple example operating system. Semaphore *in_mutex* is used to implement mutually exclusive access to *input_buffer* and *out_mutex* is used to implement mutually exclusive access to *output_buffer*.[12] Because the buffers are disjoint, it is possible for operations on *input_buffer* and *output_buffer* to proceed concurrently. Semaphores *num_cards*, *num_lines*, *free_cards*, and *free_lines* are used for condition synchronization: *num_cards* (*num_lines*) is the number of card images (line images) that have been deposited but not yet fetched from *input_buffer* (*output_buffer*); *free_cards* (*free_lines*) is the number of free slots in *input_buffer* (*output_buffer*). Executing **P**(*num_cards*) delays a process until there is a card in *input_buffer*; **P**(*free_cards*) delays its invoker until there is space to insert a card in *input_buffer*. Semaphores *num_lines* and *free_lines* play corresponding roles with respect to *output_buffer*. Note that before accessing a buffer, each process first waits for the condition required for access and then acquires exclusive access to the buffer. If this were not the case, deadlock could result. (The order in which **V** operations are performed after the buffer is accessed is not critical.)

Semaphores can be implemented by using busy-waiting. More commonly, however, they are implemented by system calls to a kernel. A *kernel* (sometimes called a *supervisor* or *nucleus*) implements processes on a processor [Dijkstra, 1968a; Shaw, 1974]. At all times, each process is either *ready* to execute on the processor or is *blocked*, waiting to complete a **P** operation. The kernel maintains a *ready list* – a queue of descriptors for ready processes – and multiplexes the processor among these processes, running each process for some period of time. Descriptors for processes that are blocked on a semaphore are stored on a queue associated with that semaphore; they are not stored on the ready list, and hence the processes will not be executed. Execution of a **P** or **V** operation causes a trap to a kernel routine. For a **P** operation, if the semaphore is positive, it is decremented; otherwise the descriptor for the executing process is moved to the semaphore's queue. For a **V** operation, if the semaphore's queue is not empty, one descriptor is moved from that queue to the ready list; otherwise the semaphore is incremented.

This approach to implementing synchronization mechanisms is quite general and is applicable to the other mechanisms that we shall discuss. Since the kernel is responsible for allocating processor cycles to processes, it can implement a synchronization mechanism without using busy-waiting. It does this by not running processes that are blocked. Of course, the names and details of the kernel calls will differ for each synchronization mechanism, but the net effects of these calls will be similar: to move processes on and off a ready list.

Things are somewhat more complex when writing a kernel for a

---

[12] In this solution, careful implementation of the operations on the buffers obviates the need for semaphores *in_mutex* and *out_mutex*. The semaphores that implement condition synchronization are sufficient to ensure mutually exclusive access to individual buffer slots.

multiprocessor or distributed system. In a multiprocessor, either a single processor is responsible for maintaining the ready list and assigning processes to the other processors, or the ready list is shared [Jones and Schwarz, 1980]. If the ready list is shared, it is subject to concurrent access, which requires that mutual exclusion be ensured. Usually, busy-waiting is used to ensure this mutual exclusion because operations on the ready list are fast and a processor cannot execute any process until it is able to access the ready list. In a distributed system, although one processor could maintain the ready list, it is more common for each processor to have its own kernel and hence its own ready list. Each kernel manages those processes residing at one processor; if a process migrates from one processor to another, it comes under the control of the other's kernel.

3.3 Conditional critical regions

Although semaphores can be used to program almost any kind of synchronization, **P** and **V** are rather unstructured primitives, and so it is easy to err when using them. Execution of each critical section must begin with a **P** and end with a **V** (on the same semaphore). Omitting a **P** or **V**, or accidentally coding a **P** on one semaphore and a **V** on another can have disastrous effects, since mutually exclusive execution would no longer be ensured. Also, when using semaphores, a programmer can forget to include in critical sections all statements that reference shared objects. This, too, could destroy the mutual exclusion required within critical sections. A second difficulty with using semaphores is that both condition synchronization and mutual exclusion are programmed using the same pair of primitives. This makes it difficult to identify the purpose of a given **P** or **V** operation without looking at the other operations on the corresponding semaphore. Since mutual exclusion and condition synchronization are distinct concepts, they should have distinct notations.

The *conditional critical region* proposal [Hoare, 1972; Brinch Hansen 1972, 1973b] overcomes these difficulties by providing a structured notation for specifying synchronization. Shared variables are explicitly placed into groups, called *resources*. Each shared variable may be in at most one resource and may be accessed only in conditional critical region (CCR) statements that name the resource. Mutual exclusion is provided by guaranteeing that execution of different CCR statements, each naming the same resource, is not overlapped. Condition synchronization is provided by explicit Boolean conditions in CCR statements.

A resource *r* containing variables $v1, v2, ..., vN$ is declared as:[13]

    resource $r : v1, v2, ..., vN$

---

[13] Our notation combines aspects of those proposed by Hoare [1972] and by Brinch Hansen [1972, 1973b].

The variables in r may only be accessed within CCR statements that name r. Such statements have the form:

region r **when** B **do** S

where B is a Boolean expression and S is a statement list. (Variables local to the executing process may also appear in the CCR statement.) A CCR statement delays the executing process until B is true; S is then executed. The evaluation of B and execution of S are uninterruptible by other CCR statements that name the same resource. Thus B is guaranteed to be true when execution of S begins. The delay mechanism is usually assumed to be fair: a process awaiting a condition B that is repeatedly true will eventually be allowed to continue.

One use of conditional critical regions is shown in Figure 4, which contains another implementation of our batch operating system example. Note how condition synchronization has been separated from mutual exclusion. The Boolean expressions in those CCR statements that access the buffers explicitly specify the conditions required for access; thus mutual exclusion of different CCR statements that access the same buffer is implicit.

Programs written in terms of conditional critical regions can be understood quite simply by using the axiomatic approach. Each CCR statement implements an operation on the resource that it names. Associated with each resource r is an *invariant relation* I_r: a predicate that is true of the resource's state after the resource is initialized and after execution of any operation on the resource. For example, in *OPSYS* of Figure 4, the operations insert and remove items from bounded buffers and the buffers *inp_buff* and *out_buff* both satisfy the invariant:

IB:
$\quad 0 \le head, tail \le N - 1$ **and**
$\quad 0 \le size \le N$ **and**
$\quad tail = (head + size) \bmod N$ **and**
$\quad slots[head]$ through $slots[(tail - 1) \bmod N]$
$\qquad$ in the circular buffer contain
$\qquad$ the most recently inserted items
$\qquad$ in chronological order

The Boolean expression B in each CCR statement is chosen so that execution of the statement list, when started in any state that satisfies I_r **and** B, will terminate in a state that satisfies I_r. Therefore the invariant is true as long as no process is in the midst of executing an operation (i.e., executing in a conditional critical region associated with the resource). Recall that execution of conditional critical regions associated with a given shared data object does not overlap. Hence the proofs of processes are interference free as long as:

(1) variables local to a process appear only in the proof of that process; and

```
program OPSYS;

    type buffer(T) = record
                slots : array [0..N − 1] of T;
                head, tail : 0..N − 1 initial (0,0);
                size : 0..N initial (0)
                end;
    var inp_buff : buffer(cardimage);
        out_buff : buffer(lineimage);
    resource ib : inp_buff; ob : out_buff;
    process reader;
        var card : cardimage;
        loop
            read card from cardreader;
            region ib when inp_buff.size < N do
                inp_buff.slots[inp_buff.tail] := card;
                inp_buff.size := inp_buff.size + 1;
                inp_buff.tail := (inp_buff.tail + 1) mod N
                end
            end
        end;
    process executer;
        var card : cardimage;
            line : lineimage;
        loop
            region ib when inp_buff.size > 0 do
                card := inp_buff.slots[inp_buff.head];
                inp_buff.size := inp_buff.size − 1;
                inp_buff.head := (inp_buff.head + 1) mod N
                end;
            process card and generate line;
            region ob when out_buff.size < N do
                out_buff.slots[out_buff.tail] := line;
                out_buff.size := out_buff.size + 1;
                out_buff.tail := (out_buff.tail + 1) mod N
                end
            end
        end;
    process printer;
        var line : lineimage;
        loop
            region ob when out_buff.size > 0 do
                line := out_buff.slots[out_buff.head];
                out_buff.size := out_buff.size − 1;
                out_buff.head := (out_buff.head + 1) mod N
                end;
            print line on lineprinter
            end
        end
    end.
```

Figure 4   Batch operating system with CCR statements.

(2)   variables of a resource appear only in assertions within conditional critical regions for that resource.

Thus, once appropriate resource invariants have been defined, a concurrent program can be understood in terms of its component sequential processes.

Although conditional critical regions have many virtues, they can be expensive to implement. Because conditions in CCR statements can contain references to local variables, each process must evaluate its own conditions.[14] On a multiprogrammed processor, this evaluation results in numerous context switches (frequent saving and restoring of process states), many of which may be unproductive because the activated process may still find the condition false. If each process is executed on its own processor and memory is shared, however, CCR statements can be implemented quite cheaply by using busy-waiting.

CCR statements provide the synchronization mechanism in the Edison language [Brinch Hansen, 1981], which is designed specifically for multiprocessor systems. Variants have also been used in Distributed Processes [Brinch Hansen, 1978] and Argus [Liskov and Scheifler, 1982].

3.4   Monitors

Conditional critical regions are costly to implement on single processors. Also, CCR statements performing operations on resource variables are dispersed throughout the processes. This means that one has to study an entire concurrent program to see all the ways in which a resource is used. Monitors alleviate both these deficiencies. A *monitor* is formed by encapsulating both a resource definition and operations that manipulate it [Dijkstra, 1968b; Brinch Hansen, 1973a; Hoare, 1974]. This allows a resource subject to concurrent access to be viewed as a module [Parnas, 1972]. Consequently, a programmer can ignore the implementation details of the resource when using it, and can ignore how it is used when programming the monitor that implements it.

3.4.1   Definition

A monitor consists of a collection of *permanent variables*, used to store the resource's state, and some procedures, which implement operations on the resource. A monitor also has permanent-variable initialization code, which is executed once before any procedure body is executed. The values of the permanent variables are retained between activations of monitor procedures and may be accessed only from within the monitor.

---

[14] When delayed, a process could instead place condition evaluating code in an area of memory accessible to other processes, but this too is costly.

Monitor procedures can have parameters and local variables, each of which takes on new values for each procedure activation. The structure of a monitor with name *mname* and procedures *op*1, ..., *opN* is shown in Figure 5.

mname : **monitor**;

    var declarations of permanent variables:

    procedure *op*1(parameters);
      var declarations of variables local to *op*1;
      begin
        code to implement *op*1
      end;

    ...

    procedure *opN*(parameters);
      var declarations of variables local to *opN*;
      begin
        code to implement *opN*
      end;

    begin
      code to initialize permanent variables
    end

Figure 5   Monitor structure.

Procedure *opJ* within monitor *mname* is invoked by executing:

call *mname.opJ* (arguments).

The invocation has the usual semantics associated with a procedure call. In addition, execution of the procedures in a given monitor is guaranteed to be mutually exclusive. This ensures that the permanent variables are never accessed concurrently.

A variety of constructs have been proposed for realizing condition synchronization in monitors. We first describe the proposal made by Hoare [1974] and then consider other proposals. A *condition variable* is used to delay processes executing in a monitor; it may be declared only within a monitor. Two operations are defined on condition variables: **signal** and **wait**. If *cond* is a condition variable, then execution of:

cond.**wait**

causes the invoker to be blocked on *cond* and to relinquish its mutually exclusive control of the monitor. Execution of:

cond.**signal**

works as follows: if no process is blocked on *cond*, the invoker continues; otherwise, the invoker is temporarily suspended and one process blocked on *cond* is reactivated. A process suspended due to a **signal** operation continues when there is no other process executing in the monitor. Moreover, signalers are given priority over processes trying to commence execution of a monitor procedure. Condition variables are assumed to be fair in the sense that a process will not forever remain suspended on a condition variable that is signaled infinitely often. Note that the introduction of condition variables allows more than one process to be in the same monitor, although all but one will be delayed at **wait** or **signal** operations.

An example of a monitor that defines a bounded buffer type is given in Figure 6. Our batch operating system can be programmed using two instances of the bounded buffer in Figure 6; these are shared by three processes, as shown in Figure 7.

At times, a programmer requires more control over the order in

```
type buffer(T) = monitor;

   var { the variables satisfy invariant IB – see Sec. 4.3 }
       slots : array [0..N − 1] of T;
       head, tail : 0..N − 1;
       size : 0..N;
       notfull, notempty : condition;

   procedure deposit( p : T);
     begin
       if size = N then notfull.wait;
       slots[tail] := p;
       size := size + 1;
       tail := (tail + 1) mod N;
       notempty.signal
     end;

   procedure fetch(var it : T);
     begin
       if size = 0 then notempty.wait;
       it := slots[head];
       size := size − 1;
       head := (head + 1) mod N;
       notfull.signal
     end;

   begin
     size := 0; head := 0; tail := 0
   end
```

Figure 6   Bounded buffer monitor.

```
program OPSYS:

  type buffer(T) = ...; { see Figure 5 }

  var inp_buff : buffer(cardimage);
      out_buff : buffer(lineimage);

  process reader;
    var card : cardimage;
    loop
      read card from cardreader;
      call inp_buff.deposit(card)
      end
    end;

  process executer;
    var card : cardimage;
        line : lineimage;
    loop
      call inp_buff.fetch(card);
      process card and generate line;
      call out_buff.deposit(line)
      end
    end;

  process printer;
    var line : lineimage;
    loop
      call out_buff.fetch(line);
      print line on lineprinter
      end
    end

end.
```

Figure 7 Batch operating system with monitors.

which delayed processes are awakened. To implement such *medium-term scheduling*,[15] the *priority* **wait** statement can be used. This statement:

cond.**wait**(*p*)

has the same semantics as *cond*.**wait**, except that in the former processes blocked on condition variable *cond* are awakened in ascending order of *p*. (Consequently, condition variables used in this way are not necessarily fair.)

---

[15] This is in contrast to *short-term scheduling*, which is concerned with how processors are assigned to ready processes, and *long-term scheduling*, which refers to how jobs are selected to be processed.

A common problem involving medium-term scheduling is 'shortest-job-next' resource allocation. A resource is to be allocated to at most one user at a time; if more than one user is waiting for the resource when it is released, it is allocated to the user who will use it for the shortest amount of time. A monitor to implement such an allocator is shown below. The monitor has two procedures:

(1) *request*(*time* : *integer*), which is called by users to request access to the resource for *time* units; and

(2) *release*, which is called by users to relinquish access to the resource:

```
shortest_next_allocator : monitor;

    var free : Boolean;
        turn : condition;

    procedure request(time : integer);
      begin
        if not free then turn.wait(time);
        free := false
      end;

    procedure release;
      begin
        free := true;
        turn.signal
      end;

    begin
      free := true
    end
```

3.4.2   Other approaches to condition synchronization

3.4.2.1   Queues and Delay/Continue.   In Concurrent PASCAL [Brinch Hansen, 1975], a slightly simpler mechanism is provided for implementing condition synchronization and medium-term scheduling. Variables of type *queue* can be defined and manipulated with the operations **delay** (analogous to **wait**) and **continue** (analogous to **signal**). In contrast to condition variables, at most one process can be suspended on a given *queue* at any time. This allows medium-term scheduling to be implemented by:

(1) defining an array of queues; and

(2) performing a **continue** operation on that queue on which the next-process-to-be-awakened has been delayed.

The semantics of **continue** are also slightly different from **signal**. Executing **continue** causes the invoker to return from its monitor call, whereas **signal** does not. As before, a process blocked on the selected queue resumes execution of the monitor procedure within which it was delayed.

It is both cheaper and easier to implement **continue** than **signal** because **signal** requires code to ensure that processes suspended by **signal** operations reacquire control of the monitor before other, newer processes attempting to begin execution in that monitor. With both **signal** and **continue**, the objective is to ensure that a condition is not invalidated between the time it is signaled and the time that the awakened process actually resumes execution. Although **continue** has speed and cost advantages, it is less powerful than **signal**. A monitor written using condition variables cannot always be translated directly into one that uses queues without also adding monitor procedures [Howard, 1976b]. Clearly, these additional procedures complicate the interface provided by the monitor. Fortunately, most synchronization problems that arise in practice can be coded using either discipline.

3.4.2.2 *Conditional Wait and Automatic Signal.*

In contrast to semaphores, **signals** on condition variables are not saved: a process always delays after executing **wait**, even if a previous **signal** did not awaken any process.[16] This can make **signal** and **wait** difficult to use correctly, because other variables must be used to record that a **signal** was executed. These variables must also be tested by a process, before executing **wait**, to guard against waiting if the event corresponding to a **signal** has already occurred.

Another difficulty is that, in contrast to conditional critical regions, a Boolean expression is not syntactically associated with **signal** and **wait**, or with the condition variable itself. Thus, it is not easy to determine why a process was delayed on a condition variable, unless **signal** and **wait** are used in a very disciplined manner. It helps if:

(1) each **wait** on a condition variable is contained in an **if** statement in which the Boolean expression is the negation of the desired condition synchronization; and

(2) each **signal** statement on the same condition variable is contained in an **if** statement in which the Boolean expression gives the desired condition synchronization.

Even so, syntactically identical Boolean expressions may have different values if they contain references to local variables, which they often do. Thus there is no guarantee that an awakened process will actually see the condition for which it was waiting. A final difficulty with **wait** and **signal**

---

[16] The limitations of condition variables discussed in this section also apply to queue variables.

is that, because **signal** is preemptive, the state of permanent variables seen by a signaler can change between the time a **signal** is executed and the time that the signaling process resumes execution.

To mitigate these difficulties, Hoare [1974] proposed the *conditional wait* statement

    wait (B)

where B is a Boolean expression involving the permanent or local variables of the monitor. Execution of **wait**(B) delays the invoker until B becomes true; no **signal** is required to reactivate processes delayed by a conditional wait statement. This synchronization facility is expensive because it is necessary to evaluate B every time any process exits the monitor or becomes blocked at a conditional wait and because a context switch could be required for each evaluation (due to the presence of local variables in the condition). However, the construct is unquestionably a very clean one with which to program.

An efficient variant of the conditional wait was proposed by Kessels [1977] for use when only permanent variables appear in B. The buffer monitor in Figure 6 satisfies this requirement. In Kessels' proposal, one declares *conditions* of the form:

    cname : **condition** B

Executing the statement *cname*.**wait** causes B, a Boolean expression, to be evaluated. If B is true, the process continues; otherwise the process relinquishes control of the monitor and is delayed on *cname*. Whenever a process relinquishes control of the monitor, the system evaluates those Boolean expressions associated with all conditions for which there are waiting processes. If one of these Boolean expressions is found to be true, one of the waiting processes is granted control of the monitor. If none is found to be true, a new invocation of one of the monitor's procedures is permitted.

Using Kessels' proposal, the buffer monitor in Figure 6 could be recoded as follows. First, the declarations of *not_full* and *not_empty* are changed to:

    not_full : **condition** *size* $< N$;
    not_empty : **condition** *size* > 0

Second, the first statement in *deposit* is replaced by

    not_full.**wait**

and the first statement in *fetch* is replaced by

    not_empty.**wait**

Finally, the **signal** statements are deleted.

The absence of a **signal** primitive is noteworthy. The implementation provides an *automatic signal,* which, though somewhat more costly, is less error prone than explicitly programmed **signal** operations. The **signal** operation cannot be accidentally omitted and never signals the wrong condition. Furthermore, the programmer explicitly specifies the conditions being awaited. The primary limitation of the proposal is that it cannot be used to solve most scheduling problems, because operation parameters, which are not permanent variables, may not appear in conditions.

3.4.2.3 Signals as Hints. Mesa [Mitchell *et al.,* 1979; Lampson and Redell, 1980] employs yet another approach to condition synchronization. Condition variables are provided, but only as a way for a process to relinquish control of a monitor. In Mesa, execution of:

> *cond*.**notify**

causes a process waiting on condition variable *cond* to resume at some time in the future. This is called *signal and continue* because the process performing the **notify** immediately continues execution rather than being suspended. Performing a **notify** merely gives a *hint* to a waiting process that it might be able to proceed.[17] Therefore, in Mesa one writes:

> **while not** *B* **do wait** *cond* **endloop**

instead of

> **if not** *B* **then** *cond*.**wait**

as would be done using Hoare's condition variables. Boolean condition *B* is guaranteed to be true upon termination of the loop, as it was in the two conditional-wait/automatic-signal proposals. Moreover, the (possible) repeated evaluation of the Boolean expression appears in the actual monitor code – there are no hidden implementation costs.

The **notify** primitive is especially useful if the executing process has higher priority than the waiting processes. It also allows the following extensions to condition variables, which are often useful when doing systems programming:

(i) A time-out interval *t* can be associated with each condition variable. If a process is ever suspended on this condition variable for longer than *t* time units, a **notify** is automatically performed by the system. The awakened process can then decide whether to perform another **wait** or to take other action.

---

[17] Of course, it is prudent to perform **notify** operations only when there is reason to believe that the awakened process will actually be able to proceed; but the burden of checking the condition is on the waiting process.

(ii) A **broadcast** primitive can be defined. Its execution causes all processes waiting on a condition variable to resume at some time in the future (subject to the mutual exclusion constraints associated with execution in a monitor). This primitive is useful if more than one process could proceed when a condition becomes true. The broadcast primitive is also useful when a condition involves local variables because in this case the signaler cannot evaluate the condition (B above) for which a process is waiting. Such a primitive is, in fact, used in UNIX [Ritchie and Thompson, 1974].

3.4.3   An axiomatic view

The valid states of a resource protected by a monitor can be characterized by an assertion called the *monitor invariant*. This predicate should be true of the monitor's permanent variables whenever no process is executing in the monitor. Thus a process must reestablish the monitor invariant before the process exits the monitor or performs a **wait**(**delay**) or **signal**(**continue**). The monitor invariant can be assumed to be true of the permanent variables whenever a process acquires control of the monitor, regardless of whether it acquires control by calling a monitor procedure or by being reactivated following a **wait** or **signal**.

The fact that monitor procedures are mutually exclusive simplifies noninterference proofs. One need not consider interleaved execution of monitor procedures. However, interference can arise when programming condition synchronization. Recall that a process will delay its progress in order to implement medium-term scheduling, or to await some condition. Mechanisms that delay a process cause its execution to be suspended and control of the monitor to be relinquished; the process resumes execution with the understanding that both some condition B and the monitor invariant will be true. The truth of B when the process awakens can be ensured by checking for it automatically or by requiring that the programmer build these tests into the program. If programmed checks are used, they can appear either in the process that establishes the condition (for condition variables and queues) or in the process that performed the **wait** (the Mesa model).

If the signaler checks for the condition, we must ensure that the condition is not invalidated between the time that the **signal** occurs and the time that the blocked process actually executes. That is, we must ensure that other execution in the monitor does not interfere with the condition. If the signaler does not immediately relinquish control of the monitor (e.g., if **notify** is used), interference might be caused by the process that established the condition in the first place. Also, if the signaled process does not get reactivated before new calls of monitor procedures are allowed, interference might be caused by some process that executes after the condition has been signaled (this can happen in

Modula [Wirth, 1977a]). Proof rules for monitors and the various signaling disciplines are discussed by Howard [1976a, 1976b].

3.4.4   Nested monitor calls

When structuring a system as a hierarchical collection of monitors, it is likely that monitor procedures will be called from within other monitors. Such nested monitor calls have caused much discussion [Haddon, 1977; Lister, 1977; Parnas, 1978; Wettstein, 1978]. The controversy is over what (if anything) should be done if a process having made a nested monitor call is suspended in another monitor. The mutual exclusion in the last monitor called will be relinquished by the process, due to the semantics of **wait** and equivalent operations. However, mutual exclusion will not be relinquished by processes in monitors from which nested cells have been made. Processes that attempt to invoke procedures in these monitors will become blocked. This has performance implications, since blockage will decrease the amount of concurrency exhibited by the system.

The nested monitor call problem can be approached in a number of ways. One approach is to prohibit nested monitor calls, as was done in SIMONE [Kaubisch et al., 1976], or to prohibit nested calls to monitors that are not lexically nested, as was done in Modula [Wirth, 1977a]. A second approach is to release the mutual exclusion on all monitors along the call chain when a nested call is made and that process becomes blocked.[18] This release-and-reacquire approach would require that the monitor invariant be established before any monitor call that will block the process. Since the designer cannot know a priori whether a call will block a process, the monitor invariant would have to be established before every call. A third approach is the definition of special-purpose constructs that can be used for particular situations in which nested calls often arise. The *manager* construct [Silberschatz et al., 1977] for handling dynamic resource allocation problems and the *scheduler monitor* [Schneider and Bernstein, 1978] for scheduling access to shared resources are both based on this line of thought.

The last approach to the nested monitor call problem, and probably the most reasonable, is one that appreciates that monitors are only a structuring tool for resources that are subject to concurrent access [Andrews and McGraw, 1977; Parnas, 1978]. Mutual exclusion of monitor procedures is only one way to preserve the integrity of the permanent variables that make up a resource. There are cases in which

---

[18] Once signaled, the process will need to reacquire exclusive access to all monitors along the call chain before resuming execution. However, if permanent monitor variables were not passed as reference parameters in any of the calls, the process could reacquire exclusive access incrementally, as it returns to each monitor.

the operations provided by a given monitor can be executed concurrently without adverse effects, and even cases in which more than one instance of the same monitor procedure can be executed in parallel (e.g., several activations of a read procedure, in a monitor that encapsulates a database). Monitor procedures can be executed concurrently, provided that they do not interfere with each other. Also, there are cases in which the monitor invariant can be easily established before a nested monitor call is made, and so mutual exclusion for the monitor can be released. Based on such reasoning, Andrews and McGraw [1977] defines a monitorlike construct that allows the programmer to specify that certain monitor procedures be executed concurrently and that mutual exclusion be released for certain calls. The Mesa language [Mitchell *et al.*, 1979] also provides mechanisms that give the programmer control over the granularity of exclusion.

3.4.5   Programming notations based on monitors

Numerous programming languages have been proposed and implemented that use monitors for synchronizing access to shared variables. Below, we very briefly discuss two of the most important: Concurrent PASCAL and Modula. These languages have received widespread use, introduced novel constructs to handle machine-dependent systems-programming issues, and inspired other language designs, such as Mesa [Mitchell *et al.*, 1979] and PASCAL-Plus [Welsh and Bustard, 1979].

3.4.5.1 Concurrent PASCAL.   Concurrent PASCAL [Brinch Hansen, 1975, 1977] was the first programming language to support monitors. Consequently, it provided a vehicle for evaluating monitors as a system-structuring device. The language has been used to write several operating systems, including Solo, a single-user operating system [Brinch Hansen, 1976a, 1976b], Job Stream, a batch operating system for processing PASCAL programs, and a real-time process control system [Brinch Hansen, 1977].

One of the major goals of Concurrent PASCAL was to ensure that programs exhibited reproducible behavior [Brinch Hansen, 1977]. Monitors ensured that pathological interleavings of concurrently executed routines that shared data were no longer possible (the compiler generates code to provide the necessary mutual exclusion). Concurrent execution in other modules (called *classes*) was not possible, due to compile-time restrictions on the dissemination of class names and scope rules for class declarations.

Concurrent PASCAL also succeeded in providing the programmer with a clean abstract machine, thereby eliminating the need for coding at the assembly language level. A systems programming language must have facilities to allow access to I/O devices and other hardware resources. In

Concurrent PASCAL, I/O devices and the like are viewed as monitors implemented directly in hardware. To perform an I/O operation, the corresponding 'monitor' is called; the call returns when the I/O has completed. Thus the Concurrent PASCAL run-time system implements synchronous I/O and 'abstracts out' the notion of an interrupt.

Various aspects of Concurrent PASCAL, including its approach to I/O, have been analyzed by Loehr [1977], Silberschatz [1977], and Keedy [1979].

3.4.5.2 Modula.   Modula was developed for programming small, dedicated computer systems, including process control applications [Wirth, 1977a, 1977b, 1977c, 1977d]. The language is largely based on PASCAL and includes processes, *interface modules*, which are like monitors, and *device modules*, which are special interface modules for programming device drivers.

The run-time support system for Modula is small and efficient. The kernel for a PDP-11/45 requires only 98 words of storage and is extremely fast [Wirth, 1977c]. It does not time slice the processor among processes, as Concurrent PASCAL does. Rather, certain kernel-supported operations – **wait**, for example – always cause the processor to be switched. (The programmer must be aware of this and design programs accordingly.) This turns out to be both a strength and weakness of Modula. A small and efficient kernel, where the programmer has some control over processor switching, allows Modula to be used for process control applications, as intended. Unfortunately, in order to be able to construct such a kernel, some of the constructs in the language – notably those concerning multiprogramming – have associated restrictions that can only be understood in terms of the kernel's implementation. A variety of subtle interactions between the various synchronization constructs must be understood in order to program in Modula without experiencing unpleasant surprises. Some of these pathological interactions are described by Bernstein and Ensor [1981].

Modula implements an abstract machine that is well suited for dealing with interrupts and I/O devices on PDP-11 processors. Unlike Concurrent PASCAL, in which the run-time kernel handles interrupts and I/O, Modula leaves support for devices in the programmer's domain. Thus new devices can be added without modifying the kernel. An I/O device is considered to be a process that is implemented in hardware. A software process can start an I/O operation and then execute a **doio** statement (which is like a **wait** except that it delays the invoker until the kernel receives an interrupt from the corresponding device). Thus interrupts are viewed as **signal** (**send** in Modula) operations generated by the hardware. Device modules are interface modules that control I/O devices. Each contains, in addition to some procedures, a *device process*, which starts I/O operations and executes **doio** statements to relinquish control of the processor (pending receipt of the corresponding I/O interrupt). The address of the interrupt vector for the device is declared in the heading of the device module, so that the compiler can do the necessary binding. Modula also has provisions for controlling the processor priority register, thus allowing a programmer to exploit the priority interrupt architecture of the processor when structuring programs.

A third novel aspect of Modula is that variables declared in interface modules can be exported. Exported variables can be referenced (but not modified) from outside the scope of their defining interface module. This allows concurrent access to these variables, which, of course, can lead to difficulty unless the programmer ensures that interference cannot occur. However, when used selectively, this feature increases the efficiency of programs that access such variables.

In summary, Modula is less constraining than Concurrent PASCAL, but requires the programmer to be more careful. Its specific strengths and weaknesses have been evaluated by Andrews [1979], Holden and Wand [1980], and Bernstein and Ensor [1981]. Wirth, Modula's designer, has gone on to develop Modula-2 [Wirth, 1982]. Modula-2 retains the basic modular structure of Modula, but provides more flexible facilities for concurrent programming and these facilities have less subtle semantics. In particular, Modula-2 provides coroutines and hence explicit transfer of control between processes. Using these, the programmer builds support for exclusion and condition synchronization, as required. In particular, the programmer can construct monitorlike modules.

3.5   Path expressions

Operations defined by a monitor are executed with mutual exclusion. Other synchronization of monitor procedures is realized by explicitly performing **wait** and **signal** operations on condition variables (or by some similar mechanism). Consequently, synchronization of monitor operations is realized by code scattered throughout the monitor. Some of this code, such as **wait** and **signal**, is visible to the programmer. Other code, such as the code ensuring mutual exclusion of monitor procedures, is not.

Another approach to defining a module subject to concurrent access is to provide a mechanism with which a programmer specifies, in *one* place in each module, all constraints on the execution of operations defined by that module. Implementation of the operations is separated from the specification of the constraints. Moreover, code to enforce the constraints is generated by a compiler. This is the approach taken in a class of synchronization mechanisms called *path expressions*.

Path expressions were first defined by Campbell and Habermann [1974]. Subsequent extensions and variations have also been proposed

[Habermann, 1975; Lauer and Campbell, 1975; Campbell, 1976; Flon and Habermann, 1976; Lauer and Shields, 1978; Andler, 1979]. Below, we describe one specific proposal [Campbell, 1976] that has been incorporated into Path PASCAL, an implemented systems programming language [Campbell and Kolstad, 1979].

When path expressions are used, a module that implements a resource has a structure like that of a monitor. It contains permanent variables, which store the state of the resource, and procedures, which realize operations on the resource. Path expressions in the header of each resource define constraints on the order in which operations are executed. No synchronization code is programmed in the procedures.

The syntax of a path expression is:

path *path_list* **end**

A *path_list* contains operation names and *path operators*. Path operators include ',' for concurrency, ';' for sequencing, '*n* : (*path_list*)' to specify up to *n* concurrent activations of *path_list*, and '[*path_list*]' to specify an unbounded number of concurrent activations of *path_list*.

For example, the path expression:

path *deposit, fetch* **end**

places no constraints on the order of execution of *deposit* and *fetch* and no constraints on the number of activations of either operation. This absence of synchronization constraints is equivalent to that specified by the path expressions

path [*deposit*], [*fetch*] **end**

or

path [*deposit, fetch*] **end**

(A useful application of the '[...]' operator will be shown later.) In contrast,

path *deposit*; *fetch* **end**

specifies that each *fetch* be preceded by a *deposit*; multiple activations of each operation can execute concurrently as long as the number of active or completed *fetch* operations never exceeds the number of completed *deposit* operations. A module implementing a bounded buffer of size one might well contain the path:

path 1 : (*deposit*; *fetch*) **end**

to specify that the first invoked operation be a *deposit*, that each *deposit* be followed by a *fetch*, and that at most one instance of the path '*deposit*; *fetch*' be active – in short, that *deposit* and *fetch* alternate and are mutually exclusive. Synchronization constraints for a bounded buffer of size N are specified by:

> **path** N : (1 : (*deposit*); 1 : (*fetch*)) **end**

This ensures that:

(i) activations of *deposit* are mutually exclusive;

(ii) activations of *fetch* are mutually exclusive;

(iii) each activation of *fetch* is preceded by a completed *deposit*; and

(iv) the number of completed *deposit* operations is never more than N greater than the number of completed *fetch* operations.

The bounded buffers we have been using for *OPSYS*, our batch operating system, would be defined by:

```
module buffer(T);

  path N : (1 : (deposit); 1 : (fetch)) end;

  var { the variables satisfy the invariant IB (see Sec. 4.3)
        with size equal to the number of executions of
        deposit minus the number of executions of fetch }
    slots : array [0..N − 1 ] of T;
    head, tail : 0..N − 1;

  procedure deposit(p : T);
    begin
      slots[tail] := p;
      tail := (tail + 1) mod N
    end;

  procedure fetch(var it : T);
    begin
      it := slots[head];
      head := (head + 1) mod N
    end;

  begin
    head := 0; tail := 0
  end
```

Note that one *deposit* and one *fetch* can proceed concurrently, which was not possible in the *buffer* monitor given in Figure 6. For this reason, there is no variable *size* because it would have been subject to concurrent access.

As a last example, consider the readers/writers problem [Courtois *et al.*, 1971]. In this problem, processes read or write records in a shared data base. To ensure that processes read consistent data, either an unbounded number of concurrent *reads* or a single *write* may be executed at any time. The path expression:

path 1 : ([*read*], *write*) **end**

specifies this constraint. (Actually, this specifies the 'weak reader's preference' solution to the readers/writers problem: readers can prevent writers from accessing the database.)

Path expressions are strongly motivated by, and based on, the operational approach to program semantics. A path expression defines all legal sequences of the operation executions for a resource. This set of sequences can be viewed as a formal language, in which each sentence is a sequence of operation names. In light of this, the resemblance between path expressions and regular expressions should not be surprising.

While path expressions provide an elegant notation for expressing synchronization constraints described operationally, they are poorly suited for specifying condition synchronization [Bloom, 1979]. Whether an operation can be executed might depend on the state of a resource in a way not directly related to the history of operations already performed. Certain variants of the readers/writers problem (e.g., writers preference, fair access for readers and writers) require access to the state of the resource – in this case, the number of waiting readers and waiting writers – in order to implement the desired synchronization. The *shortest_next_allocator* monitor of Section 3.4.1 is an example of a resource in which a parameter's value determines whether execution of an operation (*request*) should be permitted to continue. In fact, most resources that involve scheduling require access to parameters and/or to state information when making synchronization decisions. In order to use path expressions to specify solutions to such problems, additional mechanisms must be introduced. In some cases, definition of additional operations on the resource is sufficient; in other cases 'queue' resources, which allow a process to suspend itself and be reactivated by a 'scheduler,' must be added. The desire to realize condition synchronization using path expressions has motivated many of the proposed extensions. Regrettably, none of these extensions have solved the entire problem in a way consistent with the elegance and simplicity of the original proposal. However, path expressions have proved useful for specifying the semantics of concurrent computations [Shields, 1979; Shaw, 1980; Best, 1982].

4   Synchronization primitives based on message passing

Critical regions, monitors, and path expressions are one outgrowth of semaphores; they all provide structured ways to control access to shared variables. A different outgrowth is *message passing*, which can be viewed as extending semaphores to convey data as well as to implement synchronization. When message passing is used for communication and synchronization, processes send and receive messages instead of reading and writing shared variables. Communication is accomplished because a process, upon receiving a message, obtains values from some sender process. Synchronization is accomplished because a message can be received only after it has been sent, which constrains the order in which these two events can occur.

A message is sent by executing:

> **send** *expression_list*
> **to** *destination_designator.*

The message contains the values of the expressions in *expression_list* at the time **send** is executed. The *destination_designator* gives the programmer control over where the message goes, and hence over which statements can receive it. A message is received by executing:

> **receive** *variable_list*
> **from** *source_designator*

where *variable_list* is a list of variables. The *source_designator* gives the programmer control over where the message came from, and hence over which statements could have sent it. Receipt of a message causes, first, assignment of the values in the message to the variables in *variable_list* and, second, subsequent destruction of the message.[19]

Designing message-passing primitives involves making choices about the form and semantics of these general commands. Two main issues must be addressed: How are source and destination designators specified? How is communication synchronized? Common alternative solutions for these issues are described in the next two sections. Then higher level message-passing constructs, semantic issues, and languages based on message passing are discussed.

---

[19] A broadcast can be modeled by the concurrent execution of a collection of **sends**, each sending the message to a different destination. A nondestructive **receive** can be modeled by a **receive**, immediately followed by a **send**.

4.1 Specifying channels of communication

Taken together, the destination and source designators define a *communications channel*. Various schemes have been proposed for naming channels. The simplest channel-naming scheme is for process names to serve as source and destination designators. We refer to this as *direct naming*. Thus:

send *card* **to** *executer*

sends a message that can be received only by the *executer* process. Similarly:

receive *line* **from** *executer*

permits receipt only of a message sent by the executer process.

Direct naming is easy to implement and to use. It makes it possible for a process to control the times at which it receives messages from each other process. Our simple batch operating system might be programmed using direct naming as shown in Figure 8.

```
program OPSYS;

  process reader;
    var card : cardimage;
    loop
      read card from cardreader;
      send card to executer
      end
    end;

  process executer;
    var card : cardimage; line : lineimage;
    loop
      receive card from reader;
      process card and generate line;
      send line to printer
      end
    end;

  process printer;
    var line : lineimage;
    loop
      receive line from executer;
      print line on lineprinter
      end
    end

end
```

Figure 8 Batch operating system with message passing.

The batch operating system also illustrates an important paradigm for process interaction – a pipeline. A *pipeline* is a collection of concurrent processes in which the output of each process is used as the input to another. Information flows analogously to the way liquid flows in a pipeline. Here, information flows from the *reader* process to the *executer* process and then from the *executer* process to the *printer* process. Direct naming is particularly well suited for programming pipelines.

Another important paradigm for process interaction is the *client/server relationship*. Some *server* processes render a service to some *client* processes. A client can request that a service be performed by sending a message to one of these servers. A server repeatedly receives a request for service from a client, performs that service, and (if necessary) returns a completion message to that client.

The interaction between an I/O driver process and processes that use it – for example, the lineprinter driver and the *printer* process in our operating system example – illustrates this paradigm. The lineprinter driver is a server; it repeatedly receives requests to print a line on the printer, starts that I/O operation, and then awaits the interrupt signifying completion of the I/O operation. Depending on the application, it might also send a completion message to the client after the line has been printed.

Unfortunately, direct naming is not always well suited for client/server interaction. Ideally, the **receive** in a server should allow receipt of a message from any client. If there is only one client, then direct naming will work well; difficulties arise if there is more than one client because, at the very least, a **receive** would be required for each. Similarly, if there is more than one server (and all servers are identical), then the **send** in a client should produce a message that can be received by *any* server. Again, this cannot be accomplished easily with direct naming. Therefore, a more sophisticated scheme for defining communications channels is required.

One such scheme is based on the use of *global names*, sometimes called *mailboxes*. A mailbox can appear as the destination designator in any process' **send** statements and as the source designator in any process' **receive** statements. Thus messages sent to a given mailbox can be received by any process that executes a **receive** naming that mailbox.

This scheme is particularly well suited for programming client/server interactions. Clients send their service requests to a single mailbox; servers receive service requests from that mailbox. Unfortunately, implementing mailboxes can be quite costly without a specialized communications network [Gelernter and Bernstein, 1982]. When a message is sent, it must be relayed to all sites where a **receive** could be performed on the destination mailbox; then, after a message has been received, all these sites must be notified that the message is no longer available for receipt.

The special case of mailboxes, in which a mailbox name can appear as the source designator in **receive** statements in one process only, does not suffer these implementation difficulties. Such mailboxes are often called *ports* [Balzer, 1971]. Ports are simple to implement, since all **receives** that designate a port occur in the same process. Moreover, ports allow a straightforward solution to the multiple-clients/single-server problem. (The multiple-clients/multiple-server problem, however, is not easily solved with ports.)

To summarize, when direct naming is used, communication is one to one since each communicating process names the other. When port naming is used, communication can be many to one since each port has one receiver but may have many senders. The most general scheme is global naming, which can be many to many. Direct naming and port naming are special cases of global naming; they limit the kinds of interactions that can be programmed directly, but are more efficient to implement.

Source and destination designators can be fixed at compile time, called *static channel naming*, or they can be computed at run time, called *dynamic channel naming*. Although widely used, static naming presents two problems. First, it precludes a program from communicating along channels not known at compile time, and thus limits the program's ability to exist in a changing environment. For example, this would preclude implementing the I/O redirection or pipelines provided by UNIX [Ritchie and Thompson, 1974].[20] The second problem is this: if a program might *ever* need access to a channel, it must permanently have the access. In many applications, such as file systems, it is more desirable to allocate communications channels to resources (such as files) dynamically.

To support dynamic channel naming, an underlying, static channel-naming scheme could be augmented by variables that contain source or destination designators. These variables can be viewed as containing *capabilities* for the communications channel [Baskett *et al.*, 1977; Solomon and Finkel, 1979; Andrews, 1982].

4.2 Synchronization

Another important property of message-passing statements concerns whether their execution could cause a delay. A statement is *nonblocking* if its execution never delays its invoker; otherwise the statement is said to

---

[20] Although in UNIX most commands read from and write to the user's terminal, one can specify that a command read its input from a file or write its output to a file. Also, one can specify that commands be connected in a pipeline. These options are provided by a dynamic channel-naming scheme that is transparent to the implementation of each command.

be *blocking*. In some message-passing schemes, messages are buffered between the time they are sent and received. Then, if the buffer is full when a **send** is executed, there are two options: the **send** might delay until there is space in the buffer for the message, or the **send** might return a code to the invoker, indicating that, because the buffer was full, the message could not be sent. Similarly, execution of a **receive**, when no message that satisfies the source designator is available for receipt, might either cause a delay or terminate with a code, signifying that no message was available.

If the system has an effectively unbounded buffer capacity, then a process is never delayed when executing a **send**. This is variously called *asynchronous message passing* and *send no-wait*. Asynchronous message passing allows a sender to get arbitrarily far ahead of a receiver. Consequently, when a message is received, it contains information about the sender's state that is not necessarily still its current state. At the other extreme, with no buffering, execution of a **send** is always delayed until a corresponding[21] **receive** is executed; then the message is transferred and both proceed. This is called *synchronous message passing*. When synchronous message passing is used, a message exchange represents a synchronization point in the execution of both the sender and receiver. Therefore, the message received will always correspond to the sender's current state. Moreover, when the **send** terminates, the sender can make assertions about the state of the receiver. Between these two extremes is *buffered message passing*, in which the buffer has finite bounds. Buffered message passing allows the sender to get ahead of the receiver, but not arbitrarily far ahead.

The blocking form of the **receive** statement is the most common, because a receiving process often has nothing else to do while awaiting receipt of a message. However, most languages and operating systems also provide a nonblocking **receive** or a means to test whether execution of a **receive** would block. This enables a process to receive all available messages and then select one to process (effectively, to schedule them).

Sometimes, further control over which messages can be received is provided. The statement:

receive *variable_list* **from** *source_designator* **when** B

permits receipt of only those messages that make B true. This allows a process to 'peek' at the contents of a delivered message before receiving it. Although this facility is not necessary – a process can always receive and store copies of messages until appropriate to act on them, as shown in the shortest-next-allocator example at the end of this section – the

---

[21] Correspondence is determined by the source and destination designators.

conditional receive makes possible concise solutions to many synchronization problems. Two languages that provide such a facility, PLITS and SR, are described in Section 4.5.

A blocking **receive** implicitly implements synchronization between sender and receiver because the receiver is delayed until after the message is sent. To implement such synchronization with nonblocking **receive**, busy-waiting is required. However, blocking message-passing statements can achieve the same semantic effects as non-blocking ones by using what we shall call *selective communications*, which is based on Dijkstra's guarded commands [Dijkstra, 1975].

In a selective-communications statement, a *guarded command* has the form:

guard $\longrightarrow$ *statement*

The guard consists of a Boolean expression, optionally followed by a message-passing statement. The guard *succeeds* if the Boolean expression is true and executing the message-passing statement would not cause a delay; the guard *fails* if the Boolean expression is false; the guard (temporarily) neither succeeds nor fails if the Boolean expression is true but the message-passing statement cannot yet be executed without causing delay. The alternative statement:

if $G1 \longrightarrow S1$
$\square$ $G2 \longrightarrow S2$

...

$\square$ $Gn \longrightarrow Sn$
fi

is executed as follows. If at least one guard succeeds, one of them, Gi, is selected nondeterministically; the message-passing statement in Gi is executed (if present); then Si, the statement following the guard, is executed. If all guards fail, the command aborts. If all guards neither succeed nor fail, execution is delayed until some guard succeeds. (Obviously, deadlock could result.) Execution of the iterative statement is the same as for the alternative statement, except selection and execution of a guarded command is repeated until all guards fail, at which time the iterative statement terminates rather than aborts.

To illustrate the use of selective communications, we implement a *buffer* process, which stores data produced by a *producer* process and allows these data to be retrieved by a *consumer* process:[22]

---

[22] Even if message passing is asynchronous, such a buffer may still be required if there are multiple producers or consumers.

```
process buffer;

    var slots : array [0..N − 1] of T;
        head, tail : 0..N − 1;
        size : 0..N;

    head := 0;   tail := 0;   size := 0;

    do size < N; receive slots[tail] from producer →
        size := size + 1;
        tail := (tail + 1) mod N

    □ size > 0;   send slots[head] to consumer →
        size := size − 1;
        head := (head + 1) mod N

    od

    end
```

The producer and consumer are as follows:

```
process producer;
    var stuff : T;
    loop
        generate stuff;
        send stuff to buffer
        end
    end;

process consumer;
    var stuff : T;
    loop
        receive stuff from buffer;
        use stuff
        end
    end
```

If **send** statements cannot appear in guards, selective communication is straightforward to implement. A delayed process determines which Boolean expressions in guards are true, and then awaits arrival of a message that allows execution of the **receive** in one of these guards. (If the guard did not contain a **receive**, the process would not be delayed.) If both **send** and **receive** statements can appear in guards,[23] implementation is much more costly because a process needs to negotiate with other processes to determine if they can communicate, and these processes could also be in the middle of such a negotiation. For example, three processes could be executing selective-communications statements in which

---

[23] Also note that allowing only **send** statements in guards is not very useful.

any pair could communicate; the problem is to decide which pair communicates and which one remains delayed. Development of protocols that solve this problem in an efficient and deadlock-free way remains an active research area [Schwartz, 1978; Silberschatz, 1979; Bernstein, 1980; Van de Snepscheut, 1981; Schneider, 1982; Reif and Spirakis, 1982].

Unfortunately, if **send** statements are not permitted to appear in guards, programming with blocking **send** and blocking **receive** becomes somewhat more complex. In the example above, the *buffer* process above would be changed to first wait for a message from the *consumer* requesting data (a **receive** would appear in the second guard instead of the **send**) and then to send the data. The difference in the protocol used by this new *buffer* process when interacting with the *consumer* and that used when interacting with the *producer* process is misleading; a producer/consumer relationship is inherently symmetric, and the program should mirror this fact.

Some process relationships are inherently asymmetric. In client/server interactions, the server often takes different actions in response to different kinds of client requests. For example, a shortest-job-next allocator (see Section 3.4.1) that receives 'allocation' requests on a *request_port* and 'release' requests on a *release_port* can be programmed using message passing as follows:

> **process** *shortest_next_allocator*;
>
> > **var** *free* : Boolean;
> > *time* : integer;
> > *client_id* : *process_id*;
> > declarations of a priority queue and other local variables;
>
> *free* := *true*;
>
> **do** *true*; **receive** (*time, client_id*) **from** *request_port* $\longrightarrow$
> > **if** *free* $\longrightarrow$ *free* := *false*;
> > > **send** *allocation* **to** *client_id*
> > $\square$ **not** *free* $\longrightarrow$ *save client_id on priority queue ordered by time*
> > **fi**
>
> $\square$ **not** *free;* **receive** *release* **from** *release_port* $\longrightarrow$
> > **if not** *priority queue empty* $\longrightarrow$
> > > *remove client_id with smallest time from queue;*
> > > **send** *allocation* **to** *client_id*
> > $\square$ *priority queue empty* $\longrightarrow$ *free* := *true*
> > **fi**
>
> **od**
>
> **end**

A client makes a request by executing:

> **send** (*time*, *my_id*) **to** *request_port*;
> **receive** *allocation* **from** *shortest_next_allocator*

and indicates that it has finished using the resource by executing:

> **send** *release* **to** *release_port*

4.3   Higher level message-passing constructs

4.3.1   Remote procedure call

The primitives of the previous section are sufficient to program any type of process interaction using message passing. To program client/server interactions, however, both the client and server execute two message-passing statements: the client a **send** followed by a **receive**, and the server a **receive** followed by a **send**. Because this type of interaction is very common, higher level statements that directly support it have been proposed. These are termed *remote procedure call* statements because of the interface that they present: a client 'calls' a procedure that is executed on a potentially remote machine by a server.

When remote procedure calls are used, a client interacts with a server by means of a **call** statement. This statement has a form similar to that used for a procedure call in a sequential language:

> **call** *service*(*value_args*; *result_args*)

The *service* is really the name of a channel. If direct naming is used, *service* designates the server process; if port or mailbox naming is used, *service* might designate the kind of service requested. Remote **call** is executed as follows: the value arguments are sent to the appropriate server, and the calling process delays until both the service has been performed and the results have been returned and assigned to the result arguments. Thus such a **call** could be translated into a **send**, immediately followed by a **receive**. Note that the client cannot forget to wait for the results of a requested service.

There are two basic approaches to specifying the server side of a remote procedure call. In the first, the remote procedure is a declaration, like a procedure in a sequential language:[24]

---

[24] This is another reason this kind of interaction is termed 'remote procedure call.'

remote procedure *service* (**in** *value_parameters*; **out** *result_parameters*)
   body
   end

However, such a procedure declaration is implemented as a process. This process, the server, awaits receipt of a message containing value arguments from some calling process, assigns them to the value parameters, executes its body, and then returns a *reply message* containing the values of the result parameters. Note that even if there are no value or result parameters, the synchronization resulting from the implicit **send** and **receive** occurs. A remote procedure declaration can be implemented as a single process that repeatedly loops [Andrews, 1982], in which case **calls** to the same remote procedure would execute sequentially. Alternatively, a new process can be treated for each execution of **call** [Brinch Hansen, 1978; Cook, 1980; Liskov and Scheifler, 1982]; these could execute concurrently, meaning that the different instances of the server might need to synchronize if they share variables.

In the second approach to specifying the server side, the remote procedure is a statement, which can be placed anywhere any other statement can be placed. Such a statement has the general form

accept *service*(**in** *value_parameters*; **out** *result_parameters*) → *body*

Execution of this statement delays the server until a message resulting from a **call** to the *service* has arrived. Then the body is executed, using the values of the value parameters and any other variables accessible in the scope of the statement. Upon termination, a reply message, containing the values of the result parameters, is sent to the calling process. The server then continues execution.[25]

When **accept** or similar statements are used to specify the server side, remote procedure call is called a *rendezvous* [Department of Defense, 1981] because the client and server 'meet' for the duration of the execution of the body of the **accept** statement and then go their separate ways. One advantage of the rendezvous approach is that client **calls** may be serviced at times of the server's choosing; **accept** statements, for example, can be interleaved or nested. A second advantage is that the

---

[25] Different semantics result depending on whether the reply message is sent by a synchronous or by an asynchronous **send**. A synchronous **send** delays the server until the results have been received by the caller. Therefore, when the server continues, it can assert that the reply message has been received and that the result parameters have been assigned to the result arguments. Use of asynchronous **send** does not allow this, but does not delay the server, either.

server can achieve different effects for **calls** to the same service by using more than one **accept** statement, each with a different body. (For example, the first **accept** of a service might perform initialization.) The final, and most important, advantage is that the server can provide more than one kind of service. In particular, **accept** is often combined with selective communications to enable a server to wait for and select one of several requests to service [U.S. Department of Defense, 1981; Andrews, 1981]. This is illustrated in the following implementation of the bounded buffer:

```
process buffer;

    var slots : array [0..N − 1] of T;
        head, tail : 0..N − 1;
        size : 0..N;

    head := 0;   tail := 0;   size := 0;

    do size < N; accept deposit(in value : T) →
        slots[tail] := value;
        size := size + 1;
        tail := (tail + 1) mod N

    □ size > 0; accept fetch(out value : T) →
        value := slots[head];
        size := size − 1;
        head := (head + 1) mod N

    od

    end.
```

The *buffer* process implements two operations: *deposit* and *fetch*. The first is invoked by a producer by executing:

```
call deposit(stuff)
```

The second is invoked by a consumer by executing:

```
call fetch(stuff)
```

Note that *deposit* and *fetch* are handled by the *buffer* process in a symmetric manner, even though **send** statements do not appear in guards, because remote procedure calls always involve two messages, one in each direction. Note also that *buffer* can be used by multiple producers and multiple consumers.

Although remote procedure call is a useful, high-level mechanism for client/server interactions, not all such interactions can be directly programmed by using it. For example, the *shortest_next_allocator* of the previous section still requires two client/server exchanges to service allocation requests because the allocator must look at the parameters of a request in order to decide if the request should be delayed. Thus the client must use one operation to transmit the request arguments and another to wait for an allocation. If there are a small number of different scheduling priorities, this can be overcome by associating a different server operation with each priority level. Ada [U.S. Department of Defense, 1981] supports this nicely by means of arrays of operations. In general, however, a mechanism is required to enable a server to accept a **call** that minimizes some function of the parameters of the called operation. SR [Andrews, 1981] includes such a mechanism (see Section 4.5.4).

4.3.2   Atomic transactions

An often-cited advantage of multiple-processor systems is that they can be made resilient to failures. Designing programs that exhibit this fault tolerance is not a simple matter. While a discussion of how to design fault-tolerant programs is beyond the scope of this survey, we comment briefly on how fault-tolerance issues have affected the design of higher level message-passing statements.[26]

Remote procedure call provides a clean way to program client/ server interactions. Ideally, we would like a remote **call**, like a procedure call in a sequential programming notation, to have *exactly once* semantics: each remote **call** should terminate only after the named remote procedure has been executed exactly once by the server [Nelson, 1981; Spector, 1982]. Unfortunately, a failure may mean that a client is forever delayed awaiting the response to a remote **call**. This might occur if:

(i) the message signifying the remote procedure invocation is lost by the network, or

(ii) the reply message is lost, or

(iii) the server crashes during execution of the remote procedure (but before the reply message is sent).

This difficulty can be overcome by attaching a time-out interval to the remote **call**; if no response is received by the client before the time-out interval expires, the client presumes that the server has failed and takes some action.

Deciding what action to take after a detected failure can be difficult. In Case (i) above, the correct action would be to retransmit the message. In Case (ii), however, retransmittal would cause a second execution of the remote procedure body. This is undesirable unless the procedure is *idempotent*, meaning that the repeated execution has the same effect as a

---

[26] For a general discussion, the interested reader is referred to Kohler 1981.

single execution. Finally, the correct action in Case (iii) would depend on exactly how much of the remote procedure body was executed, what parts of the computation were lost, what parts must be undone, etc. In some cases, this could be handled by saving state information, called *checkpoints*, and programming special recovery actions. A more general solution would be to view execution of a remote procedure in terms of atomic transactions.

An *atomic transaction* [Lomet, 1977; Reed, 1979; Lampson, 1981] is an all-or-nothing computation – either it installs a complete collection of changes to some variables or it installs no changes, even if interrupted by a failure. Moreover, atomic transactions are assumed to be indivisible in the sense that partial execution of an atomic transaction is not visible to any concurrently executing atomic transaction. The first attribute is called *failure atomicity*, and the second *synchronization atomicity*.

Given atomic transactions, it is possible to construct a remote procedure call mechanism with *at most once* semantics – receipt of a reply message means that the remote procedure was executed exactly once, and failure to receive a reply message means the remote procedure invocation had no (permanent) effect [Liskov and Scheifler, 1982; Spector, 1982]. This is done by making execution of a remote procedure an atomic transaction that is allowed to 'commit' only after the reply has been received by the client. In some circumstances, even more complex mechanisms are useful. For example, when nested remote **calls** occur, failure while executing a higher level call should cause the effects of lower level (i.e., nested) calls to be undone, even if those calls have already completed [Liskov and Scheifler, 1982].

The main consideration in the design of these mechanisms is that it may not be possible for a process to see system data in an inconsistent state following partial execution of a remote procedure. The use of atomic transactions is one way to do this, but it is quite expensive [Lampson and Sturgis, 1979; Liskov, 1981]. Other techniques to ensure the invisibility of inconsistent states have been proposed [Lynch, 1981; Schlichting and Schneider, 1981], and this remains an active area of research.

4.4   An axiomatic view of message passing

When message passing is used for communication and synchronization, processes usually do not share variables. Nonetheless, interference can still arise. In order to prove that a collection of processes achieves a common goal, it is usually necessary to make assertions in one process about the state of others. Processes learn about each other's state by exchanging messages. In particular, receipt of a message not only causes the transfer of values from sender to receiver but also facilitates the 'transfer' of a predicate. This allows the receiver to make assertions about the state of the sender, such as about how far the sender has progressed in its computation. Clearly, subsequent execution by the sender might invalidate such an assertion. Thus it is possible for the sender to interfere with an assertion in the receiver.

It turns out that two distinct kinds of interference must be considered when message passing is used [Schlichting and Schneider, 1982a]. The first is similar to that occurring when shared variables are used: assertions made in one process about the state of another must not be invalidated by concurrent execution. The second form of interference arises only when asynchronous or buffered message passing is used. If a sender 'transfers' a predicate with a message, the 'transferred' predicate must be true when the message is received: receipt of a message reveals information about the state of the sender at the time that the message was sent, which is not necessarily the sender's current state.

The second type of interference is not possible when synchronous message passing is used, because, after sending a message, the sender does not progress until the message has been received. This is a good reason to prefer the use of synchronous **send** over asynchronous **send** (and to prefer synchronous **send** for sending the reply message in a remote procedure body). One often hears the argument that asynchronous **send** does not restrict parallelism as much as synchronous **send** and so it is preferable. However, the amount of parallelism that can be exhibited by a program is determined by program structure and not by choice of communications primitives. For example, addition of an intervening buffer process allows the sender to be executed concurrently with the receiving process. Choosing a communications primitive merely establishes whether the programmer will have to do the additional work (of defining more processes) to allow a high degree of parallel activity or will have to do additional work (of using the primitives in a highly disciplined way) to control the amount of parallelism. Nevertheless, a variety of 'safe' uses of asynchronous message passing have been identified: the 'transfer' of monotonic predicates and the use of 'acknowledgment' protocols, for example. These schemes are studied in Schlichting and Schneider [1982b], where they are shown to follow directly from simple techniques to avoid the second kind of interference.

Formal proof techniques for various types of message-passing primitives have been developed. Axioms for buffered, asynchronous message passing were first proposed in connection with Gypsy [Good *et al.*, 1979]. Several people have developed proof systems for synchronous message-passing statements – in particular the input and output commands in CSP [Apt *et al.*, 1980; Cousot and Cousot, 1980; Levin and Gries, 1981; Misra and Chandy, 1981; Soundararajan, 1981; Lamport and Schneider, 1982; Schlichting and Schneider, 1982a]. Also, several people have developed proof rules for asynchronous message passing

[Misra *et al.*, 1982; Schlichting and Schneider, 1982b], and proof rules for remote procedures and rendezvous [Barringer and Mearns, 1982; Gerth, 1982; Gerth *et al.*, 1982; Schlichting and Schneider, 1982a].

4.5 Programming notations based on message passing

A large number of concurrent programming languages have been proposed that use message passing for communication and synchronization. This should not be too surprising; because the two major message-passing design issues – channel naming and synchronization – are orthogonal, the various alternatives for each can be combined in many ways. In the following, we summarize the important characteristics of four languages: CSP, PLITS, Ada, and SR. Each is well documented in the literature and was innovative in some regard. Also, each reflects a different combination of the two design alternatives. Some other languages that have been influential – Gypsy, Distributed Processes, StarMod and Argus – are then briefly discussed.

4.5.1 Communicating Sequential Processes

Communicating Sequential Processes (CSP) [Hoare, 1978] is a programming notation based on synchronous message passing and selective communications. The concepts embodied in CSP have greatly influenced subsequent work in concurrent programming language design and the design of distributed programs.

In CSP, processes are denoted by a variant of the **cobegin** statement. Processes may share read-only variables, but use input/output commands for synchronization and communication. Direct (and static) channel naming is used and message passing is synchronous.

An *output command* in CSP has the form:

destination!expression

where *destination* is a process name and *expression* is a simple or structured value. An *input command* has the form:

source?target

where *source* is a process name and *target* is a simple or structured variable local to the process containing the input command. The commands:

Pr!expression

in process *Ps* and:

Ps?target

in process *Pr match* if *target* and *expression* have the same type. Two processes communicate if they execute a matching pair of input/output commands. The result of communication is that the expression's value is assigned to the target variable; both processes then proceed independently and concurrently.

A restricted form of selective communications statement is supported by CSP. Input commands can appear in guards of alternative and iterative statements, but output commands may not. This allows an efficient implementation, but makes certain kinds of process interaction awkward to express, as was discussed in Section 4.2.

By combining communication commands with alternative and iterative statements, CSP provides a powerful mechanism for programming process interaction. Its strength is that it is based on a simple idea – input/output commands – that is carefully integrated with a few other mechanisms. CSP is not a complete concurrent programming language, nor was it intended to be. For example, static direct naming is often awkward to use. Fortunately, this deficiency is easily overcome by using ports; how to do so was discussed briefly by Hoare [Hoare, 1978] and is described in detail by Kieburtz and Silberschatz [1979]. Recently, two languages based on CSP have also been described [Jazayeri *et al.*, 1980; Roper and Barter, 1981].

4.5.2 PLITS

PLITS, an acronym for 'Programming Language In The Sky,' was developed at the University of Rochester [Feldman, 1979]. The design of PLITS is based on the premise that it is inherently difficult to combine a high degree of parallelism with data sharing and therefore message passing is the appropriate means for process interaction in a distributed system. Part of an ongoing research project in programming language design and distributed computation, PLITS is being used to program applications that are executed on Rochester's Intelligent Gateway (RIG) computer network [Ball *et al.*, 1976].

A PLITS program consists of a number of modules; *active modules* are processes. Message passing is the sole means for intermodule interaction. So as not to restrict parallelism, message passing is asynchronous. A module sends a message containing the values of some expressions to a module *modname* by executing:

send *expressions* **to** *modname* [**about** *key*]

The 'about *key*' phrase is optional. If included, it attaches an identifying *transaction key* to the message. This key can then be used to identify the message uniquely, or the same key can be attached to several different messages to allow messages to be grouped.

A module receives messages by executing:

> **receive** *variables* [**from** *modname*]
> [**about** *key*]

If the last two phrases are omitted, execution of **receive** delays the executing module until the arrival of any message. If the phrase '**from** *modname*' is included, execution is delayed until a message from the named module arrives. Finally, if the phrase '**about** *key*' is included, the module is delayed until a message with the indicated transaction key has arrived.

By combining the options in **send** and **receive** in different ways, a programmer can exert a variety of controls over communication. When both the sending and receiving modules name each other, communication is direct. The effect of port naming is realized by having a receiving module not name the source module. Finally, the use of transaction keys allows the receiver to select a particular kind of message; this provides a facility almost as powerful as attaching '**when** *B*' to a **receive** statement.

In PLITS, execution of **receive** can cause blocking. PLITS also provides primitives to test whether messages with certain field values or transaction keys are available for receipt; this enables a process to avoid blocking when there is no message available.

PLITS programs interface to the operating systems of the processors that make up RIG. Each host system provides device access, a file system, and job control. A communications kernel on each machine provides the required support for interprocessor communication.

4.5.3   Ada

Ada[27] [US Department of Defense, 1981] is a language intended for programming embedded real-time, process-control systems. Because of this, Ada includes facilities for multiprocessing and device control. With respect to concurrent programming, Ada's main innovation is the rendezvous form of remote procedure call.

Processes in Ada are called *tasks*. A task is activated when the block containing its declaration is entered. Tasks may be nested and may interact by using shared variables declared in enclosing blocks. (No

---

[27] Ada is a trademark of the U.S. Department of Defense.

special mechanisms for synchronizing access to shared variables are provided.)

The primary mechanism for process interaction is the remote procedure call. Remote procedures in Ada are called *entries*; they are ports into a server process specified by means of an **accept** statement, which is similar in syntax and semantics to the **accept** statement described in Section 4.3.1. Entries are invoked by execution of a remote **call**. Selective communications is supported using the **select** statement, which is like an alternative statement.

Both **call** and **accept** statements are blocking. Since Ada programs might have to meet real-time response constraints, the language includes mechanisms to prevent or control the length of time that a process is delayed when it becomes blocked. Blocking on **call** can be avoided by using the *conditional entry call*, which performs a **call** only if a rendezvous is possible immediately. Blocking on **accept** can be avoided by using a mechanism that enables a server to determine the number of waiting **calls**. Blocking on **select** can be avoided by means of the **else** guard, which is true if none of the other guards are. Finally, a task can suspend execution for a time interval by means of the **delay** statement. This statement can be used within a guard of **select** to ensure that a process is eventually awakened.

In order to allow the programmer to control I/O devices, Ada allows entries to be bound to interrupt vector locations. Interrupts become **calls** to those entries and can therefore be serviced by a task that receives the interrupt by means of an **accept** statement.

Since its inception, Ada has generated controversy [Hoare, 1981], much of which is not related to concurrency. However, few applications using the concurrent programming features have been programmed, and at the time of this writing no compiler for full Ada has been validated. Implementation of some of the concurrent programming aspects of Ada is likely to be hard. A paper by Welsh and Lister [1981] compares the concurrency aspects of Ada to CSP and Distributed Processes [Brinch Hansen, 1978]; Wegner and Smolka [1983] compare Ada, CSP, and monitors.

4.5.4 SR

SR (Synchronizing Resources) [Andrews, 1981, 1982], like Ada, uses the rendezvous form of remote procedure call and port naming. However, there are notable differences between the languages, as described below. A compiler for SR has been implemented on PDP-11 processors and the language is being used in the construction of a UNIX-like network operating system.

An SR program consists of one or more *resources*.[28] The resource

---

[28] SR's resources are not to be confused with resources in conditional critical regions.

construct supports both control of process interaction and data abstraction. (In contrast, Ada has two distinct constructs for this – the task and the package.) Resources contain one or more processes. Processes interact by using *operations*, which are similar to Ada entries. Also, processes in the same resource may interact by means of shared variables.

Unlike Ada, operations may be invoked by either **send**, which is nonblocking, or **call**, which is blocking. (The server that implements an operation can require a particular form of invocation, if necessary.) Thus both asynchronous message passing and remote **call** are supported. Operations may be named either statically in the program text or dynamically by means of capability variables, which are variables having fields whose values are the names of operations. A process can therefore have a changing set of communication channels.

In SR, operations are specified by the **in** statement, which also supports selective communications. Each guard in an **in** statement has the form:

$$op\_name(parameters) \ [\textbf{and } B] \ [\textbf{by } A]$$

where B is an optional Boolean expression and A is an optional arithmetic expression. The phrase '**and** B' allows selection of the operation to be dependent on the value of B, which may contain references to parameters. The phrase '**by** A' controls which invocation of *op_name* is selected if more than one invocation is pending that satisfies B. This can be used to express scheduling constraints succinctly. For example, it permits a compact solution to the shortest-job-next allocation problem discussed earlier. Although somewhat expensive to implement because it requires reevaluation of A whenever a selection is made, this facility turns out to be less costly to use than explicitly programmed scheduling queues, if the expected number of pending invocations is small (which is usually the case).

Operations may also be declared to be *procedures*. In SR, a procedure is short-hand for a process that repeatedly executes an **in** statement. Thus such operations are executed sequentially.

To support device control, SR provides a variant of the resource called a *real resource*. A real resource is similar to a Modula device module: it can contain device-driver processes and it allows variables to be bound to device-register addresses. Operations in real resources can be bound to interrupt vector locations. A hardware interrupt is treated as a **send** to such an operation; interrupts are processed by means of **in** statements.

4.5.5 Some other language notations based on message passing

Gypsy [Good *et al.*, 1979], one of the first high-level languages based on message passing, uses mailbox naming and buffered message passing. A major focus of Gypsy was the development of a programming language well suited for constructing verifiable systems. It has been used to implement special-purpose systems for single- and multiprocessor architectures.

Distributed Processes (DP) [Brinch Hansen, 1978] was the first language to be based on remote procedure calls. It can be viewed as a language that implements monitors by means of active processes rather than collections of passive procedures. In DP, remote procedures are specified as externally callable procedures declared along with a host process and shared variables. When a remote procedure is called, a server process is created to execute the body of the procedure. The server processes created for different calls and the host process execute with mutual exclusion. The servers and host synchronize by means of a variant of conditional critical regions. An extension of DP that employs the rendezvous form of remote procedure call and thus has a more efficient implementation is described by Mao and Yeh [1980].

StarMod [Cook, 1980] synthesizes aspects of Modula and Distributed Processes: it borrows modularization ideas from Modula and communication ideas from Distributed Processes. A module contains one or more processes and, optionally, variables shared by those processes. Synchronization within a module is provided by semaphores. Processes in different modules interact by means of remote procedure call; StarMod provides both remote procedures and rendezvous for implementing the server side. In StarMod, as in SR, both **send** and **call** can be used to initiate communication, the choice being dictated by whether the invoked operation returns values.

Argus [Liskov and Scheifler, 1982] also borrows ideas from Distributed Processes – remote procedures implemented by dynamically created processes, which synchronize using critical regions – but goes much further. It has extensive support for programming atomic transactions. The language also includes exception handling and recovery mechanisms, which are invoked if failures occur during execution of atomic transactions. Argus is higher level than the other languages surveyed here in the sense that it attaches more semantics to remote **call**. A prototype implementation of Argus is nearing completion.

5 Models of concurrent programming languages

Most of this survey has been devoted to mechanisms for process interaction and programming languages that use them. Despite the resulting large variety of languages, each can be viewed as belonging to one of three classes: procedure oriented, message oriented, or operation oriented. Languages in the same class provide the same basic kinds of mechanisms for process interaction and have similar attributes.

In *procedure-oriented* languages, process interaction is based on shared variables. (Because monitor-based languages are the most widely known languages in this class, this is often called the *monitor model*.) These languages contain both active objects (processes) and shared, passive objects (modules, monitors, etc.). Passive objects are represented by shared variables, usually with some procedures that implement the operations on the objects. Processes access the objects they require directly and thus interact by accessing shared objects. Because passive objects are shared, they are subject to concurrent access. Therefore, procedure-oriented languages provide means for ensuring mutual exclusion. Concurrent PASCAL, Modula, Mesa, and Edison are examples of such languages.

Message- and operation-oriented languages are both based on message passing, but reflect different views of process interaction. *Message-oriented* languages provide **send** and **receive** as the primary means for process interaction. In contrast to procedure-oriented languages, there are no shared, passive objects, and so processes cannot directly access all objects. Instead, each object is managed by a single process, its *caretaker*, which performs all operations on it. When an operation is to be performed on an object, a message is sent to its caretaker, which performs the operation and then (possibly) responds with a completion message. Thus, objects are never subject to concurrent access. CSP, Gypsy, and PLITS are examples of message-oriented languages.

Operation-oriented languages provide remote procedure call as the primary means for process interaction. These languages combine aspects of the other two classes. As in a message-oriented language, each object has a caretaker process associated with it; as in a procedure-oriented language, operations are performed on an object by calling a procedure. The difference is that the caller of an operation and the caretaker that implements it synchronize while the operation is executed. Both then proceed asynchronously. Distributed Processes, StarMod, Ada, and SR are examples of operation-oriented languages.

Languages in each of these classes are roughly equivalent in expressive power. Each can be used to implement various types of cooperation between concurrently executing processes, including client/server interactions and pipelines. Operation-oriented languages are well suited for programming client/server systems, and message-oriented languages are well suited for programming pipelined computations.

Languages in each class can be used to write concurrent programs for uniprocessors, multiprocessors, and distributed systems. Not all three classes are equally suited for all three architectures, however. Procedure-oriented languages are the most efficient to implement on contemporary single processors. Since it is expensive to simulate shared memory if none is present, implementing procedure-oriented languages on a distributed system can be costly. Nevertheless, procedure-oriented languages can be used to program a distributed system – an individual program is written for each processor and the communications network is viewed as a shared object. Message-oriented languages can be implemented with or without shared memory. In the latter case, the existence of a communications network is made completely transparent, which frees the programmer from concerns about how the network is accessed and where processes are located. This is an advantage of message-oriented languages over procedure-oriented languages when programming a distributed system. Operation-oriented languages enjoy the advantages of both procedure-oriented and message-oriented languages. When shared memory is available, an operation-oriented language can, in many cases, be implemented like a procedure-oriented language [Habermann and Nassi, 1980]; otherwise it can be implemented using message passing. Recent research has shown that both message- and operation-oriented languages can be implemented quite efficiently on distributed systems if special software/firmware is used in the implementation of the language's mechanisms [Nelson, 1981; Spector, 1982].

In a recent paper, Lauer and Needham argued that procedure-oriented and message-oriented languages are equals in terms of expressive power, logical equivalence, and performance [Lauer and Needham, 1979]. (They did not consider operation-oriented languages, which have only recently come into existence.) Their thesis was examined in depth by Reid [1980], who reached many conclusions that we share. At an abstract level, the three types of languages are interchangeable. One *can* transform any program written using the mechanisms found in languages of one class into a program using the mechanisms of another class without affecting performance. However, the classes emphasize different styles of programming – the same program written in languages of different classes is often best structured in entirely different ways. Also, each class provides a type of flexibility not present in the others. Program fragments that are easy to describe using the mechanisms of one can be awkward to describe using the mechanisms of another. One might argue (as do Lauer and Needham) that such use of these mechanisms is a bad idea. We, however, favor programming in the style appropriate to the language.

6 Conclusion

This paper has discussed two aspects of concurrent programming: the key concepts – specification of processes and control of their interaction – and important language notations. Early work on operating systems led to the discovery of two types of synchronization: mutual exclusion and condition synchronization. This stimulated development of synchronization primitives, a number of which are described in this paper. The historical and conceptual relationships among these primitives are illustrated in Figure 9.

The difficulty of designing concurrent programs that use busy-waiting and their inefficiency led to the definition of semaphores. Semaphores were then extended in two ways:

(1) constructs were defined that enforced their structured use, resulting in critical regions, monitors, and path expressions;

(2) 'data' were added to the synchronization associated with semaphores, resulting in message-passing primitives.

Finally, the procedural interface of monitors was combined with message passing, resulting in remote procedure call.

Since the first concurrent programming languages were defined only a decade ago, practical experience has increased our understanding of how to engineer such programs, and the development of formal techniques has greatly increased our understanding of the basic concepts. Although there are a variety of different programming languages, there are only three essentially different kinds: procedure oriented, message oriented, and operation oriented. This, too, is illustrated in Figure 9.

At present, many of the basic problems that arise when constructing concurrent programs have been identified, solutions to these problems are by and large understood, and substantial progress has been made toward the design of notations to express those solutions. Much remains to be done, however. The utility of various languages – really, combinations of constructs – remains to be investigated. This requires using the languages to develop systems and then analyzing how they helped or

Figure 9 Synchronization techniques and language classes.

hindered the development. In addition, the interaction of fault tolerance and concurrent programming is not well understood. Little is known about the design of distributed (decentralized) concurrent programs. Last, devising formal techniques to aid the programmer in constructing correct programs remains an important open problem.

Acknowledgments

Numerous people have been kind enough to provide very helpful comments on earlier drafts of this survey: David Gries, Phil Kaslo, Lynn Kivell, Gary Levin, Ron Olsson, Rick Schlichting, and David Wright. Three referees, and also Eike Best and Michael Scott, provided valuable comments on the penultimate draft. Tony Wasserman has also provided helpful advice; it has been a joy to have him as the editor for this paper. Rachel Rutherford critiqued the ultimate draft and made numerous useful, joyfully picturesque comments.

References

Akkoyunlu, E. A., Bernstein, A. J., Schneider, F. B., and Silberschatz, A. 'Conditions for the equivalence of synchronous and asynchronous systems.' *IEEE Trans. Softw. Eng.* **SE-4**, 6 (Nov. 1978), 507–516.

Andler, S. 'Predicate path expressions.' In *Proc. 6th ACM Symp. Principles of Programming Languages* (San Antonio, Tex.). ACM, New York, 1979, pp. 226–236.

Andrews, G. R. 'The design of a message switching system: An application and evaluation of Modula.' *IEEE Trans. Softw. Eng.* **SE-5**, 2 (March 1979), 138–147.

Andrews, G. R. 'Synchronizing resources.' *ACM Trans. Prog. Lang. Syst.* **3**, 4 (Oct. 1981), 405–430.

Andrews, G. R. 'The distributed programming language SR – Mechanisms, design, and implementation.' *Softw. Pract. Exper.* **12**, 8 (Aug. 1982), 719–754.

Andrews, G. R., and McGraw, J. R. 'Language features for process interaction.' In *Proc. ACM Conf. Language Design for Reliable Software, SIGPLAN Not.* **12**, 3 (March 1977), 114–127.

Apt, K. R., Francez, N., and de Roever, W. P. 'A proof system for communicating sequential processes.' *ACM Trans. Prog. Lang. Syst.* **2**, 3 (July 1980), 359–385.

Aschcroft, E. A. 'Proving assertions about parallel programs.' *J. Comput. Syst.* **10** (Jan. 1975), 110–135.

Ball, E., Feldman, J., Low, J., Rashid, R., and Rovner, P. 'RIG, Rochester's intelligent gateway: System overview.' *IEEE Trans. Softw. Eng.* **SE-2**, 4 (Dec. 1976), 321–328.

Balzer, R. M. 'PORTS – A method for dynamic interprogram communication and job control.' In *Proc. AFIPS Spring Jt. Computer Conf.* (Atlantic City,

N. J., May 18–20, 1971), vol. 38. AFIPS Press, Arlington, Va., 1971, pp. 485–489.

Barringer, H., and Mearns, I. 'Axioms and proof rules for Ada tasks.' *IEE Proc.* **129**, Pt. E, 2 (March 1982), 38–48.

Baskett, F., Howard, J. H., and Montague, J. T. 'Task communication in DEMOS.' In *Proc. 6th Symp. Operating Systems Principles* (West Lafayette, Indiana, Nov. 16–18, 1977). ACM, New York, 1977, pp. 23–31.

Ben-Ari, M. *Principles of Concurrent Programming.* Prentice-Hall, Englewood Cliffs, N. J., 1982.

Bernstein, A. J. 'Output guards and nondeterminism in communicating sequential processes.' *ACM Trans. Prog. Lang. Syst.* **2**, 2 (Apr. 1980), 234–238.

Bernstein, A. J., and Ensor, J. R. 'A modification of Modula.' *Softw. Pract. Exper.* **11** (1981), 237–255.

Bernstein, A. J., and Schneider, F. B. 'On language restrictions to ensure deterministic behavior in concurrent systems.' In J. Moneta (Ed.), *Proc. 3rd Jerusalem Conf. Information Technology JCIT3.* North-Holland Publ., Amsterdam, 1978, pp. 537–541.

Bernstein, P. A., and Goodman, N. 'Concurrency control in distributed database systems.' *ACM Comput. Surv.* **13**, 2 (June 1981), 185–221.

Best, E. 'Relational semantics of concurrent programs (with some applications).' In *Proc. IFIP WG2.2 Conf.* North-Holland Publ., Amsterdam, 1982.

Bloom, T. 'Evaluating synchronization mechanisms.' In *Proc. 7th Symp. Operating Systems Principles* (Pacific Grove, Calif., Dec. 10–12, 1979). ACM, New York, 1979, pp. 24–32.

Brinch Hansen, P. 'Structured multiprogramming.' *Commun. ACM* **15**, 7 (July 1972), 574–578.

Brinch Hansen, P. *Operating System Principles.* Prentice-Hall, Englewood Cliffs, N. J., 1973. (a)

Brinch Hansen, P. 'Concurrent programming concepts.' *ACM Comput. Surv.* **5**, 4 (Dec. 1973), 223–245. (b)

Brinch Hansen, P. 'The programming language Concurrent Pascal.' *IEEE Trans. Softw. Eng.* **SE-1**, 2 (June 1975), 199–206.

Brinch Hansen, P. 'The Solo operating system: Job interface.' *Softw. Pract. Exper.* **6** (1976), 151–164. (a)

Brinch Hansen, P. 'The Solo operating system: Processes, monitors, and classes.' *Softw. Pract. Exper.* **6** (1976), 165–200. (b)

Brinch Hansen, P. *The Architecture of Concurrent Programs.* Prentice-Hall, Englewood Cliffs, N. J., 1977.

Brinch Hansen, P. 'Distributed processes: A concurrent programming concept.' *Commun. ACM* **21**, 11 (Nov. 1978), 934–941.

Brinch Hansen, P. 'Edison: A multiprocessor language.' *Softw. Pract. Exper.* **11**, 4 (Apr. 1981), 325–361.

Campbell, R. H. 'Path expressions: A technique for specifying process synchronization.' Ph.D. dissertation, Computing Laboratory, University of Newcastle upon Tyne, Aug. 1976.

Campbell, R. H., and Habermann, A. N. 'The specification of process synchronization by path expressions.' *Lecture Notes in Computer Science*, vol. 16. Springer-Verlag, New York, 1974, pp. 89–102.

Campbell, R. H., and Kolstad, R. B. 'Path expressions in Pascal.' In *Proc. 4th Int. Conf. on Software Eng.* (Munich, Sept. 17–19, 1979). IEEE, New York, 1979, pp. 212–219.

Conway, M. E. 'Design of a separable transition-diagram compiler.' *Commun. ACM* **6**, 7 (July 1963), 396–408. (a)

Conway, M. E. 'A multiprocessor system design.' In *Proc. AFIPS Fall Jt. Computer Conf.* (Las Vegas, Nev., Nov., 1963), vol. 24. Spartan Books, Baltimore, Maryland, pp. 139–146. (b)

Cook, R. P. '*MOD – A language for distributed programming.' *IEEE Trans. Softw. Eng.* **SE-6**, 6 (Nov. 1980), 563–571.

Courtois, P. J., Heymans, F., and Parnas, D. L. 'Concurrent control with "readers" and "writers".' *Commun. ACM* **14**, 10 (Oct. 1971), 667–668.

Cousot, P., and Cousot, R. 'Semantic analysis of communicating sequential processes.' In *Proc. 7th Int. Colloquium Automata, Languages and Programming (ICALP80), Lecture Notes in Computer Science*, vol. 85. Springer-Verlag, New York, 1980, pp. 119–133.

Dennis, J. B., and Van Horn, E. C. 'Programming semantics for multi-programmed computations.' *Commun. ACM* **9**, 3 (March 1966), 143–155.

Dijkstra, E. W. 'The structure of the "THE" multiprogramming system.' *Commun. ACM* **11**, 5 (May 1968), 341–346. (a)

Dijkstra, E. W. 'Cooperating sequential processes.' In F. Genuys (Ed.), *Programming Languages*. Academic Press, New York, 1968. (b)

Dijkstra, E. W. 'Guarded commands, nondeterminacy, and formal derivation of programs.' *Commun. ACM* **18**, 8 (Aug. 1975), 453–457.

Dijkstra, E. W. *A Discipline of Programming*. Prentice-Hall, Englewood Cliffs, N. J., 1976.

Dijkstra, E. W. 'An assertional proof of a program by G. L. Peterson.' EWD 779 (Feb. 1979), Nuenen, The Netherlands. (a)

Dijkstra, E. W. Personal communication, Oct. 1981. (b)

Feldman, J. A., 'High level programming for distributed computing.' *Commun. ACM* **22**, 6 (June 1979), 353–368.

Flon, L., and Habermann, A. N. 'Towards the construction of verifiable software systems.' In *Proc. ACM Conf. Data, SIGPLAN Not.* **8**, 2 (March 1976), 141–148.

Floyd, R. W. 'Assigning meanings to programs.' In *Proc. Am. Math. Soc. Symp. Applied Mathematics*, vol. 19, pp. 19–31, 1967.

Gelernter, D., and Bernstein, A. J. 'Distributed communication via global buffer.' In *Proc. Symp. Principles of Distributed Computing* (Ottawa, Canada, Aug. 18–20, 1982). ACM, New York, 1982, pp. 10–18.

Gerth, R. 'A sound and complete Hoare axiomatization of the Ada-rendezvous.' In *Proc. 9th Int. Colloquium Automata, Languages and Programming (ICALP82), Lecture Notes in Computer Science*, vol. 140. Springer-Verlag, New York, 1982, pp. 252–264.

Gerth, R., de Roever, W. P., and Roncken, M. 'Procedures and concurrency: A study in proof.' In *5th Int. Symp. Programming, Lecture Notes in Computer Science*, vol. 137. Springer-Verlag, New York, 1982, pp. 132–163.

Good, D. I., Cohen, R. M., and Keeton-Williams, J. 'Principles of proving concurrent programs in Gypsy.' In *Proc. 6th ACM Symp. Principles of Programming Languages* (San Antonio, Texas, Jan. 29–31, 1979). ACM, New York, 1979, pp. 42–52.

Habermann, A. N. 'Path expressions.' Dep. of Computer Science, Carnegie-Mellon Univ., Pittsburgh, Pennsylvania, June, 1975.

Habermann, A. N., and Nassi, I. R. 'Efficient implementation of Ada tasks.' Tech. Rep. CMU-CS-80-103, Carnegie–Mellon Univ., Jan. 1980.

Haddon, B. K. 'Nested monitor calls.' *Oper. Syst. Rev.* **11**, 4 (Oct. 1977), 18–23.

Hanson, D. R., and Griswold, R. E. 'The SL5 procedure mechanism.' *Commun. ACM* **21**, 5 (May 1978), 392–400.

Hoare, C. A. R. 'An axiomatic basis for computer programming.' *Commun. ACM.* **12**, 10 (Oct. 1969), 576–580, 583.

Hoare, C. A. R. 'Towards a theory of parallel programming.' In C. A. R. Hoare and R. H. Perrott (Eds.), *Operating Systems Techniques*. Academic Press, New York, 1972, pp. 61–71.

Hoare, C. A. R. 'Monitors: An operating system structuring concept.' *Commun. ACM* **17**, 10 (Oct. 1974), 549–557.

Hoare, C. A. R. 'Communicating sequential processes.' *Commun. ACM* **21**, 8 (Aug. 1978), 666–677.

Hoare, C. A. R. 'The emperor's old clothes.' *Commun. ACM* **24**, 2 (Feb. 1981), 75–83.

Holden, J., and Wand, I. C. 'An assessment of Modula.' *Softw. Pract. Exper.* **10** (1980), 593–621.

Holt, R. C., Graham, G. S. Lazowska, E. D., and Scott, M. A. *Structured Concurrent Programming with Operating Systems Applications*. Addison-Wesley, Reading, Mass., 1978.

Howard, J. H. 'Proving monitors.' *Commun. ACM* **19**, 5 (May 1976), 273–279. (a)

Howard, J. H. 'Signaling in monitors.' In *Proc. 2nd Int. Conf. Software Engineering* (San Francisco, Oct. 13–15, 1976). IEEE, New York, 1976, pp. 47–52. (b)

Jazayeri, M., *et al.* 'CSP/80: A language for communicating processes.' In *Proc. Fall IEEE COMPCON80* (Sept. 1980). IEEE, New York, 1980, pp. 736–740.

Jones, A. K., and Schwarz, P. 'Experience using multiprocessor systems – A status report.' *ACM Comput. Surv.* **12**, 2 (June 1980), 121–165.

Kaubisch, W. H., Perrott, R. H., and Hoare, C. A. R. 'Quasiparallel programming.' *Softw. Pract. Exper.* **6** (1976), 341–356.

Keedy, J. L. 'On structuring operating systems with monitors.' *Aust. Comput. J.* **10**, 1 (Feb. 1978), 23–27. Reprinted in *Oper. Syst. Rev.* **13**, 1 (Jan. 1979), 5–9.

Keller, R. M. 'Formal verification of parallel programs.' *Commun. ACM* **19**, 7 (July 1976), 371–384.

Kessels, J. L. W. 'An alternative to event queues for synchronization in monitors.' *Commun. ACM* **20**, 7 (July 1977), 500–503.

Kieburtz, R. B., and Silberschatz, A. 'Comments on "communicating sequential processes." ' *ACM Trans. Program. Lang. Syst.* **1**, 2 (Oct. 1979), 218–225.

Kohler, W. H. 'A survey of techniques for synchronization and recovery in decentralized computer systems.' *ACM Comput. Surv.* **13**, 2 (June 1981), 149–183.

Lamport, L. 'Proving the correctness of multiprocess programs.' *IEEE Trans. Softw. Eng.* **SE-3**, 2 (March 1977), 125–143.

Lamport, L. 'The "Hoare logic" of concurrent programs.' *Acta Inform.* **14**, 21–37. (a)

Lamport, L. 'The mutual exclusion problem.' Op. 56. SRI International, Menlo Park, Calif., Oct. 1980. (b)

Lamport, L., and Schneider, F. B. 'The "Hoare logic" of CSP, and all that.' Tech. Rep. TR 82-490, Dep. Computer Sci., Cornell Univ., May, 1982.

Lampson, B. W. 'Atomic transactions.' In *Distributed Systems – Architecture and Implementation, Lecture Notes in Computer Science*, vol. 105. Springer-Verlag, New York, 1981.

Lampson, B. W., and Redell, D. D. 'Experience with processes and monitors in Mesa.' *Commun. ACM* **23**, 2 (Feb. 1980), 105–117.

Lampson, B. W., and Sturgis, H. E. 'Crash recovery in a distributed data storage system.' Xerox Palo Alto Research Center, Apr. 1979.

Lauer, H. C., and Needham, R. M. 'On the duality of operating system structures.' In *Proc. 2nd Int. Symp. Operating Systems* (IRIA, Paris, Oct. 1978); reprinted in *Oper. Syst. Rev.* **13**, 2 (Apr. 1979), 3–19.

Lauer, P. E., and Campbell, R. H. 'Formal semantics of a class of high level primitives for coordinating concurrent processes.' *Acta Inform.* **5** (1975), 297–332.

Lauer, P. E., and Shields, M. W. 'Abstract specification of resource accessing disciplines: Adequacy, starvation, priority and interrupts.' *SIGPLAN Not.* **13**, 12 (Dec. 1978), 41–59.

Lehmann, D., Pnueli, A., and Stavi, J. 'Impartiality, justice and fairness: The ethics of concurrent termination.' *Automata, Languages and Programming, Lecture Notes in Computer Science*, vol. 115. Springer-Verlag, New York, 1981, pp. 264–277.

Levin, G. M., and Gries, D. 'A proof technique for communicating sequential processes.' *Acta Inform.* **15** (1981), 281–302.

Liskov, B. L. 'On linguistic support for distributed programs.' In *Proc. IEEE Symp. Reliability in Distributed Software and Database Systems* (Pittsburgh, July 21–22, 1981). IEEE, New York, 1981, pp. 53–60.

Liskov, B. L., and Scheifler, R. 'Guardians and actions: Linguistic support for robust, distributed programs.' In *Proc. 9th ACM Symp. Principles of Programming Languages* (Albuquerque, New Mexico, Jan. 25–27, 1982). ACM, New York, 1982, pp. 7–19.

Lister, A. 'The problem of nested monitor calls.' *Oper. Syst. Rev.* **11**, 3 (July 1977), 5–7.

Loehr, K.-P. 'Beyond Concurrent Pascal.' In *Proc. 6th ACM Symp. Operating Systems Principles* (West Lafayette, Ind., Nov. 16–18, 1977). ACM, New York, 1977, pp. 173–180.

Lomet, D. B. 'Process structuring, synchronization, and recovery using atomic transactions.' In *Proc. ACM Conf. Language Design for Reliable Software, SIGPLAN Not.* **12**, 3 (March 1977), 128–137.

Lynch, N. A. 'Multilevel atomicity – A new correctness criterion for distributed databases.' Tech. Rep. GIT-ICS-81/05, School of Information and Computer Sciences, Georgia Tech., May 1981.

Mao, T. W., and Yeh, R. T. 'Communication port: A language concept for concurrent programming.' *IEEE Trans. Softw. Eng.* **SE-6**, 2 (March 1980), 194–204.

Misra, J., and Chandy, K. 'Proofs of networks of processes.' *IEEE Trans. Softw. Eng.* **SE-7**, 4 (July 1981), 417–426.

Misra, J., Chandy, K. and Smith, T. 'Proving safety and liveness of communicating processes with examples.' In *Proc. Symp. Principles of Distributed Computing* (Ottawa, Canada, Aug. 18–20, 1982). ACM, New York, 1982, pp. 201–208.

Mitchell, J. G., Maybury, W., and Sweet, R. 'Mesa language manual, version 5.0.' Rep. CSL-79-3, Xerox Palo Alto Research Center, Apr. 1979.

Nelson, B. J. 'Remote procedure call.' Ph.D. thesis. Rep. CMU-CS-81-119, Dep. of Computer Science, Carnegie–Mellon Univ., May 1981.

Nygaard, K., and Dahl, O. J. 'The development of the SIMULA languages.' *Preprints ACM SIGPLAN History of Programming Languages Conference, SIGPLAN Not.* **13**, 8 (Aug. 1978), 245–272.

Owicki, S. S., and Gries, D. 'An axiomatic proof technique for parallel programs.' *Acta Inform.* **6** (1976), 319–340. (a)

Owicki, S. S., and Gries, D. 'Verifying properties of parallel programs: an axiomatic approach.' *Commun. ACM* **19**, 5 (May 1976), 279–285. (b)

Parnas, D. L. 'On the criteria to be used in decomposing systems into modules.' *Commun. ACM* **15**, 12 (Dec. 1972), 1053–1058.

Parnas, D. L. 'The non-problem of nested monitor calls.' *Oper. Syst. Rev.* **12**, 1 (Jan. 1978), 12–14.

Peterson, G. L. 'Myths about the mutual exclusion problem.' *Inform. Process. Lett.* **12**, 3 (June 1981), 115–116.

Reed, D. P. 'Implementing atomic actions on decentralized data.' *ACM Trans. Comput. Syst.* **1**, 1 (Feb. 1983), 3–23.

Reid, L. G. 'Control and communication in programmed systems.' Ph.D. thesis, Rep. CMU-CS-80-142, Dep. of Computer Science, Carnegie–Mellon Univ., Sept. 1980.

Reif, J. H., and Spirakis, P. G. 'Unbounded speed variability in distributed communications systems.' In *Proc. 9th ACM Conf. Principles of Programming Languages* (Albuquerque, N. M., Jan. 25–27, 1982). ACM, New York, 1982, pp. 46–56.

Ritchie, D. M., and Thompson, K. 'The UNIX timesharing system.' *Commun. ACM* **17**, 7 (July 1974), 365–375.

Roper, T. J., and Barter, C. J. 'A communicating sequential process language and implementation.' *Softw. Pract. Exper.* **11** (1981), 1215–1234.

Schlichting, R. D., and Schneider, F. B. 'An approach to designing fault-tolerant computing systems.' Tech. Rep. TR 81-479, Dep. of Computer Sci., Cornell Univ., Nov. 1981.

Schlichting, R. D., and Schneider, F. B. 'Using message passing for distributed programming: Proof rules and disciplines.' Tech. Rep. TR 82–491, Dep. of Computer Science, Cornell Univ., May 1982. (a)

Schlichting, R. D., and Schneider, F. B. 'Understanding and using asynchronous message passing primitives.' In *Proc. Symp. Principles of Distributed Computing* (Ottawa, Canada, Aug. 18–20, 1982). ACM, New York, 1982, pp. 141–147. (b)

Schneider, F. B. 'Synchronization in distributed programs.' *ACM Trans. Program. Lang. Syst.* **4**, 2 (Apr. 1982), 125–148.

Schneider, F. B., and Bernstein, A. J. 'Scheduling in Concurrent Pascal.' *Oper. Syst. Rev.* **12**, 2 (Apr. 1978), 15–20.

Schwartz, J. S. 'Distributed synchronization of communicating sequential processes.' Tech. Rep., Dep. of Artificial Intelligence, Univ. of Edinburgh, July 1978.

Shaw, A. C. *The Logical Design of Operating Systems.* Prentice-Hall, Englewood Cliffs, N. J., 1974.

Shaw, A. C. 'Software specification languages based on regular expressions.' In W. E. Riddle and R. E. Fairley (Eds.), *Software Development Tools.* Springer-Verlag, New York, 1980, pp. 148–175.

Shields, M. W. 'Adequate path expressions.' In *Proc. Int. Symp. Semantics of Concurrent Computation, Lecture Notes in Computer Science*, vol. 70. Springer-Verlag, New York, pp. 249–265.

Silberschatz, A. 'On the input/output mechanism in Concurrent Pascal.' In *Proc. COMPSAC'77 – IEEE Computer Society Computer Software and Applications Conference* (Chicago, Ill., Nov. 1977). IEEE, New York, 1977, pp. 514–518.

Silberschatz, A. 'Communication and synchronization in distributed programs.' *IEEE Trans. Softw. Eng.* **SE-5**, 6 (Nov. 1979), 542–546.

Silberschatz, A., Kieburtz, R. B., and Bernstein, A. J. 'Extending Concurrent Pascal to allow dynamic resource management.' *IEEE Trans. Softw. Eng.* **SE-3**, 3 (May 1977), 210–217.

Solomon, M. H., and Finkel, R. A. 'The Roscoe distributed operating system.' In *Proc. 7th Symp. Operating System Principles* (Pacific Grove, Calif., Dec. 10–12, 1979). ACM, New York, 1979, pp. 108–114.

Soundararajan, N. 'Axiomatic semantics of communicating sequential processes.' Tech. Rep., Dep. of Computer and Information Science, Ohio State Univ., 1981.

Spector, A. Z. 'Performing remote operations efficiently on a local computer network.' *Commun. ACM* **25**, 4 (Apr. 1982), 246–260.

U.S. Department of Defense. *Programming Language Ada: Reference Manual*, vol. 106, *Lecture Notes in Computer Science*. Springer-Verlag, New York, 1981.

Van de Snepscheut, J. L. A. 'Synchronous communication between synchronization components.' *Inform. Process. Lett.* **13**, 3 (Dec. 1981), 127–130.

van Wijngaarden, A., Mailloux, B. J., Peck, J. L., Koster, C. H. A., Sintzoff, M., Lindsey, C. H., Meertens, L. G. L. T., and Fisker, R. G. 'Revised report on the algorithm language ALGOL68.' *Acta Inform.* **5**, 1–3 (1975), 1–236.

Wegner, P., and Smolka, S. A. 'Processes, tasks and monitors: A comparative study of concurrent programming primitives.' *IEEE Trans. Softw. Eng.*, to appear, 1983.

Welsh, J., and Bustard, D. W. 'Pascal-Plus – Another language for modular multiprogramming.' *Softw. Pract. Exper.* **9** (1979), 947–957.

Welsh, J., and Lister, A. 'A comparative study of task communication in Ada.' *Softw. Pract. Exper.* **11** (1981), 257–290.

Wettstein, H. 'The problem of nested monitor cells revisited.' *Oper. Syst. Rev.* **12**, 1 (Jan. 1978), 19–23.

Wirth, N. 'Modula: A language for modular multi-programming.' *Softw. Pract. Exper.* **7** (1977), 3–35. (a)

Wirth, N. 'The use of Modula.' *Softw. Pract. Exper.* **7** (1977), 37–65. (b)

Wirth, N. 'Design and implementation of Modula.' *Softw. Pract. Exper.* **7** (1977), 67–84. (c)

Wirth, N. 'Toward a discipline of real-time programming.' *Commun. ACM* **20**, 8 (Aug. 1977), 577–583. (d)

Wirth, N. *Programming in Modula-2*. Springer-Verlag, New York, 1982.

Wulf, W. A., Russell, D. B., and Habermann, A. N. 'BLISS: A language for systems programming.' *Commun. ACM* **14**, 12 (Dec. 1971), 780–790.

PART TWO
Concurrent Programming Languages

There are now many languages that support concurrent programming, for example, Concurrent Pascal, Modula 2, *MOD, Concurrent C, Concurrent Euclid and Mesa and the Ada language. None of these was designed with concurrent programming as the fundamental programming paradigm – sequential programming being a special case of concurrent programming. Either the concurrent programming facilities were just another set of facilities put in the new language or they were grafted on to a reasonably successful existing sequential programming language.

The motivation for the latter approach is abundantly clear:

- It enhances the chances of the extended language being used in practice; it would be relatively easy to entice users of the original sequential language to try out the concurrent programming superset.

- It eases the learning and educational problems associated with the acceptance of any new language.

- With proper care, it simplifies the tasks of language design and implementation.

There is little point in looking at all languages with concurrent programming facilities, but there is much merit in examining a representative subset that includes languages based on both the shared memory and message passing models. In this section, we shall take a closer look at Concurrent Pascal, *MOD, Concurrent C and the Ada language.

2

The Programming Language Concurrent Pascal

Per Brinch Hansen
California Institute of Technology

The paper describes a new programming language for structured programming of computer operating systems. It extends the sequential programming language Pascal with concurrent programming tools called processes and monitors. Section I explains these concepts informally by means of pictures illustrating a hierarchical design of a simple spooling system. Section II uses the same example to introduce the language notation. The main contribution of Concurrent Pascal is to extend the monitor concept with an explicit hierarchy of access rights to shared data structures that can be stated in the program text and checked by a compiler.

Index terms: abstract data types, access rights, classes, concurrent processes, concurrent programming languages, hierarchical operating systems, monitors, scheduling, structured multiprogramming.

I The purpose of Concurrent Pascal

A Background

Since 1972 I have been working on a new programming language for structured programming of computer operating systems. This language is called Concurrent Pascal. It extends the sequential programming language Pascal with concurrent programming tools called processes and monitors [1]–[3].

This is an informal description of Concurrent Pascal. It uses examples, pictures, and words to bring out the creative aspects of new programming concepts without getting into their finer details. I plan to define these concepts precisely and introduce a notation for them in later

This project is supported by the National Science Foundation under Grant DCR74-17331.

papers. This form of presentation may be imprecise from a formal point of view, but is perhaps more effective from a human point of view.

B Processes

We will study concurrent processes inside an operating system and look at one small problem only: how can large amounts of data be transmitted from one process to another by means of a buffer stored on a disk?

Figure 1 shows this little system and its three components:

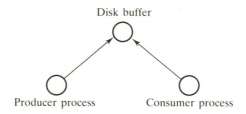

Figure 1 Process communication.

- a process that produces data;
- a process that consumes data; and
- a disk buffer that connects them.

The circles are *system components* and the arrows are the *access rights* of these components. They show that both *processes* can use the buffer (but they do not show that data flows from the producer to the consumer). This kind of picture is an *access graph*.

The next picture shows a process component in more detail (Figure 2).

Access rights
Private data
Sequential program

Figure 2 Process.

A *process* consists of a *private data* structure and a *sequential program* that can operate on the data. One process cannot operate on the private data of another process. But concurrent processes can share certain data structures (such as a disk buffer). The *access rights* of a process mention the shared data it can operate on.

Figure 3   Monitor.

C   Monitors

A disk buffer is a data structure shared by two concurrent processes. The details of how such a buffer is constructed are irrelevant to its users. All the processes need to know is that they can *send* and *receive* data through it. If they try to operate on the buffer in any other way it is probably either a programming mistake or an example of tricky programming. In both cases, one would like a compiler to detect such misuse of a shared data structure.

To make this possible, we must introduce a language construct that will enable a programmer to tell a compiler how a shared data structure can be used by processes. This kind of system component is called a monitor. A monitor can synchronize concurrent processes and transmit data between them. It can also control the order in which competing processes use shared, physical resources. Figure 3 shows a monitor in detail.

A *monitor* defines a *shared data* structure and all the operations processes can perform on it. These synchronizing operations are called *monitor procedures*. A monitor also defines an *initial operation* that will be executed when its data structure is created.

We can define a *disk buffer* as a monitor. Within this monitor there will be shared variables that define the location and length of the buffer on the disk. There will also be two monitor procedures, *send* and *receive*. The initial operation will make sure that the buffer starts as an empty one.

Processes cannot operate directly on shared data. They can only call monitor procedures that have access to shared data. A monitor procedure is executed as part of a calling process (just like any other procedure).

If concurrent processes simultaneously call monitor procedures that operate on the same shared data these procedures must be executed strictly one at a time. Otherwise, the results of monitor calls will be unpredictable. This means that the machine must be able to delay processes for short periods of time until it is their turn to execute monitor procedures. We will not be concerned about how this is done, but will just notice that a monitor procedure has *exclusive access* to shared data while it is being executed.

So the (virtual) machine on which concurrent programs run will handle *short-term scheduling* of simultaneous monitor calls. But the programmer must also be able to delay processes for longer periods of time if their requests for data and other resources cannot be satisfied immediately. If, for example, a process tries to receive data from an empty disk buffer it must be delayed until another process sends more data.

Concurrent Pascal includes a simple data type, called a *queue*, that can be used by monitor procedures to control *medium-term scheduling* of processes. A monitor can either *delay* a calling process in a queue or *continue* another process that is waiting in a queue. It is not important here to understand how these queues work except for the following essential rule: a process only has exclusive access to shared data as long as it continues to execute statements within a monitor procedure. As soon as a process is delayed in a queue it loses its exclusive access until another process calls the same monitor and wakes it up again. (Without this rule, it would be impossible for other processes to enter a monitor and let waiting processes continue their execution.)

Although the disk buffer example does not show this yet, monitor procedures should also be able to call procedures defined within other monitors. Otherwise, the language will not be very useful for hierarchical design. In the case of a disk buffer, one of these other monitors could perhaps define simple input/output operations on the disk. So a monitor can also have *access rights* to other system components (see Figure 3).

D   System design

A process executes a sequential program – it is an active component. A monitor is just a collection of procedures that do nothing until they are called by processes – it is a passive component. But there are strong similarities between a process and a monitor: both define a data structure (private or shared) and the meaningful operations on it. The main difference between processes and monitors is the way they are scheduled for execution.

It seems natural therefore to regard processes and monitors as *abstract data types* defined in terms of the operations one can perform on them. If a compiler can check that these operations are the only ones carried out on the data structures, then we may be able to build very reliable, concurrent programs in which *controlled access* to data and physical resources is guaranteed before these programs are put into operation. We have then to some extent solved the *resource protection* problem in the

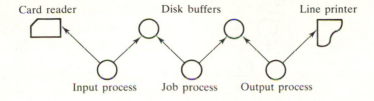

Figure 4 Spooling system.

cheapest possible manner (without hardware mechanisms and run time overhead).

So we will define processes and monitors as data types and make it possible to use several instances of the same component type in a system. We can, for example, use two disk buffers to build a *spooling system* with an input process, a job process, and an output process (Figure 4). I will distinguish between definitions and instances of components by calling them *system types* and *system components*. Access graphs (such as Figure 4) will always show system components (not system types).

Peripheral devices are considered to be monitors implemented in hardware. They can only be accessed by a single procedure *io* that delays the calling process until an input/output operation is completed. Interrupts are handled by the virtual machine on which processes run.

To make the programming language useful for stepwise system design it should permit the division of a system type, such as a disk buffer, into smaller system types. One of these other system types should give a disk buffer access to the disk. We will call this system type a *virtual disk*. It gives a disk buffer the illusion that it has its own private disk. A virtual disk hides the details of disk input/output from the rest of the system and makes the disk look like a data structure (an array of disk pages). The only operations on this data structure are *read* and *write* a page.

Each virtual disk is only used by a single disk buffer (Figure 5). A system component that cannot be called simultaneously by several other components will be called a *class*. A class defines a data structure and the possible operations on it (just like a monitor). The exclusive access of class procedures to class variables can be guaranteed completely at

Figure 5 Buffer refinement.

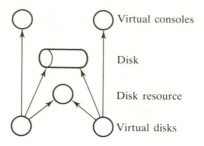

Figure 6   Decomposition of virtual disks.

compile time. The virtual machine does not have to schedule simultaneous calls of class procedures at run time, because such calls cannot occur. This makes class calls considerably faster than monitor calls.

The spooling system includes two virtual disks but only one real disk. So we need a single *disk resource* monitor to control the order in which competing processes use the disk (Figure 6). This monitor defines two procedures, *request* and *release* access, to be called by a virtual disk before and after each disk transfer.

It would seem simpler to replace the virtual disks and the disk resource by a single monitor that has exclusive access to the disk and does the input/output. This would certainly guarantee that processes use the disk one at a time. But this would be done according to the built-in short-term scheduling policy of monitor calls.

Now to make a virtual machine efficient, one must use a very simple short-term scheduling rule (such as first come, first served) [2]. If the disk has a moving access head this is about the worst possible algorithm one can use for disk transfers. It is vital that the language make it possible for the programmer to write a medium-term scheduling algorithm that will minimize disk head movements [3]. The data type *queue* mentioned earlier makes it possible to implement arbitrary scheduling rules within a monitor.

The difficulty is that while a monitor is performing an input/output operation it is impossible for other processes to enter the same monitor and join the disk queue. They will automatically be delayed by the short-term scheduler and only allowed to enter the monitor one at a time after each disk transfer. This will, of course, make the attempt to control disk scheduling within the monitor illusory. To give the programmer complete control of disk scheduling, processes should be able to enter the disk queue during disk transfers. Since *arrival* and *service* in the disk queueing system potentially are simultaneous operations they must be handled by different system components, as shown in Figure 6.

If the disk fails persistently during input/output this should be reported on an operator's console. Figure 6 shows two instances of a class type, called a *virtual console*. They give the virtual disks the illusion that they have their own private consoles.

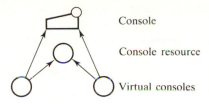

Console

Console resource

Virtual consoles

Figure 7   Decomposition of virtual consoles.

The virtual consoles get exclusive access to a single, real console by calling a *console resource* monitor (Figure 7). Notice that we now have a standard technique for dealing with virtual devices.

If we put all these system components together, we get a complete picture of a simple spooling system (Figure 8). Classes, monitors, and processes are marked *C*, *M*, and *P*.

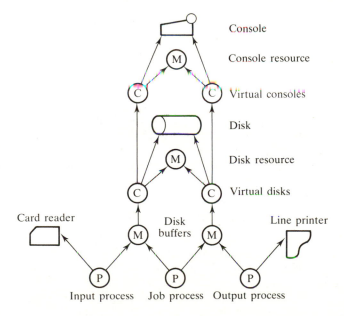

Figure 8   Hierarchical system structure.

E   Scope rules

Some years ago I was part of a team that built a multi-programming system in which processes can appear and disappear dynamically [4]. In practice, this system was used mostly to set up a fixed configuration of processes. Dynamic process deletion will certainly complicate the semantics and implementation of a programming language considerably. And since it appears to be unnecessary for a large class of real-time applications, it seems wise to exclude it altogether. So an operating system written in Concurrent Pascal will consist of a fixed number of processes, monitors, and classes. These components and their data structures will exist forever after system initialization. An operating system can, however, be extended by recompilation. It remains to be seen whether this restriction will simplify or complicate operating system design. But the poor quality of most existing operating systems clearly demonstrates an urgent need for simpler approaches.

In existing programming languages the data structures of processes, monitors, and classes would be called 'global data.' This term would be misleading in Concurrent Pascal where each data structure can be accessed by a single component only. It seems more appropriate to call them *permanent data structures.*

I have argued elsewhere that the most dangerous aspect of concurrent programming is the possibility of *time-dependent programming errors* that are impossible to locate by program testing ('lurking bugs') [2], [5], [6]. If we are going to depend on real-time programming systems in our daily lives, we must be able to find such obscure errors before the systems are put into operation.

Fortunately, a compiler can detect many of these errors if processes and monitors are represented by a structured notation in a high-level programming language. In addition, we must exclude low-level machine features (registers, addresses, and interrupts) from the language and let a virtual machine control them. If we want real-time systems to be highly reliable, we must stop programming them in assembly language. (The use of hardware protection mechanisms is merely an expensive, inadequate way of making arbitrary machine language programs behave almost as predictably as compiled programs.)

A Concurrent Pascal compiler will check that the private data of a process only are accessed by that process. It will also check that the data structure of a class or monitor only is accessed by its procedures.

Figure 8 shows that *access rights* within an operating system normally are not tree structured. Instead they form a directed graph. This partly explains why the traditional scope rules of block-structured languages are inconvenient for concurrent programming (and for sequential programming as well). In Concurrent Pascal one can state the access rights of components in the program text and have them checked by a compiler.

Since the execution of a monitor procedure will delay the execution of further calls of the same monitor, we must prevent a monitor from calling itself recursively. Otherwise, processes can become *deadlocked*. So the compiler will check that the access rights of system components are hierarchically ordered (or, if you like, that there are no cycles in the access graph).

The *hierarchical ordering* of system components has vital consequences for system design and testing [7].

A hierarchical operating system will be tested component by component, bottom up (but could, of course, be conceived top down or by iteration). When an incomplete operating system has been shown to work correctly (by proof or testing), a compiler can ensure that this part of the system will continue to work correctly when new untested program components are added on top of it. Programming errors within new components cannot cause old components to fail because old components do not call new components, and new components only call old components through well-defined procedures that have already been tested.

(Strictly speaking, a compiler can only check that single monitor calls are made correctly; it cannot check sequences of monitor calls, for example whether a resource is always reserved before it is released. So one can only hope for compile time assurance of *partial correctness*.)

Several other reasons besides program correctness make a hierarchical structure attractive:

(1) a hierarchical operating system can be studied in a stepwise manner as a sequence of *abstract machines* simulated by programs [8];

(2) a partial ordering of process interactions permits one to use *mathematical induction* to prove certain overall properties of the system (such as the absence of deadlocks) [2];

(3) *efficient resource utilization* can be achieved by ordering the program components according to the speed of the physical resources they control (with the fastest resources being controlled at the bottom of the system) [8];

(4) a hierarchical system designed according to the previous criteria is often *nearly decomposable* from an analytical point of view. This means that one can develop stochastic models of its dynamic behavior in a stepwise manner [9].

F   Final remarks

It seems most natural to represent a hierarchical system structure, such as Figure 8, by a two-dimensional picture. But when we write a concurrent program we must somehow represent these access rules by linear text. This limitation of written language tends to obscure the simplicity of the original structure. That is why I have tried to explain the purpose of Concurrent Pascal by means of pictures instead of language notation.

The class concept is a restricted form of the class concept of Simula 67 [10]. Dijkstra suggested the idea of monitors [8]. The first structured language notation for monitors was proposed in [2], and illustrated by examples in [3]. The queue variables needed by monitors for process scheduling were suggested in [5] and modified in [3].

The main contribution of Concurrent Pascal is to extend monitors with explicit access rights that can be checked at compile time. Concurrent Pascal has been implemented at Caltech for the PDP 11/45 computer. Our system uses sequential Pascal as a job control and user programming language.

II   The use of Concurrent Pascal

A   Introduction

In Section I the concepts of Concurrent Pascal were explained informally by means of pictures of a hierarchical spooling system. I will now use the same example to introduce the language notation of Concurrent Pascal. The presentation is still informal. I am neither trying to define the language precisely nor to develop a working system. This will be done in other papers. I am just trying to show the flavor of the language.

B   Processes

We will now program the system components in Figure 8 one at a time from top to bottom (but we could just as well do it bottom up).

Although we only need one *input process*, we may as well define it as a general system type of which several copies may exist:

```
type inputprocess = process(buffer : diskbuffer);
var block : page;
cycle
    readcards(block);
    buffer.send(block);
end
```

An input process has access to a *buffer* of type *diskbuffer* (to be defined later). The process has a private variable block of type *page*. The data type *page* is declared elsewhere as an array of characters:

```
type page = array(.1..512.) of char
```

A process type defines a *sequential program* – in this case, an endless cycle that inputs a block from a card reader and sends it through the buffer to another process. We will ignore the details of card reader input.

The *send* operation on the buffer is called as follows (using the block as a parameter):

buffer.send(*block*)

The next component type we will define is a *job process*:

```
type jobprocess = process(input, output : diskbuffer);
var block : page;
cycle
    input.receive(block);
    update(block);
    output.send(block);
end
```

A job process has access to two disk buffers called *input* and *output*. It receives blocks from one buffer, updates them, and sends them through the other buffer. The details of updating can be ignored here.

Finally, we need an *output process* that can receive data from a disk buffer and output them on a line printer:

```
type outputprocess = process(buffer : diskbuffer);
var block : page;
cycle
    buffer.receive(block);
    printlines(block);
end
```

The following shows a declaration of the main system components:

```
var buffer1, buffer2 : diskbuffer;
    reader : inputprocess;
    master : jobprocess;
    writer : outputprocess;
```

There is an input process, called the *reader*, a job process, called the *master*, and an output process, called the *writer*. Then there are two disk buffers, *buffer1* and *buffer2*, that connect them.

Later I will explain how a disk buffer is defined and initialized. If we assume that the disk buffers already have been initialized, we can initialize the input process as follows:

```
init reader(buffer1)
```

The *init* statement allocates space for the *private variables* of the reader process and starts its execution as a sequential process with access to *buffer*1.

The *access rights* of a process to other system components, such as *buffer*1, are also called its *parameters*. A process can only be initialized once. After initialization, the parameters and private variables of a process exist forever. They are called *permanent variables*.

The *init* statement can be used to start concurrent execution of several processes and define their access rights. As an example, the statement:

> **init** *reader*(*buffer*1), *master*(*buffer*1, *buffer*2),
>   *writer*(*buffer*2)

starts concurrent execution of the *reader* process (with access to *buffer*1), the *master* process (with access to both buffers), and the *writer* process (with access to *buffer*2).

A process can only access its own parameters and private variables. The latter are not accessible to other system components. Compare this with the more liberal scope rules of block-structured languages in which a program block can access not only its own parameters and local variables, but also those declared in outer blocks. In Concurrent Pascal, all variables accessible to a system component are declared within its type definition. This access rule and the *init* statement make it possible for a programmer to state access rights explicitly and have them checked by a compiler. They also make it possible to study a system type as a self-contained program unit.

Although the programming examples do not show this, one can also define constants, data types, and procedures within a process. These objects can only be used within the process type.

C   Monitors

The *disk buffer* is a monitor type:

```
type diskbuffer =
monitor(consoleaccess, diskaccess : resource;
    base, limit : integer);

var disk : virtualdisk; sender, receiver : queue;
    head, tail, length : integer;

procedure entry send(block : page);
begin
    if length = limit then delay(sender);
    disk.write(base + tail, block);
```

```
    tail := (tail + 1) mod limit;
    length := length + 1;
    continue(receiver);
end;

procedure entry receive(var block : page);
begin
    if length = 0 then delay(receiver);
    disk.read(base + head, block);
    head := (head + 1) mod limit;
    length := length - 1;
    continue(sender);
end;

begin "initial statement"
    init disk(consoleaccess, diskaccess);
    head := 0; tail := 0; length := 0;
end
```

A disk buffer has access to two other components, *consoleaccess* and *diskaccess*, of type resource (to be defined later). It also has access to two integer constants defining the *base* address and *limit* of the buffer on the disk.

The monitor declares a set of *shared variables*: the *disk* is declared as a variable of type *virtualdisk*. Two variables of type queue are used to delay the *sender* and *receiver* processes until the buffer becomes *nonfull* and *nonempty*. Three integers define the relative addresses of the *head* and *tail* elements of the buffer and its current *length*.

The monitor defines two *monitor procedures*, *send* and *receive*. They are marked with the word *entry* to distinguish them from local procedures used within the monitor (there are none of these in this example).

Receive returns a page to the calling process. If the buffer is empty, the calling process is *delayed* in the receiver queue until another process sends a page through the buffer. The *receive* procedure will then read and remove a page from the head of the disk buffer by calling a *read* operation defined within the virtual disk type:

    disk.read(base + head, block)

Finally, the *receive* procedure will *continue* the execution of a sending process (if the latter is waiting in the sender queue).

Send is similar to *receive*.

The queuing mechanism will be explained in detail in the next section.

The *initial statement* of a disk buffer initializes its virtual disk with access to the console and disk resources. It also sets the buffer length to zero. (Notice, that a disk buffer does not use its access rights to the console and disk, but only passes them on to a virtual disk declared within it.)

The following shows a declaration of two system components of type resource and two integers defining the base and limit of a disk buffer:

    var *consoleaccess, diskaccess* : *resource*;
      base, limit : *integer*;
      buffer : *diskbuffer*;

If we assume that these variables already have been initialized, we can initialize a disk buffer as follows:

    init *buffer*(*consoleaccess, diskaccess, base, limit*)

The *init* statement allocates storage for the parameters and shared variables of the disk buffer and executes its initial statement.

A monitor can only be initialized once. After initialization, the parameters and shared variables of a monitor exist forever. They are called *permanent variables*. The parameters and local variables of a monitor procedure, however, exist only while it is being executed. They are called *temporary variables*.

A monitor procedure can only access its own temporary and permanent variables. These variables are not accessible to other system components. Other components can, however, call procedure entries within a monitor. While a monitor procedure is being executed, it has *exclusive access* to the permanent variables of the monitor. If concurrent processes try to call procedures within the same monitor simultaneously, these procedures will be executed strictly one at a time.

Only monitors and constants can be permanent parameters of processes and monitors. This rule ensures that processes only communicate by means of monitors.

It is possible to define constants, data types, and local procedures within monitors (and processes). The local procedures of a system type can only be called within the system type. To prevent *deadlock* of monitor calls and ensure that access rights are hierarchical the following rules are enforced:

- a procedure must be declared before it can be called;
- procedure definitions cannot be nested and cannot call themselves;
- a system type cannot call its own procedure entries.

The absence of recursion makes it possible for a compiler to determine the store requirements of all system components. This and the use of permanent components make it possible to use *fixed store allocation* on a computer that does not support paging.

Since system components are permanent they must be declared as permanent variables of other components.

D Queues

A monitor procedure can delay a calling process for any length of time by executing a *delay* operation on a queue variable. Only one process at a time can wait in a queue. When a calling process is delayed by a monitor procedure it loses its exclusive access to the monitor variables until another process calls the same monitor and executes a continue operation on the queue in which the process is waiting.

The *continue* operation makes the calling process return from its monitor call. If any process is waiting in the selected queue, it will immediately resume the execution of the monitor procedure that delayed it. After being resumed, the process again has exclusive access to the permanent variables of the monitor.

Other variants of process queues (called 'events' and 'conditions') are proposed in [3], [5]. They are multi-process queues that use different (but fixed) scheduling rules. We do not yet know from experience which kind of queue will be the most convenient one for operating system design. A single-process queue is the simplest tool that gives the programmer complete control of the scheduling of individual processes. Later, I will show how multi-process queues can be built from single-process queues.

A queue must be declared as a permanent variable within a monitor type.

E Classes

Every disk buffer has its own virtual disk. A virtual disk is defined as a class type:

```
type virtualdisk = class(consoleaccess, diskaccess : resource);

var terminal : virtualconsole; peripheral : disk;

procedure entry read(pageno : integer; var block : page);
var error : boolean;
begin
  repeat
    diskaccess.request;
    peripheral.read(pageno, block, error);
    diskaccess.release;
    if error then terminal.write('disk failure');
  until not error;
end;

procedure entry write(pageno : integer; block : page);
begin "similar to read" end;

begin "initial statement"
  init terminal(consoleaccess), peripheral;
end
```

A virtual disk has access to a console resource and a disk resource. Its permanent variables define a virtual console and a disk. A process can access its virtual disk by means of *read* and *write* procedures. These procedure entries *request* and *release* exclusive access to the real disk before and after each block transfer. If the real disk fails, the virtual disk calls its virtual console to report the error.

The *initial statement* of a virtual disk initializes its virtual console and the real disk.

Section II-C shows an example of how a virtual disk is declared and initialized (within a disk buffer).

A class can only be initialized once. After initialization, its parameters and private variables exist forever. A class procedure can only access its own temporary and permanent variables. These cannot be accessed by other components.

A class is a system component that cannot be called simultaneously by several other components. This is guaranteed by the following rule:

- a class must be declared as a permanent variable within a system type;
- a class can be passed as a permanent parameter to another class (but not to a process or monitor).

So a chain of nested class calls can only be started by a single process or monitor. Consequently, it is not necessary to schedule simultaneous class calls at run time – they cannot occur.

F   Input/Output

The real *disk* is controlled by a class:

    type *disk* = **class**

with two procedure entries:

    read(*pageno, block, error*)
    write(*pageno, block, error*)

The class uses a standard procedure:

    io(*block, param, device*)

to transfer a block to or from the disk device. The *io* parameter is a record:

    var *param* : **record**
                operation : *iooperation*;
                result : *ioresult*;
                pageno : *integer*
        end

that defines an input/output operation, its result, and a page number on the disk. The calling process is delayed until an *io* operation has been completed.

A *virtual console* is also defined as a class:

```
type virtualconsole = class(access : resource);
var terminal : console;
```

It can be accessed by read and write operations that are similar to each other:

```
procedure entry read(var text : line);
begin
  access.request;
  terminal.read(text);
  access.release;
end
```

The real *console* is controlled by a class that is similar to the disk class.

G Multiprocess scheduling

Access to the console and disk is controlled by two monitors of type *resource*. To simplify the presentation, I will assume that competing processes are served in first-come, first-served order. (A much better disk scheduling algorithm is defined in [3]. It can be programmed in Concurrent Pascal as well, but involves more details than the present one.)

We will define a multiprocess queue as an array of single-process queues:

```
type multiqueue = array(0..qlength − 1) of queue
```

where *qlength* is an upper bound on the number of concurrent processes in the system.

A first-come, first-served scheduler is now straightforward to program:

```
type resource = monitor
var free : boolean; q : multiqueue;
  head, tail, length : integer;
```

```
procedure entry request;
var arrival : integer;
begin
  if free then free := false else
  begin
    arrival := tail;
    tail := (tail + 1) mod qlength;
    length := length + 1;
    delay (q(.arrival.));
  end;
end;

procedure entry release;
var departure : integer;
begin
  if length = 0 then free := true else
  begin
    departure := head;
    head := (head + 1) mod qlength;
    length := length − 1;
    continue (q(.departure.));
  end;
end;

begin "initial statement"
  free := true; length := 0;
  head := 0; tail := 0;
end
```

H   Initial process

Finally, we will put all these components together into a concurrent program. A Concurrent Pascal program consists of nested definitions of system types. The outermost system type is an anonymous process, called the initial process. An instance of this process is created during system loading. It initializes the other system components.

The initial process defines system types and instances of them. It executes statements that initialize these system components. In our example, the initial process can be sketched as follows (ignoring the problem of how base addresses and limits of disk buffers are defined):

```
type
  resource = monitor...end;
  console = class...end;
  virtualconsole = class(access : resource);...end;
  disk = class...end;
```

```
virtualdisk = class(consoleaccess, diskaccess : resource);...end
diskbuffer = monitor(consoleaccess, diskaccess : resource;
    base, limit : integer);...end;
inputprocess = process(buffer : diskbuffer);...end;
jobprocess = process(input, output : diskbuffer);...end;
outputprocess = process(buffer : diskbuffer);...end;
var
    consoleaccess, diskaccess : resource;
    buffer1, buffer2 : diskbuffer;
    reader : inputprocess;
    master : jobprocess;
    writer : outputprocess;
begin
    init consoleaccess, diskaccess,
        buffer1(consoleaccess, diskaccess, base1, limit1),
        buffer2(consoleaccess, diskaccess, base2, limit2),
        reader(buffer1),
        master(buffer1, buffer2),
        writer(buffer2);
end
```

When the execution of a process (such as the initial process) terminates, its private variables continue to exist. This is necessary because these variables may have been passed as permanent parameters to other system components.

Acknowledgments

It is a pleasure to acknowledge the immense value of continuous exchange of ideas with C. A. R. Hoare on structured multiprogramming. I also thank my students L. Medina and R. Varela for their helpful comments on this paper.

References

[1]   N. Wirth. 'The programming language Pascal,' *Acta Informatica*, **1**, 1, pp. 35–63, 1971.
[2]   P. Brinch Hansen. *Operation System Principles*. Englewood Cliffs, N. J.: Prentice-Hall, July 1973.
[3]   C. A. R. Hoare. 'Monitors: An operating system structuring concept,' *Commun. Ass. Comput. Mach.*, **17**, 549, Oct. 1974.

[4]   P. Brinch Hansen. 'The nucleus of a multiprogramming system,' *Commun. Ass. Comput. Mach.*, **13**, pp. 238–250, Apr. 1970.

[5]   —. 'Structured multiprogramming,' *Commun. Ass. Comput, Mach.*, **15**, pp. 574–578, July 1972.

[6]   —.'Concurrent programming concepts,' *Ass. Comput. Mach Comput. Rev.*, **5**, pp. 223–245, Dec. 1974.

[7]   —.'A programming methodology for operating system design.' In: *1974 Proc. IFIP Congr.* Stockholm, Sweden: North-Holland, Aug. 1974, pp. 394–397.

[8]   E. W. Dijkstra. 'Hierarchical ordering of sequential processes,' *Acta Informatica*, **1**, 2, pp. 115–138, 1971.

[9]   H. A. Simon. 'The architecture of complexity.' In: *Proc. Amer. Philosophical Society*, **106**, 6, 1962, pp. 468–482.

[10]   O.-J. Dahl and C. A. R. Hoare. 'Hierarchical program structures.' In: *Structured Programming*, O.-J. Dahl, E. W. Dijkstra, and C. A. R. Hoare, New York: Academic, 1972.

3

*MOD – A Language for Distributed Programming

Robert P. Cook
University of Wisconsin

Distributed programming is characterized by high communications costs and the inability to use shared variables and procedures for interprocessor synchronization and communication. *MOD is a high-level language system which attempts to address these problems by creating an environment conducive to efficient and reliable network software construction. Several of the *MOD distributed programming constructs are discussed as well as an interprocessor communication methodology. Examples illustrating these concepts are drawn from the areas of network communication and distributed process synchronization.

Index terms: computer networks, distributed programming, Modula, processor module, programming languages.

I Introduction

*MOD (Starmod), a language derived from Modula [35]–[37], is intended for systems or application programming in a network environment. The *MOD design is based on experience with our PDP-11/VAX Modula compiler [7] and was inspired by Brinch Hansen's 'distributed processes' concepts [3]. A *distributed program* can be characterized as an algorithm which requires multiple processors for its implementation, whereas a *concurrent program* requires multiple processes for its implementation. A *sequential program* is an algorithm which is implemented using only procedural constructs.

This work was supported in part by the U.S. Army under Contract DAAG29-75-C-0024 and in part by the National Science Foundation under Grant MCS-7903947.

It is interesting to observe that after 25 years of experience with sequential programming, there is still no consensus on language features. The current discussions involving Ada [19], [20] provide a case in point. Since even less is known about the requirements for distributed and concurrent programs, *MOD was developed as an experimentation media and is not presented here as the ultimate solution. The primary design criteria were transparency, extensibility, and program adaptability.

Following Parnas' definition [29], a language is *transparent* with respect to a given computer system if any system state and any sequence of system states which could be obtained by programming the component machines could also be obtained by using the high-level language. For instance, experimentation would be severely hampered if the language were inflexible with respect to process definition and scheduling. Therefore, *MOD provides low-level operations which can be extended by the programmer to define high-level abstractions appropriate to a particular machine environment. *MOD programs can also adapt to changes in workload or response time requirements. The language is designed so that a library module could be upgraded from a collection of procedures to a collection of processes without changing any of its users' programs. Finally, *MOD permits the user to organize his/her program to reflect the structure of the physical processors and the connectivity of the network.

This paper discusses the rationale behind the design of the *MOD system and contrasts the language features chosen with those of the Department of Defense (DoD) Ada language [19], Hoare's communicating sequential processes (CSP) [18], Feldman's PLITS [1], [13], and Brinch Hansen's 'distributed processes' [3]. In particular, we address the distributed programming problem areas of interprocessor communication, software testing, and kernel efficiency. The *MOD design decisions in other areas such as data abstraction [8] and synchronization [9] are described elsewhere.

II Program organization

Before proceeding further with a more detailed discussion of the *MOD distributed programming mechanisms, the *module* concept of Modula [35] will be considered as a focal point for network software development. A module usually corresponds to a program abstraction and consists of an external interface specification, data structure definitions, procedures, processes, and an optional initialization part. In *MOD, a module can be used as a type definition or to delineate a lexical scope as in Modula; therefore, both the information-hiding properties proposed by Parnas [28] and the flexibility of the Simula [10] 'class' mechanism are maintained.

In Modula, if the prefix 'device' or 'interface' is used before the 'module' keyword, the semantics of the module change. For instance, 'interface' denotes a module which semantically is similar to a monitor [17]. *MOD extends the Modula prefix notation to provide the user with the following module types:

PROGRAM ::= **network module** *IDENTIFIER* [= *LINKLIST*];
          [*MODULEBODY*]
          end *IDENTIFIER*.

PROCESSORDECLARATION ::= **processor module** *IDENTIFIER*
          [*REPLICATIONCOUNT*];
          [*MODULEBODY*]
          [**begin** *STATEMENTLIST*]
          end *IDENTIFIER*

MODULETYPEDECLARATION ::= **type** *IDENTIFIER* =
          [MODULETYPE] **module**;
          [*MODULEBODY*]
          [**begin** *STATEMENTLIST*]
          end *IDENTIFIER*

MODULEDECLARATION ::= [*MODULETYPE*] **module** *IDENTIFIER*;
          [[*MODULEBODY*]
          [**begin** *STATEMENTLIST*]
          end *IDENTIFIER*]

MODULETYPE ::= *MODULETYPEID*
LINKLIST ::= *LINK* [,*LINK*] ...
LINK ::= (*PROCESSORVAR* [,*PROCESSORVAR*] ...)
REPLICATIONCOUNT ::= '[' *EXPRESSION* ']'

A network module is required to define processor connectivity and to declare any types, constants, procedures, or processes which are global to the processor modules. The *LINKLIST* details the communication paths among processor modules in terms of a source specification and a list of destinations. Variable declarations and the initialization *STATEMENTLIST* are prohibited at the network level since there is no instruction or data storage outside of a physical processor. Procedures and processes are allowed within network modules for global standardization but are copied automatically by the compiler into each processor module. Figure 1 gives an example of a five processor module 'star' system.

Processor modules were introduced as part of the *MOD design to allow the programmer to partition a computation into collections of processes. All procedures and processes within a processor module can directly access shared variables, whereas interprocessor references must be in the form of messages. By using combinations of processes and the ability to specify processor modules, a *MOD user can take full advantage of the physical hardware available in order to exploit the

```
network module star = (center,pr),(pr,center);
    const NOPROCESSORS = 4;
    processor module center;
        define communicator;
        process communicator(...);
                    .

                    .

                    .
            pr[i].communicator(...); (*call processor i*)
                    .

                    .

                    .
        end communicator;
        begin (*initialization*)
        end center;

    processor module pr[NOPROCESSORS]; (*four peripheral processors*)
        define communicator;
        import center;
        process communicator(...);
                    .

                    .

                    .
            center.communicator(...); (*call center*)
                    .

                    .

                    .
        end communicator;
        begin (*initialization*)
        end pr
    end star.
```

Figure 1

inherent parallelism in his/her algorithm. In some situations, an algorithm may contain more processor modules than the number of physical processors available. In this case, a mechanism such as Jones' 'task force' language [21] must be used to *map* the *MOD virtual processor set on to the physical network. It may also be advantageous to use a mapping specification for networks with nonuniform communication costs. In addition, the performance of processes within a processor module can be improved by mapping the module to a multiprocessor. We should also point out that the availability of a hardware multiprocessor to implement a particular processor module should be regarded as a fortuitous circumstance and should not be counted on by the programmer.

The *MODULETYPEDECLARATION* can be used to define a

module as an extended type, such as 'complex' or 'stack.' The variables in the module represent the type's data structures and the exported procedures define the operators for the new type. If a *MODULETYPE* name is used as a prefix in a *MODULEDECLARATION*, the module body declared with the *MODULETYPE* is replicated as the body for the new module. The first option, which is similar to the Simula [10] 'class' notation, duplicates data while sharing the type module's procedures. The second option duplicates both data and code. For instance, a communications module might be declared as a 'type' which could then be replicated for each use. Next, the syntax of a *MODULEBODY* will be illustrated:

MODULEBODY ::= *EXTERNALINTERFACE*
                  BLOCKHEADING

EXTERNALINTERFACE ::= [**define** *ELEMENT* [,*ELEMENT*] ... ;]
                        [**export** *ELEMENT* [,*ELEMENT*] ... ;]
                        [**pervasive** *ELEMENT* [,*ELEMENT*] ... ;]

BLOCKHEADING ::= [**import** *IDENTIFIER* [,*IDENTIFIER*] ... ;]
                   [*DECLARATIONLIST*]

ELEMENT ::= *IDENTIFIER* [(**readonly** | **protected**)]

A module boundary delineates a closed lexical scope which can only be superseded by the explicit specification of 'define,' 'export,' 'import,' or 'pervasive.' The external interface for a processor module usually lists any message types and process names which are used for communication.

An *IDENTIFIER* specified in an 'import' list causes a declaration from a global lexical scope to be made accessible within the module. The 'export' attribute allows a local declaration to be visible at the enclosing lexical level, while 'pervasive' makes the *IDENTIFIER* known at the enclosing and all nested levels where the same name is not already declared. The latter option is most useful for making functions appear to their users as 'builtin' to the language. For instance, the 'sine' and 'cosine' functions are declared as 'pervasive' in the math library module; therefore, any use of that library automatically imports the math routines into the enclosed scopes.

The 'define' statement is provided as an alternative to 'export.' It gives the user the ability to list those *IDENTIFIERS* which can be referenced externally, but only by prefixing the reference with the module name as in the Simula [10] 'class' notation. 'Define' is used to reduce the size of 'import' lists since 'import'ing a module name permits references to any of its 'define'd symbols. Secondly, a qualified reference to a 'define'd name serves a useful documentation function. The ability to specify the external interface for each module is becoming a standard feature of modern programming as is demonstrated by its use in Mesa [14], Euclid [23], Alphard [32], Ada [19], etc.

The *MOD user can also restrict variables and types to read-only access or to no access. These restrictions are not applied within the exporting module. Since the access checking is enforced by the compiler, it can be maintained even across distributed processors. The only exception is that any restricted variable or instance of a restricted type can be passed as an argument to a procedure exported from the defining module.

III   Language concepts

From the *MOD viewpoint, a computer network can be characterized as an arbitrary collection of processors with fixed communication paths for interprocessor message transfer. We have adopted the traditional [33] definitions that a **processor** executes commands or instructions, a **procedure** is a sequence of instructions for a processor, and a **process** is one or more procedures together with the state vector which controls and defines the virtual processor on which the process runs. It should be noted that a procedure cannot execute except as part of a process. Since *MOD programs are intended to run on a bare machine, a *MOD process is a *much simpler* entity than the processes found in most operating systems. For instance, the state vector for a UNIX [30] process on a PDP-11 contains over 1000 bytes of information while the *MOD kernel for the same computer uses 32 bytes for a process' state vector. Processes in the same processor module can communicate using shared variables or messages; however, interprocessor communication can only consist of messages.

Messages are assumed to range from no content (signal or interrupt) to arbitrary data structures. We will refer to the recipient of a message as the *message handler*, or handler. Furthermore, *MOD enforces strong type checking on messages both within and across processors to maintain system consistency. Finally, any communication mechanisms presented should be efficient and should not constrain the options of the programmer. In the next sections, the *MOD design will be discussed along with a detailed analysis of the alternatives, advantages, and disadvantages.

A   Message handlers

A procedure is a simple example of an intraprocessor message handler. Since a message can be an arbitrary data structure composed of many subfields, the syntax for the argument list and returned value was expanded to permit record and array types. Thus, the familiar argument list notation is used to represent the component fields of a message:

PROCEDUREDECLARATION ::=
  procedure IDENTIFIER [(FORMALS)] [: TYPEID];
    BLOCKHEADING
    [**begin** STATEMENTLIST]
    end IDENTIFIER

PROCEDUREREFERENCE ::= PROCEDUREID [(ARGUMENTS)]

A procedure is an example of a *dependent* service in that the procedure's activation record must be attached to the activation record stack of an existing process, usually the caller, in order to execute. *MOD does not permit procedures as interprocessor message handlers. As an alternative, *MOD uses a process-oriented communication methodology.

1 Processes

Each 'processor module' consists of one or more concurrent processes declared as follows:

PROCESSDECLARATION ::=

  process IDENTIFIER [(FORMALS)] ['['PRIORITY']'] : TYPEID;
    BLOCKHEADING
    [**begin** STATEMENTLIST]
    end IDENTIFIER

PROCESSREFERENCE ::= PROCESSID [(ARGUMENTS)]

Except for the keyword 'process' and the optional PRIORITY expression, the declaration is identical to that of a procedure. This correspondence was made intentionally to make it easier for a programmer to convert a sequential program to a concurrent or distributed program. A PRO-CESSREFERENCE must specify a list of arguments corresponding exactly in type and number to the FORMALS. Every procedure call creates a new activation record; however, a PROCESSREFERENCE creates a new activation record stack and state vector. Thus, each process can have multiple activations all executing in parallel.

The returned value for a functional process is set by assignment to the process identifier and must match the specified TYPEID. A reference to a functional process within the same processor is the same as a procedure reference. However, an interprocessor functional reference implies independent execution for the called process; the caller must wait. Also, the compiler will flag a process reference as an error if there are no direct communication links between the caller and handler processes.

The optional PRIORITY must evaluate to a compile-time constant which specifies the initial (default zero) priority of the process. The initial priority can be modified by altering the value of the pseudo-variable 'priority.' Priority can be used to improve the performance or response time of an algorithm by establishing precedence relationships among its processes.

Consider the following execution options for a process as a message handler:

(1)   execute in parallel with caller   no reply message
(2)   execute in parallel with caller   reply message
(3)   caller waits for completion   no reply message
(4)   caller waits for completion   reply message.

Option 1 is implemented by a *MOD process which does not return a value while option 4 is represented by a functional process. The reply message is the returned value which can range from a simple variable to an arbitrary record. Option 3 is easily programmed by using option 4 to return a completion indication. Option 2, which corresponds to Conway's [5] 'fork' and 'join' methodology, is available using the 'port' mechanism described in Section III-A2.

The example in Figure 2 illustrates these concepts with a ring network version of Dijkstra's Dining Philosophers [11] problem. As in the original version, five philosophers are each trying to eat from a plate of special spaghetti which has been placed in the middle of a round table. The spaghetti is special since each philosopher requires two forks to eat it. In our example, each philosopher can directly control only the right-hand fork; to get the left fork, the philosopher to the left must be consulted. However, each philosopher is also restricted to conversation with the right neighbor only; therefore, messages must be sent around the ring (table) to get permission to use the left-hand fork and to give it back. The algorithm is based on an ordered resource allocation strategy developed by Havender [16] which prevents deadlock and starvation.

Each philosopher is required to call *getforks* to start eating and *putforks* to stop. The lower level protocol as well as the problem restrictions and network topology are completely hidden from the user. The *get* process accepts fork requests and either passes the request to the right in the ring or else gets control of its own fork and sends an acknowledgment to the *who* philosopher. *pid* is a built-in function which identifies each processor by its index value. *'got'* acknowledges fork allocations and *put* frees forks. The algorithm works correctly without process priority but we have specified a higher priority for the *got* process to illustrate how performance can be *tuned* by such assignments. Note that every message in the ring activates a parallel process; thus, the performance of the algorithm can also be improved by using multiprocessors for the nodes of the ring.

```
network module diningroom = (phil [1],phil [2]),(phil [2],phil [3]),
                            (phil [3],phil [4]),(phil [4],phil [5]),
                            (phil [5],phil [1]);   (*ring network*)

  processor module phil [5];
    define get, put, got;      (*communication processes*)
    module at_table;
      export get, put, got, getforks, putforks;
      import phil;
      var myfork, gotone : semaphore;

      process get(who, fork : integer);      (*get "fork" for "who"*)
        begin
        if fork < > pid then phil [pid mod 5 + 1].get(who, fork)
                      else p(myfork);      got(who)
                      end if
        end get;

      process put( fork : integer);      (*give "fork" back*)
        begin
        if fork < > pid then phil [pid mod 5 + 1].put( fork)
                      else v(myfork)
                      end if
        end put;

      process got(who : integer) [1];      (*let "who" use fork*)
        begin
        if who < > pid then phil [pid mod 5 + 1].got(who)
                      else v(gotone)
                      end if
        end got;

      procedure getforks;      (*philosopher waits for both forks*)
        begin   get(if pid = 1 then 1 else pid − 1);   p(gotone);
                get(if pid = 1 then 5 else pid);        p(gotone)
        end getforks;

      procedure putforks;      (*give forks back and don't wait*)
        begin   put(pid);
                put(if pid = 1 then 5 else pid − 1)
        end putforks;
      end at_table;

    begin loop
            (*think*)   getforks;
            (*eat  *)   putforks
            end loop
    end phil
end diningroom.
```

Figure 2

2   Ports

In addition to the call/return form of message communication described in Section III-Al, it is often desirable to implement coroutine [6], rendezvous [19], or multiple handler protocols. We have integrated Balzer's [2] port mechanism into the *MOD design to provide these facilities:

PORTDECLARATION ::= **port** IDENTIFIER [(FORMALS)] [:TYPEID];
PORTREFERENCE ::= PORTID [(ARGUMENTS)]

A procedure provides a dependent message handler; a process is an independent message handler; and a port is a message queue which is independent of a handler. Thus, a port can be thought of as a queue of procedure or process messages (argument lists) waiting for execution. With a procedure or process, the caller initiates execution; with a port, only the handler can initiate execution as follows:

REGIONSTATEMENT ::= **region** PORTID [,PORTID] ...;
                    [PORTBODY]
                    end region

PORTBODY ::= STATEMENTLIST | PORTCASE [;PORTCASE] ...
PORTCASE ::= PORTID : **begin** STATEMENTLIST
                    end PORTID

If only a single PORTID is present, the PORTBODY must be a STATEMENTLIST; otherwise, a PORTCASE is required for each PORTID listed. The latter option permits a process to service requests with nondeterministic arrival times. The region statement copies the selected message into the current activation record and reserves a return value cell if the port is a function. When an 'exit' from the region occurs, the returned value, if present, is transmitted to the PORTREFERENCE statement. As with processes, the caller only waits if the port returns a value. At compile-time, the scope of the argument list is opened on region entry and closed on region exit for a single port. For multiple ports, a scope is opened and closed for each PORTCASE. When the region statement is executed, the executing process will wait until a message is present at one of the listed ports. If multiple regions are waiting for the same port when a message arrives, the region to execute is chosen nondeterministically. If a region is waiting for several ports which simultaneously receive messages, the arrival order determines the processing order. Also, an 'awaited' function is provided to test the status of a port.

Figure 3 illustrates an implementation of the previous example using ports. The first example uses a process for every message which provides the maximum parallelism. In the port implementation, only one

```
network module diningroom = (phil [1], phil [2]),(phil [2], phil [3]),
                            (phil [3], phil [4]),(phil [4], phil [5]),
                            (phil [5], phil [1]);   (*ring network*)
  processor module phil [5];
    define get, put, got;
    module at_table;
      export get, put, got, getforks, putforks;
      import phil;
      var myfork, gotone : semaphore;
      port get(who, fork : integer);     (*get "fork" for "who"*)
      port got(who : integer);           (*let "who" know*)
      port put( fork : integer);         (*give "fork" back*)
      process waitrep(who : integer);    (*local rep. for "who"*)
        begin p(myfork); got(who)
        end waitrep;
      process communicator;
        begin loop
               region get, put, got;
    get:           begin
                   if fork < > pid then phil [pid mod 5 + 1].get(who, fork)
                                     else waitrep(who)
                                     end if

                   end get;
    put :          begin
                   if fork < > pid then phil [pid mod 5 + 1].put( fork)
                                     else v(myfork)
                                     end if

                   end put;
    got :          begin
                   if who < > pid then phil [pid mod 5 + 1].got(who)
                                    else v(gotone)
                                    end if

                   end got
               end region
           end loop
       end communicator;
      procedure getforks;   (*philosopher waits for both forks*)
        begin   get(if pid = 1 then 1 else pid − 1);   p(gotone);
                get(if pid = 1 then 5 else pid );       p(gotone)
        end getforks;
      procedure putforks;   (*give forks back and don't wait*)
        begin   put(pid );
                put(if pid = 1 then 5 else pid − 1)
        end putforks;
      begin   communicator
      end at_table;
    begin loop
          (*think*) getforks;   (*eat*) putforks
          end loop
    end phil
end diningroom.
```

Figure 3

communication process is created for each processor and the messages are handled sequentially. However, multiple 'communicator' processes could still be invoked to increase parallelism.

B Processor communication

In *MOD, processes, ports and procedures are all referenced with the same syntax; thus, the user of a module's services need never know how the service is provided. The advantage is that the implementation can be easily modified to adapt to changes in workload or response time requirements. The only restriction on such changes is that procedures cannot be used for interprocessor communication.

A procedure invocation implies the creation of an activation record which is added to the stack of the calling process. However, for an interprocessor call, the stack of the calling process is not available. The alternative is to attach the procedure's activation record to the stack of a randomly selected process in the called processor. We rejected this choice because the selected process could not continue execution until the procedure's activation record was removed. A more serious problem occurs if the process controls a resource needed by the procedure; in this case, deadlock could result. Therefore, *MOD provides only ports and processes for interprocessor communication.

A process provides parallel execution for each message handler but requires a storage allocation operation to create its stack. A port, or multiple ports, can be handled by a single process which remains permanently active; thus, a port communication involves only a context switch which can be performed very quickly with modern hardware. If the handler execution time is considerably longer than process creation time, a process is the appropriate implementation choice. Otherwise, a port will provide the fastest response time.

C Comparison with other languages

*MOD integrates Brinch Hansen's [3] 'distributed processes' (DP) concepts with the modular programming philosophy of Wirth [35]–[37]. Figure 4 illustrates the compatibility of a DP 'process' with a *MOD 'processor module'. *MOD also provides the user with network and processor modules, ports, processes, and synchronization abstractions [9]. DP is oriented towards a single process per processor while *MOD is intended as a general-purpose language for distributed programming.

1 Ada

Ada [19], [20] is a language proposed by the Department of Defense for universal use; therefore, it should be instructive to compare an Ada 'task'

```
process distributed
  <own variables>
  proc name(input params#output params)
    <local variables>
    <statement>
  <initial statement>

processor module *MODdistributed;
  define name, nametype;
  <own variables>
  type nametype = record
                    output params
                  end record;
  process name(input params) : nametype;
    <local variables>
    begin <statement>
    end name;
  begin <initial statement>
end *MODdistributed;
```

Figure 4

with a *MOD 'process'. In *MOD as in Modula, a 'process' cannot be declared inside other processes or procedures. An Ada task 'may be
declared local to other task bodies, packages, subprograms, and blocks'
and a 'thread of control' is maintained between a task and its parent. In
addition, 'any subprogram, module, or block containing task declarations cannot be left until all local tasks have terminated.' Furthermore,
tasks can contain procedures which can be called by other tasks. Thus,
tasks within blocks or procedures must be able to share activation record
stacks and tasks which call procedures in other tasks must be able to share
the procedure's global variable space. *MOD avoids these addressing and
protection problems by allowing shared access only to global variables.
*MOD also avoids maintenance of the 'thread of control' information.
All of these Ada conventions are even more difficult to implement across
processors.

It is an error to initiate more than one instance of an Ada task; the
user can declare vectors of tasks but each element must be individually
addressed. Ada provides ports in the form of 'entry' declarations which
are restricted to a task body. Therefore, to communicate with a task, the
user must name an entry point. If multiple instances of tasks with the
same name were allowed, the entry point could not be named without
ambiguity. *MOD avoids this restriction by requiring *port* declarations
to occur outside of processes; thus, any *port* can be serviced by any
process. This is not possible in Ada.

The Ada 'accept' statement is equivalent to a *MOD 'region' but
always requires the caller to wait until the body of the 'accept' completes

execution. Thus, Ada does not have a direct equivalent to *MOD functional ports, functional processes, or multiple processes. Procedures, processes, and ports are referenced identically in *MOD; only procedure and entry references are similar in Ada.

2 Mesa

Mesa [27] includes both processes and ports in a format similar to *MOD. Mesa allows a procedure body to be called as a process by using the 'fork/join' statements. The 'join' statement allows the returned value to be retrieved after the call. We decided not to use this methodology because it would require changes to all user programs if a handler were changed from a procedure to a process. As pointed out in a recent paper [22], the 'join' construct is infrequently used compared to the 'detached' process option which is similar to the *MOD design. Ports in Mesa were designed to implement coroutines; procedures must have a special 'start' phase, be 'connect'ed to a port and then 'restart'ed. The Mesa port mechanism is so complex because it was designed to set up a coroutine relationship between two or more procedures within the same process. The *MOD port is a more general mechanism which has a variety of uses including connecting processes as coroutines.

3 CSP and PLITS

Hoare's CSP [18] and Feldman's [1], [13] PLITS languages are oriented toward end-user programming on top of an operating system. PLITS, for instance, performs automatic routing and flow control of messages; these would be user-implemented services in *MOD. CSP is strongest in its exploration of nondeterministic programming features while PLITS is more completely specified with respect to distributed programming. Both languages are port oriented. Hoare's processes can be created dynamically as in *MOD; however, the relationship between two communicating processes is symmetrical and requires both of them to name the other. Communication is asymmetrical in *MOD so that in hierarchical systems, handlers can be created without knowing the identities of their callers.

4 CLU

Liskov [24] has recently proposed some distributed computing extensions to CLU [25]. A CLU 'guardian' is similar to a *MOD 'processor module' but is restricted to ports for communication. There is no equivalent to a 'network module' for processor organization. Ports are global to processes as in *MOD and include timeout and error detection notation. The major difference between the two proposals arises because of the integrated definitions of procedures, processes, and ports in *MOD. All of the languages that we have examined, including CLU, have a special syntax for one or more of these constructs; thus, any change to a library program may require changes to all user programs.

IV   Software testing

In order to test software in the distributed environment, it must be possible to experiment both with software algorithms and hardware organizations. The advent of high-level languages has greatly enhanced algorithm development but the same flexibility is not present for hardware. The virtual machine approach [15] was a step in the right direction but was primarily oriented towards the construction of multi-programmed, single processor software. The VM environment has been suggested [34] as suitable for the development of network software but the user is still given a bare machine as a starting point.

Our proposal consists of a two-level approach:

(1)   a VHLN (virtual high-level language network) *MOD environment for network software development and testing on a single host computer (a PDP-11 or VAX in the current implementation effort); and

(2)   a compiler capable of producing code for a number of different machines.

The VHLN system is a run-time package which executes all of the processor modules on a single processor. The package also provides debugging, simulation, and performance analysis aids. It is much more economical to develop software tools for one host development computer than for each target machine. Once a software system has been tested, it can be moved to the network for production use. We have used this methodology to construct operating systems for virtual processors, file systems, and simulations of the Ethernet [26] and DCS [12] networks.

The VHLN system also has some disadvantages. The simulated, multiple processor environment provided by the *MOD test system is unrealistic in the sense that events will not have a real-time correspondence to the performance of systems running on bare machines. However, even this problem can be solved by using the techniques proposed by Canon [4]. As we gain experience with the system, it will be possible to draw more definitive conclusions regarding the ease of moving from a simulated to a real network.

V   The *MOD kernel

The code generated by the *MOD compiler is independent of its execution environment. For example, we have several bare machine kernels for different PDP-11s, a kernel for simulation, and a kernel which allows *MOD programs to run on UNIX [30]. The bare machine kernels are used for real-time testing, the simulation kernel for performance evaluation, and the UNIX kernel for system development and debugging. Except for simulation statements, the same *MOD program could be executed with any of the kernels. Next, the *MOD bare machine kernel will be described.

The *MOD kernel performs message transmission and synchronization functions only; any routing, scheduling, or flow control operations are the domain of the systems programmer. A process loses control of a hardware processor only by terminating, blocking, lowering its priority, or by receipt of a message for a higher priority process.

The compiler generates a list which details the processes and ports referenced by a processor module together with their processor addresses. In addition, a similar list is created for local ports or processes that have been exported or defined. When an external process or port call occurs, the kernel constructs a message from the argument list as follows:

```
var message : record
         arg₁ : TYPE₁;
             :
         argₙ : TYPEₙ;
         end record
```

The processor address for the destination is available from the kernel tables to control message transmission. For a functional call, the originating kernel changes the process' status to indicate that it is waiting for a reply message from the target processor. When a reply arrives, its origin is verified against the saved value in the process' control block; the reply is appended to the process' activation record; and the process' status is changed to 'ready'. It will resume execution when it is the highest priority, 'ready' process.

In *MOD, each interrupt or message is sent to either a port or a process. A message to a process creates a new process activation record stack. The new process' priority and start address are taken from the kernel control table. A process switch occurs only if the new process has a higher priority than any of the executing processes. A message to a port is logged if no process is waiting; otherwise, a process switch decision based on priority is made. Port communication only requires a process switch while a process call requires both the creation of an activation record and a process switch. The critical question is how quickly these operations can be performed. Table I lists the number of instructions executed for process/port communication on our PDP-11 standalone and UNIX kernels.

The UNIX kernel copies each process' stack segment from high core to a save area on every process switch. The standalone kernel has less

Table I

Operation	Standalone	Unix Kernel
process create (N arguments)	39 + 7N + A + S	31 + 2N + A + S
process delete	71 + B + S	10 + 5E + B + S
port call (no arguments)	18 + S	14 + S
port call (N arguments)	24 + 7N + S	20 + B + A + 2N + S
(A) allocate memory	45	20 + 10C
(B) free memory	5	22 + 6D
(S) process switch	32	36 + B + A + 2F + 2G
(C) number of free list cells of smaller size		
(D) number of free list cells at a smaller address		
(E) number of processes in scheduling list		
(F) old process' stack size		
(G) new process' stack size		

work to do on context switches because there is no copying, although the state vector is more complicated. Also, the initial stack space for new processes is fixed in size which means that the allocate/free operations can be executed in constant time.

VI Summary

The *MOD system represents an exploration of the design decisions necessary to apply the modular programming philosophy of Wirth to the development of distributed software and to propose an environment conducive to the construction and testing of such systems. This paper would not have been written but for the impetus and inspiration of Brinch Hansen's article [3] on distributed processes.

The current design was developed by experimenting with extensions to our Modula compiler which is written in C [31] and runs on Version 7 UNIX. The compiler generates either PDP-11 or VAX11/780 machine code. A separate *MOD compiler is currently under development.

References

[1] J. E. Ball, G. J. Williams, and J. R. Low, 'Preliminary ZENO language description,' Univ. Rochester, Rep. TR41, Jan. 1979.

[2] R. M. Balzer, 'PORTS – A method for dynamic interprogram communication and job control," in *Proc. AFIPS SJCC Comput. Conf.*, **39**, 1971, pp. 485–489.

[3] P. Brinch Hansen, 'Distributed processes: A concurrent programming concept,' *Commun. Ass. Comput. Mach.*, **21**, pp. 934–941, Nov. 1978.

[4] M. D. Canon *et al.*, 'A virtual machine emulator for performance evaluation,' *Commun. Ass. Comput. Mach.*, **23**, pp. 71–80, Feb. 1980.

[5] M. E. Conway, 'A multiprocessor system design,' in *Proc. AFIPS Fall Joint Comput. Conf.*, **24**, 1963, pp. 139–146.

[6] —, 'Design of a separable transition-diagram compiler,' *Commun. Ass. Comput. Mach.*, **6**, pp. 396–408, July 1963.

[7] R. P. Cook, 'An introduction to modular programming for Pascal users,' Univ. Wisconsin-Madison, Tech. Rep. 372, Nov. 1979.

[8] —, 'Data abstraction in *MOD,' in preparation.

[9] —, 'Schedulers as abstractions – An operating system structuring concept,' Univ. Wisconsin-Madison, Tech. Rep. 393, July 1980.

[10] O. J. Dahl *et al.*, 'Simula 67 common base language,' Norwegian Comput. Center, Oslo, May 1968.

[11] E. W. Dijkstra, 'Cooperating sequential processes,' in *Programming Languages*, F. Genuys, Ed. New York: Academic, 1968, pp. 43–112.

[12] D. Farber *et al.*, 'The distributed computing system,' in *Proc. COMPCON 73*, IEEE Comput. Soc., Feb. 1973, pp. 31–34.

[13] J. A. Feldman, 'High level programming for distributed computing,' *Commun. Ass. Comput. Mach.*, **22**, pp. 353–368, June 1979.

[14] C. M. Geschke, J. H. Morris, Jr. and E. H. Satterthwaite, 'Early experience with Mesa,' *Commun. Ass. Comput. Mach.*, **20**, pp. 540–553, Aug. 1977.

[15] R. P. Goldberg, 'Survey of virtual machine research,' *Computer*, **6**, pp. 34–44, June 1974.

[16] J. W. Havender, 'Avoiding deadlock in multitasking systems,' *IBM Syst. J.*, **7**, pp. 74–84, 1968.

[17] C. A. R. Hoare, 'Monitors: An operating system structuring concept,' *Commun. Ass. Comput. Mach.*, **17**, pp. 549–557, Oct. 1974.

[18] —, 'Communicating sequential processes,' *Commun. Ass. Comput. Mach.*, **21**, pp. 666–677, Aug. 1978.

[19] Honeywell, Inc. and Cii Honeywell Bull, 'Reference manual for the ADA programming language,' *SIGPLAN Notices*, **14**, part A, June 1979.

[20] —, 'Rationale for the design of the ADA programming language,' *SIGPLAN Notices*, **14**, part B, June 1979.

[21] A. Jones and K. Schwans, 'TASK Forces: Distributed software for solving problems of substantial size,' in *Proc. 4th Int. Conf. Software Eng.*, SIGSOFT-ACM, Sept. 1979, pp. 315–330.

[22] B. W. Lampson and D. D. Redell, 'Experience with processes and monitors in MESA,' *Commun. Ass. Comput. Mach.*, **23**, pp. 105–117, Feb. 1980.

[23] B. W. Lampson *et al.*, 'Report on the programming language Euclid,' *SIGPLAN Notices*, **12**, Feb. 1977.

[24] B. Liskov *et al.*, 'CLU reference manual,' Comput. Structures Group Memo 161, Lab. Comput. Sci., M.I.T., Cambridge, July 1978.

[25] B. Liskov, 'Primitives for distributed computing,' in *Proc. 7th Symp. Operating Syst. Principles*, Pacific Grove, CA, pp. 33–42, Dec. 1979.

[26] R. Metcalfe and D. Boggs, 'Ethernet: Distributed packet switching for local computer networks,' *Commun. Ass. Comput. Mach.*, **19**, pp. 395–404, July 1976.

[27] J. G. Mitchell, W. Maybury, and R. Sweet, 'Mesa language manual,' Xerox PARC Tech. Rep. CSL-79-3, Apr. 1979.

[28] D. L. Parnas, 'A technique for software module specification with examples,' *Commun. Ass. Comput. Mach.*, **15**, pp. 330–336, May 1972.

[29] D. L. Parnas and D. L. Siewiorek, 'Use of the concept of transparency in the design of hierarchically structured systems,' *Commun. Ass. Comput. Mach.*, **18**, pp. 401–408, July 1975.

[30] D. M. Ritchie and K. Thompson, 'The UNIX time-sharing system,' *Commun. Ass. Comput. Mach.*, **17**, pp. 365–375, July 1974.

[31] D. M. Ritchie, 'C reference manual,' Bell Labs., Jan. 1974.

[32] M. Shaw, W. A. Wulf, R. L. London, 'Abstraction and verification in Alphard: Defining and specifying iteration and generators,' *Commun. Ass. Comput. Mach.*, **20**, pp. 553–564, Aug. 1977.

[33] R. W. Watson, *Timesharing System Design Concepts*. New York: McGraw-Hill, 1970.

[34] J. M. Winett, 'Virtual machines for developing systems software,' in *Proc. IEEE Comput. Soc. Conf.*, Boston, MA, Sept. 1971.

[35] N. Wirth, 'Modula: A language for modular multiprogramming.' *Software – Practice and Experience*, **7**, pp. 3–35, 1977.

[36] —, 'The use of Modula,' *Software–Practice and Experience*, **7**, pp. 36–65, 1977.

[37] —, 'Design and implementation of Modula,' *Software–Practice and Experience*, **7**, pp. 67–84, 1977.

4

Concurrent C

N. H. Gehani and W. D. Roome
AT & T Bell Laboratories

Concurrent programming is becoming increasingly important because multicomputers, particularly networks of microprocessors, are rapidly becoming attractive alternatives to traditional maxicomputers. Effective utilization of such network computers requires that programs be written with components that can be executed in parallel. The C programming language does not have concurrent programming facilities. Our objective is to enhance C so that it can be used to write concurrent programs that can run efficiently on both single computers and multicomputers. Our concurrent programming extensions to C are based on the *rendezvous* concept. These extensions include mechanisms for the declaration and creation of processes, for process synchronization and interaction, and for process termination and abortion. We give a rationale for our decisions and compare Concurrent C extensions with the concurrent programming facilities in Ada. Concurrent C has been implemented on the UNIX system running on a single processor. A distributed version of Concurrent C is being implemented.

Key words: concurrent programming, C, distributed systems.

Introduction

Concurrent programming is becoming increasingly important because multicomputer architectures, particularly networks of microprocessors, are rapidly becoming attractive alternatives to traditional maxicomputers. Concurrent programming is important for many reasons [1]:

- Concurrent programming facilities are notationally convenient and conceptually elegant when used for writing systems in which many events occur concurrently, for example, in operating systems, real-time systems and database systems.
- Inherently concurrent algorithms are best expressed when the concurrency is stated explicitly; otherwise, the structure of the algorithm may be lost.

- Efficient utilization of multiprocessor architectures requires concurrent programming.
- Concurrent programming can reduce program execution time even on uniprocessors, by allowing input/output operations to run in parallel with computation.

The C programming language [2] does not have facilities for concurrent programming. In this paper, we describe an upward-compatible extension of C, called Concurrent C, that provides concurrent programming facilities. We chose C as the base language because it is a small language that can be implemented efficiently, even on microcomputers, and because the use of the C language has spread rapidly in the last few years. Concurrent C is based on the synchronous message passing model that has been discussed in detail in the literature [3][4].

We had two main objectives in enhancing C with concurrent programming facilities:

(1) To provide a concurrent programming language that can be used for writing systems on genuinely parallel hardware, such as a network of microprocessors or workstations.

(2) To provide a test bed for experimenting with a variety of high-level concurrent programming facilities and distributed programming.

Selection of the concurrent programming model

Synchronous message passing

In Concurrent C, programmers define processes that interact via synchronous ('blocking send' and 'blocking receive') message passing. Synchronous message passing primitives combine process synchronization with information transfer. Two processes interact first by synchronizing, then by transferring information, and finally by continuing their individual activities. This synchronization is called a *rendezvous*.

In a *simple* rendezvous, the exchange of information is unidirectional – from the message sender to the receiver. However, many process interactions, such as a client process requesting service from a server process, require bidirectional information transfer, and hence require two simple rendezvous. In the first rendezvous, the client gives a description of the request to the server. The server performs the request, and then, if necessary, does a second rendezvous with the client to give it the results of executing the request.

We selected the *extended rendezvous* or *transaction* concept for Concurrent C. An extended rendezvous allows bidirectional information transfer using only one rendezvous [4][5]. After the rendezvous is established, information is copied from the process requesting service –

the client – to the server. The client process is then forced to wait while the server process performs the requested service. Upon completion of the service, the results, if any, are returned to the client, which is then free to resume execution. From the client's viewpoint, an extended rendezvous is just like a function call.

Although Concurrent C and Ada are both based on the extended rendezvous model, there are important differences between the concurrent programming facilities in the two languages. These differences are summarized later.

Why this model?

Initially, we considered several categories of concurrent programming models:

(1)   Those based on shared memory.

(2)   Those based on asynchronous (non-blocking) message passing.

(3)   Those based on synchronous (blocking) message passing.

(4)   A combination of message passing and shared memory [6][7].

We immediately rejected the shared memory models, because we wanted Concurrent C programs to run efficiently on non-shared memory multicomputers, such as a network of workstations connected by a local area network.

That left us with asynchronous and synchronous message passing models. In one sense, these two models are equivalent, in that either set of primitives can be implemented in terms of the other. We finally selected a synchronous model for the following reasons:

- Most inter-process interactions are synchronous: the client requests a service, and waits for it. This matches the synchronous model perfectly. Thus, while the asynchronous model is more flexible, few people would actually use this extra flexibility.

- A synchronous model can be implemented more efficiently than an asynchronous model. For example, an asynchronous model requires message buffers and a sizable message controller [5][8]; data must always be copied into a message buffer and then out. For the synchronous model, data can be copied directly from the client process to the server, without going through an intermediate buffer, and the server's reply can be copied directly to the client. Thus the synchronous model saves space and saves time.

Some final comments about shared memory are in order. First and foremost, we wanted Concurrent C to allow (and encourage!) programmers to write portable programs that will run efficiently on multiprocessors with or without shared memory. This is why we choose a message passing model, and why we have not added any language constructs for dealing with shared memory or for simulating shared variables in a non-shared-memory environment.

On the other hand, we did not want to forbid programmers from using shared memory altogether, as long as they accept the resulting limitations on portability. If we tried to prevent the use of shared memory in a shared memory multiprocessor, programmers would just refuse to use Concurrent C. Therefore Concurrent C does not forbid processes from referencing global variables, nor does Concurrent C forbid processes from exchanging pointers. However, programmers do so at their own risk; such programs will not work as expected unless run on a computer with shared memory.

Concurrent C

The following description of Concurrent C assumes that the reader is somewhat familiar with the C programming language [2][9].

Processes, process types and transactions

First, some terminology. A *process definition* consists of two parts: a *type* (or *specification*) and a *body* (or *implementation*). A *process* is an instantiation of a process definition. Each process has its own flow-of-control; it executes in parallel with other processes. The existence of a process definition does not automatically create a process. Instead, the programmer must explicitly create each process at run-time.

One can think of each process as having its own stack, machine registers, program counter, etc. Most implementations will have some underlying scheduler that runs these processes on the available processors. Concurrent C does not define the scheduling policy, except to say that the scheduling policy should be fair; scheduling is regarded as an implementation detail.

The process type is the public part of a process definition. Only the information specified in the process type is visible to other processes. A process body contains the code (and associated declarations and definitions) that is executed by a process of that type; it is analogous to a function body, which it resembles. Details of the process body are not visible to other processes. The process type and body are described in detail later.

Recall that the extended rendezvous model has a 'client' process, which initiates an interaction, and a 'server' process, which waits for an interaction. The process type defines the kinds of extended rendezvous for which this process can act as a server. Each kind of rendezvous is called a *transaction*.[†] For each transaction, the process type defines the name of the transaction, the types of the arguments passed by the client, and the type of the value returned to the client. For example, a buffer manager process might have a `put` transaction, which places a character in the buffer, and a `get` transaction, which gets a character from the buffer.

In an extended rendezvous interaction, we will refer to the client process as *calling* a transaction of the server process, and we will refer to the rendezvous itself as a *transaction call*. Thus a client of a buffer manager process calls the buffer's `get` transaction. That client is blocked until the buffer process indicates that it is willing to *accept* a call for the `get` transaction.

A simple example

Before presenting Concurrent C in detail, we will first give an example of a simple buffer manager process to illustrate the flavor of Concurrent C. The process type of the buffer manager process, given below, indicates that it has one parameter, `max`, which is the maximum size of the buffer, and two transactions, `get` and `put`:

```
process spec buffer(int max)/* buffer holds max char */
{
   trans void put(char c);     /* put c into buffer; wait if full */
   trans char get();           /* return next char; wait if empty */
};
```

Here is a (trivial!) example of code segment in a client that creates a buffer process, puts the character 'a' into the buffer, and then retrieves that character:

```
char c;
process buffer b;        /* id for a process of type buffer */
b = create buffer(128);  /* start new buffer process, */
                         /* and save id in variable b */
b.put('a');              /* put 'a' into buffer */
c = b.get();             /* get next char, save in c */
c_abort(b);              /* destroy process b */
```

Variable `b` is a process variable; it holds an identifier (alias) for a process of type `buffer`. The declaration for `b` does not automatically create a process. Instead we must use the `create` operator to create a new process of type `buffer`. `create` returns an alias for the new

---

[†] An extended rendezvous can be thought of as an atomic operation done by a server process; the client is blocked until the server process accepts the request and performs the operation. Hence the term 'transaction,' as in an atomic set of updates in a database.

process, which we save in b. (A process variable is analogous to a pointer variable, and `create` is analogous to the storage allocation function `malloc`.)

The construct b.put('a') is the client's side of a transaction call. Note that it looks like a function call with a two-part name: an identifier for a process, and the name of one of that process's transactions. The put transaction returns no value, so the call appears as a statement by itself. The get transaction returns a char value, which is saved in the variable c. In general, b.get can be used wherever an expression of type char is allowed. Note that when the client makes a transaction call, it is blocked until process b accepts the call.

Here is the body of the buffer process:

```
process body buffer(max)
{
  char *buf;                           /* circular buffer of max bytes */
  int n = 0;                           /* number of characters in buffer */
  int in = 0;                          /* index of next available empty slot */
  int out = 0;                         /* index of next available character */
  buf = malloc(max);                   /* allocate buffer */
  for (;;)                             /* forever, */
    select {                           /* wait for next transaction */
      (n < max):                       /* when buffer has space, */
        accept put(c)                  /* accept put transaction */
            {buf[in] = c;}             /* copy argument character */
        n++;                           /* update count and index, */
        in = (in + 1) % max;           /* in parallel with client */
      or (n > 0):                      /* when buffer has data, */
        accept get()                   /* accept get transaction */
          {treturn buf[out];}          /* return next char */
        n--;                           /* update count and index, */
        out = (out + 1) % max;         /* in parallel with client */
    }
}
```

After declaring the buffer control variables and allocating a buffer array, the process repeatedly waits for either a put or a get transaction. The select statement has two guarded alternatives: the first accepts a put transaction whenever the buffer has space for another character, and the second accepts a get transaction whenever the buffer has data. Once one of those alternatives is taken, all statements in that alternative are executed; the other alternative is skipped. Because this select statement is in a 'forever' loop, the buffer process then executes the select statement again.

Initially, only the first guard is true; the select statement waits for the client to execute the statement b.put() (if it hasn't already, of course). At that point, the buffer process executes the first accept statement. The client process is suspended while the buffer process executes the single statement in the block following the accept statement. Parameter c is a local variable of the block, and is initialized to the value of the argument supplied by the client. The client process remains suspended until the buffer process completes executing the block. Afterwards, the client becomes free to resume, and the buffer process continues with the next two statements. The buffer process then skips over the second alternative and loops back to the `select` statement. Now both guards are true, so the buffer process waits for the next `put` or `get` transaction call. The next transaction call issued by the client is `b.get()`, so the buffer process will take the second alternative of the `select` statement. This is similar to the first alternative, except that the buffer process executes a `treturn` statement; this simultaneously returns a value to the client process, and causes an exit from the `accept` block.

Note that the buffer process accepts a pending transaction call only when it is at the `select` statement. If a call arrives at some other time, the call is held (and the client is suspended) until the buffer process executes the `select` statement and takes the corresponding alternative. The buffer process is never interrupted by the arrival of a transaction call.

Process types and transaction declarations

A process type has the general form:[†]

```
process spec process-type-name(parameter-declarations)
    { transaction declarations };
```

where *parameter-declarations* is a comma-separated list of parameter declarations, as in:

```
process spec multiplexor(int number, int max_size)
```

If a process has no transactions, the type can be written as:

```
process spec process-type-name(parameter-declarations);
```

As discussed earlier, Concurrent C processes synchronize and communicate by means of transactions. A process type must have a transaction declaration for each transaction for which this process can act as a server. A transaction declaration is like a function declaration except that it is preceded by the keyword `trans`, and that the parameter types are explicitly specified. The form is:

```
trans return-type tname(parameter-declarations);
```

[†] The keyword spec in the process type declaration represents the fact that a process type can also be viewed as the syntactic specification of a process.

This declares a transaction named *tname*, which returns a value of type *return-type*. The *parameter-declarations* is a comma-separated list of parameter declarations. The parameters represent the data that a client gives to the server; the return type is the type of the data that the server returns to the client.

The same transaction name can be used in several process types, and those transactions can have different argument types and return value types. Thus a transaction name is only meaningful in the context of a specific process type. In short, transaction names are to process types as structure member names are to structure types.

Process bodies

A process body has the form:

```
process body process-type-name(process-parameter-names)
    statement
```

The process body specifies the statements to be executed by each process of that type. Each process is a sequential program component that runs independently and in parallel with other processes. The statement in the process body can be a compound statement with automatic variables; each process of that type will get its own set of variables. Process parameters are used in the process body just as function parameters are used in function bodies. The types for the process parameters are given in the process type; to avoid unnecessary verbosity, they are not repeated in the process body. Values for the process parameters are supplied when each instance of this process is created (see the `create` operator, below).

Process bodies can contain any legal C statement, plus several Concurrent C extensions, such as the `accept` and `select` statements. These will be described later. Process bodies can call functions; the function is considered to be executing on behalf of that process. Any function can be called by a process of any type.

In a process body, the `return` statement terminates the process that executes it. This is equivalent to running off the end of the process body. Note that a process cannot return any value.

Process-valued expressions and process variables

The `create` operator is used to create (instantiate) a new process of the specified type with appropriate values for the process parameters. For example, given the declaration:

```
process spec buffer(int max) { ... };
```

the expression:

```
create buffer(128)
```

creates a new process of type buffer, with 128 for the value of the parameter max. The create operator returns a *process value* for this process type; in this case, a value of type process buffer. A process value is an identifier, or alias, for a specific process. A process value can be stored in a process variable of the same type:

```
process buffer b;
b = create buffer(128);
```

Concurrent C programs can have arrays of process values, structures whose members are process values, or pointers to process values, as in:

```
process buffer bufarr[10], *pb;
```

If the same process value is stored in several process variables, then all these variables refer to the same process. As with pointer values, care must be taken to avoid dangling references.

Provided that the types match, process values can be used in the following ways:

- as parameters to functions, transactions, or processes
- as values returned by functions or transactions
- in assignment to process variables
- in equality or inequality tests.

The predefined type process anytype is a 'wild card' process type: it is an alias for a process of an unknown type. It is used for declaring objects that may be associated with different processes types during program execution. For example, it is used to declare the type of the formal parameter of function c_abort, which can be used to abort a process of any type. As another example, the built-in function c_mypid() returns the process value of the process executing it; c_mypid() is declared as returning process anytype.

In general, any specific process-valued expression can be used wherever a process anytype value is expected; for example, a value of type process buffer can be assigned to a process anytype variable. Going the other way, a process anytype value can be used wherever a specific process type is expected; Concurrent C generates an implicit cast to the target type. Thus a process anytype value can be assigned to a process type variable, but cannot be used to specify the process in a transaction call. Concurrent C guarantees that if a value of type process x is converted to process anytype, it can be safely converted back to type `process x`. However, if the value is converted back to a different type `process y`, then the results of using this value are undefined. The `process anytype` mechanism provides an escape from type checking. For example, it allows us to write a general 'process name server,' which maintains a table of pairs of process values and symbolic names, without having to know in advance the types of all processes that will be in the table.

The predefined constant `c_nullpid` is a null (invalid) process value. It is of type `process anytype`, so that it can be assigned to, or compared against, a process variable of any type. Thus `c_nullpid` is to process values as `null` is to pointers.

Process creation and priority

As mentioned before, the `create` operator creates and activates a new process. The created process becomes eligible for execution immediately. The created process is called a *child* process of the creating, or *parent*, process. Processes that have the same parent process are called *sibling* processes. The `create` operator has the general form:[†]

        create *process-type-name*(*initial-values*) [`priority`(*p*)]

The `create` operator either returns a process value identifying the created process, or else returns `c_nullpid` if a new process could not be created. The integer expression *p* specifies the new process's priority relative to some standard priority. Positive values give the new process higher priority; negative values give it lower priority. If the priority is omitted, then the new process is assigned the standard priority.

The process scheduler is free to schedule processes subject to the following rules:

(1) If two processes that are ready for execution have different priorities, then the one with the higher priority is given preference for execution.

(2) No process should be indefinitely denied execution because of processes at the same or lower priority level.

Priorities should be used to give more execution time to some processes at the expense of others but *not* for synchronizing processes. For example, programmers should *not* assume that a higher priority process will immediately preempt all lower priority processes.

There are several built-in functions that manipulate process priorities:

[†] Expression [*a*], with the meta brackets [and], denotes the optional occurrence of item *a*.

c_setpriority(*pid*, *p*)	sets the absolute priority of process *pid* to value *p*.
c_changepriority(*pid*, *p*)	changes the current priority of process *pid* by the signed integer value *p*.
c_getpriority (*pid*)	returns the current priority of the process *pid*.

The initial process

When a Concurrent C program starts executing, there is only one process running. This process calls the function named main, which must then create all other processes. This initial process is part of the Concurrent C run-time system and does not have any transactions associated with it.

Process states and process termination

A process can be in one of the following three states:

- Active: A process becomes *active* upon creation and remains in this state while executing the statements specified in the corresponding process body.

- Completed: A process becomes *completed* when it executes a return statement in its process body, or when it reaches the end of its body.

- Terminated: A process becomes *terminated* when it has completed and all the processes created by it have terminated or it executes a terminate alternative defined in the section on the select statement.

A process can also be explicitly terminated by means of the c_abort function, i.e., the call c_abort(p) aborts process p. Aborting an active or completed process forces it to become terminated. That is, c_abort terminates all children (and grandchildren, etc.) of the indicated process. Aborting a terminated process has no effect.

Transaction calls

A transaction call is the caller's side of a transaction. The format is similar to a function call:

> *process-value.transaction-name*(*actual-parameters*)

Process-value is a process-valued expression designating a specific process. The type of that process must have a transaction named *transaction-name*, and the types of the arguments must match that transaction's parameter types. Like C function arguments, transaction arguments are passed by value. The transaction call expression has the type returned by the transaction. In general, a transaction call can be used wherever an expression of that type is allowed.

The calling process is delayed until the called process accepts the transaction (see the `accept` statement, below). The called process is given the values for transaction parameters specified by the caller. The calling process then remains suspended until the called process returns a value. This returned value becomes the value of the transaction-call expression.

Accept statements

The `accept` statement is the called process's side of a transaction. An `accept` statement has the form:

> `accept` transaction-name(parameter-names) [`suchthat` (e)] [`by` (ae)]
> [statement]

where e is a boolean expression and ae is an arithmetic expression; these expressions must involve the parameters of the `accept` statement. The compound statement is the body of the `accept` statement. An `accept` statement can only appear in the body of a process whose process type has a corresponding transaction declaration.

Which transaction call to accept

First consider an `accept` statement without a `suchthat` or `by` clause. If a process has one or more transaction calls outstanding for a transaction named `t`, then an `accept` statement for `t` accepts one of them immediately. Transaction calls are accepted in first-in-first-out (FIFO) order. If there are no outstanding transaction calls for `t`, then the `accept` statement waits until such a call arrives.

If a `suchthat` clause is present, then the `accept` statement considers only those transaction calls for which the expression e is true (non-zero). If there is no `by` clause, then these calls are accepted in FIFO order. If e is false for all the outstanding transaction calls, then execution of the `accept` statement is delayed until an appropriate transaction call arrives. Outstanding transaction calls for which e is false are not discarded; they are held, and may be accepted at some later time. As an example, the following accepts the first `get_lock` call for a free identifier:

> `accept get_lock(id) suchthat(isfree(id)){ ... }`

If there is a `by` clause, then the arithmetic expression ae is evaluated for each outstanding transaction call, and the call with the minimum value is accepted. Of course, if there is a suchthat clause, only those calls for which the suchthat expression is true are considered. For example, in a disk driver process, the following accepts the diskop transaction that is for the cylinder that is closest to the current position of the disk arm:

```
accept diskop(cyl,...) by(abs(cyl-curpos)){ ... }
```

The suchthat and by expressions can contain function calls. However, there are no guarantees on how often these expressions will be evaluated, so side-effects should be avoided. Transaction calls and process creation are not allowed within the suchthat and by expressions.

Accepting a transaction call

Once a transaction call has been accepted, the body of the accept statement is executed. Within the accept statement body, the parameter names represent variables that are initialized to the parameter values given by the transaction caller. The scope of a parameter variable is limited to the body of the accept statement. To retain a parameter value beyond the scope of the accept statement body, the parameter value must be stored in a variable with a larger scope.

The calling process is delayed until the accept statement terminates by completing execution of its body or by executing a treturn statement of the form:

```
treturn [expression];
```

The value of the treturn expression is returned to the calling process. The type of *expression* must conform to the result type of the corresponding transaction. If the result type is void, then no value is returned to the calling process, i.e., a treturn statement without an associated expression is used. After executing the treturn statement, the process containing the accept statement goes on to execute the next statement after the body of the accept, while the process issuing the transaction call becomes free to resume execution.[†]

An accept statement can only be used in a process body; it cannot appear in a function. We made this restriction so that the compiler can know the type of the process that is executing the accept statement, and can verify that the process has such a transaction.

[†] Both processes compete for the available processors; the scheduler can activate them in any order it sees fit.

Delay statements

A process can delay itself by executing a statement of the form:

    delay *duration*;

where *duration* is a floating-point expression specifying the amount of the delay in seconds. The actual delay may be more, but not less, than the requested delay.

Select statements

The select statement allows a process to wait for the first of several events. The syntax is:

    select {
      [(*guard*₁) :]   *alternative*₁
    or
      [(*guard*₂) :]   *alternative*₂
    or
      ...
    or
      [(*guard*ₙ) :]   *alternative*ₙ
    }

A *guard* is a boolean expression. The order in which guards will be evaluated is unspecified, and there is no guarantee that all the guards will be evaluated. Consequently, side-effects should be avoided in guards. As in the case of suchthat and by expressions, transaction calls and process creation are not allowed within guards.

An *alternative* is a set of Concurrent C statements. The first statement determines the type of the alternative:

(1) An accept statement, optionally followed by other statements (an accept alternative).

(2) A delay statement, optionally followed by other statements (a delay alternative).

(3) The keyword terminate followed by a semicolon (a terminate alternative). Or

(4) A list of statements, not beginning with any of the above (an *immediate* alternative).

The select statement executes one and only one of the alternatives. Once chosen, all statements in that alternative are executed, and flow resumes after the select statement. The following rules determine which alternative will be taken:

(1) If there is an `accept` alternative with a true guard (non-zero or omitted), and if there is a pending call for that transaction, accept that call and take that alternative. If the `accept` statement has a `suchthat` clause, take the alternative only if there is a call that satisfies the `suchthat` clause.

(2) Otherwise, if there is an *immediate* alternative with a true guard, take it.

(3) Otherwise, if there is a `terminate` alternative with a true guard, and there are no open `delay` alternatives, then wait until:

  (i) a transaction arrives that can be accepted; or
  (ii) all other processes have completed or terminated or are waiting at a `terminate` alternative – if this happens, then the entire Concurrent C program will terminate normally.

(4) Otherwise, let x be the lowest delay specified by a `delay` alternative with a true guard, or infinity if there are no such `delay` alternatives. The `delay` alternative is selected unless a transaction call for an `accept` alternative with a true guard arrives within x seconds.

If none of the `select` guards is true then an error condition occurs and the user is notified at run time.

The `terminate` alternative provides a simple mechanism for 'automatic' program termination because of 'collective process termination'. To make the implementation of the `terminate` alternative as simple as possible, we impose the following restriction: if the choice is between a `terminate` alternative that cannot be selected immediately and a `delay` alternative with true guards, then the result is undefined in the sense that the `select` statement semantics do not state which alternative will be taken.

Note that a `terminate` alternative is never chosen in the presence of an open immediate alternative.

We will conclude discussion of the `select` statement with a few notes:

• Concurrent C implementations are free to select any strategy for implementing the `select` statement, provided the semantics are equivalent to those described above. For example, an implementation might not evaluate all the guards.

• The `accept` statement for an `accept` alternative may have `suchthat` and/or `by` clauses. The `accept` alternative will be chosen only if the `suchthat` expression, if any, is satisfied. Once that `accept` alternative has been chosen, the `by` clause determines which of the outstanding calls will be accepted. The `by` clause does *not* determine whether or not the alternative is taken.

Timed transaction calls

The timed transaction call allows the 'client' process to withdraw a transaction call if the 'server' process named does not accept the call within the specified period. A timed transaction call is an expression of the form:

within *duration* ? *p.t(actual-parameters)* : *expr*

where *duration* is floating point expression, *p* is a process-valued expression and *t* is a transaction name. If the process *p* accepts this transaction call within *duration* seconds, the value returned by *p* becomes the value of the timed call expression. In this case, expression *expr* is not evaluated. Otherwise, the transaction call is withdrawn, *expr* is evaluated, and its value becomes that of the timed call expression. The transaction call is withdrawn atomically: Concurrent C guarantees that the server process *never* accepts a call that has been withdrawn by the client.

The timeout period *duration* refers to the waiting time until the server *accepts* the call, not to the time until the server returns the result. Once accepted, a transaction call cannot be withdrawn. Note that *duration* is a lower bound on the waiting time before a call can be withdrawn. That is, the client may wait for more than *duration* time units before withdrawing the call, but will never wait for less time.

Transaction pointers

A transaction pointer refers to a specific transaction associated with a specific process. Transaction pointers are similar to function pointers, except that their declarations are prefixed by the keyword trans:[†]

trans *type-specifier trans–ptr–declarator*₁, ..., *trans–ptr–declarator*ₙ;

trans–ptr–declarator is identical to declarators derived from function pointers [9]. Transaction pointer declarations specify the result type and parameter types associated with the transaction, but are independent of the process type. For example:

```
trans void (*tp)(char);
```

[†] Our syntax does not allow the direct declaration of a pointer to a transaction that returns a transaction pointer. However, this can be done in two steps, using an intermediate typedef statement to define the return-value type:

```
typedef trans int (*tp_type) (int, int);
trans tp_type (*xtp)(int);
```

declares t p as a pointer to a transaction that takes one c h a r parameter
and returns no value, and:

```
trans int (**ptp)(float, float);
```

declares p t p as a pointer to a transaction pointer that takes two f l o a t
parameters and returns an i n t value.

Provided the parameter and return value types match, an expression
of the form *p.t*, where *p* is a process-valued expression and *t* is the name of
one of *p*'s transactions, can be used wherever a transaction pointer value
is expected. For example, the following sets t p to point to the p u t
transaction of process b:

```
tp = b.put;
```

The expression:

```
(*tp)('a');
```

calls the transaction to which t p points, giving the character 'a' as an
argument. The syntax of a transaction call using a transaction pointer is
identical to that used for calling a function referred to by a function
pointer.

As an example, consider the function g e t l i n e, which calls a
transaction, using a transaction pointer, to 'read' a line into an array:

```
    /* Read from *getp to new-line, saving characters in arr. */
getline (getp, arr)
    trans char (*getp)();
    char arr[];
{
    int i = 0; char c;
    do {
        c = (*getp)();
        arr[i++] = c;
        } while (c != '\n')
    arr[i] = '\0';
}
```

Given a buffer process with a g e t transaction, we can use g e t l i n e to
read a line from that buffer:

```
process spec buffer(int max) {trans char get(); ...};
process buffer b;
char linebuf[100];
...
getline(b.get, linebuf);
```

We can give `getline` any appropriate transaction pointer to read a line. Instead of a transaction pointer, we could have passed a process value to `getline` but this has the following disadvantage: to read a line using a process of a type other than `buffer` requires writing a new `getline` for this process type. The transaction pointer lets us 'factor out' the process type. Because a transaction pointer does not include the process type, a transaction pointer can refer to transactions of different processes types, provided these transactions have the same parameter types and return-value type.

Process scheduling

The points at which the scheduler is invoked (for processes on the same machine) is left to the implementation. For example, an implementation may use a round-robin scheduling strategy modified to take into account process priorities.

When a new process is to be scheduled, the process with the highest priority is always the first one to be scheduled. If there is more than one process with the same high priority, then one of these processes is arbitrarily selected.

Interrupts and transactions

Interrupts can be associated with transactions; when that interrupt occurs, Concurrent C generates a call to the associated transaction. The implementation-dependent library function `c_associate` does the association; one of the parameters is a transaction pointer. The other parameters define the interrupt, and are obviously implementation dependent.

Number of outstanding transaction calls

The pseudo-function `c_transcount` returns the number of outstanding calls for a specific transaction, i.e., the call:

```
c_transcount(tp)
```

returns the number of outstanding calls associated with transaction referred to by the transaction pointer *tp*. The value returned by `c_transcount` includes outstanding timed transaction calls. Because these can be withdrawn by the calling process, the returned value is only an approximate indication of the number of outstanding calls.

Process states

The following library functions test the status of a process value. In each case, *p* is of type:

```
process anytype.
```

c_active (*p*)	returns 1 if process *p* is active; otherwise it returns 0.
c_completed (*p*)	returns 1 if process *p* has completed; otherwise it returns 0.
c_valid (*p*)	returns 1 if *p* refers to an active or completed process; otherwise it returns 0 (the process has terminated or *p* is an invalid value).

Examples

This section gives two examples of complete Concurrent C programs. The first is a solution of the dining philosophers problem. This problem has been studied extensively in the computer science literature, and is used as a benchmark to check the appropriateness of concurrent programming facilities. It is interesting because, despite its apparent simplicity, it illustrates many of the problems, such as shared resources and deadlock, encountered in concurrent programming. The forks are the resources shared by the philosophers who are represented by the concurrent processes.

The second example is a lock manager, and is representative of a real concurrent programming problem that occurs in databases and operating systems. It also illustrates the suchthat clause in Concurrent C.

The mortal dining philosophers

Five philosophers [1] spend their lives eating spaghetti and thinking. They eat at a circular table in a dining room. The table has five chairs around it and chair number i has been assigned to philosopher number i ($0 \leq i \leq 4$). Five forks have also been laid out on the table so that there is precisely one fork between every adjacent two chairs. Consequently there is one fork to the left of each chair and one to its right. Fork number i is to the left of chair number i.

Before eating, a philosopher must enter the dining room and sit in the chair assigned to her. A philosopher must have two forks to eat (the forks placed to the left and right of every chair). If the philosopher cannot get two forks immediately, then she must wait until she can get them. The forks are picked up one at a time. When a philosopher is finished eating (after a finite amount of time), she puts the forks down and leaves the room.

Each of the five philosophers and five forks is implemented as a process. On activation, each philosopher is given an identification number (0–4) and the process values of the forks she is supposed to use. Each philosopher is mortal and passes on to the next world soon after having eaten 100 000 times (about three times a day for 90 years).

The types of the philosopher and fork processes are:

```
process spec fork()
{
  trans void pick_up();
  trans void put_down();
};


process spec philosopher(int id, process fork left, process
fork right);
```

The bodies of the philosopher and fork processes are:

```
#define LIFE_LIMIT  100000

process body philosopher(id, left, right)
{
  int times_eaten;

  for (times_eaten = 0; times_eaten != LIFE_LIMIT; times_eaten++) {
    /* think; then enter dining room */
    /* pick up forks */
      right.pick_up();
      left.pick_up();
    /* eat */
      printf("Philosopher %d : *burp*\n", id);
    /* put down forks */
      left.put_down();
      right.put_down();
    /* get up and leave dining room */
  }
  printf("Philosopher %d : See you in the next world.\n", id);
}

process body fork()
{
  for (;;)
    select {
      accept pick_up();
      accept put_down();
    or
      terminate;
    }
}
```

```
main()
{
  process fork f[5];
  int j;
  /* first create the forks, then create the philosophers */
      for (j = 0; j < 5; j++)
        f[j] = create fork();
      for (j = 0; j < 5; j++)
        create philosopher(j,f[j], f[(j + 1) % 5]);
}
```

Once the philosophers have terminated, the forks have nothing else to do; because each fork is waiting at a `select` statement with a terminate alternative, and the parent process (i.e., `main`) has completed, they all terminate. This allows the `main` process to terminate, which completes execution of the Concurrent C program.

The program given above will deadlock if each philosopher picks up one fork. One way of avoiding deadlock is to allow at most four philosophers to sit at the table at any given time. This can be enforced by a 'gatekeeper' process.

Note that the output of the philosophers can get mixed up if two of them write to standard output at the same time.

Lock manager

This example presents a process that manages locks for a large collection of items. Client processes can get and release locks on these items. If an item is already locked, a process requesting a lock on that item waits until that item is available. Here is the type for the lock manager process (items are identified by a value of type `lockid`):

```
process spec lock_mngr()
{
  trans void get_lock(lockid id);
  trans void release_lock(lockid id);
};
```

Clients call `get_lock` to lock an item, and `release_lock` to release an item they have previously locked.

Here is the body of the lock manager process. Note how we use the `suchthat` clause to accept a `get_lock` if and only if the requested item is unlocked. The functions `isfree`, `lock`, and `unlock` manipulate a lock table:

```
process body lock_mngr()
{
  lockid xid;
  for (;;)
    select {
      accept get_lock(id) suchthat (isfree(id))
        {xid = id;}
      lock(xid);
    or
      accept release_lock(id)
        {xid = id;}
      unlock(xid);
      }
}
/* isfree(id) returns true if id is unlocked */
/* lock(id) locks id */
/* unlock(id) unlocks id */
```

Concurrent C design decisions

This section discusses the rationale for several of the design decisions that we made for Concurrent C. The most important decision, of course, was the choice of the rendezvous model; this was discussed earlier.

Language extensions versus library functions

A major question was, why provide language extensions at all? A simpler alternative would be to write a function package that provides some form of concurrent processing [10]. However, such a library package would have the following limitations:

(1)   It would be clumsy and inelegant to provide some of the facilities of Concurrent C, e.g., the select statement.

(2)   The concurrent parts of a program would not be easily identifiable – either to a compiler or to another programmer.

(3)   It is difficult to design a set of functions that can be implemented efficiently on a wide class of machines.

(4)   A compiler may not be easily able to optimize concurrent programs well, since it will be tuned to optimizing sequential programs [11].

Transaction pointers

Transaction pointers were included because they allow the dynamic specification of process interaction points. For example, a server manager process can give a client process a transaction pointer which is to be used by the client to call the process that will actually perform the service. The client does not need to know the type of the server process.

Because transaction pointers are very similar to function pointers, we could have used function pointers to refer to transactions also. We decided against this for the following reasons:

(1) Using function pointers to point to transactions would have a negative impact on program clarity. It would not be possible, in general, to statically determine whether a function pointer referred to a function or a transaction.

(2) It would complicate the implementation because it would force us to determine at run-time whether a function pointer value really points to a function, or to a transaction pointer. Moreover, it might make it necessary to use an additional byte or word to implement the extended function pointers.

Suchthat clause

At first, we resisted adding a suchthat clause to the accept statement, because of the complexity and potential inefficiency. What changed our minds was the lock manager example given above. Our first lock manager did not use suchthat, and was extremely complicated; we discovered the suchthat clause greatly simplified the lock manager and the interaction with it. (The first lock manager required a separate process for each locked item, and each lock and release request required several transaction calls.)

Types in accept statements

In their stripped form, Concurrent C accept statements (i.e., without the suchthat or by clauses) are similar to those in Ada. The major difference is that Ada requires the return value and parameter types to be repeated in the accept statement, while our accept statement gives just the parameter names. We originally required the types; like the Ada designers [5], we felt that the redundancy was useful. This was fine for our first examples, which had only one or two simple parameters, and which returned simple types. However, for practical programs, with transactions with five parameters of complicated types, the accept statements became unreadable. The return value type obscured the transaction name, and the parameter names were buried in the type declarations. Furthermore, we found that the parameter declarations ran off the right edge of the page, because accept statements generally appear inside loops or if statements, and are already indented. For these reasons, we (reluctantly) decided to omit types from accept statements.

Nested processes

We decided not to allow processes to be syntactically nested within functions within other processes. This is in the spirit of the C language, which does not allow nested functions. This allows each process to have its own independent stack, which greatly simplified the implementation. We did not really appreciate this simplification until we saw how Ada processes needed 'cactus stacks.'

Process anytype

Process values in Concurrent C are strongly typed. We have found this very helpful when interacting with processes. However, we also found that the strong typing got in the way when performing general operations on an arbitrary process. We added the built-in type `process anytype` to solve these problems. To see the difficulty, consider the built-in function `c_mypid` , which returns the process value of the calling process. In the current version of Concurrent C, `c_mypid` is an ordinary function that returns a `process anytype` value. However, before we added `process anytype`, `c_mypid` was a pseudo-function, in that it was only allowed inside a process body, and the compiler made the return type match that of the enclosing process body. This was unsatisfactory first because `c_mypid` could not be called from a function, and second because the compiler had to treat `c_mypid` specially. We ran into similar problems with the parameter types for the functions which abort processes or which manipulate process priorities; it was annoying to change the compiler each time we added such a function. The `process anytype` concept provided a neat, extensible solution to these problems.

Open issues

There are several areas where we feel that Concurrent C could be extended or improved:

(1) Concurrent C does not provide facilities for data abstraction. There is another research project, C++ [12][13] which is investigating how to add data abstraction facilities to C, and we did not want to duplicate that effort. We considered basing our work on C++ instead of C. However, C++ is also a research project, and might change very quickly; designing extensions to a rapidly evolving language can be a nightmare. We certainly feel that the features in C++ would be useful in a concurrent programming language; when C++ becomes more stable, we intend to investigate merging Concurrent C with C++.

(2) Currently `accept` statements can only appear inside process bodies (Ada has a similar restriction). In theory, at least, it would be nice to allow them to appear inside arbitrary functions. However, recall that an `accept` statement gives just the transaction name. This is ambiguous without the name of the process type containing that

transaction. We could extend the `accept` statement, perhaps by allowing *processtype.transname* for the transaction name. However, this raises several questions, such as what is to be done if the function was not called by a process of the specified type.

Instead of trying to answer those questions immediately – and perhaps making an unfortunate choice – we instead decided to disallow `accept` statements in functions, and see how painful this restriction would be. As it turns out, it has not been a significant limitation: we have not seen any programs that this feature would simplify. The typical structure of a process is a single `select` statement in a loop, with `accept` alternatives for that process's transactions, and guards expressing when each transaction can be accepted. These alternatives then call functions as necessary (e.g., see the lock manager example).

(3)   Our automatic process termination mechanism – the `terminate` alternative in the `select` statement – is modeled after Ada's mechanism for process termination. We are not quite happy with this mechanism because its semantics are complicated and are not easy to describe. We are exploring other mechanisms.

(4)   As in C functions, transaction arguments are always passed by value. In C functions, programmers can effectively pass arguments by reference by passing their *addresses*. However, this technique will not work for transaction arguments in a distributed, non-shared memory implementation. Thus Concurrent C needs some argument passing mechanism that will allow the called process to change the values of arguments supplied by the calling process. We are currently considering a value-result mechanism. The transaction declaration in the process type will indicate the value-result parameters. When a call is accepted, the argument to be passed by value-result will be copied into some work area owned by the receiving process; at the end of the transaction, the final value will be copied back. Of course, if the two processes share an address space, then the run-time system will just pass the argument address, instead of copying the data. However, we are still looking for a solution that has the proper combination of simplicity, efficiency, and flexibility in the context of C, our base language.

Differences between Concurrent C and Ada

The concurrent programming facilities in Ada and Concurrent C are both based on the rendezvous concept. However, the implementation of the rendezvous concept in Concurrent C is quite different from that in Ada. Although many of the differences are minor (e.g., syntax changes), some of the differences are major and can have a significant impact on the programming style and implementation efficiency:

Transaction calls

In Concurrent C, transaction calls are similar to function calls. In Ada, they are similar to procedure calls. Thus in Concurrent C, transaction calls can be used in arbitrary expressions, while in Ada they can only occur as statements.

Ordering of transaction calls

The Concurrent C `by` clause allows the programmer to specify the order in which transaction calls are accepted. In Ada, calls are always accepted in FIFO order. This difference effects how schedulers are designed in the two languages. For example, in Ada, a process that must run transactions in non-FIFO order requires two rendezvous for each service request [1]. In Concurrent C, such a process only needs one rendezvous per service request. It is true that the Concurrent C `by` clause incurs some extra overhead. However, this is not significant if the number of outstanding transaction calls is small. Furthermore, accomplishing the same thing in Ada requires an extra rendezvous, which is more expensive than the extra overhead of the Concurrent C `by` clause.

Selective acceptance of transaction calls

The `suchthat` clause can be used to restrict the set of acceptable transaction requests. Only transaction calls with parameters that satisfy the `suchthat` expression are considered for acceptance. There is no comparable mechanism in Ada.

The select statement

Concurrent C allows *immediate* alternatives in `select` statements; Ada does not. This restriction is one of the reasons why Ada has a polling bias [14].

Transaction pointers

There is no mechanism in Ada for specifying a pointer to a transaction. Consequently, it is not possible for a process to specify dynamically a process interaction point to other processes.

Arrays of transactions

Ada provides arrays of entries; Concurrent C does not. In Ada, entry arrays are generally used to implement a non-FIFO scheduling policy. The by and suchthat clauses make array entries unnecessary in Concurrent C. Furthermore, Ada's array entries can require polling, which is wasteful of system resources [14].

Process parameters

Concurrent C processes can be parameterized, allowing the initialization of processes at creation time. Process initialization at creation time is not possible in Ada; consequently, initialization parameters must be supplied explicitly to the process after it has been activated. The overhead involved includes declaring an entry that is used for initialization, and one rendezvous for supplying the initial values.

Process activation

Process activation is implicit in Ada, while in Concurrent C it is explicit. Thus in Concurrent C, the programmer has more control over when processes are instantiated. However, the programmer must explicitly instantiate each process (by using the create operator).

Process ownership

In Concurrent C, processes are owned by the process which created them; in Ada they are owned by the program unit, i.e., a block, subprogram or process, that created them.

Process nesting

Ada allows nested processes; Concurrent C processes cannot be nested. This is in the spirit of C, which does not allow nested functions.

Process declaration

In Concurrent C, process types must be declared in order to declare processes. In Ada, processes can be declared directly, in addition to using process types.

Priority specification

In Concurrent C, the priority is specified when a process is created; different processes of the same process type can have different priorities. Moreover, process priorities can be changed dynamically. In Ada, all processes instantiated from a process type must have the same priority, because the priority is associated with the process type.

Interrupts and transaction calls

In Ada, interrupts are statically associated with transaction calls, via declarations. Concurrent C is much more flexible; it allows interrupts to be dynamically associated with transaction calls, using a library function and transaction pointers. Moreover, this allows associations to be changed or discontinued, which is not possible in Ada.

Conclusions

The concurrency model in Concurrent C is based on the rendezvous concept. Many of the differences between Concurrent C and Ada are a result of trying to eliminate the polling bias in Ada [14], to increase programmer control of scheduling, and to provide the programmer with more control of the concurrency (process parameterization and explicit process activation).

Concurrent C can be used for a variety of applications:

(1) Implementing parallel algorithms, such as simulation programs and protocols.
(2) To write genuinely distributed applications, such as distributed databases.
(3) To write real-time programs.
(4) To write dedicated programs, such as device drivers, that execute on a bare machine.
(5) To implement operating systems.

Concurrent C has been used for writing several applications, e.g., hardware simulation and design, discrete event simulation, a credit card caller, a distributed version of the UNIX make [15] command, the control program for a terminal driver board, and teaching. It has also been used as a target language for generating executable programs from protocol specifications.

The concurrent programming facilities in Concurrent C are subject to revision. We hope that writing real programs in Concurrent C will lead to an evaluation of these facilities followed by modifications of these facilities as necessary.

We have implemented Concurrent C on the UNIX system running on a single processor. Implementation of a distributed version of Concurrent C, which will allow a Concurrent C program to run on multiple processors, is in progress. The distributed implementation will give us a vehicle to explore issues involved in a multicomputer implementation, such as:

(1) How should the multicomputer computer architecture be conveyed to the Concurrent C compiler?

(2) Should the programmer specify on which computers the different processes are to be executed, or should the compiler decide on its own?

(3) Should groups of processes be allowed to share global data in a controlled manner, or should processes be prohibited from sharing data?

The target architecture for the first distributed implementation consists of several identical computers connected by Ethernet. We have made decisions for the issues mentioned above, although we have not yet had a chance to explore their ramifications. For example, the programmer must explicitly specify the processor on which a process is to execute. Only processes on the same computer can share global data.

Acknowledgments

B. W. Ballard, T. A. Cargill, R. F. Cmelik, M. D. Durand, A. R. Feuer, D. Gay, D. D. Hill, B. W. Kernighan, M. D. P. Leland, N. Ostrove, D. E. Perry, R. Mascitti, J. Schwartz, B. Smith-Thomas, D. Swartwout, and some anonymous referees gave us detailed comments. We are grateful for their suggestions and criticisms.

References

[1] Gehani, Narain. *Ada: Concurrent Programming.* Prentice-Hall, 1984.

[2] Kernighan, B. W. and D. M. Ritchie. *The C Programming Language.* Prentice-Hall, 1978.

[3] Hoare, C. A. R. Communicating Sequential Processes. *CACM*, **21**, 8, pp. 666–677, August 1978.

[4] *Reference Manual for the Ada Programming Language.* United States Department of Defense, January 1983.

[5] *Rationale for the Design of the Ada Programming Language. SIGPLAN Notices*, **14**, 6, part B, June 1979.

[6] Andrews, G. R. Synchronizing Resources. *TOPLAS*, **3**, 4, pp. 405–430, October 1981.

[7] Andrews, G. R. The Distributed Programming Language SR – Mechanisms, Design and Implementation. *Software – Practice and Experience*, **12**, pp. 719–753, 1982.

[8]   Gentleman, W. M. Message Passing Between Sequential Processes: The Reply Primitive and the Administrator Concept. *Software – Practice and Experience*, **11**, pp. 435–466, 1981.

[9]   Ritchie, D. M. The C Programming Language – Reference Manual. AT&T Bell Labs, September 1980.

[10] Wirth N. 1982. *Programming in Modula-2*. Springer–Verlag.

[11] Pratt, V. Five Paradigm Shifts in Programming Language Design and Their Realization in Viron, a Dataflow Programming Environment. *Conference Record of the Tenth Annual ACM Symposium on Principles of Programming Languages*, Austin, Texas, January 1983.

[12] Stroustrup, B. Adding Classes to the C Language: An Exercise in Language Evolution. *Software – Practice and Experience*, **13**, pp. 139–161, 1983.

[13] Stroustrup, B. The C++ Reference Manual. Computing Science Technical Report No. 108, AT&T Bell Laboratories, January 1984.

[14] Gehani, N. H. and Cargill, T. A. Concurrent Programming in the Ada Language: The Polling Bias. *Software – Practice and Experience*, **14**, 5, pp. 413–427, May 1984.

[15] Feldman, S. I. `Make` – A Program for Maintaining Computer Programs. *Software – Practice and Experience*, **9**, pp. 255–265, 1979.

5

Parallel Processing in Ada

Olivier Roubine
CISI-Ingénierie

Jean-Claude Heliard
ALSYS

---

1 Introduction

Real-time systems often deal with the control of several activities that are relatively independent of each other. For such systems, as in the case of operating systems, the notion of parallel processes represents an important design concept. Although far from being new, this notion has become all the more appealing with the advent of low-cost microprocessors and the growth of distributed systems. It is therefore important, when designing a model for parallel programming, to anticipate its use on a variety of architectures: monoprocessors, multiprocessors with shared memory, or truly distributed systems. In the design of a language for which *portability* is a major issue, the applicability to a wide variety of architectures must be a primary concern.

Another concern is *simplicity*: parallel programs tend to be far more complicated to write and understand than their sequential counterparts. The user must not be plagued by a variety of primitives, each of which serves a particular purpose, but also interferes with the other ones. This concern for simplicity is reinforced by considerations of *efficiency*: a multitude of primitives, however easy to implement, makes for a multitude of run-time routines, and ultimately for a fairly large nucleus.

And lastly, the major concern should be one of *methodology*: a programming language must encourage the use of abstraction whenever possible. In the case of sequential programs, notions such as subprograms, packages, types, constitute as many tools to foster abstraction. The same should hold for parallel programs.

142

We shall now see how Ada was designed to meet the criteria set forth above.

The next section presents the evolution of ideas on parallelism, and shows how they led to the present formulation. This formulation is then detailed in the following section. The two final sections contain a substantial example and a discussion of various issues related to the present design.

2 Background

Several issues must be considered with respect to parallel processes (or tasks, as they are called in Ada): declaration/elaboration, activation and termination, synchronisation and communication, of which the latter two are by far the most important. A special case of synchronisation, namely mutual exclusion, deserves special attention. A quick review of past primitives can show their inadequacies, as they are obviously oriented towards solving a particular problem. For instance, semaphores [Dijkstra 1968], signals, path expressions [Campbell and Habermann 1974] are clearly concerned with synchronisation. Messages [Brinch Hansen 1970], or pipes [Thompson and Ritchie 1974] are more oriented towards communication. Critical regions and monitors [Hoare 1974] are especially adapted to mutual exclusion.

Although still placing an emphasis on communication, boxes [Ichbiah *et al.* 1978] can also be used to express synchronisation. Close to them, Hoare's system of Communicating Sequential Processes [Hoare 1978] introduces some order by recognising the fact that, in order to communicate with each other, two processes must be synchronised. An additional advantage of this scheme is that, by emphasising the importance of explicit communication between tasks, it renders implicit communication (in the form of access to shared variables) rather unnecessary. In fact, the intention is that the primitives of CSP be suitable for a distributed architecture with no shared memory.

The primitives of CSP introduce the basic idea of a *rendezvous* between two processes, whereby, in order to communicate with each other, both processes must have expressed the desire to do so. However, what happens at the time of the rendezvous is essentially limited to the transmission of data from one process to the other. The case where a request is made (possibly requiring some information to accompany the request) and must be acknowledged (possibly requiring some information to be passed back to the requester) before the requester may proceed, appears to be rather frequent in real-time systems or operating systems. In addition, in loosely coupled systems, the time overhead for synchronising two processes is likely to be incommensurate with the amount of processing that can be performed at one node of the system.

These considerations have led to the desire to be able to perform arbitrary computations while two processes are synchronised. Such a notion corresponds to an *extended rendezvous*: one task waits for another at a given location, and when the meeting occurs, the two tasks walk together for a while, before parting each on its own way.

This kind of interaction was present in the concept of 'Distributed Processes' [Brinch Hansen 1978], that is intended mostly 'for real-time applications controlled by microcomputer networks with distributed storage'. This proposal had a substantial appeal in terms of ease of use and reliability, and was a source of inspiration in the design of the Ada tasking facilities.

3   The Ada tasking facilities

3.1   The notion of task

In Ada, the notion of **task** corresponds informally to an independent flow of control, i.e., a part of a program whose execution can proceed independently of other parts. As a consequence, there can be several tasks in a program, which correspond to different flows of control that can be in existence simultaneously.

This dynamic view of the notion of task is expressed textually through a specific program unit: the *task*. A task in the static sense is the representation of a potential flow of control, in the same manner as the declaration of a procedure is the representation of the potential execution of the corresponding sequence of code.

Like other Ada units, a task declaration consists of two parts: the *specification* and the *body*. The specification describes the possible actions that other program parts can have on a task, whereas the body describes the actual behaviour of the executing task.

A task specification, however, has two unique features that have no equivalent in other Ada units: first of all, if it is intended for a task to describe several possible flows of control of the same nature, one will declare a *task type*. Actual flows of control will then be created by declaring variables of that type, or by dynamic allocation of objects of that type. The declaration of a single task is a degenerate case in the same way as the declaration of an array object with an anonymous array type. Second, a task is the only Ada unit that can contain an *entry* declaration; in fact, this is the only form of declaration that can appear in a task specification. Entries are the primary means of cooperation between tasks, and are described in detail below.

Example 1

```
task type MAILBOX is
    -- this is the specification of the task; it may contain only
    -- declarations of entries.
    entry send (M : in STRING);
    entry receive (M : out STRING);
    entry is_empty (Status : out BOOLEAN);
    entry is_full (Status : out BOOLEAN);
end MAILBOX;

task body MAILBOX is
    -- this declarative part may contain any declaration; all the entities
    -- declared here are not accessible to outside units.
    First_Mesg, Last_Mesg : INTEGER;

begin
    -- this statement part contains the description of the execution of the task.
    ...

end MAILBOX;
```

There are several aspects related to tasks that are of interest, and in particular the *lifetime* of a task, i.e., the conditions upon which a flow of control comes to existence, remains active or ceases to exist, and the means for cooperation between tasks, especially in terms of *synchronisation* and *communication*; these aspects are considered in the following sections.

0.2   Task activation and termination

Given the declaration of a task type, tasks of that type can be *created* by creating objects, either by variable declaration or dynamic allocation. Once the task object has been created, it becomes possible for other tasks to attempt to communicate with that task; it does not mean, however, that the task will immediately start executing: this latter notion is known as the *activation* of the task, and follows some specific rules, namely:

- a task object created by a variable declaration will be activated 'after passing the reserved word **begin** following the declarative part';
- a task object created by an allocator will be activated immediately after the allocation has been performed.

The main reason for the first rule is that it is often the case that a complete subsystem, consisting of several tasks, has to be initiated: in this case, it is important that all tasks forming that subsystem be launched at the same time to be in a consistent state.

The counterpart of activation is the notion of *termination* when a task will end its execution. A task that has terminated can no longer execute any instruction, but it may still be visible to other program parts that are within the scope of the task declaration. Termination can occur in one of four different ways:

- the 'normal' way for a task to terminate is by executing the last instruction in its body;
- a task can also be terminated if an exception is raised or propagated in the body and is not handled there;
- a task can be terminated unconditionally by another task, using the instruction **abort**;
- lastly, there is a provision for a 'passive' termination, which is induced indirectly by the termination of other program units; this feature is detailed later (see **terminate**).

Furthermore, it is important to realize that tasks, like other units, have access to all objects which are in the same or an enclosing scope; as a consequence, any unit that contains tasks may not be exited until all the inner tasks have terminated. This rule deserves some qualification: a unit is said (in that sense) to 'contain tasks' if:

- its declarative part contains task declarations, or declarations of objects of a composite type that has some task components, or
- its declarative part contains the declaration of an access type to a task type (in that case, the unit will contain tasks if any object of that type has been dynamically created).

3.3   Interaction between active tasks

As was discussed earlier, the interactions between parallel tasks consist of *synchronisation* actions and *communication* actions. We first consider how synchronisation is achieved, and how the basic mechanism for synchronisation (the **entry**) also covers communication.

3.3.1   The entry

One of the salient characteristics of a task in Ada is that it is the only kind of unit that may contain entry declarations. Inside other tasks, an entry can be used (i.e., called) just like a procedure; it has however a synchronising effect.

Inside the task that contains an entry declaration, **accept statements** are used to specify the actions to be performed in response to an entry call; they also have a synchronising effect.

Synchronisation   Consider the following two tasks A and B:

Example 2

```
task A is                task B;
    entry check_point;
end A;

task body A is           task body B is
begin                    begin
    ...                      ...
    accept check_point;      A.check_point;
    ...                      ...
end A;                   end B;
```

The purpose is to let the two tasks execute in parallel up to a certain point, and to proceed in parallel past this point, but with the guarantee that no task can proceed past the check point before the other one has reached it.

To this end, task A declares an entry CHECK_POINT. Within its body, B calls this entry by the statement 'A.CHECK_POINT', which is exactly similar to a subprogram call. The body of A, on the other hand, contains an 'accept statement' for the entry CHECK_POINT (an accept statement for an entry can only appear in the statement part of the body of the task that contains the entry declaration). Once activated, the two tasks will execute in parallel. A will eventually reach the accept statement, and B will eventually reach the entry call. Two cases are possible: A reaches the accept statement before B reaches the entry call, or conversely. In either case, the task that gets to its check point first will be blocked until the second one reaches it. When the second one gets there, a *rendezvous* occurs, at the end of which the two interacting tasks may again proceed in parallel.

As presented here, a parameterless entry acts as a blocking signal.

Communication   Entries also provide the means to exchange data between tasks: similarly to procedures, entries can have formal parameters, and an entry call provides the actual values for these parameters.

In the case of a procedure, the parameters are accessible only within the procedure body. In the case of entries, there must be a way to ensure that the value of **in** parameters have already been provided, and that the binding to **out** or **in out** parameters is still meaningful. This is provided by associating a sequence of statements with an accept statement, such that these statements can be executed only once the entry has been called, and the task calling the accept statement may not proceed until that sequence of statements has been executed. During execution of that sequence of statements, the two tasks involved *remain* synchronised, and we talk of an *extended rendezvous*. During the rendezvous, **in** and **in out** parameters can be acted upon, and **out** and **in out** parameters can receive values.

Example 3

Building up on the previous scheme, assume that once synchronised, A must receive some information from B, and pass some other information back to B.

```
task A is
   entry check_point
         (Input : INTEGER; Output : out INTEGER);      task B;
end A;

task body A is                                          task body B is
   Local : INTEGER;                                        To_A, From_A : INTEGER;
begin                                                    begin
   ...                                                      To_A := ... ;
   accept check_point                                       ...
         (Input : INTEGER; Output : out INTEGER) do       A.check_point (To_A, From_A);
      Local := Input;                                       ...
      Output := f (Input);                               end B;
   end check_point;
   ...
end A;
```

Mutual exclusion   The notion of rendezvous can conveniently be used to express problems of mutual exclusion in a form similar to monitors or critical regions.

Note first that several tasks may call the same entry of a given task. However, when an accept statement is reached, a rendezvous is achieved with only one task, the first one to call or have called the entry without having rendezvoused with it. Thus, one has the guarantee that the body of an accept statement is executed in mutual exclusion with the caller, and with any other task having called an entry of the task containing the accept statement.

We illustrate this aspect of the language by the example of a buffer manager: a buffer is defined as an abstract object which can be filled with items, or from which items can be removed. There is a fixed number of such buffers, that are allocated on demand. Allocation of free buffers must be performed in mutual exclusion.

This example requires some explanation about the treatment of exceptions raised whilst engaged in a rendezvous: since a rendezvous is a sequence of code that is really executed on behalf of two tasks, it is quite understandable that an exception that is propagated within this rendezvous could be of potential interest to either the caller or the callee. For this reason, when an exception is raised inside a rendezvous, the rendezvous is terminated, and the exception is propagated BOTH to the caller, as would be the case with a procedure call, and to the task containing the accept statement in a way similar to the propagation of an exception out of a nested block. In the above example, the exception X_NO_BUFFER_AVAILABLE is essentially of interest to the caller to indicate that there was no free buffer at the time of the call.

Example 4

```
package BUFFER_POOL is
   type BUFFER is limited private;

   procedure allocate (B : out BUFFER);
   ... -- other buffer manipulation routines
       -- that do not require mutual exclusion

   X_NO_BUFFER_AVAILABLE : exception;

private
   N_BUFFERS : constant := 16;
   type BUFFER is range 1..N_BUFFERS;
end BUFFER_POOL;

package body BUFFER_POOL is
   BUFFER_SIZE : constant := 256;
   type BUFFER_TYPE is
      array (1..BUFFER_SIZE) of ITEM;
   type BUFFERS is
      array (BUFFER) of BUFFER_TYPE;
   type FLAGS is
      array (BUFFER) of BOOLEAN;

   Pool : BUFFERS;
   Is_Free : FLAGS := (BUFFER => TRUE);

   task Allocator is
      entry get_a_buffer (Buf : out BUFFER);
   end Allocator;

   procedure allocate (B : out BUFFER) is
   begin
      Allocator.get_a_buffer (B);
   end allocate;

   task body Allocator is
   begin
      loop
         begin   -- this inner block to catch exceptions
            accept get_a_buffer (Buf: out BUFFER) do
               for Index in BUFFER loop
                  if Is_Free (Index) then
                     Is Free (Index) := FALSE;
                     Buf := Index;
                     exit;
                  elsif Index = BUFFER'LAST then
                     raise X_NO_BUFFER_AVAILABLE;
                  end if;
               end loop;
            end get_a_buffer;
         exception
            when X_NO_BUFFER_AVAILABLE =>
                        delay 5.0;
         end;
      end loop;
   end Allocator;
end BUFFER_POOL;
```

The example also introduces another feature that is specific of the tasking facilities: the **delay** statement, which causes the task that executes it to be blocked for a certain amount of time, expressed in seconds.

3.3.2   The select statement

We have seen constructs of the language that provide for synchronisation, communication and mutual exclusion. The basic mechanism presented for these purposes lacks an important capability: that of conditional execution.

In systems involving parallel processes, it is often the case that one must respond to several possible requests, with no particular preference for one rather than another. If several such requests have occurred, which one is serviced first may be irrelevant. If none has been made, one probably wants to honour the first one that gets issued, no matter which one.

This capability is provided in Ada by the *select statement*, which specifies a synchronisation with several possible callers. A select statement combines several alternatives which describe possible actions. These alternatives may correspond to accepting calls to certain entries, to waiting for specific periods of time, or possibly to waiting for an entry call to be accepted by another task. When a select statement is reached, one considers if some of the alternatives could be executed immediately, meaning that a rendezvous is immediately possible; if this is the case, one of the alternatives is selected for execution as if it had appeared in the code without being embedded within the select statement (if more than one alternative is possible, which one will be selected is not specified). On the other hand, if no alternative is immediately possible, the task is suspended until the first event that will make an alternative possible, be it a call to one of the entries mentioned, or the expiration of one of the possible delays, or the acceptance of the entry call mentioned (it is a rule of the language that there cannot be both an alternative with an entry call and an alternative with an accept statement in the same select, and that there can be only one alternative with an entry call in a given select).

We can consider, as an illustration, a bid arbitrator: various agents can bid for a resource by submitting a proposal, or they can look at the current highest bid; if no operation has occurred within a certain period of time, the bid is adjudicated to the highest bidder:

Example 5

```
task BID is
    entry raise_bid (From : BIDDER_ID; By : NATURAL);
    entry look_at (Value : out NATURAL);
end BID;

task body BID is
    Current_Bid : NATURAL := 0;
    Last_Bidder : BIDDER_ID;
begin
    -- We must first accept at least one bid
    accept raise_bid (From : BIDDER_ID; By : NATURAL) do
        Last_Bidder := From;
        Current_Bid := Current_Bid + By;
    end raise_bid;

    loop
        select
            accept raise_bid (From : BIDDER_ID; By : NATURAL) do
                Last_Bidder := From;
                Current_Bid := Current_Bid + By;
            end raise_bid;
        or
            accept look_at (Value : out NATURAL) do
                Value := Current_Bid;
            end look_at;
        or
            delay 10.0;
            exit;
        end select;
    end loop;
    -- sold to last bidder
end BID;
```

Guards   Given the basic functionality of the select statement, its power and flexibility is enhanced by the possibility of *guarding* any of the alternatives by a Boolean condition: the guarded alternative will only be considered for a potential selection if the condition evaluates to TRUE; thus, in our bid adjudicator, we may want to adjudicate the bid only after a certain 'reserve' value has been reached. This is achieved by guarding the delay clause as follows:

Example 5a

```
select
   accept raise_bid ...

or
   accept look_at ...

or when Current_Bid >= Reserve_Value =>
   delay 10.0;
   exit;
end select;
```

The COUNT attribute   Although not specific to the select statement, there are a number of attributes that are connected to the notion of task or entry. One such attribute, COUNT, indicates the number of waiting callers for a particular entry. For instance, it can be used to prevent the value of the current bid to be examined if there is any new bid pending (this essentially results in giving priority to RAISE_BID in the servicing):

Example 5b

```
select
   accept raise_bid ...

or when raise_bid'COUNT = 0 =>
   accept look_at ...

or when Current_Bid >= Reserve_Value =>
   delay 10.0;
   exit;
end select;
```

The else part   A select statement may contain an *else clause* which indicates actions to be executed if no other alternative can be selected immediately, i.e., when all entries with guards that are TRUE have not been called, and the guards on delay alternatives (if any) all evaluate to FALSE. The above variation could have been programmed differently using an else clause:

Example 5c

```
select
    accept raise_bid ...

else
    select
        accept raise_bid ...

    or
        accept look_at ...

    or when Current_Bid >= Reserve_Value =>
        delay 10.0;
        exit;
    end select;
end select;
```

The terminate alternative   Finally, a select statement can also be used to induce a 'passive termination': it is often the case that tasks that provide a *service* are programmed to wait for any request (expressed as an entry call). Such tasks have no reason to remain in existence if there is no more task to call them, but on the other hand, it may be tedious or even unsafe to rely on an explicit termination of these servers.

A select statement may contain a **terminate** alternative which indicates that if no other task is willing to emit a call to this task, the task can terminate. The notion 'no other task is willing' may seem strange or imprecise, but it is in fact very simple to translate in executable terms: in order to emit a call, a task must have visibility on the task it is trying to call; this reduces the number of tasks that 'may be willing'. Furthermore, in order to emit a call, a task that has visibility on another one must also be active; therefore, the notion actually means that any task that has visibility on (i.e., could potentially call) the task of concern is either terminated, or at its end, waiting for some inner task to terminate, or is itself in a similar state at a select statement with a terminate alternative.

When a terminate alternative is selected, the task will actually terminate. This feature is used in the complete example treated in the following section.

4   A process control example

4.1   Problem

Assume two processes A and B: A reads data from the outside world and stores them in a buffer area, whilst B processes the data found in the buffer area according to some algorithm. It is further assumed that A and B interact in the following specific way.

The buffer is organised as a *double-buffer*, i.e., after one of its two areas has been filled by process A, process B is notified and starts to read out of the buffer. Process A continues by depositing data in the second buffer area. If this fills up, A will try to deposit data in the first buffer again. Process B, in turn, notifies process A after having read a complete buffer area.

It is illegal to read a buffer area which has not been previously filled, and to write into a buffer area which has not been completely read (except in the initialisation phase).

It shall also be possible to terminate processes A and B at any time, without losing data, i.e., so that all data that have been entered in a buffer will be processed fully.

4.2 Overview of the solution

The solution presented here shows the flexibility and power of the Ada tasking facilities. It is somewhat unconventional, in that each buffer is controlled by a separate task. The proper handling of multiple buffers is achieved exclusively by task synchronisation.

The tasks A and B are defined inside the package BUFFERS. The buffer size and maximum number of buffers are also defined there and could be modified (i.e., the solution will work for an arbitrary number of buffers).

Each buffer is controlled by a task of the type BUFFER; each such task takes the initiative of passing its buffer successively to A for filling, and to B for utilizing the data. Both the filling and use of the buffer is done by A or B *while in a rendezvous with the buffer task*. This effects most of the synchronisation. The two buffers are also synchronised with each other as follows: once one buffer is full, it notifies the other by calling its entry RELEASE. This signals the other buffer that it can start its cycle.

Task B repeatedly receives a buffer through its entry UTILIZE. The actual number of elements is also passed as a parameter; thus, if the buffer is not full, this is an indication that B should terminate after having processed the remaining data.

Termination is handled as follows: the signal to terminate is sent to A through its entry STOP; when this signal is received while filling a buffer, the rendezvous ends, and the buffer is returned incompletely filled. If the stop signal is received while not filling a buffer, the next buffer will be returned empty. After having returned an empty or incomplete buffer, A will terminate. The incomplete buffer will be transmitted to B which will in turn terminate, but will also propagate an exception in the buffer task. This exception will cause the buffer task to terminate, and as a result, the other buffer task, which contains a select with terminate, will also terminate.

```
package BUFFERS is
   N_BUFFERS : constant := 2;
   BUFFER_SIZE : constant := 512;

   type BUFFER_TYPE is array (1..BUFFER_SIZE) of CHARACTER;
   task A is
      entry stop;
      entry fill (Buf : in out BUFFER_TYPE;
                  Buf_Length : in out NATURAL);
   end A;

   task B is
      entry stop;
      entry utilize (Buf : in out BUFFER_TYPE;
                     Buf_Length : NATURAL);
   end B;
end BUFFERS;

package body BUFFERS is

   type BUFFER;

   type BUFFER_REF is access BUFFER;

   task type BUFFER is
      entry release;
      entry initialize (Buf : BUFFER_REF);
   end BUFFER;

   task body A is
      Finishing : BOOLEAN := FALSE;
   begin
      loop
         select
            accept fill (Buf : in out BUFFER_TYPE;
                         Buf_Length : in out NATURAL) do
               if not Finishing then
                  -- fill the buffer
                  for I in 1..BUFFER_SIZE loop
                     select
                        accept stop;
                        Buf_Length := I − 1;
                        Finishing := TRUE;
                        exit;
                     else
                        -- get next character
                        Buf (I) := next character;
                     end select;
                  end loop;
                  if not Finishing then
                     Buf_Length := BUFFER_SIZE;
                  end if;
               end if;
            end fill;
            exit when Finishing;
```

```
      or when not Finishing =>
        accept stop;
        Finishing := TRUE;
      end select;
    end loop;
  end A;

  task body B is
    begin
      loop
        select
          accept utilize (Buf : in out BUFFER_TYPE;
                          Buf_Length : NATURAL) do
            -- consume the buffer
            if Buf_Length < BUFFER_SIZE then
              raise TASKING_ERROR;
              -- this exception will be propagated to the caller;
              -- it will also serve to terminate task B.
            end if;
          end utilize;
        or
          accept stop;
          exit;
        end select;
      end loop;
  end B;

  task body BUFFER is
    Next : BUFFER_REF;
    My_Store : BUFFER_TYPE;      -- this is the actual buffer
    N_Elems : NATURAL;
  begin
    accept initialize (Buf : BUFFER_REF) do
      Next := Buf;
    end initialize;

    loop
      select
        accept release;
      or
        terminate;
      end select;

      N_Elems := 0;
      A.fill (My_Store, N_Elems);

      Next.release;

      B.utilize (My_Store, N_Elems);
    end loop;
    -- termination is handled as follows:
    -- either A, B, or NEXT is dead, and TASKING_ERROR will be raised
    -- when any of these tasks is called, thus killing the caller.
    -- It may also be the case that A, B, and all the other buffers die while this
```

```
        -- one is waiting for a call to its entry RELEASE;
        -- in this case, the 'terminate' clause will do the job.
    end BUFFER;

begin
    -- we initialize the system by allocating the desired number of buffers, and
    -- passing to each one an access to the next one.
    declare
        First, Previous, Next : BUFFER_REF;
    begin
        First := new BUFFER;
        Previous := First;
        for I in 2..N_BUFFERS loop
            Next := new BUFFER;
            Next.initialize (Previous);
            Previous := Next;
        end loop;
        First.initialize (Previous);
        First.release;      -- trigger first buffer
    end;
end BUFFERS;
```

5 Miscellaneous issues

Within the framework of Ada's multitasking facilities, several design issues can be addressed. In this section, we cover the questions of fairness, of scheduling, the semantics of guard evaluation, and some consequences of the naming scheme.

5.1 Naming convention

In Ada, a task must name another one when issuing an entry call (i.e., it must know the identity of the called task), whereas the task accepting an entry call need not (and in general does not) know the identity of the caller. This asymmetry is actually well-suited to the very common case of *servers*, that is tasks that provide assistance to whoever requests it. The fully symmetric notation of CSP seems overly restrictive, whereas a totally anonymous convention often leads to more complex protocols in order to exchange task identities before starting an interaction.

5.2 Scheduling

The notion of scheduling covers the arbitration of computing resources among the various tasks that are ready for execution. Ada dictates only partially how such an arbitration should be done, by allowing the programmer to specify a *priority* for a given task: tasks with a higher priority will always execute in preference to tasks with a lower priority; on the other hand, Ada does not specify what happens to tasks at the same priority level, or when a scheduling decision should be made. This not only gives more freedom to the implementation, which can, but is not forced to, provide a time-slicing scheduling, as an example, but it also makes it more difficult for the programmer to rely on implicit assumptions about the order of execution of different tasks. Thus, whenever such an order is an integral part of the solution developed in the program, then this order should be enforced by explicit synchronization commands. This provides for more readable and more reliable programs.

With respect to priorities, an interesting question is that of the priority at which a given accept statement should be executed: the issue is that since priorities indicate a degree of urgency, it could be problematic to have an urgent task slowed down because it calls a lower-priority one, or conversely, because it has been called by a lower-priority one. Therefore, it is a rule of the language that a rendezvous should be executed with *at least* the higher of the priorities of the two tasks involved. The possibility of executing with a higher priority allows for some efficient optimizations at run time.

5.3 Fairness

When several alternatives of a select statement can be executed, the language does not specify how the choice is made. In this respect, the language does not guarantee the fairness of the selection, in that a caller may be delayed indefinitely on an entry while other calls are accepted. Hoare's comments on this particular problem are of interest [Hoare 1978]:

> "The question arises: Should a programming language definition specify that an implementation must be fair? Here, I am fairly sure that the answer is NO. [...] I would therefore suggest that it is the programmer's responsibility to prove that his program terminates correctly – without relying on the assumption of fairness in the implementation. [...]
>
> Nevertheless, I suggest that an efficient implementation should try to be reasonably fair and should ensure that an output command is not delayed unreasonably often after it first becomes executable."

The concept of fairness is important in a scheduler whose responsibility it is to ensure that the execution of parallel tasks in an environment that restricts the amount of actual parallelism will not be noticeably different from a perfect execution where each task has a processor of its own. These considerations do not apply to a concept such as the select statement, which is precisely intended to control the amount of true parallelism.

5.4 Semantics of guard evaluation

When reaching a select statement, all guards are evaluated first, and those alternatives with true guards are then selected for further consideration. If the task is suspended because no call to one of these entries has been issued, there is no guarantee that the condition expressed in the guard will still hold when the call is accepted.

An alternative semantics would be to evaluate the guard only when an entry call has occurred. Thus, when a select statement is reached, the guards of all entries for which a call is pending are evaluated, and one is chosen out of those with true guards. If no call is pending for an entry, or if all those that have been called have false guards, then the task is suspended, and all alternatives whose guards have not yet been evaluated are considered as potential choices. When a call to one of the corresponding entries occurs, the guard is then evaluated, and the call accepted only if the guard evaluates to true; otherwise, that alternative is removed from consideration. This semantics does not guarantee that the value of guards will not change; it merely ensures that the guard was true at the time the call was accepted. Nothing can be stated during actual execution of the accept statement, however, so little seems to have been gained. On the other hand, the consequences on efficiency would be rather disastrous, since when a call arrives, a context switch must occur in order to evaluate the guard, possibly to no avail if this guard evaluates to FALSE.

Another annoying consequence is that the order in which guards are evaluated could no longer be guaranteed, which is incompatible with the presence of side-effects.

Yet another problem would be that all guards may end up evaluating to FALSE. Whereas in the current scheme this is either a programming error or an intended effect, it would be deprived of meaning in the alternative scheme, since some of the guards that had originally evaluated to FALSE may have become TRUE in the meantime.

Of course, the ideal solution, which resembles that suggested in [Brinch Hansen 1978], would be to re-evaluate a guard as soon as anything happens in the system that may cause its value to change. This solution has the unfortunate drawback of stretching the demands on the implementation beyond acceptable limits.

6 Conclusion

The tasking primitives of Ada can be considered as both simple, by their small number, and extremely powerful, as they provide in essentially one concept all the forms of interactions between parallel processes. In addition, the concept of rendezvous permits the definition of abstractions in the same sense as procedures do. This concept is a major jump to a higher level, compared with previous primitives to deal with parallelism.

In spite of this high level, the features can be implemented efficiently on a variety of architectures, and fit nicely in the overall design of Ada.

References

Brinch Hansen, P. (1970): 'The Nucleus of a Multiprogramming System'. *Communications of the ACM*, **13**, No. 4.

Brinch Hansen, P. (1978): 'Distributed Processes: A Concurrent Programming Concept'. *Communications of the ACM*, **21**, No. 11.

Campbell, P.H., and Habermann, A.N. (1974): 'The Specification of Process Synchronisation by Path Expressions', in: *Lecture Notes in Computer Sciences*, **16**, Springer-Verlag.

Dijkstra, E.W. (1968): 'Cooperating Sequential Processes', in: *Programming Languages*, F. Genuys, ed., Academic Press.

Hoare, C.A.R. (1974): 'Monitors: an Operating System Structuring Concept'. *Communications of the ACM*, **17**, No. 10.

Hoare, C.A.R. (1978): 'Communicating Sequential Processes'. *Communications of the ACM*, **21**, No. 8.

Ichbiah, J.D., Barnes, J.G.P., Heliard, J.-C., Krieg-Brueckner, B., Roubine, O., and Wichmann, B.A. (1978): 'Preliminary Reference Manual for the GREEN Programming Language'. Honeywell Inc. and Cii-Honeywell Bull.

Kahn, G. (1974): 'The Semantics of a Simple Language for Parallel Programming', in: *Proceedings of IFIP Congress '74*, North Holland.

Thompson, K., and Ritchie, D.M. (1974): 'The UNIX Time-Sharing System'. *Communications of the ACM*, **17**, No. 7.

PART THREE
Concurrent Programming Models

In the previous section we looked at some specific concurrent programming languages. In this section, we step back and examine the abstract models that serve as the basis of these and other concurrent programming languages. These models are often inspired by the underlying hardware and reflect current technology or technology that is likely to be available in the future. Most, such as the 'monitor' and 'communicating sequential process' models, are based on the notion that the number of activities going on in parallel is relatively small – say in the tens or even hundreds – but certainly not in the thousands or hundreds of thousands. The parallelism considered by these models may be classified as 'coarse' and is not 'massive' parallelism. On the other hand, the dataflow and array processing models focus on 'fine grain' parallelism and the parallelism that may be achieved with these models can be potentially massive. For example, dataflow computer architecture designers envisage that dataflow computers will eventually have hundreds of thousands – or even more – processors.

PART THREE
Customer Representation

6

Data Flow Languages

William B. Ackerman
Massachusetts Institute of Technology

In a data flow language, locality of effect is easily achieved. But obtaining freedom from side effects requires a fundamental alteration in the execution model of the language.

The exploitation of parallelism is a primary goal for the architects of multiprocessor, vector machine, and array processor computer systems. Over the years, attempts have been made to design compilers that optimize programs written in conventional languages (e.g., 'vectorizing' compilers for Fortran). There have also been various language designs developed to facilitate the use of these systems, such as concurrent Pascal for multiprocessors [1]. In order to utilize the features of the systems directly, researchers have even developed highly specialized languages like Glypnir for the Illiac IV array processor [2] and the various 'vector' dialects of Fortran [3]. These languages almost always make the multiprocessor, vector, or array properties of the computer visible to the programmer, that is, they are actually vehicles that the programmer can use to help the compiler uncover parallelism. Many of these languages or dialects are 'unnatural' in the sense that they closely reflect the behavior of the systems for which they were designed, rather than the manner in which programmers normally think about problem solving.

Data flow computer design also seeks to take advantage of parallelism. The parallelism in a data flow computer is both microscopic (much more so than in a multiprocessor) and all-encompassing (much more so than in a vector processor). Like other forms of parallel computers, data flow computers are best programmed in special languages: most data flow designs would be extremely inefficient if programmed in conventional languages such as Fortran or PL/1. However, languages suitable for data flow computers can be very elegant. The language properties that a data flow computer requires are beneficial in and of themselves and are very similar to some of the properties (e.g., disciplined control structures and orderly module interactions) that are known to facilitate understandable and maintainable software. In fact, languages with many of these properties existed long before data flow computers were conceived. When discussing data flow, some of the relevant properties to keep in mind are:

(1) Freedom from side effects. This property is all-important. The (pure) Lisp language [4–6] is perhaps the best known example of a language without side effects. 'Functional' languages such as FP [7] also fit in this category.[†] The connection between freedom from side effects and efficient parallel computation has been known for many years [8].

(2) Locality of effect. Data flow languages generally exhibit considerable locality.

(3) Equivalence of instruction scheduling constraints with data dependencies. This means that all of the information needed to execute a program is contained in its 'data flow graph.' Since the data flow graph is, in effect, the machine code for a data flow computer, this property is what makes a language suitable for such a computer.

(4) A 'single assignment' convention. A variable may appear on the left side of an assignment only once within the area of the program in which it is active. This is a notational convention that is widely accepted.

(5) A somewhat unusual notation for iterations, necessitated by (1) and (4).

(6) A lack of 'history sensitivity' in procedures. Procedures have no state variables that retain data from one invocation to the next, so they cannot 'remember.' While this is generally observed for ordinary procedures (as required by (1) and (2)), history-sensitive procedures are often permitted.

To see why data flow computers require languages free of side effects, we must examine the nature of data flow computation and the nature of side effects. A detailed description of the mechanism of data flow computers is beyond the scope of this article but may be found elsewhere [9–15]. The two data flow languages touched on here, Val [16]

[†] The term 'functional' is often used, along with 'applicative,' to describe a language that operates by application of functions to values. This implies freedom from side effects. There is also a narrower meaning of the term in which 'functional language' denotes a language such as FP, where all control structures are replaced by combining operators that manipulate functions directly, without ever appearing to explicitly manipulate data. The difference between such a language and the data flow languages discussed in this article is simply a difference in the notation used to route data through functions. The languages in this article are 'functional' in the first sense only.

and Id [10], were developed by the data flow projects at the MIT and the University of California at Irvine, respectively. Lucid [17] and FP [7] were developed for their attractive mathematical properties and their amenability to program verification, rather than for programming data flow computers, but are nevertheless suitable languages for data flow computation.

Data flow analysis

Let us begin by examining a simple sequence of assignment statements written in a conventional language such as Fortran:

(1) $P = X + Y$
(2) $Q = P/Y$
(3) $R = X * P$
(4) $S = R - Q$
(5) $T = R * P$
(6) RESULT $= S/T$

A straightforward analysis of this program will show that many of these instructions can be executed concurrently, as long as certain constraints are met. These constraints can be represented by a graph in which nodes represent instructions and an arrow from one instruction to another means that the second may not be executed until the first has been completed. So the permissible computation sequences include, among others, (1,3,5,2,4,6), (1,2,3,5,4,6), and (1,[2 and 3 simultaneously], [4 and 5 simultaneously],6).

This type of analysis (commonly called data flow analysis, a term which long predates data flow computers) is frequently performed at runtime in the arithmetic processing units of high performance conventional computers such as the IBM 360/91 and at compile time in optimizing compilers. In optimizing compilers, data flow analysis yields improved utilization of temporary memory locations. For example, on a computer with high-speed general-purpose or floating-point registers, this program can be compiled to use the registers instead of main memory for P, Q, R, S, and T, if it can be determined that they will not be used again. (This determination is very difficult, principally because of GOTOs, which is one of the reasons why it is very difficult to write optimizing compilers for languages such as Fortran.)

In the graph representation, an instruction can be executed as soon as all the instructions with arrows pointing into it have completed. On a multiprocessor system, we would allocate a processor for each instruction, with appropriate instructions (such as semaphore operations [18]) to enforce the sequencing constraints, but execution would be hopelessly inefficient because the parallelism of this example is far too 'fine grained' for a multiprocessor. The overhead in the process scheduling and in the *wait* and *signal* instructions would be many times greater than the execution time of the arithmetic operations. A data flow computer, on the other hand, is designed to execute algorithms with such a fine grain of parallelism efficiently. In these machines, parallelism is exploited at the level of individual instructions, as in the above example, and at all coarser levels as well. In most programs there are typically many sections, often far removed from each other, at which computations may proceed simultaneously.

To exploit parallelism at all levels, the instruction sequencing constraints must be deducible from the program itself. The sequencing constraints in Figure 1a are given by arrows. It is not difficult to see that these arrows coincide with data transmission from one instruction to its successor through variables. In fact, the graph could be redrawn with the arrows labeled by the variables that they represent (Figure 1b).

In a data flow computer, the machine-level program is essentially represented as a graph with pointers between nodes, the pointers representing both the flow of data and the sequencing constraints. The status of each instruction is kept in a special memory that is capable of 'firing' (executing) the instruction when all of the necessary data values have arrived, and using the result to update the status of the destination instructions.[†] The programming language for a data flow computer must therefore satisfy two criteria: it must be possible to deduce the data dependencies of the program operations; and the sequencing constraints must always be exactly the same as the data dependencies, so that the instruction firing rule can be based simply on the availability of data.[‡] A language can meet these criteria if it utilizes the general properties of locality of effect and freedom from side effects.

Locality of effect

Locality of effect means that instructions do not have unnecessary far-reaching data dependencies. For example, the Fortran program fragment given previously appears to use variables P, Q, R, S, and T only as

---

[†] Although the language concepts presented in this article assume that the computer exploits parallelism at a microscopic level, not all data flow or data-driven computers do so. Designs of data flow computers that exploit parallelism only at the subroutine level may be found in Davis [19] and Rumbaugh [20].

[‡] Not all designs for data flow computers accept the second of these criteria or its consequences. The LAU language [21] is intended for execution on a data flow computer, but it was designed to support conventional forms of data-base updating and retrieval, so it has side effects on certain operations. The sequencing of these operations must therefore be constrained by means other than data dependencies, and so it does not satisfy the second criterion. The extra constraints in LAU are specified by path expressions [22] written into the source program.

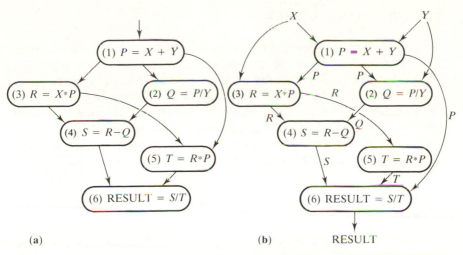

Figure 1   (a) Sequencing constraints in Fortran assignment statements; (b) constraints with variables represented.

temporaries. A similar fragment appearing elsewhere in the program might use the same temporaries for some unrelated computation, and the logic of the program might allow the two fragments to be executed concurrently were it not for this duplication of names. (Unfortunately, many conventional languages encourage this style of programming in the name of 'saving space.') Any attempt to execute the fragments concurrently would be impossible because of the apparent data dependencies arising from the duplication of these temporaries, unless the compiler can deduce that the conflict is not real and remove it by using different sets of temporaries.

In languages such as Fortran and PL/1, this deduction is not an easy one to make. A reference to a variable in one part of the program does not necessarily imply dependence on the value computed in another part: the variable might be overwritten before it is next read. Careful analysis is required to determine whether a variable is actually transmitting data or is 'dead.' This analysis is made much more difficult if unrestricted GOTOs or other undisciplined control structures are allowed. Of course, existing optimizing compilers can do a very good job of analyzing the various types of dependencies in reasonably well-structured programs [23], but the languages being proposed in this article make that unnecessary.

The problem can be simplified by assigning every variable a definite 'scope,' or region of the program in which it is active, and carefully restricting the entry to and exit from the blocks that constitute scopes. It is also helpful to deny procedures access to any data items that are not transmitted as arguments, though this is not really necessary if global variables are avoided and procedure definitions are carefully block structured as in Pascal.

Side effects

Freedom from side effects is necessary to ensure that the data dependencies are the same as the sequencing constraints. It is much more difficult to achieve than locality of effect because locality only requires superficial restrictions on the language, whereas freedom from side effects requires fundamental changes in the way the language's 'virtual machine' processes data. Side effects come in many forms – the most well-known examples arise in procedures that modify variables in the calling program, as in this Pascal example:

```
procedure GETRS(X, Y : real);
begin RS := X * X + Y * Y; (* RS is declared in an outer block *)
end;
```

Absence of global or 'common' variables and careful control of the scopes of variables make it possible for a compiler to prohibit this sort of thing, but a data flow computer imposes much stricter prohibitions against side effects: a procedure may not even modify its own arguments. In a sense nothing may ever be modified at all.

If we prohibit global variables and modification of arguments, simple side effect problems such as the above can be cured, but problems will remain that could interfere with concurrent computation. These more serious side effects do not arise in the manipulation of simple (scalar) data, but only from the processing of data structures such as arrays and records. More precisely, they arise from the way data structures are manipulated in conventional languages. The solution is to manipulate data structures in the same way scalars are manipulated.

Consider the following procedure, which modifies its arguments by a conventional 'call by reference' mechanism. $SORT2$ is a procedure to sort two elements, the Jth and the $J + 1$st, of array A into ascending order by exchanging them if necessary:

```
procedure SORT2(var A : array[1..10] of real; J : integer);
var T : real;
begin if A[J] > A[J + 1] begin
        T := A[J];
        A[J] := A[J + 1];
        A[J + 1] := T;
        end;
    end;
(1)  SORT2(AA, J);
(2)  SORT2(AA, K);
(3)  P := AA[L];
```

Statements 1 and 2 might interfere with each other and with statement 3. Since the values of J, K, and L are not known to the compiler, it must assume that the statements will conflict, and execute them in the exact order specified. Any attempt at parallel execution might result in the incorrect results, depending on J, K, L, and unpredictable fluctuations in timing.

A phenomenon known as 'aliasing' makes the problem even more difficult. This occurs when different formal parameters to a procedure refer to the same actual parameter, that is, they are 'aliases' of each other:

```
procedure REVERSE (var A, B : array[1..10] of real);
begin for J := 1 to 10 do
  B[J] := A[11 − J];
end;
```

In this program it would appear that since A and B are different arrays, all 10 assignments could proceed concurrently or in any order. However, if this were part of a larger program and *REVERSE* were invoked in the statement '*REVERSE(Q, Q)*;' arrays A and B would actually be the same, and the assignments would seriously interfere with each other. Languages such as Fortran and PL/1, in which external procedures are not available to the compiler when the calling program is being compiled, make the problem harder still. Facilities for manipulating data structures by pointers, such as the pointer data type in PL/1 and Pascal, make it possible for all of these problems to arise without using procedures – the 'call by reference' mechanism is not at fault here. Even if procedures and pointers are not used, the sequencing constraints may be far from clear, as in:

(1) $A[J] := 3$;
(2) $X := A[K]$;

If the convention is adopted that any statement modifying any element of an array constitutes a 'writing' of the array, statement 1 clearly passes array A to statement 2. But then a statement such as the assignment in:

```
for J := 1 to 10 do
  A[J + 1] := A[J] + 1;
```

depends on itself!

All of this leads to one inescapable conclusion: if arrays and records exist as global objects in memory and are manipulated by statements and passed as pointers or procedure parameters, it is virtually impossible to tell, at the time an array element is modified, what effects that modification may have elsewhere in the program.

One way to solve some of these problems is to use 'call by value' instead of the more common 'call by reference.' This solves the aliasing problem and the problem of procedures modifying their arguments. In a 'call by value' scheme, a procedure copies its arguments (even if they are arrays). Thus it can never modify the actual argument in the calling program. Call by reference has traditionally been used instead of call by value because it is a more faithful way of modeling computation, and is more efficient, on von Neumann computers.

Applicative languages

A scheme is used for data flow languages which goes far beyond call by value: all arrays are values rather than objects and are treated as such at all times, not just when being passed as procedure arguments. Arrays are not modified by subscripted assignment statements such as '$A[J] := S;$' but are processed by operators which create new array values. The simplest operator to perform the applicative equivalent of modifying an array takes three arguments: an array, an index, and a new data value. The result of the operation is a new array, containing the given data value at the given index, and the same data as the original array at all other indices. In the Val language this elementary operator appears as '$A[J:S]$', while in the Id language it is '$A + [J] S$'. This operation does not modify its argument. Hence, in this Val program:

(1) $B := A[J:S];$
(2) $C := A[K:T];$
(3) $P := A[L];$
(4) $Q := B[M];$
(5) $R := C[N];$

statements 1 and 2 do not interfere with each other or with array A. Statement 3 may be executed immediately, whether 1 and/or 2 have completed or not, since they would have no effect on statement 3 anyway. Statement 4 can be executed as soon as statement 1 completes, whether statement 2 has completed or not. In fact, the sequencing constraints are those shown in Figure 2. This situation is similar to the one in our first

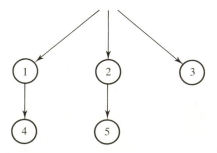

Figure 2   Sequencing constraints in a Val program.

simple Fortran example: the sequencing constraints are exactly the same as the data dependencies, which is the property we seek for data flow. Note that an assignment like '$A := A[J : S]$' makes no sense conceptually, and the single assignment rule will in fact forbid it.

An operator-based handling of arrays and records automatically accomplishes call by value. In a call by value scheme, a routine such as the $SORT2$ given previously would not accomplish its purpose. $SORT2$ must return the new array as its value. It would be written in simplified Val as:

```
function SORT2(A, J)
   if A[J] < A[J + 1] then A
   else (A[J : A[J + 1]]) [J + 1 : A[J]]     %No temporary variable needed
                                             %during this exchange because
                                             %A is not modified.

   end;
end;
```

Note that the array construction operator may be composed with itself and with other operators in the same way as arithmetic operators.

In conventional languages, procedures do most, if not all, of their work through side effects: a procedure might be designed to alter dozens of variables in the calling program. Functions, on the other hand, typically return a single value, which is usually not an array or record. To make functions as powerful and flexible as the procedures of conventional languages, applicative languages often allow functions to return several values, entire records or arrays, or both. If a function returns several values, its invocation can be used in a 'multiple assignment' such as

$$X, Y, Z := FUNC(P, Q, R) \qquad \%FUNC\ returns\ 3\ values$$

Perhaps the most profound difference in the way people must think when writing programs in data flow languages as opposed to conventional languages lies in regarding arrays and records as values instead of objects. The customary view of arrays as objects residing in static locations of memory and being manipulated by statements that are executed in some sequence is incompatible with detection of parallelism among the statements. Viewing arrays and records as values manipulated by operations (as scalar values are) allows the parallelism among the operators to be deduced from the data dependencies, again as is the case with scalar values.

The value-oriented approach to arrays is, at first, confusing to some, but it need not be. An integer array can be thought of as a string of integers, just as an integer can be thought of as a string of digits. If J has the value 31416, the statement '$K := J - 400$;' leaves K equal to 31016; no programmer would expect the value of J to be affected. If A is an array with elements [3, 1, 4, 1, 6], the statement '$B := A[3 : 0]$' is completely analogous; it leaves B with elements [3, 1, 0, 1, 6] and does not change A.

Languages that perform all processing by means of operators applied to values are called applicative languages, and are thus the natural languages for data flow computation. Lisp is the earliest well-known applicative language to be implemented on a computer. (It is applicative only if *RPLACA*, *RPLACD*, and all other functions with side effects are avoided; this subset of the language is often called 'pure' Lisp.) The connection between applicative languages and the detection of parallelism has been reported by Tesler and Enea [8] and more recently by Friedman and Wise [24]. The Tesler/Enea paper, and the development of Lisp and other applicative languages, all predate the data flow computer concept by several years. In even more 'historical' terms, the concept of computation by applicative evaluation of expressions actually goes back to the invention of the lambda calculus in 1941 [25].

Definitional languages and the single assignment rule

Having accepted an applicative programming style and a value-oriented rather than object-oriented execution model, let us examine the implications of this style as they relate to the meaning of assignment statements. Except in iterations (which will be discussed later), an assignment statement has no effect except to provide a value and bind that value to the name appearing on its left side. The result of the assignment is accessible only in later expressions in which that name appears. If the language uses blocks in which all variables are local to the block for which they are declared, the places where a variable is used can be determined by inspection. If the expression on the right side of an assignment is substituted for the variable on the left side everywhere within the block, the resultant program will be completely equivalent. (Note in the example below that the program on the left is clearly more efficient, requiring only two additions instead of four. I am not proposing the substitution be made in practice):

$$S := X + Y;$$
$$D := 3 * S;$$
$$E := S/2 + F(S);$$

is equivalent to:

$$D := 3 * (X + Y);$$
$$E := (X + Y)/2 + F(X + Y);$$

Now this situation is the same as a system of mathematical equations. If a system of equations contains '$S = X + Y$', it is clear that $3 * S$ and $3 * (X + Y)$ are equivalent. Hence the statement '$S := X + Y;$'

means the same thing in the program that the equation '$S = X + Y$' means in a system of equations, namely that within the scope of these variables S is the sum of X and Y. The correspondence can be thought of as holding for all time; it is not necessary to consider the statements as being executed at particular instants. (In fact, perhaps the word 'variable' is an appropriate term.) Of course, the addition of X and Y to form S must take place before any of the operations that use S can be performed, but the programmer does not need to be directly concerned with this.

In short, the statement '$S := X + Y$' should be thought of as a *definition*, not an assignment. Languages which use this interpretation of assignments are called *definitional languages* as opposed to conventional imperative languages. Definitional languages are well suited to program verification because the assertions made in proving correctness are exactly the same as the definitions appearing in the program itself. In conventional languages one must follow the flow of control to determine where in the program text assertions such as '$S = X + Y$' are true, because the variables S, X, and Y can be changed many times, and assertions must therefore be associated with points in the program. In a definitional language, however, the situation is extremely simple. If a program block contains the statement '$S := X + Y$;' then the assertion '$S = X + Y$' is true. Of course, care must be taken to prevent a system of circular definitions such as:

$$X := Y;$$
$$Y := X + 3;$$

Such circular definitions can easily be checked by the compiler. The simplest way is to require that every name be defined (appear on the left side of a definition) before it appears on the right side of any definition, and that it be defined only once. So the actual proof rule is: if a program block contains the statement '$S := X + Y$;' and the program compiles correctly, then '$S = X + Y$' is true. Strictly speaking, it is true only in statements after the one defining S, but since S could not have appeared in earlier statements, the assertion can be treated as being true throughout the block.

The power of definitional languages for program verification is well-known outside the data flow field. Lucid [17] is an example of an applicative definitional language designed expressly for ease of program verification. A language proposed by Kessels [26] would allow a program to be a mixture of modules, some imperative and some definitional.

There is one problem that could ruin the elegance of definitional languages: multiple definition of the same name. Definitional languages almost invariably obey the single assignment rule, which prevents program constructs which imply mathematical abominations such as '$J := J + 1$;'. Since the appearance of J on the right side precedes the actual definition of J, it implies an inconsistent statement sequence that the compiler would diagnose. The prevention of such abominations is necessary if the definitions in the program are to be carried directly into assertions used to prove correctness, since the assertion '$J = J + 1$' is absurd.

But it is not actually necessary for a data flow language to conform to the single assignment rule. A data flow language could be designed with multiple assignments in which the scope of a variable extends only from one definition to the next, which, in effect, introduces a new variable that simply happens to have the same name. A program written this way can easily be transformed into one obeying the single assignment rule by simply choosing a new name for any redefined variable, and changing all subsequent references to the new name. However, the advantages of single assignment languages, namely, clarity and ease of verification, generally outweigh the 'convenience' of reusing the same name.

Iterations

In spite of the previous discussions, one area remains in which statements in conventional languages, such as:

$$I := I - 1;$$

or

$$A := A[J : X + Y];$$

seem to be explicitly or implicitly necessary, and that is in iterations. The technique of renaming variables to make a program conform to the single assignment rule works only for straight-line programs. If a statement appears in a loop, renaming its variables will not preserve the programmer's intentions. For example:

    for I := 1 to 10 do
        J := J + 1;

cannot be transformed to:

    for I := 1 to 10 do
        J1 := J + 1;

If the language allows general **GOTO**s, with the resulting possibility of complex and unstructured loops, the problem becomes difficult indeed. But data flow languages have no **GOTO** statement, and require loops to be created only by specific program structures (such as the 'while ... do ... ' and similar statements found in PL/1 and Pascal). This makes the problem easy to solve, and allows for simple and straightforward iterations.

To develop the data flow equivalent of a 'while ... do ... ' type of iteration, we must consider what the '**do**' part of such a structure contains. Since there are no side effects, the only state information in an iteration is in the bindings of the loop variables, and the only activity that can take place is the redefinition of those variables through functional operators. An iteration therefore consists of:

(1) Definitions of the initial values of the loop variables,

(2) A test to determine, for any given values of the loop variables, whether the loop is to terminate or to cycle again,

(3) If it is to terminate, some expression giving the value(s) to be returned (these values typically depend on the current values of the loop variables), and

(4) If it is to cycle again, some expressions giving the new values to be assigned to the loop variables. These also typically depend on the current values of the loop variables.

An iteration to compute the factorial of N could be written in simplified Val as follows:

```
for J,K := N,1;   %Give loop variables J and K initial
                  %values N and 1, respectively. J will
                  %count downward. K will keep the
                  %accumulated product.

do if J = 0       %Decide whether to terminate.
    then K        %Yes, final result is current K.
   else iter J,K := J − 1, K * J;   %No, compute new values of J and K,
      end;                          %and cycle again.
end;
```

It could be written in Id (with a similar representation in Lucid) as:

```
(initial J ← N; K ← 1
while J ≠ 0 do
   new J ← J − 1;
   new K ← K * J;
return K)
```

Although the values of the loop variables do change, they change only between one iteration cycle and the next. The single assignment rule, with its prohibition against things like '$J = J − 1$', is still in force within any one cycle. All redefinitions take place precisely at the boundary between iteration cycles (though they need not actually occur simultaneously). This is enforced in Val by allowing redefinitions only after the word *iter*, which is the command to begin a new iteration cycle. In Id and Lucid, the 'new' values become the 'current' values at the boundary between cycles.

Since the single assignment rule is obeyed and names have single values, the mathematical simplicity of assertions about values still exists within any single iteration cycle. The assertions typically take the form 'In any cycle, $S = X + Y$' and assertions used in proving correctness of an iteration are usually proved inductively. Because the assertions take a simple form, such proofs are usually simpler than in conventional languages. For example, the assertion '$J \geq 0$ and $K * (J!) = N!$' is the 'invariant' used to prove correctness of the factorial program. Note that a loop invariant is not something that is true only at certain places in the loop (e.g., at its beginning), but is true throughout the body of the loop. An invariant has a different interpretation during different iteration cycles because the values of the iteration variables change from one cycle to another. It must be proved for each cycle, typically by induction from the preceding cycle.

In the factorial program, the basis of the induction is that the invariant is true for the initial values $J = N$ (assuming $N \geq 0$) and $K = 1$. The induction step is that, if another cycle is started with the values $J - 1$ and $K * J$ substituted for J and K, respectively, these values will obey the assertion, that is, '$J - 1 \geq 0$ and $(K * J) * ((J - 1)!) = N!$'. This is clearly true if we observe that a new cycle will only be started if $J > 0$ and, hence, $J - 1 \geq 0$. The next step is to examine the value returned when and if the iteration terminates. Since $J = 0$ at that time, we will have $K * (0!) = N!$, or $K = N!$ Since K is the value returned, it is $N!$. Finally, we must show that the iteration will terminate, meaning that within a finite number of steps the termination condition will be satisfied – that condition is $J = 0$, which is clearly satisfied after N cycles.

Parallelism demands that sequential computations be held to a minimum. The iteration constructs just described seem to imply a sequential execution of the various cycles. If the values of the iteration variables in one cycle depend on those in the previous cycles (as they do in the factorial example), nothing can be done, although a data flow computer can often execute part of a cycle before the previous one has completed. If the values in one cycle do not depend on those of the previous cycles, the cycles can be performed in parallel. In Val this is done with a FORALL program construct that does not allow one cycle to depend on another and directs the computer to perform all cycles simultaneously. In Id the same effect is achieved when the cycles do not depend on each other by an automatic 'unfolding' of the iteration that permits the cycles to be performed simultaneously.

Errors and exceptional conditions

Locality of effect requires that errors such as arithmetic overflow be handled by error values rather than by program interruptions or manipulation of global status flags. If an error occurs in an operation, that fact must be transmitted only to the destinations of that operation. This can easily be accomplished by enlarging the set of values to include error values such as overflow, underflow, or zero-divide.

If the intent is to abort the computation when an error occurs, it can be achieved by making the error values propagate: if an argument to an arithmetic operation is an error, the result is an error. When an error propagates to the end of an iteration body, that iteration always terminates rather than cycling again. In this way the entire computation will quickly come to a stop, yielding an error value as its result. If the computer keeps a record of every error generation and propagation, that record will tell us when and where the error occurred, and what iterations and procedures were active.

If the intent is to correct an error when it occurs (perhaps keeping a list of such errors in some array), that can be accomplished through operations that test for errors. For example, a program to set Z to the quotient of X and Y, or to zero when an error occurs, could be written in Val as follows:

```
ZZ := X/Y;
Z  := if is_error (ZZ) then 0 else ZZ end;
```

History sensitive computation

While the mechanism described thus far is universal in a theoretical sense, it exhibits a glaring shortcoming in performing real-time computation. Consider the problem of printing the cumulative totals of a series of input values.

Inputs:	1	3	-2	7	5
Outputs:	1	4	2	9	14

It is, of course, easy to write a function that transforms the input as an array to the output array shown above, but this will not work if each output value needs to be seen immediately after the corresponding input value is entered. If each output depended only on the corresponding input instead of on the corresponding input and all earlier inputs, the problem would be trivial – trivial because the same function could be repeatedly invoked, once per input, and the result of each invocation then printed. This is the normal mode of operation of an abstract interactive system, such as the read/eval/print loop of Lisp.

The problem can therefore be seen as one of providing a history-sensitive function: a function that 'remembers' its past inputs. In the cumulative sum example, the function would have to keep the sum of its past inputs and add to that sum each input when it arrives. Another way to view the problem is to think of the function as operating on a stream of values [10, 27–29]. A stream is like an array handled so that its values can be transmitted in real time. Of course, any function that operates on streams instead of arrays must obey certain restrictions to avoid obvious violations of causality. For example, an output value, once written, may not be erased. Programs that manipulate streams may be written in a recursive style [27, 29] in which a stream is treated like a list in Lisp, or in an iterative style [10] in which the rebinding of an iteration variable denoting a stream causes that stream to advance to the next element. Either method enforces the causality constraint if certain rules are followed regarding the permissible recursions or iterations.

The cumulative sum function could be written (in an iterative style) in Id as:

```
(initial SUM ← 0
for each T in INPUT_DATA do
     !INPUT_DATA is the incoming stream
  new SUM ← SUM + T
return all SUM)
     !Produce each cumulative sum as a stream item
```

This approach can be used to solve general data-base query and update problems. In such an application, the entire data base would be one or more loop variables that are redefined in response to items in the input stream.

In addition to history sensitivity, functions that manipulate streams have another property that makes them indispensable for real-time input/output operation: they can emit more (or fewer) outputs than their inputs. A typical example would be a function to remove all ⟨newline⟩ characters from its input or to insert a ⟨newline⟩ after every 80 characters. Operations of this sort are commonly performed by coroutines. A data flow program using streams is a network of parallel communicating processes, a computational model that has been of some theoretical interest in the last few years [30–32].

Methods of achieving high speed

When programs written in applicative languages are to be run on data flow computers or other supercomputers, care must be taken to exploit the maximum amount of parallelism whenever arrays are involved. The problem is that there is an apparent data dependency, and therefore a scheduling constraint, between any array-construction operation and any fetch operation that uses the resultant array, even if the element it fetches is not the one that was added. In a program written in a conventional language that allows concurrency and nondeterminacy (concurrent Pascal, for example), a knowledgeable programmer might be able to explicitly specify parallelism, and make the program run more efficiently than in the applicative system. Consider the conventional program:

(1) $A[J] := S$;
(2) $A[K] := T$;
(3) $P := A[M]$;
(4) $Q := A[N]$;

If the programmer knows that J and M will always be even, and K and N always odd, then statements 1 and 3 interact only with each other, as do 2 and 4. Statements 1 and 2 could be executed simultaneously, 3 need only follow 1, and 4 would only need to follow 2. If the programmer has the ability to control parallelism explicitly, he could exactly specify those constraints. This would produce a program that would appear (to the compiler) to be nondeterminate, although the programmer would know that it is determinate. Such an explicit specification of scheduling constraints in disagreement with the apparent data dependencies is not possible in a data flow language, but simultaneous execution could still be realized by writing the program as follows (using the programmer's knowledge that J and M are even while K and N are odd):

$B0 := A0[J : S]$; %$A0$ and $B0$ are constructed
$B1 := A1[K : T]$; %with the even elements,
$P \ := B0[M]$;   %$A1$ and $B1$ with the
$Q \ := B1[N]$;   %odd ones.

This exploits the parallelism exactly.

Lenient Cons

The data dependency problem also arises in a much more general context. If function 'F' creates an array value by filling the array one element at a time and then passes the array to 'G,' which reads the elements one at a time, G cannot begin until F completes. In many instances this delay is unnecessary, and a number of techniques have been proposed for eliminating it without departing from the principle that the sequencing constraints are exactly the data dependencies. These techniques are variously called lenient Cons [24] or I-structures [33]. The array-construction operation 'computes' its result as soon as the array argument is available, even if the index and data arguments are not. It fills the unknown array positions with a special code indicating that the datum at that position is not yet available. The computation of each datum proceeds concurrently, and, when it completes, that datum goes into the array, replacing the special code. Any attempt to read an array position containing such a code waits until the actual datum is available. Using lenient Cons, when the function F is to fill an array, the array comes back almost instantly, whether or not it contains useful data. From this point on, when function G attempts to use an element of the array, it only needs to wait for that element to be computed. (Note that a computer with lenient Cons automatically takes care of the problem in the previous example.)

The lenient Cons principle is somewhat similar to a computational principle called lazy evaluation [34]. Under lazy evaluation, an operation is not performed until its result is actually demanded by another operation, so there is a flow of 'demands' upward through the data flow graphs as well as a flow of data downward. With this method, even infinite arrays can be 'created,' such as an array containing all prime numbers. Whenever a reference to an element is made, its prime number is computed. A form of lenient Cons and lazy evaluation is used in a data flow computer proposed by Keller, Lindstrom, and Patil [14].

Streams

The ability of a stream to act as an array that is fragmented in time makes streams suitable for the data dependency problem. The output of F and the input of G could be a stream. G would receive each element as soon as F created it, and G would be processing the Nth element while F computes the $N + 1$st, resulting in parallel pipelined computation of F and G. The same language constraints that prevent streams from violating causality will force G to process the elements in the order in which they were produced by F, and will generally prevent random access to streams.

Conclusion

There have recently been calls to realize the enormous potential of VLSI technology [7] by abandoning traditional von Neumann computer architecture. There has also been widespread recognition of the fact that proper language design is essential if the high cost of software is to be brought under control, and that most existing languages are seriously deficient in this area.

Fortunately, the implications of these two trends for language design are similar: languages must avoid an execution model (the von Neumann model) that involves a global memory whose state is manipulated by the sequential execution of commands. Such a global memory makes realization of the potential of VLSI technology difficult because it creates a bottleneck between the computer's control unit and its memory. Languages that use a global memory in their execution model also exacerbate the software problem by allowing program modules to interact with each other in ways that are difficult to understand, rather than through simple transmission of argument and result values. Language designs based on concepts of applicative programming should be able to help control the high cost of software and meet the needs of future computer designs.

Acknowledgments

This research was supported in part by the Lawrence Livermore National Laboratory of the University of California under contract no. 8545403, in part by the National Science Foundation under research grant DCR75-04060, and in part by the Advanced Research Projects Agency of the Department of Defense under Office of Naval Research contract no. N00014-75-C-0661.

References

[1] P. Brinch Hansen, 'The Programming Language Concurrent Pascal,' *IEEE Trans. Software Eng.*, **SE-1**, 2, June 1975, pp. 199–207.

[2] D. H. Lawrie, T. Layman, D. Baer, and J. M. Randal, 'Glypnir – A Programming Language for Illiac IV,' *Comm. ACM,* **18**, 3, Mar. 1975, pp. 157–164.

[3] J. T. Martin, R. G. Zwakenberg, and S. V. Solbeck, 'LRLTRAN Language Used with the CHAT and STAR Compilers,' Livermore Time-Sharing System Manual, Chapter 207, Lawrence Livermore National Laboratory, edition 4, Dec. 11, 1974.

[4] J. McCarthy, 'Recursive Functions of Symbolic Expressions and their Computation by Machine,' *Comm. ACM*, 3, 4, Apr. 1960, pp. 185–195.

[5] J. McCarthy *et al.*, 'LISP 1.5 Programmer's Manual,' MIT Press, 1966.

[6] P. H. Winston and B. K. P. Horn, *LISP*, Addison-Wesley, Reading, Mass., 1981.

[7] J. Backus, 'Can Programming be Liberated from the von Neumann Style? A Functional Style and Its Algebra of Programs,' *Comm. ACM*, **21**, 8, Aug. 1978, pp. 613–641.

[8] L. G. Tesler and H. J. Enea, 'A Language Design for Concurrent Processes,' *AFIPS Conf. Proc.*, **32**, 1968 SJCC, pp. 403–408.

[9] Arvind and K. P. Gostelow, 'Dataflow Computer Architecture: Research and Goals,' Department of Information and Computer Science Technical Report TR-113, University of California, Irvine, Feb. 1978.

[10] Arvind, K. P. Gostelow, and W. Plouffe, 'An Asynchronous Programming Language and Computing Machine,' Department of Information and Computer Science Technical Report 114a, University of California, Irvine, Dec. 1978.

[11] J. B. Dennis, 'Data Flow Supercomputers,' *Computer*, **13**, 11, Nov. 1980, pp. 48–56.

[12]   J. B. Dennis, D. P. Misunas, and C. K. C. Leung, 'A Highly Parallel Processor Using a Data Flow Machine Language,' Computation Structures Group Memo 134, Laboratory for Computer Science, MIT, Cambridge, Mass., Jan. 1977.

[13]   J. Gurd, I. Watson, and J. Glauert, 'A Multilayered Data Flow Computer Architecture,' Department of Computer Science, University of Manchester, Manchester, England, July 1978.

[14]   R. M. Keller, G. Lindstrom, and S. Patil, 'A Loosely-Coupled Applicative Multi-Processing System,' *AFIPS Conf. Proc.*, **48**, 1979 NCC, pp. 613–622.

[15]   A. Plas, D. Comte, O. Gelly, and J. C. Syre, 'LAU System Architecture: A Parallel Data Driven Processor Based on Single Assignment,' *Proc. 1976 Int'l Conf. Parallel Processing*, Aug. 1976, pp. 293–302.

[16]   W. B. Ackerman and J. B. Dennis, 'VAL – A Value-Oriented Algorithmic Language: Preliminary Reference Manual,' MIT Laboratory for Computer Science Technical Report TR-218, MIT, Cambridge, Mass., June 1979.

[17]   E. A. Ashcroft and W. W. Wadge, 'Lucid, a Non-procedural Language with Iteration,' *Comm. ACM*, **20**, 7, July 1977, pp. 519–526.

[18]   E. W. Dijkstra, 'Cooperating Sequential Processes,' *Programming Languages*, F. Genuys, ed., Academic Press, New York, 1968.

[19]   A. L. Davis, 'The Architecture and System Method of DDM1: A Recursively Structured Data Driven Machine,' *Proc. Fifth Ann. Symp. Computer Architecture*, Apr. 1978, pp. 210–215.

[20]   J. E. Rumbaugh, 'A Data Flow Multiprocessor,' *IEEE Trans. Computers*, **C-26**, 2, Feb. 1977, pp. 138–146.

[21]   D. Comte, G. Durrieu, O. Gelly, A. Plas, and J. C. Syre, 'Parallelism, Control and Synchronization Expressions in a Single Assignment Language,' *Sigplan Notices*, **13**, 1, Jan. 1978, pp. 25–33.

[22]   R. H. Campbell, 'Path Expressions: A Technique for Specifying Process Synchronization,' Department of Computer Science Report UIUCDCS-R-77-863, University of Illinois at Urbana-Champaign, Urbana, Ill., 1977.

[23]   D. J. Kuck *et al.*, 'Dependence Graphs and Compiler Optimizations,' *Conf. Record Eighth ACM Symp. Principles of Programming Languages*, Jan. 1981, pp. 207–218.

[24]   D. P. Friedman and D. S. Wise, 'The Impact of Applicative Programming on Multiprocessing,' *Proc. 1976 Int'l Conf. Parallel Processing*, Aug. 1976, pp. 263–272.

[25]   A. Church, 'The Calculi of Lambda-Conversion,' *Ann. Math. Studies*, Vol. 6, Princeton University Press, Princeton, N.J., 1941.

[26]   J. L. W. Kessels, 'A Conceptual Framework for a Non-procedural Programming Language,' *Comm. ACM*, **20**, 12, Dec. 1977, pp. 906–913.

[27]   J. B. Dennis, 'A Language Design for Structured Concurrency,' *Design and Implementation of Programming Languages: Proceedings of a DoD Sponsored Workshop*, J. H. Williams and D. A. Fisher, eds., *Lecture Notes in Computer Science*, Vol. 54, Oct. 1976; also in Computation Structures Group Note 28-1, Feb. 1977, Laboratory for Computer Science, MIT, Cambridge, Mass.

[28] J. B. Dennis and K-S. Weng, 'An Abstract Implementation for Concurrent Computation with Streams,' *Proc. 1979 Int'l Conf. Parallel Processing,* Aug. 1979, pp. 35–45; also in Computation Structures Group Memo 180, Laboratory for Computer Science, MIT, Cambridge, Mass., July 1979.

[29] K-S Weng, 'Stream-Oriented Computation in Recursive Data Flow Schemas,' Laboratory for Computer Science Technical Manual TM-68, MIT, Cambridge, Mass., Oct. 1975.

[30] C. A. R. Hoare, 'Communicating Sequential Processes,' *Comm. ACM,* **21,** 8, Aug. 1978, pp. 666–677.

[31] G. Kahn, 'The Semantics of a Simple Language for Parallel Programming,' *Proc. IFIP Congress 74,* pp. 471–475.

[32] G. Kahn and D. MacQueen, 'Coroutines and Networks of Parallel Processes,' *Proc. IFIP Congress 77,* pp. 993–998.

[33] Arvind and R. E. Thomas, 'I-Structures: An Efficient Data Type for Functional Languages,' MIT Laboratory for Computer Science Technical Manual TM-178, MIT, Cambridge, Mass., Sept. 1980.

[34] P. Henderson and J. Morris, Jr., 'A Lazy Evaluator,' *Conf. Record Third ACM Symp. Principles of Programming Languages,* Jan. 1976, pp. 95–103.

7

Synchronizing Resources

Gregory R. Andrews
University of Arizona

A new proposal for synchronization and communication in parallel programs is presented. The proposal synthesizes and extends aspects of procedures, coroutines, critical regions, messages, and monitors. It provides a single notation for parallel programming with or without shared variables and is suited for either shared or distributed memory architectures. The essential new concepts are operations, input statements, and resources. The proposal is illustrated by the solutions of a variety of parallel programming problems; its relation to other parallel programming proposals is also discussed.

Key words and phrases: parallel programming, processes, synchronization, process communication, monitors, distributed processing, programming languages, operating systems, databases.

CR categories: 4.20, 4.22, 4.32, 4.35.

1 Introduction

There is by now widespread agreement on a few basic concepts of sequential programming: assignment, composition (e.g., ;), alternation (e.g., **if**), iteration (e.g., **do**), and procedures. There is also widespread agreement that the process is a basic concept of parallel programming and that process communication and process synchronization are the two other fundamental issues. However, there is not yet agreement on the appropriate mechanisms for parallel programming. This results from the rapid changes in the field, the lack of a widely recognized set of selection criteria, the immense variety of applications and hardware architectures, and the diversity of philosophies about how systems should be structured.

This work was supported in part by National Science Foundation grants MCS 77-07554 and MCS 80-01668.

Processes can communicate in two basic ways: directly by exchanging messages or indirectly by reading and writing shared variables. Processes can also synchronize in two basic ways: directly by explicit signaling or indirectly by testing and setting shared variables. Numerous communication and synchronization mechanisms have been proposed, each of which combines the above possibilities in different ways: semaphores [9], conditional critical regions [6, 21], messages [3, 6, 12–14, 27], event counts and sequencers [33], monitors [5, 20, 28], modules [36], path expressions [7, 16], managers [23], input/output commands [19], common procedures [4], and entries [32]. Underlying each choice of mechanism is a different philosophy about the relationship between processes. The various mechanisms and philosophies can be illustrated by considering the characteristics of and differences among those that are based on monitors, those that are based on buffered messages, and those that are based on synchronous (unbuffered) messages.

Monitors have been used as the process interaction mechanism in Concurrent Pascal [5], Mesa [28], and Modula [36] (which calls them interface modules). Programs in these languages contain active processes, which execute statements, and passive monitors, which define procedural operations and protect shared variables from concurrent access. Processes communicate by calling monitor procedures and synchronize (within monitors) by explicit signaling. Because monitors are passive, they are best suited for hardware architectures where one or more processors share memory. The advantage of monitors is that they support hierarchically organized systems that consist of levels of abstract machines. With respect to process interaction, the essential difference between Concurrent Pascal on the one hand and Mesa and Modula on the other is that Concurrent Pascal prohibits simultaneous access to shared variables, whereas the other two do not. Mesa and Modula are examples of languages that provide a tool for mutual exclusion but give the programmer the freedom to allow concurrent access when the situation warrants.

Buffered messages have been used as the process interaction mechanism in actors [3], Gypsy [14], PLITS [12, 13], and a recent proposal by Liskov [27]. In such languages, processes are largely self-contained modules that communicate solely by exchanging messages. Since messages are passed by value and no shared variables are allowed, these languages are readily suited to hardware architectures where processors do not share memory [12, 27]. (They can, of course, also be implemented on shared memory architectures.) Since messages are buffered, processes synchronize only when a process attempts to send a message and buffer space is exhausted or when a process attempts to receive a message and none is available.

The final class of proposals consists of those based on synchronous (unbuffered) message passing. These include communicating sequential processes (CSP) [19], distributed processes (DP) [4], and Ada [32]. In CSP, processes interact by means of input/output commands. Communication is synchronized by delaying an input (output) command in one process until a matching output (input) command is executed by another process. Since input commands are executable statements, a key attribute of CSP is that each process can explicitly control when it will accept an input command. DP differs from CSP in that processes in DP communicate by means of common (shared) procedures, which may return results, rather than by the more primitive input/output commands of CSP. In essence, CSP integrates processes and message passing, whereas DP integrates processes and monitors. Ada combines and generalizes aspects of CSP and DP; processes communicate by shared variables, shared procedures, or entries. Entries are basically procedures that are declared and executed by one process when called by another. Synchronization in Ada is similar to that in CSP; a process can explicitly control when it will accept entry calls. Each of these languages is suited to distributed computations; Ada is also suited to conventional systems that share variables. An interesting aspect of each of these languages is that synchronization is controlled by statements based on Dijkstra's guarded commands; the author(s) of each language have independently decided that, for synchronization, Boolean expressions are preferable to explicit signals (e.g., semaphores or condition variables).

Each of the above proposals and underlying philosophies is adequate for its intended purpose. However, each has a restricted domain of application. This paper presents a new proposal, called Synchronizing Resources (SR), which unifies and generalizes the above approaches, and, consequently, is suited to both conventional and distributed systems. It is the result of a search for a common denominator that is primitive enough to be easily understood and implemented yet powerful enough to provide a high-level, structured solution to a wide variety of parallel programming problems.

The remainder of this paper is organized as follows. Section 2 presents the philosophy, structure, and mechanisms of SR. Sections 3–5 present solutions to numerous parallel programming problems; many are familiar communication and scheduling problems, but others are included to illustrate the range of application. Section 6 examines the relationship between SR and other programming concepts, including procedures and classes as well as other synchronization proposals, and discusses semantic and implementation issues. Finally, Section 7 makes a few concluding remarks.

2 Basic concepts

The main contribution of SR is to provide a small, integrated set of mechanisms for programming a wide variety of parallel systems. The essential ideas are the following:

(1) A system, hence a program, consists of a set of resources that define operations. Resources may be loosely connected, as in a distributed system, or closely related, as in a hierarchically organized system.

(2) Internally, a resource consists of one or more processes that implement operations together with the variables, if any, that they share. Processes in different resources interact only by means of operations; processes in the same resource cooperate using operations or shared variables.

(3) Operations are a generalization of procedures and message passing. They are defined by **in** statements, which are based on Dijkstra's guarded commands [10] and are activated by either **send** statements, which are like message sends, or **call** statements, which are like procedure calls.

(4) Processes synchronize and schedule their execution of operations by means of Boolean expressions and arithmetic expressions, respectively. No explicit signaling mechanism and no explicit queues are required.

Each of these ideas is now described in detail.

2.1 Programs

A program consists of global type declarations and one or more resources. It has the form

```
[type_declarations;]
resource {resource}
```

where the brackets indicate that the enclosed unit is optional and the braces denote zero or more repetitions of the enclosed unit. Many view parallel systems as consisting of levels (or layers) of virtual machines. At each level, a programmer implements a set of resources by employing operations defined by lower levels. For example, the kernel level of an operating system is implemented by employing hardware operations and in turn provides a set of logical resources and operations for use by other portions of the operating system and by user programs. Using SR, one can program *any* of the levels, including those that interface to hardware. In short, the SR philosophy is that parallel programs provide, contain, and are implemented in terms of resources.

2.2 Resources

A resource is a collection of processes and the variables they share. It has the form:

```
resource name["["range"]"];
  [define operation_list;]
  [variable_declarations;]
  [statement_list;]

  process {process}
  end name
```

A resource contains at least one process; it optionally contains permanent (ALGOL **own**) variables shared by the processes, as well as statements to initialize the permanent variables. Its purpose is to encapsulate its permanent variables and processes. It does so by constructing a wall around them such that operations provide the only gates through the wall. Operations are declared within processes (see Section 2.4); those named in the **define** clause are exported from the resource. Processes external to the resource can invoke the exported operations; processes internal to the resource can invoke operations exported by other resources. (Processes in a resource can also invoke operations declared by other processes in the same resource, as described in Section 2.3.)

The **define** clause has the form:

$$\textbf{define} \quad \text{operation}_1["["\text{range}_1"]"]["\{"\text{restrictor}_1"\}"],$$
$$\vdots$$
$$\text{operation}_n["["\text{range}_n"]"]["\{"\text{restrictor}_n"\}"]$$

For each exported operation, the range and restrictor are optional. The range is used to denote that a family of identical operations, one per element of the range, is being exported; it is used when an operation is declared within a process family (see Section 2.4). The restrictor is used to specify a restriction on the way in which the operation may be invoked. The possible restrictor specifications are {**call**}, {**send**}, or {**call**, **send**}; the default is {**call**, **send**}, which imposes no restrictions.

If a range is specified in the resource heading, a family of identical resources is created, one for each value in the specified range. A specific instance is denoted by *name*[*i*] where *name* is the resource name and *i* is a value in the range. Within an instance, the special variable *myresource* contains the identity of the resource.

If a resource contains one process, that process has exclusive access to the permanent variables of the resource. When a greater degree of concurrency or a finer degree of mutual exclusion is required, a resource may contain more than one process, and the processes may share resource variables. It has become fashionable to preclude all concurrent access to variables, but doing so precludes efficiently solving numerous parallel programming problems such as readers/writers [8], in-place buffer access [20], and on-the-fly garbage collection [11, 15]. Although concurrent access should occur only when it is both beneficial and safe, it seems overly restrictive and unnecessary to prohibit it. SR allows concurrent access but *only* within a resource and *only* with respect to the permanent variables. The extent of sharing is therefore localized and identifiable. The one critical assumption is that each reference (read or write) to a permanent scalar variable (integer, etc.) or scalar component of an array or record is atomic (i.e., indivisible).

2.3   Processes

A process contains a set of variables and a sequence of statements. It has the form:

```
process name["["range"]"];
    [variable_declarations;]
    statement_list
end name
```

A process executes one statement at a time and terminates when its statement list terminates. The variables declared within a process are local to it and hence can be accessed only by the statements within the process. Processes can also declare operations by means of input statements (see Section 2.4). Operations are automatically exported from the process; they can be invoked by processes in the same resource, and, if exported from the resource, they can be invoked by processes in other resources. Together, processes and input statements allow mutually exclusive operations to be programmed. In fact, processes are the *sole mechanism* needed for mutual exclusion.

If a range is specified in the process heading, a *family* of identical processes is created, one for each value in the range. Within an instance, the special variable *myprocess* contains the identity of the process.

2.4   Statements

Six kinds of statements are used in SR programs: four for sequential programming and two for communication and synchronization. The sequential statements are the following:

null:	**skip**
assignment:	variable := expression
alternation:	**if** guarded_command {□ guarded_command} **fi**
repetition:	**do** guarded_command {□ guarded_command} **od**

The null statement does not change the value of any variable and always terminates. The assignment statement computes the value of the expression and terminates after assigning it to the indicated variable.

The alternative and repetitive statements are Dijkstra's [10]. Each contains one or more guarded commands of the form:

Boolean_expression $\rightarrow$ statement_list

A guarded command can be executed if its guard (Boolean expression) is true.

An alternative statement specifies that exactly one of the guarded commands is to be executed. If at least one of the guards is true, an arbitrary one of the corresponding statement lists is executed, and the alternative statement terminates; if all guards are false, the statement aborts, and the executing process terminates abnormally.

A repetitive statement specifies that its constituent commands are to be executed repeatedly until it is no longer possible. On each iteration, if at least one of the guards is true, an arbitrary one of the corresponding statement lists is executed; if all guards are false, the statement terminates.

Processes communicate and synchronize by means of two kinds of statements:

invocation: **call** operation_denotation([actual_parameters])
              send operation_denotation([actual_parameters])
input: **in** operation_command {□ operation_command} **ni**

An operation denotation has the form:

resource_name[resource_index].operation_name[process_index]

The resource name and index identify the resource that defined the operation; they may be omitted if there is no ambiguity. The operation name and process index identify the specific operation; the process index is omitted if the operation is implemented by a single process.

An invocation statement requests execution of the named operation and specifies a set of actual parameters. If the operation is invoked by **call**, the invoking process delays until the operation has been executed by the process that declares it (see below). If the operation is invoked by **send**, the invoking process may proceed as soon as the actual parameter values have been saved or transmitted. The invoking process controls whether or not it wishes to be delayed, subject to possible restrictions specified with **define** (see Section 2.2). If the operation returns results through its parameters, however, the results are lost if the operation is invoked by **send**. (It is assumed that **send** is implemented by theoretically unbounded buffering, which implies that a sending process can never know if it is delayed due to buffer congestion.)

Input statements declare, synchronize, and schedule operations. Each operation command in an input statement has the form:

operation_name([formal_parameters]) [**and** Boolean_expression]
    [**by** arithmetic_expression] → statement_list

The *operation guard* consists of the operation name and Boolean expression. The guard is true if there is at least one pending invocation of the named operation and the corresponding Boolean expression is true (if omitted, the Boolean expression is implicitly true). If there are two or more pending invocations of the named operation for which the corresponding Boolean expression is true, the invocations are ordered by the values of the arithmetic expression, with the minimum value first (if the **by** phrase is omitted, the order is undefined). The guard determines whether or not *any* invocation of the operation can be executed; the arithmetic expression determines *which* invocation is to be executed first. Therefore, the guard specifies a correctness constraint, and the arithmetic expression specifies a scheduling constraint that applies once the correctness constraint is satisfied.

Execution of an input statement proceeds as follows. If at least one of the operation guards is true, an arbitrary one is chosen, the first of the pending invocations is selected (as determined by the arithmetic expression), and the corresponding statement list is executed. Otherwise, the input statement is *delayed* until at least one of the operation guards becomes true. The input statement terminates when one of the operation commands has been executed; if the operation was called, the appropriate **call** statement also terminates.

Operation parameter passing is assumed to have value or value/result (for **var** parameters) semantics. In particular, the value of each formal parameter becomes that of the corresponding actual parameter when an invoked operation is selected, and, if the operation was called, the value of each actual result parameter becomes that of the corresponding **var** formal parameter when the invocation terminates. It is assumed that actual **var** parameters do not overlap. Parameter passing is therefore semantically equivalent to executing multiple assignment statements on invocation and return. Formal parameters are assumed to be declared in the same manner as in Pascal procedures [37].

Operations are declared *within* executable input statements rather than as procedures because this allows one to implement and enforce orders on the execution of operations. (They can, in fact, be declared in more than one input statement, as is shown below.) Synchronization conditions are specified by Boolean expressions rather than explicit signaling since this leads to more comprehensible programs [22, 24]; explicit synchronization by signaling, if required, can be built using input and invocation. Scheduling constraints are specified by arithmetic expressions associated with operations in order to provide a concise tool for selecting among a set of operations that vary only in the values of their parameters.

Example 2.1

in $P(\ )$ **and** $sem > 0 \rightarrow sem := sem - 1$
$\square\ V(\ ) \rightarrow sem := sem + 1$
ni

Waits until P is invoked and $sem > 0$ or until V is invoked. Then the value of sem is either decremented or incremented by one. If embedded in a nonterminating loop, this statement defines and implements the semaphore P and V operations [9], assuming that P is invoked by **call**. Note that, as given, the **in** statement only preserves the invariant $sem > 0$; it does not specify any constraint on which of P or V is executed if both operation guards are true. Scheduling constraints can be programmed using the techniques shown in Examples 2.4 and 2.5.

Example 2.2

in $deposit(m1 : message) \rightarrow box := m1$ **ni**;
in $fetch(\textbf{var}\ m2 : message) \rightarrow m2 := box$ **ni**

These two input statements implement a single-slot mailbox [17]. The first statement puts a message in the box when deposit is invoked (by **send** or **call**). The second statement returns the contents of the box when fetch is invoked (by **call**). Note that special variables, such as an empty flag, do not appear in this solution; the order of *deposit* and *fetch* is controlled by the order of the two input statements. Achieving the synchronization is the responsibility of the implementation.

Example 2.3

in $getforks(i : integer)$ **and** $\neg eating[i \oplus 1]$
    and $\neg eating[i \ominus 1] \rightarrow eating[i] := \textbf{true}$
$\square\ releaseforks(i : integer) \rightarrow eating[i] := \textbf{false}$
ni

This statement implements the allocator in a solution to the dining philosophers problem [9], assuming that *getforks* is invoked by **call**. *Eating* records the status of each philosopher, and $\oplus$ and $\ominus$ are modulo addition and subtraction. Note that the Boolean expression in the *getforks* operation references the value of i, the actual parameter.

Example 2.4

in *request*(*amount* : *integer*) **by** *amount* → *skip*
ni

Waits until *request* is invoked (by **call**). Pending requests are ordered by the values of their actual parameters; when *request* is selected, an invocation with the minimum value for *amount* is executed. This statement implements a shortest-job-next scheduler (or a first-come, first-served scheduler if *amount* is a clock value).

2.5   Variables and expressions

Variables are assumed to be declared analogously to the way they are declared in Pascal [37]. The examples in subsequent sections will use basic types, such as Boolean and integer, and structured types, such as arrays.

Expressions in statements can refer to any variable local to the process containing the expression, the permanent variables of the enclosing resource, or, in the case of input statements, any formal parameter in the operation command containing the expression. Expressions within a process can also reference one special attribute that is implicitly associated with each operation declared by the process: *?operation_name* – the number of pending invocations of the named operation. This allows a programmer to test for the presence of an invocation; one use is shown below. (It is assumed that reading and changing the value of *?operation_name* are atomic operations.)

Example 2.5

in $P(\ )$ **and** $sem > 0 \longrightarrow sem := sem - 1$
$\square\ V(\ )$ **and** ($sem = 0$ **or** $?P = 0$) $\longrightarrow sem := sem + 1$
ni

This statement modifies Example 2.1 (semaphores) to give preference to *P* operations. An invocation of *V* is executed only if *sem* = 0 (in which case *P* cannot be executed) or if there are no pending invocations of *P*.

2.6   Initialization and termination

Execution of an SR program begins with the concurrent execution of the initialization statements in each resource. Once this has been completed, each process is executed concurrently with the others. It is assumed that, if a process is not locked, it eventually gets to execute, namely, it gets a chance to make progress. A process is blocked if it is delayed at a **call** or **in** statement.

A program terminates when every process either has terminated or is blocked. A process terminates normally if it completes execution of its statement list; it terminates abnormally if all guards in an alternative command are false. It is the programmer's responsibility to program for termination. In some applications it may be desirable to program so that each process completes its statement list. In others, such as operating system utilities, it may be desirable to have some service processes repeatedly wait for input and block permanently when all users of the service have terminated. In short, if some processes are blocked when a program terminates, it may have been intended, or it may indicate the existence of deadlock.

3 Communication

Two processes communicate directly if one defines an operation that the other invokes. Direct communication is either synchronous and un-buffered, if the operation is called, or asynchronous and potentially buffered, if the operation is sent. Synchronous communication is employed when the invoking process needs to wait for the operation to be completed before proceeding, for example, when the operation returns results. Asynchronous communication is employed when the invoking process merely passes on a value, for example, in a pipelined computation such as the coroutine examples described in [19]. These two basic communication facilities can also be combined to implement more complex communication protocols. This section presents implementations of two such protocols.

3.1 Parallel bounded buffer [17]

Suppose that one or more producer processes wish to send messages to several consumer processes and that any consumer can receive any message sent by a producer. (For example, the consumers provide identical services.) The problem is to program a buffer resource with a bound of, say, 10 slots. Producer processes deposit messages in the buffer; consumer processes receive messages from the buffer when they are available. To minimize delays, *deposit* and *receive* should be able to access the buffer concurrently when possible.

Solution

```
resource Buffer;
   define deposit, receive{call};
   var buf: array[0..9] of message;
      slots, msgs : integer;
   slots := 10; msgs := 0
```

```
process put;
  do true →
    in deposit(m : message) and (slots − msgs) > 0 →
      buffer[msgs mod 10] := m;
      msgs := msgs + 1
    ni
  od
  end put

process get;
  do true →
    in receive(var m : message) and (slots − msgs) < 10 →
      m := buffer[slots mod 10];
      slots := slots + 1
    ni
  od
  end get

end Buffer
```

This solution illustrates a resource having two processes that share common variables (*buffer*, *slots*, and *msgs*). *Deposit* can be executed when the buffer is not full; *receive* can be executed when the buffer is not empty. Since *deposit* is declared in one process, *deposits* are mutually exclusive (at most one at a time can be executed); the same is true of *receive*. Since *deposit* and *receive* are implemented by different processes, however, they may execute concurrently when there are both free slots and available messages. The solution works correctly, since it is assumed that references to the shared variables are atomic and neither process invalidates the synchronization constraint of the other. Although one could place *deposit* and *receive* in the same process and thereby make them mutually exclusive, it is not necessary to do so. A basic tenet of SR is to allow the solution that is most appropriate for a given application or hardware architecture to be programmed. One must take care when processes are allowed to share variables, but many problems such as this one can be correctly, efficiently, and clearly solved by using shared variables.

3.2 Client/server rendezvous

Suppose there are several clients that require service from any one of several identical servers (e.g., file servers or command processes). When a client needs service, it calls *GetService*, passing appropriate parameters and receiving a rendezvous number as a return value. At some later time, the client calls *WaitDone* to await completion of the requested service; the rendezvous number is passed to *WaitDone*, and appropriate results are returned. The problem is to outline the actions of the servers and to program a rendezvous resource that coordinates the clients and servers.

Solution

```
resource Server[1..N];
  process service;
    do true →
      call GetTask(task_parameters, rendezvousid);
      perform task;
      send TaskDone(result_parameters, rendezvousid)
    od
    end service
  end Server

resource Rendezvous;
  define GetService{call},
         WaitDone{call},
         GetTask{call},
         TaskDone;

  process StartService;
    var rid : integer;
    rid := 0;
    do true →
      in GetService(client_params; var rid1 : integer) →
        in GetTask(var server_params; var rid2 : integer) →
          server_params := client_params;
          rid1 := rid;
          rid2 := rid;
          rid := rid + 1
        ni
      ni
    od
    end StartService

  process Completion;
    do true →
      in TaskDone(results1; rid1 : integer) →
        in WaitDone(var results2; rid2 : integer)
          and rid1 = rid2 →
            results2 := results1
        ni
      ni
    od
    end Completion

end Rendezvous
```

This problem illustrates the use of nested input statements to co-ordinate operations invoked by different processes. In *StartService*, a client and server rendezvous as soon as there are calls to both *GetService* and *GetTask*. Once the rendezvous has occurred, parameters are passed, and a rendezvous number (*rid*) is returned to both the client and the server. The *Completion* process synchronizes the completion of service and the return of results. As programmed, it can only process one completion at a time, since it waits for the client of rendezvous *rid*1 to call *WaitDone*. As a result, the solution given delays other clients who may be waiting for an already completed task. This can be remedied by having the *Completion* process store the rendezvous numbers of completed tasks so that it can accept calls to *WaitDone* for any completed task. Alternately, if clients are in identical resources, they could each define and accept (by means of **in**) a completion operation that is called directly by the server (assuming the client's index is passed to the server).

4   Scheduling and allocation

Efficient scheduling and allocation of shared resources is one of the most important concerns of parallel systems. In this section, three familiar scheduling and allocation problems are considered: readers/writers, database transactions, and a disk head scheduler. They illustrate different uses of processes and input statements and different kinds of scheduling disciplines.

4.1   Readers/Writers

Two groups of processes, readers and writers, share a database. To protect the integrity of the database, at most one writer at a time may access it, and no reader may examine the database while a writer is altering it; readers however, may access the database concurrently. To ensure eventual access, no reader or writer should be delayed indefinitely. The assumed user interface and implementation of the allocator are described following the solution:

Solution

```
resource ReadersWriters;
    define read[1..M]{call}, write[1..M];
    var database : array[1..N] of item;

    process RW[1..M];
        do true →
            in read(var v : item; i : (1..N)) →
                call startread( );
                v := database[i];
                send endread( )
            □ write(v : item; i : (1..N)) →
                call startwrite( );
                database[i] := v;
                send endwrite( )
            ni
        od
        end RW
```

```
process allocator;
    var state : integer; writerlast : Boolean;
    state := 0; writerlast := false;

do true →
    in startread( ) and state > 0
        and (writerlast or ?startwrite = 0) →
            state := state + 1; writerlast := false
    □ endread( ) → state := state − 1
    □ startwrite( ) and state = 0
        and (¬writerlast or ?startread = 0) →
            state := −1; writerlast := true
    □ endwrite( ) → state := 0
    ni
od
end allocator

end ReadersWriters
```

It is assumed that there is one instance *j* of process *RW* for each user of the database. To access the database, a user process calls *read*[*j*] or *write*[*j*]. Each *read* operation first calls *startread* (and is therefore delayed until it is safe to read), reads the appropriate item (identified by parameter *i*), and then sends an *endread* operation (since no delay need be incurred). *Write* is similar. The *allocator* process enforces the specified access constraints. Its local variable, *state*, records how the database is being accessed (*state* $= 0 =>$ no readers or writers, *state* $= -1 =>$ one writer, *state* $> 0 =>$ *state* readers); Boolean variable *writerlast* indicates whether a writer was the last to start. The synchronization conditions in the allocator's input statement ensure the required exclusion, allow concurrent reading, and preclude starvation. (Note the use of ?*startread* and ?*startwrite* to test for pending *reads* and *writes*.)

An important attribute of this solution which is not present in numerous other proposed solutions [4, 8, 20] is that the *ReadersWriters* resource encapsulates the use of the database. Outside *ReadersWriters*, processes only see *read* and *write* operations; inside, instances of the *RW* process provide the required concurrency and use the allocator to guarantee that access is correctly scheduled.

4.2 Database transactions

The previous example considered ways to synchronize the reading and writing of *single* database records. In database applications, however, processing a user transaction may require reading or writing *several* records. In order to ensure the integrity and consistency of the database, it is necessary to synchronize entire transactions, not just individual reads and writes. Assume that processing a transaction consists of first requesting read or write access to the database, then invoking (possibly several) read or write operations, and finally releasing control of the database. The problem is to modify the *ReadersWriters* resource of the previous example to meet these constraints and to ensure that the database is requested before it is accessed.

Solution

resource *Transactions*;
  define *reqread*[1..*M*] {**call**},
        read[1..*M*] {**call**},
        relread[1..*M*],
        reqwrite[1..*M*] {**call**},
        write[1..*M*],
        relwrite[1..*M*];
  var *database* : **array**[1..*N*] **of** *item*;

process *R*[1..*M*];
var *reading* : *Boolean*;
do true →
  in *reqread*( ) → **call** *startread*( );
    reading := **true**
  ni;
  do *reading* →
    in *read*(**var** *v* : *item*; *i* : (1..*N*)) →
      v := *database*[*i*]
    □ *relread*( ) → **send** *endread*( );
      reading := **false**
    ni
    od
  od
  end *R*

process *W*[1..*M*];
  var *writing* : *Boolean*;
  do true →
    in *reqwrite*( ) → **call** *startwrite*( );
      writing := **true**
    ni;
    do *writing* →
      in *write*(*v* : *item*; *i* : (1..*N*)) →
        database[*i*] := *v*
      □ *relwrite*( ) → **send** *endwrite*( );
        writing := **false**
      ni
    od
  od
  end *W*

process *allocator*;
  (* body as in Section 4.1 *)
  end *allocator*

end *Transactions*

Again, this solution encapsulates the database. In addition, it illustrates the utility of being able to accept input operations at different places in the body of a process, in this case to ensure that each user of *Transactions* first does request, then access the database, and then releases it. The solution also illustrates how the **process** construct can be used to specify a family of coroutines, one for each user of *Transactions*. The reader is encouraged to use these techniques to program a solution to the buffer allocation problem described in [20, pp. 554–555].

4.3   Disk scheduling

A different kind of scheduling problem occurs with a moving-head disk. Assume that a disk resource defines a *doIO* operation that is invoked when processes wish to read from or write to the disk. In order to utilize the disk efficiently, it is necessary to reduce excessive head movement, which means it is necessary to be able to order the execution of *doIO* operations when more than one is pending. Assume that one parameter to *doIO* is c, the index of the cylinder to be accessed. To minimize head movement, the disk should select the invocation of *doIO* for which c is closest to the current head position.

> *Solution*
> ```
> resource disk;
>     define doIO;
>     var buffers, etc.;
>
>     process driver;
>         var position : (1..maxcylinder);
>         position := 1;
>         do true →
>             in doIO(c : (1..maxcylinder); ...)
>                 by abs(c − position) →
>                     position := c;
>                     start I/O on disk;
>                     wait for interrupt
>             ni
>         od
>         end driver
>
>     end disk
> ```

In the above solution, the driver schedules itself; no separate scheduling process is required. The specific scheduling desired is specified by the arithmetic expression $abs(c - position)$, which results in the execution of the invocation of *doIO* closest to the current head position.

Although the above solution minimizes head movement and is

generally preferred, it can lead to starvation (some pending invocation of *doIO* may be repeatedly bypassed if traffic is heavy). Several other scheduling algorithms which preclude starvation have been proposed [35]. The more popular are CSCAN, which services requests 'ahead' of the current position until there are no more and then starts over at position 1, and SCAN (elevator), which services requests in one direction until there are no more and then reverses direction. To use CSCAN instead of the above minimum-seek-time scheduling algorithm, *all* that is changed is the scheduling expression, which becomes **by** ($c - position$) **mod** *maxcylinder* (assuming **mod** can take negative arguments). The reader is encouraged to write a scheduling expression that implements the elevator algorithm. (Hint: use the function *sign* (n), which returns 1 if $n \geq 0$ and -1 if $n < 0$.)

5   Miscellaneous

The previous examples presented solutions to a variety of typical operating system and database problems. Since SR is intended to be useful for programming parallel computations ranging from device control to user utilities, this section presents two final examples: a CRT controller and a parallel sorting algorithm.

5.1   CRT display

As an example of hardware control, consider a CRT that displays on a screen points stored in a grid array. A refresh process within the CRT controller continuously writes points on the screen; in parallel, another process accepts update operations and alters the grid. The refresh and update processes can execute in parallel, since a new update merely overwrites the screen. Assume that *writept* initiates writing a point on the screen and that the CRT generates an interrupt after each point is written.

Solution

```
resource CRT;
   define update;
   var grid : array[1..M, 1..N] of intensity;
   grid := "blank"; (* for all elements *)

   process up;
      do true →
         in update(i : (1..M); j : (1..N); v : intensity) →
            grid[i, j] := v
         ni
      od
      end up
```

```
process refresh;
  var i, j : integer;
  do true →
    i := 1; j := 1;
    do i ≤ M and j ≤ N →
        writept;
        call waitint("CRT ");
        j := j + 1
    □ i ≤ M and j > N →
        i := i + 1; j := 1
    od
  od
  end refresh
end CRT

resource IntHandler;
  define interrupt, (* "invoked" by the device *)
        waitint{call};
  var done : array[deviceid] of Boolean;
  done := false (* for all device ids *)

  process IH;
    do true →
      in interrupt(d : deviceid) → done[d] := true
      □ waitint(d : deviceid) and done[d] →
            done[d] := false
      ni
    od
    end IH

end IntHandler
```

This solution illustrates a general approach to device control and interrupt handling. After writing a point, *refresh* calls the interrupt handler operation *waitint*. Assuming the actual I/O interrupts cause the interrupt operation to be invoked (by a run-time kernel), the *IH* process in *IntHandler* synchronizes *waitint* with the interrupt.

5.2 Parallel sorting

Sorting is a canonical example of a library program, and many parallel sorting algorithms have recently been proposed [18]. One specific algorithm that sorts an array of size $N (0 < N ≤ 100)$ into ascending order in linear time using N processes is shown below. The solution illustrates pipelined communication among instances of a **process** family.

Solution

```
resource Arraysort;
  define sort{call};
  var B : arrayof T;
      N : integer;
```

```
process starter;
  var temp : T; i : integer;
  do true →
    in sort (var A : arrayof T; size : integer) →
      N := size;
      B[1] := A[1]; i := 2;
      do i ≤ N →
        if B[1] ≤ A[i] → send next[2](A[i])
        □ B[1] > A[i] → temp := B[1];
                        B[1] := A[i];
                        send next[2](temp)
        fi;
        i := i + 1
      od
      in done( ) → A := B
      ni
    ni
  od
  end starter
process sorter[2..100];
  var i : integer; temp : T;
  do true →
    in next(v : T) → B[myprocess] := v
    ni;
    i := myprocess;
    do i < N →
      in next(v : T) →
        if B[myprocess] ≤ v → send next[myprocess + 1](v)
        □ B[myprocess] > v → temp := B[myprocess];
                             B[myprocess] := v;
                             send next[myprocess + 1](temp)
        fi
      ni;
      i := i + 1
    od;
    if myprocess = N → send done( )
    □ myprocess ≠ N → skip
    fi
  od
  end sorter

end Arraysort
```

In the above solution, the *starter* process defines the *sort* operation, which takes an array and *size* as parameters. The *starter* process looks at each element of the array, stores the smallest element in $B[1]$, and sends all other elements to the first instance of *sorter*. Each *sorter* process accepts a stream of elements from its predecessor, saves the smallest (in $B[myprocess]$), and sends all others on to its successor. When the last instance of *sorter* (the one with $myprocess = N$) receives an array element, sorting is complete; so *starter* is sent a *done* signal. *Starter* returns the sorted array; then it waits for another call of *sort*.

6   Discussion

The most important aspects of any parallel programming language are:

(1)   the nature of and relations among its modules; and

(2)   its mechanisms for communication and synchronization.

In these areas, SR presents three new constructs:

- resources,
- operations, and
- input statements.

In this section, the characteristics of these constructs and their relationship to other language proposals are discussed. In addition, semantic issues are discussed, and an implementation is outlined.

6.1   Resources

The resource construct is the means for encapsulating processes and the variables they share. Its name and internal structure are both indicative of its correspondence to physical resources, since both software and hardware systems contain groups of processes (processors) that share variables (memory) and are connected by communication paths (lines). At one extreme, a resource (or collection of resources) can be used to implement a large object such as a node in a computer network; at the other, it can implement a small object such as a semaphore.

The structure of a resource is similar to that of Ada's task modules [32] and Liskov's guardians [27]. The main difference is that resources and processes cannot be arbitrarily nested. The reason for this restriction is to make it easier to identify shared variables and thereby to make it easier to understand their use. In the author's opinion, the relationship between resources, namely, the ways in which they are connected by communication paths, is easier to understand if it is described by something like Concurrent Pascal's access rights [5] rather than by lexical nesting. Whether this approach is adequate for constructing complex systems remains to be seen.

6.2   Processes

The process construct combines the conventional concept of a process as an active program with the concept of a coroutine. Processes can execute independently, have master/slave relationships, form a pipeline, or interact as coroutines. For example, the processes within the *Rendezvous* resource (Section 3.2) and *CRT* resource (Section 5.1) execute independently; the *driver* process in the *disk* resource (Section 4.3) is a slave of its users; the *sorter* processes in *Arraysort* (Section 5.2) form a pipeline; and the *R* and *W* processes in the *Transactions* resource (Section 4.2) are coroutines with respect to their users.

Process families provide a way for several other processes to share the same set of concurrently executing operations. The construct is similar to those in [4, 19, 32]. Because processes in a resource can share permanent resource variables, process families also provide the means for allowing identical resource operations to access shared storage concurrently. Operations in process families can therefore be used like procedures. Unlike Distributed Processes or Ada, however, SR does not contain procedures. The reason is that it does not make much sense to have nonlocal procedures in a distributed environment, since they must be implemented by a process or similar construct anyway. In short, the process concept appears to be the essential one for distributed computations.

Together, resources and processes generalize the concepts of monitors [5, 20, 28], classes [5], and modules [36]. If a resource contains only one process, it is like a monitor, since only that one process can access the resource variables. If a resource has permanent variables and contains a process family, it is like a regular (i.e., noninterface) Modula module [36], since there are several concurrently executing instances of the process that share the variables. If a resource contains one process family but has no permanent variables, it is like a Concurrent Pascal class [5], since there are several instances of the process but each has access only to its own private variables. Since a resource may contain permanent variables and *more* than one process, however, other combinations of mutual exclusion and concurrency can also be implemented. This was illustrated by examples such as the parallel bounded buffer (Section 3.1), readers/writers (Section 4.1), database transactions (Section 4.2), and CRT controller (Section 5.1).

6.3   Operations

As mentioned in Section 1, there are three basic kinds of process interaction mechanisms: monitors, buffered messages, and unbuffered messages. Although Lauer and Needham [25] have shown that these methods are duals in the sense that each can be used to implement the others, each has its particular advantages. Monitors are useful when a process must be delayed until the action implemented by a monitor procedure has been completed or when results are to be returned; they are well suited to building hierarchical systems on machines with shared memory. By contrast, message passing is well suited to programming systems of basically independent modules that do not share memory but requires that all passing of information between modules be by value. Unbuffered messages do not require intermediate storage for messages but do necessitate delaying the sender of a message until the message has been received; buffered messages are just the opposite. The reason for choosing one method over the other depends on the nature of the application and the hardware on which it is to execute. Since there is a wide variety of applications and hardware architectures, no single one of these methods is always ideal.

To overcome these limitations and give the designer of a system the option of choosing the approach that is best suited for a specific problem, operations combine aspects of both procedures and message passing. Operations are declared in the same way as procedures: they have formal parameters, some of which may return results, and a statement list. Operations can also be invoked in the same way as procedures using the **call** statement; this allows the invoking process to delay until the operation has completed (when it is necessary to do so) and to receive results from the operation if there are any. Operations also contain aspects of message passing, since they cause information to be passed from one process to another and may be sent when it is not necessary to wait for a reply.

6.4   Input statements

The final new idea of SR is the input statement. The input statement allows a process to wait for (possibly) several operations, to control which of the operations can be executed (using Boolean expressions for synchronization), and to control the order in which multiple invocations of the same operation are executed (using arithmetic expressions for scheduling). An input statement is therefore like a collection of conditional critical regions [6, 21]. Since operations are declared within statements, however, the declaring process can order the operations sequentially as well as synchronize them. This was used to advantage in the mailbox (Example 2.2) and database transactions (Section 4.2) solutions. In addition, the same operation name can appear in more than one input statement, which capability was used in the sorting program (Section 5.2) to do initialization on the first invocation of operation *next*.

Input statements are similar to Ada select/accept statements [32]. They are more expressive, however, since they allow formal parameters to be referenced in the synchronization expression and may include scheduling expressions. As illustrated by the dining philosophers problem (Example 2.3), shortest-job-next scheduler (Example 2.4), and disk scheduler (Section 4.3), this leads to a concise specification of synchronization and scheduling constraints and avoids the need for programming scheduling queues (which, however, must exist in the implementation, as described in Section 6.6). The idea behind using arithmetic expressions for scheduling is to have a programming notation for scheduling that is as convenient and expressive as Boolean expressions are for synchronization. The actual mechanism is similar to that proposed in [34]. Here scheduling expressions have been limited to simple arithmetic expressions; were the language to include functions, the scheduling expression could in general contain function calls, which would allow complex scheduling decisions to be made.

Input statements also provide a means for implementing path expressions, which are a way to specify allowable sequences of operations [7, 16]. Operations can be sequentially ordered by defining them in sequentially ordered input statements; operations can be repeated by enclosing them in a loop; and operations can be concurrently executed by defining them in separate processes. SR shares with path expressions the philosophy that flexible combinations of concurrency and synchronization should be allowed; it differs in that it reflects the view that complex synchronization and scheduling requirements are best expressed with the operations (but not within them as is the case with monitors) rather than separately.

6.5   Semantic concepts

A contemporary rule of thumb in language design is that, if a language construct has a complex proof rule, then it is undoubtedly difficult to understand and to use. Although formal proof rules for SR have not yet been developed, the concern for being able to develop clear proof rules has influenced the language design. The sequential statements are those used by Dijkstra; so they have the same axioms and rules as his do [10] Since processes have the same form as in other languages, they also have the same effect; in particular, the effect of a process is the composition of the effects of its component statements. The new constructs for which proof rules need to be developed are invocation statements, input statements, and resources. In addition, means for combining the proofs of processes and resources need to be developed. The next few paragraphs identify the main issues that must be addressed and present some preliminary ideas.

To the invoking process, a **call** statement has the effect of a procedure call: values are passed to the operation, the caller waits for the operation to be executed, and results are returned. The proof rule for **call** should therefore be similar to that for a procedure call with value/result parameter passing semantics. The difference is that the operation could be implemented by more than one input statement, perhaps with different bodies. If this is the case, the visible effect of the operation assumed by the caller must be satisfied by the process that implements it.

This undoubtedly requires a proof concept similar to satisfaction [26] or cooperation [2], which is also needed to develop proofs of programs written in CSP.

The other invocation statement, **send**, has no visible effect in the invoking process since the message is buffered in a theoretically infinite buffer. Formally, this means that the postcondition (result assertion) of **send** must be implied by its precondition. (Since an actual implementation has to impose some bound on the amount of buffer storage, however, a run-time exception could occur as the result of buffer overflow; this is similar to the fact that integers are theoretically unbounded, but, when implemented, they are of finite size.)

The other new statement is the input statement, which is the most powerful and complex of the statements. The effect of an input statement is a combination of the effects of procedures, alternation, and ordering. With respect to partial correctness, an input statement can execute when one of its guards is true; its execution results in possible changes to parameters and other variables global to the operation. Suppose an input statement has the form:

> **in** op_1(formals$_1$) **and** $B_1 \longrightarrow S_1$
> □ ...
> □ op_n (formals$_n$) **and** $B_n \longrightarrow S_n$
> **ni**

Let P be the precondition for **in** and R_i be an assertion about the input values of formals$_i$. Then the effect of **in** is described by the proof rule:

$$\frac{\{P \text{ and } R_i \text{ and } B_i\}\, S_i\, \{Q \text{ and } T_i\}\ 1 \leq i \leq n}{\{P\}\, \textbf{in} \ldots \textbf{ni}\, \{Q\}}$$

where Q is an assertion about variables global to **in** and T_i is an assertion about the output values of the result parameters. This rule says that each operation must produce the same postcondition Q with respect to variables accessible outside **in** but that each operation may have a different effect, T_i, with respect to result parameters.

The above rule only addresses partial correctness. The other correctness properties of interest are absence of deadlock and absence of starvation or other scheduling properties. (Termination of **in** depends only on termination of each S_i and absence of deadlock.) An input statement deadlocks if no guard becomes true. To show absence of deadlock of an entire program is in general a difficult task that requires a technique like the one that Levin has developed for CSP [26].

To prove formally that an input statement meets specified scheduling properties is an even more difficult task. In SR, scheduling constraints can be expressed by use of the **by** phrase; so in general its use affects scheduling properties. Note, however, that **by** only affects selection among multiple, acceptable invocations of an operation; hence it does not affect partial correctness or lead to blocking. The most promising approach to dealing with scheduling properties is temporal logic [30, 31], but the use of temporal logic is still in its infancy and is just now being applied to concurrent programs.

Given axioms and proof rules, a proof for each process can be developed. Unfortunately, the axioms and rules can be applied only if the statements in the process meet certain atomicity constraints with respect to access to shared variables. If processes are disjoint, as in CSP [19], then there are no shared variables; so every reference to a variable is automatically atomic since no other process can reference it. In SR, however, processes can directly reference permanent resource variables. In addition, the special variable *?opname* associated with each operation is also a shared variable, since it is incremented whenever *opname* is invoked and decremented whenever *opname* is executed by an input statement. In Section 2, it was stated that each reference to such a shared variable is assumed to be atomic.

In order for the assignment axiom and the proof rules for the other statements to be meaningful, however, it is also necessary to impose further atomicity restrictions on assignment statements and expression evaluation. One could assume that every assignment or expression is an indivisible operation (as seen by other processes), but this restriction is overly harsh since it limits concurrency and imposes high execution overhead. A weaker restriction is to require that every assignment or expression refer at most once to at most one variable that could be altered by another process [29]. This restriction is not quite strong enough for **if**, **do**, and **in** statements, however. Consider the statement:

$$\begin{aligned}
&\textbf{if } B \longrightarrow S_1 \\
&\square \; \neg B \longrightarrow S_2 \\
&\textbf{fi}
\end{aligned}$$

where B contains one reference to a shared variable. If the shared variable does not change during execution of **if**, this statement does not abort, since either B or $\neg B$ is true. However, if B is evaluated and found to be false and then the shared variable is changed, $\neg B$ could now be false! What is required is that every **if**, **do**, or **in** statement access each shared variable in Boolean guards at most once per execution of the statement (or per iteration in the case of **do**).

Given proofs of each process, the remaining concern is showing noninterference [29]. Two proofs interfere if an assertion in one can be invalidated by an assignment statement in the other. Since processes in different resources are disjoint, they cannot interfere except in the use of *?opname* or auxiliary variables that are introduced in the proof [29]. Within a resource, however, processes can interfere in their use of permanent resource variables. In practice, this means that no process can assume that a shared variable has a specific, single value; rather, a process can only contain weaker assertions about the possible values each shared variable could have. For example, in Section 3.1, it may be assumed that (*slots* − *msgs*) > 0 at the start of *deposit* (since *fetch* only increments *slots*) but not that *slots* has any specific value. This observation also holds true for references to ?*opname*; if a process finds that ?*opname* has a value, say zero, it may assume in subsequent statements only that ?*opname* is greater than or equal to zero, since another process could have invoked *opname* after ?*opname* was evaluated.

6.6 Implementation

The remaining issue of concern when a new language notation is proposed is how efficiently it can be implemented. An experimental translator, which produces Modula code, was implemented two years ago and used for initial experiments [1]. A compiler for a full language built around the mechanisms described here is currently near completion. (The full language adds data type, dynamic access control, device control, and separate compilation mechanisms.) Implementation of the four sequential statements is straightforward. The challenge is to implement invocation and input statements, processes, and resources. An implementation of these constructs is outlined below. First, a single processor implementation is described, and then the extensions needed to support multiple processors are discussed.

Each process has local data and code segments. Processes in the same resource also share a segment containing permanent resource variables (if there are any). Global to all processes are a communication area, operation queues, and a kernel. The communication area is used to store operation parameters and is subdivided into two parts: one for **call** parameters and one for (buffered) **send** parameters. Each process has its own call area, which is statically allocated; processes share the **send** area, which is dynamically allocated. There is one operation queue per operation; it contains a linked list of pending invocations. The kernel schedules processes and provides primitives for process synchronization as well as for manipulating the **send** area and the operation queues. The specific kernel primitives are identified below.

A **call** statement is implemented as follows. First, the actual parameters are evaluated and stored in the calling process' part of the **call** communication area (the size of which is determined at compile time and is sufficient for any **call** the process makes). Then the process executes the kernel invoke primitive, passing the address of its communication area, the identity of the invoked operation, and the kind of invocation ('call'). The invoke primitive links the parameters onto the appropriate operation queue, blocks the calling process, awakens the process that implements the invoked operation (if it is blocked and is waiting for the operation), and schedules a new process for execution. The calling process remains blocked until the operation has been executed (see below). Once awakened, it retrieves result parameters, if any, from its **call** communication area and continues execution.

send is implemented in a similar fashion. The differences are that a kernel primitive to allocate buffer space is called before the actual parameters are stored in the communication area, that invoke does not block the sending process, and that there are no result parameters. (The allocate primitive may need to block the process, however, if there is not sufficient free buffer storage at present.)

The invocation statement is not only the most powerful and semantically complex, it is also the most complex to implement! For each input statement in a process, the compiler generates a mask that identifies the operations within the input statement and produces code that works as follows. For each operation indicated by the mask, the process checks the operation queue. If the queue is not empty, the Boolean expression is evaluated to see if any operation on the queue can be executed. If one can, the first or appropriate one (if **by** is present) is selected and executed (see below). If the operation queue is empty or if no pending operation satisfies the Boolean expression, the next operation in the input statement is checked as above. If no operation can be executed, the process calls the kernel wait primitive and is blocked until there is a possibility it can proceed, which usually results from a new invocation of an operation for which it is waiting. (Without going into detail, suffice it to say that care has been taken to awaken a blocked process only if it could possibly execute the invoked operation.)

Once an executable operation has been found, the body of the operation is executed. The actual parameters remain in the global communication area, however; formal parameters are merely a template over the communication area. After the body of the operation has been executed, the kernel reply primitive is called. If the executed operation was invoked by **call**, the calling process is awakened; if the operation was invoked by **send**, the buffer area containing the parameters is deallocated (which may result in awakening a process waiting to execute **send**).

The chief source of overhead in this implementation is the searching and testing involved in finding and scheduling an executable operation in an input statement. This overhead does not appear to be excessive, although final judgment cannot be made until the implementation is completed and measurements are performed. In any case, searching and testing is done outside the kernel and is extensive only when an input statement contains complex synchronization or scheduling expressions. Less expressive mechanisms are less expensive to implement, but they require that a programmer explicitly build and maintain queues in order to solve scheduling problems. Since queues duplicate information already present in the above implementation, we conjecture that our implementation will be nearly as efficient as a hand-coded one. If so, there is a net gain for the programmer.

The above implementation can be readily extended to support multiple processors. If the processors share memory, the only changes are to the kernel, which then must be executed as a critical section and must be able to schedule processes on several processors. If the processors do not share memory but rather are connected by a communications network, the major change is to add mechanisms to support interprocessor communication. Our plan is to implement resources, processes, and input statements as above, which implies that each resource is implemented on one processor in the network. Invocation of operations local to the processor will also be handled as above. To support remote invocations, there will be two communication processes, which will be automatically loaded with the kernel on each processor. One communication process will handle output messages that result from **call**, **send**, or replies. The other will handle incoming messages. In the invoking process, an invocation statement will be implemented the same way whether it is local or remote. The difference is that a remote invocation will be inserted on an operation queue for the communication process that handles output. The communication process will subsequently send a message, which contains the identity of the invocation and its parameters, to the appropriate destination processor, where it will be received by that processor's input communication process and inserted on the appropriate operation queue as if it had been invoked within the other processor. Replies and result parameters will come back in a similar way. Again, the overhead incurred in this implementation is not yet known but will be measured as soon as the implementation is completed in mid-1981.

7 Concluding remarks

This paper has presented a new approach to parallel programming. Equally important, it has also attempted to explain the philosophy on which the choice of language mechanisms is based. The use of the mechanisms has been illustrated by the solutions of a variety of parallel programming problems, and the main language concepts have been related to other language proposals. The examples considered here are only a small subset of those that have been programmed.

Although the focus has been on illustrating the use and hence the expressive power of the mechanisms, concern for semantic and implementation issues has also influenced their design, as discussed in Section 6. As mentioned, a full programming language built around the concepts has been designed and is currently being implemented. In addition, work on developing a formal semantics of the language is underway.

Acknowledgments

This work was begun while the author was at Cornell University. Art Bernstein, David Gries, Carl Hauser, Gary Levin, Tom Murtah, Richard Reitman, and especially Fred Schneider provided very helpful feedback on the language concepts and written comments on an earlier draft of this paper; Mike Ingber and John Thalhamer implemented the experimental translator. Subsequently, the referees and editors asked many probing questions and made numerous suggestions that helped clarify both the language concepts and their presentation.

References

[1] Andrews, G.R., Ingber, M.A., and Thalhamer, J.T. An implementation of Synchronizing Resources. Tech. Rep., Deps. Computer Science, Univ. Arizona, Tucson, Ariz., and Cornell Univ., Ithaca, N.Y., Nov. 1979.

[2] Apt, K.R., Francez, N., and de Roever, W.P. A proof system for communicating sequential processes. *ACM Trans. Program. Lang. Syst.* **2**, 3 (July 1980), 359–385.

[3] Atkinson, R., and Hewitt, C. Synchronization in actor systems. In Conf. Rec., 4th ACM Symp. Principles of Programming Languages, Los Angeles, Calif., Jan. 17–19, 1977, pp. 267–280.

[4] Brinch Hansen, P. Distributed processes: A concurrent programming concept. *Commun. ACM* **21**, 11 (Nov. 1978), 934–941.

[5] Brinch Hansen, P. The programming language Concurrent Pascal. *IEEE Trans. Softw. Eng.* **SE-1**, 2 (June 1975), 199–207.

[6] Brinch Hansen, P. *Operating System Principles.* Prentice-Hall, Englewood Cliffs, N.J., 1973.

[7] Campbell, R.H., and Habermann, A.N. The specification of process synchronization by path expressions. In *Lecture Notes in Computer Science*, **16**: Proc. Int. Symp. Operating Systems, Paris, April 1974. Springer-Verlag, New York, 1974, pp. 89–102.

[8] Courtois, P.J., Heymans, F., and Parnas, D.L. Concurrent control with 'readers' and 'writers.' *Commun. ACM* **14**, 10 (Oct. 1971), 667–668.

[9] Dijkstra, E.W. Cooperating sequential process. In *Programming Languages*, F. Genuys (Ed.). Academic Press, New York, 1968, pp. 43–112.

[10] Dijkstra, E.W. Guarded commands, nondeterminacy and formal derivation of programs. *Commun. ACM* **18**, 8 (Aug. 1975), 453–457.

[11] Dijkstra, E.W. Lamport, L., Martin, A.J., Scholten, C.S., and Steffens, E.F.M. On-the-fly garbage collection: An exercise in cooperation. *Commun. ACM* **21**, 11 (Nov. 1978), 966–975.

[12]   Feldman, J.A. High level programming for distributed computing. *Commun. ACM* **22**, 6 (June 1979), 353–368.

[13]   Feldman, J.A. A programming methodology for distributed computing (among other things). Tech. Rep. TR9, Computer Science Dep., Univ. Rochester, Rochester, N.Y., Jan. 1977.

[14]   Good, D.I., Cohen, R.M., and Keeton-Williams, J. Principles of proving concurrent programs in Gypsy. In Conf. Rec., 6th Ann. ACM Symp. Principles of Programming Languages, San Antonio, Tex., Jan. 29–31, 1979, pp. 42–52.

[15]   Gries, D. An exercise in proving parallel programs correct. *Commun. ACM* **20**, 12 (Dec. 1977), 921–930.

[16]   Habermann, A.N. Path expressions. Tech. Rep., Carnegie-Mellon Univ., Pittsburgh, Pa., June 1975.

[17]   Habermann, A.N. Synchronization of communicating processes. *Commun. ACM* **15**, 3 (March 1972), 171–176.

[18]   Hirschberg, D.S. Fast parallel sorting algorithms. *Commun. ACM* **21**, 8 (Aug. 1978), 657–661.

[19]   Hoare, C.A.R. Communicating sequential processes. *Commun. ACM* **21**, 8 (Aug. 1978), 666–677.

[20]   Hoare, C.A.R. Monitors: An operating system structuring concept. *Commun. ACM* **17**, 10 (Oct. 1974), 549–557.

[21]   Hoare, C.A.R. Towards a theory of parallel programming. In *Operating Systems Techniques*, C.A.R. Hoare and R.H. Perrott (Eds.). Academic Press, New York, 1972, pp. 61–71.

[22]   Howard, J.H. Signalling in monitors. In Proc. 2d Int. Conf. Softw. Eng., San Francisco, Calif., Oct. 1976, pp. 47–52.

[23]   Jammel, A.J., and Stiegler, H.G. Managers versus monitors. In *Information Processing 77*, B. Gilchrist (Ed.). Elsevier North-Holland, New York, 1977, pp. 827–830.

[24]   Kessels, J.L.W. An alternative to event queues for synchronization in monitors. *Commun. ACM* **20**, 7 (July 1977), 500–503.

[25]   Lauer, H.C., and Needham, R.M. On the duality of operating system structures. In Proc. 2d Int. Symp. Operating Systems, IRIA, Le Chesnay, France, Oct. 1978; reprinted in *Oper. Syst. Rev.* **13**, 2 (April 1979), 3–19.

[26]   Levin, G.M. Proof Rules for Communicating Sequential Processes. Ph.D. dissertation, Dep. Computer Science, Cornell Univ., Ithaca, N.Y., Aug. 1980.

[27]   Liskov, B. Primitives for distributed computing. In Proc. 7th Symp. Operating Systems Principles (Pacific Grove, Calif., Dec. 10–12, 1979). ACM, New York, 1979, pp. 33–42.

[28]   Mitchell, J.G., Maybury, W., and Sweet, R. Mesa language manual, version 5.0. Rep. CSL-79-3, Xerox PARC, Palo Alto, Calif., April 1979.

[29]   Owicki, S., and Gries, D. An axiomatic proof technique for parallel programs. *Acta Inf.* **6**, 4 (1976), 319–340.

[30]   Owicki, S., and Lamport, L. Proving liveness properties of concurrent programs. Tech. Rep., Computer Systems Lab., Stanford Univ., Stanford, Calif., Oct. 1980.

[31]   Pneuli, A. The temporal logic of programs. In Proc. 18th Symp. Foundations of Computer Science, Providence, R.I., Nov. 1977.

[32] Preliminary Ada Reference Manual. *SIGPLAN Notices* (*ACM*) **14**, 6 (June 1979), part A.

[33] Reed, D.P., and Kanodia, R.K. Synchronization with eventcounts and sequencers. *Commun. ACM* **22**, 2 (Feb. 1979), 115–123.

[34] Schneider, F.B., and Bernstein, A.J. Mechanisms for specifying scheduling policies. Tech. Rep. 79-365, Dep. Computer Science, Cornell Univ., Ithaca, N.Y., Jan. 1979.

[35] Teorey, T.J., and Pinkerton, T.B. A comparative analysis of disk scheduling policies. *Commun. ACM* **15**, 3 (March 1972), 177–184.

[36] Wirth, N. Modula: A programming language for modular multiprogramming. *Softw. Pract. Exper.* **7**, 1 (Jan. 1977), 3–35.

[37] Wirth, N. The programming language Pascal. *Acta Inf.* **1**, 1 (1971), 35–63.

Distributed Processes: A Concurrent Programming Concept

Per Brinch Hansen
University of Southern California

A language concept for concurrent processes without common variables is introduced. These processes communicate and synchronize by means of procedure calls and guarded regions. This concept is proposed for real-time applications controlled by microcomputer networks with distributed storage. The paper gives several examples of distributed processes and shows that they include procedures, coroutines, classes, monitors, processes, semaphores, buffers, path expressions, and input/output as special cases.

Key words and phrases: concurrent programming, distributed processes, microprocessor networks, nondeterminism, guarded regions, programming languages, process communication and scheduling, sorting arrays, coroutines, classes, monitors, processes, semaphores, buffers, path expressions, input/output.

CR categories: 3.8, 4.2, 4.22, 4.32, 5.24.

I   Introduction

This paper introduces *distributed processes* – a new language concept for concurrent programming. It is proposed for real-time applications controlled by microcomputer networks with distributed storage. The paper gives several examples of distributed processes and shows that they include procedures, coroutines, classes, monitors, processes, semaphores, buffers, path expressions and input/output as special cases.

Real-time applications push computer and programming technology to its limits (and sometimes beyond). A real-time system is

This work was partially supported by the Office of Naval Research under Contract NR049-415.

216

expected to monitor simultaneous activities with critical timing constraints continuously and reliably. The consequences of system failure can be serious.

Real-time programs must achieve the ultimate in simplicity, reliability, and efficiency. Otherwise one can neither understand them, depend on them, nor expect them to keep pace with their environments. To make real-time programs manageable it is essential to write them in an abstract programming language that hides irrelevant machine detail and makes extensive compilation checks possible. To make real-time programs efficient at the same time will probably require the design of computer architectures tailored to abstract languages (or even to particular applications).

From a language designer's point of view, real-time programs have these characteristics:

(1) A real-time program interacts with an environment in which many things happen simultaneously at high speeds.

(2) A real-time program must respond to a variety of *nondeterministic requests* from its environment. The program cannot predict the order in which these requests will be made but must respond to them within certain time limits. Otherwise, input data may be lost or output data may lose their significance.

(3) A real-time program controls a computer with a fixed configuration of processors and peripherals and performs (in most cases) a fixed number of concurrent tasks in its environment.

(4) A real-time program never terminates but continues to serve its environment as long as the computer works. (The occasional need to stop a real-time program, say at the end of an experiment, can be handled by ad hoc mechanisms, such as turning the machine off or loading another program into it.)

What is needed then for real-time applications is the ability to specify a fixed number of concurrent tasks that can respond fast to nondeterministic requests. The programming languages *Concurrent Pascal* and *Modula* come close to satisfying the requirements for abstract concurrent programming [1, 2, 10]. Both of them are based on the *monitor* concept [3, 7]. Modula, however, is primarily oriented towards multiprogramming on a single processor. And a straightforward implementation of Concurrent Pascal requires a single processor or a multiprocessor with a common store. In their present form, these languages are not ideal for a microcomputer network with distributed storage only.

It may well be possible to modify Concurrent Pascal to satisfy the constraints of distributed storage. The ideas proposed here are more attractive, however, because they unify the monitor and process concepts and result in more elegant programs. The new language concepts for real-time applications have the following properties:

(1) A real-time program consists of a fixed number of concurrent processes that are started simultaneously and exist forever. Each process can access its *own variables* only. There are no common variables.

(2) A process can call *common procedures* defined within other processes. These procedures are executed when the other processes are waiting for some conditions to become true. This is the only form of process communication.

(3) Processes are synchronized by means of nondeterministic statements called *guarded regions* [4, 8].

These processes can be used as program modules in a multiprocessor system with common or distributed storage. To satisfy the real-time constraints each processor will be dedicated to a single process. When a process is waiting for some condition to become true then its processor is also waiting until an external procedure call makes the condition true. This does not represent a waste of resources but rather a temporary lack of useful work for that processor. Parameter passing between processes can be implemented either by copying within a common store or by input/output between separate stores.

The problems of designing verification rules and computer architectures for distributed processes are currently being studied and are not discussed. This paper also ignores the serious problems of performance evaluation and fault tolerance.

2   Language concepts

A concurrent program consists of a fixed number of sequential processes that are executed simultaneously. A *process* defines its own variables, some common procedures, and an initial statement:

```
process name
own variables
common procedures
initial statement
```

A process may only access its *own variables*. There are no common variables. But a process may call *common procedures* defined either within itself or within other processes. A procedure call from one process to another is called an *external request*.

A process performs two kinds of *operations* then: the *initial statement* and the *external requests* made by other processes. These operations are executed one at a time by *interleaving*. A process begins by executing its initial statement. This continues until the statement either terminates or waits for a condition to become true. Then another operation is started (as the result of an external request). When this operation in turn terminates or waits the process will either begin yet another operation (requested by another process) or it will resume an earlier operation (as the result of a condition becoming true). This interleaving of the initial statement and the external requests continues forever. If the initial statement terminates, the process continues to exist and will still accept external requests.

So the interleaving is controlled by the program (and *not* by clock signals at the machine level). A process switches from one operation to another only when an operation terminates or waits for a condition within a guarded region (introduced later).

A process continues to execute operations except when all its current operations are delayed within guarded regions or when it makes a request to another process. In the first case, the process is idle until another process calls it. In the second case, the process is idle until the other process has completed the operation requested by it. Apart from this nothing is assumed about the order in which a process performs its operations.

A process guarantees only that it will perform *some* operations as long as there are any unfinished operations that can proceed. But only the programmer can ensure that *every* operation is performed within a finite time.

A *procedure* defines its input and output parameters, some local variables perhaps, and a statement that is executed when it is called:

```
proc name (input param # output param)
local variables
statement
```

A process P can call a procedure R defined within another process Q as follows:

```
call Q.R (expressions, variables)
```

Before the operation R is performed the expression values of the call are assigned to the *input* parameters. When the operation is finished the values of the *output* parameters are assigned to the variables of the call. Parameter passing between processes can therefore be implemented either by copying within a common store or by input/output between processors that have no common store.

In this paper processes can call procedures within one another without any restrictions. In a complete programming language additional notation would be added to limit the access rights of individual processes. It may also be necessary to eliminate recursion to simplify verification and implementation. But these are issues that will not concern us here.

Nondeterminism will be controlled by two kinds of statements called *guarded commands* and *guarded regions*. A guarded region can delay an operation, but a guarded command cannot.

A guarded command [6] enables a process to make an arbitrary choice among several statements by inspecting the current state of its variables. If none of the alternatives are possible in the current state the guarded command cannot be executed and will either be skipped or cause a program exception.

The guarded commands have the following syntax and meaning:

if $B1 : S1 \mid B2 : S2 \mid$ ... **end**
do $B1 : S1 \mid B2 : S2 \mid$ ... **end**

- *If statement*   If some of the conditions $B1$, $B2$, ..., are true then select one of the true conditions Bi and execute the statement Si that follows it; otherwise, stop the program.

   (If the language includes a mechanism whereby one process can detect the failure of another process, it is reasonable to let an exception in a process stop that process only. But, if recovery from programming errors is not possible then it is more consistent to stop the whole program. This paper does not address this important issue.)

- *Do statement*   While some of the conditions are true select one of them arbitrarily and execute the corresponding statement.

   A guarded region [4, 8] enables a process to wait until the state of its variables makes it possible to make an arbitrary choice among several statements. If none of the alternatives are possible in the current state the process postpones the execution of the guarded region.

   The guarded regions have the following syntax and meaning:

   when $B1 : S1 \mid B2 : S2 \mid$ ... **end**
   cycle $B1 : S1 \mid B2 : S2 \mid$ ... **end**

- *When statement*   Wait until one of the conditions is true and execute the corresponding statement.

- *Cycle statement*   Endless repetition of a **when** statement.

   If several conditions are true within a guarded command or region it is unpredictable which one of the corresponding statements the machine will select. This uncertainty reflects the nondeterministic nature of real-time applications.

   The *data types* used are either integers, Booleans, or characters, or they are finite sets, sequences, and arrays with at most n elements of some type T:

```
int        bool       char
set[n]T    seq[n]T    array[n]T
```

The following statement enumerates all the elements in a data structure:

for x **in** $y : S$ **end**

- *For statement*   For each element x in the set or array y execute the statement S. A **for** statement can access and change the values of array elements but can only read the values of set elements.

Finally, it should be mentioned that the empty statement is denoted *skip* and the use of semicolons is optional.

3   Process communication

The following presents several examples of the use of these language concepts in concurrent programming. We will first consider communication between processes by means of procedure calls.

Example: semaphore

A general semaphore initialized to zero can be implemented as a process *sem* that defines *wait* and *signal* operations:

```
process sem; s : int
proc wait when s > 0 , s := s - 1  end
proc signal; s := s + 1
s := 0
```

The initial statement assigns the value zero to the semaphore and terminates. The process, however, continues to exist and can now be called by other processes:

call sem.wait   **call** sem.signal

Example: message buffer

A buffer process stores a sequence of characters transmitted between processes by means of *send* and *receive* operations:

```
process buffer; s : seq[n]char
proc send(c : char) when not s.full : s.put(c) end
proc rec(# v : char) when not s.empty : s.get(v) end
s := []
```

The initial statement makes the buffer empty to begin with. The buffer operations are called as follows:

call buffer.send(x)   **call** buffer.rec(y)

The semaphore and buffer processes are similar to *monitors*: They define the representation of a shared data structure and the meaningful operations on it. These operations take place one at a time. After initialization, a monitor is idle between external calls.

Example: character stream

A process inputs punched cards from a card reader and outputs them as a sequence of characters through a buffer process. The process deletes *spaces* at the end of each card and terminates it by a *newline* character.

```
process stream
b : array[80]char; n, i : int
do true :
   call cardreader.input(b)
   if b = blankline : skip |
      b ≠ blankline : i := 1; n := 80
         do b[n] = space : n := n − 1 end
         do i ≤ n : call buffer.send(b[i]); i := i + 1 end
   end
   call buffer.send(newline)
end
```

This use of a process is similar to the traditional *process* concept: the process executes an initial statement only. It calls common procedures within other processes, but does not define any within itself. Such a process does not contain guarded regions because other processes are unable to call it and make the conditions within it true.

The example also illustrates how *peripheral devices* can be controlled by distributed processes. A device (such as the card reader) is associated with a single process. Other processes can access the device only through common procedures. So a peripheral device is just another process.

While a process is waiting for input/output, no other operations take place within it. This is a special case of a more general rule: When a process P calls a procedure R within another process Q then R is considered an indivisible operation within process P, and P will not execute any other operation until R is finished (see Section 2).

Notice, that there is no need for *interrupts* even in a real-time language. Fast response to external requests is achieved by dedicating a processor to each critical event in the environment and by making sure that these processors interact with a small number of neighboring processors only (to prevent them from being overloaded with too many requests at a time).

Exercise

Write a process that receives a sequence of characters from a buffer process and outputs them line by line to a printer. The process should output a *formfeed* after every 60 lines.

4   Resource scheduling

We will now look at a variety of scheduling problems solved by means of guarded regions. It should perhaps be mentioned that resource schedulers are by nature *bottlenecks*. It would therefore be wise in a real-time program to make sure that each resource either is used frequently by a small number of processes or very infrequently by a larger number of processes. In many applications it is possible to avoid resource scheduling altogether and dedicate a resource to a single process (as in the card reader and line printer examples).

Example: resource scheduler

A set of user processes can obtain exclusive access to an abstract resource by calling request and release operations within a scheduling process:

```
process resource; free : bool
proc request when free : free := false end
proc release if not free : free := true end
free := true

call resource.request ... call resource.release
```

The use of the Boolean *free* forces a strict alternation of request and release operations. The program stops if an attempt is made to release a resource that already is free.

In this example, the scheduler does not know the identity of individual user processes. This is ideal when it does not matter in which order the users are served. But, if a scheduler must enforce a particular scheduling policy (such as *shortest job next*) then it must know the identity of its users to be able to grant the resource to a specific user. The following example shows how this can be done.

Example: shortest job next scheduler

A scheduler allocates a resource among *n* user processes in shortest-job-next order. A request enters the identity and service time of a user process in a queue and waits until that user is selected by the scheduler. A release makes the resource available again.

The scheduler waits until one of two situations arise:

(1) A process enters or leaves the queue: the scheduler will scan the queue and select the next user (but will not grant the resource to it yet).

(2) The resource is not being used and the next user has been selected: the scheduler will grant the resource to that user and remove it from the queue.

User processes identify themselves by unique indices 1, 2, ..., n. The constant *nil* denotes an undefined process index.

The scheduler uses the following variables:

queue	the indices of waiting processes
rank	the service times of waiting processes
user	the index of the current user (if any)
next	the index of the next user (if any)

```
process sjn
queue : set[n] int; rank : array[n]int
user, next, min : int
proc request(who, time : int)
begin queue.include(who); rank[who] := time
   next := nil; when user = who : next := nil end
end
proc release; user := nil

begin queue := [ ]; user := nil; next := nil
   cycle
     not queue.empty & (next = nil) :
       min := maxinteger
       for i in queue :
         if rank[i] > min : skip |
           rank[i] ≤ min : next := i; min := rank[i]
         end
       end |
     (user = nil) & (next ≠ nil) :
       user := next; queue.exclude(user)
   end

 end
```

In a microprocessor network where each processor is dedicated to a single process it is an attractive possibility to let a process carry out computations *between* external calls of its procedures. The above scheduler takes advantage of this capability by selecting the next user while the resource is still being used by the present user. It would be simpler (but less efficient) to delay the selection of the next user until the previous one has released the resource.

The scheduling of individual processes is handled completely by means of guarded regions without the use of synchronizing variables, such as semaphores or event queues.

The periodic evaluation of a synchronizing condition, such as 'user = who,' might be a serious load on a *common* store shared by other processors. But it is quite acceptable when it only involves the *local* store of a single processor that has nothing else to do. This is a good example of the influence of hardware technology on abstract algorithms.

Exercise

Write a first-come, first-served scheduler.

Example: readers and writers

Two kinds of processes, called readers and writers, share a single resource. The readers can use the resource simultaneously, but each writer must have exclusive access to it. The readers and writers behave as follows:

call resource.startread	**call** resource.startwrite
read	write
call resource.endread	**call** resource.endwrite

A variable s defines the current resource *state* as one of the following:

$s = 0$	1 writer uses the resource
$s = 1$	0 processes use the resource
$s = 2$	1 reader uses the resource
$s = 3$	2 readers use the resource
...	...

This leads to the following solution [4]:

```
process resource; s : int
proc startread when s ≥ 1 : s := s + 1 end
proc endread if s > 1 : s := s − 1 end
proc startwrite when s = 1 : s := 0 end
proc endwrite if s = 0 : s := 1 end
s := 1
```

Exercise

Solve the same problem with the additional constraint that further reader requests should be delayed as long as some writers are either waiting for or are using the resource.

Example: alarm clock

An alarm clock process enables user processes to wait for different time intervals. The alarm clock receives a signal from a timer process after each time unit. (The problems of representing a clock with a finite integer are ignored here.)

```
process alarm; time : int
proc wait(interval : int)
due : int
begin due := time + interval
   when time = due : skip end
end
proc tick; time := time + 1
time := 0
```

5   Process arrays

So far we have only used one instance of each process. The next example uses an array of n identical processes [9]:

```
process name[n]
```

A standard function *this* defines the identity of an individual process within the array ($1 \le$ this $\le n$).

Example: dining philosophers

Five philosophers alternate between thinking and eating. When a philosopher gets hungry, he joins a round table and picks up two forks next to his plate and starts eating. There are, however, only five forks on the table. So a philosopher can eat only when none of his neighbors are eating. When a philosopher has finished eating he puts down his two forks and leaves the table again.

```
process philosopher[5]
do true : think
   call table.join(this); eat; call table.leave(this)
end

process table; eating : set[5]int
proc join(i : int)
when ([i ⊖ 1, i ⊕ 1] & eating) = [ ] : eating.include(i) end
proc leave(i : int); eating.exclude(i)
eating := [ ]
```

This solution does not prevent two philosophers from starving a philosopher between them to death by eating alternately.

Exercise

Solve the same problem without starvation.

Example: sorting array

A process array sorts m data items in time $O(m)$. The items are input through sort process 1 that stores the smallest item input so far and passes the rest to its successor sort process 2. The latter keeps the second smallest item and passes the rest to its successor sort process 3, and so on. When the m items have been input they will be stored in their natural order in sort processes 1, 2, ..., m. They can now be output in increasing order through sort process 1. After each output the processes receive the remaining items from their successors.

A user process behaves as follows:

```
A : array[m] int
for x in A : call sort[1].put(x) end
for x in A : call sort[1].get(x) end
```

The sorting array can sort n elements or less ($m \leq n$). A sorting process is in equilibrium when it holds one item only. When the equilibrium is disturbed by its predecessor, a process takes the following action:

(1)   If the process holds two items, it will keep the smallest one and pass the largest one to its successor.

(2)   If the process holds no items, but its successor does, then the process will fetch the smallest item from its successor.

A sorting process uses the following variables:

here   the items stored in this process ($0 \leq$ here.length ≤ 2)
rest   the number of items stored in its successors

A standard function *succ* defines the index of the successor process (succ = this + 1).

```
process sort[n]
here : seq[2]int; rest, temp : int
proc put(c : int) when here.length < 2 : here.put(c) end
proc get(#v : int) when here.length = 1: here.get(v) end

begin here := [ ]; rest := 0
  cycle
    here.length = 2 :
      if here[1] ≤ here[2] : temp := here[2]; here := [here[1]] |
         here[1] > here[2] : temp := here[1]; here := [here[2]]
      end
```

```
            call sort[succ].put(temp); rest := rest + 1 |
        (here.length = 0) & (rest > 0) :
            call sort[succ].get(temp); rest := rest − 1
            here := [temp]
    end
end
```

A hardware implementation of such a sorting array could be used as a very efficient form of a priority scheduling queue.

Exercise

Program a process array that contains $N = 2^n$ numbers to begin with and which will add them in time $(\log_2 N)$.

Since a process can define a common procedure it obviously includes the *procedure* case as a special case. In [9] Hoare shows that a process array also can simulate a *recursive* procedure with a fixed maximum depth of recursion.

Exercise

Write a process array that computes a Fibonacci number by recursion.

6   Abstract data types

A process combines a data structure and all the possible operations on it into a single program module. Since other processes can perform these operations only on the data structure, but do not have direct access to it, it is called an *abstract* data structure.

We have already seen that a process can function as a *monitor* – an abstract data type that is shared by several processes. The next example shows that a process also can simulate a *class* – an abstract data type that is used by a single process only.

Example: vending machine

A vending machine accepts one coin at a time. When a button is pushed the machine returns an item with change provided there is at least one item left and the coins cover the cost of it; otherwise, all the coins are returned.

```
    process vending_machine
    items, paid, cash : int
    proc insert(coin : int) paid := paid + coin
```

```
proc push (#change, goods : int)
if (items > 0) & (paid ≥ price) :
    change := paid − price; cash := cash + price
    goods := 1; items := items − 1; paid := 0 |
  (items = 0) or (paid < price) :
    change := paid; goods := 0; paid := 0
end
begin items := 50; paid := 0; cash := 0 end
```

7   Coroutines

Distributed processes can also function as coroutines. In a coroutine relationship between two processes P and Q only one of them is running at a time. A resume operation transfers control from one process to the other. When a process is resumed it continues at the point where it has transferred control to another process.

```
process P; go : bool
proc resume; go := true

begin go := false
   ...
   call Q.resume
   when go : go := false end
   ...
end
```

Process Q is very similar.

8   Path expressions

Path expressions define meaningful *sequences* of operations $P, Q, ... ,$ [5]. A path expression can be implemented by a scheduling process that defines the operations $P, Q, ... ,$ as procedures and uses a state variable s to enforce the sequence in which other processes may invoke these procedures.

Suppose, for example, that the operation P only can be followed by the operation Q as shown by the graph below:

$$\rightarrow P \longrightarrow Q \rightarrow$$

To implement this path expression one associates a distinct state a, b, and c with each arrow in the graph and programs the operations as follows:

```
proc P if s = a : ... s := b end
proc Q if s = b : ... s := c end
```

If P is called in the state $s = a$ it will change the state to $s = b$ and make Q possible. Q, in turn, changes the state from b to c. An attempt to perform P or Q in a state where they are illegal will cause a program exception (or a delay if a *when* statement is used within the operation).

The next path expression specifies that either P or Q can be performed. This is enforced by means of two states a and b:

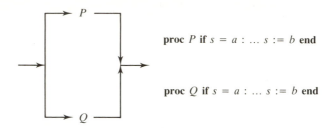

proc P **if** $s = a$: ... $s := b$ **end**

proc Q **if** $s = a$: ... $s := b$ **end**

If an operation P can be performed zero or more times then the execution of P leaves the state $s = a$ unchanged as shown below:

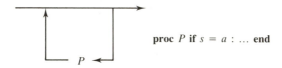

proc P **if** $s = a$: ... **end**

The simple resource scheduler in Section 4 implements a composite path expression in which the sequence *request* ... *release* is repeated zero or more times.

The readers and writers problem illustrates the use of a state variable to permit some operations to take place *simultaneously* while other operations are temporarily *excluded* (in this case, simultaneous reading by several processes excludes writing). Each simultaneous operation P is surrounded by a pair of scheduling operations, *startP* and *endP*. The state variable counts the number of P operations in progress.

9 Implementation hints

The following outlines the general nature of an implementation of distributed processes but ignores the details which are currently being studied.

In a well-designed concurrent program one may assume that each process communicates with a small number of neighboring processes only. For if the interactions are not strongly localized one cannot expect to gain much from concurrency. (A few resource schedulers may be an exception to this rule.)

Each processor will contain a distributed process P and a small, fixed number of anonymous processes which are the *representatives* of those distributed processes that can call process *P*. Additional notation in the language should make it possible for a compiler to determine the number of processes which call a particular process.

Whenever a processor is idle it activates a local representative which then waits until it receives a request with input data from another processor. The representative now calls the local procedure requested with the available input. When the procedure terminates, its output data are returned to the other processor and the representative becomes passive again. The switching from one *quasiconcurrent* process to another within a processor takes place as described in Section 2.

Since processes are permanent and procedures are nonrecursive, a compiler can determine the maximum storage required by a distributed process and the local representatives of its environment. So the storage allocation is *static* within each processor.

The parameter passing between two processors requires a single *input* operation before a procedure is executed and a single *output* operation when it terminates.

The speed of process switching within a single processor will probably be crucial for its real-time response.

The technique of representing the environment of a processor by local processes synchronized with external processes seems conceptually attractive. Although these processes are anonymous in this proposal one could design a language in which the store of a single processor is shared by local quasiconcurrent processes which communicate with nonlocal processes by input/output only.

10   Final remarks

It would certainly be feasible to adapt the processes and monitors of Concurrent Pascal to multiprocessor networks with distributed storage by restricting the parameter passing mechanism as proposed here. All the examples discussed here could then be programmed in that language – but not nearly as elegantly!

What then are the merits of distributed processes? Primarily, that they are a combination of *well-known* programming concepts (processes, procedures, and conditional critical regions) which *unify* the class, monitor, and process concepts. They include a surprising number of basic programming concepts as special cases:

- procedures
- coroutines
- classes
- monitors
- processes

- semaphores
- buffers
- path expressions
- input/output

Since there is a common denominator for all these concepts, it may well be possible to develop common proof rules for them. The use of a single concept will certainly simplify the language implementation considerably.

The Concurrent Pascal machine distinguishes between 15 virtual instructions for classes, monitors, and processes. This number would be reduced by a factor of three for distributed processes. In addition, numerous special cases would disappear in the compiler.

It is also encouraging that distributed processes can be used to write elegant algorithms both for the more well-known concurrent problems and for some new ones that are non-trivial.

A recent proposal by Hoare has the same pleasant properties [9]. Both proposals attack the problem of concurrency without shared variables and recognize the need for nondeterminacy within a single process.

Hoare's *communicating sequential processes* can be created and terminated dynamically, A single data transfer from one process to another is the communication mechanism. A process synchronizes itself with its environment by guarded input commands which are executed when a Boolean expression is true *and* input is available from another process. The relationship between two communicating processes is symmetrical and requires both of them to name the other. The brief and nonredundant notation does not require declarations of communication channels but depends (conceptually) on dynamic type checking to recognize matching input and output commands in two processes.

In their present form communicating sequential processes seem well-suited to a theoretical investigation of concurrency and as a concise specification language that suppresses minor details. However, as Hoare points out, the language concepts and the notation would have to be modified to make them practical for program implementation.

The proposal for *distributed processes* is intended as a first step toward a practical language for networks. The proposal recognizes that the exchange of input and output in one operation is a frequent case, particularly for peripheral devices which return a result after each operation. The notation is redundant and enables a compiler to determine the number of processes and their storage requirements. The relationship between two communicating processes is asymmetrical and requires only that the caller of an operation name the process that performs it. This asymmetry is useful in hierarchical systems in which servants should be unaware of the identities of their masters.

Distributed processes derive much of their power from the ability to delay process interactions by means of Boolean expressions which may involve both the global variables of a process *and* the input parameters from other processes (as illustrated by the *sjn* scheduler and the alarm clock). The price for this flexibility is the need for quasiconcurrent processes in the implementation. A more restricted form of Hoare's proposal might be able to implement process synchronization by the simpler method of polling a number of data channels until one of them transmits data.

But more work remains to be done on verification rules and network architectures for these new concepts. And then the ideas must be tested in *practice* before a final judgment can be made.

Acknowledgments

I am grateful to Nissim Francez, Wolfgang Franzen, Susan Gerhart, Charles Hayden, John Hennessy, Tony Hoare, David Lomet, David MacQueen, Johannes Madsen, David Musser, Michel Sintzoff, Jørgen Staunstrup and the referees for their constructive comments.

References

[1]   Brinch Hansen, P. The programming language Concurrent Pascal. *IEEE Trans. Software Eng.* **1**, 2 (June 1975), 199–207.

[2]   Brinch Hansen, P, *The Architecture of Concurrent Programs*. Prentice-Hall, Englewood Cliffs, N.J., 1977.

[3]   Brinch Hansen, P. *Operating System Principles*. Prentice-Hall, Englewood Cliffs, N.J., 1973.

[4]   Brinch Hansen, P., and Staunstrup, J. Specification and implementation of mutual exclusion. Comptr. Sci. Dept., U. of Southern California, Los Angeles, Sept. 1977.

[5]   Campbell, R.H., and Habermann, A.N. The specification of process synchronization by path expressions. *Lecture Notes in Computer Science 16*, Springer-Verlag, 1974, pp. 89–102.

[6]   Dijkstra, E.W. Guarded commands, nondeterminacy, and formal derivation of programs. *Comm. ACM* **18**, 8 (Aug. 1975), 453–57.

[7]   Hoare, C.A.R. Monitors: an operating system structuring concept. *Comm. ACM* **17**, 10 (Oct. 1974), 549–57.

[8]   Hoare, C.A.R. Towards a theory of parallel programming. In *Operating Systems Techniques*, Academic Press, New York, 1972.

[9]   Hoare, C.A.R. Communicating sequential processes. Comptr. Sci. Dept., Queen's U., Belfast, N. Ireland, March 1977.

[10] Wirth, N. Modula: A programming language for modular multiprogramming. *Software – Practice and Experience* **7**, 1 (Jan. 1977), 3–35.

Broadcasting Sequential Processes (BSP)

Narain H. Gehani
AT & T Bell Laboratories

Communication in a broadcast protocol multiprocessor (BPM) is inherently different from that in distributed systems formed by explicit links between processors. A message *broadcast* by a processor in a BPM is received directly by all other processors in the network instead of being restricted to only one processor. Broadcasting is an inexpensive way of communicating with a large number of processors on a BPM. In this paper I will describe a new approach to user-level distributed programming called *broadcast programming*, i.e., distributed programs written as cooperating broadcasting sequential processes (BSP). Existing concurrent programming languages do not provide facilities to exploit the broadcast capability of a BPM. The idea of distributed programs written as BSP is tailored to exploiting a BPM architecture but is not restricted to such an architecture – however, implementation of the broadcast capability may not be as efficient on other architectures.

I will illustrate the utility and convenience of broadcast programming with many examples. These examples will also be used to explore the suitability and advantages of BSP and to determine appropriate facilities for BSP.

I Introduction

A *broadcast protocol multiprocessor* (BPM), such as Ethernet [17], is a network of computers that uses a broadcast protocol to communicate.

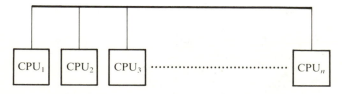

Communication in a broadcast protocol multiprocessor is inherently different from that in distributed systems formed by explicit links between processors. A message *broadcast* by a processor in a BPM is received directly by all other processors in the network instead of being restricted to only one processor. Broadcasting is an inexpensive way of communicating with a large number of processors.

A BPM is a local area network in which broadcasting is used for interprocessor communication. Unlike wide area networks, local area networks are characterized by extremely fast communication speeds (Mbits/s), have very low rates of error (1 bit in 10^{11} bits), and preserve the order in which the messages are sent. These characteristics have a profound impact on the way local area networks may be used. For example, even trivial services can be requested from other machines [18].

Motivated by the characteristics of a BPM and local area networks, I will describe a new approach to user-level distributed programming called *broadcast programming*, i.e., distributed programs written as cooperating *broadcasting sequential processes* (BSP). A message broadcast by one process can be received by all other processes. Programs will be written as a collection of closely coupled processes cooperating to accomplish a common objective – not loosely coupled processes with individual objectives.

I shall show that the ability to broadcast can be used to advantage in designing certain kinds of distributed programs or computer systems.[†] Existing concurrent programming languages do not provide a mechanism by which a process can *directly* broadcast to all other processes. Consequently, a broadcast capability, if provided by the underlying hardware, cannot be efficiently utilized.

By providing a user-level broadcast capability, there is no intent of making the underlying architecture and communication protocols visible to the user. Instead, the intent is to explore a new way of programming at a user level. Although broadcast programming is tailored to exploit a BPM architecture or an architecture in which it is relatively easy and cheap to send the same message to a large number of processors, e.g., other kinds of local area networks [15], [18] it is not restricted to such architectures. If the underlying architecture happens to be a BPM or one suitable for broadcasting (such architectures are becoming increasingly common with the popularity of BPMs such as Ethernet), then the implementation of the broadcast primitives will be efficient; otherwise their implementation may be very inefficient.

A BSP program consists of a set of closely coupled processes that can communicate by broadcasting. Processes in a BSP program cooperate to implement *one* program. Although I envision each process of a BSP

[†] *Distributed programs* are *concurrent programs* in which each process is executed by a dedicated physical processor.

program as running on a different node of a network, i.e., each process is executed by a dedicated computer on the network, there is no reason why several processes may not reside on the same computer.

In the examples given later, I assume that the individual processors are not overloaded, since the processes do not require much processing, and that the processes may call upon one another even for very simple tasks. These assumptions are economically viable because of recent advances in hardware technology such as VLSI [16].

II   Utility of broadcast programming – some examples

Consider, as an example, an *administrator* process managing a group of *worker* processes. The administrator can broadcast a message to all the worker processes requesting that a free worker volunteer for work; it then selects the first worker to respond. The administrator does not have to keep track of the free workers. Worker processes can be added or deleted without having to modify the administrator process. The use of the *administrator concept* in designing concurrent programs has been recommended as a good concurrent programming discipline [12].

Another example is taken from artificial intelligence. In the implementation of the parallel version of the alpha-beta algorithm [9] (used in game playing programs), a finite set of *slave* processes is used to evaluate the alternative moves. This parallel alpha-beta algorithm has to keep track of the free slaves. The BSP parallel alpha-beta algorithm will not have to keep track of the free slaves since it can broadcast a message to all the slaves requesting volunteers – one of the volunteers is then selected to do the specified task. An additional advantage is that slaves can be added and deleted dynamically without requiring modification of the parallel alpha-beta algorithm.

One final example is the use of BSP to implement a distributed relational database, with different processes taking care of different relations or even different parts of relations [5]. Database queries are broadcast to all the processes which respond with answers to the queries vis-à-vis their local relations.

III   Advantages of broadcast programming

Broadcast programming has several advantages over concurrent programming in which processes communicate on a one-to-one basis with each other:

(1) *No explicit knowledge of other processes is required*   A process does not have to specify explicitly the names of processes it communicates with because a message broadcast by it is received by all processes. Every process in the network can listen to this message.

The name of the broadcasting process can be determined from the broadcast message.

(2) *No need for internal management of interacting processes*   Certain kinds of programs, such as *administrator of work processes* can be designed elegantly without the need to account for worker processes explicitly. A request is broadcast to all worker processes and all workers in an appropriate state respond.

(3) *Additional processes can be added and deleted dynamically*   Since a process *P* does not explicitly need to know the names of processes it interacts with, additional processes that interact with *P* can be added and others deleted, dynamically, without the need for modifying *P*. For example, the number of worker processes can be increased or decreased without the need to modify the administrator.

(4) *Activity monitoring*   Monitoring of activity in a BSP program and analysis of the broadcast messages can be done without having to modify the monitored processes. A process can be added to monitor the broadcasts.

(5) *BPM efficiency*   Broadcasting, not point-to-point communication, is an appropriate mechanism for the efficient use of an underlying BPM architecture.

IV Facilities in other concurrent programming languages and notations

Concurrent language notations such as CSP [13] and languages with concurrent facilities such as Ada [8], [10] do not provide a facility to broadcast messages. Communication between processes is less restrictive in Ada than in CSP where both the sending and receiving processes must be named. In Ada only the receiving process must be named – to allow the building of libraries of processes. (Although names of interacting processes need not be known in concurrent languages or notations in which processes communicate via channels or ports, the channel and port names must be known instead [16]; one exception is the *pipe* concept in the UNIX operating system [23].)

When implementing an administrator process in CSP, worker process names must be known to the administrator – a severe disadvantage – and broadcasting must be done by sending an individual message to each worker, a very inefficient scheme if the underlying computer is a BPM.

In Ada, instead of the administrator knowing the names of the worker processes, the administrator name can be built in to the workers. This scheme requires that worker processes call the administrator for a message. The worker processes will remain in a blocked state, ready to accept messages from the administrator until they get a message. Moreover, the worker processes will not be able to offer their services to two or more administrators at the same time since they can be blocked with respect to only one administrator at a time.

To summarize, existing concurrent programming languages do not provide a facility for broadcasting. Moreover, implementing broadcasting by sending each process a message, besides being inefficient, requires that the names of interacting processes be known.

V Assumptions and notation

I will assume that the underlying broadcast protocols provide an error free environment – messages are received without errors and in the order sent. Protocols with such properties have been proposed [4], [21] and I will not discuss them in this paper. Broadcast protocols can be implemented directly if the underlying hardware provides a broadcast capability or indirectly by using point-to-point communication – of course, the former will be much more efficient than the latter.

Derivatives of Dijkstra's guarded commands [7] and notation from Hoare's CSP [13] will be used to illustrate the idea of BSP. Only notation sufficient to illustrate the ideas of BSP will be presented here.

The guarded *if* statement has the form:

```
if guard → statement list
   □ guard → statement list
   ⋮
   □ guard → statement list
fi
```

where *guard* is a Boolean expression. The guard **else** may be used as a convenient abbreviation for the Boolean expression that is **true** when all the specified guards are **false**. These expressions are called *guards* because they guard the associated statement lists from execution until the expression becomes **true**.

The statement list corresponding to one of the *guards* that evaluates to **true** is executed. If more than one *guard* is **true**, then the statement list executed is selected nondeterministically, i.e., randomly, from the statement lists with **true** guards. At least one of the *guards* must be **true**; otherwise execution of the *if* statement will result in an error.

The guarded *do* statement has the form:

```
do guard → statement list
   □ guard → statement list
   ⋮
   □ guard → statement list
od
```

The *do* statement is executed as long as one of the *guards* is **true**. The statement list corresponding to one of the *guards* that evaluates to **true** is executed. If more than one *guard* is **true**, then the statement list to be executed is selected nondeterministically.

VI   Broadcast programming primitives – asynchronous

Broadcasting is an asynchronous communication mechanism. Broadcasting cannot be synchronous because it is unrealistic to expect a broadcasting process to wait until all other processes in the network are ready to receive the broadcast. Moreover, the broadcasting process may not even know about the existence of the receiving processes. Processes that are not ready to receive the message just miss the message – programs must be designed taking this into account.

A timeout facility is necessary because, after having broadcast a message, the process has no idea of how long to wait to receive all the responses. A broadcasting process has no way of even knowing whether its message was received or missed by the receiving processes. The broadcasting process must, if necessary, be able to rebroadcast its message or to perform some alternative action.

A   Notation

Each message m sent by one process to other processes (broadcast or otherwise) will contain the following information (adapted from the notation used by Schneider, Gries, and Schlichting [21]):

m.sender   name of the process sending message m

m.info   information component of message m

B   Early broadcasting primitives

Two broadcast programming primitives SHOUT and LISTEN have been proposed by Levitan [14].

The primitive SHOUT *attempts* to broadcast a message on the BPM. This attempt may or may not be successful – the next message in the BPM must be examined to try to determine if the attempt to broadcast was successful or not. (A broadcast message is received by the broadcasting process also.)

The primitive LISTEN is used to receive the message most recently broadcast on the BPM. Messages not listened to by a process are lost.

As described and used, these primitives makes no attempt at hiding the underlying BPM architecture – they are used in the context of timeslots for broadcasting. These primitives have been used to write programs to manipulate values held at different computers on the network – computing the maximum and the minimum, sorting the values, and finding a spanning tree [14]. The primitives are rather low level in nature and by themselves are inconvenient to use.

C   High level broadcasting facilities

Two different types of broadcast commands are necessary and appropriate for different applications: *buffered broadcast* and *unbuffered broadcast*. These two broadcast commands have an analogy in everyday life. For example, a radio announcement or a teacher requesting a volunteer from the class corresponds to an unbuffered broadcast. If the radio announcement or the teacher's request is not heard, then the message is lost. In case of the teacher's request, if no student responds, the request can be repeated by the teacher. The request may be repeated several times before a student responds or the teacher gives up. On the other hand, mass mailings, such as those sent out by prospective political candidates and by publishers soliciting subscriptions, correspond to a buffered broadcast.

I will now propose additional primitives and facilities to facilitate broadcast programming. Although these primitives are derived from SHOUT and LISTEN, they are higher level and can be implemented easily in hardware.

As mentioned earlier, two versions of the broadcast primitive – unbuffered and buffered, designated by $\bigcirc$ and $\otimes$, respectively – are proposed with the purpose of exploring their utility. Broadcast messages are received by means of the *receive* command designated by the symbol $\textcircled{?}$.

all$\bigcirc i$ *Unbuffered Broadcast*   Execution of this command by a process results in a *broadcast*, to all *other* processes, of a message m with $m.info = i$ and $m.sender = name\ of\ the\ executing\ process$.

Execution of the *unbuffered broadcast* command, designated by $\bigcirc$, is delayed until it is possible to broadcast a message on the network. The message broadcast by this command is lost if not received immediately by a process, i.e., the message is not buffered for the receiving process.

Execution of the unbuffered broadcast $\bigcirc$ results in a message being broadcast whereas execution of SHOUT represents only an attempt to broadcast a message – the attempt may or may not be successful. The command **all**$\bigcirc i$ may be informally defined in terms of SHOUT(i) as:

SHOUT(i)

do not successful in broadcasting $\longrightarrow$ SHOUT(i) **od**

If a message is to be received by a subset of processes, say $p_1, p_2, \ldots, p_n$, then it is advisable to *multicast*:

$$[p_1, p_2, \ldots, p_n] \bigcirc i$$

instead of broadcasting to avoid errors and to improve program readability.

The command:

$$p \bigcirc i$$

is equivalent to an asynchronous unbuffered point-to-point communication between the executing process and process p.

all$\otimes i$ *Buffered Broadcast* The buffered broadcast is very similar to the unbuffered broadcast except that the message broadcast is buffered for each receiving process, if necessary. The buffer size is considered to be infinite (of course, in practice only a finite number of messages can be buffered).

Like the unbuffered broadcast, the buffered broadcast can be multicast or used to send a message to one process.

any$\bigcirc m$ *Receive* The *receive* command is used to receive all broadcast messages. Its semantics depend upon the kind of broadcast mechanism used, i.e., unbuffered or buffered.

In the case of the unbuffered broadcast, execution of the command is delayed until a message m is received. The message received is assigned to m.

Irrelevant messages can be screened out by specifying restrictions on the contents of the message or the names of the senders. For example, the command:

any$(\text{info} = i)\bigcirc m$

ignores all messages until one is received with its information component equal to i. The command:

any$(\text{sender} = [p_1, p_2, \ldots, p_n])\bigcirc m$

ignores all messages until a message broadcast by one of the processes $p_1, p_2, \ldots, p_n$ is received. If only one process is of interest, then the square brackets may be left out.

Of course, both kinds of restrictions can be specified together as in:

any$(\text{info} = i, \text{sender} = [p_1, p_2, \ldots, p_n])\bigcirc m.$

In the case of the buffered broadcast, execution of the command results in the first message from the queue of waiting broadcast messages being assigned to *m*. If the queue is empty, then execution of the command is delayed until a message is received.

Restrictions in the *receive* command cause all messages not satisfying the restrictions to be discarded. If none of the messages in the buffer satisfy the restrictions or if the buffer is empty, then execution of the *receive* command awaits the arrival of a message satisfying the restrictions.

The unbuffered broadcast is simpler to implement than the buffered broadcast, but it suffers from the disadvantage that a message may be lost if a receiving process is not ready to receive the message when it is broadcast.

D   Timeout mechanism

The *delay* command:

delay(*d*)

executes successfully after a delay of at least *d* seconds. The *delay* command can be used in extended guarded commands (next section) allowing a process to give up waiting for a response after a finite time period, i.e., to timeout.

VII   Synchronized communication primitives

Synchronized communication will be used for communication between two processes. The semantics of the first two primitives are similar to their counterparts in CSP [13] with one important exception – a variable containing the name of a process can be used in the synchronization primitives instead of the process name itself (as in [11]).

p!i Output Command   Execution of this command results in a message *m* with *m.info* = *i* and *m.sender* = *name of the executing process* being sent to the process *p*. Execution of this *output* command will be delayed until *p* is ready to accept the message.

p?m Input Command   Execution of this command results in a message *m* being received from process *p*. Execution of this *input* command is delayed until process *p* sends a message.

any*?m General Input Command*   Similar to *p?m* except that a message can be accepted from any process instead of the named process *p*. Multiple *output* commands by several processes directed to one process are queued and accepted in FIFO order.

Restrictions can be specified in the *input* commands in a manner similar to the specification of restrictions in the *receive* command.

The *input* command is used in conjunction with the *output* command while the *receive* command is used in conjunction with broadcasts. Although the *input* and *receive* commands could have been combined, they have been kept separate because they correspond to different message sending commands, and because they have different semantics (synchronous versus asynchronous execution), and to enhance program readability.

VIII Integration with guarded commands

To allow a process to select from a set of possible interactions, the guarded commands are now extended to include the specification of the *receive, input,* and *delay* commands as part of the guard.

The extended guarded *if* and *do* statements have the form:

if extended guard $\longrightarrow$ statement list
    □ extended guard $\longrightarrow$ statement list
    ⋮
    □ extended guard $\longrightarrow$ statement list
fi

and:

do extended guard $\longrightarrow$ statement list
    □ extended guard $\longrightarrow$ statement list
    ⋮
    □ extended guard $\longrightarrow$ statement list
od

where *extended guard* is of the form:

guard | guard; command | command

and where *command* is a *delay* command, a *receive* command or an *input* command.

I will now informally define the semantics of the extended *if* and *do* statements.

An *extended guard* is *open* if its guard, if any, evaluates to **true** and its associated command, if any, can he immediately executed. An extended guard is *closed* if its guard is **false**. An extended guard is *pending evaluation* when its guard, if any, is **true**, but its associated command cannot be immediately executed.

If an extended guard, with a true guard, contains a *receive* command with restrictions, then a broadcast message that does not satisfy these restrictions is discarded only after determining that it does not satisfy a *receive* command in the other extended guards with a true guard.

Execution of the *if* statement results in an error if all the guards are closed. If there are one or more open guards, then a statement list corresponding to one of the open guards is executed. If there are no open guards but there are some guards pending evaluation, then execution of the *if* statement is delayed until one of the guards opens up. A *delay(d)* command successfully executes with a delay of at least d seconds after its guard was determined to be pending evaluation.

For the *do* statement, execution of its body continues until all its guards are closed. The alternative to be executed is selected as in the *if* statement.

IX Examples

The purpose of these examples is to show how BSP programs are written and to show that a variety of programs can be written using BSP. Early attempts to program these examples lead to modifications of the broadcast capability, distinction between the buffered and unbuffered broadcasts, and addition of a timeout facility integrated with the guarded commands.

Curly brackets are used as delimiters for comments in the programming examples.

A A stack of *N* elements

A stack of N elements is implemented by using N 'element processes' – each process holding one element. Elements can be added, inspected, and deleted by the following messages:

```
<add, 5>
<delete, null>
<top, null>
```

Each message is a record consisting of two fields: *oper* and *value*.
The ith stack element process is defined as:

```
stack_size := 0
any⑦m
do true →
   if m.info.oper = add →
      if i = stack_size − 1 → element := m.info.value {my turn to store}
         □ else → skip
      fi
      stack_size := stack_size + 1
   □ m.info.oper = top and i = stack_size → m.sender!element
   □ m.info.oper = delete → stack_size := stack_size − 1
   fi
   any⑦m
od
```

This stack implementation has the nice property of being a fully distributed solution, i.e., loss of some elements in the stack does not destroy the integrity of the rest of the stack. Some disadvantages of the above implementation are that the element numbers are *hard wired* into the processes and each process keeps track of how many elements are currently in the stack.

The first disadvantage can be easily eliminated by requesting a free element process every time an element is to be added to the stack (see example on sets). The second disadvantage can be eliminated by giving the element holding the top element a special marker which it passes on to the next element when it is being deleted (but the solution is then no longer fully distributed).

Use of the unbuffered broadcast by the process broadcasting the stack operations is dangerous since it relies on the execution speed of the element processes for them to receive the messages. Use of the buffered broadcast would be safer since program correctness would then be independent of execution speeds of the element processes. Note that more than one process can manipulate the set.

B   A set

A set is implemented by dedicating a process for each element of a set, All operations on the set are channeled via a process SET which interacts with the element processes. As in case of the stack example, each message sent to the element processes is a record of the form ⟨oper, value⟩.

Each element process is of the form:

```
free := true; m := null
do true →
   any⑦m
   if m.info.oper = are_you_free and free → m.sender!yes
      □ m.info.oper = add and free →
            element := m.info.value; free := false
      □ m.info.oper = delete and not free →
         if m.info.value = element → free := true; m.sender!deleted
            □ else → m.sender!cannot
         fi
      □ m.info.oper = in and not free →
         if m.info.value = element → m.sender!i_have_it
            □ else → m.sender!dont_have_it
         fi
      □ else → skip
   fi
od
```

I will briefly describe program segments from the process SET that are used for manipulating the set. Process SET keeps track of the number of elements to avoid exceeding the maximum set size *max_size* (also the maximum number of element process) from being exceeded and to keep track of how many responses to expect. An element x is added to the set by requesting the free element processes to volunteer to store the element. The first volunteering process is selected and the element sent to it. Responses of the other volunteers are ignored.

```
if cur_size < max_size →
  all⊗are_you_free
  any(info = yes)? m → m.sender⊗<add, x>;
                cur_size := cur_size + 1
  i := 0
  do i < max_size – cur_size; any(info = yes)? m →
    i := i + 1
  od
    {ignore the other volunteers}
fi
```

An element x is deleted by broadcasting an appropriate message and then examining the responses to see if x was actually deleted (which happens if x was in the set) or not:

```
all⊗<delete, x>
i := 0; n := cur_size
do i ⩽ n →        {n responses expected}
  if any(info = deleted) → cur_size := cur_size − 1
    □ any(info = cannot) → skip
  fi
  i := i + 1
od
```

The above program segments have one undesirable property – each response by an element process is explicitly accepted by SET. This is necessary to avoid incorrectly interpreting a response to an earlier request as a response to a later request. All responses associated with a request are accepted prior to broadcasting the next request – an inefficient solution since all but one response is of interest.

This undesirable property can be eliminated by using sequence numbers to ensure correct association of responses with requests. When making a request, a request number is also broadcast. This request number is used by the element process when responding. For example, the program segment to add an element to the set is modified as:

```
if cur_size < max_size →
  request# := request# + 1
  all⊗<are_you_free, request#>
  if any(info = <yes, request#>)? m →
    m.sender⊗<add, x>; cur_size := cur_size + 1 fi
fi
```

Old responses still pending acceptance are discarded when SET waits for a response to a request.

An asynchronous response using a buffered broadcast, instead of a synchronous response via an output command, is used in each element process so that it does not have to wait, until the next request has been broadcast by SET, to find out that it was not needed for an earlier request.

$$\vdots$$

if m.info.oper = are_you_free **and** free $\longrightarrow$ m.sender $\otimes$<yes, m.info.value>
{m.info.value is the request number}

C The dining philosophers who shout (i.e., broadcast)

Five philosophers spend their lives eating spaghetti and thinking. They eat at a circular table in a dining room. The table has five chairs around it and a chair number i is assigned to philosopher number $i (1 \leqslant i \leqslant 5)$. There is a bowl of spaghetti that is replenished every so often to ensure that it is never empty. Five plates have been placed on the table – one for each philosopher. Five forks have also been laid out on the table so that there is one fork between every two chairs. Consequently there is one fork to the left of each chair and one to its right. Fork number i is to the left of chair number i.

Each philosopher sits in the chair assigned to him in order to be able to eat. A philosopher must have two forks to eat – the forks to his left and right. The philosophers *shout* (i.e., broadcast) an appropriate message whenever they want a fork. If the philosopher cannot get two forks immediately, then he must wait until he gets them before he can eat. The forks are picked up one at a time with the left fork being picked up first.

When a philosopher is finished eating (after a finite amount of time), he puts the forks down and starts thinking.

The dining philosophers problem was posed by E. W. Dijkstra [6] and has been studied extensively in the computer science literature [1], [2], [6]. It is used as a benchmark problem to check the appropriateness of concurrent programming facilities in a programming language and of proof techniques for concurrent programs. It is interesting, because, despite its apparent simplicity, it illustrates many of the problems encountered in concurrent programming, particularly shared resources and *deadlock*. The forks are the resources shared by the philosophers who represent the concurrent processes.

Each of the five philosophers P_i and forks F_i $(1 \leqslant i \leqslant 5)$ is represented as a process on a BPM. Messages *request_fork$_i$* and *return_fork$_i$* from philosophers P_i or $P_{i+1 \bmod 5}$ are destined for fork F_i, indicating a request to grant use of fork i and that fork i is being returned, respectively. Message *take_fork$_i$* from F_i is destined for either philosopher P_i or $P_{i \bmod 5+1}$, indicating that fork i can be picked up.

Philosopher P_i is represented by the process:

```
do true →
   {wait for fork i}
   allОrequest_fork_i
   do any(info = take_fork_i)⑦m1 → exit
   {exit causes termination of the loop}
      □ delay(d) → allОrequest_fork_i
   od

   {wait for fork i mod 5 + 1}
   allОrequest_fork_i mod 5+1)
   do any(info = take_fork_i mod 5+1)⑦m2 → exit
      □ delay(d) → allОrequest_fork_i mod 5+1
   od

   Eat

   {return the forks}
   m1.sender!return_fork_i
   m2.sender!return_fork_i mod 5+1

   Think
od
```

Fork F_i is represented by the process:

```
do any(info = request_fork_i)⑦m →
   m.senderОtake_fork_i
   m.sender?m1
od
```

The availability of a broadcast facility allows the philosopher processes to be built without requiring a knowledge of fork processes. Since the names of the fork processes are not known to the philosopher processes, message content is used as a protocol to route the message to appropriate processes. The programming technique is more flexible than one relying on explicit knowledge of process names, e.g., the program can be changed so that all forks are handled by one process without requiring any change to the philosophers.

Note that the philosophers can deadlock! Deadlock can be easily avoided by requiring that every philosopher pick up an odd fork first [3].

There is still another problem – starvation of an individual philosopher. It is possible that when a philosopher requests a fork, his neighbor is using it. The request is missed by the appropriate fork process since it is waiting for a message indicating return of the fork. The philosopher waits d s for a reply. During this period, the neighbor returns the fork, requests it again and then receives it. Starvation of the philosopher occurs if the neighbor does this repeatedly. Starvation can be avoided by using the buffered broadcast instead of the unbuffered broadcast because this will ensure that the hungry philosopher's request is queued and that he will be the next one to get the fork. The buffered solution also turns out to be simpler.

Philosopher P_i is represented by the process:

```
do true →
    {wait for fork i}
    all⊗request_fork_i
    any?m1

    {wait for fork i mod 5 + 1}
    all⊗request_fork_{i mod 5+1}
    any?m2

    Eat

    {return the forks}
    m1.sender!return_fork_i
    m2.sender!return_fork_{i mod 5+1}

    Think
od
```

Fork F_i is represented by the process:

```
do any(info = request_fork_i)⑦m →
    m.sender!take_fork_i
    m.sender?m1
od
```

D   The administrator concept

A process *printer administrator* manages one or more *printer worker* processes. Whenever the printer administrator needs to fulfill a printing request, it requests that a *printer* process volunteer to print the next job. If a printer process does not respond within a specified period, then the administrator re-broadcasts its request.

The printer processes are defined as:

```
do
    any(info = request_for_printer)⑦m ⟶ m.sender○free
    □ m.sender?work ⟶ print work
od
```

The appropriate program segment in the printer administrator is:

```
all○request_for_printer
do any(info = free)⑦m ⟶ exit
    □ delay(d) ⟶ all○request_for_printer
od
m.sender!stuff_to_be_printed
```

E   A relational database

A relational database can be implemented on a BPM with each site storing some relations. A relation can be fragmented in that parts of it may be at different sites. I will briefly illustrate the idea of using BSP for such a database. Assume there are N sites. To determine the *union* of two relations A and B, the requesting process executes the following program segment:

```
result := local union of A and B, if A or B is stored locally; otherwise φ
all⊗<union, A, B>
i := 0
do any(info = no)? m ⟶ i := i + 1
    □ any(info ≠ no)? m ⟶ i := i + 1; result := result ∪ m.info
    □ i = N ⟶ exit
od
```

The sites execute code similar to the following program segment:

```
any⑦m
if m.info.oper = union ⟶ if we have relations m.info.R1
    or m.info.R2 then m.sender!R1 ∪ R2 otherwise
    m.sender!no
    ⋮
fi
```

If the number of sites is not known *a priori*, then timeouts must be used.

F   A resource server [11]

The *resource server* process has the form:

```
free := true
do any(info = i_want_it)⑦m and free →
     m.sender!go_ahead; free := false
□ any(info = i_want_it)⑦m and not free → put m.sender in queue
□ any(info = resource_free)? m and queue empty → free := true
□ any(info = resource_free)? m and queue not empty →
                    select process p from queue; p!go_ahead
od
```

The process requesting use of the resource executes a program segment of the form:

```
all⊗i_want_it
any(info = go_ahead)? m
⋮
use resource
⋮
m.sender!resource_free
```

The requesting process does not initially need to know the name of the resource server. Upon receiving permission to use the resource, it determines the name of the resource server from the message which it then uses in sending a message informing the server that it has finished using the resource. Extraneous messages must be screened out, e.g., the message *i_want_it* may not be of any interest to the processes other than the server.

X   Some comments on broadcast programming

Although broadcast programming has many advantages, it also has some disadvantages. These disadvantages can be easily avoided by using an appropriate programming style as follows.

(1)   No knowledge of the names or number of interacting processes

If the broadcasting process does not know the names or the number of interacting processes, then how can it determine that all appropriate processes have received the broadcast message (i.e., a message was not missed by a receiving process because it was busy with something else)?

Or how can the broadcasting process determine that it has received all answering messages – the broadcasting process cannot wait forever; it will eventually have to timeout.

The solutions to the above problems lie in program design appropriate for broadcast programming. A distributed BSP program should be designed using one or more of the following rules:

- Buffered broadcasts should be used for critical messages. For example, buffered broadcasts were used in the dining philosophers' problem to avoid starvation.

- The broadcasting process should know exactly how many responses it should get. In the example illustrating the implementation of a set, process SET knows exactly how many responses it must wait for before it is sure that an element is deleted.

- The broadcasting process relies only on a minimum number of responses to a broadcast message. If the minimum number of responses is not received within some specific time period, then the message is rebroadcast. For example, the printer administrator requires only one worker process at a time to volunteer for new work. If no worker responds to a broadcast message within a specified time period, then the message is rebroadcast. On the other hand, if more than one worker process responds, one process is arbitrarily selected and all worker processes are informed of the decision (if necessary).

- The broadcasting process does not rely on the number of responses it gets. In the BSP version of a relational database, an answer to a query may depend upon the number of processes responding – an approximate database.

Of course, there is no requirement that a broadcasting process must be oblivious of the processes it interacts with. However, this knowledge is often not necessary and can result in a centralized solution. Names of interacting processes should not be built-in to the solution; if this knowledge is necessary, it should be dynamically collected. For example, in a BSP version of the distributed telephone system [22], every telephone process must inform the site administrator when it is joining the telephone network – to allow the site administrator to maintain a list of current users, to perform accounting, and the like.

(2) Flood of responses

A broadcasting process may be inundated with responses causing some responses to be lost because the broadcasting process was not able to digest them fast enough. This problem can be avoided by avoiding unbuffered broadcasts when responding and instead using:

(a) buffered broadcasts and

(b) synchronized communication to respond to a broadcast message (sending processes are queued).

(3) Extraneous messages

A message broadcast by a process can be received by every other process. Consequently, every process must screen out irrelevant messages.

XI Conclusions

In this paper I have tried to illustrate the concept of BSP. I have not attempted to give a complete programming language notation and syntax for BSP – that is the subject of future work as are the exact semantics of BSP, detailed implementation considerations, and an implementation.

Plans for future work also include investigation of additional facilities to support broadcast programming. For example, if the number of processes that comprise a BSP program is known statically, then it would be possible to provide a primitive that will be **true** if all processes have replied to a broadcast and *false* otherwise – such a primitive would be convenient to have.

As mentioned before, BSP has many parallels in everyday life. Broadcasting is used to establish communication and then the analog of synchronized communication is used for further communication. For example, a manager addressing a group of employees may ask for a volunteer to perform a task (by broadcasting). If some employee volunteers, then further communication occurs directly between the manager and volunteer. If no employee volunteers, then the manager may make the request again or take some alternative action.

Broadcasting introduces another avenue for making errors in concurrent programming – just as concurrent programming introduced a class of errors not found in sequential programs. Appropriate broadcasting primitives, programming discipline, and experience with broadcast programming will solve this problem. For example, once communication has been established via the broadcast primitive between two processes, synchronized communication should be used in preference to broadcasting to minimize chances of errors and for better program reliability.

Which one of the two broadcasting paradigms should be used – unbuffered or buffered? Unbuffered broadcasting is simple to implement, whereas buffered broadcasting makes the implementation somewhat more complex. However, does buffering just push the lost message problem of unbuffered broadcasting one level further? What happens when the buffer is full? Is the message lost or is the broadcast delayed until every process can receive the message? Should specification of the restrictions on the *receive* and *input* commands be made more elaborate? Answers to these questions merit further study.

Acknowledgments

I am grateful for the comments and criticisms of my colleagues T. A. Cargill, D. E. Comer, J. DeTreville, A. R. Feuer, J. O. Limb, M. D. McIlroy, D. K. Sharma, W. D. Sincoskie, C. S. Wetherell, and P. Wolper.

Initially, I hesitated to include buffered broadcasting, limiting BSP to unbuffered broadcasts, so as to keep a potential implementation of BSP as simple as possible. However, P. Wolper convinced me that the advantages of including them would outweigh an additional implementation complexity.

The detailed comments of D. E. Comer, M. D. McIlroy, C. Wetherell, and P. Wolper were an important factor in refining BSP and its presentation.

References

[1]   M. Ben-Ari, *Principles of Concurrent Programming*. Englewood Cliffs, NJ: Prentice-Hall, 1982.

[2]   P. Brinch Hansen, *Operating System Principles*. Englewood Cliffs, NJ: Prentice-Hall, 1973.

[3]   T. A. Cargill, 'A robust distributed solution to the dining philosophers problem,' *Software Practice Exper.*, **10**, Oct. 1982.

[4]   J. M. Chang and N. F. Maxemchuck, 'Reliable broadcast protocols,' submitted for publication.

[5]   J. D. DeTreville and W. D. Sincoskie, 'Program transformations that trade data structure for control structure in a local distributed environment,' Bell Lab., Holmdel, NJ, Intern. Memo., 1982.

[6]   E. W. Dijkstra, 'Hierarchical ordering of sequential processes,' *Acta Inform.*, **1**, pp. 115–138, 1971.

[7]   ——, *A Discipline of Programming*. Englewood Cliffs, NJ: Prentice-Hall, 1976.

[8]   *Reference Manual for the Ada Programming Language,* U.S. Dep. Defense, 1983.

[9]   R. A. Finkel and J. P. Fishburn, 'Parallelism in alpha-beta search,' *Artificial Intell.*, **19**, pp. 89–106, 1982.

[10]   N. Gehani, *Ada: An Advanced Introduction*. Englewood Cliffs, NJ: Prentice-Hall, 1983.

[11]   D. Gelernter and A. J. Bernstein, 'Distributed communication via global buffer,' *Proc. ACM SIGACT-SIGOPS Symp. Priniciples Distributed Comput.*, Ottawa, Canada, Aug. 1982.

[12]   W. M. Gentleman, 'Message passing between sequential processes: The reply primitive and the administrator concept,' *Software Practice Exper.*, **1**, pp. 435–466, 1981.

[13] C. A. R. Hoare, 'Communicating sequential processes,' *Commun. Ass. Comput. Mach.*, **21**, pp. 666–677, Aug. 1978.

[14] S. P. Levitan, 'Algorithms for a broadcast protocol multiprocessor,' In: *Proc. 3rd Int. Conf. Distributed Comput. Syst.*, Miami/Fort Lauderdale, FL, Oct. 1982, pp. 666–671.

[15] J. O. Limb and C. Flores, 'Description of Fasnet – A unidirectional local area communications network,' *Bell Syst. Tech. J.*, **61**, pp. 1413–1440, Sept. 1982.

[16] Y. M. Mao and R. T. Yeh, 'Communication port: A language concept for concurrent programming,' *IEEE Trans. Software Eng.*, SE-6, pp. 194–204, Mar. 1980.

[17] R. M. Metcalfe and D. R. Boggs, 'Ethernet: Distributed packet switching for local computer networks,' *Commun. Ass. Comput. Mach.*, **19**, July 1976.

[18] R. M. Needham and A. J. Herbert, *The Cambridge Distributing Computing System*. Reading, MA: Addison-Wesley, 1982.

[19] F. B. Schneider, 'Broadcasts: A paradigm for distributed programs,' Dep. Comput. Sci., Cornell Univ., Ithaca, NY, Tech. Rep. 80–440.

[20] ——, 'Synchronization in distributed programs,' *TOPLAS*, **4**, 2, 1982.

[21] F. B. Schneider, D. Gries, and R. D. Schlichting, 'Fast reliable broadcasts ,' Dep. Comput. Sci., Cornell Univ., Ithaca, NY, Tech. Rep. 82–519.

[22] W. D. Sincoskie, private communcation, Dec. 1982.

[23] T. A. Dolotta, S. B. Olsson, and A. G. Petrucelli, *UNIX User's Manual*, Bell Lab., Murray Hill, NJ, June 1980.

[24] P. Wolper, private communication, Jan. 1983.

Monitors: An Operating System Structuring Concept

C. A. R. Hoare
The Queen's University of Belfast

This paper develops Brinch Hansen's concept of a monitor as a method of structuring an operating system. It introduces a form of synchronization, describes a possible method of implementation in terms of semaphores and gives a suitable proof rule. Illustrative examples include a single resource scheduler, a bounded buffer, an alarm clock, a buffer pool, a disk head optimizer, and a version of the problem of readers and writers.

Key words and phrases: monitors, operating systems, scheduling, mutual exclusion, synchronization, system implementation languages, structured multiprogramming.

CR categories: 4.31, 4.22

1   Introduction

A primary aim of an operating system is to share a computer installation among many programs making unpredictable demands upon its resources. A primary task of its designer is therefore to construct resource allocation (or scheduling) algorithms for resources of various kinds (main store, drum store, magnetic tape handlers, consoles, etc.). In order to simplify his task, he should try to construct separate schedulers for each class of resource. Each scheduler will consist of a certain amount of local administrative data, together with some procedures and functions which are called by programs wishing to acquire and release resources. Such a collection of associated data and procedures is known as a *monitor*; and a suitable notation can be based on the *class* notation of SIMULA67 [6].

```
monitorname : monitor
    begin ... declarations of data local to the monitor;
        procedure procname (... formal parameters ...);
            begin ... procedure body ... end;
```

... declarations of other procedures local to the monitor;
... initialization of local data of the monitor ...
   end;

Note that the procedure bodies may have local data, in the normal way.

In order to call a procedure of a monitor, it is necessary to give the name of the monitor as well as the name of the desired procedure, separating them by a dot:

monitorname.procname(... actual parameters ...);

In an operating system it is sometimes desirable to declare several monitors with identical structure and behavior, for example to schedule two similar resources. In such cases, the declaration shown above will be preceded by the word **class**, and the separate monitors will be declared to belong to this class:

monitor 1, *monitor* 2 : *classname*;

Thus the structure of a class of monitors is identical to that described for a data representation in [13], except for addition of the basic word *monitor*. Brinch Hansen uses the word *shared* for the same purpose [3].

The procedures of a monitor are common to all running programs, in the sense that any program may at any time attempt to call such a procedure. However, it is essential that only one program at a time actually succeed in entering a monitor procedure, and any subsequent call must be held up until the previous call has been completed. Otherwise, if two procedure bodies were in simultaneous execution, the effects on the local variables of the monitor could be chaotic. The procedures local to a monitor should not access any nonlocal variables other than those local to the same monitor, and these variables of the monitor should be inaccessible from outside the monitor. If these restrictions are imposed, it is possible to guarantee against certain of the more obscure forms of time-dependent coding error; and this guarantee could be underwritten by a visual scan of the text of the program, which could readily be automated in a compiler.

Any dynamic resource allocator will sometimes need to delay a program wishing to acquire a resource which is not currently available, and to resume that program after some other program has released the resource required. We therefore need: a '*wait*' operation, issued from inside a procedure of the monitor, which causes the calling program to be delayed; and a '*signal*' operation, also issued from inside a procedure of the same monitor, which causes exactly one of the waiting programs to be resumed immediately. If there are no waiting programs, the signal has no effect. In order to enable other programs to release resources during a wait, a wait operation must relinquish the exclusion which would otherwise prevent entry to the releasing procedure. However, we decree that a signal operation be followed immediately by resumption of a waiting program, without possibility of an intervening procedure call from yet a third program. It is only in this way that a waiting program has an absolute guarantee that it can acquire the resource just released by the signalling program without any danger that a third program will interpose a monitor entry and seize the resource instead.

In many cases, there may be more than one reason for waiting, and these need to be distinguished by both the waiting and the signalling operation. We therefore introduce a new type of 'variable' known as a '*condition*'; and the writer of a monitor should declare a variable of type *condition* for each reason why a program might have to wait. Then the wait and signal operations should be preceded by the name of the relevant condition variable, separated from it by a dot:

> *condvariable.wait*;
> *condvariable.signal*;

Note that a condition 'variable' is neither true nor false; indeed, it does not have any stored value accessible to the program. In practice, a condition variable will be represented by an (initially empty) queue of processes which are currently waiting on the condition; but this queue is invisible both to waiters and signallers. This design of the condition variable has been deliberately kept as primitive and rudimentary as possible, so that it may be implemented efficiently and used flexibly to achieve a wide variety of effects. There is a great temptation to introduce a more complex synchronization primitive, which may be easier to use for many purposes. We shall resist this temptation for a while.

As the simplest example of a monitor, we will design a scheduling algorithm for a single resource, which is dynamically acquired and released by an unknown number of customer processes by calls on procedures:

> **procedure** *acquire*;
> **procedure** *release*;

A variable[†]:

> *busy* : *Boolean*

[†] As in Pascal [15], a variable declaration is of the form: *<variable identifier>* : *<type>*;

determines whether or not the resource is in use. If an attempt is made to acquire the resource when it is busy, the attempting program must be delayed by waiting on a variable:

nonbusy : *condition*

which is signalled by the next subsequent release. The initial value of busy is false. These design decisions lead to the following code for the monitor:

```
single resource : monitor
    begin busy : Boolean;
        nonbusy : condition;
      procedure acquire;
        begin if busy then nonbusy.wait;
                busy := true
        end;

      procedure release;
        begin busy := false;
                nonbusy.signal
        end;
        busy := false; comment initial value;
    end single resource;
```

Notes

(1) In designing a monitor, it seems natural to design the procedure headings, the data, the conditions, and the procedure bodies, in that order. All subsequent examples will be designed in this way.

(2) The *acquire* procedure does not have to retest that *busy* has gone false when it resumes after its wait, since the *release* procedure has guaranteed that this is so; and as mentioned before, no other program can intervene between the signal and the continuation of exactly one waiting program.

(3) If more than one program is waiting on a condition, we postulate that the signal operation will reactivate the longest waiting program. This gives a simple neutral queuing discipline which ensures that every waiting program will eventually get its turn.

(4) The single resource monitor simulates a Boolean semaphore [7] with *acquire* and *release* used for *P* and *V* respectively. This is a simple proof that the monitor/condition concepts are not in principle less powerful than semaphores, and that they can be used for all the same purposes.

2 Interpretation

Having proved that semaphores can be implemented by a monitor, the next task is to prove that monitors can be implemented by semaphores.

Obviously, we shall require for each monitor a Boolean semaphore '*mutex*' to ensure that the bodies of the local procedures exclude each other. The semaphore is initialized to 1; a $P(mutex)$ must be executed on entry to each local procedure, and a $V(mutex)$ must usually be executed on exit from it.

When a process signals a condition on which another process is waiting, the signalling process must wait until the resumed process permits it to proceed. We therefore introduce for each monitor a second semaphore '*urgent*' (initialized to 0), on which signalling processes suspend themselves by the operation P (*urgent*). Before releasing exclusion, each process must test whether any other process is waiting on *urgent*, and if so, must release *urgent* instead by a $V(urgent)$ instruction. We therefore need to count the number of processes waiting on *urgent*, in an integer '*urgentcount*' (initially zero). Thus each exit from a procedure of a monitor should be coded:

> **if** *urgentcount* $>$ 0 **then** $V(urgent)$ **else** $V(mutex)$

Finally, for each condition local to the monitor, we introduce a semaphore '*condsem*' (initialized to 0), on which a process desiring to wait suspends itself by a $P(condsem)$ operation. Since a process signalling this condition needs to know whether anybody is waiting, we also need a count of the number of waiting processes held in an integer variable '*condcount*' (initially 0). The operation '*cond.wait*' may now be implemented as follows (recall that a waiting program must release exclusion before suspending itself):

> *condcount* := *condcount* + 1;
> **if** *urgentcount* $>$ 0 **then** $V(urgent)$ **else** $V(mutex)$;
> $P(condsem)$;
> **comment** This will always wait;
> *condcount* := *condcount* − 1

The signal operation may be coded:

> *urgentcount* := *urgentcount* + 1;
> **if** *condcount* $>$ 0 **then** $\{V(condsem); P(urgent)\}$;
> *urgentcount* := *urgentcount* − 1

In this implementation, possession of the monitor is regarded as a privilege which is explicitly passed from one process to another. Only when no one further wants the privilege is *mutex* finally released.

This solution is not intended to correspond to recommended 'style' in the use of semaphores. The concept of a condition-variable is intended as a substitute for semaphores, and has its own style of usage, in the same way that while-loops or coroutines are intended as a substitute for jumps.

In many cases, the generality of this solution is unnecessary, and a significant improvement in efficiency is possible.

(1) When a procedure body in a monitor contains no wait or signal, exit from the body can be coded by a simple $V(mutex)$, since *urgentcount* cannot have changed during the execution of the body.

(2) If a *cond.signal* is the last operation of a procedure body, it can be combined with monitor exit as follows:

> **if** *condcount* > 0 **then** $V(condsem)$
> **else if** *urgentcount* > 0 **then** $V(urgent)$ **else** $V(mutex)$

(3) If there is no other wait or signal in the procedure body, the second line shown above can also be omitted.

(4) If *every* signal occurs as the last operation of its procedure body, the variables *urgentcount* and *urgent* can be omitted, together with all operations upon them. This is such a simplification that O-J. Dahl suggests that signals should always be the last operation of a monitor procedure; in fact, this restriction is a very natural one, which has been unwittingly observed in all examples of this paper.

Significant improvements in efficiency may also be obtained by avoiding the use of semaphores, and by implementing conditions directly in hardware, or at the lowest and most uninterruptible level of software (e.g., supervisor mode). In this case, the following optimizations are possible.

(1) *urgentcount* and *condcount* can be abolished, since the fact that someone is waiting can be established by examining the representation of the semaphore, which cannot change surreptitiously within noninterruptible mode.

(2) Many monitors are very short and contain no calls to other monitors. Such monitors can be executed wholly in noninterruptible mode, using, as it were, the common exclusion mechanism provided by hardware. This will often involve *less* time in noninterruptible mode than the establishment of separate exclusion for each monitor.

I am grateful to J. Bezivin, J. Horning, and R.M. McKeag for assisting in the discovery of this algorithm.

3   Proof rules

The analogy between a monitor and a data representation has been noted in the introduction. The mutual exclusion on the code of a monitor ensures that procedure calls follow each other in time, just as they do in sequential programming; and the same restrictions are placed on access to nonlocal data. These are the reasons why the same proof rules can be applied to monitors as to data representations.

As with a data representation, the programmer may associate an invariant $\mathscr{I}$ with the local data of a monitor, to describe some condition which will be true of this data before and after every procedure call. $\mathscr{I}$ must also be made true after initialization of the data, and before *every* wait instruction; otherwise the next following procedure call will not find the local data in a state which it expects.

With each condition variable b the programmer may associate an assertion B which describes the condition under which a program waiting on b wishes to be resumed. Since other programs may invoke a monitor procedure during a wait, a waiting program must ensure that the invariant $\mathscr{I}$ for the monitor is true beforehand. This gives the proof rule for waits:

$$\mathscr{I}\{b.wait\}\,\mathscr{I}\,\&\,B$$

Since a signal can cause immediate resumption of a waiting program, the conditions $\mathscr{I}\,\&\,B$ which are expected by that program must be made true before the signal; and since B may be made false again by the resumed program, only $\mathscr{I}$ may be assumed true afterwards. Thus the proof rule for a signal is:

$$\mathscr{I}\,\&\,B\,\{b.signal\}\,\mathscr{I}$$

This exhibits a pleasing symmetry with the rule for waiting.

The introduction of condition variables makes it possible to write monitors subject to the risk of deadly embrace [7]. It is the responsibility of the programmer to avoid this risk, together with other scheduling disasters (thrashing, indefinitely repeated overtaking, etc. [11]). Assertion-oriented proof methods cannot prove absence of such risks; perhaps it is better to use less formal methods for such proofs.

Finally, in many cases an operating system monitor constructs some 'virtual' resource which is used in place of actual resources by its 'customer' programs. This virtual resource is an abstraction from the set of local variables of the monitor. The program prover should therefore define this abstraction in terms of its concrete representation, and then express the intended effect of each of the procedure bodies in terms of the abstraction. This proof method is described in detail in [13].

4 Example: Bounded buffer

A bounded buffer is a concrete representation of the abstract idea of a sequence of portions. The sequence is accessible to two programs running in parallel: the first of these (the producer) updates the sequence by appending a new portion x at the end; and the second (the consumer) updates it by removing the first portion. The initial value of the sequence is empty. We thus require two operations:

(1) *append*(x : *portion*);

which should be equivalent to the abstract operation:

$$sequence := sequence \cap <x>;$$

where $<x>$ is the sequence whose only item is x and $\cap$ denotes concatenation of two sequences.

(2) *remove*(**result** x : *portion*);

which should be equivalent to the abstract operations:

$$x := first(sequence); sequence := rest(sequence);$$

where *first* selects the first item of a sequence and *rest* denotes the sequence with its first item removed. Obviously, if the sequence is empty, *first* is undefined; and in this case we want to ensure that the consumer waits until the producer has made the sequence non-empty.

We shall assume that the amount of time taken to produce a portion or consume it is large in comparison with the time taken to append or remove it from the sequence. We may therefore be justified in making a design in which producer and consumer can both update the sequence, but not simultaneously.

The sequence is represented by an array:

$$buffer : \textbf{array } 0..N - 1 \textbf{ of } portion;$$

and two variables:

(1) *lastpointer* : $0..N - 1$;

which points to the buffer position into which the next append operation will put a new item; and

(2) *count* : $0..N$;

which always holds the length of the sequence (initially 0).

We define the function:

$$seq(b, l, c) =_{df} \textbf{if } c = 0 \textbf{ then } empty$$
$$\textbf{else } seq(b, l \ominus 1, c - 1) \cap \langle b[l \ominus 1] \rangle$$

where the circled operations are taken modulo N. Note that if $c \neq 0$:

$$first(seq(b, l, c)) = b[l \ominus c]$$

and:

$$rest(seq(b, l, c)) = seq(b, l, c - 1)$$

The definition of the abstract sequence in terms of its concrete representation may now be given:

$$sequence =_{df} seq(buffer, lastpointer, count)$$

Less formally, this may be written:

$$sequence =_{df} <buffer[lastpointer \ominus count],$$
$$buffer[lastpointer \ominus count \oplus 1],$$
$$...,$$
$$buffer[lastpointer \ominus 1]>$$

Another way of conveying this information would be by an example and a picture, which would be even less formal.

The invariant for the monitor is:

$$0 \leq count \leq N \ \& \ 0 \leq lastpointer \leq N - 1$$

There are two reasons for waiting, which must be represented by condition variables:

$$nonempty : condition;$$

means that the count is greater than 0, and:

$$nonfull : condition;$$

means that the count is less than N.

With this constructive approach to the design [8], it is relatively easy to code the monitor without error.

```
bounded buffer : monitor
  begin buffer : array 0..N − 1 of portion;
        lastpointer : 0..N − 1;
        count : 0..N;
        nonempty, nonfull : condition;

    procedure append(x : portion);
      begin if count = N then nonfull.wait;
            note 0 ≤ count < N;
            buffer[lastpointer] := x;
            lastpointer := lastpointer ⊕ 1;
            count := count + 1;
            nonempty.signal
      end append;

    procedure remove(result x : portion);
      begin if count = 0 then nonempty.wait;
            note 0 < count ≤ N;
            x := buffer[lastpointer ⊖ count];
            nonfull.signal
      end remove;
      count := 0; lastpointer := 0;
  end bounded buffer;
```

A formal proof of the correctness of this monitor with respect to the stated abstraction and invariant can be given if desired by techniques described in [13]. However, these techniques seem not capable of dealing with subsequent examples of this paper.

Single-buffered input and output may be regarded as a special case of the bounded buffer with $N = 1$. In this case, the array can be replaced by a single variable, the *lastpointer* is redundant, and we get:

```
iostream : monitor
begin buffer : portion;
      count : 0..1;
      nonempty, nonfull : condition;

  procedure append(x : portion);
    begin if count = 1 then nonfull.wait;
      buffer := x;
      count := 1;
      nonempty.signal
    end append;

  procedure remove(result x : portion);
    begin if count = 0 then nonempty.wait;
      x := buffer;
      count := 0;
      nonfull.signal
    end remove;
    count := 0;
end iostream;
```

If physical output is carried out by a separate special purpose channel, then the interrupt from the channel should simulate a call of *iostream.remove*(x); and similarly for physical input, simulating a call of *iostream.append*(x).

5 Scheduled waits

Up to this point, we have assumed that when more than one program is waiting for the same condition, a signal will cause the longest waiting program to be resumed. This is a good simple scheduling strategy, which precludes indefinite overtaking of a waiting process.

However, in the design of an operating system, there are many cases when such simple scheduling on the basis of first-come-first-served is not adequate. In order to give a closer control over scheduling strategy, we introduce a further feature of a conditional wait, which makes it possible to specify as a parameter of the wait some indication of the priority of the waiting program, e.g.:

busy.wait(p);

When the condition is signalled, it is the program that specified the lowest value of p that is resumed. In using this facility, the designer of a monitor must take care to avoid the risk of indefinite overtaking; and often it is advisable to make priority a nondecreasing function of the time at which the wait commences.

This introduction of a 'scheduled wait' concedes to the temptation to make the condition concept more elaborate. The main justifications are:

(1) It has no effect whatsoever on the *logic* of a program, or on the formal proof rules. Any program which works without a scheduled wait will work with it, but possibly with better timing characteristics.

(2) The automatic ordering of the queue of waiting processes is a simple fast scheduling technique, except when the queue is exceptionally long – and when it is, central processor time is not the major bottleneck.

(3) The maximum amount of storage required is one word per process. Without such a built-in scheduling method, each monitor may have to allocate storage proportional to the number of its customers; the alternative of dynamic storage allocation in small chunks is unattractive at the low level of an operating system where monitors are found.

I shall yield to one further temptation, to introduce a Boolean function of conditions:

condname.queue

which yields the value true if anyone is waiting on *condname* and false otherwise. This can obviously be easily implemented by a couple of instructions, and affords valuable information which could otherwise be obtained only at the expense of extra storage, time, and trouble.

A trivially simple example is an *alarmclock* monitor, which enables a calling program to delay itself for a stated number n of time-units, or '*ticks*'. There are two entries:

procedure *wakeme*(n : *integer*);
procedure *tick*;

The second of these is invoked by hardware (e.g., an interrupt) at regular intervals, say ten times per second. Local variables are:

now : *integer*;

which records the current time (initially zero) and

wakeup : *condition*;

on which sleeping programs wait. But the *alarmsetting* at which these programs will be aroused is known at the time when they start the wait; and this can be used to determine the correct sequence of waking up.

```
alarmclock : monitor
begin now : integer;
      wakeup : condition;

   procedure wakeme(n : integer);
      begin alarmsetting : integer;
         alarmsetting := now + n;
         while now < alarmsetting do wakeup.wait(alarmsetting);
         wakeup.signal;
         comment In case the next process is due to wake up at the same time;
      end;

   procedure tick;
      begin now := now + 1;
         wakeup.signal
      end;
   now := 0
end alarmclock
```

In the program given above, the next candidate for wakening is actually woken at every tick of the clock. This will not matter if the frequency of ticking is low enough, and the overhead of an accepted signal is not too high.

I am grateful to A. Ballard and J. Horning for posing this problem.

6   Further examples

In proposing a new feature for a high-level language it is very difficult to make a convincing case that the feature will be both easy to use efficiently and easy to implement efficiently. Quality of implementation can be proved by a single good example, but ease and efficiency of use require a great number of realistic examples; otherwise it can appear that the new feature has been specially designed to suit the examples, or vice versa. This section contains a number of additional examples of solutions of familiar problems. Further examples may be found in [14].

6.1   Buffer allocation

The bounded buffer described in Section 4 was designed to be suitable only for sequences with small portions, for example, message queues. If the buffers contain high volume information (for example, files for pseudo offline input and output), the bounded buffer may still be used to store the *addresses* of the buffers which are being used to hold the information. In this way, the producer can be filling one buffer while the consumer is emptying another buffer of the same sequence. But this requires an allocator for dynamic acquisition and relinquishment of *buffer addresses*. These may be declared as a type:

   type *bufferaddress* = 1..*B*;

where *B* is the number of buffers available for allocation.

   The buffer allocator has two entries:

   procedure *acquire*(**result** *b* : *bufferaddress*);

which delivers a free *bufferaddress b*; and

   procedure *release*(*b* : *bufferaddress*);

which returns a *bufferaddress* when it is no longer required. In order to keep a record of free buffer addresses the monitor will need:

   freepool : **powerset** *bufferaddress*;

which uses the Pascal **powerset** facility to define a variable whose values range over all sets of *buffer addresses*, from the empty set to the set containing all *buffer addresses*. It should be implemented as a *bitmap* of *B* consecutive bits, where the *i*th bit is 1 if and only if *i* is in the set. There is only one condition variable needed:

nonempty : *condition*;

which means that *freepool* ≠ *empty*. The code for the allocator is:

```
buffer allocator : monitor
begin freepool : powerset bufferaddress;
      nonempty : condition;

   procedure acquire (result b : bufferaddress);
      begin if freepool = empty then nonempty.wait;
        b := first(freepool);
        comment Any one would do;
        freepool := freepool − {b};
        comment Set subtraction;
      end acquire;

   procedure release(b : bufferaddress);
      begin freepool := freepool − {b};
        nonempty.signal
      end release;
      freepool := all buffer addresses

end buffer allocator
```

The action of a producer and consumer may be summarized:

```
producer :    begin b : bufferaddress; ...
                while not finished do
                   begin bufferallocator.acquire(b);
                   ... fill buffer b ...;
                   bounded buffer.append(b)
                   end; ...
                end producer;

consumer :   begin b : bufferaddress; ...
                while not finished do
                   begin bounded buffer.remove(b);
                   ... empty buffer b ...;
                   buffer allocator.release(b)
                   end; ...
                end consumer;
```

This buffer allocator would appear to be usable to share the buffers among several streams, each with its own producer and its own consumer, and its own instance of a bounded buffer monitor. Unfortunately, when the streams operate at widely varying speeds, and when the freepool is empty, the scheduling algorithm can exhibit persistent undesirable behavior. If two producers are competing for each buffer as it becomes free, then the first-come-first-served discipline of allocation will ensure (apparently fairly) that each gets alternate buffers; and they will consequently begin to produce at equal speeds. But if one consumer is a 1000 lines/min printer and the other is a 10 lines/min teletype, the faster consumer will be eventually reduced to the speed of the slower, since it cannot forever go faster than its producer. At this stage nearly all buffers will belong to the slower stream, so the situation could take a long time to clear.

A solution to this is to use a scheduled wait, to ensure that in heavy load conditions the available buffers will be shared reasonably fairly between the streams that are competing for them. Of course, inactive streams need not be considered, and streams for which the consumer is currently faster than the producer will never ask for more than two buffers anyway. In order to achieve fairness in allocation, it is sufficient to allocate a newly freed buffer to that one among the competing producers whose stream currently owns fewest buffers. Thus the system will seek a point as far away from the undesirable extreme as possible.

For this reason, the entries to the allocator should indicate for what stream the buffer is to be (or has been) used, and the allocator must keep a count of the current allocation to each stream in an array:

   count : **array** *stream* **of** *integer*;

The new version of the allocator is:

```
bufferallocator : monitor
   begin free pool : powerset bufferaddress;
         nonempty : condition;
         count : array stream of integer;

      procedure acquire(result b : bufferaddress; s : stream);
         begin if freepool = empty then nonempty.wait(count[s]);
            count[s] := count[s] + 1;
            b := first(freepool);
            freepool := freepool − {b}
         end acquire;

      procedure release(b : bufferaddress; s : stream);
         begin count[s] := count[s] − 1;
            freepool := freepool − {b};
            nonempty.signal
         end;
         freepool := all buffer addresses;
         for s : stream do count[s] := 0
   end bufferallocator
```

Of course, if a consumer stops altogether, perhaps owing to mechanical failure, the producer must also be halted before it has acquired too many buffers, even if no one else currently wants them. This can perhaps be most easily accomplished by appropriate fixing of the size of the bounded buffer for that stream and/or by ensuring that at least two buffers are reserved for each stream, even when inactive. It is an interesting comment on dynamic resource allocation that, as soon as resources are heavily loaded, the system must be designed to fall back toward a more static regime.

I am grateful to E.W. Dijkstra for pointing out this problem and its solution [10].

6.2 Disk head scheduler

On a moving head disk, the time taken to move the heads increases monotonically with the distance traveled. If several programs wish to move the heads, the average waiting time can be reduced by selecting, first, the program which wishes to move them the shortest distance. But unfortunately this policy is subject to an instability, since a program wishing to access a cylinder at one edge of the disk can be indefinitely overtaken by programs operating at the other edge or the middle.

A solution to this is to minimize the frequency of change of direction of movement of the heads. At any time, the heads are kept moving in a given direction, and they service the program requesting the nearest cylinder in that direction. If there is no such request, the direction changes, and the heads make another sweep across the surface of the disk. This may be called the 'elevator' algorithm, since it simulates the behavior of a lift in a multi-storey building.

There are two entries to a disk head scheduler:

(1) *request*(*dest* : *cylinder*);

where
type *cylinder* = 0..*cylmax*;

which is entered by a program just *before* issuing the instruction to move the heads to cylinder *dest*.

(2) *release*;

which is entered by a program when it has made all the transfers it needs on the current cylinder.

The local data of the monitor must include a record of the current headposition, *headpos*, the current direction of *sweep*, and whether the disk is *busy*:

headpos : *cylinder*;
direction : (*up, down*);
busy : *Boolean*

We need two conditions, one for requests waiting for an *upsweep* and the other for requests waiting for a *downsweep*:

upsweep, downsweep : condition;

diskhead : **monitor**
begin *headpos* : *cylinder*;
    direction : (*up, down*);
    busy : *Boolean*;
    upsweep, downsweep : *condition*;

    procedure *request*(*dest* : *cylinder*);
      begin if *busy* **then**
        {**if** *headpos* < *dest* ∨ *headpos* = *dest* & *direction* = *up*
        then *upsweep.wait*(*dest*)
        else *downsweep.wait*(*cylmax* – *dest*)};
        busy := *true*; *headpos* := *dest*
      end *request*;

    procedure *release*;
      begin *busy* := *false*;
      if *direction* = *up* **then**
        {**if** *upsweep.queue* **then** *upsweep.signal*
                 else {*direction* := *down*;
                          downsweep.signal}}
        else if *downsweep.queue* **then** *downsweep.signal*
                   else {*direction* := *up*;
                       upsweep.signal}
      end *release*;
    headpos := 0; *direction* := *up*; *busy* := *false*

end *diskhead*;

6.3 Readers and writers

As a more significant example, we take a problem which arises in on-line real-time applications such as airspace control. Suppose that each aircraft is represented by a record, and that this record is kept up to date by a number of 'writer' processes and accessed by a number of 'reader' processes. Any number of 'reader' processes may simultaneously access the same record, but obviously any process which is updating (writing) the individual components of the record must have exclusive access to it, or chaos will ensue. Thus we need a class of monitors; an instance of this class local to *each* individual aircraft record will enforce the required discipline for that record. If there are many aircraft, there is a strong motivation for minimizing local data of the monitor; and if each read or write operation is brief, we should also minimize the time taken by each monitor entry.

When many readers are interested in a single aircraft record, there is a danger that a writer will be indefinitely prevented from keeping that record up to date. We therefore decide that a new reader should not be permitted to start if there is a writer waiting. Similarly, to avoid the danger of indefinite exclusion of readers, all readers waiting at the end of a write should have priority over the next writer. Note that this is a very different scheduling rule from that propounded in [4], and does not seem to require such subtlety in implementation. Nevertheless, it may be more suited to this kind of application, where it is better to read stale information than to wait indefinitely!

The monitor obviously requires four local procedures:

startread	entered by reader who wishes to read.
endread	entered by reader who has finished reading.
startwrite	entered by reader who wishes to write.
endwrite	entered by reader who has finished writing.

We need to keep a count of the number of users who are reading, so that the last reader to finish will know this fact:

   readercount : *integer*

We also need a *Boolean* to indicate that someone is actually writing:

   busy : *Boolean*;

We introduce separate conditions for readers and writers to wait on:

   OKtoread, OKtowrite : *condition*;

The following annotation is relevant:

   $OKtoread \equiv \neg busy$
   $OKtowrite \equiv \neg busy \ \& \ readercount = 0$
   invariant : $busy \Rightarrow readercount = 0$

   class *readers and writers* : **monitor**
      begin *readercount* : *integer*;
            busy : *Boolean*;
            OKtoread, OKtowrite : *condition*;

         procedure *startread*;
            begin if *busy* $\vee$ *OKtowrite.queue* **then** *OKtoread.wait*;
               readercount := *readercount* + 1;
               OKtoread.signal;
               comment Once one reader can start, they all can;
            end *startread*;

```
procedure endread;
  begin readercount := readercount − 1;
    if readercount = 0 then OKtowrite.signal
  end endread;

procedure startwrite;
  begin
    if readercount ≠ 0 ∨ busy then OKtowrite.wait;
    busy := true
  end startwrite;

procedure endwrite;
  begin busy := false;
    if OKtoread.queue then OKtoread.signal
                      else OKtowrite.signal
  end endwrite;
  readercount := 0;
  busy := false;

end readers and writers;
```

I am grateful to Dave Gorman for assisting in the discovery of this solution.

7 Conclusion

This paper suggests that an appropriate structure for a module of an operating system, which schedules resources for parallel user processes, is very similar to that of a data representation used by a sequential program. However, in the case of monitors, the bodies of the procedures must be protected against re-entrance by being implemented as critical regions. The textual grouping of critical regions together with the data which they update seems much superior to critical regions scattered through the user program, as described in [7, 12]. It also corresponds to the traditional practice of the writers of operating system supervisors. It can be recommended without reservation.

However, it is much more difficult to be confident about the condition concept as a synchronizing primitive. The synchronizing facility which is easiest to use is probably the conditional *wait* [2, 12]:

wait(B);

where B is a general Boolean expression (it causes the given process to wait until B becomes true); but this may be too inefficient for general use in operating systems, because its implementation requires re-evaluation of the expression B after every exit from a procedure of the monitor. The condition variable gives the programmer better control over efficiency and over scheduling; it was designed to be very primitive, and to have a simple proof rule. But perhaps some other compromise between convenience and efficiency might be better. The question whether the signal should always be the last operation of a monitor procedure is still open. These problems will be studied in the design and implementation of a pilot project operating system, currently enjoying the support of the Science Research Council of Great Britain.

Another question which will be studied will be that of the disjointness of monitors: Is it possible to design a separate isolated monitor for each kind of resource, so that it will make sensible scheduling decisions for that resource, using only the minimal information about the utilization of that resource, and using no information about the utilization of any resource administered by other monitors? In principle, it would seem that, when more knowledge of the status of the entire system is available, it should be easier to take decisions nearer to optimality. Furthermore, in principle, independent scheduling of different kinds of resource can lead to deadly embrace. These considerations would lead to the design of a traditional 'monolithic' monitor, maintaining large system tables, all of which can be accessed and updated by any of the procedures of the monitor.

There is no a priori reason why the attempt to split the functions of an operating system into a number of isolated disjoint monitors should succeed. It can be made to succeed only by discovering and implementing good scheduling algorithms in each monitor. In order to avoid undesirable interactions between the separate scheduling algorithms, it appears necessary to observe the following principles:

(1) Never seek to make an optimal decision; merely seek to avoid persistently pessimal decisions.

(2) Do not seek to present the user with a virtual machine which is better than the actual hardware; merely seek to pass on the speed, size, and flat unopiniated structure of a simple hardware design.

(3) Use preemptive techniques in preference to non-preemptive ones where possible.

(4) Use 'grain of time' [9] methods to secure independence of scheduling strategies.

(5) Keep a low variance (as well as a low mean) on waiting times.

(6) Avoid fixed priorities; instead, try to ensure that every program in the system makes reasonably steady progress. In particular, avoid indefinite overtaking.

(7) Ensure that when demand for resources outstrips the supply (i.e., in overload conditions), the behavior of the scheduler is satisfactory (i.e., thrashing is avoided).

(8) Make rules for the correct and sensible use of monitor calls, and assume that user programs will obey them. Any checking which is necessary should be done not by a central shared monitor, but rather by an algorithm (called 'user envelope') which is local to each process executing a user program. This algorithm should be implemented at least partially in the hardware (e.g., base and range registers, address translation mechanisms, capabilities, etc.).

It is the possibility of constructing separate monitors for different purposes, and of separating the scheduling decisions embodied in monitors from the checking embodied in user envelopes, that may justify a hope that monitors are an appropriate concept for the structuring of an operating system.

Acknowledgments

The development of the monitor concept is due to frequent discussions and communications with E.W. Dijkstra and P. Brinch Hansen. A monitor corresponds to the 'secretary' described in [9], and is also described in [1, 3].

Acknowledgment is also due to the support of IFIP WG.2. 3., which provides a meeting place at which these and many other ideas have been germinated, fostered, and tested.

References

[1]   Brinch Hansen, P. Structured multiprogramming. *Comm. ACM* **15**, 7 (July 1972), 574–577.

[2]   Brinch Hansen, P. A comparison of two synchronizing concepts. *Acta Informatica* **1** (1972), 190–199.

[3]   Brinch Hansen, P. *Operating System Principles*. Prentice-Hall, Englewood Cliffs, N.J., 1973.

[4]   Courtois, P.J., Heymans, F., Parnas, D.L. Concurrent control with readers and writers. *Comm. ACM* **14**, 10 (Oct. 1971), 667–668.

[5]   Courtois, P.J., Heymans, F., Parnas, D.L. Comments on [2]. *Acta Informatica* **1** (1972), 375–376.

[6]   Dahl, O.J. Hierarchical program structures. In *Structured Programming*. Academic Press, New York, 1972.

[7]   Dijkstra, E.W. Cooperating Sequential Processes. In *Programming Languages* (Ed. F. Genuys). Academic Press, New York, 1968.

[8]   Dijkstra, E.W. A constructive approach to the problem of program correctness. *BIT* **8** (1968), 174–186.

[9]   Dijkstra, E.W. Hierarchical ordering of sequential processes. In *Operating Systems Techniques*. Academic Press, New York, 1972.

[10]   Dijkstra, E.W. Information streams sharing a finite buffer. *Information Processing Letters* **1**, 5 (Oct. 1972), 179–180.

[11]   Dijkstra, E.W. A class of allocation strategies inducing bounded delays only. Proc AFIPS 1972 SJCC, **40**, AFIPS Press, Montvale, N.J., pp. 933–936.

[12]   Hoare, C.A.R. Towards a theory of parallel programming. In *Operating Systems Techniques*. Academic Press, New York, 1972.

[13]   Hoare, C.A.R. Proof of correctness of data representations. *Acta Informatica* **1** (1972), 271–281.

[14]   Hoare, C.A.R. A structured paging system. *Computer J.* **16**, 3 (1973), 209–215.

[15]   Wirth, N. The programming language PASCAL. *Acta Informatica* **1**, 1 (1971), 35–63.

11

Communicating Sequential Processes

C. A. R. Hoare
The Queen's University of Belfast

This paper suggests that input and output are basic primitives of programming and that parallel composition of communicating sequential processes is a fundamental program structuring method. When combined with a development of Dijkstra's guarded command, these concepts are surprisingly versatile. Their use is illustrated by sample solutions of a variety of familiar programming exercises.

Key words and phrases: programming, programming languages, programming primitives, program structures, parallel programming, concurrency, input, output, guarded commands, nondeterminacy, coroutines, procedures, multiple entries, multiple exits, classes, data representations, recursion, conditional critical regions, monitors, iterative arrays.

CR categories: 4.20, 4.22, 4.32.

1   Introduction

Among the primitive concepts of computer programming, and of the high-level languages in which programs are expressed, the action of assignment is familiar and well understood. In fact, any change of the internal state of a machine executing a program can be modeled as an assignment of a new value to some variable part of that machine. However, the operations of input and output, which affect the external environment of a machine, are not nearly so well understood. They are often added to a programming language only as an afterthought.

Among the structuring methods for computer programs, three basic constructs have received widespread recognition and use: A repetitive

---

This research was supported by a Senior Fellowship of the Science Research Council.

construct (e.g. the **while** loop), an alternative construct (e.g. the conditional **if..then..else**), and normal sequential program composition (often denoted by a semicolon). Less agreement has been reached about the design of other important program structures, and many suggestions have been made: subroutines (Fortran), procedures (Algol 60 [15]), entries (PL/I), coroutines (UNIX [17]), classes (SIMULA 67 [5]), processes and monitors (Concurrent Pascal [2]), clusters (CLU [13]), forms (ALPHARD [19]), actors (Hewitt [1]).

The traditional stored program digital computer has been designed primarily for deterministic execution of a single sequential program. Where the desire for greater speed has led to the introduction of parallelism, every attempt has been made to disguise this fact from the programmer, either by hardware itself (as in the multiple function units of the CDC 6600) or by the software (as in an I/O control package, or a multiprogrammed operating system). However, developments of processor technology suggest that a multiprocessor machine, constructed from a number of similar self-contained processors (each with its own store), may become more powerful, capacious, reliable, and economical than a machine which is disguised as a monoprocessor.

In order to use such a machine effectively on a single task, the component processors must be able to communicate and to synchronize with each other. Many methods of achieving this have been proposed. A widely adopted method of communication is by inspection and updating of a common store (as in Algol 68 [18], PL/I, and many machine codes). However, this can create severe problems in the construction of correct programs and it may lead to expense (e.g. crossbar switches) and unreliability (e.g. glitches) in some technologies of hardware implementation. A greater variety of methods has been proposed for synchronization: semaphores [6], events (PL/I), conditional critical regions [10], monitors and queues (Concurrent Pascal [2]), and path expressions [3]. Most of these are demonstrably adequate for their purpose, but there is no widely recognized criterion for choosing between them.

This paper makes an ambitious attempt to find a single simple solution to all these problems. The essential proposals are:

(1) Dijkstra's guarded commands [8] are adopted (with a slight change of notation) as sequential control structures, and as the sole means of introducing and controlling nondeterminism.

(2) A parallel command, based on Dijkstra's *parbegin* [6], specifies concurrent execution of its constituent sequential commands (processes). All the processes start simultaneously, and the parallel command ends only when they are all finished. They may not communicate with each other by updating global variables.

(3) Simple forms of input and output command are introduced. They are used for communication between concurrent processes.

(4) Such communication occurs when one process names another as destination for output *and* the second process names the first as source for input. In this case, the value to be output is copied from the first process to the second. There is *no* automatic buffering: In general, an input or output command is delayed until the other process is ready with the corresponding output or input. Such delay is invisible to the delayed process.

(5) Input commands may appear in guards. A guarded command with an input guard is selected for execution only if and when the source named in the input command is ready to execute the corresponding output command. If several input guards of a set of alternatives have ready destinations, only one is selected and the others have *no* effect; but the choice between them is arbitrary. In an efficient implementation, an output command which has been ready for a long time should be favored; but the definition of a language cannot specify this since the relative speed of execution of the processes is undefined.

(6) A repetitive command may have input guards. If all the sources named by them have terminated, then the repetitive command also terminates.

(7) A simple pattern-matching feature, similar to that of [16], is used to discriminate the structure of an input message, and to access its components in a secure fashion. This feature is used to inhibit input of messages that do not match the specified pattern.

The programs expressed in the proposed language are intended to be implementable both by a conventional machine with a single main store, and by a fixed network of processors connected by input/output channels (although very different optimizations are appropriate in the different cases). It is consequently a rather static language: The text of a program determines a fixed upper bound on the number of processes operating concurrently; there is no recursion and no facility for process-valued variables. In other respects also, the language has been stripped to the barest minimum necessary for explanation of its more novel features.

The concept of a communicating sequential process is shown in Sections 3–5 to provide a method of expressing solutions to many simple programming exercises which have previously been employed to illustrate the use of various proposed programming language features. This suggests that the process may constitute a synthesis of a number of familiar and new programming ideas. The reader is invited to skip the examples which do not interest him.

However, this paper also ignores many serious problems. The most serious is that it fails to suggest any proof method to assist in the development and verification of correct programs. Secondly, it pays no attention to the problems of efficient implementation, which may be particularly serious on a traditional sequential computer. It is probable that a solution to these problems will require:

(1) imposition of restrictions in the use of the proposed features;

(2) reintroduction of distinctive notations for the most common and useful special cases;

(3) development of automatic optimization techniques; and

(4) the design of appropriate hardware.

Thus the concepts and notations introduced in this paper (although described in the next section in the form of a programming language fragment) should not be regarded as suitable for use as a programming language, either for abstract or for concrete programming. They are at best only a partial solution to the problems tackled. Further discussion of these and other points will be found in Section 7.

2   Concepts and notations

The style of the following description is borrowed from Algol 60 [15]. Types, declarations, and expressions have not been treated; in the examples, a Pascal-like notation [20] has usually been adopted. The curly braces { } have been introduced into BNF to denote none or more repetitions of the enclosed material. (Sentences in parentheses refer to an implementation: they are not strictly part of a language definition.)

```
<command> ::= <simple command>|<structured command>
<simple command> ::= <null command>|<assignment command>
     |<input command>|<output command>
<structured command> ::= <alternative command>
     |<repetitive command>|<parallel command>
<null command> ::= skip
<command list> ::= {<declaration>;|<command>;} <command>
```

A command specifies the behavior of a device executing the command. It may succeed or fail. Execution of a simple command, if successful, may have an effect on the internal state of the executing device (in the case of assignment), or on its external environment (in the case of output), or on both (in the case of input). Execution of a structured command involves execution of some or all of its constituent commands, and if any of these fail, so does the structured command. (In this case, whenever possible, an implementation should provide some kind of comprehensible error diagnostic message.)

A null command has no effect and never fails.

A command list specifies sequential execution of its constituent commands in the order written. Each declaration introduces a fresh variable with a scope which extends from its declaration to the end of the command list.

2.1 Parallel commands

<parallel command> ::= [<process>{‖<process>}]
<process> ::= <process label> <command list>
<process label> ::= <empty>|<identifier> ::
        |<identifier>(<label subscript>{,<label subscript>}) ::
<label subscript> ::= <integer constant>|<range>
<integer constant> ::= <numeral>|<bound variable>
<bound variable> ::= <identifier>
<range> ::= <bound variable>:<lower bound>..<upper bound>
<lower bound> ::= <integer constant>
<upper bound> ::= <integer constant>

Each process of a parallel command must be *disjoint* from every other process of the command, in the sense that it does not mention any variable which occurs as a target variable (see Sections 2.2 and 2.3) in any other process.

A process label without subscripts, or one whose label subscripts are all integer constants, serves as a name for the command list to which it is prefixed; its scope extends over the whole of the parallel command. A process whose label subscripts include one or more ranges stands for a series of processes, each with the same label and command list, except that each has a different combination of values substituted for the bound variables. These values range between the lower bound and the upper bound inclusive. For example, $X(i : 1..n) :: \text{CL}$ stands for:

$$X(1) :: \text{CL}_1 \| X(2) :: \text{CL}_2 \| ... \| X(n) :: \text{CL}_n$$

where each CL_j is formed from CL by replacing every occurrence of the bound variable i by the numeral j. After all such expansions, each process label in a parallel command must occur only once and the processes must be well formed and disjoint.

A parallel command specifies concurrent execution of its constituent processes. They all start simultaneously and the parallel command terminates successfully only if and when they have all successfully terminated. The relative speed with which they are executed is arbitrary.

Examples

(1) [cardreader?cardimage‖lineprinter!lineimage]

Performs the two constituent commands in parallel, and terminates only when both operations are complete. The time taken may be as low as the longer of the times taken by each constituent process, i.e. the sum of its computing, waiting, and transfer times.

(2)   [west :: DISASSEMBLE‖X :: SQUASH‖east :: ASSEMBLE]

The three processes have the names 'west,' 'X,' and 'east.' The capitalized words stand for command lists which will be defined in later examples.

(3)   [room :: ROOM‖fork(i : 0..4) :: FORK‖phil(i : 0..4) :: PHIL]

There are eleven processes. The behavior of 'room' is specified by the command list ROOM. The behavior of the five processes fork(0), fork(1), fork(2), fork(3), fork(4), is specified by the command list FORK, within which the bound variable i indicates the identity of the particular fork. Similar remarks apply to the five processes PHIL.

2.2   Assignment commands

<assignment command> ::= <target variable> ::= <expression>
<expression> ::= <simple expression>|<structured expression>
<structured expression> ::= <constructor>(<expression list>)
<constructor> ::= <identifier>|<empty>
<expression list> ::= <empty>|<expression>{,<expression>}
<target variable> ::= <simple variable>|<structured target>
<structured target> ::= <constructor>(<target variable list>)
<target variable list> ::= <empty>|<target variable>
     {,<target variable>}

An expression denotes a value which is computed by an executing device by application of its constituent operators to the specified operands. The value of an expression is undefined if any of these operations are undefined. The value denoted by a simple expression may be simple or structured. The value denoted by a structured expression is structured; its constructor is that of the expression, and its components are the list of values denoted by the constituent expressions of the expression list.

An assignment command specifies evaluation of its expression, and assignment of the denoted value to the target variable. A simple target variable may have assigned to it a simple or a structured value. A structured target variable may have assigned to it a structured value, with the same constructor. The effect of such assignment is to assign to each constituent simpler variable of the structured target the value of the corresponding component of the structured value. Consequently, the value denoted by the target variable, if evaluated *after* a successful assignment, is the same as the value denoted by the expression, as evaluated *before* the assignment.

An assignment fails if the value of its expression is undefined, or if that value does not *match* the target variable, in the following sense: A *simple* target variable matches any value of its type. A *structured* target variable matches a structured value, provided that:

(1)   they have the same constructor,

(2)   the target variable list is the same length as the list of components of the value,

(3)   each target variable of the list matches the corresponding component of the value list. A structured value with no components is known as a 'signal.'

Examples

(1)	$x := x + 1$	the value of x after the assignment is the same as the value of $x + 1$ before.
(2)	$(x, y) := (y, x)$	exchanges the values of x and y.
(3)	$x ::= \text{cons}(\text{left}, \text{right})$	constructs a structured value and assigns it to x.
(4)	$\text{cons}(\text{left}, \text{right}) := x$	fails if x does not have the form $\text{cons}(y, z)$; but if it does, then y is assigned to left, and z is assigned to right.
(5)	$\text{insert}(n) := \text{insert}(2*x + 1)$	equivalent to $n := 2*x + 1$.
(6)	$c := P( )$	assigns to c a 'signal' with constructor P, and no components.
(7)	$P( ) := c$	fails if the value of c is not $P( )$; otherwise has no effect.
(8)	$\text{insert}(n) := \text{has}(n)$	fails, due to mismatch.

Note: Successful execution of both (3) and (4) ensures the truth of the postcondition $x = \text{cons}(\text{left}, \text{right})$; but (3) does so by changing x and (4) does so by changing left and right. Example (4) will fail if there is *no* value of left and right which satisfies the postcondition.

2.3   Input and output commands

```
<input command> ::= <source>?<target variable>
<output command> ::= <destination>!<expression>
<source> ::= <process name>
<destination> ::= <process name>
<process name> ::= <identifier>|<identifier>(<subscripts>)
<subscripts> ::= <integer expression>{,<integer expression>}
```

Input and output commands specify communication between two concurrently operating sequential processes. Such a process may be implemented in hardware as a special-purpose device (e.g., cardreader or lineprinter), or its behavior may be specified by one of the constituent processes of a parallel command. Communication occurs between two processes of a parallel command whenever:

(1)   an input command in one process specifies as its source the process name of the other process;

(2)   an output command in the other process specifies as its destination the process name of the first process; and

(3)   the target variable of the input command matches the value denoted by the expression of the output command. On these conditions, the input and output commands are said to *correspond*. Commands which correspond are executed simultaneously, and their combined effect is to assign the value of the expression of the output command to the target variable of the input command.

An input command fails if its source is terminated. An output command fails if its destination is terminated or if its expression is undefined.

(The requirement of synchronization of input and output commands means that an implementation will have to delay whichever of the two commands happens to be ready first. The delay is ended when the corresponding command in the other process is also ready, or when the other process terminates. In the latter case the first command fails. It is also possible that the delay will never be ended, for example, if a group of processes are attempting communication but none of their input and output commands correspond with each other. This form of failure is known as a deadlock.)

Examples

(1) cardreader?cardimage	from cardreader, read a card and assign its value (an array of characters) to the variable cardimage.
(2) lineprinter!lineimage	to lineprinter, send the value of lineimage for printing.
(3) $X?(x, y)$	from process named X, input a pair of values and assign them to x and y.
(4) $DIV!(3*a + b, 13)$	to process DIV, output the two specified values.

Note: If a process named DIV issues command (3), and a process named X issues command (4), these are executed simultaneously, and have the same effect as the assignment: $(x, y) := (3*a + b, 13)$ $(\equiv x := 3*a + b; y := 13)$.

(5) console(i)?c from the ith element of an array of consoles, input a value and assign it to c.

(6) console$(j - 1)$!"A"   to the $(j - 1)$th console, output character "A".

(7) $X(i)$?V( )   from the ith of an array of processes X, input a signal V( ); refuse to input any other signal.

(8) sem!P( )   to sem output a signal P( ).

2.4 Alternative and repetitive commands

<repetitive command> ::= *<alternative command>
<alternative command> ::= [<guarded command>
        {□<guarded command>}]
<guarded command> ::= <guard> → <command list>
        |(<range>{,<range>})<guard> → <command list>
<guard> ::= <guard list>|<guard list>;<input command>
        |<input command>
        <guard list> ::= <guard element>{;<guard element>}
<guard element> ::= <boolean expression>|<declaration>

A guarded command with one or more ranges stands for a series of guarded commands, each with the same guard and command list, except that each has a different combination of values substituted for the bound variables. The values range between the lower bound and upper bound inclusive. For example, $(i : 1..n)G \rightarrow CL$ stands for:

$$G_1 \rightarrow CL_1 \square G_2 \rightarrow CL_2 \square ... \square G_n \rightarrow CL_n$$

where each $G_j \rightarrow CL_j$ is formed from $G \rightarrow CL$ by replacing every occurrence of the bound variable i by the numeral j.

A guarded command is executed only if and when the execution of its guard does not fail. First its guard is executed and then its command list. A guard is executed by execution of its constituent elements from left to right. A Boolean expression is evaluated: If it denotes false, the guard fails; but an expression that denotes true has no effect. A declaration introduces a fresh variable with a scope that extends from the declaration to the end of the guarded command. An input command at the end of a guard is executed only if and when a corresponding output command is executed. (An implementation may test whether a guard fails simply by trying to execute it, and discontinuing execution if and when it fails. This is valid because such a discontinued execution has no effect on the state of the executing device.)

An alternative command specifies execution of exactly one of its constituent guarded commands. Consequently, if all guards fail, the alternative command fails. Otherwise an arbitrary one with successfully executable guard is selected and executed. (An implementation should take advantage of its freedom of selection to ensure efficient execution and good response. For example, when input commands appear as guards, the command which corresponds to the earliest ready and matching output command should in general be preferred; and certainly, no executable and ready output command should be passed over unreasonably often.)

A repetitive command specifies as many iterations as possible of its constituent alternative command. Consequently, when all guards fail, the repetitive command terminates with no effect. Otherwise, the alternative command is executed once and then the whole repetitive command is executed again. Consider a repetitive command when all its true guard lists end in an input guard. Such a command may have to be delayed until either:

(1) an output command corresponding to one of the input guards becomes ready; or

(2) all the sources named by the input guards have terminated.

In case (2), the repetitive command terminates. If neither event ever occurs, the process fails (in deadlock).

Examples

(1) $[x \geq y \longrightarrow m := x \square y \geq x \longrightarrow m := y]$

If $x \geq y$, assign x to m; if $y \geq x$ assign y to m; if both $x \geq y$ and $y \geq x$, either assignment can be executed.

(2) $i := 0; *[i < \text{size}; \text{content}(i) \neq n \longrightarrow i := i + 1]$

The repetitive command scans the elements content(i), for $i = 0, 1,$ ... , until either $i \geq$ size, or a value equal to n is found.

(3) $*[c : \text{character}; \text{west}?c \longrightarrow \text{east}!c]$

This reads all the characters output by west, and outputs them one by one to east. The repetition terminates when the process west terminates.

(4) $*[(i : 1..10)\text{continue}(i); \text{console}(i)?c \longrightarrow X!(i, c); \text{console}(i)!\text{ack}( );$
    $\text{continue}(i) := (c \neq \text{sign off})]$

This command inputs repeatedly from any of ten consoles, provided that the corresponding element of the Boolean array continue is true. The bound variable i identifies the originating console. Its value, together with the character just input, is output to X, and an acknowledgment signal is sent back to the originating console. If the character indicated 'sign off', continue(i) is set false, to prevent further input from that console. The repetitive command terminates when all ten elements of continue are false. (An implementation should ensure that no console which is ready to provide input will be ignored unreasonably often.)

(5) $*[n$: integer; $X?\text{insert}(n) \longrightarrow$ INSERT
     $\Box n$: integer; $X?\text{has}(n) \longrightarrow$ SEARCH; $X!(i < \text{size})$
     ]

(Here, and elsewhere, capitalized words INSERT and SEARCH stand as abbreviations for program text defined separately.)
     On each iteration this command accepts from X *either*:

(a) a request to 'insert(n),' (followed by INSERT); or
(b) a question 'has(n),' to which it outputs an answer back to X.

The choice between (a) and (b) is made by the next output command in X. The repetitive command terminates when X does. If X sends a nonmatching message, deadlock will result.

(6) $*[X?\text{V}(\ ) \longrightarrow \text{val} := \text{val} + 1$
     $\Box \text{val} > 0; Y?\text{P}(\ ) \longrightarrow \text{val} := \text{val} - 1$
     ]

     On each iteration, accept *either* a V( ) signal from X and increment val, *or* a P( ) signal from Y, and decrement val. But the second alternative cannot be selected unless val is positive (after which val will remain invariantly nonnegative). (When val > 0, the choice depends on the relative speeds of X and Y, and is not determined.) The repetitive command will terminate when both X and Y are terminated, or when X is terminated and val ≤ 0.

3 Coroutines

In parallel programming coroutines appear as a more fundamental program structure than subroutines, which can be regarded as a special case (treated in the next section).

3.1 Copy

Problem

Write a process X to copy characters output by process west to process east.

> **Solution**
>
> $X :: *[c$: character; west?$c \longrightarrow$ east!$c]$

Notes

(1) When west terminates, the input 'west?*c*' will fail, causing termination of the repetitive command, and of process *X*. Any subsequent input command from east will fail.

(2) Process *X* acts as a single-character buffer between west and east. It permits west to work on production of the next character, before east is ready to input the previous one.

3.2 Squash

Problem

Adapt the previous program to replace every pair of consecutive asterisks '**' by an upward arrow '↑'. Assume that the final character input is not an asterisk.

Solution

```
X :: *[c : character; west?c →
    [c ≠ asterisk → east!c
    □c = asterisk → west?c;
            [c ≠ asterisk → east!asterisk; east!c
            □c = asterisk → east!upward arrow
    ]]       ]
```

Notes

(1) Since west does not end with asterisk, the second 'west?*c*' will not fail.

(2) As an exercise, adapt this process to deal sensibly with input which ends with an odd number of asterisks.

3.3 Disassemble

Problem

To read cards from a cardfile and output to process *X* the stream of characters they contain. An extra space should be inserted at the end of each card.

Solution

```
*[cardimage : (1..80)character; cardfile?cardimage →
     i : integer, i := 1;
     *[i ≤ 80 → X!cardimage(i); i := i + 1]
     X!space
]
```

Notes

(1) '(1..80) character' declares an array of 80 characters, with subscripts ranging between 1 and 80.

(2) The repetitive command terminates when the cardfile process terminates.

3.4 Assemble

Problem

To read a stream of characters from process X and print them in lines of 125 characters on a lineprinter. The last line should be completed with spaces if necessary.

Solution

```
lineimage : (1..125)character;
i : integer, i := 1;
*[c : character; X?c →
      lineimage(i) := c;
      [i ≤ 124 → i := i + 1
      □i = 125 → lineprinter!lineimage; i := 1
]    ];
[i = 1 → skip
□i > 1 → *[i ≤ 125 → lineimage(i) := space; i := i + 1];
      lineprinter!lineimage
]
```

Note

When X terminates, so will the first repetitive command of this process. The last line will then be printed, if it has any characters.

3.5 Reformat

Problem

Read a sequence of cards of 80 characters each, and print the characters on a lineprinter at 125 characters per line. Every card should be followed by an extra space, and the last line should be completed with spaces if necessary.

Solution

[west :: DISASSEMBLE ‖ X :: COPY ‖ east :: ASSEMBLE]

Notes

(1) The capitalized names stand for program text defined in previous sections.

(2) The parallel command is designed to terminate after the cardfile has terminated.

(3) This elementary problem is difficult to solve elegantly without coroutines.

3.6 Conway's problem [4]

Problem

Adapt the above program to replace every pair of consecutive asterisks by an upward arrow.

Solution

[west :: DISASSEMBLE‖X :: SQUASH‖east :: ASSEMBLE]

4   Subroutines and data representations

A conventional nonrecursive subroutine can be readily implemented as a coroutine provided that:

(1) its parameters are called 'by value' and 'by result'; and

(2) it is disjoint from its calling program.

Like a Fortran subroutine, a coroutine may retain the values of local variables (*own* variables, in Algol terms) and it may use input commands to achieve the effect of 'multiple entry points' in a safer way than PL/I. Thus a coroutine can be used like a SIMULA class instance as a concrete representation for abstract data.

A coroutine acting as a subroutine is a process operating concurrently with its user process in a parallel command: [subr :: SUB-ROUTINE‖X :: USER]. The SUBROUTINE will contain (or consist of) a repetitive command: *[X?(value params) → ...; X!(result params)], where ... computes the results from the values input. The subroutine will terminate when its user does. The USER will call the subroutine by a pair of commands: subr!(arguments); ...; subr?(results). Any commands between these two will be executed concurrently with the subroutine.

A multiple–entry subroutine, acting as a representation for data [11], will also contain a repetitive command which represents each entry by an alternative input to a structured target with the entry name as constructor. For example:

```
*[X?entry1(value params) → ...
□X?entry2(value params) → ...
]
```

The calling process X will determine which of the alternatives is activated on each repetition. When X terminates, so does this repetitive command. A similar technique in the user program can achieve the effect of multiple exits.

A recursive subroutine can be simulated be an array of processes, one for each level of recursion. The user process is level zero. Each activation communicates its parameters and results with its predecessor and calls its successor if necessary:

[recsub(0) :: USER‖recsub(i : 1..reclimit) :: RECSUB].

The user will call the first element of

recsub : recsub(1)!(arguments); ... ; recsub(1)?(results);.

The imposition of a fixed upper bound on recursion depth is necessitated by the 'static' design of the language.

This clumsy simulation of recursion would be even more clumsy for a mutually recursive algorithm. It would not be recommended for conventional programming; it may be more suitable for an array of microprocessors for which the fixed upper bound is also realistic.

In this section, we assume each subroutine is used only by a *single* user process (which may, of course, itself contain parallel commands).

4.1   Function: Division with remainder

Problem

Construct a process to represent a function-type subroutine, which accepts a positive dividend and divisor, and returns their integer quotient and remainder. Efficiency is of no concern.

Solution

```
[DIV :: *[x, y : integer; X?(x, y) →
        quot,rem : integer; quot := 0; rem := x;
        *[rem ≥ y → rem := rem − y; quot := quot + 1];
        X!(quot,rem)
        ]
‖X :: USER
]
```

4.2   Recursion: Factorial

Problem

Compute a factorial by the recursive method, to a given limit.

Solution

[fac(*i* : 1..limit) ::
*[*n* : integer; fac(*i* − 1)?*n* →
  [*n* = 0 → fac(*i* − 1)!1
   ☐*n* > 0 → fac(*i* + 1)!*n* − 1;
     r : integer; fac(*i* + 1)?*r*; fac(*i* − 1)!(*n* ∗ *r*)
  ]]
‖fac(0) :: USER
]

Note

This unrealistic example introduces the technique of the 'iterative array' which will be used to a better effect in later examples.

4.3   Data representation: Small set of integers [11]

Problem

To represent a set of not more than 100 integers as a process, S, which accepts two kinds of instruction from its calling process X:

(1)   S!insert(*n*), insert the integer *n* in the set, and

(2)   S!has(*n*); ...; S?*b*, *b* is set true if *n* is in the set, and false otherwise. The initial value of the set is empty.

Solution

S ::
content : (0..99)integer; size : integer; size := 0;
∗[*n* : integer; *X*?has(*n*) → SEARCH; *X*!(*i* < size)
☐*n* : integer; *X*?insert(*n*) → SEARCH;
     [*i* < size → skip
     ☐*i* = size; size < 100 →
        content (size) := *n*; size := size + 1
]   ]

where SEARCH is an abbreviation for:

i : integer; *i* := 0;
∗[*i* < size; content(*i*) ≠ *n* → *i* := *i* + 1]

Notes

(1)   The alternative command with guard 'size < 100' will fail if an attempt is made to insert more than 100 elements.

(2)   The activity of insertion will in general take place concurrently with the calling process. However, any subsequent instruction to S will be delayed until the previous insertion is complete.

4.4   Scanning a set

Problem

Extend the solution to 4.3 by providing a fast method for scanning all members of the set without changing the value of the set. The user program will contain a repetitive command of the form:

```
    S!scan( ); more : boolean; more := true;
*[more; x : integer; S?next(x) → ... deal with x ... .
□more; S?noneleft( ) → more := false
]
```

where S!scan( ) sets the representation into a scanning mode. The repetitive command serves as a **for** statement, inputting the successive members of x from the set and inspecting them until finally the representation sends a signal that there are no members left. The body of the repetitive command is *not* permitted to communicate with S in any way.

Solution

Add a third guarded command to the outer repetitive command of S:

```
...□X?scan( ) → i : integer; i := 0;
                *[i < size → X!next(content(i)); i := i + 1];
                X!noneleft( )
```

4.5   Recursive data representation: Small set of integers

Problem

Same as above, but an array of processes is to be used to achieve a high degree of parallelism. Each process should contain at most one number. When it contains no number, it should answer 'false' to all inquiries about membership. On the first insertion, it changes to a second phase of behavior, in which it deals with instructions from its predecessor, passing some of them on to its successor. The calling process will be named S(0). For efficiency, the set should be sorted, i.e., the ith process should contain the ith largest number.

Solution

$S(i : 1..100) ::$

$*[n : \text{integer}; S(i - 1)?\text{has}(n) \longrightarrow S(0)!\text{false}$
$\square n : \text{integer}; S(i - 1)?\text{insert}(n) \longrightarrow$
$\qquad *[m : \text{integer}; S(i - 1)?\text{has}(m) \longrightarrow$
$\qquad\quad [m \leq n \longrightarrow S(0)!(m = n)$
$\qquad\quad \square m > n \longrightarrow S(i + 1)!\text{has}(m)$
$\qquad\quad]$

$\qquad \square m : \text{integer}; S(i - 1)?\text{insert}(m) \longrightarrow$
$\qquad\quad [m < n \longrightarrow S(i + 1)!\text{insert}(n); n := m$
$\qquad\quad \square m = n \longrightarrow \text{skip}$
$\qquad\quad \square m > n \longrightarrow S(i + 1)!\text{insert}(m)$
$]\qquad]]$

Notes

(1) The user process S(0) inquires whether n is a member by the commands $S(1)!\text{has}(n); ...; [(i : 1..100)S(i)?b \longrightarrow \text{skip}]$. The appropriate process will respond to the input command by the output command in line 2 or line 5. This trick avoids passing the answer back 'up the chain.'

(2) Many insertion operations can proceed in parallel, yet any subsequent 'has' operation will be performed correctly.

(3) All repetitive commands and all processes of the array will terminate after the user process S(0) terminates.

4.6   Multiple exits: Remove the least member

Problem

Extend the above solution to respond to a command to yield the least member of the set and to remove it from the set. The user program will invoke the facility by a pair of commands:

$S(1)!\text{least}( ); [x : \text{integer}; S(1)?x \longrightarrow ... \text{deal with } x ...$
$\qquad\qquad\quad \square S(1)?\text{noneleft}( ) \longrightarrow ...$
$\qquad\qquad\quad]$

or, if he wishes to scan and empty the set, he may write:

$S(1)!\text{least}( ); \text{more} : \text{boolean}; \text{more} := \text{true};$
$\qquad\quad *[\text{more}; x : \text{integer}; S(1)?x \longrightarrow ... \text{deal with } x ...; S(1)!\text{least}( )$
$\qquad\quad \square \text{more}; S(1)?\text{noneleft}( ) \longrightarrow \text{more} := \text{false}$
$\qquad\quad]$

Hint

Introduce a Boolean variable, *b*, initialized to true, and prefix this to all the guards of the inner loop. After responding to a !least( ) command from its predecessor, each process returns its contained value *n*, asks its successor for its least, and stores the response in *n*. But if the successor returns 'noneleft( ),' *b* is set false and the inner loop terminates. The process therefore returns to its initial state (solution due to David Gries).

5   Monitors and scheduling

This section shows how a monitor can be regarded as a single process which communicates with more than one user process. However, each user process must have a different name (e.g., producer, consumer) or a different subscript (e.g., $X(i)$) and each communication with a user must identify its source or destination uniquely.

Consequently, when a monitor is prepared to communicate with *any* of its user processes (i.e., whichever of them calls first) it will use a guarded command with a range. For example: $*[(i : 1..100)X(i)?(value parameters) \rightarrow ...; X(i)!(results)]$. Here, the bound variable *i* is used to send the results back to the calling process. If the monitor is not prepared to accept input from some particular user (e.g., $X(j)$) on a given occasion, the input command may be preceded by a Boolean guard. For example, two successive inputs from the same process are inhibited by $j = 0$; $*[(i : 1..100)i \neq j; X(i)?(values) \rightarrow ...; j := i]$. Any attempted output from $X(j)$ will be delayed until a subsequent iteration, after the output of some other process $X(i)$ has been accepted and dealt with.

Similarly, conditions can be used to delay acceptance of inputs which would violate scheduling constraints – postponing them until some later occasion when some other process has brought the monitor into a state in which the input can validly be accepted. This technique is similar to a conditional critical region [10] and it obviates the need for special synchronizing variables such as events, queues, or conditions. However, the absence of these special facilities certainly makes it more difficult or less efficient to solve problems involving priorities – for example, the scheduling of head movement on a disk.

5.1   Bounded buffer

Problem

Construct a buffering process *X* to smooth variations in the speed of output of portions by a producer process and input by a consumer process. The consumer contains pairs of commands $X!more( ); X?p$, and the producer contains commands of the form $X!p$. The buffer should contain up to ten portions.

Solution

```
X ::
buffer : (0..9) portion;
in,out : integer; in := 0; out := 0;
comment 0 ≤ out ≤ in ≤ out + 10;
    *[in < out + 10; producer?buffer(in mod 10) → in := in + 1
    □out < in; consumer?more( ) → consumer!buffer(out mod 10);
       out := out + 1
    ]
```

Notes

(1) When out < in < out + 10, the selection of the alternative in the repetitive command will depend on whether the producer produces before the consumer consumes, or vice versa.

(2) When out = in, the buffer is empty and the second alternative cannot be selected even if the consumer is ready with its command $X!$more( ). However, after the producer has produced its next portion, the consumer's request can be granted on the next iteration.

(3) Similar remarks apply to the producer, when in = out + 10.

(4) X is designed to terminate when out = in and the producer has terminated.

5.2   Integer semaphore

Problem

To implement an integer semaphore, S, shared among an array $X(i : 1..100)$ of client processes. Each process may increment the semaphore by S!V( ) or decrement it by S!P( ), but the latter command must be delayed if the value of the semaphore is not positive.

Solution

```
S :: val : integer; val := 0;
    *[(i : 1..100)X(i)?V( ) → val := val +1
    □(i : 1..100)val > 0; X(i)?P( ) → val := val − 1
    ]
```

Notes

(1) In this process, no use is made of knowledge of the subscript i of the calling process.

(2) The semaphore terminates only when all hundred processes of the process array X have terminated.

5.3   Dining philosophers

Problem

Five philosophers spend their lives thinking and eating. The philosophers share a common dining room where there is a circular table surrounded by five chairs, each belonging to one philosopher. In the center of the table there is a large bowl of spaghetti, and the table is laid with five forks (see Figure 1). On feeling hungry, a philosopher enters the dining room, sits in his own chair, and picks up the fork on the left of his place. Unfortunately, the spaghetti is so tangled that he needs to pick up and use the fork on his right as well. When he has finished, he puts down both forks, and leaves the room. The room should keep a count of the number of philosophers in it.

Solution

The behavior of the ith philosopher may be described as follows:

```
PHIL = *[... during ith lifetime ... →
        THINK;
        room!enter( );
        fork(i)!pickup( ); fork((i + 1) mod 5)!pickup( );
        EAT;
        fork(i)!putdown( ); fork((i + 1) mod 5)!putdown( );
        room!exit( )
        ]
```

The fate of the ith fork is to be picked up and put down by a philosopher sitting on either side of it:

```
FORK =
  *[phil(i)?pickup( ) → phil(i)?putdown( )
  □phil((i − 1)mod 5)?pickup( ) → phil((i − 1) mod 5)?putdown( )
  ]
```

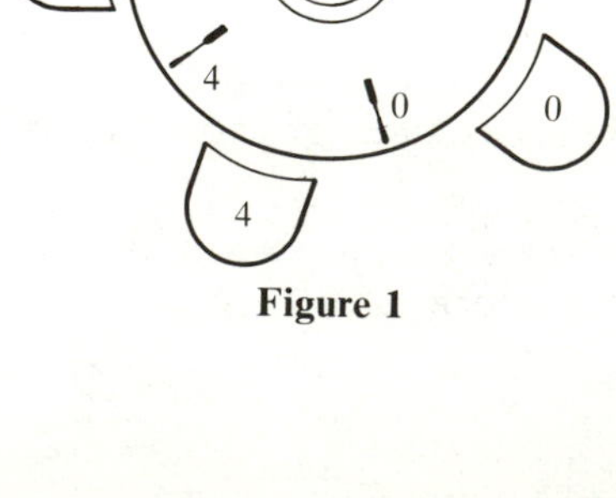

Figure 1

The story of the room may be simply told:

ROOM = occupancy : integer; occupancy := 0;
  *[(*i* : 0..4)phil(*i*)?enter( ) → occupancy := occupancy + 1
  □(*i* : 0..4)phil(*i*)?exit( ) → occupancy := occupancy − 1
  ]

All these components operate in parallel:

[room :: ROOM‖fork(*i* : 0..4) :: FORK‖phil(*i* : 0..4) :: PHIL].

Notes

(1) The solution given above does not prevent all five philosophers from entering the room, each picking up his left fork, and starving to death because he cannot pick up his right fork.

(2) Exercise: Adapt the above program to avert this sad possibility. *Hint*: Prevent more than four philosophers from entering the room. (Problem and solution due to E. W. Dijkstra.)

6   Miscellaneous

This section contains further examples of the use of communicating sequential processes for the solution of some less familiar problems; a parallel version of the sieve of Eratosthenes, and the design of an iterative array. The proposed solutions are even more speculative than those of the previous sections, and in the second example, even the question of termination is ignored.

6.1   Prime numbers: The sieve of Eratosthenes [14]

Problem

To print in ascending order all primes less than 10 000. Use an array of processes, SIEVE, in which each process inputs a prime from its predecessor and prints it. The process then inputs an ascending stream of numbers from its predecessor and passes them on to its successor, suppressing any that are multiples of the original prime.

Solution

[SIEVE(*i* : 1..100) ::
  p,mp : integer;
  SIEVE(*i* − 1)?*p*;
  print!*p*;
  mp := *p*; *comment mp* is a multiple of *p*;

```
*[m : integer, SIEVE(i − 1)?m →
    *[m > mp → mp := mp + p];
    [m = mp → skip
    □m < mp → SIEVE(i + 1)!m
]    ]
‖SIEVE(0) :: print!2; n : integer; n := 3;
        *[n < 10000 → SIEVE(1)!n; n := n + 2]
‖SIEVE(101) :: *[n : integer; SIEVE(100)?n → print!n]
‖print :: *[(i : 0..101) n : integer; SIEVE(i)?n → ...]
]
```

Notes

(1) This beautiful solution was contributed by David Gries.
(2) It is algorithmically similar to the program developed in [7, pp. 27–32].

6.2 An iterative array : Matrix multiplication

Problem

A square matrix A of order 3 is given. Three streams are to be input, each stream representing a column of an array IN. Three streams are to be output, each representing a column of the product matrix IN × A. After an initial delay, the results are to be produced at the same rate as the input is consumed. Consequently, a high degree of parallelism is required. The solution should take the form shown in Figure 2. Each of the nine nonborder nodes inputs a vector component from the west and a partial sum from the north. Each node outputs the vector component to its east, and an updated partial sum to the south. The input data is produced by the west border nodes, and the desired results are consumed by south border nodes. The north border is a constant source of zeros and the east border is just a sink. No provision need be made for termination nor for changing the values of the array A.

Solution

There are twenty-one nodes, in five groups, comprising the central square and the four borders:

```
[M(i : 1..3,0) :: WEST
‖M(0, j : 1..3) :: NORTH
‖M(i : 1..3,4) :: EAST
‖M(4, j : 1..3) :: SOUTH
‖M(i : 1..3, j : 1..3) :: CENTER
]
```

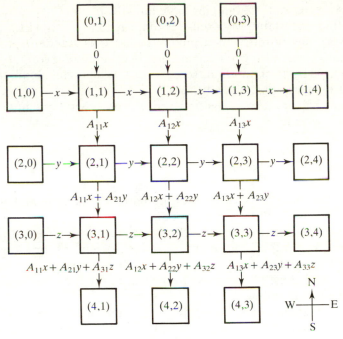

Figure 2

The WEST and SOUTH borders and processes of the user program; the remaining processes are:

NORTH = *[true → M(1, j)!0]
EAST = *[x : real; M(i, 3)?x → skip]
CENTER = *[x : real; M(i, j − 1)?x →
    M(i, j + 1)!x; sum : real;
    M(i − 1, j)?sum; M(i + 1, j)!(A(i, j)*x + sum)
]

7 Discussion

A design for a programming language must necessarily involve a number of decisions which seem to be fairly arbitrary. The discussion of this section is intended to explain some of the underlying motivation and to mention some unresolved questions.

7.1 Notations

I have chosen single-character notations (e.g., !,?) to express the primitive concepts, rather than the more traditional boldface or underlined English words. As a result, the examples have an APL-like brevity, which some readers find distasteful. My excuse is that (in contrast to APL) there are only a very few primitive concepts and that it is standard practice of mathematics (and also good coding practice) to denote common primitive concepts by brief notations (e.g., $+$, $\times$). When read aloud, these are replaced by words (e.g., plus, times).

Some readers have suggested the use of assignment notation for input and output:

> \<target variable\> := \<source\>
> \<destination\> := \<expression\>

I find this suggestion misleading: it is better to regard input and output as distinct primitives, justifying distinct notations.

I have used the same pair of brackets ([...]) to bracket all program structures, instead of the more familiar variety of brackets (**if..fi**, **begin..end**, **case..esac**, etc.). In this I follow normal mathematical practice, but I must also confess to a distaste for the pronunciation of words like **fi**, **od**, or **esac**.

I am dissatisfied with the fact that my notation gives the same syntax for a structured expression and a subscripted variable. Perhaps tags should be distinguished from other identifiers by a special symbol (say #).

I was tempted to introduce an abbreviation for combined declaration and input, e.g., $X?(n : \text{integer})$ for $n : \text{integer}; X?n$.

7.2   Explicit naming

My design insists that every input or output command must name its source or destination explicitly. This makes it inconvenient to write a library of processes which can be included in subsequent programs, independent of the process names used in that program. A partial solution to this problem is to allow one process (the *main* process) of a parallel command to have an empty label, and to allow the other processes in the command to use the empty process name as source or destination of input or output.

For construction of large programs, some more general technique will also be necessary. This should at least permit substitution of program text for names defined elsewhere – a technique which has been used informally throughout this paper. The Cobol COPY verb also permits a substitution for formal parameters within the copied text. But whatever facility is introduced, I would recommend the following principle: Every program, after assembly with its library routines, should be printable as a text expressed wholly in the language, and it is this printed text which should describe the execution of the program, independent of which parts were drawn from a library.

Since I did not intend to design a complete language, I have ignored the problem of libraries in order to concentrate on the essential semantic concepts of the program which is actually executed.

7.3 Port names

An alternative to explicit naming of source and destination would be to name a *port* through which communication is to take place. The port names would be local to the processes, and the manner in which pairs of ports are to be connected by channels could be declared in the head of a parallel command.

This is an attractive alternative which could be designed to introduce a useful degree of syntactically checkable redundancy. But it is semantically equivalent to the present proposal, provided that each port is connected to exactly one other port in another process. In this case each channel can be identified with a tag, together with the name of the process at the other end. Since I wish to concentrate on semantics, I preferred in this paper to use the simplest and most direct notation, and to avoid raising questions about the possibility of connecting more than two ports by a single channel.

7.4 Automatic buffering

As an alternative to synchronization of input and output, it is often proposed that an outputting process should be allowed to proceed even when the inputting process is not yet ready to accept the output. An implementation would be expected automatically to interpose a chain of buffers to hold output messages that have not yet been input.

I have deliberately rejected this alternative, for two reasons:

(1) it is less realistic to implement in multiple disjoint processors; and

(2) when buffering is required on a particular channel, it can readily be specified using the given primitives.

Of course, it could be argued equally well that synchronization can be specified when required by using a pair of buffered input and output commands.

7.5 Unbounded process activation

The notation for an array of processes permits the same program text (like an Algol recursive procedure) to have many simultaneous 'activations'; however, the exact number must be specified in advance. In a conventional single-processor implementation, this can lead to inconvenience and wastefulness, similar to the fixed-length array of Fortran. It would therefore be attractive to allow a process array with no *a priori* bound on the number of elements; and to specify that the exact number of elements required for a particular execution of the program should be determined dynamically, like the maximum depth of recursion of an Algol procedure or the number of iterations of a repetitive command.

However, it is a good principle that every actual run of a program with unbounded arrays should be identical to the run of some program with all its arrays bounded in advance. Thus the unbounded program should be defined as the 'limit' (in some sense) of a series of bounded programs with increasing bounds. I have chosen to concentrate on the semantics of the bounded case – which is necessary anyway and which is more realistic for implementation on multiple microprocessors.

7.6 Fairness

Consider the parallel command:

$$[X :: Y!\text{stop}(\,) \| Y :: \text{continue} : \text{boolean}; \text{continue} := \text{true};$$
$$*[\text{continue}; X?\text{stop}(\,) \rightarrow \text{continue} := \text{false}$$
$$\Box \text{continue} \rightarrow n := n + 1$$
$$]$$
$$].$$

If the implementation always prefers the second alternative in the repetitive command of Y, it is said to be *unfair*, because although the output command in X could have been executed on an infinite number of occasions, it is in fact always passed over.

The question arises: Should a programming language definition specify that an implementation must be *fair*? Here, I am fairly sure that the answer is NO. Otherwise, the implementation would be obliged to successfully complete the example program shown above, in spite of the fact that its nondeterminism is unbounded. I would therefore suggest that it is the programmer's responsibility to prove that his program terminates correctly – without relying on the assumption of fairness in the implementation. Thus the program shown above is incorrect, since its termination cannot be proved.

Nevertheless, I suggest that an efficient implementation should try to be reasonably fair and should ensure that an output command is not delayed unreasonably often after it first becomes executable. But a proof of correctness must not rely on this property of an efficient implementation. Consider the following analogy with a sequential program: An efficient implementation of an alternative command will tend to favor the alternative which can be most efficiently executed, but the programmer must ensure that the logical correctness of his program does not depend on this property of his implementation.

This method of avoiding the problem of fairness does not apply to programs such as operating systems which are intended to run forever because in this case termination proofs are not relevant. But I wonder whether it is ever advisable to write or to execute such programs. Even an operating system should be designed to bring itself to an orderly conclusion reasonably soon after it inputs a message instructing it to do so. Otherwise, the *only* way to stop it is to 'crash' it.

7.7 Functional coroutines

It is interesting to compare the processes described here with those proposed in [12]; the differences are most striking. There, coroutines are strictly deterministic: No choice is given between alternative sources of input. The output commands are automatically buffered to any required degree. The output of one process can be automatically fanned out to any number of processes (including itself!) which can consume it at differing rates. Finally, the processes there are designed to run forever, whereas my proposed parallel command is normally intended to terminate. The design in [12] is based on an elegant theory which permits proof of the properties of programs. These differences are not accidental – they seem to be natural consequences of the difference between the more abstract applicative (or functional) approach to programming and the more machine-oriented imperative (or procedural) approach, which is taken by communicating sequential processes.

7.8 Output guards

Since input commands may appear in guards, it seems more symmetric to permit output commands as well. This would allow an obvious and useful simplification in some of the example programs, for example, in the bounded buffer (5.1). Perhaps a more convincing reason would be to ensure that the externally visible effect and behavior of every parallel command can be modeled by come sequential command. In order to model the parallel command:

$$Z :: [X!2 \parallel Y!3]$$

we need to be able to write the sequential alternative command:

$$Z :: [X!2 \rightarrow Y!3 \square Y!3 \rightarrow X!2]$$

Note that this *cannot* be done by the command:

$$Z :: [\text{true} \rightarrow X!2; \ Y!3 \square \text{true} \rightarrow Y!3; \ X!2]$$

which can fail if the process Z happens to choose the first alternative, but the processes Y and X are synchronized with each other in such a way that Y must input from Z before X does, e.g.:

$$Y :: Z?y; X!go( )$$
$$\|X :: Y?go( ); Z?x$$

7.9 Restriction: repetitive command with input guard

In proposing an unfamiliar programming language feature, it seems wiser at first to specify a highly restrictive version rather than to propose extensions – especially when the language feature claims to be primitive. For example, it is clear that the multidimensional process array is not primitive, since it can readily be constructed in a language which permits only single-dimensional arrays. But I have a rather more serious misgiving about the repetitive command with input guards.

The automatic termination of a repetitive command on termination of the sources of all its input guards is an extremely powerful and convenient feature but it also involves some subtlety of specification to ensure that it is implementable; and it is certainly not primitive, since the required effect can be achieved (with considerable inconvenience) by explicit exchange of 'end( )' signals. For example, the subroutine DIV(4.1) could be rewritten:

```
[DIV :: continue : boolean; continue := true;
*[continue; X?end( ) → continue := false
□continue; x, y : integer; X?(x, y) → ...; X!(quot,rem)
‖X :: USER PROG; DIV!end( )
]
```

Other examples would be even more inconvenient.

But the dangers of convenient facilities are notorious. For example, the repetitive commands with input guards may tempt the programmer to write them without making adequate plans for their termination; and if it turns out that the automatic termination is unsatisfactory, reprogramming for explicit termination will involve severe changes, affecting even the interfaces between the processes.

8 Conclusion

This paper has suggested that input, output, and concurrency should be regarded as primitives of programming, which underlie many familiar and less familiar programming concepts. However, it would be unjustified to conclude that these primitives can wholly replace the other concepts in a programming language. Where a more elaborate construction (such as a procedure or a monitor) is frequently useful, has properties which are more simply provable, and can also be implemented more efficiently than the general case, there is a strong reason for including in a programming language a special notation for that construction. The fact that the construction can be defined in terms of simpler underlying primitives is a useful guarantee that its inclusion is logically consistent with the remainder of the language.

Acknowledgments

The research reported in this paper has been encouraged and supported by a Senior Fellowship of the Science Research Council of Great Britain. The technical inspiration was due to Edsger W. Dijkstra [9], and the paper has been improved in presentation and content by valuable and painstaking advice from D. Gries, D.Q.M. Fay, Edsger W. Dijkstra, N. Wirth, Robert Milne, M.K. Harper, and its referees. The role of IFIP W.G.2.3. as a forum for presentation and discussion is acknowledged with pleasure and gratitude.

References

[1] Atkinson, R., and Hewitt, C. Synchronisation in actor systems. Working Paper 83, M.I.T., Cambridge, Mass., Nov. 1976.

[2] Brinch Hansen, P. The programming language Concurrent Pascal. *IEEE Trans. Software Eng.* **1**, 2 (June 1975), 199–207.

[3] Campbell, R.H., and Habermann, A.N. The specification of process synchronisation by path expressions. *Lecture Notes in Computer Science* **16**, Springer, 1974, pp. 89–102.

[4] Conway, M.E. Design of a separable transition-diagram compiler. *Comm. ACM* **6**, 7 (July 1963), 396–408.

[5] Dahl, O-J., *et al.* SIMULA 67, common base language. Norwegian Computing Centre, Forskningveien, Oslo, 1967.

[6] Dijkstra, E.W. Co-operating sequential processes. In *Programming Languages*, F. Genuys, Ed., Academic Press, New York, 1968, pp. 43–112.

[7] Dijkstra, E.W. Notes on structured programming. In *Structured Programming*, Academic Press, New York, 1972, pp. 1–82.

[8] Dijkstra, E.W. Guarded commands, nondeterminacy, and formal derivation of programs. *Comm. ACM* **18**, 8 (Aug. 1975), 453–457.

[9] Dijkstra, E.W. Verbal communication, Marktoberdorf, Aug. 1975.

[10] Hoare, C.A.R. Towards a theory of parallel programming. In *Operating Systems Techniques*, Academic Press, New York, 1972, pp. 61–71.

[11] Hoare, C.A.R. Proof of correctness of data representations. *Acta Informatica* **1**, 4 (1972), 271–281.

[12] Kahn, G. The semantics of a simple language for parallel programming. In *Proc. IFIP Congress* **74**, North Holland, 1974.

[13] Liskov, B.H. A note on CLU. Computation Structures Group Memo. 112, M.I.T., Cambridge, Mass., 1974.

[14]   McIlroy, M.D. Coroutines. Bell Laboratories, Murray Hill, N.J., 1968.

[15]   Naur, P., Ed. Report on the algorithmic language ALGOL 60. *Comm. ACM* **3**, 5 (May 1960), 299–314.

[16]   Reynolds, J.C. COGENT. ANL-7022, Argonne Nat. Lab., Argonne, Ill., 1965.

[17]   Thompson, K. The UNIX command language. In *Structured Programming*, Infotech, Nicholson House, Maidenhead, England, 1976, pp. 375–384.

[18]   van Wijngaarden, A. Ed. Report on the algorithmic language ALGOL 68. *Numer. Math.* **14**, (1969), 79–218.

[19]   Wulf, W.A., London, R.L., and Shaw, M. Abstraction and verification in ALPHARD. Dept. of Comptr. Sci., Carnegie–Mellon U., Pittsburgh, Pa., June 1976.

[20]   Wirth, N. The programming language PASCAL. *Acta Informatica* **1**, 1 (1971), 35–63.

12

Guardians and Actions: Linguistic Support for Robust, Distributed Programs

Barbara Liskov and Robert Scheifler

Massachusetts Institute of Technology

An overview is presented of an integrated programming language and system designed to support the construction and maintenance of distributed programs: programs in which modules reside and execute at communicating, but geographically distinct, nodes. The language is intended to support a class of applications concerned with the manipulation and preservation of long-lived, on-line, distributed data. The language addresses the writing of robust programs that survive hardware failures without loss of distributed information and that provide highly concurrent access to that information while preserving its consistency. Several new linguistic constructs are provided; among them are atomic actions, and modules called guardians that survive node failures.

Categories and subject descriptors: C.2.4 [**Computer-Communication Networks**]: Distributed Systems – distributed applications; distributed databases; D.1.3 [**Programming Techniques**]: Concurrent Programming; D.3.3 [**Programming Languages**]: Language Constructs – abstract data types; concurrent programming structures; modules, packages; D.4.5 [**Operating Systems**]: Reliability – checkpoint/restart; fault-tolerance; H.2.4 [**Database Management**]: System – distributed systems; transaction processing.

General terms: languages, reliability.

Additional key words and phrases: atomicity, nested atomic actions, remote procedure call.

A preliminary version of this paper appeared in the Conference Record of the Ninth Annual Symposium on Principles of Programming Languages, January 1982 [18].

This research was supported in part by the Advanced Research Projects Agency of the Department of Defense, monitored by the Office of Naval Research under contract N00014-75-C-0661, and in part by the National Science Foundation under grant MCS 79-23769.

1 Introduction

Technological advances have made it cost effective to construct large systems from collections of computers connected via networks. To support such systems, there is a growing need for effective ways to organize and maintain *distributed programs*: programs in which modules reside and execute at communicating, but geographically distinct, locations. In this paper we present an overview of an integrated programming language and system, called Argus, that was designed for this purpose.

Distributed programs run on *nodes* connected (only) via a communications network. A node consists of one or more processors, one or more levels of memory, and any number of external devices. Different nodes may contain different kinds of processors and devices. The network may be long haul or short haul, or any combination, connected by gateways. Neither the network nor any nodes need be reliable. However, we do assume that all failures can be detected as explained in [15]. We also assume that message delay is long relative to the time needed to access local memory and therefore that access to nonlocal data is significantly more expensive than access to local data.

The applications that can make effective use of a distributed organization differ in their requirements. We have concentrated on a class of applications concerned with the manipulation and preservation of long-lived, on-line data. Examples of such applications are banking systems, airline reservation systems, office automation systems, database systems, and various components of operating systems. In these systems, real-time constraints are not severe, but reliable, available, distributed data is of primary importance. The systems may serve a geographically distributed organization. Our language is intended to support the implementation of such systems.

The application domain, together with our hardware assumptions, imposes a number of requirements:

- *Service* A major concern is to provide continuous service of the system as a whole in the face of node and network failures. Failures should be localized so that a program can perform its task as long as the particular nodes it needs to communicate with are functioning and reachable. Adherence to this principle permits an application program to use replication of data and processing to increase availability.

- *Reconfiguration* An important reason for wanting a distributed implementation is to make it easy to add and reconfigure hardware to increase processing power, decrease response time, or increase the availability of data. It also must be possible to implement logical systems that can be reconfigured. To maintain continuous service, it must be possible to make both logical and physical changes *dynamically*, while the system continues to operate.

- *Autonomy*   We assume that nodes are owned by individuals or organizations that want to control how the node is used. For example, the owner may want to control what runs at the node, or to control the availability of services provided at the node. Further, a node might contain data that must remain resident at that node; for example, a multinational organization must abide by laws governing information flow among countries. The important point here is that the need for distribution arises not only from efficiency considerations, but from political and sociological considerations as well.

- *Distribution*   The distribution of data and processing can have a major impact on overall efficiency, in terms of both responsiveness and cost-effective use of hardware. Distribution also affects availability. To create efficient, available systems while retaining autonomy, the programmer needs explicit control over the placement of modules in the system. However, to support a reasonable degree of modularity, changes in the location of modules should have limited, localized effects on the actual code.

- *Concurrency*   Another major reason for choosing a distributed implementation is to take advantage of the potential concurrency in an application, thereby increasing efficiency and decreasing response time.

- *Consistency*   In almost any system where on-line data is being read and modified by ongoing activities, there are consistency constraints that must be maintained. Such constraints apply not only to individual pieces of data, but to distributed sets of data as well. For example, when funds are transferred from one account to another in a banking system, the net gain over the two accounts must be zero. Also, data that is replicated to increase availability must be kept consistent.

Of the above requirements, we found consistency the most difficult to meet. The main issues here are the coordination of concurrent activities (permitting concurrency but avoiding interference) and the masking of hardware failures. Thus, to support consistency we had to devise methods for building a reliable system on unreliable hardware. Reliability is an area that has been almost completely ignored in programming languages (with the exception of [22, 25, 28]). Yet our study of applications convinced us that consistency is a crucial requirement: an adequate language must provide a modular, reasonably automatic method for achieving consistency.

Our approach is to provide *atomicity* as a fundamental concept in the language. The concept of atomicity is not original with our work, having been used extensively in database applications [4–6, 8–10]. However, we believe the integration into a programming language of a general mechanism for achieving atomicity is novel.

The remainder of the paper is organized as follows. Atomicity is discussed in the next section. Section 3 presents an overview of Argus. The main features are *guardians*, the logical unit of distribution in our system, and atomic *actions*. Section 4 illustrates many features of the language with a simple mail system. The final section discusses what has been accomplished.

2   Atomicity

Data consistency requires, first of all, that the data in question be resilient to hardware failures, so that a crash of a node or storage device does not cause the loss of vital information. Resiliency is accomplished by means of redundancy. We believe the most practical technique using current technology is to keep data on stable storage devices [15].[†] Of course, stable storage, in common with any other technique for providing resiliency, cannot guarantee that data survive all failures, but it can guarantee survival with extremely high probability.

Data resiliency only ensures data survival in a quiescent environment. Our solution to the problem of maintaining consistent distributed data in the face of concurrent, potentially interfering activities, and in the face of system failures such as node crashes and network disruptions while these activities are running, is to make activities *atomic*.

The state of a distributed system is a collection of data objects that reside at various locations in the network. An activity can be thought of as a process that attempts to examine and transform some objects in the distributed state from their current (initial) states to new (final) states, with any number of intermediate state changes. Two properties distinguish an activity as being atomic: indivisibility and recoverability. By *indivisibility* we mean that the execution of one activity never appears to overlap (or contain) the execution of any other activity. If the objects being modified by one activity are observed over time by another activity, the latter activity will either always observe the initial states or always observe the final states. By *recoverability* we mean that the overall effect of the activity is all-or-nothing: either all of the objects remain in their initial state, or all change to their final state. If a failure occurs while an activity is running, it must be possible either to complete the activity or to restore all objects to their initial states.

[†] We need merely assume that stable storage is accessible to every node in the system; it is not necessary that every node have its own local stable storage devices.

2.1 Actions

We call an atomic activity an *action*. An action may complete either by *committing* or by *aborting*. When an action aborts, the effect is as if the action had never begun: all modified objects are restored to their previous states. When an action commits, all modified objects take on their new states.

One simple way to implement the indivisibility property is to force actions to run sequentially. However, one of our goals is to provide a high degree of concurrency. The usual method of providing indivisibility in the presence of concurrency, and the one we have adopted, is to guarantee *serializability* [6]; namely, actions are scheduled in such a way that their overall effect is as if they had been run sequentially in some order. To prevent one action from observing or interfering with the intermediate states of another action, we need to synchronize access to shared objects. In addition, to implement the recoverability property, we need to be able to undo the changes made to objects by aborted actions.

Since synchronization and recovery are likely to be somewhat expensive to implement, we do not provide these properties for all objects. For example, objects that are purely local to a single action do not require these properties. The objects that do provide these properties are called *atomic objects*, and we restrict our notion of atomicity to cover only access to atomic objects. That is, atomicity is guaranteed only when the objects shared by actions are atomic objects.

Atomic objects are encapsulated within *atomic abstract data types*. An abstract data type consists of a set of objects and a set of primitive operations; the primitive operations are the only means of accessing and manipulating the objects [21]. Atomic types have operations just like normal data types, except that the operations provide indivisibility and recoverability for the calling actions. Some atomic types are built in, while others are user defined. Argus provides, as built-in types, atomic arrays, records, and variants, with operations nearly identical to those on the normal arrays, records, and variants provided in CLU [20]. In addition, objects of built-in scalar types, such as characters and integers, are atomic, as are structured objects of built-in immutable types, such as strings, whose components cannot change over time.

Our implementation of (mutable) built-in atomic objects is based on a fairly simple locking model. There are two kinds of locks: read locks and write locks. Before an action uses an object, it must acquire a lock in the appropriate mode. The usual locking rules apply: multiple readers are allowed, but readers exclude writers, and a writer excludes readers and other writers. When a write lock is obtained, a *version* of the object is made, and the action operates on this version. If, ultimately, the action commits, this version will be retained, and the old version discarded. If the action aborts, this version will be discarded, and the old version retained. For example, atomic records have the usual component selection and update operations but selection operations obtain a read lock on the record (not the component), and update operations obtain a write lock and create a version of the record the first time the action modifies the record.

All locks acquired by an action are held until the completion of that action, a simplification of standard two-phase locking [9]. This rule avoids the problem of *cascading* aborts: if a lock on an object could be released early, and the action later aborted, any action that had observed the new state of that object would also have to be aborted.

Within the framework of actions, there is a straightforward way to deal with hardware failures at a node: they simply force the node to crash, which in turn forces actions to abort. As was mentioned above, we make data resilient by storing it on stable storage devices. Furthermore, we do not actually copy information to stable storage until actions commit. Therefore, versions made for a running action and information about locks can be kept in volatile memory. This volatile information will be lost if the node crashes. If this happens, the action must be forced to abort. To ensure that the action will abort, a standard two-phase commit protocol [8] is used. In the first phase, an attempt is made to verify that all locks are still held, and to record the new state of each modified object on stable storage. If the first phase is successful, then in the second phase the locks are released, the recorded states become the current states, and the previous states are forgotten. If the first phase fails, the recorded states are forgotten and the action is forced to abort, restoring the objects to their previous states.

Turning hardware failures into aborts has the merit of freeing the programmer from low-level hardware considerations. It also reduces the probability that actions will commit. However, this is a problem only when the time to complete an action approaches the mean time between failures of the nodes. We believe that most actions will be quite short compared to realistic mean time between failures for hardware available today.

It has been argued that indivisibility is too strong a property for certain applications because it limits the amount of potential concurrency [14]. We believe that indivisibility is the desired property for most applications, *if* it is required only at the appropriate levels of abstraction. Argus provides a mechanism for *user-defined* atomic data types. These types present an external interface that supports indivisibility but that can offer a great deal of concurrency as well. We do not present our mechanism here; user-defined atomic types are discussed in [30].

2.2   Nested actions

So far we have presented actions as monolithic entities. In fact, it is useful to break down such entities into pieces; to this end we provide hierarchically structured, *nested* actions. Nested actions, or subactions, are a mechanism for coping with failures, as well as for introducing concurrency within an action. An action may contain any number of subactions, some of which may be performed sequentially, some concurrently. This structure cannot be observed from outside; that is, the overall action still satisfies the atomicity properties. Subactions appear as atomic activities with respect to other subactions of the same parent. Subactions can commit and abort independently, and a subaction can abort without forcing its parent action to abort. However, the commit of a subaction is conditional: even if a subaction commits, aborting its parent action will abort it. Further, object versions are written to stable storage only when top-level actions commit.

Nested actions aid in composing (and decomposing) activities in a modular fashion. This allows a collection of existing actions to be combined into a single, higher level action, and to be run concurrently within that action with no need for additional synchronization. For example, consider a database replicated at multiple nodes. If only a majority of the nodes need to be read or written for the overall action to succeed, this is accomplished by performing the reads or writes as concurrent subactions, and committing the overall action as soon as a majority of the subactions commit, even though some of the other subactions are forced to abort.

Nested actions have been proposed by others [4,10,26]; our model is similar to that presented in [23]. To keep the locking rules simple, we do not allow a parent action to run concurrently with its children. The rule for read locks is extended so that an action may obtain a read lock on an object provided every action holding a write lock on that object is an ancestor. An action may obtain a write lock on an object provided every action holding a (read or write) lock on that object is an ancestor. When a subaction commits, its locks are inherited by its parent; when a subaction aborts, its locks are discarded.

Note that the locking rules permit multiple writers, which implies that multiple versions of objects are needed. However, since writers must form a linear chain when ordered by ancestry, and actions cannot execute concurrently with their subactions, only one writer can ever actually be executing at one time. Hence, it suffices to use a stack of versions (rather than a tree) for each atomic object. On commit, the top version becomes the new version for the parent; on abort, the top version is simply discarded. Since versions become permanent only when top-level actions commit, the two-phase commit protocol is used only for top-level actions. A detailed description of locking and version management in a system supporting nested actions is presented in [23].

In addition to nesting subactions inside other actions, it is sometimes useful to start a new top action inside another action. Such a 'nested' top action, unlike a subaction, has no special privileges relative to its parent; for example, it is not able to read an atomic object modified by its parent. Furthermore, the commit of a nested top action is not relative to its parent; its versions are written to stable storage, and its locks are released, just as for normal top actions. Nested top actions are useful for benevolent side effects. For example, in a naming system a name lookup may cause information to be copied from one location to another, to speed up subsequent lookups of that name. Copying the data within a nested top action ensures that the changes remain in effect even if the parent action aborts.

2.3   Remote procedure call

Perhaps the single most important application of nested actions is in masking communication failures. Logical nodes (described in Section 3) in Argus communicate via messages. We believe that the most desirable form of communication is the paired send and reply: for every message sent, a reply message is expected. In fact, we believe the form of communication that is needed is *remote procedure call*, with *at-most-once* semantics, namely, that (effectively) either the message is delivered and acted on exactly once, with exactly one reply received, or the message is never delivered and the sender is so informed.

   The rationale for the high-level, at-most-once semantics of remote procedure call is presented in [16] (see also [29]). Briefly, we believe the system should mask from the user low-level issues, such as packetization and retransmission, and that the system should make a reasonable attempt to deliver messages. However, we believe the possibility of long delays and of ultimate failure in sending a message cannot and should not be masked. In such a case, the communication would fail.[†] The sender can then cope with the failure according to the demands of the particular application. However, coping with the failure is much simpler if it is guaranteed that in this case the remote procedure call had no effect.

   The all-or-nothing nature of remote procedure call is similar to the recoverability property of actions, and the ability to cope with communication failures is similar to the ability of an action to cope with the failures of subactions. Therefore, it seems natural to implement a remote procedure call as a subaction: communication failures will force the subaction to abort, and the caller has the ability to abort the subaction on demand. However, as mentioned above, aborting the subaction does not force the parent action to abort. The caller is free to find some other

---

[†] For example, the system would cause the communication to fail if it is unable to contact the remote node. We believe the system, and not the programmer, should take on this kind of responsibility, because the programmer would find it very difficult to define reasonable timeouts.

means of accomplishing its task, such as communicating with some other node.

2.4 Remarks

In our model, there are two kinds of actions: subactions and top-level actions. We believe these correspond in a natural way to activities in the application system. Top-level actions correspond to activities that interact with the external environment, or, in the case of nested top actions, to activities that should not be undone if the parent aborts. For example, in an airline reservation system, a top-level action might correspond to an interaction with a clerk who is entering a related sequence of reservations. Subactions, on the other hand, correspond to internal activities that are intended to be carried out as part of an external interaction; a reservation on a single flight is an example.

Not all effects of an action can be undone by aborting that action, since a change to the external environment, for example, printing a check, cannot be undone by program control alone. But as long as all effects can be undone, the user of our language does not need to write any code to undo or compensate for the effects of aborted actions.

Before doing something like printing a check, the application program should make sure that printing the check is the right thing to do. One technique for ensuring this is to break an activity into two separate, sequential top-level actions. All changes to the external environment are deferred to the second action, to be executed only if the first action is successful. Such a technique will greatly decrease the likelihood of actions having undesired effects that cannot be undone.

The commit of a top-level action is irrevocable. If that action is later found to be in error, actions that compensate for the effects of the erroneous action (and of all later actions that read its results) must be defined and executed by the user. Compensation must also be performed for effects of aborted actions that cannot be undone. Note that, in general, there is no way that such compensation could be done automatically by the system, since extrasystem activity is needed (e.g., cancelling already issued checks).

Given our use of a locking scheme to implement atomic objects, it is possible for two (or more) actions to *deadlock*, each attempting to acquire a lock held by the other. Although in many cases deadlock can be avoided with careful programming, certain deadlock situations are unavoidable. Rather than having the system prevent, or detect and break, deadlocks, we rely on the user to time out and abort top-level actions. These timeouts generally will be very long, or will be controlled by someone sitting at a terminal. Note that such timeouts are needed even without deadlocks, since there are other reasons why a top action may be too slow (e.g., contention).

A user can retry a top action that aborted because of a timeout or crash, but Argus provides no guarantee that progress will be made. Argus will be extended if needed (e.g., by raising the priority of a top action each time it is repeated [27] or by using checkpoints [10]).

3   Linguistic constructs

In this section we describe the main features of Argus. The most novel features are the constructs for implementing guardians, the logical nodes of the system, and for implementing actions, as described in the previous section. To avoid rethinking issues that arise in sequential languages, we have based Argus on an existing sequential language. CLU [17, 20] was chosen because it supports the construction of well-structured programs through abstraction mechanisms and because it is an object-oriented language, in which programs are naturally thought of as operating on potentially long-lived objects.

3.1   Overview

In Argus, a distributed program is composed of a group of *guardians*. A guardian encapsulates and controls access to one or more resources, for example, databases or devices. A guardian makes these resources available to its users by providing a set of operations called *handlers,* which can be called by other guardians to make use of the resources. The guardian executes the handlers, synchronizing them and performing access control as needed.

Internally, a guardian contains data objects and processes. The processes execute handlers (a separate process is spawned for each call) and perform background tasks. Some of the data objects, for example, the actual resources, make up the *state* of the guardian; these objects are shared by the processes. Other objects are local to the individual processes.

A guardian runs at a single node but can survive crashes of this node (with high probability). Thus, the guardians themselves are resilient. A guardian's state consists of *stable* and *volatile* objects. Resiliency is accomplished by writing the stable objects to stable storage when a top action commits; only those objects that were modified by the committing action need be written. The probability of loss of volatile objects is relatively high, so these objects must contain only redundant information if the system as a whole is to avoid loss of information. Such redundant information is useful for improving efficiency, for example, an index into a database for fast access.

After a crash of the guardian's node, the language support system re-creates the guardian with the stable objects as they were when last written to stable storage. A process is started in the guardian to recreate the volatile objects. Once the volatile objects have been restored, the guardian can resume background tasks and can respond to new handler calls.

Guardians allow a programmer to decompose a problem into units of tightly coupled processing and data. Within a guardian, processes can share objects directly. However, direct sharing of objects between guardians is not permitted. Instead, guardians must communicate by calling handlers, and the arguments to handlers are passed by value: it is impossible to pass a reference to an object in a handler call. This rule ensures that objects local to a guardian remain local, and thus ensures that a guardian retains control of its own objects. It also provides the programmer with a concept of what is expensive: local objects are close by and inexpensive to use, while nonlocal objects are more expensive to use. A handler call is performed using a message-based communication mechanism. The language implementation takes care of all details of constructing and sending messages (see [11]).

Guardians are created dynamically. The programmer specifies the node at which a guardian is to be created; in this way individual guardians can be placed at the most advantageous locations within the network. The (name of the) guardian and (the names of) its handlers can be communicated in handler calls. Once (the name of) a guardian or one of its handlers has been received, handler calls can be performed on that guardian. Handler calls are location independent, however, so one guardian can use another without knowing its location. In fact, handler calls will continue to work even if the called guardian has changed its location, allowing for ease of system reconfiguration.

Guardians and handlers are an abstraction of the underlying hardware of a distributed system. A guardian is a logical node of the system, and interguardian communication via handlers is an abstraction of the physical network. The most important difference between the logical system and the physical system is reliability: the stable state of a guardian is never lost (to a very high probability), and the at-most-once semantics of handler calls ensures that the calls either succeed completely or have no effect.

3.2 Guardian structure

The syntax of a guardian definition is shown in Figure 1.[†] A guardian definition implements a special kind of abstract data type whose operations are handlers. The name of this type, and the names of the handlers, are listed in the guardian header. In addition, the type provides one or more

---

[†] In the syntax, optional clauses are enclosed with [ ], zero or more repetitions are indicated with { }, and alternatives are separated by |.

creation operations, called *creators*, that can be invoked to create new guardians of the type; the names of the creators are also listed in the header. Guardians may be *parameterized*, providing the ability to define a class of related abstractions by means of a single module. Parameterized types are discussed in [17, 20].

> *name* = **guardian** [*parameter-decls*] **is** *creator-names*
>   **handles** *handler-names*
> {*abbreviations*}
> { [**stable**] *variable-decls-and-inits*}
> [**recover** *body* **end**]
> [**background** *body* **end**]
> {*creator-handler-and-local-routine-definitions*}
> **end** *name*

Figure 1   Guardian structure.

The first internal part of a guardian is a list of abbreviations for types and constants. Next is a list of variable declarations, with optional initializations, defining the guardian state. Some of these variables can be declared as **stable** variables; the others are volatile variables.

The stable state of a guardian consists of all objects *reachable* from the stable variables; these objects, called stable objects, have their new versions written to stable storage by the system when top-level actions commit. Argus, like CLU, has an object-oriented semantics. Variables name (or refer to) objects residing in a heap storage area. Objects themselves may refer to other objects, permitting recursive and cyclic data structures without the use of explicit pointers. The set of objects reachable from a variable consists of the object that variable refers to, any objects referred to by that object, and so on.[†]

Guardian instances are created dynamically by invoking creators of the guardian type. For example, suppose a guardian type named *spooler* has a creator with a header of the form:

> *create* = **creator**(*dev* : *printer*) **returns** (*spooler*)

When a process executes the expression:

> *spooler*$*create*(*pdev*)

a guardian object is created at the same physical node where the process is executing and (the name of) the guardian is returned as the result of the

---

[†] In languages that are not object oriented, the concept of reachability would still be needed to accommodate the use of explicit pointers.

call.[†] Guardians can also be created at other nodes. Given a variable *home* naming some node:

> *spooler$create*(*pdev*) @ *home*

creates a guardian at the specified node.

When a creator is invoked, a new guardian instance is created, and any initializations attached to the variable declarations of the guardian state are executed. The body of the creator is then executed; typically, this code will finish initializing the guardian state and then return the guardian object. (Within the guardian, the expression **self** refers to the guardian object.)

Aside from creating a new guardian instance and executing state-variable initializations, a creator has essentially the same semantics as a handler, as described in the next section. In particular, a creator call is performed within a new subaction of the caller, and the guardian will be destroyed if this subaction or some parent action aborts. The guardian becomes permanent (i.e., survives node crashes) only when the action in which it was created commits to the top level. A guardian cannot be destroyed from outside the guardian (except by aborting the creating action). Once a guardian becomes permanent, only the guardian can destroy itself, using a **destroy** primitive.

The **recover** section runs after a crash. Its job is to recreate a volatile state that is consistent with the stable state. This may be trivial, for example, creating an empty cache, or it may be a lengthy process, for example, creating a database index.

After a crash, the system recreates the guardian and restores its stable objects from stable storage. Since updates to stable storage are made only when top-level actions commit, the stable state has the value it had at the latest commit of a top-level action before the guardian crashed. The effects of actions that had executed at the guardian prior to the crash, but had not yet committed to the top level, are lost, and the actions are aborted.

After the stable objects have been restored, the system creates a process in the guardian to first execute any initializations attached to declarations of volatile variables of the guardian state and then execute the **recover** section. This process runs as a top-level action. Recovery succeeds if this action commits; otherwise, the guardian crashes, and recovery is retried later.

After the successful completion of a creator, or of the **recover** section after a crash, two things happen inside the guardian: a process is created to run the **background** section, and handler invocations may be executed.

[†] As in CLU, the notation *t$op* is used to name the *op* operation of type *t*.

The **background** section provides a means of performing periodic (or continuous) tasks within the guardian; examples are given in Section 4. The **background** section is not run as an action, although generally it creates top-level actions to execute tasks, as explained in Section 3.4.[†]

3.3 Handlers

Handlers (and creators), like procedures in CLU, are based on the termination model of exception handling [19]. A handler can terminate in one of a number of conditions: one of these is considered to be the 'normal' condition, while others are 'exceptional' and are given user-defined names. Results can be returned in both the normal and exceptional cases; the number and types of results can differ among conditions. The header of a handler definition lists the names of all exceptional conditions and defines the number and types of results in all cases. For example:

$$files\_ahead\_of = \textbf{handler}(entry\_id : int) \textbf{ returns } (int)$$
$$\textbf{signals } (printed(date))$$

might be the header of a spooler handler used to determine how many requests are in front of a given queue entry. Calls of this handler either terminate normally, returning an integer result, or exceptionally in condition *printed* with a *date* result. In addition to the named conditions, any handler can terminate in the *failure* condition, returning a string result; failure termination may be caused explicitly by the user code, or implicitly by the system when something unusual happens, as explained further below.

A handler executes as a subaction. As such, in addition to returning or signaling, it must either commit or abort. We expect committing to be the most common case, and, therefore, execution of a **return** or **signal** statement within the body of a handler indicates commitment. To cause an abort, the **return** or **signal** is prefixed with **abort**.

Given a variable x naming a guardian object, a handler h of the guardian may be referred to as $x.h$. Handlers are invoked using the same syntax as for procedure invocation, for example:

$$x.h(\text{"read"}, 3, false)$$

However, whereas procedures are always executed locally within the current action, and always have their arguments and results passed by

---

[†] A process that is not running as an action is severely restricted in what it can do. For example, it cannot call operations on atomic objects or call handlers without first creating a top-level action.

sharing,[†] handlers are always executed as new subactions, usually in a different guardian, and always have their arguments and results passed by value.

Let us examine a step-by-step description of what the system does when a handler is invoked:

(1) A new subaction of the calling action is created.

(2) A message containing the arguments is constructed. Since part of building this message involves executing user-defined code (see [11]), message construction may fail. If so, the subaction aborts and the call terminates with a *failure* exception.

(3) **The system suspends the calling process and sends the message to the target guardian. If that guardian no longer exists, the subaction aborts, and the call terminates with a *failure* exception.**

(4) The system makes a reasonable attempt to deliver the message, but success is not guaranteed. The reason is that it may not be sensible to guarantee success under certain conditions, such as a crash of the target node. In such cases, the subaction aborts, and the call terminates with a *failure* exception. The meaning of such a failure is that there is a very low probability of the call succeeding if it is repeated immediately.

(5) The system creates a process and a subaction (of the subaction in step (1)) at the receiving guardian to execute the handler. Note that multiple instances of the same handler may execute simultaneously. The system takes care of locks and versions of atomic objects used by the handler in the proper manner, according to whether the handler commits or aborts.

(6) When the handler terminates, a message containing the results is constructed, the handler action terminates, the handler process is destroyed, and the message is sent. If the message cannot be sent (as in step (2) or (4) above), the subaction created in step (1) aborts, and the call terminates with a *failure* exception.

(7) The calling process continues execution. Its control flow is affected by the termination condition as explained in [19]. For example:

> *count* : *int* := *spool. files_ahead_of* (*ent*) % normal return
> **except when** *printed*(*at* : *date*) : ...   % exceptional returns
>   **when** *failure*(*why* : *string*) : ...
>   **end**

Since a new process is created to perform an incoming handler call, guardians have the ability to execute many requests concurrently. Such

---

[†] Somewhat similar to passing by reference. See [17].

an ability helps to avoid having a guardian become a bottleneck. Of course, if the guardian is running on a single-processor node, then only one process will be running at a time. However, a common case is that in executing a handler call another handler call to some other guardian is made. It would be unacceptable if the guardian could do no other work while this call was outstanding.

The scheduling of incoming handler calls is performed by the system. Therefore, the programmer need not be concerned with explicit scheduling, but instead merely provides the handler definitions to be executed in response to the incoming calls. An alternative structure for a guardian would be a single process that multiplexed itself and explicitly scheduled execution of incoming calls. We think our structure is more elegant, and no less efficient since our processes are cheap: creating a new process is only slightly more expensive than calling a procedure.

As was mentioned above, the system does not guarantee message delivery; it merely guarantees that, if message delivery fails, there is a very low probability of the call succeeding if it is repeated immediately. Hence, there is no reason for user code to retry handler calls. Rather, as mentioned earlier, user programs should make progress by retrying top-level actions, which may fail because of node crashes even if all handler calls succeed.

3.4   In-line actions

Top-level actions are created by means of the action statement:

> **enter topaction** *body* **end**

This causes the *body* to execute as a new top-level action. It is also possible to have an in-line subaction:

> **enter action** *body* **end**

This causes the *body* to run as a subaction of the action that executes the **enter**.

When the body of an in-line action completes, it must indicate whether it is committing or aborting. Since committing is assumed to be most common, it is the default; the qualifier **abort** can be prefixed to any termination statement to override this default. For example, an in-line action can execute:

> **leave**

to commit and cause execution to continue with the statement following the **enter** statement; to abort and have the same effect on control, it executes:

abort leave

Falling off the end of the *body* causes the action to commit.

3.5 Concurrency

The language as defined so far allows concurrency only between top actions originating in different guardians. The following statement form provides more concurrency:

coenter {*coarm*} **end**

where:

coarm ::= *armtag* [**foreach** *decl-list* **in** *iter-invocation*]
　　　　body
armtag ::= **action** | **topaction**

The process executing the **coenter**, and the action on whose behalf it is executing, are suspended; they resume execution after the **coenter** is finished.

A **foreach** clause indicates that multiple instances of the coarm will be activated, one for each item (a collection of objects) yielded by the given iterator invocation.[†] Each such coarm will have local instances of the variables declared in the *decl-list*, and the objects constituting the yielded item will be assigned to them. Execution of the **coenter** starts by running each of the iterators to completion, sequentially, in textual order. Then all coarms are started simultaneously as concurrent siblings. Each coarm instance runs in a separate process, and each process executes within a new top-level action or subaction, as specified by the *armtag*.

A simple example making use of **foreach** is in performing a write operation concurrently at all copies of a replicated database:

```
coenter
    action foreach db : db_copy in all_copies(...)
        db.write(...)
    end
```

This statement creates separate processes for the guardian objects yielded by *all_copies*, each process having a local variable *db* bound to a particular guardian. Each process runs in a newly created subaction and makes a handler call.

[†] An iterator is a limited kind of coroutine that provides results to its caller one at a time [17, 20].

A coarm may terminate without terminating the entire **coenter** either by falling off the end of its *body* or by executing a **leave** statement. As before, **leave** may be prefixed by **abort** to cause the completing action to abort; otherwise, the action commits.

A coarm also may terminate by transferring control outside the **coenter** statement. Before such a transfer can occur, all other active coarms of the **coenter** must be terminated. To accomplish this, the system forces all coarms that are not yet completed to abort. A simple example where such early termination is useful is in performing a read operation concurrently at all copies of a replicated database, where a response from any single copy will suffice:

```
coenter
    action foreach db : db_copy in all_copies(...)
        result := db.read(...)
        exit done
    end except when done : ... end
```

Once a read has completed successfully, the **exit** will commit the read and abort all remaining reads. The aborts take place immediately; in particular, it is not necessary for the handler calls to finish before the subactions can be aborted. (Such aborts can result in *orphan* handler processes that continue to run at the called guardians and elsewhere. We have developed algorithms for dealing with orphans, but they are beyond the scope of this paper.)

There is another form of **coenter** for use outside of actions, as in the **background** section of a guardian. In this form the *armtag* can be **process** or **topaction**. The semantics is as above, except that no action is created in the **process** case.

3.6   Program development and reconfiguration

Argus, like CLU, provides separate compilation of modules with complete type checking at compile time (see [17]). Separate compilation is performed in the context of a program library, which contains information about abstractions (e.g., guardian types).

Before creating a guardian at a node, it is first necessary to load the code of that guardian at that node. Once the code image has been loaded, any number of guardians of that type can be created at that node. It is also possible to load a different code image of the same guardian type at the node, and then create guardians that run that code.

To build a code image of a guardian definition, it is necessary to select implementations for the data, procedural, and iteration abstractions that are used, but not for other guardian abstractions. In other words, each guardian is linked and loaded separately. In fact, each guardian is independent of the implementation of all other guardians, because our method of communicating data values between guardians is implementation independent (see [11]). A guardian is also independent of all abstractions except for those it actually uses. New abstractions can be added to the library, and new implementations can be written for both old and new abstractions, without affecting any running guardian.

Guardians are constrained to communicate with other guardians only via handlers whose types were known when the guardian was compiled. Communication via handlers of unknown type is not sensible; the situation is exactly analogous to calling a procedure of unknown type. Of course, a guardian or handler argument of known type but unknown value can be very useful. We *do* provide this: guardians and handlers can be used as arguments in local procedure calls and in handler calls.

Compile-time type checking does *not* rule out dynamic reconfiguration. By receiving guardians and handlers dynamically in handler calls, a guardian can communicate with new guardians as they are created or become available. For example, the Argus system contains a distributed *catalog* that registers guardians and handlers according to their type. The catalog would respond to a request for printer guardians by returning all guardians of type 'printer' that previously had been registered.

In many applications it will be necessary to change the implementations of running guardians. We are investigating a replacement strategy that permits new implementations to be provided for running guardians without affecting the users of these guardians [2]. This system also allows for certain kinds of changes in guardian type (e.g., additional handlers).

4 A simple mail system

In this section we present a simple mail system, designed somewhat along the lines of Grapevine [1]. This is a pedagogical example: we have chosen inefficient or inadequate implementations for some features, and have omitted many necessary and desirable features of a real mail system. However, we hope it gives some idea of how a real system could be implemented in Argus.

The interface to the mail system is quite simple. Every user has a unique name (*user_id*) and a mailbox. However, mailbox locations are hidden from the user. Mail can be sent to a user by presenting the mail system with the user's user_id and a *message*; the message will be appended to the user's mailbox. Mail can be read by presenting the mail system with a user's *user_id*; all messages are removed from the user's mailbox and are returned to the caller. For simplicity, there is no protection on this operation: any user may read another user's mail. Finally, there is an operation for adding new users to the system, and there are operations for dynamically extending the mail system.

All operations are performed within the action system. For example, a message is not really added to a mailbox unless the sending action commits, messages are not really deleted unless the reading action commits, and a user is not really added unless the requesting action commits.

The mail system is implemented out of three kinds of guardians: mailers, maildrops, and registries. *Mailers* act as the front end of the mail system: all use of the system occurs through calls of mailer handlers. To achieve high availability, many mailers are used, for example, one at each physical node. All mailers would be registered in the catalog for dynamic lookup. A *maildrop* contains the mailboxes for some subset of users. Individual mailboxes are not replicated, but multiple, distributed maildrops are used to reduce contention and to increase availability, in that the crash of one physical node will not make all mailboxes unavailable. The mapping from user_id to maildrop is provided by the *registries*. Replicated registries are used to increase availability, in that at most one registry need be accessible to send or read mail. Each registry contains the complete mapping for all users. In addition, registries keep track of all other registries.

Two built-in atomic types are used in implementing the mail system: *atomic_array* and *struct*. Atomic arrays are one-dimensional and can grow and shrink dynamically. Of the array operations used in the mail system, *new* creates an empty array, *addh* adds an element to the high end, *trim* removes elements, *elements* iterates over the elements from low to high, and *copy* makes a complete copy of an array. A read lock on the entire array is obtained by *new*, *elements*, and *copy*, and a write lock is obtained by *addh* and *trim*. Structs are immutable (hence atomic) records: new components cannot be stored in a struct object once it has been created. However, the fact that a struct is immutable does not prevent its component objects from being modified if they are mutable.

The mailer guardian is presented in Figure 2. Each mailer is given a registry when created; this registry is the mailer's stable reference to the entire mail system. The mailer also keeps a volatile reference, representing the 'best' access path into the system. The **background** code periodically polls all registries; the first to respond is used as the new best registry.

A mailer performs a request to send or read mail by first using the best registry to look up the maildrop for the specified user and then forwarding the request to that maildrop. A mailer adds a new user by first calling the registry *select* handler to make sure the user is not already present and to choose a maildrop; then, concurrently, the new user/maildrop pair is added to each registry, and the new user is added to the chosen maildrop. A maildrop (or registry) is added by creating the maildrop (or registry) and then concurrently adding it to all registries. A new mailer is created with the current best registry for its stable reference.

```
mailer = guardian is create
                    handles send_mail, read_mail, add_user,
                            add_maildrop, add_registry, add_mailer
reg_list = atomic_array[registry]
msg_list = atomic_array[message]
stable some : registry   % stable reference to some registry
best : registry          % volatile reference to some registry
recover
    best := some         % reassign after a crash
    end

background
  while true do
    enter topaction
        regs : reg_list := best.all_registries( )
        coenter
          action foreach reg : registry in reg_list$elements(regs)
              reg.ping( )   % see if it responds
              best := reg  % make it best
              exit done    % abort all others
            end except when done : end
          end except when failure(*) : end
      sleep(...)   % some amount of time
      end
  end

create = creator(reg : registry) returns (mailer)
    some := reg
    best := reg
    return(self)
    end create

send_mail = handler(user : user_id, msg : message) signals (no_such_user)
    drop : maildrop := best.lookup(user)
      resignal no_such_user
    drop.send_mail(user, msg)
    end send_mail

read_mail = handler(user : user_id) returns (msg_list) signals (no_such_user)
    drop : maildrop := best.lookup(user)
      resignal no_such_user
    return(drop.read_mail(user))
    end read_mail

add_user = handler(user : user_id) signals (user_exists)
    drop : maildrop := best.select(user)
      resignal user_exists
    regs : reg_list := best.all_registries( )
```

Figure 2   Mailer guardian

```
      coenter
        action
          drop.add_user(user)
        action foreach reg : registry in reg_list$elements(regs)
          reg.add_user(user, drop)
        end
      end add_user

  add_maildrop = handler(home : node)
    drop : maildrop := maildrop$create( ) @ home
    regs : reg_list := best.all_registries( )
      coenter
        action foreach reg : registry in reg_list$elements(regs)
          reg.add_maildrop(drop)
        end
      end add_maildrop

  add_registry = handler(home : node)
    new : registry := best.new_registry(home)
    regs : reg_list := best.all_registries( )
      coenter
        action foreach reg : registry in reg_list$elements(regs)
          reg.add_registry(new)
        end
      end add_registry

  add_mailer = handler(home : node) returns (mailer)
    m : mailer := mailer$create(best) @ home
    return(m)
    end add_mailer

  end mailer
```

Figure 2   Mailer guardian (contd).

Figure 3 shows the registry guardian. The state of a registry consists
of an atomic array of registries together with a *steering list* associating an
array of users with each maildrop. When a registry is created, it is given
the current steering list and an array of all other registries, to which array
it adds itself. The *lookup* handler uses linear search to find the given
user's maildrop. The *select* handler uses linear search to check if a user
already exists, and then chooses some existing maildrop. The *add_user*
handler uses linear search to find the specified maildrop and then
appends the user to the associated user list. The *add_user, add_maildrop,*
and *add_registry* handlers perform no error checking because correctness
is guaranteed by the mailer guardian.

```
registry = guardian is create
                    handles lookup, select, all_registries, ping,
                            add_user, add_maildrop, new_registry,
                            add_registry
reg_list   = atomic_array[registry]
steer_list = atomic_array[steering]
steering   = struct[users : user_list,   % users with mailboxes
                    drop : maildrop]   % at this maildrop
user_list = atomic_array[user_id]
stable regs : reg_list      % all registries
stable steers : steer_list   % all users and maildrops
create = creator(rlist : reg_list, slist : steer_list) returns (registry)
   reg_list$addh(rlist, self)   % add self to list
   regs := rlist
   steers := slist
   return(self)
   end create

lookup = handler(user : user_id) returns (maildrop) signals (no_such_user)
   for steer : steering in steer_list$elements(steers) do
      for usr : user_id in user_list$elements(steer.users) do
         if usr = user then return(steer.drop) end
         end
      end
   signal no_such_user
   end lookup

select = handler(user : user_id) returns (maildrop) signals (user_exists)
   for steer : steering in steer_list$elements(steers) do
      for usr : user_id in user_list$elements(steer.users) do
         if usr = user then signal user_exists end
         end
      end
   return(...)   % choose, for example, maildrop with least users
   end select

all_registries = handler( ) returns (reg_list)
   return(regs)
   end all_registries

ping = handler( )
   end ping

add_user = handler(user : user_id, drop : maildrop)
   for steer : steering in steer_list$elements(steers) do
      if steer.drop = drop
         then user_list$addh(steer.users, user)   % append user
            return
         end
      end
   end add_user
```

Figure 3   Registry guardian

```
add_maildrop = handler(drop : maildrop)
    steer : steering := steering${users : user_list$new( ),
                                        drop : drop}
    steer_list$addh(steers, steer)
    end add_maildrop

new_registry = handler(home : node) returns (registry)
    reg : registry := registry$create(regs, steers) @ home
    return(reg)
    end new_registry

add_registry = handler(reg : registry)
    reg_list$addh(regs, reg)
    end add_registry

end registry
```

Figure 3 Registry guardian (contd).

The maildrop guardian is given in Figure 4. The state of a maildrop consists of an atomic array of mailboxes; a mailbox is represented by a struct containing a user_id and an atomic array of messages. A maildrop is created with no mailboxes. The *add_user* handler is used to add a mailbox. Note that this handler does not check to see if the user already exists since the mailer will have already performed this check. The *send_mail* and *read_mail* handlers use linear search to find the correct mailbox. When the mailbox is found, *send_mail* appends a message to the end of the message array; *read_mail* first copies the array, then deletes all messages, and, finally, returns the copy. Both handlers assume the user exists; again, the mailer guarantees this.

Now that we have all of the pieces of the mail system, we can show how the initial configuration of the mail system is created:

```
reg : registry := registry$create(reg_list$new( ), steer_list$new( )) @ home1
m : mailer := mailer$create(reg) @ home2
```

where *reg_list* and *steer_list* are defined as in the registry. The resulting mailer can then be placed in the catalog and used to add maildrops and users, as well as more registries and mailers.

Finally, we show a simple use of the mail system, namely, sending a message to a group of users, with the constraint that the message be delivered either to all of the users or to none of them:

```
enter action
    coenter
        action foreach user : user_id in user_group("net")
            m.send_mail(user, msg)
        end except when no_such_user, failure(*) :   % ignore failure string
                            abort leave
                        end
    end
```

```
maildrop = guardian is create
                      handles send_mail, read_mail, add_user
box_list = atomic_array[mailbox]
mailbox = struct[mail : msg_list,    % messages for
                 user : user_id]     % this user
msg_list = atomic_array[message]

stable boxes : box_list := box_list$new( )

create = creator( ) returns (maildrop)
   return(self )
   end create

send_mail = handler(user : user_id, msg : message)
   for box : mailbox in box_list$elements(boxes) do
      if box.user = user
         then msg_list$addh(box.mail, msg)   % append message
            return
         end
      end
   end send_mail

read_mail = handler(user : user_id) returns (msg_list)
   for box : mailbox in box_list$elements(boxes) do
      if box.user = user
         then mail : msg_list := msg_list$copy(box.mail)
            msg_list$trim(box.mail, 1, 0)   % delete messages
            return(mail)
         end
      end
   end read_mail

add_user = handler(user : user_id)
   box : mailbox := mailbox${mail : msg_list$new( ),
                            user : user}
   box_list$addh(boxes, box)
   end add_user

end maildrop
```

Figure 4   Maildrop guardian.

The message is sent to all users simultaneously. A nonexistent user or a failure to send a message transfers control outside the **coenter**, forcing termination of all active coarms; the outer action is then aborted, guaranteeing that none of the messages is actually delivered.

4.1 Remarks

One obvious problem with the mailers as implemented is that, if the best registry for a mailer goes down, the mailer effectively goes down as well, since every task the mailer performs (including choosing a new *best* registry) requires communication with that registry. A better implementation might be for each mailer to have stable and volatile references to multiple registries, and for mailer handlers to try several registries (sequentially) before giving up.

Close examination of the mail system reveals places where the particular choice of data representation leads to less concurrency than might be expected. For example, in the maildrop guardian, since both *send_mail* and *read_mail* modify the message array in a mailbox, either operation will lock out all other operations on the same mailbox until the executing action commits to the top level. Even worse, since both *send_mail* and *read_mail* read the mailbox array, and *add_user* modifies that array, an *add_user* operation will lock out all operations on all mailboxes at that maildrop. In the registry guardian, an *add_user* operation will lock out *lookup* operations on all users with mailboxes at the given maildrop, and an *add_maildrop* operation will lock out all *lookup* operations.

In a traditional mail system this lack of concurrency might be tolerable, but there are other, similar systems where it would not be acceptable. What is needed are data types that allow more concurrency than do atomic arrays. For example, an associative memory that allowed concurrent insertions and lookups could replace the mailbox array in maildrops and the steering list in registries; a queue with a 'first-commit first-out' semantics, rather than a 'first-in first-out' semantics, could replace the message arrays in maildrops. Such types can be built as user-defined atomic types, although we do not present implementations here.

The concurrency that *is* built in to the mail system can lead to a number of deadlock situations. For example, in the registry guardian, any two concurrent *add_user* or *add_registry* requests will almost always deadlock, and two *add_maildrop* requests can deadlock by modifying registries in conflicting orders. Some of these deadlocks would disappear if data representations allowing more concurrency were used. For example, the use of a highly concurrent associative memory for the steering list would allow all *add_maildrop* requests to run concurrently, as well as all *add_user* requests for distinct users. Other deadlocks can be eliminated simply by reducing concurrency. To avoid deadlocks between *add_registry* requests, all *new_registry* calls could be made to a distinguished registry, and *new_registry* could obtain a write lock on the registry list before creating the new registry.

It may be argued that the strict serialization of actions enforced by the particular implementation we have shown is not important in a real mail system. This does not mean that actions are inappropriate in a mail system, just that the particular granularity of actions we have chosen may not be the best. For example, if an action discovers that a user does (or does not) exist, it may not be important that the user continues to exist (or not to exist) for the remainder of the overall action. It is possible to build such 'loopholes' through appropriately defined abstract types. As another example, it might not be important for all registries to have the most up-to-date information, provided they receive all updates eventually. In particular, when adding a user, it may suffice to guarantee that all registries eventually will be informed of that user. This could be accomplished by keeping appropriate information in the stable state of one of the registries, and using a background process in that registry to (eventually) inform all other registries.

5   Summary and conclusions

Argus has two main concepts: guardians and actions. Guardians maintain local control over their local data. The data inside a guardian are truly local; no other guardian has the ability to access or manipulate the data directly. The guardian provides access to the data via handler calls, but the actual access is performed inside the guardian. It is the guardian's job to guard its data in three ways: by synchronizing concurrent access to the data, by requiring that the caller of a handler have the authorization needed to do the access, and by making enough of the data stable so that the guardian as a whole can survive crashes without loss of information.

While guardians are the unit of modularity, actions are the means by which distributed computation takes place. A top-level action starts at some guardian. This action can perform a distributed computation by making handler calls to other guardians; those handler calls can make calls to still more guardians; and so on. Since the entire computation is an atomic action, it is guaranteed that the computation is based on a consistent distributed state and that, when the computation finishes, the state is still consistent, assuming in both cases that user programs are correct.

Argus is quite different from other languages that address concurrent or distributed programs (e.g., [3, 7, 12, 24]). Those languages tend to provide modules that bear a superficial resemblance to guardians, and some form of communication between modules based on message passing. For the most part, however, the modules have no internal concurrency and contain no provision for data consistency or resiliency. Indeed, the languages completely ignore the problem of hardware failures. In the area of communication, either a low-level, unreliable mechanism is provided, or reliability is ignored, implying that the mechanism is completely reliable, with no way of actually achieving such reliability.

Although a great many details have been omitted, we hope enough of the language has been described to show how Argus meets the requirements stated in the introduction. Consistency, service, distribution, concurrency, and extensibility are all well supported in Argus. However, there are two areas that are not well supported. One is protection. Guardians could check for proper authorization before performing requests, for example, by requiring principal IDs as arguments to handler calls. But, there is no way within the language to express constraints as to where and when guardians may be created. For example, the owner of a node may wish to allow a particular guardian to be created at that node but disallow that guardian from creating other guardians at the node. These kinds of protection issues are under investigation.

Another area that may need work is support for scheduling. Within a guardian a separate process is automatically created for each handler call. This structure provides no direct support for scheduling incoming calls. If one wanted to give certain incoming calls priority over others, this could be done explicitly (by means of a shared monitorlike [13] object). If one wanted certain incoming calls to take priority over calls currently being executed, this could be done (very awkwardly) by programming handlers to relinquish control periodically. However, if one wanted to make priorities global to an entire node, rather than just within a single guardian, there would be no way to accomplish this in Argus. We are not convinced that priorities are required frequently enough to justify any additional mechanism. We prefer to adopt a 'wait-and-see' attitude, although we are investigating priority mechanisms.

Supporting atomic activities as part of the semantics of a programming language imposes considerable implementation difficulties. We have completed a preliminary, centralized implementation of the language, ignoring difficult problems such as lock propagation and orphan detection. We are working on a real, distributed implementation. At this point it is unclear how efficient such an implementation can be.

The approach to resiliency taken in Argus represents an engineering compromise given the current state of hardware. If ultrareliable hardware does become practical, it may no longer be necessary to compensate for hardware failures in software. This would simplify the structure of guardians since stable objects and the recover section would no longer be needed. Furthermore, the implementation of Argus would become more efficient.

However, regardless of advances in hardware, we believe atomic actions are necessary and are a natural model for a large class of applications. If the language/system does not provide actions, the user will be compelled to implement them, perhaps unwittingly reimplementing them with each new application, and may implement them incorrectly. For some applications, actions simply may be a convenient tool, not a strictly necessary one. We believe that actions can be implemented efficiently enough that they will be used in applications even when they are not strictly necessary. We expect to get a much more realistic idea of the strengths and weaknesses of the language once the distributed implementation is complete and we can run applications.

Acknowledgments

The authors gratefully acknowledge the contributions made by members of the Argus design group, especially Maurice Herlihy, Paul Johnson, and Bill Weihl. The paper was improved by the comments of the referees and many others.

References

[1]   Birrell, A.D., Levin, R., Needham, R.M., and Schroeder, M.D. Grapevine: An exercise in distributed computing. *Commun. ACM* **25**, 4 (Apr. 1982), 260–274.

[2]   Bloom, T. Dynamic Module Replacement in a Distributed Programming Environment. Ph.D. dissertation, Laboratory for Computer Science, Massachusetts Inst. of Technology, Cambridge, Mass., to appear.

[3]   Brinch Hansen, P. Distributed processes: A concurrent programming concept. *Commun. ACM* **21**, 11 (Nov.1978), 934–941.

[4]   Davies, C.T. Data processing spheres of control. *IBM Syst. J.* **17**, 2 (1978), 179–198.

[5]   Davies, C.T., Jr. Recovery semantics for a DB/DC system. In *Proceedings, ACM 73: Annual Conference,* Aug. 1973, pp. 136–141.

[6]   Eswaran, K.P., Gray, J.N., Lorie, R.A., and Traiger, I.L. The notions of consistency and predicate locks in a database system. *Commun. ACM* **19**, 11 (Nov. 1976), 624–633.

[7]   Feldman, J.A. High level programming for distributed computing. *Commun. ACM* **22**, 6 (June 1979), 353–368.

[8]   Gray, J.N. Notes on data base operating systems. In *Lecture Notes in Computer Science,* **60**: *Operating Systems, An Advanced Course,* R. Bayer, R.M. Graham, G. Seegmüller (Eds.). Springer-Verlag, New York, 1978, pp. 393–481.

[9]   Gray, J.N., Lorie, R.A., Putzolu, G.F., and Traiger, I.L.. Granularity of locks and degrees of consistency in a shared data base. In *Modeling in Data Base Management Systems,* G.M. Nijssen (Ed.). Elsevier North-Holland, New York, 1976.

[10] Gray, J., McJones, P., Blasgen, M., Lindsay, B., Lorie, R., Price, T., Putzolu, F., and Traiger, I. The recovery manager of the System R database manager. *Comput. Surv. (ACM)* **13**, 2 (June 1981), 223–242.

[11] Herlihy, M., and Liskov, B. A value transmission method for abstract data types. *ACM Trans. Program. Lang. Syst.* **4**, 4 (Oct. 1982), 527–551.

[12] Hoare, C.A.R. Communicating sequential processes. *Commun. ACM* **21**, 8 (Aug. 1978), 666–677.

[13] Hoare, C.A.R. Monitors: An operating system structuring concept. *Commun. ACM* **17**, 10 (Oct. 1974), 549–557.

[14] Lamport, L. Towards a theory of correctness for multi-user data base systems. Rep. CA-7610-0712, Massachusetts Computer Associates, Wakefield, Mass., Oct. 1976.

[15] Lampson, B., and Sturgis, H. Crash recovery in a distributed data storage system. Xerox PARC, Palo Alto, Calif., Apr. 1979.

[16] Liskov, B. On linguistic support for distributed programs. In Proceedings, IEEE Symposium on Reliability in Distributed Software and Database Systems, Pittsburgh, Pa., July 1981, pp. 53–60.

[17] Liskov, B., Atkinson, R., Bloom, T., Moss, E., Schaffert, J.C., Scheifler, R., and Snyder, A. *Lecture Notes in Computer Science,* **114**: *CLU Reference Manual.* Springer-Verlag, New York, 1981.

[18] Liskov, B., and Scheifler, R. Guardians and actions: Linguistic support for robust, distributed programs. In Conference Record of the 9th Annual ACM Symposium on Principles of Programming Languages, Albuquerque, N.M., Jan. 25–27, 1982, pp. 7–19.

[19] Liskov, B., and Snyder, A. Exception handling in CLU. *IEEE Trans. Softw. Eng.* **SE-5**, 6 (Nov. 1979), 546–558.

[20] Liskov, B., Snyder, A., Atkinson, R., and Schaffert, C. Abstraction mechanisms in CLU. *Commun. ACM* **20**, 8 (Aug. 1977), 564–576.

[21] Liskov, B., and Zilles, S.N. Programming with abstract data types. In Proceedings, ACM SIGPLAN Conference on Very High Level Languages. *SIGPLAN Notices* (ACM) **9**, 4 (Apr. 1974), 50–59.

[22] Lomet, D. Process structuring, synchronization, and recovery using atomic actions. In Proceedings of an ACM Conference on Language Design for Reliable Software. *SIGPLAN Notices* (ACM) **12**, 2 (Mar. 1977).

[23] Moss, J.E.B. Nested Transactions: An Approach to Reliable Distributed Computing. Ph.D. dissertation and Tech. Rep. MIT/LCS/TR-260, Laboratory for Computer Science, Massachusetts Inst. of Technology, Cambridge, Mass., 1981.

[24] Preliminary Ada Reference Manual. *SIGPLAN Notices* (ACM) **14**, 6 (June 1979), pt. A.

[25] Randell, B. System structure for software fault tolerance. *IEEE Trans. Softw. Eng.* **SE-1**, 2 (June 1975), 220–232.

[26] Reed, D.P. Naming and Synchronization in a Decentralized Computer System. Ph.D. dissertation and Tech. Rep. MIT/LCS/TR-205, Laboratory for Computer Science, Massachusetts Inst. of Technology, Cambridge, Mass., 1978.

[27] Rosenkrantz, D.J., Stearns, R.E., and Lewis, P.M., II. System level concurrency control for distributed database systems. *ACM Trans. Database Syst.* **3**, 2 (June 1978),178–198.

[28] Shrivastava, S.K., and Banatre, J.P. Reliable resource allocation between unreliable processes. *IEEE Trans. Softw. Eng.* **SE-4**, 3 (May 1978), 230–240.

[29] Spector, A.Z., Performing remote operations efficiently on a local computer network. *Commun. ACM* **25**, 4 (Apr. 1982), 246–260.

[30] Weihl, W., and Liskov, B. Specification and implementation of resilient, atomic data types. Computation Structures Group Memo 223, Laboratory for Computer Science, Massachusetts Inst. of Technology, Cambridge, Mass., Dec. 1982.

13

Design Considerations for Array Processing Languages

Charles Wetherell

University of California at Davis

The Department of Energy (DoE) has a long history of large-scale scientific calculation on the most advanced 'number-crunching' computers. Recently, an effort to improve communications and software sharing among DoE laboratories has been underway. One result of this sharing is a project to design and implement a common language. That language turns out to be FORTRAN 77 significantly extended with new data structures, control structures and array processing. The data used to design the array processing feature is surprising and likely to be of use to others working in scientific language design; it is reported here so that others may profit from DoE's experience.

Key words: array processing, FORTRAN 77, language design, vector processing, scientific computation.

Large scientific programs dominate computer usage at Lawrence Livermore Laboratory (LLL) and at many of the other laboratories and institutions supported by the Department of Energy (DoE). The larger laboratories with the most pressing needs have banded together as the

---

This work was performed under the auspices of the U.S. Department of Energy by the Lawrence Livermore Laboratory under contract number W-7405-ENG-48.

Advanced Computing Committee (ACC) in an effort to improve service and to share resources among their sites. ACC spawned a child, the Language Working Group (LWG), chartered to provide users with a powerful common language and language support services. LWG has developed an extension of FORTRAN 77 to meet the needs of ACC and will report on the new language during 1980. But the process of research and development was interesting in itself; this paper discusses that process and some of the more surprising conclusions, particularly concerning array processing.

Some LWG history

Before LWG had been long in existence, it laid down some guidelines for its own work:

(1) Instead of trying to standardize the varying practices of the individual laboratories, LWG would develop a new *common* language for use at all ACC sites.

(2) Although other purposes will be served by the common language (particularly systems programming), scientific applications are the most important.

(3) Because DoE laboratories regularly purchase the largest state-of-the-art computer systems (also the most expensive), the common language must take advantage of powerful and exotic architectural features.

(4) The common language must draw on the vast accumulation of programs and experience already available at the laboratories.

As a result, LWG proposed and ACC accepted the principle that FORTRAN 77, suitably extended to meet DoE's advanced needs, should be the common language. This is a particularly attractive decision for three reasons: FORTRAN 77 will certainly be common not only to DoE but to a larger community; FORTRAN 77 is quite amenable to extensions; and ACC laboratories have considerable experience in extending earlier FORTRANs.

Of the extensions under consideration, array processing is perhaps the most important and it is certainly the most complicated. Almost all scientific programs contain extensive array processing sections, either because of the need to solve explicit linear equations or because there is a quantity of data to be analysed in parallel. Further, novel architectures (CDC STAR, Cray CRAY-1, Burroughs BSP, add-on vector boxes, etc.) attempt to improve machine performance by providing hardware support to array processing. Languages with some array or vector features abound; APL, BASIC, PL/I and LLL's LRLTRAN are four in DoE use. But these languages suffer from a variety of defects including inefficient implementation, inappropriate structure for very large (100 000 lines) program systems, and *ad hoc* definition and support. Although each suggests possible array processing features, none of these four, nor any other language with which LWG is conversant, solves DoE's array processing difficulties.

Early in its life, LWG surveyed computer usage at ACC sites. LWG found that all sites share a need to allocate different amounts of storage at each program invocation *without recompilation* (dynamic data sizing) and that many programs need to change the size of arrays during execution (dynamic array allocation). Since FORTRAN (either 66 or 77) is notoriously deficient in dynamic memory allocation, Richard Zwakenberg and Richard Potter (no longer a member of LWG) proposed dynamic allocation extensions as an LWG enhancement. After critical comment by LWG, John Williams (then of Cornell University and now of IBM) and by the Language Group at LLL, Zwakenberg and Potter's ideas were accepted in principle by the LWG.

At this time, I joined LWG and prepared a thorough expansion and revision of the Zwakenberg–Potter paper. Simultaneously, Lester Petrie of Oak Ridge National Laboratory wrote and presented a short summary of array processing features which might be of interest to LWG. The two papers generated spirited discussion at two meetings of LWG. In preparation for decisions to be made in June 1978 on the future of all the array processing proposals, Zwakenberg and I asked our users what array processing features they would like to see. The surprising answers, which are discussed at length later, were presented to LWG and now form the basis of our planning in the area of array processing. In addition, the results have been discussed (once at very great length) with about half a dozen groups and individuals interested in high-speed computation and array processing. So far, the results of our informal survey have generated some shock but no rebuttals.

What users want from array processing

Zwakenberg and I were quite informal in our survey. First, we reviewed notes Zwakenberg, Potter and Williams had made when asking users about the development of a dynamic allocation feature. At the same time we recalled the arguments for the several vector processing features of LRLTRAN. Then we interviewed several representative programmers from LLL and the DoE Magnetic Fusion Energy Computer Center (MFECC). When all of these sources pointed to the same rough conclusions, we decided that we had enough information to report local consensus to LWG. Had we realized how generally applicable the conclusions were, we might well have been more careful in our survey. I will defer discussion of why I feel the results to be generally applicable until after the results have been presented.

Before we went to the users, we made several observations which interviews confirmed:

(1) 'Dynamic data sizing' is very important. Most applications try to use all the available memory on every machine on which they run. Since interior data structure sizes depend on input data in complicated ways, the fitting to memory must be done when the data is available at run-time. The fixed size structures used in standard FORTRAN are awkward and inefficient, or (commonly) unable to provide such fitting.

(2) Although dynamic allocation during a program run is slightly less pressing, many programs run in distinct phases, each phase with its own storage needs. This implies that the programmer should have control of allocation during program execution, not just at program initiation.

(3) Users like array processing arithmetic statements for two distinct reasons. First, parallel computations and loop controls can often be collapsed into single statements. Such simplified statements make both the flow of data and the flow of control obvious to the reader. Some quite large programs can have almost all their control statements eliminated this way.

(4) Second, array processing exposes parallel operations so that a compiler may exploit the parallelism. Rather than rely on a 'vectorizer' to discover possible optimizations, the user is confident that the parallelism is visible. Since many large computers use vector and array hardware, lightening the compiler's task this way can be a significant aid to efficient object code generation.

At the beginning of each interview, we told the subject that DoE was planning to extend FORTRAN 77 with array processing operations and that the extensions would certainly include some kind of 'executable' DIMENSION statement to allocate storage dynamically. We then asked the subject to reflect on:

- the vector operations in LRLTRAN,
- the array operations used in linear algebra texts,
- the array operations identifiable in current application programs,
- the array operation available in subroutine and macro packages used in current applications,
- the array operations in APL.[†]

[†] APL operations are at the outer limit of generality, at least as extensions to FORTRAN. In addition, APL is widely known at LLL, is available on the time-sharing system, even if not heavily used, and was once the subject of a compiler effort to provide array operations to large applications.

After the preamble, the user was then invited to describe the operations he would like to see, regardless of expense or difficulty of implementation.

The answers given were well-nigh unanimous.

First, all agreed that array-valued arithmetic expressions and array assignments are absolutely essential. But the arithmetic chosen is element-by-element, *not* matrix arithmetic. Hence $A * B$ should have as its ij-th element $A_{ij} \cdot B_{ij}$, not the dot product of row i of A and column j of B. Arrays combined under an operator should be the same 'shape' (definitions of conformity varied in detail); two arrays would be legitimate operands if scalars of the same type would combine legally under the operator. Under this interpretation, *all* FORTRAN scalar operators are extended to element-by-element operators. The desire for addition of 'traditional' matrix operators like dot product, matrix multiply, inverse, trace and so on is small.

Users also wanted the common mathematical functions to operate element-by-element. The functions named include sin, cos, tan, exp, log, sqrt and so on. In fact, no reason has been found to exclude any of the FORTRAN 77 intrinsic functions from extension. A few of the functions may have ambiguous definitions – does MAX(A, B) return an array which is the element-by-element maximum of A and B (which must be the same shape) or simply the largest single element in A or B (where there is no shape restriction)? Both interpretations are valuable; a new function will be necessary to compute the interpretation not chosen. Notice that all the type conversion functions are among the extended intrinsics.

When a scalar appears in an array expression, it should be coerced into an array of the necessary shape for completion of the operation. This coercion is called *broadcasting*. For example, if F is a scalar, $F + A$ yields a result whose ij-th element is $F + A_{ij}$. Particularly for multiplication, broadcasting seems to be a natural coercion.

The extended array operators include relational and logical operators which may be used to construct logical arrays. Although logical arrays are useful in their own right, users emphasize their value in controlling other array operations. The most desired controlled operation is *conditional array assignment* – elements of the target array receive new values only where the controlling array contains .TRUE. in the corresponding element. The masking function can be used to combine arrays into one target or to avoid undesirable computations (for example, division by zero).

The last array operations users' desire are compression and expansion. *Compression* packs an array into a vector, squeezing out those elements not selected by a controlling logical array. *Expansion* reverses compression, moving contiguous vector elements back into selected array locations; naturally, a compressed array need not be expanded back to the same host or locations. Compression may be used to select a series of elements which go through common processing denied to the rest of the array or to construct more compact storage for some array elements.

Obviously, users want a variety of array operations; perhaps the surprise is that the desired operations are generally quite simple. In contrast to this simplicity, users asked for a variety of sophisticated ways to rename and slice arrays. Originally, we investigated renaming as an extension of FORTRAN EQUIVALENCE for dynamic arrays; it quickly became obvious that we were really being asked to add new ways to *section* arrays. Eventually five distinct sectioning methods emerged.

The first sectioning method is borrowed from PL/I (and other languages, no doubt). All the subscript positions along one dimension may be taken by placing a special marker in that subscript. For example, $A(*, I)$ might select the I-th *column* of A – that is, all elements with a second subscript of I and any possible first subscript. As with the next two sectioning methods, use of a section selector does not reduce the dimensionality of the selected objects; use of an ordinary subscript does. Hence, $A(*, I)$ is a vector or 1-dimensional array. Also, most agree that the upper and lower bounds of the dimension selected this way should be the same as the bounds of the original array along the dimension.

The second sectioning method is called by LWG *triplet notation*. It uses an abbreviated DO-loop to select subscript values along one dimension of a host array. For example, $A(1 : N: 2, I)$ would select every other element of column I of A. Details of evaluation of the selector triplet need to be settled, but the basic idea is well-accepted. The bounds along the selected dimension run from 1 to the number of elements selected; otherwise, using the selector indices might leave holes in the index set of the section.

Subscripting with a vector is the third sectioning method desired. If **V** is a vector with values 2, 4, 1 and 2, then $A(V, I)$ is also a vector with elements $A(2, I)$, $A(4, I)$, $A(1, I)$ and $A(2, I)$ (again). Unlike the first two sectioning methods, the number of elements along a selected dimension may be more than the number of elements along the same dimension in the host array. Users report that *vector subscripts* are handy for parallel table lookup and readout.

The last two sectioning methods differ from the first three because their effect runs over several statements (depending on the program, of course) and is not restricted to a single mention. The simpler of the two is *range setting*. Normally the shape of an array is determined from its declaration (or allocation, if allocation is available) and that shape is used to control all whole array operations. Range setting causes the high or low bounds of an array to be temporarily set inwards. If a general array is viewed as a rectangular parallelepiped, range setting shrinks the array to a smaller inner parallelepiped. The actual storage of the array is *not* affected, only the portion to be used in whole array operations. Range settings stay in effect until another setting is made or the original bounds are reset. Processing the blocks of a block diagonal matrix in turn might be a good use of range setting.

Mapping appears to be the dynamic equivalent of FORTRAN EQUIVALENCE, but it is possible to select more exotic subsets of arrays by mapping. A mapping between a mapped array and a host array is set up by specifying a set of host array subscripts for every possible mapped array subscript set. An example of a common mapping is:

$$D(I) \longrightarrow B(I, I)$$

where D is mapped onto the diagonal of B. Any indexing function might be allowed to be specified for the host array, but functions which are linear polynomials in the mapped array subscripts seem to be all that are necessary for our users. These also have the virtue of generating simple linear subscripting functions for the mapped array.

The idea of mapping provides no explicit bounds for a mapped array. When one attempts to derive such bounds from the host array bounds, it is easy to find cases where equations with multiple roots are generated. But by setting the ranges of a mapped array, bounds are known; hence range setting is regarded as a prerequisite for mapping. As an additional note, both range setting and mapping expressions might have free variables in them; users suggest that these variables should be evaluated once when the range or mapping is selected rather than left free to vary the section selected by side effects.

If all these different ways to select an array section are available, users demand that it be possible to pass such a section to a procedure just as one might pass an ordinary array. Unfortunately, FORTRAN takes advantage of the fact that arrays are stored contiguously in its argument passage semantics. Hence, any passage of sections (which are not normally contiguous) will have to contend with this difficulty. LWG, for example, will allow passage of any array object but has not settled on a resolution of the conflict with FORTRAN 77.

As mentioned before, there is not much desire for elaborate matrix operators, although matrix multiply and dot product should not be spurned. If user functions which may return arbitrarily shaped arrays are available, there is even less need for elaborate operators since such operators may be user programmed. Array-valued functions do not excite a great deal of interest, but some users would find them of value.

Our final user desired feature concerns FORTRAN COMMON. In theory, a COMMON block is a largely amorphous block of storage which each routine may rename and restructure almost at will. In fact, scientific applications usually import exactly the same names and structure into every routine which uses a given COMMON block. This technique creates a global name space (or its simulacrum) within FORTRAN; however, properties of variables are not really carried across routine boundaries. This can be confusing to programmers. Although global naming is not strictly an array processing feature, users commonly mention the need for better naming to make array processing more valuable.

Conclusion

APL is the most widely used array processing language; it is remarkable for the power and sophistication of its operators. When we began this study, we felt it likely that our users, most of whom are familiar with APL, would ask for these elaborate operators to be included in any new array processing language. Instead, they asked only for quite simple computational operators. But to our surprise, users requested powerful data manipulation and selection operators. There is no doubt that the emphasis was on data organization rather than calculation.

These findings have been filtered through my prejudices and through a number of heated language design meetings. It is unlikely that any one user would recognize the result as a direct reflection of that one user's needs. Yet I believe that the findings are generally applicable because:

(1) Taken together, they are harmonious.

(2) It is possible to design a coherent language incorporating all the desired features.

(3) The most successful features of current languages fall in our list.

(4) Although the emphasis on data manipulation is surprising, it accords with my 'gut' feeling that data structures are at the heart of any language.

(5) When a précis of these findings has been presented to others contemplating array processing, there has often been surprise at the emphasis on data manipulation, but there has been no countervailing evidence that this emphasis is misplaced.

No doubt this is not the final word on array processing even within DoE; I hope it may be of some use to those contemplating array processing language design. I also hope that computer architects will take some heed.

Acknowledgments

The contributions of Rich Zwakenberg, Rick Potter, John Williams and Les Petrie are very large. Members of the LLL Language Group and of LWG spent a great deal of time in fruitful discussion with me and in group meetings. Users obviously provided the raw material. However, none of these people is responsible for my presentation or opinions, nor is this an official DoE policy paper. Conclusions drawn are mine alone.

References

Although a number of language manuals were waved about in discussion, it is fair to say that all the items presented here are original in combination.

FORTRAN Language Requirements; Fourth Report of the Language Working Group of the Advanced Computing Committee. Available from Paul Messina, Argonne National Laboratory, Argonne, IL. Undated draft. C. Wetherall, *Array Processing for FORTRAN*, 2nd edn., Lawrence Livermore Laboratory, UCID-30175, rev. 1. January, 1980.

PART FOUR
Assessment of Concurrent Programming Languages

The assessment of concurrent programming languages is important for identifying their strengths and weaknesses. In the short-term, language evaluation can lead to improvements in existing concurrent programming languages and to better designs for the future. In the long-term, language evaluation can eventually lead to a set of criteria that can be used to design 'good, expressive and efficient' concurrent programming facilities.

Here is a partial list of criteria that can be used for assessment:

- The clarity, precision and simplicity of the language definition and constructs.
- The success of the language in meeting its design goal.
- The ability to express well known concurrent programming paradigms.
- Experience with the language.
- Implementation efficiency and error detection.

These and other criteria are used in this section to evaluate languages such as Concurrent Pascal, the Ada language and Mesa, and Hoare's concurrent programming model 'communicating sequential processes'.

14

An Assessment of Concurrent Pascal

D. Coleman, R. M. Gallimore, J. W. Hughes and M. S. Powell

University of Manchester Institute of Science and Technology

This paper assesses Concurrent Pascal against its design aims. The language is shown to be suitable for writing reliable non-trivial concurrent applications programs and operating systems. The major weakness of the language is its inability to provide an environment for other Concurrent Pascal programs. A new language construct, group, is proposed to remedy this difficulty.

Key words: concurrent Pascal, concurrent applications programs, operating systems.

Introduction

The programming language Concurrent Pascal [1] was designed by Per Brinch Hansen to allow the development of concurrent programs in a structured language. The following objectives are seen as centrally important to its development:

(1) to produce a language for building large, reliable concurrent programs from trivial modules;

(2) to make a compiler that checks the correctness of accesses between program modules;

(3) to allow programs to be developed and systematically tested bottom-up, by the incremental addition and testing of new modules;

(4) to build useful minicomputer operating systems exclusively by means of this language [2].

Brinch Hansen and his staff at California Institute of Technology implemented Concurrent Pascal on the DEC PDP-11/45. The

Concurrent Pascal System has been widely distributed and includes compilers for Concurrent Pascal and for Sequential Pascal [3], both written in Sequential Pascal, together with a single-user operating system, Solo [4], written in Concurrent Pascal. Solo provides an environment for the development of Sequential and Concurrent Pascal programs. Both compilers produce code for a virtual Pascal machine [5], provided by a small kernel and interpreter written in assembly code. Almost all machine dependent features of the system are isolated in the virtual machine. An implementation of the system on a CTL Modular-1 [6] has been available at UMIST for over a year. During this time Concurrent Pascal has been used both as an applications language and for the development of operating systems.

The following sections outline the main features of Concurrent Pascal and assess its usefulness in the light of Brinch Hansen's published uses [7] and the authors' experiences with the language in the problem areas mentioned above.

Programming in Concurrent Pascal

This section describes the principal features of Concurrent Pascal and attempts to convey the way in which it is used for concurrent programming. As the name implies Concurrent Pascal is an extension of (sequential) Pascal. It therefore inherits most of the features of that language: simplicity, machine independence, data abstraction and a high degree of compile time checking. In addition it provides facilities required in particular by operating systems programs, i.e., the facility to express concurrent processes, their communication, the sharing and protection of data and the execution of arbitrary sequential user programs.

A *process* type defines a sequential program module which operates on private data. A Concurrent Pascal program comprises a fixed number of processes which execute concurrently and communicate by means of *monitors* which operate on shared data on behalf of processes.

Monitor procedures provide exclusive access to shared data structures so that they can never be accessed while in some arbitrary partially updated state – the Pascal machine handles the *short term scheduling* of processes by enforcing this mutual exclusion.

Medium term scheduling is achieved by means of the simple data type *queue*. A monitor procedure may *delay* a calling process in a queue, or *continue* a process waiting in a queue. A delayed process loses its exclusive access to the shared data until it is continued by another process calling the monitor. Processes may execute simultaneously but since their short and medium term scheduling is controlled, their speeds are immaterial.

A *class* type defines an abstract data type by declaring private variables and the operations which may be performed on them using *class entry* procedures. Class type variables are local to the system component (monitor, class or process) in which they are declared.

A *program* declaration allows a Sequential Pascal program to be loaded and executed as part of a process. Thus, for example, a general input process may load and execute different peripheral driver programs and similarly a job process may load and execute different sequential user programs. A sequential program may be given access to routines local to the process in which it is declared, but is otherwise completely self-contained.

System components, instances of system types, are declared as variables and initialized by means of *init* statements. Processes and monitors may only be initialized in the initial process (the outermost level of a Concurrent Pascal program). *Init* statements establish the connections between components by specifying the access rights for each component. An *init* statement also causes execution of the initial statement of a system component. The initial statement of a process type is the process body. Thus the initialization of a process starts its execution.

The Concurrent Pascal compiler supports this modularity and compile-time protection ensures that program components use one another properly. The compiler checks that:

(1) shared data is only accessed via monitor procedures;

(2) no other data is shared;

(3) the implementation details of class and monitor types are hidden;

(4) components only use each other according to their access rights.

Consequently, once a system component has been implemented correctly, no other components can make it fail. This leads to greatly improved program reliability and aids systematic testing. A large program can be developed bottom-up in the knowledge that the addition of a new untested component cannot make any old and tested component fail. Testing is carried out in machine independent terms. The behaviour of a component under test is reproducible and the overall procedure does not rely on the use of octal memory dumps, switch registers and the like. Systematic testing is a powerful tool for the development of reliable concurrent programs.

In summary, Concurrent Pascal allows the encapsulation of private data types in classes and shared data types in monitors. Processes are expressed as self-contained sequential programs with private variables and access to shared data defined by parameters on initialization. Processes may load and execute self-contained sequential programs. This encapsulation allows concurrent programs to be constructed from small, relatively trivial modules. The compiler performs extensive checking of access rights. This allows large concurrent programs to be reliably developed bottom-up using systematic testing.

Real Concurrent Pascal programs

To assess the usefulness of Concurrent Pascal it is necessary to consider the main characteristics of those concurrent programs which have been successfully written in the language. After a description of the model operating systems written by Per Brinch Hansen, this section discusses the authors' experiences in using Concurrent Pascal to write general purpose applications programs and to develop new operating systems.

The model operating systems

Brinch Hansen [7] used Concurrent Pascal to write three model operating systems:

(1)   Solo – a single user operating system;
(2)   A Job Stream system for small user jobs;
(3)   A Real-time Scheduler for process control.

The Solo system is the most important and best known of these as it is the central part of the Concurrent Pascal distribution system. As described earlier, Solo is a useful, reliable, well-documented operating system. In addition to the Sequential and Concurrent Pascal compilers it supports a comprehensive range of other utilities. In all the system amounts to 110K words of code. However, Solo makes extensive use of the program facility; only 4% of the system is written in Concurrent Pascal – most of the system (92%) consists of utilities written in Sequential Pascal. Thus the Solo Concurrent Pascal program must be distinguished from the Solo operating system.

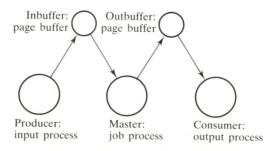

Figure 1   Solo pipeline.

The Solo program itself is only 1300 lines long. At the heart of Solo is a *job process* which executes Sequential Pascal programs, e.g., a pass of the compiler, or a user program. The job process communicates with an *input process* and an *output process*, as shown in Figure 1, whose purpose is to route data between the job process and peripheral devices. They also use the program facility to load and execute sequential peripheral driver programs.

The Job Stream system compiles and executes a stream of Sequential Pascal user programs. Its structure is similar to that of the Solo system.

The Real-time Scheduler was built for process control applications in which a fixed number of concurrent tasks are carried out periodically with frequencies chosen by a human operator. The Real-time Scheduler is written entirely in Concurrent Pascal. The program is 600 lines long, but only provides a rudimentary skeleton of a real-time system.

Thus Brinch Hansen's published use of Concurrent Pascal has been mainly to provide a framework of concurrency for executing Sequential Pascal programs.

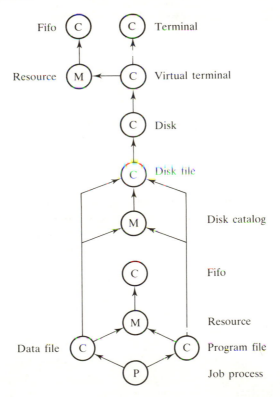

Figure 2   Simplified structure of the Solo file system.

The model operating systems further illustrate the use of Concurrent Pascal to build a multiprogram as a hierarchy of simple modules. For instance, the Solo program consists of 1300 lines of text, divided into 23 modules. Each module is roughly one page of text (57 lines on average). Each module contains on average 5 small routines. This internal structure makes modules readily comprehensible. On the other hand, the Solo program is non-trivial and the way in which the models are connected is not so easy to comprehend. Diagrams such as Figure 2 are used in the documentation to express the hierarchy of interconnections. The circles are program modules (processes, monitors and classes); the arrows show how they are connected (call one another).

This information about the interconnection of modules is not readily discernible from the text of the Solo program. The problem appears not to stem from any intrinsic weakness in Concurrent Pascal but from trying to express a non-tree structured hierarchy of modules in a program text. The effects of this problem can be limited in practice by keeping hierarchical interconnections of modules as simple as possible.

Operating system development in Concurrent Pascal

The usefulness of Concurrent Pascal for developing general purpose operating systems is being investigated at UMIST in anticipation of the need for reliable software for the CYBA-M [9] multiprocessor research machine.

The first project undertaken was the development of a terminal system which gives each user the facilities of a mini-Solo system. Such a medium sized operating system is suggested by Brinch Hansen as being worthy of consideration and expressible in Concurrent Pascal [7].

A straightforward approach to the development of such a system is to have several instances of the Solo pipeline running in parallel. Each pipeline is initialized to provide a Solo-like capability on a distinct user terminal. This approach is conceptually simple and is easily accomplished by declaring extra variables of the appropriate types, e.g., job process, page buffer. Extra resource managers are introduced to ensure exclusive access to non-shareable resources such as the cardreader or lineprinter for which competition may arise. As Brinch Hansen predicted, the resulting program is 'more of the same' when compared with Solo and emphasizes the expressive power of Concurrent Pascal as an operating system language.

However, in practical terms, the main store required for a terminal system using n Solo pipelines is approximately n times the store required by Solo itself (~40K). The excessive store requirements arise because the program store within processes which is used to receive the Sequential Pascal programs cannot be shared and managed as a resource. Thus it is impossible to run such a system on a mini-computer unless the Pascal virtual machine provides a large virtual memory through dynamic allocation of main store. This is generally not feasible without paging hardware.

Thus writing minicomputer operating systems by using Concurrent Pascal to provide the framework of concurrency for Sequential Pascal utilities is only really suited to single user systems. The problem can be eased to some extent if the larger and more frequently used sequential utility programs are replaced by Concurrent Pascal system types since multiple instances of a type use only one copy of its code. The extended program is much larger than the Solo program, consisting of several thousand lines of text structured into small (roughly one page) modules. Consequently the hierarchical program structure is complex and not readily discernible. Readability can be improved by grouping together functionally related modules, e.g., an editing group and a file-handling group. Despite the extra size and complexity, program development is manageable by the incremental addition of components and the use of systematic testing.

Concurrent Pascal is being used in this way to develop several related operating systems. Prototype terminal systems have been written which provide limited editing and file handling capabilities to on-line users. A foreground–background system is being built which provides terminal editing and file handling in the foreground and a compilation stream in the background and runs on a loosely coupled two-processor system. It would also be a straightforward matter to replace each user terminal by a suitable microcomputer configuration (e.g., DEC PDP-11/03) to provide a local filestore with edit and copy facilities.

Concurrent Pascal as an applications language

Over the last year Concurrent Pascal has been used as the implementation language for a research project into design methods for multiprograms [8]. A number of applications programs have been designed as pipelines of translations, individual translations being implemented as processes. This technique of problem decomposition results in small, simple, functionally independent components which are consequently relatively error free, easy to understand and to test systematically by incrementally building the pipeline. Concurrent Pascal has proved a very satisfactory implementation language. It has been used to write multiprograms in the following applications areas:

(1) Data processing;
(2) Assemblers/compilers;
(3) Operational research.

The first problem that an applications programmer encounters when using Concurrent Pascal arises because Concurrent Pascal programs do not run under an operating system but on the bare Pascal machine. Consequently, every applications program must contain modules to provide facilities normally provided by the operating system, e.g., a filing system.

The 'operating system' part of a program can be organized as a standard prefix of type definitions of modules to be concatenated with the applications modules prior to compilation. The prefix performs the necessary resource management and mappings between abstract and concrete data representations required by the abstract applications program. Many of the modules recur in different applications programs and it is possible to reduce the effort needed to build a new prefix by exploiting this re-usability. The prefix of an applications program that processes COBOL-like fixed format records is around 1000 lines long. Complete textual separation of the prefix and applications modules is impossible. The initial process, which declares and initializes system components, must refer to both operating systems and applications modules. The need to provide an 'operating system prefix' in every Concurrent Pascal applications program makes these programs more complicated and less readable than they would otherwise be.

In summary, Concurrent Pascal possesses the attractions of standard Pascal and substantially satisfies Brinch Hansen's original design goals. Overall the language has proved an excellent tool for building multiprograms. The modularity and abstraction supported by the language allows programs to be expressed in a largely readable and machine independent form. The extensive compile time checking of access rights permits the systematic testing of programs. This technique is of great value in the development of reliable programs. However, its use for writing general purpose operating systems and applications programs has highlighted a number of shortcomings:

(1)   It is not practicable to use the program facility in system types of which several instances are declared.

(2)   Programs run on the bare Pascal machine so that applications programs need a large number of modules to provide facilities normally provided by an operating system. These modules cannot be textually separated from the applications modules because the initial process refers to both.

(3)   It is not possible to use Concurrent Pascal to write an operating system which supports Concurrent Pascal user programs. This is unfortunate as we have found Concurrent Pascal highly suited to the expression of programs for a wide variety of applications.

A proposed language extension – 'groups'

The shortcomings listed at the end of the previous section result in non-trivial programs, whether multi-user operating system or applications program, being over-complex and unwieldy. A means is needed to separate functionally groups of modules in a large multi-program. The functional separation could be achieved on a loosely coupled multiprocessor system by separately compiling each group of modules onto a separate processor with inter-program communications accomplished at the Pascal machine level. The disadvantage is that one program becomes a collection of programs with a hidden communication mechanism. Concurrent Pascal itself provides no way of expressing a large program as a collection of distinct groups of functionally related system components. We propose that the language should be extended to provide a new system type, the *group*, which will allow large Concurrent Pascal programs to be built from structured subprograms no larger and no more complex than the Solo program. Since the proposal is an extension to the language, existing Concurrent Pascal programs would still be valid in the extended language.

In most respects a *group* corresponds to a conventional Concurrent Pascal program. Each group declares the system types from which it is constructed. Components are declared as variables at the outermost level of a group. **Init** statements are used in the initial process of a group to initialize the components and to specify the way they are connected together. In addition each group has access to external objects which it uses to communicate with the outside world. Thus groups can be allowed to communicate by giving them access to a shared external object such as a data buffer.

The group structure is used to best advantage if groups can be compiled separately. This solves the problem of having to incorporate a prefix of operating system modules in every Concurrent Pascal program. The run-time link-loading of groups would allow Concurrent Pascal

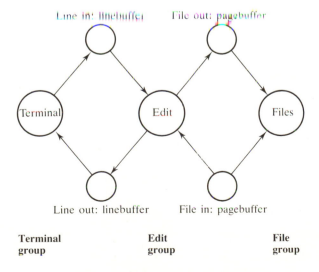

Figure 3   Structure of a text editing system.

operating systems to support concurrent user programs. The operating system would consist of one or more fixed groups. A Concurrent Pascal user program then corresponds to a group which is loaded dynamically and linked with the operating system groups prior to its execution.

These ideas are reflected in Figure 3 which represents a concurrent program for interactive text editing. The program comprises three major sub-systems: an edit system, a file system and a terminal system to handle communication with the user. The system components of each sub-system are organized into a group. The groups execute concurrently and communicate via shared buffer monitors as shown.

The main characteristics of the construction of groups are illustrated in Figure 4 which outlines the type definition of the file group. The

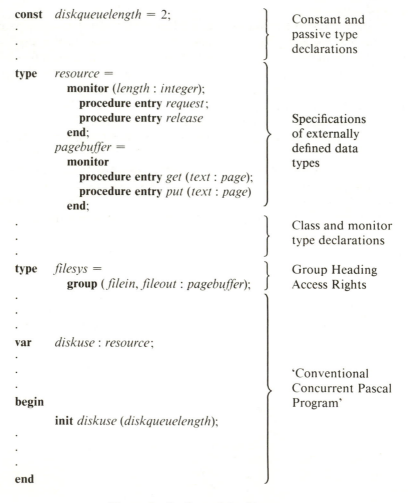

```
const   diskqueuelength = 2;                          Constant and
    .                                                 passive type
    .                                                 declarations
    .

type    resource =
            monitor (length : integer);
                procedure entry request;
                procedure entry release              Specifications
            end;                                     of externally
            pagebuffer =                             defined data
            monitor                                  types
                procedure entry get (text : page);
                procedure entry put (text : page)
            end;
    .                                                Class and monitor
    .                                                type declarations
    .

type    filesys =                                    Group Heading
            group ( filein, fileout : pagebuffer);   Access Rights
    .
    .

var     diskuse : resource;
    .
    .                                                'Conventional
    .                                                Concurrent Pascal
begin                                                Program'
            init diskuse (diskqueuelength);
    .
    .
    .

end
```

Figure 4   Outline of the file group.

internal structure of the group module is not described in detail but is handled within that part of the module text labelled 'Conventional Pascal Program'.

Access to external objects is specified in a parameter list which follows the group heading. Monitor type components are used to implement shared data structures used for communication between groups.

A new kind of program module is introduced called the *initial module* of a Concurrent Pascal program. Its purpose is derived from that of the initial process of a conventional Concurrent Pascal program. System component variables are declared as instances of system types (groups, processes, monitors and classes) and are initialized by means of **init** statements. Group type variables may only be initialized in the initial module. Figure 5 outlines the initial module for the interactive text edit system of Figure 3.

The **init** statements establish the connections between system components by specifying the actual parameters of each component. In Figure 5 the same instances of type *pagebuffer* are passed to both edit and file, hence the two groups are connected by shared data buffers. An **init** statement also causes the execution of the initial statement of a system component. For each group type component this corresponds to the execution of the local initial process which occurs at its outermost level. In turn this establishes the internal structure of the group and initializes the locally declared system components.

The initial module contains the type declarations for global data types. In addition to the data types for shared data structures used to connect groups, global definitions are provided for other standard types. For instance in the case of a widely used private data type, unnecessary duplication of text and code in groups is avoided by providing a global definition of the appropriate data type in the initial module.

So that each group can be compiled separately and instances of groups linked together at run-time, each group contains a description of its interface with the outside world in the form of a *type specification* for each globally defined data type. Each specification details the assumption which the components make about the data type in question: what operations can be performed on the data type, what form do the parameters of the respective calls take, etc. The specifications may take the form of a prefix which is related to the global type definitions in the initial module and which is standard to all groups. When compiling a group module the compiler can use this information to ensure that components in the group only use instances of globally defined types in ways which are consistent with their type specification.

Similarly, the initial module contains a description of the externally defined groups that it uses so that it can be compiled separately from them. This description takes the form of *group specifications* which are used by the compiler to check that the access rights granted to a group type component are consistent with the requirements stated in its group specification.

In practical terms the introduction of the proposed system type,

```
const    buffersize =
         .
         .
         .

type     pagebuffer =
         .
         .

type     terminalsys =
             group (inline, outline : linebuffer);
         editsys =
             group (inline : linebuffer);
         filesys =
             group (infile, outfile : pagebuffer);

         .

         .

         .
var

             linein, lineout : linebuffer;
             filein, fileout : pagebuffer;
             edit : editsys;
             terminal : terminalsys;
             files : filesys;

         .

         .

         .

begin
         .

         .

         .
init
             linein, lineout, filein, fileout,
         .

         .

         .

             terminal (linein, lineout),
             edit (linein, lineout, filein, fileout),
             files (filein, fileout),

         .

         .

         .

end
```

Constant and
passive type
declarations

Global monitor
and class type
declarations

Group
specifications

Declarations including instances
of groups and
monitors used for
communication

Initialization
of monitors
and groups

Figure 5 Outline of the initial module for the text editing system.

group, into Concurrent Pascal does not increase the complexity of the language, requiring only a small extension to the language definition. To implement the group construct requires only small changes to the Concurrent Pascal compiler and the Pascal machine. These changes are compatible with existing Concurrent Pascal since the proposed language represents a superset of the original. A preliminary study has shown that the introduction of groups would increase the general usability of the language. It results in less complex programs and allows the language to be used for a wider range of applications.

Conclusion

It is our experience that Concurrent Pascal substantially fulfils its original design aims. Overall it is an excellent language for writing reliable non-trivial concurrent programs. We have confirmed that the modular approach to concurrent program design in terms of processes, monitors and classes can be used successfully for both applications programs and operating systems. Systematic testing has proved a highly successful way of testing concurrent programs, resulting in highly reliable programs. Its use promotes a greater understanding of the dynamic behaviour of the developed program and hence greater confidence in its correctness.

The language should be extended to allow the expression of a program as a collection of groups of functionally related program modules. The introduction of the *group* construct makes Concurrent Pascal generally more useful. It avoids the otherwise inevitable complexity of large concurrent programs and allows Concurrent Pascal operating systems to support concurrent user programs. With this extension and the inherent modularity and encapsulation in the language, Concurrent Pascal should prove a suitable general purpose, abstract programming language for use on systems which exhibit parallelism as exemplified by CYBA-M with its multimicroprocessor architecture.

References

[1]   P. Brinch Hansen, 'The programming language Concurrent Pascal', *IEEE Transactions on Software Engineering*, **1**, 2, 199–207 (1975).

[2]   P. Brinch Hansen, 'Experience with modular concurrent programming', *IEEE Transactions of Software Engineering*, **3**, 2, 156–159 (1977).

[3]   P. Brinch Hansen and A. C. Hartman, 'Sequential PASCAL report', *Information Science, California Institute of Technology* (1975).

[4]   P. Brinch Hansen, 'The SOLO operating system', *Software – Practice and Experience*, **6**, 2, 141–207 (1976).

[5]   P. Brinch Hansen, 'Concurrent PASCAL machine', *Information Science, California Institute of Technology* (1975).

[6] M. S. Powell, 'Experience of transporting and using the SOLO operating system', *Software – Practice and Experience*, **9**, 7, 561–569 (1979).

[7] P. Brinch Hansen, *The Architecture of Concurrent Programs*, Prentice-Hall Inc., Englewood Cliffs, New Jersey, 1977.

[8] D. Coleman, J. W. Hughes and M. S. Powell, 'Developing a programming methodology for multiprograms', *Department of Computation Report No. 218*, UMIST (1978).

[9] E. L. Dagless, 'A multimicroprocessor – CYBA-M', *IFIP Congress Proceedings*, North Holland Publishing Co., 1977.

15

Concurrent Programming in the Ada Language: The Polling Bias

N. H. Gehani and T. A. Cargill

AT & T Bell Laboratories

The *rendezvous* is an important concept in concurrent programming – two processes need to synchronize, i.e., rendezvous, to exchange information. The Ada programming language is the first programming language to use the rendezvous as the basis of its concurrent programming facilities.

Our experience with rendezvous facilities in the Ada language shows that these facilities lead to and encourage the design of programs that poll. Polling is generally, but not always, undesirable because it is wasteful of system resources.

We illustrate and examine the reasons for polling bias in the Ada language. We give suggestions on how to avoid polling programs, and suggest changes to the rendezvous facilities to eliminate the polling bias. The ramifications of these changes to the implementation of the Ada language are also discussed.

Although we have focused on the rendezvous facilities in the Ada language our analysis is also applicable to other languages. A polling bias can occur in any concurrent programming language based on the rendezvous mechanism if it does not provide appropriate facilities.

1   Introduction

One important notion of process interaction arises from viewing process synchronization and communication as inseparable activities [1] [2]. Two parallel processes interact by first synchronizing, then exchanging information and finally continuing their individual activities. This synchronization or meeting to exchange information is called the *rendezvous.*

Ada is the first programming language to use the rendezvous concept as the basis of its concurrent programming facilities. These facilities are based on Hoare's concurrent programming proposal *Communicating*

Sequential Processes [3]. Facilities similar to those in the Ada programming language have never been tried out in any other programming language. Consequently, only experience in using these facilities will indicate their appropriateness.

Our experience with concurrent programming in the Ada language points to inadequacies in the facilities provided for the rendezvous mechanism which lead to and encourage the design of programs that poll. Polling is generally, but not always, undesirable because it is wasteful of system resources.

2   Concurrency in the Ada language – the rendezvous

Parallel processes are called *tasks* in the Ada language. A task may have *entries* which are called by other tasks. Two tasks A and B *rendezvous* at entry E of B when A calls entry E and the entry call is accepted by B. If A calls entry E before B is ready to accept the entry call, then A waits until B is ready. Similarly, if B is ready to accept an entry call, then it must wait until some task issues that entry call. A rendezvous is a transaction in which two tasks – the task making the entry call and the task accepting the entry call – can exchange information.

Tasks synchronize and communicate with each other by means of the rendezvous.[†] As an example, consider a task BUFFER that buffers communication between two tasks PRODUCED and CONSUMER. Its specification is:

```
task BUFFER is
    entry WRITE(C : in CHARACTER); -- add character to buffer
    entry READ(C : out CHARACTER); -- get character from buffer
end BUFFER;
```

BUFFER can be called with requests to rendezvous at entries WRITE or READ. The skeleton of the body of task BUFFER is:

```
task body BUFFER is
⋮
-- local declarations
⋮
begin
  loop
    select
      when buffer not full =>
        accept WRITE(C : in CHARACTER) do
```

_____

[†] The rendezvous is the primary means of communication between tasks. However, tasks can also communicate via shared variables.

```
            store character C in buffer
        end WRITE;
        do book-keeping

    or
      when buffer not empty =>
          accept READ(C : out CHARACTER) do
              store the next character from the buffer in C
          end READ;
          do book-keeping
      end select;
   end loop;
end BUFFER;
```

The notation for entry calls is syntactically similar to that of procedure calls, e.g.:

```
BUFFER.WRITE(X);
BUFFER.READY(Y);
```

These entry calls are accepted in the task BUFFER by the **accept** statements. A call to WRITE will be accepted only if the buffer is not full and a call to READ will be accepted only if the buffer is not empty. Calls to a specific entry are accepted in first-in first-out order. In the above example, if the buffer is neither full nor empty then either a call to WRITE or a call to READ may be accepted – the execution of the **select** statement is non-deterministic.

3   Rendezvous statements

In this section we will briefly describe two of the statements used for task interaction. For a complete description the reader is referred to the *Reference Manual for the Ada Programming Language* [4].

3.1   The selective wait statement

The *selective wait* statement is used for waiting and for selection from one or more alternatives. It has the form[†]:

[†] Extended BNF notation, as used in the *Reference Manual for the Ada Programming Language*, is used to specify the syntax: [a] specifies the optional occurrence of item a and {a} specifies 0 or more occurrences of item a. Bold and bigger characters will be used for the BNF meta symbols **[ ]** and **{ }** to distinguish them from Ada language characters.

```
select
   [when condition =>] selective_wait_alternative
{or
   [when condition =>] selective_wait_alternative}
[else
   sequence_of_statements]
end select;
```

A selective_wait_alternative can be an **accept** or a **delay** statement followed by a sequence of statements, or the **terminate** alternative [4].

Execution of the selective wait statement will be briefly explained now. Complete details of the semantics of the selective wait statement can be found in Reference 4.

An alternative is said to be *open* if no condition is associated with it or if the associated condition is true; otherwise it is said to be closed. Assume that there is an open alternative. The selective_wait_alternative executed is non-deterministically selected from the set of open **accept** alternatives, if non-empty, for which a corresponding rendezvous is immediately possible.[†] If a rendezvous is not immediately possible and there is no **else** part then the task waits until such an open **accept** alternative can be selected. An open **delay** alternative will be selected if no **accept** alternative can be selected before the specified delay has elapsed. If none of the selective_wait_alternative in this set can be immediately executed (e.g., a rendezvous is not immediately possible) then the **else** part is executed.

If there is no open alternative and there is no **else** part in the selective wait statement then the exception PROGRAM_ERROR is raised.

3.2   The conditional entry call

A *conditional entry call* is an entry call that is cancelled if a rendezvous is not immediately possible; an alternative action is performed instead:

```
select
   entry_call_statement [sequence_of_statements]
else
   sequence_of_statements
end select;
```

Although the syntax of a conditional entry call is similar to that of a selective wait statement, they are semantically quite different, the first being used for making entry calls and the second for accepting entry calls.

[†] Non-deterministic selection will be possible only if the set of open **accept** alternatives has more than one element; otherwise, selection will be deterministic.

4 Polling

A task which needs to communicate with another task must either block until the other is ready to communicate or make repeated attempts to establish communication.

Polling is characterized by a task actively and repeatedly checking for the occurrence of an event that originates outside the task. Formally, we can offer no generalized definition of polling applicable to concurrent programming as a whole. However, if we restrict our attention to tasks communicating pairwise by means of the rendezvous, we can capture the intuitive notion of polling and distinguish two kinds of polling: *rendezvous polling* and *information polling*.

Definition of rendezvous polling

Take A *rendezvous polls* task B with respect to entry E if the rendezvous can be preceded by an unbounded number of attempts by A to rendezvous. An attempt may be an unsuccessful entry call or a failure to select an **accept** alternative in a **select** statement.

Definition of information polling

Task A *information polls* task B with respect to entry E if A and B can rendezvous an unbounded number of times before the desired information is transferred.

Consider the program segment of a task A that wants to access some resource managed by a resource manager task RM:

```
    ⋮
FREE := FALSE;
while not FREE loop
  RM.REQUEST(FREE);
end loop;
    ⋮
```

Task A calls entry REQUEST of task RM repeatedly rendezvousing with RM until FREE is set to TRUE, indicating that A can go ahead and use the resource. The polling performed by task A is of the second kind, i.e., information polling and not rendezvous polling.

Of course, it is possible that polling in a program may actually be some combination of rendezvous and information polling. For example, rendezvous polling may be nested inside information polling.

While polling, a task may or may not do useful work – leading to the notion of *busy waiting*. A polling task *busy waits* if between (attempted) rendezvous no useful action is performed, i.e., there is no computational progress.

Both kinds of polling are generally, but not always, undesirable because they are wasteful of system resources – polling burns up CPU cycles. Even if a task is assigned a dedicated CPU in a computer network, polling can be undesirable because it may generate unnecessary traffic on the network.

In the Ada language, both the calling task and the called task can poll – using the conditional entry call and selective wait statement with the *else* part, respectively. This can lead to a dangerous situation when two tasks try to rendezvous with each other by polling – the rendezvous may never happen.

4.1 Example of a desirable polling program

Polling programs may be desirable in cases where non-polling programs result in additional overhead, such as extra statements or rendezvous, which may result in real-time constraints being violated.

The following example (adapted from Reference 5) illustrates a polling program that is more desirable than a non-polling program simply because it is more efficient. The problem is to display the position of a moving point on a screen (e.g., an aeroplane on a radar screen) based on the supplied co-ordinates or from computations based on the most recent co-ordinates and velocity available. The point position is to be displayed *as fast as possible* so that it is tracked accurately. If an updated position of the point is not available, then a new position should be computed before displaying the point position:

```
loop
   select
      accept UPDATE(coordinates and velocity of point) do
         record X, Y, VX, VY;
      end UPDATE;
   else
      compute new position using old coordinates and velocity;
   end select;
   display point position on screen
end loop;
```

The critical thing is to display, as fast as possible, the latest position of a point – regardless of whether the position of the point is new or one computed using its old position and velocity. The time required to compute a new position is much less than the average interval between updates of point position.

Rendezvous polling in the task represented by the above program segment can be avoided by rewriting it alternatively as two or more tasks. However, the resulting non-polling program will not be as efficient as the above polling version because resources will be expended in scheduling the multiple tasks and in task communication.

5   Bias towards rendezvous polling

We will now examine the specific causes of the undesirable and often needless polling that results from the rendezvous mechanism in the Ada language. The tendency towards rendezvous polling results from the lack of some facilities, from some restrictions and from the presence of some facilities.

5.1   Conditional entry call

The *conditional entry call* should be used with care as it can easily lead to unnecessary polling. For example, the *Reference Manual for the Ada Programming Language* [4] contains the following example illustrating the use of a conditional entry call:

```
procedure SPIN(R : RESOURCE) is
begin
  loop
    select
      R.SEIZE;
      return;
    else
      null;    -- busy waiting
    end select;
  end loop;
end;
```

This is a poor example of a conditional entry call because the above subprogram involves rendezvous polling which can be easily avoided by just calling the entry:

```
procedure SPIN(R : RESOURCE) is
begin
  R.SEIZE;
end;
```

Better examples of the use of a conditional entry call are the polling solution to the problem of displaying the position of a moving point or the following program segment [6].

```
loop
  accept FIRE_LOCATION(X : LOCATION);
  select
    OPERATOR.CALL("Put Out Fire at Location", X);
  else
    FIRE_STATION.CALL(X);
  end select;
end loop;
```

which calls the fire station if the operator cannot accept the call immediately. Note that this example does not poll.

5.2   Handling an entry family and subsets of it

The general way of handling calls to an entry family (or a subset of the entry family) involves polling [7]. For example, consider the entry family UP, with N members, declared as:

```
entry UP(FLOORS);
```

where FLOORS is a discrete range declared as:

```
subtype FLOORS is INTEGER range 1..N;
```

The skeleton of a program segment accepting calls to all members of the entry family UP is:

```
loop
  for l in FLOORS loop
    select
      accept UP(l) do ... end;
    else
      null;
    end select;
  end loop;
end loop;
```

Polling can be avoided by explicitly writing **accept** statements for each member of the entry family UP:

```
loop
  select
    accept UP(1) do ... end;
  or
    accept UP(2) do ... end;
  or
    accept UP(3) do ... end;
```

```
        or
            ⋮
        or
            accept UP(N) do ... end;
        end select;
    end loop;
```

This alternative way of handling an entry family is feasible only if N is known at the time the program is written and convenient only if N is small.

Alternatively, if possible, the entry family may be replaced by a single entry with an additional parameter. However, this may not be a viable alternative in all cases.

The use of entry families is necessary in some situations, e.g., to implement a general scheduling strategy [1, 6]. Implementation of a general scheduling strategy requires that the tasks requesting service call two entries in the scheduler. The first entry call, called the sign-in, is used by the requestor to get an index of an entry family, in the scheduler, which it must then call to get service.

Calls to the entry family are accepted by the scheduler in an order that reflects the desired scheduling strategy. The simplest way of accepting calls to an entry family is by polling. However, in this case polling can be avoided by careful programming – use is made of information such as the number of tasks that have signed in but have not received service as yet, and the entry family indices given to the requestors.

5.3 Restrictions on the selective wait statement

Some bias towards polling can be directly attributed to restrictions on the selective wait statement.

5.3.1 Not allowing a when condition followed by a sequence of non-tasking statements as a select alternative

Alternatives in the selective wait statement can be either an **accept**, a **delay** or a **terminate** alternative. An alternative cannot be the optional **when** condition followed by a sequence of non-tasking statements, e.g., a sequence of assignment statements.

Consider the following priority scheduler abstract program segment [7]:

```
    loop -- illegal form
        select
            accept REQUEST(request details) do
                add request to waiting set;
            end REQUEST;
            next_user := unknown;
```

```
       or
          when current_user = no_one and next_user /= unknown =>
             accept ACQUIRE ... specify next_user ... end ACQUIRE;
             current_user := next_user; next_user := unknown;
             delete current_user from the waiting set;

       or
          when current_user /= no_one =>
             accept RELEASE;
             current_user := no_one;

       or
          when next_user = unknown and waiting set is not empty =>
             next_user := highest priority user in waiting set;
       end select;
   end loop;
```

This program segment is illegal in the Ada language because the last alternative is not a **delay**, a **terminate** or an **accept** alternative. Welsh and Lister suggest that the above program might be written alternatively using the **else** clause as:

```
   loop
      select
         ⋮
      else
         if next_user = unknown and waiting set is not empty then
            next_user := highest priority user in waiting set;
         end if;
      end select;
   end loop;
```

However, this program formulation results in busy waiting since in the absence of any feasible user interaction, the **else** clause is executed to no effect. In many practical applications, busy waiting within a scheduler task is unacceptable. Busy waiting can be avoided by rewriting the program segment to eliminate the **else** clause [7]. The code in the **else** clause is moved to some other place.

A very simple strategy that avoids polling and does not require rewriting of the program segment would be to use a **delay** statement with a zero time period:

```
   loop
      select
         ⋮
      or
         when next_user = unknown and waiting set is not empty =>
            delay 0.0;
            next_user := highest priority user in waiting set;
      end select;
   end loop;
```

5.3.2 Lack of a selective call statement and not allowing an entry call as a selective wait alternative

The Ada language does not have a selective call statement corresponding to the selective wait statement. Consequently a program segment of the form:

```
loop   -- illegal form
   select
      call entry X.E
   or
      call entry Y.F
   end select;
end loop;
```

must be expressed alternatively as the polling program segment:

```
loop
   select
      call entry X.E
   else
      select
         call entry Y.F
      else
         null;
      end select;
   end select;
end loop;
```

The above polling alternative is not quite equivalent to its non-polling counterpart since it gives preference to calling entry X.E. In fact, in discussing the lack of a selective call alternative, an article in *Ada Letters* [8] suggested a polling alternative similar to the one given above.

An entry call statement is not allowed as a selective wait alternative. This restriction can also result in polling. As an example, consider the situation when a task X is prepared to accept entry calls E_i from other tasks when the associated conditions B_i are satisfied and would also like to call entry F of Y if the associated condition C is satisfied:

```
loop   -- illegal form
   select
      when B₁ => accept call to entry E₁
   or
      ⋮
   or
      when Bₙ => accept call to entry Eₙ
   or
      when C => call entry Y.F
   end select;
end loop;
```

The **select** statement in the above program statement is not legal in the Ada language because an entry call is not allowed as a selective wait alternative. This program segment can be written using rendezvous polling with the aid of a conditional entry call:

```
loop
  select
    when B₁ => accept call to entry E₁
  or
  ⋮
  or
    when Bₙ => accept call to entry Eₙ
  else
    if C then
      select
        call entry Y.F
      else
        null;
      end select;
    end if;
  end select;
end loop;
```

If X and Y are symmetrical tasks, then this design can lead to a situation when both X and Y are polling each other simultaneously – a potentially disastrous situation since they may never establish a rendezvous.

Alternatively, if the entry call Y.F involves information flow from X to Y only, then this polling can be avoided by using an intervening buffer task B with the following form:

```
loop
  call entry X.G to get information for Y
  call entry Y.F to pass on the information
end loop;
```

where G is now an entry in task X which is modified so that it now looks like:

```
loop
  select
    when B₁ => accept call to entry E₁
  or
  ⋮
  or
    when Bₙ => accept call to entry Eₙ
  or
    when C => accept call to entry G
  end select;
end loop;
```

Such a situation actually arose in the following problem. Consider two terminals T_1 and T_2 being used for communication with each other. Every character typed in at T_1 is echoed on T_1's display and upon completion of the line, the line is sent to T_2 for display where it is displayed in between lines being typed in by the user. T_2 is symmetrical to T_1 (see Figure 1).

Figure 1

The body of T_1 can be described abstractly as:

```
loop
  select
    Accept a line from T₂ and display it
  or
    when internal buffer is empty =>
      Accept a character from the keyboard, echo and
      store in internal buffer
      while character not end of line loop
        Accept a character from the keyboard, echo and
        store in internal buffer
      end loop;
  or
    when internal buffer has a complete line =>
      Send line to T₂ by calling an entry of T₂
  end select;
end loop;
```

The characters typed in by the user are collected in the internal buffer and echoed back at the same time. When the internal buffer has a complete line, it is sent to T_2 for display.

Since an entry call cannot be a select alternative, a polling solution was considered. In this case, a polling solution would not be viable since T_2 would be symmetrical to T_1. If two tasks poll each other to communicate, they may never communicate! The problem was solved by means of intervening buffer tasks (see Figure 2).

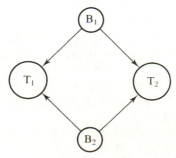

Figure 2   (Arrows indicate entry calls and not message flow).

The buffer tasks make entry calls to take lines from one task and deliver them to the other task. The entry call in T_1, as described above, is now replaced by an **accept** statement. The body of T_1, is modified so that a line is accepted from T_2 via the buffer task B_2 and a line is delivered to task T_2 via buffer task B_1:

```
loop
   select
      Accept a call from buffer B₂ to receive a line from task T₂, and
      display it
   or
      when internal buffer is empty =>
         Accept a character from the keyboard, echo and
         store in internal buffer
         while character not end of line loop
            Accept a character from the keyboard, echo and
            store in internal buffer
         end loop;
   or
      when internal buffer has a complete line =>
         Accept a call from buffer B₁ to send a line to task T₂
   end select;
end loop;
```

Buffer task B_1 can be described abstractly as:

```
loop
   Call T₁ to get a line
   Call T₂ to deliver the line
end loop;
```

Tasks T_2 and B_2 are similar to tasks T_1 and B_1, respectively.

A more elegant solution than this solution can be arrived at by devoting one task to each of the keyboards and the display. A terminal is really two devices!

5.4 *else* clause in the selective wait statement

The use of the **else** clause in the selective wait statement is a clear temptation to write polling programs (especially for the novice). The **else** clause allows an alternative action to be performed if no alternative of the selective wait statement is open. It seems to make it natural to do 'something else' when a rendezvous is not possible, i.e., poll. An example of this is the use of the **else** clause in the first attempt to write the scheduling program shown earlier.

The programmer should consider carefully if this alternative action is part of the task or if it should be encapsulated in another task which could result in the elimination of the polling. Alternatively, rearrange-ment of the code should be considered to avoid polling.

5.5   Careful program design

Consider the following abstract version of the body of a task that controls the motion of an elevator [9]:

```
loop
    Accept calls for elevator service

    if no requests then move car towards home floor
    elsif requests and (car at home floor or arriving at destination) then
        Compute new destination, etc.
    else
        select
            Accept signal to keep elevator moving
        else
            null;
        end select;
    end if;
end loop;
```

This task represents a first attempt in the design of a program to control an elevator. This is not a very good design since the task performs three functions – handles all the calls for elevator service, stores service request information and actually controls the elevator motion. Because the task must accept calls for elevator service also, it does not wait to receive a signal from the elevator to keep it moving. Instead it polls; if the signal has not come then it goes on to accept requests for service.

A better design, which is also non-polling, would be to replace this task by three tasks – one for each function. One task accepts the calls, the second is a database task and the third is the elevator control task. The first task supplies information to the database task; the third task gets information, such as pending requests and the new destination, from the database task to control the elevator.

A good design principle to follow is to dedicate a task to each function or job to be done in a program instead of letting a task perform several functions (the same design strategy is recommended for designing procedures in sequential programs).

6   Suggestions and implementation considerations

The bias towards polling programs in the Ada language can be eliminated by incorporating the following simple extensions which have no impact on the rest of the language:

(1) Allow **when** conditions followed by a sequence of non-tasking statements as select alternatives – this extension should result in no semantic change or implementation overhead at all. A trivial way to implement it would be to treat it as a **delay** alternative with a zero delay.

(2) Include a selective call statement and/or allow entry calls as selective wait alternatives – the selective call statement was not included by the designers of the Ada language as a fundamental design decision [1]. The designers felt that such a statement would complicate the implementation by resulting in a task being placed in more than one entry queue – one for each entry call in the selective call statement. It is not clear whether any thought was given to the fact that this decision would result in a bias towards polling.

Allowing entry calls in a selective wait statement will increase the implementation complexity because a task may have to be placed in more than one queue and for other reasons [10]. Entry calls correspond to **output** statements of Hoare's Communicating Sequential Processes and **accept** statements correspond to **input** statements [3]. Hoare had not allowed output statements to be used in a statement that parallels the **select** statement. However, Hoare did feel that this restriction should be removed from the point of symmetry and programming ease, as did Bernstein [10], who also suggested a rather straightforward implementation for this extension.

(3) Allow the specification of ranges in the **select** statement to handle entry families – for example:

```
loop
    accept UP(FLOORS) do ... end;
end loop;
```

Specification of ranges also eliminates the unnecessary sequencing that results from handling calls to an entry family by polling.

Implementation of an **accept** statement that accepts the whole entry family or its subsets is rather straightforward. If the specified range is static, then one can do a simple macro expansion into a list of **accept** statements for each of the entries in the range, as was done manually in the example given earlier. If the range is dynamic, then code will have to be generated to examine the queues associated with the individual members of the entry family.

This extension results in one programming problem. Inside the **accept** statement for an entry family (or a subset of it), it will not be possible to identify the member of the entry family whose call was accepted. Two simple ways of solving this problem are:

(i) Define a new attribute INDEX for every entry family. When used inside an **accept** statement for an entry family E,

E'INDEX yields the value of the index of the member of the entry family whose call was accepted, e.g.:

> **accept** UP(FLOORS) **do** ... UP'INDEX ... **end**;

(ii) Extend the syntax further to allow the specification of a local variable that has the value equal to the index of the entry family member whose call was accepted, e.g., in:

> **accept** UP(I in FLOORS) **do** ... I ... **end**;

the local variable I, inside the body of the **accept** statement, has a value equal to the index of the entry whose call was accepted.

7 Conclusions

The Ada language is the first programming language to use the rendezvous concept as the basis for its concurrent programming facilities. Consequently, only experience with concurrent programming in the Ada language will lead us to finding the facilities most appropriate for the rendezvous concept.

Two kinds of polling can occur with the rendezvous mechanism in the Ada language – rendezvous polling and information polling. Occurrence of rendezvous polling depends heavily on the facilities provided in a programming language whereas information polling, on the other hand, depends wholly on program design.

The bias towards rendezvous polling results from many decisions made in the design of the Ada language. We feel that the changes and extensions we have suggested will enhance the usability of the Ada language in expressing concurrent programs. However, we are somewhat hesitant about advocating the incorporation of all the suggestions, primarily because the Ada language is large and some of these extensions would further increase its complexity – both from the implementor's and the user's viewpoints. Suggestions 1 and 3 in Section 6 do not complicate the implementation in any way. However, suggestion 2, proposing the selective call statement and an extension allowing an entry call alternative in the selective wait statement, will make the implementation of the concurrent facilities somewhat more complicated.

It is likely that the Ada language will not be modified, at least in the near future. Consequently, it is important that a programmer recognize the bias towards rendezvous polling in Ada. Care should be taken in the design of programs in the Ada language to avoid unnecessary polling.

We have suggested ways in which polling can be eliminated. For example, since **when** conditions followed by a sequence of non-tasking statements are not allowed as **select** alternatives, a **delay** statement with a zero delay should be used instead of the **else** part. Programs should reflect the structure of the problem.

Polling programs may result from poor program design. Polling may arise if a programmer attempts to use too few tasks (as in the terminal communication or the elevator problems). As mentioned earlier, a good design principle to follow is to dedicate a task to each function or job to be done in a program instead of letting one task perform several functions.

Although we have focused on rendezvous facilities in the Ada language our analysis carries over to other languages that may be based on the rendezvous mechanism. Lack of appropriate facilities to support the rendezvous mechanism can result in a polling bias in any concurrent programming language based on the rendezvous mechanism.

Acknowledgments

We thank the referees for their insights and constructive comments. We are also grateful to A. R. Feuer, B. W. Kernighan, D. D. Hill, J. O. Limb, R. H. McCullough and C. S. Wetherell for their comments and suggestions.

References

[1]   'Rationale for the design of the Ada programming language', *Sigplan Notices*, **14** (6), part B (1979).

[2]   M. E. Conway, 'Design of a separable transition diagram compiler', *CACM*, 396–408 (1963).

[3]   C. A. R. Hoare, 'Communicating sequential processes', *CACM*, **21** (8), 666–677 (1978).

[4]   *Reference Manual for the Ada Programming Language*, United States Department of Defense, January 1983.

[5]   R. B. Kieburtz and A. Silberschatz, 'Comments on "Communicating Sequential Processes" ', *TOPLAS*, **1** (2), 218–225 (1979).

[6]   J. G. P. Barnes, *Programming in Ada*, Addison-Wesley, 1982.

[7]   J. Welsh and A. Lister, 'A comparative study of task communication in Ada', *Software – Practice and Experience*, **11**, 257–290 (1981).

[8]   G. Booch, *Ada Letters*, **II** (3), (1982).

[9]   N. Gehani, *Ada: An Advanced Introduction*, Prentice-Hall, 1983.

[10]   A. J. Bernstein, 'Output guards and nondeterminism in "communicating sequential processes" ', *ACM TOPLAS*, **2** (2), 234–238 (1980).

[11]   W. M. Gentleman, 'Message passing between sequential processes: the reply primitive and the administrator concept', *Software – Practice and Experience*, **11**, 435–466 (1981).

16

Comments on 'Communicating Sequential Processes'

Richard B. Kieburtz
State University of New York at Stony Brook

Abraham Silberschatz
University of Texas at Dallas

In his recent paper, 'Communicating Sequential Processes' (*Comm. ACM* 21, 8 (Aug. 1978), 666–677), C.A.R. Hoare outlines a programming language notation for interprocess communication in which processes are synchronized by the messages they exchange. The notation carries with it certain implications for the synchronization protocols required in a message transfer. These are not at all obvious and are made explicit here. An alternative convention is suggested in which communication and synchronization are partially uncoupled from one another

Key words and phrases: concurrency, interprocess communication, message passing, synchronization.

CR categories: 4.20, 4.22, 4.32.

In 'Communicating Sequential Processes' (CSP) [1], Hoare has given us the outline of a new programming style, designed to cater to the needs of concurrent programming. As with any new concept, there are several aspects that seem to deserve further exploration and discussion.

This work was supported in part by the National Science Foundation under Grants MCS7681087 and MCS7702463.

1   Causality, synchronization, and automatic buffering

The activities of parallel processes are synchronized by interprocess communications. The fundamental law of causality requires that a communication cannot be received before it is sent.

In CSP, it is further required that a source process cannot send a communication until a destination process is ready to accept it. Obviously, this restriction means that the parallel execution of CSP programs will be less than that of a system in which processes are synchronized only by the causality constraint. Furthermore, the additional synchronization is in a sense implicit, as it is an effect accompanying the explicit action of delivering output. Implicit synchronization that restricts parallel execution does not seem to meet any of the stated design goals of CSP, and we should examine carefully the reasons for its inclusion.

One reason stated for this restriction is that otherwise an output message would need to be buffered automatically for subsequent input at its destination. It is argued that automatic buffering is not a primitive operation and should not be mandated by the programming language, since it can always be accomplished (if desired) by software buffering at the destination, or by interposing a buffering process between the ultimate source and destination. We can think of three objections to this argument.

(1)   In order to program software buffering at the destination, the structure of a destination process must usually be somewhat complicated in order to anticipate input messages before they are to be acted upon.

(2)   Underlying the notion that buffered communications are not primitive is the assumption that memoryless communications channels are the norm, rather than channels with memory. Although this may be true of many current computer architectures, it need not be true of future architectures. Specifically, communication via a time-shared, common bus provides no in-channel memory. However, direct processor-to-processor links can easily have memory, and memory is inherent when indirect, store-and-forward transmission is used. With current LSI technology, these kinds of channels are reasonable alternatives to a common bus, and in VLSI technology, they may be greatly preferred.

(3)   A further assumption is that all communications are of such importance that none may be lost. This depends upon the application. For an example in which a few communications can be overlooked, consider a pair of processes: one which computes the location of a moving point to be presented on a display screen, and one which continuously refreshes the display.

```
Update :: [x, y : integer;
              *[compute coordinates of the point;
                 Display!(x, y);
              ]  ]
‖ Display :: [u, v : integer; j : 0..Nlines;
                *[ j := 0;
                    *[ j < Nlines  ⟶  [Update?(u, v) ⟶ skip
                                    ☐ true ⟶ refresh the jth line, using
                                             (u, v) as the current position
                                             of the point; j := j + 1
                                      ]
                    ]  ]  ]
```

In this example, it is unimportant whether a particular set of coordinates is lost or not. If one set is lost, it will shortly be replaced by a more recent estimate of the position of the point. In fact, the process *Update* will make better use of its time by beginning the computation of a new set of position coordinates immediately rather than by waiting to transmit a set of data already inaccurate.

2   Clean termination of processes

A CSP process is a unit of activity which is intended to terminate after some finite time. A process terminates when execution reaches the end of its command list, with no further activity specified. A process may, of course, contain repetitive commands. A repetitive command terminates when all of its component commands fail in an attempt to execute it one more time. However, since an unfulfilled output (input) command does not fail immediately, simply because no corresponding input (output) is ready, it is necessary to provide for the exigency in which the partner process named in an I/O command has already terminated. When this happens, the I/O command is said to fail, and the process does not wait further for it to be completed. Thus it is necessary, in an interprocess communication of CSP, that each process be afforded a glimpse of the state of its communication partner, and herein lies a potential problem.

It can easily happen that a process will be able to terminate only after one or more of its partner processes has terminated. CSP provides very little support for the programmer to assure himself that the processes of a parallel command will always terminate in an orderly and predictable manner. In fact, it appears to be fraught with possibilities for deadlocking processes, and this seems to us a great weakness. For instance, consider:

```
[ [A :: [B!msg1 ( ); C!msg2 ( )]
‖ [B :: [C?msg3 ( ); A?msg1 ( )]
‖ [C :: [A?msg2 ( ); B!msg3 ( )]
```

which is a deadlocking parallel command in CSP, but would be deadlock free if a source process could continue execution immediately upon executing an output command.

In Section 7.9 of [1], Hoare has briefly discussed an important aspect of the clean termination problem, but the restriction he proposes there seems to run counter to the definition he gives in Section 2.4.

3   Communication and the process state

It has been mentioned that some information about the state of each process must be exchanged in the course of executing an I/O command, in order to determine when and whether communication can take place. Let us examine the states of a process, relative to a single input command. We are only interested in a projection of the total state vector of the process, reflecting state changes that occur as a direct consequence of requesting and accepting an input message. The state transition diagram of Figure 1 is illustrative of the case in which an input command appears in a guard. Circles in the diagram represent states of the destination process:

R – ready to receive input;
A – active, but not ready to receive;
T – terminated.

The state-transition arcs are labeled to indicate the steps in the execution of an input command that bring them about. An A-to-R transition occurs when an input command is encountered in the execution sequence of a process. An R-to-A transition occurs if either the communication is successfully completed, or if it is aborted. Abortion of an input command can occur in either of two ways:

(1) If the source process has terminated, then the input command fails; or

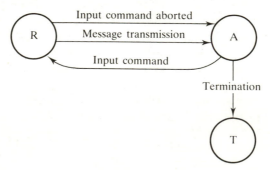

Figure 1

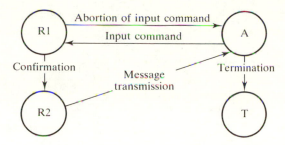

Figure 2

(2)   When the input command occurs in a guard, and execution of the guard of some other component of the same guarded command succeeds, then the as yet unsatisfied command is aborted.

In case (2) the R-to-A transition occurs 'spontaneously,' without any signal from the source process. The states of a source process are similar, but there is no 'spontaneous' R-to-A transition for a source, as an output command cannot occur within a guard.

The effective signaling that takes place between a source and a destination process must establish that both are ready to proceed. Unfortunately, this is complicated by the possibility of a spontaneous R-to-A transition by the destination. For an effective rendezvous, the R state of the destination process must be split, as shown in Figure 2. This resolves the problem, since the only R2-to-A transition is by completion of the communication. However, it requires an additional signal, here called confirmation, to be exchanged. At the time the destination process sends a confirmation signal and makes the transition R1 to R2, the input command has succeeded in the sense that it cannot subsequently be aborted by either of the communicating processes. Thus, if the input command happens to be within a guard, the guard can be said to succeed at that point in time.

In the signaling diagram of Figure 3, the initial input request is presumed to contain the 'pattern' that is to be matched by the output command. The request for confirmation and the confirmation itself are both pure signals, incorporated into the sequence solely for the purpose of exchanging state information. Thus, insofar as these signals carry no information relevant to the particular program, they may be regarded as overhead of the communications channel. (If the signaling were assumed to be initiated by a source, rather than by a destination process, then the initial message-request signal shown in Figure 3 would be omitted, and the pattern which gives the message type would accompany the first signal sent by the source process. A confirmation signal from the destination is still necessary, however.)

Note, however, that the illustration is independent of any assumptions about architecture or implementation; it demonstrates the inherent

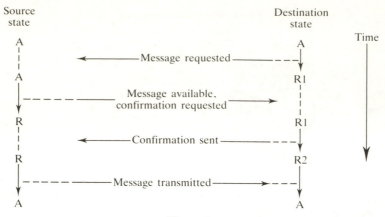

Figure 3

complexity of the communications scheme. And if output commands were allowed to appear in guards, a possibility suggested in Section 7.8 of [1], then a spontaneous R-to-A transition would also be possible for source processes. In consequence, a reliable rendezvous could no longer be accomplished by fixed-message signals exchanged between finite-state controls! In order for asynchronous processes to rendezvous, one process or the other must honor a commitment not to change the state it has reflected to the partner process, until the partner has had an opportunity to arrive at the expected rendezvous and complete the anticipated transaction.

4   Topology of interprocess communications channels

One of the more powerful aspects of the language notation presented in CSP is the ability to define an indexed array of processes. A source or a destination process for a communications command can then be identified merely by specifying a value for the index of a process. If an index is specified by a constant expression (or by an expression that differs by at most a constant from the index of the process in whose code the command appears), then the binding of the communications channel is clearly static, and this is the use made of indexed processes in the examples given by Hoare. However, the notation appears to allow the use of more complex indexing expressions, which could be used to simulate dynamic binding of a source or a destination process as well. Also, even in examples 4.5, 5.2, and 6.1 given in [1], we find instances of static bindings of communications between a single process and all the other processes of an indexed set.

The ability to specify static bindings of input or output channels to an arbitrary number of partner processes, or to simulate dynamic bindings of I/O channels, should give us cause to reflect on the intended use of the language. If it were meant only to specify multiprocess execution on a multiplexed, single processor, then it would be easy to accept this very flexible communications topology, for we would expect that it could be realized by the use of shared memory segments, with the sharing managed by an operating system kernel. But the language notation is also meant to be applicable to multiprocessing with multiple processors, each having independent memory. With such a configuration, each communications channel between processors must be explicitly provided by some mixture of hardware and software technology. In the latter case, it is not presently feasible to presume an arbitrary interprocess communications topology among more than a handful of participating processes. A language notation that imposes no restriction on the communications topology provides little help to the programmer in distinguishing between that which is implementable, and that which is not.

5   Summary of objections

To summarize, CSP gives us a crisp and clean concept of process, in which the states of processes are isolated from one another, except at explicit communications points. This allows us to specify systems in which processes are driven by their inputs and synchronized by their outputs. However, the required synchronization at output commands seems very likely to degrade the performance of parallel systems, relative to their potential. Clean termination of processes is not always easy to assure in CSP programs and is left as a problem for the applications programmer to cope with. The communications mechanism turns out to require some unsuspected signals to be exchanged, and extension of the language to allow the inclusion of output commands in guards is not as simple as it might at first appear. The use of indexed process arrays allows one to specify interprocess communications of arbitrary topology, which may not be implementable in a multiprocessor configuration.

6   Alternatives

It is admittedly easier to voice criticism than it is to create a clean and elegant structure for others to criticize. Nevertheless, a critic should be willing to try to suggest alternatives to those aspects with which he finds fault. Let us consider one in particular.

I/O ports with memory

Within the framework of CSP, better isolation of process states can be obtained if communications are routed through ports. By allowing a port to have sufficient memory to hold a single message, we can relax the strict synchronization of outputs with inputs. The states of a port are illustrated in Figure 4.

Ports can be declared in a parallel command, and the scope of a port declaration is the entire parallel command. Each port name can be used by only a single pair of processes, one of which may use it in output commands, and the other in input commands. A port may be closed by a destination process executing a terminal input command (denoted by ??) or marked to be closed by an output process executing a terminal output (!!). An input (output) command fails if the port to which it is directed is closed.

This convention avoids the need to reflect the state of one process to its communication partners in order to secure clean termination of a parallel command. Neither a source nor a destination needs to exchange confirmation signals with a port, because a port, once ready to accept output or deliver input, cannot 'spontaneously' undergo a state transition. Concurrent execution of processes is limited only by the synchronization requirement of causality, unless a programmer explicitly specifies more synchronization. Ports can readily be implemented either in hardware as an interprocessor data pipe, or in software by the use of shared memory.

At this point we should realize that we have given up the principal synchronizer available for use in CSP by stripping the synchronization requirement from the output command. An explicit synchronization primitive can readily be provided. Let us define a Boolean-valued synchronizing function *When-empty*( ). If the state of the port given as its argument is *Empty*, then *When-empty*( ) evaluates to true; if the state of its argument is *Closed* then it evaluates to false, and its evaluation is delayed if the port is in any other state. Through the use of this synchronizer, the activity of a source process can be delayed until a destination process at the other terminal of a port has accepted a message previously placed there.

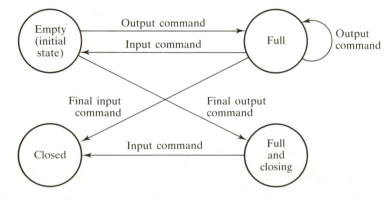

Figure 4

The alternative of port-directed I/O is appealing because it further isolates the states of processes, consistent with the design goal of CSP, still allows all process synchronization to be activated through the interprocess communications, yet distinguishes the message transmission function from the synchronization aspect of communication and allows the programmer to specify exactly that which is needed. It further offers the programmer better means by which to assure that processes will terminate cleanly, by allowing the state of a port to be controlled and tested, rather than relying on the implicit communication of information about process states.

A further consideration is the required overhead of the communications facility. Communication through a port can be accomplished without the use of 'hidden' signals. The communications facility offered by CSP not only mandates such signals in each communication, but further requires of a terminating process that it either remain active, in order to respond to its nonterminated partners that it can no longer participate in a communication, or else broadcast to all of its partners a notice of its demise. A process communicating through a port needs only to close the port at the time of its last communication.

As to the allowable interprocess communication topology, we have no patent solution. However, it seems reasonable that the expressions used to specify indices of communicating processes should be restricted to reflect the concept of proximity in an architecture on which the process array is to exist. Perhaps the topology should be reflected in a set of functions that can be particularized for any given hardware architecture. For instance, given a two-dimensional iterative array architecture one might allow two-dimensional process arrays and restrict the index expressions that can be used in an input or output command to use only the expressions that can be formed by use of functions *Successor* and *Predecessor*, relative to the index of the process in which the command appears. Further study of the problem of communications topology seems to be desirable.

Reference

[1]   Hoare, C.A.R. Communicating sequential processes. *Comm. ACM* **21**, 8 (Aug. 1978), 666–677.

17

Experience with Processes and Monitors in Mesa

Butler W. Lampson
Xerox Palo Alto Research Center

David D. Redell
Xerox Business Systems

The use of monitors for describing concurrency has been much discussed in the literature. When monitors are used in real systems of any size, however, a number of problems arise which have not been adequately dealt with: the semantics of nested monitor calls; the various ways of defining the meaning of WAIT; priority scheduling; handling of timeouts, aborts and other exceptional conditions; interactions with process creation and destruction; monitoring large numbers of small objects. These problems are addressed by the facilities described here for concurrent programming in Mesa. Experience with several substantial applications gives us some confidence in the validity of our solutions.

Key words and phrases: concurrency, condition variable, deadlock, module, monitor, operating system, process, synchronization, task.

CR categories: 4.32, 4.35, 5.24.

1 Introduction

In early 1977 we began to design the concurrent programming facilities of Pilot, a new operating system for a personal computer [18]. Pilot is a fairly large program itself (24 000 lines of Mesa code). In addition, it must support a variety of quite large application programs, ranging from database management to inter-network message transmission, which are heavy users of concurrency; our experience with some of these applications is discussed later in the paper. We intended the new facilities to be used at least for the following purposes:

- *Local concurrent programming*   An individual application can be implemented as a tightly coupled group of synchronized processes to express the concurrency inherent in the application.

- *Global resource sharing*   Independent applications can run together on the same machine, cooperatively sharing the resources; in particular, their processes can share the processor.

- *Replacing interrupts*   A request for software attention to a device can be handled directly by waking up an appropriate process, without going through a separate interrupt mechanism (e.g., a forced branch).

Pilot is closely coupled to the Mesa language [17], which is used to write both Pilot itself and the applications programs it supports. Hence it was natural to design these facilities as part of Mesa; this makes them easier to use, and also allows the compiler to detect many kinds of errors in their use. The idea of integrating such facilities into a language is certainly not new; it goes back at least as far as PL/I [1]. Furthermore the invention of monitors by Dijkstra, Hoare, and Brinch Hansen [3, 5, 8] provided a very attractive framework for reliable concurrent programming. There followed a number of papers on the integration of concurrency into programming languages, and at least one implementation [4].

We therefore thought that our task would be an easy one: read the literature, compare the alternatives offered there, and pick the one most suitable for our needs. This expectation proved to be naive. Because of the large size and wide variety of our applications, we had to address a number of issues which were not clearly resolved in the published work on monitors. The most notable among these are listed below, with the sections in which they are discussed:

(1) *Program structure*   Mesa has facilities for organizing programs into modules which communicate through well-defined interfaces. Processes must fit into this scheme (see Section 3.1).

(2) *Creating processes*   A set of processes fixed at compile-time is unacceptable in such a general-purpose system (see Section 2). Existing proposals for varying the amount of concurrency were limited to concurrent elaboration of the statements in a block, in the style of Algol 68 (except for the rather complex mechanism in PL/I).

(3) *Creating monitors*   A fixed number of monitors is also unacceptable, since the number of synchronizers should be a function of the amount of data, but many of the details of existing proposals depended on a fixed association of a monitor with a block of the program text (see Section 3.2).

(4) *WAIT in a nested monitor call* This issue had been (and has continued to be) the source of a considerable amount of confusion, which we had to resolve in an acceptable manner before we could proceed (see Section 3.1).

(5) *Exceptions* A realistic system must have timeouts, and it must have a way to abort a process (see Section 4.1). Mesa has an UNWIND mechanism for abandoning part of a sequential computation in an orderly way, and this must interact properly with monitors (see Section 3.3).

(6) *Scheduling* The precise semantics of waiting on a condition variable had been discussed [10] but not agreed upon, and the reasons for making any particular choice had not been articulated (see Section 4). No attention had been paid to the interaction between monitors and priority scheduling of processes (see Section 4.3).

(7) *Input-output* The details of fitting I/O devices into the framework of monitors and condition variables had not been fully worked out (see Section 4.2).

Some of these points have also been made by Keedy [12], who discusses the usefulness of monitors in a modern general-purpose mainframe operating system. The Modula language [21] addresses (2) and (7), but in a more limited context than ours.

Before settling on the monitor scheme described below, we considered other possibilities. We felt that our first task was to choose either shared memory (i.e., monitors) or message passing as our basic interprocess communication paradigm.

Message passing has been used (without language support) in a number of operating systems; for a recent proposal to embed messages in a language, see [9]. An analysis of the differences between such schemes and those based on monitors was made by Lauer and Needham [14]. They conclude that, given certain mild restrictions on programming style, the two schemes are duals under the transformation:

message $\longleftrightarrow$ process
process $\longleftrightarrow$ monitor
send/reply $\longleftrightarrow$ call/return

Since our work is based on a language whose main tool of program structuring is the procedure, it was considerably easier to use a monitor scheme than to devise a message-passing scheme properly integrated with the type system and control structures of the language.

Within the shared memory paradigm, we considered the possibility of adopting a simpler primitive synchronization facility than monitors. Assuming the absence of multiple processors, the simplest form of mutual exclusion appears to be a nonpreemptive scheduler; if processes only yield the processor voluntarily, then mutual exclusion is insured between yield-points. In its simplest form, this approach tends to produce very delicate programs, since the insertion of a yield in a random place can introduce a subtle bug in a previously correct program. This danger can be alleviated by the addition of a modest amount of 'syntactic sugar' to delineate critical sections within which the processor must not be yielded (e.g., pseudo monitors). This sugared form of nonpreemptive scheduling can provide extremely efficient solutions to simple problems, but was nonetheless rejected for four reasons:

(1) While we were willing to accept an implementation which would not work on multiple processors, we did not want to embed this restriction in our basic semantics.

(2) A separate preemptive mechanism is needed anyway, since the processor must respond to time-critical events (e.g., I/O interrupts) for which voluntary process switching is clearly too sluggish. With preemptive process scheduling, interrupts can be treated as ordinary process wakeups, which reduces the total amount of machinery needed and eliminates the awkward situations which tend to occur at the boundary between two scheduling regimes.

(3) The use of nonpreemption as mutual exclusion restricts programming generality within critical sections; in particular, a procedure that happens to yield the processor cannot be called. In large systems where modularity is essential, such restrictions are intolerable.

(4) The Mesa concurrency facilities function in a virtual memory environment. The use of nonpreemption as mutual exclusion forbids multiprogramming across page faults, since that would effectively insert preemptions at arbitrary points in the program.

For mutual exclusion with a preemptive scheduler, it is necessary to introduce explicit locks, and machinery which makes requesting processes wait when a lock is unavailable. We considered casting our locks as semaphores, but decided that, compared with monitors, they exert too little structuring discipline on concurrent programs. Semaphores do solve several different problems with a single mechanism (e.g., mutual exclusion, producer/consumer) but we found similar economies in our implementation of monitors and condition variables (see Section 5.1).

We have not associated any protection mechanism with processes in Mesa, except what is implicit in the type system of the language. Since the system supports only one user, we feel that the considerable protection offered by the strong typing of the language is sufficient. This fact contributes substantially to the low cost of process operations.

2 Processes

Mesa casts the creation of a new process as a special procedure activation which executes concurrently with its caller. Mesa allows *any* procedure (except an internal procedure of a monitor; see Section 3.1) to be invoked in this way, at the caller's discretion. It is possible to later retrieve the results returned by the procedure. For example, a keyboard input routine might be invoked as a normal procedure by writing:

buffer ← ReadLine[terminal]

but since *ReadLine* is likely to wait for input, its caller might wish instead to compute concurrently:

p ← FORK ReadLine[terminal];
... <concurrent computation> ...
buffer ← JOIN p;

Here the types are:

ReadLine : PROCEDURE [Device] RETURNS [Line];
p : PROCESS RETURNS [Line].

The rendezvous between the return from *ReadLine* which terminates the new process and the JOIN in the old process is provided automatically. *ReadLine* is the *root* procedure of the new process.

This scheme has a number of important properties:

(1)   It treats a process as a first-class value in the language, which can be assigned to a variable or an array element, passed as a parameter, and in general treated exactly like any other value. A process value is like a pointer value or a procedure value which refers to a nested procedure, in that it can become a dangling reference if the process to which it refers goes away.

(2)   The method for passing parameters to a new process and retrieving its results is exactly the same as the corresponding method for procedures, and is subject to the same strict type checking. Just as PROCEDURE is a generator for a family of types (depending on the argument and result types), so PROCESS is a similar generator, slightly simpler since it depends only on result types.

(3)   No special declaration is needed for a procedure which is invoked as a process. Because of the implementation of procedure calls and other global control transfers in Mesa [13], there is no extra execution cost for this generality.

(4) The cost of creating and destroying a process is moderate, and the cost in storage is only twice the minimum cost of a procedure instance. It is therefore feasible to program with a large number of processes, and to vary the number quite rapidly. As Lauer and Needham [14] point out, there are many synchronization problems which have straightforward solutions using monitors only when obtaining a new process is cheap.

Many patterns of process creation are possible. A common one is to create a *detached* process, which never returns a result to its creator, but instead functions quite independently. When the root procedure *p* of a detached process returns, the process is destroyed without any fuss. The fact that no one intends to wait for a result from *p* can be expressed by executing:

Detach[*p*]

From the point of view of the caller, this is similar to freeing a dynamic variable – it is generally an error to make any further use of the current value of *p*, since the process, running asynchronously, may complete its work and be destroyed at any time. Of course the design of the program may be such that this cannot happen, and in this case the value of *p* can still be useful as a parameter to the *Abort* operation (see Section 4.1).

This remark illustrates a general point: Processes offer some new opportunities to create dangling references. A process variable itself is a kind of pointer, and must not be used after the process is destroyed. Furthermore, parameters passed by reference to a process are pointers, and if they happen to be local variables of a procedure, that procedure must not return until the process is destroyed. Like most implementation languages, Mesa does not provide any protection against dangling references, whether connected with processes or not.

The ordinary Mesa facility for exception handling uses the ordering established by procedure calls to control the processing of exceptions. Any block may have an attached exception handler. The block containing the statement which causes the exception is given the first chance to handle it, then its enclosing block, and so forth until a procedure body is reached. Then the caller of the procedure is given a chance in the same way. Since the root procedure of a process has no caller, it must be prepared to handle any exceptions which can be generated in the process, including exceptions generated by the procedure itself. If it fails to do so, the resulting error sends control to the debugger, where the identity of the procedure and the exception can easily be determined by a programmer. This is not much comfort, however, when a system is in operational use. The practical consequence is that while any procedure suitable for forking can also be called sequentially, the converse is not generally true.

3   Monitors

When several processes interact by sharing data, care must be taken to properly synchronize access to the data. The idea behind monitors is that a proper vehicle for this interaction is one which unifies:

- The synchronization,
- The shared data,
- The body of code which performs the accesses.

The data is *protected* by a *monitor*, and can only be accessed within the body of a *monitor procedure*. There are two kinds of monitor procedures: *entry procedures*, which can be called from outside the monitor, and *internal procedures*, which can only be called from monitor procedures. Processes can only perform operations on the data by calling entry procedures. The monitor ensures that at most one process is executing a monitor procedure at a time; this process is said to be *in* the monitor. If a process is in the monitor, any other process which calls an entry procedure will be delayed. The monitor procedures are written textually next to each other, and next to the declaration of the protected data, so that a reader can conveniently survey all the references to the data.

As long as any order of calling the entry procedures produces meaningful results, no additional synchronization is needed among the processes sharing the monitor. If a random order is not acceptable, other provisions must be made in the program outside the monitor. For example, an unbounded buffer with *Put* and *Get* procedures imposes no constraints (of course a *Get* may have to wait, but this is taken care of within the monitor, as described in the next section). On the other hand, a tape unit with *Reserve*, *Read*, *Write*, and *Release* operations requires that each process execute a *Reserve* first and a *Release* last. A second process executing a *Reserve* will be delayed by the monitor, but another process doing a *Read* without a prior *Reserve* will produce chaos. Thus monitors do not solve all the problems of concurrent programming; they are intended, in part, as primitive building blocks for more complex scheduling policies. A discussion of such policies and how to implement them using monitors is beyond the scope of this paper.

3.1   Monitor modules

In Mesa the simplest monitor is an instance of a *module*, which is the basic unit of global program structuring. A Mesa module consists of a collection of procedures and their global data, and in sequential programming is used to implement a data abstraction. Such a module has PUBLIC procedures which constitute the external interface to the abstraction, and PRIVATE procedures which are internal to the implementation and cannot be called from outside the module; its data is normally entirely private. A MONITOR module differs only slightly. It has three kinds of procedures: *entry*, *internal* (private), and *external* (nonmonitor procedures). The first two are the monitor procedures, and execute with the monitor lock held. For example, consider a simple storage allocator with two entry procedures, *Allocate* and *Free*, and an external procedure *Expand* which increases the size of a block.

```
StorageAllocator : MONITOR = BEGIN
  availableStorage : INTEGER;
  moreAvailable : CONDITION;

  ...
  Allocate : ENTRY PROCEDURE [size : INTEGER]
  RETURNS [p : POINTER] = BEGIN
    UNTIL availableStorage ≥ size
      DO WAIT moreAvailable ENDLOOP;
    p ← <remove chunk of size words & update availableStorage>
  END;

  Free : ENTRY PROCEDURE [p : POINTER, size : INTEGER]
      = BEGIN
    <put back chunk of size words & update availableStorage>;
    NOTIFY moreAvailable END;

  Expand : PUBLIC PROCEDURE [pOld : POINTER,
    size : INTEGER]
  RETURNS [pNew : POINTER] = BEGIN
    pNew ← Allocate[size];
    <copy contents from old block to new block>;
    Free[pOld] END;

END.
```

A Mesa module is normally used to package a collection of related procedures and protect their private data from external access. In order to avoid introducing a new lexical structuring mechanism, we chose to make the scope of a monitor identical to a module. Sometimes, however, procedures which belong in an abstraction do not need access to any shared data, and hence need not be entry procedures of the monitor; these must be distinguished somehow.

For example, two asynchronous processes clearly must not execute in the *Allocate* or *Free* procedures at the same time; hence, these must be entry procedures. On the other hand, it is unnecessary to hold the monitor lock during the copy in *Expand*, even though this procedure logically belongs in the storage allocator module; it is thus written as an external procedure. A more complex monitor might also have internal procedures, which are used to structure its computations, but which are inaccessible from outside the monitor. These do not acquire and release the lock on call and return, since they can only be called when the lock is already held.

If no suitable block is available, *Allocate* makes its caller wait on the *condition* variable *moreAvailable*. *Free* does a NOTIFY to this variable whenever a new block becomes available; this causes some process waiting on the variable to resume execution (see Section 4 for details). The WAIT releases the monitor lock, which is reacquired when the waiting process reenters the monitor. If a WAIT is done in an internal procedure, it still releases the lock. If, however, the monitor calls some other procedure which is outside the monitor module, the lock is not released, even if the other procedure is in (or calls) another monitor and ends up doing a WAIT. The same rule is adopted in Concurrent Pascal [4].

To understand the reasons for this, consider the form of a correctness argument for a program using a monitor. The basic idea is that the monitor maintains an *invariant* which is always true of its data, except when some process is executing in the monitor. Whenever control leaves the monitor, this invariant must be established. In return, whenever control enters the monitor the invariant can be assumed. Thus an entry procedure must establish the invariant before returning, and monitor procedures must establish it before doing a WAIT. The invariant can be assumed at the start of an entry procedure, and after each WAIT. Under these conditions, the monitor lock ensures that no one can enter the monitor when the invariant is false. Now, if the lock were to be released on a WAIT done in another monitor which happens to be called from this one, the invariant would have to be established before making the call which leads to the WAIT. Since in general there is no way to know whether a call outside the monitor will lead to a WAIT, the invariant would have to be established before every such call. The result would be to make calling such procedures hopelessly cumbersome.

An alternative solution is to allow an *outside block* to be written inside a monitor, with the following meaning: on entry to the block the lock is released (and hence the invariant must be established); within the block the protected data is inaccessible; on leaving the block the lock is reacquired. This scheme allows the state represented by the execution environment of the monitor to be maintained during the outside call, and imposes a minimal burden on the programmer: to establish the invariant before making the call. This mechanism would be easy to add to Mesa; we have left it out because we have not seen convincing examples in which it significantly simplifies the program.

If an entry procedure generates an exception in the usual way, the result will be a call on the exception handler from within the monitor, so that the lock will not be released. In particular, this means that the exception handler must carefully avoid invoking that same monitor, or a deadlock will result. To avoid this restriction, the entry procedure can restore the invariant and then execute:

RETURN WITH ERROR[<arguments>]

which returns from the entry procedure, thus releasing the lock, and then generates the exception.

3.2 Monitors and deadlock

There are three patterns of pairwise deadlock that can occur using monitors. In practice, of course, deadlocks often involve more than two processes, in which case the actual patterns observed tend to be more complicated; conversely, it is also possible for a single process to deadlock with itself (e.g., if an entry procedure is recursive).

The simplest form of deadlock takes place inside a single monitor when two processes do a WAIT, each expecting to be awakened by the other. This represents a localized bug in the monitor code and is usually easy to locate and correct.

A more subtle form of deadlock can occur if there is a cyclic calling pattern between two monitors. Thus if monitor M calls an entry procedure in N, and N calls one in M, each will wait for the other to release the monitor lock. This kind of deadlock is made neither more nor less serious by the monitor mechanism. It arises whenever such cyclic dependencies are allowed to occur in a program, and can be avoided in a number of ways. The simplest is to impose a partial ordering on resources such that all the resources simultaneously possessed by any process are totally ordered, and insist that if resource r precedes s in the ordering, then r cannot be acquired later than s. When the resources are monitors, this reduces to the simple rule that mutually recursive monitors must be avoided. Concurrent Pascal [4] makes this check at compile time; Mesa cannot do so because it has procedure variables.

A more serious problem arises if M calls N, and N then waits for a condition which can only occur when another process enters N through M and makes the condition true. In this situation, N will be unlocked, since the WAIT occurred there, but M will remain locked during the WAIT in N. This kind of two-level data abstraction must be handled with some care. A straightforward solution using standard monitors is to break M into two parts: a monitor M' and an ordinary module O which implements the abstraction defined by M, and calls M' for access to the shared data. The call on N must be done from O rather than from within M'.

Monitors, like any other interprocess communication mechanism, are a *tool* for implementing synchronization constraints chosen by the programmer. It is unreasonable to blame the tool when poorly chosen constraints lead to deadlock. What is crucial, however, is that the tool makes the program structure as understandable as possible, while not restricting the programmer too much in his choice of constraints (e.g., by forcing a monitor lock to be held much longer than necessary). To some extent, these two goals tend to conflict; the Mesa concurrency facilities attempt to strike a reasonable balance and provide an environment in which the conscientious programmer can avoid deadlock reasonably easily. Our experience in this area is reported in Section 6.

3.3 Monitored objects

Often we wish to have a collection of shared data objects, each one representing an instance of some abstract object such as a file, a storage volume, a virtual circuit, or a database view, and we wish to add objects to the collection and delete them dynamically. In a sequential program this is done with standard techniques for allocating and freeing storage. In a concurrent program, however, provision must also be made for serializing access to each object. The straightforward way is to use a single monitor for accessing all instances of the object, and we recommend this approach whenever possible. If the objects function independently of each other for the most part, however, the single monitor drastically reduces the maximum concurrency which can be obtained. In this case, what we want is to give each object its own monitor; all these monitors will share the same code, since all the instances of the abstract object share the same code, but each object will have its own lock.

One way to achieve this result is to make multiple instances of the monitor module. Mesa makes this quite easy, and it is the next recommended approach. However, the data associated with a module instance includes information which the Mesa system uses to support program linking and code swapping, and there is some cost in duplicating this information. Furthermore, module instances are allocated by the system; hence the program cannot exercise the fine control over allocation strategies which is possible for ordinary Mesa data objects. We have therefore introduced a new type constructor called a *monitored record*, which is exactly like an ordinary record, except that it includes a monitor lock and is intended to be used as the protected data of a monitor.

In writing the code for such a monitor, the programmer must specify how to access the monitored record, which might be embedded in some larger data structure passed as a parameter to the entry procedures. This is done with a LOCKS clause which is written at the beginning of the module:

    MONITOR LOCKS *file*↑
        USING *file* : POINTER TO *FileData*;

if the *FileData* is the protected data. An arbitrary expression can appear in the LOCKS clause; for instance, LOCKS *file.buffers*[*currentPage*] might be appropriate if the protected data is one of the buffers in an array which is part of the *file*. Every entry procedure of this monitor, and every internal procedure that does a WAIT, must have access to a *file*, so that it can acquire and release the lock upon entry or around a WAIT. This can be accomplished in two ways: the *file* may be a global variable of the module, or it may be a parameter to *every* such procedure. In the latter case, we have effectively created a separate monitor for each object, without limiting the program's freedom to arrange access paths and storage allocation as it likes.

Unfortunately, the type system of Mesa is not strong enough to make this construction completely safe. If the value of *file* is changed within an entry procedure, for example, chaos will result, since the return from this procedure will release not the lock which was acquired during the call, but some other lock instead. In this example we can insist that *file* be read-only, but with another level of indirection aliasing can occur and such a restriction cannot be enforced. In practice this lack of safety has not been a problem.

3.4   Abandoning a computation

Suppose that a procedure P_1 has called another procedure P_2, which in turn has called P_3 and so forth until the current procedure is P_n. If P_n generates an exception which is eventually handled by P_1 (because P_2 ... P_n do not provide handlers), Mesa allows the exception handler in P_1 to abandon the portion of the computation being done in P_2 ... P_n and continue execution in P_1. When this happens, a distinguished exception called UNWIND is first generated, and each of P_2 ... P_n is given a chance to handle it and do any necessary cleanup before its activation is destroyed.

This feature of Mesa is not part of the concurrency facilities, but it does interact with those facilities in the following way. If one of the procedures being abandoned, say P_i, is an entry procedure, then the invariant must be restored and the monitor lock released before P_i is destroyed. Thus if the logic of the program allows an UNWIND, the programmer must supply a suitable handler in P_i to restore the invariant; Mesa will automatically supply the code to release the lock. If the programmer fails to supply an UNWIND handler for an entry procedure, the lock is *not* automatically released, but remains set; the cause of the resulting deadlock is not hard to find.

4   Condition variables

In this section we discuss the precise semantics of WAIT, and other details associated with condition variables. Hoare's definition of monitors [8] requires that a process waiting on a condition variable must run immediately when another process *signals* that variable, and that the signaling process in turn runs as soon as the waiter leaves the monitor. This definition allows the waiter to assume the truth of some predicate stronger than the monitor invariant (which the signaler must of course establish), but it requires several additional process switches whenever a process continues after a WAIT. It also requires that the signaling mechanism be perfectly reliable.

Mesa takes a different view: When one process establishes a condition for which some other process may be waiting, it *notifies* the corresponding condition variable. A NOTIFY is regarded as a *hint* to a waiting process; it causes execution of some process waiting on the condition to resume at some convenient future time. When the waiting process resumes, it will reacquire the monitor lock. There is no guarantee that some other process will not enter the monitor before the waiting process. Hence nothing more than the monitor invariant may be assumed after a WAIT, and the waiter must reevaluate the situation each time it resumes. The proper pattern of code for waiting is therefore:

    WHILE NOT <OK to proceed> DO WAIT *c*
    ENDLOOP.

This arrangement results in an extra evaluation of the <OK to proceed> predicate after a wait, compared to Hoare's monitors, in which the code is:

    IF NOT <OK to proceed> THEN WAIT *c*.

In return, however, there are no extra process switches, and indeed no constraints at all on when the waiting process must run after a NOTIFY. In fact, it is perfectly all right to run the waiting process even if there is not any NOTIFY, although this is presumably pointless if a NOTIFY is done whenever an interesting change is made to the protected data.

It is possible that such a laissez-faire attitude to scheduling monitor accesses will lead to unfairness and even starvation. We do not think this is a legitimate cause for concern, since in a properly designed system there should typically be no processes waiting for a monitor lock. As Hoare, Brinch Hansen, Keedy, and others have pointed out, the low level scheduling mechanism provided by monitor locks should not be used to implement high level scheduling decisions within a system (e.g., about which process should get a printer next). High level scheduling should be done by taking account of the specific characteristics of the resource being scheduled (e.g., whether the right kind of paper is in the printer). Such a scheduler will delay its client processes on condition variables after recording information about their requirements, make its decisions based on this information, and notify the proper conditions. In such a design the data protected by a monitor is never a bottleneck.

The verification rules for Mesa monitors are thus extremely simple: The monitor invariant must be established just before a return from an entry procedure or a WAIT, and it may be assumed at the start of an entry procedure and just after a WAIT. Since awakened waiters do not run immediately, the predicate established before a NOTIFY cannot be assumed after the corresponding WAIT, but since the waiter tests explicitly for <OK to proceed>, verification is actually made simpler and more localized.

Another consequence of Mesa's treatment of NOTIFY as a hint is that many applications do not trouble to determine whether the exact condition needed by a waiter has been established. Instead, they choose a very cheap predicate which implies the exact condition (e.g., some change has occurred), and NOTIFY a *covering* condition variable. Any waiting process is then responsible for determining whether the exact condition holds; if not, it simply waits again. For example, a process may need to wait until a particular object in a set changes state. A single condition covers the entire set, and a process changing any of the objects broadcasts to this condition (see Section 4.1). The information about exactly which objects are currently of interest is implicit in the states of the waiting processes, rather than having to be represented explicitly in a shared data structure. This is an attractive way to decouple the detailed design of two processes; it is feasible because the cost of waking up a process is small.

4.1   Alternatives to NOTIFY

With this rule it is easy to add three additional ways to resume a waiting process:

- *Timeout*   Associated with a condition variable is a timeout interval t. A process which has been waiting for time t will resume regardless of whether the condition has been notified. Presumably in most cases it will check the time and take some recovery action before waiting again. The original design for timeouts raised an exception if the timeout occurred; it was changed because many users simply wanted to retry on a timeout, and objected to the cost and coding complexity of handling the exception. This decision could certainly go either way.

- *Abort*   A process may be aborted at any time by executing *Abort*[p]. The effect is that the next time the process waits, or if it is waiting now, it will resume immediately and the *Aborted* exception will occur. This mechanism allows one process to gently prod another, generally to suggest that it should clean up and terminate. The aborted process is, however, free to do arbitrary computations, or indeed to ignore the abort entirely.

- *Broadcast* Instead of doing a NOTIFY to a condition, a process may do a BROADCAST, which causes *all* the processes waiting on the condition to resume, instead of simply one of them. Since a NOTIFY is just a hint, it is always correct to use BROADCAST. It is better to use NOTIFY if there will typically be several processes waiting on the condition, and it is known that any waiting process can respond properly. On the other hand, there are times when a BROADCAST is correct and a NOTIFY is not; the alert reader may have noticed a problem with the example program in Section 3.1, which can be solved by replacing the NOTIFY with a BROAD-CAST.

None of these mechanisms affects the proof rule for monitors at all. Each provides a way to attract the attention of a waiting process at an appropriate time.

Note that there is no way to stop a runaway process. This reflects the fact that Mesa processes are cooperative. Many aspects of the design would not be appropriate in a competitive environment such as a general-purpose time-sharing system.

4.2   Naked NOTIFY

Communication with input/output devices is handled by monitors and condition variables much like communication among processes. There is typically a shared data structure, whose details are determined by the hardware, for passing commands to the device and returning status information. Since it is not possible for the device to wait on a monitor lock, the updating operations on this structure must be designed so that the single-word atomic read and write operations provided by the memory are sufficient to make them atomic. When the device needs attention, it can NOTIFY a condition variable to wake up a waiting process (i.e., the interrupt handler); since the device does not actually acquire the monitor lock, its NOTIFY is called a *naked* NOTIFY. The device finds the address of the condition variable in a fixed memory location.

There is one complication associated with a naked NOTIFY: Since the notification is not protected by a monitor lock, there can be a race. It is possible for a process to be in the monitor, find the <OK to proceed> predicate to be FALSE (i.e, the device does not need attention), and be about to do a WAIT, when the device updates the shared data and does its NOTIFY. The WAIT will then be done and the NOTIFY from the device will be lost. With ordinary processes, this cannot happen, since the monitor lock ensures that one process cannot be testing the predicate and preparing to WAIT, while another is changing the value of <OK to proceed> and doing the NOTIFY. The problem is avoided by providing the familiar wakeup-waiting switch [19] in a condition variable, thus turning it into a binary semaphore [8]. This switch is needed only for condition variables that are notified by devices.

We briefly considered a design in which devices would wait on and acquire the monitor lock, exactly like ordinary Mesa processes; this design is attractive because it avoids both the anomalies just discussed. However, there is a serious problem with any kind of mutual exclusion between two processes which run on processors of substantially different speeds: The faster process may have to wait for the slower one. The worst-case response time of the faster process therefore cannot be less than the time the slower one needs to finish its critical section. Although one can get higher throughput from the faster processor than from the slower one, one cannot get better worst-case real-time performance. We consider this a fundamental deficiency.

It therefore seemed best to avoid any mutual exclusion (except for that provided by the atomic memory read and write operations) between Mesa code and device hardware and microcode. Their relationship is easily cast into a producer-consumer form, and this can be implemented, using linked lists or arrays, with only the memory's mutual exclusion. Only a small amount of Mesa code must handle device data structures without the protection of a monitor. Clearly a change of models must occur at some point between a disk head and an application program; we see no good reason why it should not happen within Mesa code, although it should certainly be tightly encapsulated.

4.3 Priorities

In some applications it is desirable to use a priority scheduling discipline for allocating the processor(s) to processes which are not waiting. Unless care is taken, the ordering implied by the assignment of priorities can be subverted by monitors. Suppose there are three priority levels (3 highest, 1 lowest), and three processes P_1, P_2, and P_3, one running at each level. Let P_1, and P_3 communicate using a monitor M. Now consider the following sequence of events:

P_1 enters M.
P_1 is preempted by P_2.
P_2 is preempted by P_3.
P_3 tries to enter the monitor, and waits for the lock.
P_2 runs again, and can effectively prevent P_3 from running, contrary to the purpose of the priorities.

A simple way to avoid this situation is to associate with each monitor the priority of the highest-priority process which ever enters that monitor. Then whenever a process enters a monitor, its priority is temporarily increased to the monitor's priority. Modula solves the problem in an even simpler way – interrupts are disabled on entry to M, thus effectively giving the process the highest possible priority, as well as supplying the monitor lock for M. This approach fails if a page fault can occur while executing in M.

The mechanism is not free, and whether or not it is needed depends on the application. For instance, if only processes with adjacent priorities share a monitor, the problem described above cannot occur. Even if this is not the case, the problem may occur rarely, and absolute enforcement of the priority scheduling may not be important.

5   Implementation

The implementation of processes and monitors is split more or less equally among the Mesa compiler, the runtime package, and the underlying machine. The compiler recognizes the various syntactic constructs and generates appropriate code, including implicit calls on built-in (i.e., known to the compiler) support procedures. The runtime implements the less heavily used operations, such as process creation and destruction. The machine directly implements the more heavily used features, such as process scheduling and monitor entry/exit.

Note that it was primarily frequency of use, rather than cleanliness of abstraction, that motivated our division of labor between processor and software. Nonetheless, the split did turn out to be a fairly clean layering, in which the birth and death of processes are implemented on top of monitors and process scheduling.

5.1   The processor

The existence of a process is normally represented only by its stack of procedure activation records or *frames*, plus a small (10-byte) description called a *ProcessState*. Frames are allocated from a *frame heap* by a microcoded allocator. They come in a range of sizes which differ by 20% to 30%; there is a separate free list for each size up to a few hundred bytes (about 15 sizes). Allocating and freeing frames are thus very fast, except when more frames of a given size are needed. Because all frames come from the heap, there is no need to preplan the stack space needed by a process. When a frame of a given size is needed but not available, there is a *frame fault*, and the fault handler allocates more frames in virtual memory. Resident procedures have a private frame heap which is replenished by seizing real memory from the virtual memory manager.

The *ProcessStates* are kept in a fixed table known to the processor; the size of this table determines the maximum number of processes. At any given time, a *ProcessState* is on exactly one *queue*. There are four kinds of queue:

- *Ready queue*   There is one ready queue, containing all processes which are ready to run.
- *Monitor lock queue*   When a process attempts to enter a locked monitor, it is moved from the ready queue to a queue associated with the monitor lock.
- *Condition variable queue*   When a process executes a WAIT, it is moved from the ready queue to a queue associated with the condition variable.
- *Fault queue*   A fault can make a process temporarily unable to run; such a process is moved from the ready queue to a fault queue, and a fault-handling process is notified.

Queues are kept sorted by process priority. The implementation of queues is a simple one-way circular list, with the queue-cell pointing to the *tail* of the queue (see Figure 1). This compact structure allows rapid access to both the head and the tail of the queue. Insertion at the tail and removal at the head are quick and easy; more general insertion and deletion involve scanning some fraction of the queue. The queues are usually short enough that this is not a problem. Only the ready queue grows to a substantial size during normal operation, and its patterns of insertions and deletions are such that queue scanning overhead is small.

The queue cell of the ready queue is kept in a fixed location known to the processor, whose fundamental task is to always execute the next instruction of the highest priority ready process. To this end, a check is made before each instruction, and a process switch is done if necessary. In particular, this is the mechanism by which interrupts are serviced. The machine thus implements a simple priority scheduler, which is preemptive between priorities and FIFO within a given priority.

Queues other than the ready list are passed to the processor by software as operands of instructions, or through a trap vector in the case of fault queues. The queue cells are passed by reference, since in general they must be updated (i.e., the identity of the tail may change.) Monitor

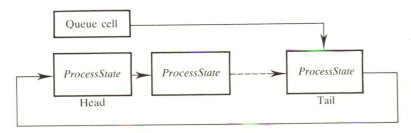

Figure 1   A process queue.

locks and condition variables are implemented as small records containing their associated queue cells plus a small amount of extra information: in a monitor lock, the actual lock; in a condition variable, the timeout interval and the wakeup-waiting switch.

At a fixed interval (~20 times per second) the processor scans the table of *ProcessStates* and notifies any waiting processes whose timeout intervals have expired. This special NOTIFY is tricky because the processor does not know the location of the condition variables on which such processes are waiting, and hence cannot update the queue cells. This problem is solved by leaving the queue cells out of date, but marking the processes in such a way that the next normal usage of the queue cells will notice the situation and update them appropriately.

There is no provision for time-slicing in the current implementation, but it could easily be added, since it has no effect on the semantics of processes.

5.2   The runtime support package

The *Process* module of the Mesa runtime package does creation and deletion of processes. This module is written (in Mesa) as a monitor, thus utilizing the underlying synchronization machinery of the processor to coordinate the implementation of FORK and JOIN as the built-in entry procedures *Process.Fork* and *Process.Join*, respectively. The unused *ProcessStates* are treated as essentially normal processes which are all waiting on a condition variable called *rebirth*. A call of *Process.Fork* performs appropriate 'brain surgery' on the first process in the queue and then notifies *rebirth* to bring the process to life; *Process.Join* synchronizes with the dying process and retrieves the results. The (implicitly invoked) procedure *Process.End* synchronizes the dying process with the joining process and then commits suicide by waiting on *rebirth*. An explicit cell on *Process.Detach* marks the process so that when it later calls *Process.End*, it will simply destroy itself immediately.

The operations *Process.Abort* and *Process.Yield* are provided to allow special handling of processes which wait too long and compute too long, respectively. Both adjust the states of the appropriate queues, using the machine's standard queueing mechanisms. Utility routines are also provided by the runtime for such operations as setting a condition variable timeout and setting a process priority.

5.3   The compiler

The compiler recognizes the syntactic constructs for processes and monitors and emits the appropriate code (e.g., a MONITORENTRY instruction at the start of each entry procedure, an implicit call of *Process.Fork* for each FORK). The compiler also performs special static checks to help avoid certain frequently encountered errors. For example, use of WAIT in an external procedure is flagged as an error, as is a direct call from an external procedure to an internal one. Because of the power of the underlying Mesa control structure primitives, and the care with which concurrency was integrated into the language, the introduction of processes and monitors into Mesa resulted in remarkably little upheaval inside the compiler.

5.4 Performance

Mesa's concurrent programming facilities allow the intrinsic parallelism of application programs to be represented naturally; the hope is that well-structured programs with high global efficiency will result. At the same time, these facilities have nontrivial local costs in storage and/or execution time when compared with similar sequential constructs; it is important to minimize these costs, so that the facilities can be applied to a finer 'grain' of concurrency. This section summarizes the costs of processes and monitors relative to other basic Mesa constructs, such as simple statements, procedures, and modules. Of course, the relative efficiency of an arbitrary concurrent program and an equivalent sequential one cannot be determined from these numbers alone; the intent is simply to provide an indication of the relative costs of various local constructs.

Storage costs fall naturally into data and program storage (both of which reside in swappable virtual memory unless otherwise indicated). The minimum cost for the existence of a Mesa module is 8 bytes of data and 2 bytes of code. Changing the module to a monitor adds 2 bytes of data and 2 bytes of code. The prime component of a module is a set of procedures, each of which requires a minimum of an 8-byte activation record and 2 bytes of code. Changing a normal procedure to a monitor entry procedure leaves the size of the activation record unchanged, and adds 8 bytes of code. All of these costs are small compared with the program and data storage actually needed by typical modules and procedures. The other cost specific to monitors is space for condition variables; each condition variable occupies 4 bytes of data storage, while WAIT and NOTIFY require 12 bytes and 3 bytes of code, respectively.

The data storage overhead for a process is 10 bytes of resident storage for its *Process.State*, plus the swappable storage for its stack of procedure activation records. The process itself contains no extra code, but the code for the FORK and JOIN which create and delete it together occupy 13 bytes, as compared with 3 bytes for a normal procedure call and return. The FORK/JOIN sequence also uses 2 data bytes to store the process value. In summary:

Construct	Space (bytes) data	code
module	8	2
procedure	8	2
call + return	–	3
monitor	10	4
entry procedure	8	10
FORK + JOIN	2	13
process	10	0
condition variable	4	–
WAIT	–	12
NOTIFY	–	3

For measuring execution times we define a unit called a *tick*: The time required to execute a simple instruction (e.g., on a 'one-MIP' machine, one tick would be one microsecond). A tick is arbitrarily set at one-fourth of the time needed to execute the simple statement '$a \leftarrow b + c$' (i.e., two loads, an add, and a store). One interesting number against which to compare the concurrency facilities is the cost of a normal procedure call (and its associated return), which takes 30 ticks if there are no arguments or results.

The cost of calling and returning from a monitor entry procedure is 50 ticks, about 70% more than an ordinary call and return. In practice, the percentage increase is somewhat lower, since typical procedures pass arguments and return results, at a cost of 2–4 ticks per item. A process switch takes 60 ticks; this includes the queue manipulations and all the state saving and restoring. The speed of WAIT and NOTIFY depends somewhat on the number and priorities of the processes involved, but representative figures are 15 ticks for a WAIT and 6 ticks for a NOTIFY. Finally, the minimum cost of a FORK/JOIN pair is 1100 ticks, or about 38 times that of a procedure call. To summarize:

Construct	Time (ticks)
simple instruction	1
call + return	30
monitor call + return	50
process switch	60
WAIT	15
NOTIFY, no one waiting	4
NOTIFY, process waiting	9
FORK + JOIN	1100

On the basis of these performance figures, we feel that our implementation has met our efficiency goals, with the possible exception of FORK and JOIN. The decision to implement these two language constructs in software rather than in the underlying machine is the main reason for their somewhat lackluster performance. Nevertheless, we still regard this decision as a sound one, since these two facilities are considerably more complex than the basic synchronization mechanism, and are used much less frequently (especially JOIN, since the detached processes discussed in Section 2 have turned out to be quite popular).

6   Applications

In this section we describe the way in which processes and monitors are used by three substantial Mesa programs: an operating system, a calendar system using replicated databases, and an internetwork gateway.

6.1   Pilot: A general-purpose operating system

Pilot is a Mesa-based operating system [18] which runs on a large personal computer. It was designed jointly with the new language features, and makes heavy use of them. Pilot has several autonomous processes of its own, and can be called by any number of client processes of any priority, in a fully asynchronous manner. Exploiting this potential concurrency requires extensive use of monitors within Pilot; the roughly 75 program modules contain nearly 40 separate monitors.

The Pilot implementation includes about 15 dedicated processes (the exact number depends on the hardware configuration); most of these are event handlers for three classes of events:

- *I/O interrupts*   Naked notifies as discussed in Section 4.2.

- *Process faults*   Page faults and other such events, signaled via fault queues as discussed in Section 5.1. Both client code and the higher levels of Pilot, including some of the dedicated processes, can cause such faults.

- *Internal exceptions*   Missing entries in resident databases, for example, cause an appropriate high level 'helper' process to wake up and retrieve the needed data from secondary storage.

There are also a few 'daemon' processes, which awaken periodically and perform housekeeping chores (e.g., swap out unreferenced pages). Essentially all of Pilot's internal processes and monitors are created at system initialization time (in particular, a suitable complement of interrupt-handler processes is created to match the actual hardware configuration, which is determined by interrogating the hardware). The running system makes no use of dynamic process and monitor creation, largely because much of Pilot is involved in implementing facilities such as virtual memory which are themselves used by the dynamic creation software.

The internal structure of Pilot is fairly complicated, but careful placement of monitors and dedicated processes succeeded in limiting the number of bugs which caused deadlock; over the life of the system, somewhere between one and two dozen distinct deadlocks have been discovered, all of which have been fixed relatively easily without any global disruption of the system's structure.

At least two areas have caused annoying problems in the development of Pilot:

(1) *The lack of mutual exclusion in the handling of interrupts*   As in more conventional interrupt systems, subtle bugs have occurred due to timing races between I/O devices and their handlers. To some extent, the illusion of mutual exclusion provided by the casting of interrupt code as a monitor may have contributed to this, although we feel that the resultant economy of mechanism still justifies this choice.

(2) *The interaction of the concurrency and exception facilities*   Aside from the general problems of exception handling in a concurrent environment, we have experienced some difficulties due to the specific interactions of Mesa signals with processes and monitors (see Sections 3.1 and 3.4). In particular, the reasonable and consistent handling of signals (including UNWINDS) in entry procedures represents a considerable increase in the mental over-head involved in designing a new monitor or understanding an existing one.

6.2   Violet: A distributed calendar system

The Violet system [6, 7] is a distributed database manager which supports replicated data files, and provides a display interface to a distributed calendar system. It is constructed according to the hierarchy of abstraction in Figure 2. Each level builds on the next lower one by calling procedures supplied by it. In addition, two of the levels explicitly deal with more than one process. Of course, as any level with multiple processes calls lower levels, it is possible for multiple processes to be executing procedures in those levels as well.

The user interface level has three processes: *Display*, *Keyboard*, and *DataChanges*. The *Display* process is responsible for keeping the display of the database consistent with the views specified by the user and with changes occurring in the database itself. It is notified by the other processes when changes occur, and calls on lower levels to read

Level

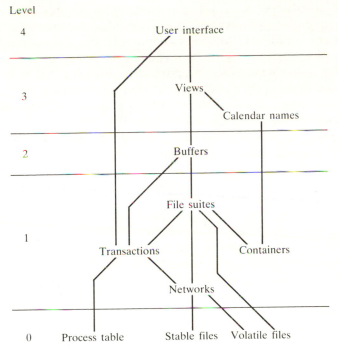

Figure 2   The internal structure of Violet.

information for updating the display. *Display* never calls update operations in any lower level. The other two processes respond to changes
initiated either by the user (*Keyboard*) or by the database (*DataChanges*).
The latter process is FORKED from the *Transactions* module when data
being looked at by Violet changes, and disappears when it has reported
the changes to *Display*.

A more complex constellation of processes exists in *FileSuites*,
which constructs a single *replicated file* from a set of *representative* files,
each containing data from some version of the replicated file. The
representatives are stored in a transactional file system [11], so that each
one is updated atomically, and each carries a version number. For each
FileSuite being accessed, there is a monitor which keeps track of the
known representatives and their version numbers. The replicated file is
considered to be updated when all the representatives in a *write quorum*
have been updated; the latest version can be found by examining a *read
quorum*. Provided the sum of the read quorum and the write quorum is as
large as the total set of representatives, the replicated file behaves like a
conventional file.

When the *FileSuite* is created, it FORKS and detaches an *inquiry*
process for each representative. This process tries to read the representative's version number, and if successful, reports the number to the

monitor associated with the file suite and notifies the condition *CrowdLarger*. Any process trying to read from the suite must collect a read quorum. If there are not enough representatives present yet, it waits on *CrowdLarger*. The inquiry processes expire after their work is done.

When the client wants to update the *FileSuite*, he must collect a write quorum of representatives containing the current version, again waiting on *CrowdLarger* if one is not yet present. He then FORKS an *update* process for each representative in the quorum, and each tries to write its file. After FORKING the update processes, the client JOINS each one in turn, and hence does not proceed until all have completed. Because all processes run within the same transaction, the underlying transactional file system guarantees that either all the representatives in the quorum will be written, or none of them.

It is possible that a write quorum is not currently accessible, but a read quorum is. In this case the writing client FORKS a *copy* process for each representative which is accessible but is not up to date. This process copies the current file suite contents (obtained from the read quorum) into the representative, which is now eligible to join the write quorum.

Thus as many as three processes may be created for each representative in each replicated file. In the normal situation when the state of enough representatives is known, however, all these processes have done their work and vanished; only one monitor call is required to collect a quorum. This potentially complex structure is held together by a single monitor containing an array of representative states and a single condition variable.

6.3   Gateway: An internetwork forwarder

Another substantial application program which has been implemented in Mesa using the process and monitor facilities in an internetwork gateway for packet networks [2]. The gateway is attached to two or more networks and serves as the connection point between them, passing packets across network boundaries as required. To perform this task efficiently requires rather heavy use of concurrency.

At the lowest level, the gateway contains a set of device drivers, one per device, typically consisting of a high priority interrupt process, and a monitor for synchronizing with the device and with noninterrupt level software. Aside from the drivers for standard devices (disk, keyboard, etc.) a gateway contains two or more drivers for Ethernet local broadcast networks [16] and/or common-carrier lines. Each Ethernet driver has two processes, an interrupt process, and a background process for autonomous handling of timeouts and other infrequent events. The driver for common-carrier lines in similar, but has a third process which makes a collection of lines resemble a single Ethernet by iteratively simulating a broadcast. The other network drivers have much the same structure; all drivers provide the same standard network interface to higher level software.

The next level of software provides packet routing and dispatching functions. The *dispatcher* consists of a monitor and a dedicated process. The monitor synchronizes interactions between the drivers and the dispatcher process. The dispatcher process is normally waiting for the completion of a packet transfer (input or output); when one occurs, the interrupt process handles the interrupt, notifies the dispatcher, and immediately returns to await the next interrupt. For example, on input the interrupt process notifies the dispatcher, which dispatches the newly arrived packet to the appropriate *socket* for further processing by invoking a procedure associated with the socket.

The *router* contains a monitor which keeps a *routing* table mapping network names to addresses of other gateway machines. This defines the next 'hop' in the path to each accessible remote network. The router also contains a dedicated housekeeping process which maintains the table by exchanging special packets with other gateways. A packet is transmitted rather differently than it is received. The process wishing to transmit to a remote socket calls into the router monitor to consult the routing table, and then the same process calls directly into the appropriate network driver monitor to initiate the output operation. Such asymmetry between input and output is particularly characteristic of packet communication, but is also typical of much other I/O software.

The primary operation of the gateway is now easy to describe: When the arrival of a packet has been processed up through the level of the dispatcher, and it is discovered that the packet is addressed to a remote socket, the dispatcher forwards it by doing a normal transmission; i.e., consulting the routing table and calling back down to the driver to initiate output. Thus, although the gateway contains a substantial number of asynchronous processes, the most critical path (forwarding a message) involves only a single switch between a pair of processes.

Conclusion

The integration of processes and monitors into the Mesa language was a somewhat more substantial task than one might have anticipated, given the flexibility of Mesa's control structures and the amount of published work on monitors. This was largely due to the fact that Mesa is designed for the construction of large, serious programs, and that processes and monitors had to be refined sufficiently to fit into this context. The task has been accomplished, however, yielding a set of language features of sufficient power that they serve as the only software concurrency mechanism on our personal computer, handling situations ranging from input/output interrupts to cooperative resource sharing among unrelated application programs.

References

[1]   *American National Standard Programming Language PL/I.* X3.53, American Nat. Standards Inst., New York, 1976.

[2]   Boggs, D. R., *et al.* Pup: An internetwork architecture. *IEEE Trans. on Communications* **28**, 4 (April 1980).

[3]   Brinch Hansen, P. *Operating System Principles.* Prentice-Hall, Englewood Cliffs, New Jersey, July 1973.

[4]   Brinch Hansen, P. The programming language Concurrent Pascal. *IEEE Trans. on Software Eng.* **1**, 2 (June 1975), 199–207.

[5]   Dijkstra, E. W. Hierarchical ordering of sequential processes. In *Operating Systems Techniques,* Academic Press, New York, 1972.

[6]   Gifford, D. K. Weighted voting for replicated data. *Operating Systs. Rev.* **13**, 5 (Dec. 1979), 150–162.

[7]   Gifford, D. K. Violet, an experimental decentralized system. Integrated Office Syst. Workshop, IRIA, Rocquencourt, France, Nov. 1979 (also available as CSL Rep. 79–12, Xerox Res. Ctr., Palo Alto. Calif.).

[8]   Hoare, C. A. R. Monitors: An operating system structuring concept. *Comm. ACM* **17**, 10 (Oct. 1974), 549–557.

[9]   Hoare, C. A. R. Communicating sequential processes. *Comm. ACM* **21**, 8 (Aug. 1978), 666–677.

[10] Howard, J. H. Signaling in monitors. Second Int. Conf. on Software Eng., San Francisco, Calif., Oct. 1976, pp. 47–52.

[11] Israel, J. E., Mitchell, J. G., and Sturgis, H. E. Separating data from function in a distributed file system. Second Int. Symp. on Operating Systs., IRIA, Rocquencourt, France, Oct. 1978.

[12] Keedy, J. J. On structuring operating systems with monitors. *Australian Comptr. J.* **10**, 1 (Feb. 1978), 23–27 (reprinted in *Operating Systs. Rev.* **13**, 1 (Jan. 1979), 5–9).

[13] Lampson, B. W., Mitchell, J. G., and Satterthwaite, E. H. On the transfer of control between contexts. In *Lecture Notes in Computer Science* **19**, Springer-Verlag, New York, 1974, pp. 181–203.

[14] Lauer, H. E., and Needham, R. M. On the duality of operating system structures. Second Int. Symp. on Operating Systems, IRIA, Rocquencourt, France, Oct. 1978 (reprinted in *Operating Systs. Rev.* **13**, 2 (April 1979), 3–19).

[15] Lister, A. M., and Maynard, K. J. An implementation of monitors. *Software – Practice and Experience* **6**, 3 (July 1976), 377–386.

[16] Metcalfe, R. M., and Boggs, D. G. Ethernet: Packet switching for local computer networks. *Comm. ACM* **19**, 7 (July 1976), 395–403.

[17] Mitchell, J. G., Maybury, W., and Sweet, R. Mesa Language Manual. Xerox Res. Ctr., Palo Alto, Calif., 1979.

[18] Redell D., *et al.* Pilot: An operating system for a personal computer. *Comm. ACM* **23**, 2 (Feb. 1980).

[19] Saltzer, J. H. Traffic control in a multiplexed computer system. Th., MAC-TR-30, MIT, Cambridge, Mass., July 1966.

[20] Saxena, A. R., and Bredt, T. H. A structured specification of a hierarchical operating system. SIGPLAN Notices **10**, 6 (June 1975), 310–318.

[21] Wirth, N. Modula: A language for modular multiprogramming. *Software – Practice and Experience* **7**, 1 (Jan. 1977), 3–36.

18

A Comparative Survey of Concurrent Programming Languages

P. David Stotts
University of Virginia

1 Introduction

In the past decade, development of a body of theory for parallel computation has fostered research into the design of programming languages intended to facilitate expression of concurrent computations. Referred to in this report as concurrent languages, or parallel languages, their number is not nearly as great as that of strictly sequential languages. Many, however, are available for academic study and general use, and their number is increasing yearly.

A graduate seminar at the University of Virginia on the design of parallel programming languages includes a survey of some of the currently used languages. Design features of each are compared, and the applicability of each language to various programming tasks is examined. A summary of the survey from a recent seminar is presented in this report.

2 Concurrent language design issues

In the design process of any language, many issues must be resolved, issues that ultimately determine the nature of the language. In addition, the design of a parallel language requires consideration of several issues unique to concurrent computations. The following sections detail the most important of these design issues. As the discussions illustrate, many of the topics are interrelated. Some of the issues are presented briefly in [1].

2.1 Language orientation

Though some sequential languages are termed general-purpose, they rarely prove to be equally applicable to all classes of problems. This lack of generality is compounded in the design of parallel languages. For any particular design, the various types of concurrency and supporting machine architectures that are available for consideration make some issues important and others irrelevant. The number and power of available processing elements affects the granularity of the concurrency that may be achieved by programs in a parallel language, and so affects the design of language features to express concurrency. Often the language designer tries to present a model of computation that closely represents the underlying machine architecture. Two commonly used models are synchronous and asynchronous. In the synchronous model, explicit synchronization primitives are usually absent from the language, as the hardware provides the necessary facilities to maintain lock-step operation of the processing elements. Machines designed for this model, often called SIMD (single instruction stream, multiple data stream) architectures, include most array machines (ILLIAC IV, MPP, DAP). A parallel language based on an asynchronous computation model requires that the designer provide facilities allowing programmers to properly sequence concurrent computations. Architectures supporting this model require more complex control software; they include multiprocessors, uniprocessors, homogeneous and heterogeneous computer networks.

In addition to the model of computation presented, parallel languages can be classified by the nature of the concurrency they provide. The most unrestricted (and so easiest to implement) concurrent activity is access of processes to a shared store. The memory hardware of the machine provides mutual exclusion on single bytes or words. The fine grain, while permitting maximum parallelism, is difficult to fully exploit for several reasons. First, effective human reasoning is difficult for such small execution units as assignment statements and operand references; there are too many possible access sequences in any but the most trivial programs for a programmer to be certain that his code functions correctly in a concurrent (and possibly nondeterminate) environment. Secondly, to overcome this limitation, software aids like monitors are often designed. Such packages enhance reasoning about correctness, but they limit the inherent parallelism by forcing sequential behavior on large blocks of code.

Another approach to concurrency is message passing: processes share nothing in such a scheme, but rather pass all data among themselves and store it locally in their private stores. Problems of concurrent memory accesses are traded off for ones of contention for communication channels and bandwidth. A third type of concurrency, that of the dataflow, or actor, languages, is a fine grained version of message passing.

Computations proceed as soon as all required operands are available to the operator, or actor; no explicit synchronization of activity is usually given to the programmer, as the availability of data solely determines the order of expression evaluation. Dataflow languages tend to be functional in nature and as such are free from side effects in evaluation, providing a high degree of inherent concurrency.

A parallel language designed with no particular architecture or class of machines in mind is a rarity. In describing the effects of architecture on design, one researcher makes this observation [2]:

- a *concurrent program* requires multiple (conceptual) processes for its implementation;
- a *distributed program* requires multiple hardware processing elements for its implementation.

Note that a distributed program is also a concurrent one. The distinction lies in the underlying machine architecture. Some designers try to keep this distinction transparent to the programmer; others allow it to be reflected in the language design in hopes that a programmer can use the information to optimize program performance.

The class of problems to which a language is intended to be applied also affects the syntactic and semantic features of a design. Writers of operating systems software are best served by a language that effectively models splitting of systems into macroscopic processes that may be executed concurrently, one in which the elements of concurrency are not too small to be useful reasoning and organization tools. Such languages are usually intended for implementation on machines with one or more general-purpose processing units. On the other hand, many matrix analysis problems can benefit from architectures that have vast numbers of less powerful, less general-purpose processing elements: the computation model presented by a parallel language for such problems must have small elements of concurrency, perhaps even on the level of arithmetic operations (as in dataflow computation). Finally, languages that are intended as stand-alone systems for dedicated programming work stations must operate without the normal support provided by an operating system; as such, the language must provide some facilities for both concurrent processes and device interfacing.

2.2 Synchronization and communication mechanisms

Concurrent processes require a method of conveying data to one another, that is to communicate; they also need at times to interact in such a way as to force a particular sequence on their executions, that is to synchronize. The mechanisms designed into a language to accomplish these closely interrelated activities depend heavily on the target architecture. Communication by global variables may be more efficient on a machine with shared memory than on one without it. Languages for SIMD machines may not need explicit process synchronization, since parallelism comes from replication of data; communication facilities, though, would be required to ship this data through the machine.

To meet these goals, many different primitive operations are presented in current parallel languages. For synchronization, some use valueless variables (signals, conditions) which are explicitly sent and awaited: others rely on the synchronization that is implicit in the semantics of coroutine calls and process invocations. In contrast to implicit techniques, a language may offer explicit expression of synchronization in specifications separate from executable code; the most notable example is the *path expression* as realized in Path Pascal [3, 4]. Compilers for such languages automatically surround processes with lower level synchronization primitives like **P** and **V** on semaphores to ensure that the proper number and sequence of code instances is maintained.

Communication methods are equally as varied. Shared variables are prevalent, especially in older languages. Often these variables are protected by a monitor or other construction designed to provide mutual exclusion on its data. Processes communicate indirectly by calling monitor procedures that safely update the shared variables on behalf of the caller. Direct process communication by message passing appears to be the choice of newer designs; the basic technique has several variations. Some languages have processes send data that is copied into the recipient's private store. Others pass the communication privileges themselves as data; a process with a certain privilege may communicate with others possessing compatible privileges. Ports (channels) provide another message passing variant; a process may be passed the ability to read, write, or read/write a port, establishing a communication network that is dynamic (see Section 2.5).

2.3   Program modularity

The ability to aid the programmer in abstracting the functional features of a program away from the implementation of the algorithm is a necessity for a parallel language. Sequential languages provide the procedure/subroutine concept for this purpose, but the added complexity of concurrent and possibly time-dependent reasoning requires more extensive facilities to support program modularity and abstraction. Several concurrent languages have some concept of a module, that is a protective fence around a collection of processes, procedures, and data. The module may alter the normal scope of identifiers, thereby restricting access to the contents in some well-defined way. It may also provide mutual exclusion on shared data, creating a rudimentary form of data abstraction that may be exploited by the programmer. Modules also provide an attractive means of isolating the hardware dependent sections of code in programs that deal directly with input/output devices and process control equipment.

A feature of newer parallel languages that further encourages construction of modular programs is separate (but not independent) compilation of program subunits, with full type checking maintained across unit boundaries. Subunits are composed of an interface specification section (*package* in Ada [5], *definition module* in Modula-2 [6]) and a corresponding code section (*package body* in Ada, *implementation module* in Modula-2). The information in the specification sections is kept in a data base to be used during compilation of other specifications (in proper order – the information must be provided before it is needed). Compilation of corresponding code sections may then be done at any time, in any order. Such facilities greatly enhance the ability of a language to support development of a large software project by many programmers.

Algorithms that exploit concurrency effectively are difficult to design and program, partly because dividing the target problem into subtasks that may safely be computed in parallel, and correctly synchronizing the chosen subtasks, is not a straightforward procedure; this is termed the partitioning problem. A rich collection of features for code modularity and abstraction in a language has the bonus effect of aiding the programmer in solving this problem in program design.

2.4 Process creation

Another degree of freedom for the parallel language designer is the manner in which concurrent processes are created. A program's set of parallel processes can be a static one, in which the number, type, and identification of each process is known and fixed at compile time. Alternatively, concurrent processes can be dynamically created. Statically created processes are easier to reason about; dynamically created processes prohibit determination of their number and space requirements prior to run-time. They also may preclude static flow analysis, hindering one form of program verification – demonstration of the absence of process deadlock and starvation (which is not an easy job even with a static set of processes).

Dynamic process creation has two forms. A process can be defined in a program, then instantiated one or more times during execution. In this form, each instance of the process has a shared code space and a separate data space, but they all have the same process name. The second form of dynamic process creation occurs in languages in which processes can be types and process-valued variables can be created at run time. Parallel processes of the same type again share code and have separate data spaces, but the names are different and, in the dynamic case, either are not known or are not bindable until program execution.

Finally, static/dynamic process creation should be distinguished from the related topic of static/dynamic process topology. In the latter, the issue is whether existing concurrent processes have time-varying interconnections, whereas with the former the question concerns the initial existence of these processes.

2.5   Process network topology specification

The communication and synchronization interconnections among parallel processes in a concurrent program is called a process network topology. Within any one language, topologies differ from program to program, and are highly dependent on the class of problem under solution. An array manipulation program may use a matrix-like process network topology, with connections from each process to four, six, even eight or more other processes that become its neighbors in computation. In contrast, a program to solve a resource sharing problem (epitomized by the dining philosophers problem) may perform best with a ring topology, in which a process is linked only to one or two others.

The issue facing the language designer is then one of providing a means of specifying a particular topology that the programmer has decided is best for solving his problem. In most current parallel languages, the process network topology is established implicitly, buried in the communication primitives or module constructs of each program. At least one language designer has experimented with explicit topology definition [7], in which the process network structure is indicated in a special section of the program. Whether explicitly or implicitly defined, however, the languages in this report share a common feature in their approach to process network topology: all have internal specifications. Interprocess links, if they exist, are a part of the program source code. An alternative technique that is being researched [8] is the definition of process topologies separate from the process definitions, that is as an activity external to program construction. A programmer using this method could write the concurrent processes needed to solve a problem, then, without altering the code, study the performance of various process interconnection schemes.

Another question deserving consideration is whether the topology, regardless of how it is specified, is static or dynamic. A dynamic topology has process connections that change during program execution; a static topology, once established, does not. Note that dynamic process creation does not entail a dynamic topology. New processes can be created at run time, but if their potential interconnections are fixed at compile time then the topology is static. Conversely, in a language like Gypsy [9] in which communication capabilities may be passed around as parameters to processes, a static set of processes can exhibit a dynamic topology. Dynamic topologies can also arise in languages that have process- or monitor-valued variables, since the exact entity represented by such a variable name at any point during execution cannot necessarily be determined statically.

2.6 Process scheduling strategy

The scheduling of concurrent processes for execution is a topic dependent on the architectural model underlying the parallel language. A machine with enough hardware for each process to have a dedicated processor requires little scheduling logic. However, many machines have far fewer processors than programs have processes; indeed, as is discussed above, many languages either do not or cannot limit the number of processes a program can have. A scheduling strategy must then be created that will insure fair execution sequences for parallel processes. Good schedules will not starve any process, that is no process awaiting a processor will be forever denied execution. Similarly, a good scheduler also will try to avoid creating execution sequences that cause the network of processes in a program to deadlock on some shared resource; complete avoidance, though, often is more expensive than deadlock detection and correction. One final consideration in process scheduling is whether all process executions are scheduled autonomously by the language implementation, or whether the programmer may have some explicit control over the execution sequence. Real-time programs often require this kind of scheduler override facility (see Section 2.12).

2.7 Processor binding strategy

One of the major difficulties in automatic management of concurrent processes is called the assignment problem. It involves the determination of the optimal binding of processes to physical processors for execution. Concurrent processes can be assigned to processors at compile time, but such a strategy may create bottlenecks by grouping several slow processes on one processor. Effective determination of optimal groupings without programmer aid (i.e., source code hints) is very nearly impossible, since information about the relative execution speeds of processes is required. An alternative strategy is to wait until run time to assign a process to a processor, giving it to any that is free when the process is ready to execute. This strategy can eliminate poor grouping, but it is infeasible on many architectures, since even in languages with static topologies, the physical communication paths change and must be managed. Processor binding is more generally considered an implementation problem, but it is nonetheless one that the language designer cannot ignore.

2.8 Process termination

Important to the issues of verification and fair scheduling is the manner in which processes terminate. A parallel process can be said to terminate when all of its code has been executed; this most often occurs in languages that have synchronization primitives requiring acknowledgment of receipt of a signal, or completion of the requested process (i.e., coroutines). In such languages, a process that is invoked from another process is executed as a slave, and terminates before the calling process continues to execute. However, languages in which processes may invoke ancillary processes but do not wait for their termination usually have a different definition of process termination. To avoid ill-formed parallel process graphs, a parent process is not said to terminate until all of its children (processes that it invoked) have terminated. The resulting tree structure of process births and deaths considerably simplifies correctness proofs of parallel programs in languages supporting this hierarchy.

2.9 Nondeterminate execution

A nondeterminate computation is one which, for two runs on one set of input data, can produce two distinct sets of output data. Nondeterminate constructs in a parallel language design afford programmers an extra measure of freedom by shifting onto the implementation some of the trivial decision making in 'don't care' situations. The extra freedom costs little in added complexity and verification difficulty, and it simplifies algorithm design by providing effective modeling of one of the major effects of concurrency directly in the language. Most current parallel languages include nondeterminate features in their designs. Some have explicit nondeterminate statements, the semantics of which express unpredictable execution sequences. Others exhibit nondeterminate behavior due to the action of some anonymous scheduler in allowing processes to execute.

2.10 Exception handling

Exception handling facilities allow the user to define some action (perhaps override implementation defined actions) to be taken on occurrence of run time errors or other unusual events. Exception handlers provide robustness by preventing common errors from locking up a system. Though not unique to parallel languages, such facilities are emerging as a feature of many well designed programming languages, especially ones intended for real-time applications.

2.11 Ease of verification

The increasing complexity and expanding range of application of computer software carry with them a greater cost of software system failure. Program proving is a difficult discipline, even for sequential languages.

Concurrent and distributed programs have an additional inherent complexity that requires parallel languages, if not to provide active aids, at least not to hinder program verification. Several researchers have developed parallel program proof techniques that involve demonstration of the correctness of the problem solving logic as well as proof that the network of concurrent processes is free of deadlock and starvation [10, 11, 12].

The complexity of program proofs can be controlled by the language designer's careful choice of communication and synchronization primitives, ones with well defined semantics and restricted use patterns. Owicki and Gries have extended the Hoare axiomatic technique to allow demonstration on non-interference among concurrent processes, using an illustrative language with specifically defined concurrency structures [13]. Wirth attacked the difficulties of time dependent reasoning by outlining a real-time programming discipline that enables execution time bounds to be determined for concurrent activities in a parallel program [14]. The semantics of the device and interface modules in Modula [15, 16, 17] are the basis for the technique. Assertions and process specifications are other features that can be designed into a language to aid in program verification. The designers of Gypsy employ this technique in conjunction with a theorem prover to verify code at compile time [11].

2.12   Real-time support

Many tasks that can be easily modeled with a parallel language come from the realm of real-time programming and process control. Such problems require that languages sufficient for programming their solutions have features for real-time support. Although a comprehensive list of support features would be difficult to compile (and defend), some common facilities can be identified from languages that have been used to write real-time software. Explicit programmer control over the order of process execution is essential. A related feature that provides a limited degree of scheduling control is a process priority scheme. By having a preemptable default scheduling policy a language helps to ensure critical timing constraints; processes requiring completion in critically small amounts of time get the hardware as soon as possible after they are scheduled. One language designer attempts to ensure critical timing by dedicating a processor to each executing process [18].

Another support feature that real-time programming requires is a concept of timeout in process communication. A process that sends a message and awaits a reply must assume a catastrophic occurrence and take appropriate action if the desired response is not received within a set amount of time. Necessarily implied is access to some (at least relative time) clock. Absence of timeout admits to a program (even a verified one) the possibility of process deadlock from an undetected hardware failure.

Timeout may be viewed as one of many exception handling facilities (see Section 2.10).

Real-time languages should also be able to communicate directly with hardware devices in the environment. Interrupts generated by peripherals can be confined to interact only with well-defined language constructs (such as the *device module* of Modula), thereby making the semantics of interrupts more clear.

2.13   Ease of use

Though the topic is subjective, a language's ease of use is nonetheless the area deserving perhaps the greatest consideration in design, for a language that is abysmally painful to use, whatever else it may have going for it, will not be used. Excessive syntax and duplicated capabilities afford a programmer too many alternatives in program structure. Uncommon or unavailable character sets require extra hardware that many installations will not purchase. Pairing of common syntax with uncommon semantics fosters programmer frustration. Designers who refuse to adequately examine human factors in their designs produce languages that are confusing, bulky, and less powerful than they could be.

3   Concurrent language summaries

Considering the wide spectrum of design features discussed in the previous section, the languages represented in this report are from a restricted domain. None are of the dataflow or functional types; in addition, all are procedural languages. All present a view of parallelism consisting of a loosely coupled collection of macroscopic processes that execute asynchronously and concurrently. For this reason, they are best suited for implementation on MIMD machines (or simulation by multiplexing on a uniprocessor). Languages that are specifically designed for SIMD architectures (e.g., IVTRAN for ILLIAC IV) are not represented in our study.

Thirteen concurrent languages were examined. No general discussion of each language is given here, though notes of interest on many are presented. Tables 3.1 and 3.2 summarize the results of the comparison. Language features considered generally follow the design issues discussed in the first half of the report:

- *Communication method*   The manner in which concurrent processes communicate data among themselves; the most commonly employed methods are message passing, unprotected shared (global) variables, shared data protected by modules or monitors, and the rendezvous [5].

- *Synchronization method*   The manner in which concurrent processes enforce sequencing restrictions among themselves; represented methods are signals, synchronized send [19], buffers, path expressions [3], events, conditions, queues, guarded regions, rendezvous, and explicit coroutine transfer.

- *Unprotected shared variables*   The oldest form of data communication (and possibly process synchronization). Some languages exclude unprotected shared variables, considering them to be contrary to the goals of the language design.

- *Buffers/User defined length*   Message buffers (possibly infinite in length) exist in a language as a predefined data type. Buffers are created as program variables, perhaps with user specified lengths.

- *Process creation*   Concurrent processes are either all created statically at the beginning of program execution, or they are each instantiated dynamically at the time of call during execution. Static creation usually entails processes that do not go out of existence, whereas dynamically created processes usually vanish on termination.

- *Process topology*   A static process interconnection scheme is one in which communication links among processes either do not change during execution, or if processes are added (or deleted) dynamically, then the links added (or deleted) are predictable at compile-time. Dynamic topology indicates communication links that may change during execution in ways that cannot be known prior to run-time.

- *Code-valued variables*   Some languages allow a procedure or process to be a type, so that variables may be declared with code for their values, or pointers to executable units generated dynamically.

- *Nondeterminate execution/explicit expression*   This feature indicates the ability of a language to express possibly nondeterminate computations, meaning that a program run twice on the same input data may produce two distinct sets of output data. Some languages have special statements for expressing explicit nondeterminate computation. In others, the action of a process scheduler or queuing mechanism that the programmer cannot directly control is responsible.

- *Separate compilation*   The language provides the ability to compile a code module without having all the code for the rest of the program. Often some specifications for other modules are required to allow strong type checking across module boundaries, but the actual code to implement those modules' functions is not needed.

- *Real-time support*   As discussed in Section 2.12, a language can include features that make real-time programming easier and more reliable.

Table 3.1

Feature	Ada	CSP	Concur. Pascal	DP	Edison	Gypsy	Mesa
				Concurrent Language Characteristics			
communication	rendez	message	monitor	module	monitor	message	monitor
synchronization	rendez	sync.send	queue	guard.reg	condition	buffer	condition
shared vars	yes	no	no	no	yes	no	yes
buffers/user	no	no	no	no	no	yes/yes	no
process creation	dynamic	dynamic	static	static	dynamic	dynamic	dynamic
process topology	dynamic	static	dynamic	static	static	dynamic	dynamic
code-valued vars	yes	no	yes	no	no	no	yes
nondeterm/explicit	yes/yes	yes/yes	yes/no	yes/yes	yes/no	yes/no	yes/no
separate compile	yes	no	no	no	no	no	yes
real-time	yes	no	yes	yes	yes	no	yes
abstraction	+++	-	+	+	+	-	++
exceptions	yes	no	no	no	no	yes	yes
proof support	-	-	+	-	-	+++	-

Table 3.2

Concurrent Language Characteristics

Feature	Modula	McCalla-2	Parlance	Path Pascal	PLITS	PL/1
communication	monitor	module	message	monitor	message	globals
synchronization	signals	transfer	sync.send	path.exp	buffer	event
shared vars	yes	yes	no	yes	no	yes
buffers/user	no	no	no	no	yes/no	no
process creation	dynamic	dynamic	static	dynamic	dynamic	dynamic
process topology	static	dynamic	static	dynamic	dynamic	dynamic
code-valued vars	no	yes	no	yes	yes	yes
nondeterm/explicit	yes/no	yes/no	no	yes/no	yes/no	yes/no
separate compile	no	yes	yes	no	yes	yes
real-time	yes	yes	no	no	no	no
abstraction	+	++	+	+	+	–
exceptions	no	no	no	no	yes	yes
proof support	–	–	+	–	++	– –

- *Procedure/data abstraction* Facilities for achieving abstraction include monitors, modules, packages, process-valued variables, generic procedures, abstract data types, and separate module compilation with consistency checking. If a language has at least one such feature, easily used, it rates a '+'.

- *Exception handling* As discussed in Section 2.10, a language can have facilities for programmer-defined action on occurrence of exceptional conditions at run-time.

- *Proof support* A language may have as part of its definition features that help either the programmer or an automated verifier to determine the logical correctness of code. Such features may be explicit syntactic constructions, including formal process specifications and variable-value assertions. Less obvious are semantic support features like process or monitor calling conventions that restrict communicating instances to non-recursive, tree structured hierarchies.

3.1 Notes

(1) Distributed Processes (DP) [18] is oriented toward implementation on a network of microcomputers, for process control and other real-time applications. Each process is intended to be executed on its own dedicated hardware processor. Code-valued variables are not allowed, but process names may be subscripted, permitting an array of processes with a common declaration; the number of process elements in such an array must be able to be bounded at compile time.

(2) The queues used to ensure synchronization in Concurrent Pascal [20] may contain only one process at a time; as such, they are equivalent to conditions and events.

(3) Unlike many other languages, Communicating Sequential Processes (CSP) [19] requires both communicants in a message exchange to know the other's name. Synchronization by message passing is possible because the messages are unbuffered and force the earlier communicant to wait for its partner. This full naming convention also disallows easy construction of process libraries. In CSP, no code-valued variables are allowed, but process names may be subscripted if the maximum number can be determined by the compiler. Finally, the language is not entirely symmetric in that output commands (send message) may not appear in guards.

(4) Modula [15] and Modula-2 [6] are both oriented toward implementation on a uniprocessor. In addition, Modula-2 has no real processes actually in the language, only coroutines. The standard module library contains a module that implements concurrent

processes and scheduling as in Modula. Synchronization of co-routines is achieved by explicit transfer of control.

(5) Parlance [7] is an experimental language designed to investigate the feasibility of explicit process topology specification separate from the executable portions of a program. Unlike the other languages in this report, networks of concurrent processes in Parlance are constructed so that nondeterminate computations are impossible to program.

(6) The Programming Language in the Sky (PLITS) project [21] is a collection of concepts on using processes and message passing effectively, with no particular preferred syntax. An example system is presented in extended Pascal and another is mentioned using SAIL [22] as a base language.

(7) The predefined buffer types in Gypsy [9] represent the capability to communicate. Processes may declare buffers to other processes and pass them around as parameters, creating a topology that would be dynamic even if the set of processes were static (which it is not).

(8) In addition to the proof aids of procedure specifications and in-code assertions. Gypsy disallows aliasing via procedure and process parameters. The restriction is enforced with both compile-time and run-time checks.

(9) Many languages do not have processes as separate syntactic entities from procedures. Rather they provide calling conventions that de-tach for concurrency the execution of any of the declared procedure bodies. For example, Mesa [23, 24] uses the *fork* operation to create a process (a similar operation is provided so that procedures may be used as coroutines as well), and Edison [25, 26, 27] specifies that procedure calls inside of *cobegin/coend* brackets are concurrently executed.

(10) Even though objects (and so monitors) can be types in Path Pascal [4], assignment to variables of object type is forbidden. Pointers to objects, however, are not similarly restricted, hence the potentially dynamic process communication topology.

(11) Monitors are not actually part of the languages Edison and Path Pascal, but their implementation by *when* statement and *path expression* respectively is trivial, requiring no explicit semaphore variables.

References

[1] G. R. Andrews, 'Synchronizing Resources,' *ACM Transactions on Programming Languages and Systems*, **3**(4), pp. 405–431 (October 1981).

[2] B. Liskov, 'Primitives for Distributed Computing,' Computation Structures Group Memo 175, MIT Laboratory for Computer Science (May 1979).

[3] R. H. Campbell and A. N. Habermann, 'The Specification of Process Synchronization by Path Expressions,' pp. 89–102. In: *Lecture Notes in Computer Science*, ed. J. Hartmanis, Springer-Verlag (1974).

[4] R. H. Campbell and R. B. Kolstad, 'An Overview of Path Pascal's Design and Path Pascal User Manual,' *SIGPLAN Notices*, **15**(9), pp. 13–24 (September 1980).

[5] 'Reference Manual for the Ada Programming Language,' United States Department of Defense (November 1980).

[6] N. Wirth, 'Modula-2,' Technical Report 36, ETH, Institut für Informatik, Zurich (March 1980).

[7] P. F. Reynolds, Jr., 'Parallel Processing Structures: Languages, Schedules, and Performance Results,' Ph.D. Thesis, University of Texas, Austin (1979).

[8] P. F. Reynolds, Jr., private communication, May 1982.

[9] D. I. Good, R. M. Cohen, and L. W. Hunter, 'A Report on the Development of Gypsy,' Certifiable Minicomputer Project Report ICSCA-CMP-13, The Institute for Computing Science and Computer Applications, the University of Texas at Austin (October 1978).

[10] K. M. Chandy and J. Misra, 'Deadlock Absence Proofs for Networks of Communicating Processes,' *Information Processing Letters*, **9**(4), pp. 185–189 (November 1979).

[11] D. I. Good, R. M. Cohen, and J. Keeton-Williams, 'Principles of Proving Concurrent Programs in Gypsy,' Certifiable Minicomputer Project Report ICSCA-CMP-15, The Institute for Computing Science and Computer Applications, the University of Texas at Austin (January 1979).

[12] D. Gries, 'An Exercise in Proving Parallel Programs Correct,' *Communications of the ACM*, **20**(12), pp. 921–930 (December 1977).

[13] S. Owicki and D. Gries, 'Axiomatic Proof Techniques for Parallel Programs,' *Acta Informatica*, **6**, pp. 319–340 (June 1976).

[14] N. Wirth, 'Toward a Discipline of Real-Time Programming,' *Communications of the ACM*, **20**(8), pp. 577–583 (August 1977).

[15] N. Wirth, 'Modula: A Language for Modular Multiprogramming,' *Software – Practice and Experience*, **7**, pp. 3–35 (1979).

[16] N. Wirth, 'The Use of Modula,' *Software – Practice and Experience*, **7**, pp. 37–65 (1979).

[17] N. Wirth, 'Design and Implementation of Modula,' *Software – Practice and Experience*, **7**, pp. 67–84 (1979).

[18] P. Brinch Hansen, 'Distributed Processes: A Concurrent Programming Concept,' *Communications of the ACM*, **21**(11), pp. 934–940 (November 1978).

[19] C. A. R. Hoare, 'Communicating Sequential Processes,' *Communications of the ACM*, **21**(8), pp. 666–677 (August 1978).

[20] P. Brinch Hansen, 'The Programming Language Concurrent Pascal,' *IEEE Transactions on Software Engineering*, **1**(2), pp. 199–207 (June 1975).

[21] J. A. Feldman, 'High Level Programming for Distributed Computing,' *Communications of the ACM*, **22**(6), pp. 353–368 (June 1979).

[22] J. A. Feldman, J. R. Low, D. Swinehart, and R. Taylor, 'Recent Developments in SAIL, an Algol-based Language for Artificial Intelligence,' *Proceedings of the AFIPS 1972 FJCC*, pp. 1193–1202, AFIPS Press (1972).

[23] J. G. Mitchell, W. Maybury, and R. Sweet, 'Mesa Language Manual, version 5.0,' Xerox Palo Alto Research Center (April 1979).

[24] B. Lampson and D. Redell, 'Experience with Processes and Monitors in Mesa,' *Communications of the ACM*, **23**(2), pp. 105–117 (February 1980).

[25] P. Brinch Hansen, 'Edison – A Multiprocessor Language,' *Software – Practice and Experience*, **11**(4), pp. 325–361 (April 1981).

[26] P. Brinch Hansen, 'The Design of Edison,' *Software – Practice and Experience*, **11**(4), pp. 363–396 (April 1981).

[27] P. Brinch Hansen, 'Edison Programs,' *Software – Practice and Experience*, **11**(4), pp. 397–414 (April 1981).

19

Task Management in Ada – A Critical Evaluation for Real-Time Multiprocessors

Eric S. Roberts, Arthur Evans, Jr. and C. Robert Morgan
Bolt Beranek and Newman Inc

Edmund M. Clarke
Harvard University

As the cost of processor hardware declines, multiprocessor architectures become increasingly cost-effective and represent an important area for future research. In order to exploit the full potential of multiprocessors, however, it is necessary to understand how to design software which can make effective use of the available parallelism. This paper considers the impact of multiprocessor architecture on the design of high-level programming languages and, in particular, evaluates the language Ada in the light of the special requirements of real-time multiprocessor systems. We conclude that Ada does not, as currently designed, meet the needs for real-time embedded systems.

1   Introduction

The possibility of using multiprocessor architecture as the basis for a powerful computing system is an attractive one for several reasons. First, a multiprocessor system can achieve significantly increased computational speed by allowing parallelism in its task structure. Second, multiprocessor architecture offers the potential for achieving system reliability through the redundancy of its processing elements. Third, as the cost of processing components (particularly the LSI-based microprocessor) declines, the cost of adding processors to a system becomes less significant in relation to the overall system cost. In the light of these advantages, interest in multiprocessor architectures has grown significantly over the past decade, and it is clear that multiprocessors are likely to become increasingly cost-effective in years to come. It is also clear that the use of multiprocessor technology has an effect on software methodology which must be considered in the design of any programming language system intended for use in a real-time multiprocessor-based environment.

In this paper, we are particularly concerned with the impact of multiprocessors on the programming language Ada [1] which was developed by Cii Honeywell Bull for the U.S. Department of Defense and is intended to serve as a programming standard for *embedded computer applications* (i.e., command and control, communications, avionics, shipboard applications, etc.). As a consequence of its projected application domain, the language contains facilities for parallel and real-time programming in addition to the usual control and data structuring facilities of conventional languages such as Pascal. Moreover, since Ada is designed to be used in applications which are well-suited to multiprocessor systems, we believe that a study of Ada from the point of view of multiprocessor systems is a particularly relevant area of research.

Section 2 of this paper examines the nature of a typical multiprocessor system and briefly outlines various differences between applications which are well adapted to multiprocessors and those intended for more conventional uniprocessor architectures. Section 3 outlines the parallel control facility provided by Ada and provides a framework for a more detailed discussion of the implications of that design. Section 4 presents an evaluation of Ada's parallel processing facility giving special consideration to the unique requirements imposed by multiprocessor systems. To the extent that the primitives provided by Ada are judged to be inadequate for use in the environment of a practical multiprocessor, alternative structures and extended facilities which would relieve the major problems are discussed. These are presented as general conclusions in Section 5.

We recognize that the Ada language is still under development and that the language definition reported in Reference 1 must be viewed as a preliminary document. In fact, there are indications that changes are being incorporated into the Ada design which solve some of the problems addressed in this paper. We believe that it is important to bring some of the questions related to parallel control in Ada before a wider audience and that the results presented in this paper will be of use in evaluating the designs of tasking mechanisms in general, even if the specific critique of Ada becomes dated through changes in the language definition.

2 The nature of multiprocessor applications

As part of our evaluation of Ada as a language for multiprocessors, we feel that it is important to consider not only the characteristics of multiprocessors themselves but also the nature of the applications which are typically encountered in a multiprocessor environment. From our experience with existing multiprocessor systems, we believe that multi-processor applications tend to have much more stringent requirements for run-time efficiency than do most applications developed for uni-processor environment. This increased requirement for efficiency arises, in part, from the observation that it is considerably more difficult to design software for a multiprocessor system than for a more traditional uniprocessor. To a large extent this increase in difficulty is related to the fact that multiprocessors represent a relatively new form of system architecture. When compared to the experience which has been as-sembled for single processor systems and sequential algorithms, very little is known about the problems involved in multiprocessor design and parallel programming.

The fundamental implication of the increased difficulty in software development is quite simple: multiprocessor systems will rarely be used for practical applications unless the use of a multiprocessor is required by the constraints of the application. Multiprocessors have significant advantages over conventional uniprocessors in three distinct areas:

(1) Multiprocessors are capable of increased effective throughput be-cause they allow independent tasks within the application to operate in parallel.

(2) Multiprocessors can be designed to include software reliability structures which exploit the inherent redundancy in the hardware to dynamically alter the system configuration in response to hardware failures.

(3) Multiprocessors can be expanded gracefully as the requirements of the application change.

Of the three factors above, the need to provide efficiency through parallelism has, in our experience, proven to be the most important. Applications chosen for use with multiprocessors tend, therefore, to have:

(1) Strict requirements for run-time efficiency; and

(2) Highly parallel internal task structures which permit them to take advantage of the multiprocessor design.

The need to produce highly efficient code is well understood by those who have experience in designing real-time applications and is reflected in the technical requirements for a common high order language which directed the development of Ada. Section 1D of the Steelman requirements [2] specifies that language 'features should be chosen to have a simple and efficient representation in many object machines'. Moreover, Steelman recognizes that the tasking facility is particularly subject to such efficiency considerations in its requirement (Section 9B) that the 'parallel processing facility shall be designed to minimize execution time and space'.

We believe that concern for efficiency leads to the following general conclusions:

(1) The use of constructs which have no efficient representation must not be required by the language design.

(2) If two different constructs display a significant variation in their efficiency depending on the application environment, both should be supplied in order to provide maximum flexibility and allow the programmer to achieve the required level of efficiency.

(3) Low-level facilities must be provided to achieve higher levels of efficiency than are attainable with any general mechanism.

It is important to note that the impact on overall efficiency from the use of an inappropriate mechanism for parallel control can be extremely high when compared to the efficiency cost generally associated with programming in a high-level language. While the techniques available for optimizing serial code are highly developed and quite successful in practice, relatively little is known about the problem of optimizing the global task structure and the internal synchronization process. Based on our experience with multiprocessor systems, we believe that these problems are extremely hard and well beyond the current state of software technology. This fact increases the importance of allowing greater flexibility in the task structure than might be required in the non-parallel aspects of a language.

3 An overview of process control in Ada

In this section, we present a brief overview of the parallel processing facilities in the Ada programming language to provide a background for the evaluation of those features presented in Section 4. For the most part, we have not attempted to cover the structure of the language in its entirety and have chosen to concentrate on the tasking facility alone. In the light of the similarity between Ada and conventional programming languages such as Pascal, the reader should have no difficulty following the examples of this section in spite of the absence of a full description of the language. To increase the readability of the examples, we have attempted to write code so as to maximize readability and to use comments whenever the intent of the code might be unclear. In Ada, comments are introduced by '--' and extend to the end of the line.

3.1 The general structure of parallel tasks

Ada uses the term 'task' to refer to the basic syntactic unit for process definition. A *task* consists of two parts: a *specification part* which describes the external behaviour of the task, and a *task body* which describes its internal behaviour. The specification part consists of a header which gives the name of the task and a declarative part which describes those features of the task which are visible to the outside world. Included in the declarative part are the declarations of those constants, types, subprograms, exceptions, and entries which are associated with the task and must be externally visible.

An example of a task specification is shown below:

```
task BUFFER is
   PACKET_SIZE : constant INTEGER := 256;
   type PACKET is array (1..PACKET_SIZE) of CHARACTER;
   entry READ (V : out PACKET);
   entry WRITE (E : in PACKET);
end BUFFER;
```

Entries are used for communication between tasks and look externally like procedures.

The task body consists of a declarative part which describes local data structures and a sequence of statements which implement the **entry** declarations described in the specification part. For the BUFFER example the task body is:

```
task body BUFFER is
   BUFSIZE   : constant INTEGER := 10;
   BUF       : array (1..BUFSIZE) of PACKET;
   IN, OUT   : INTEGER range 1..BUFSIZE := 1;
   COUNT     : INTEGER range 1..BUFSIZE := 0;
begin
   - - statements for entries READ and WRITE - -
end BUFFER;
```

The statements implementing the buffer operations READ and WRITE are given later in the chapter after additional features of Ada have been described.

The term 'thread of control' is used to describe the execution of a task. When a thread of control enters a scope containing task declarations, the elaboration of each declaration creates a new potential thread of control. The *parent* of a task is the task whose thread of control elaborates the task declaration. In order to cause the task body to be executed, the task name must be explicitly named in an **initiate** statement, e.g.:

```
initiate PRODUCER, CONSUMER, BUFFER;
```

The tasks named in the initiate statement are activated and run in parallel with each other and with the parent task. Note that the parent of a task may be different from the task which initiated it, although both must have access to the task's name. Consider:

```
task body T1 is
  task T2 is
    ...
  end T2;
  task body T2 is
    ...
  end T2;

  task T3 is
    ...
  end T3;

  task body T3 is
    ...
    initiate T2;
    ...
  end T3;

begin
  ...
  initiate T3;
end T1;
```

Here, T1 is the parent of T2, but T2 was initiated by T3 instead of T1.

Normal termination of a task occurs when control reaches the end of the task body. If the terminating task is a parent, then it may have to be delayed until all of its offsprings have terminated. Tasks may also be terminated by means of an explicit abort statement. For example, the statement:

```
abort T1, T2;
```

causes tasks T1 and T2 plus any descendent tasks to be terminated unconditionally. In this case a TASKING_ERROR exception is raised in those tasks which were communicating with the aborted task or its descendents.

Facilities are also provided for determining the status of a task. The system attribute T'PRIORITY may be used to determine the priority that has been assigned to task T by the scheduling algorithm which allocates available processors to tasks. The priority of a task may be changed by means of a call on the procedure SET_PRIORITY to reflect a change in the urgency of process execution.

Ada also provides arrays of tasks called *task families* to handle those situations in which it is necessary to construct a large number of similar tasks. A typical use for task families occurs when there are multiple copies of some physical device such as a console terminal and a distinct copy of the same task is necessary to drive each device; i.e.:

```
task TELETYPE_DRIVER (1..100) is
   type LINE is array (1..132) of CHARACTER;
   entry WRITELINE (TEXT : in LINE);
   entry READLINE (TEXT : out LINE);
end TELETYPE_DRIVER;

task body TELETYPE_DRIVER is
   - - statements to implement WRITELINE and READLINE - -
end TELETYPE_DRIVER;
```

Individual copies of the task may be referred to by appending the appropriate subscript to the task name. Thus the statement:

```
initiate TELETYPE_DRIVER (3);
```

will cause the third copy of task TELETYPE_DRIVER to become active.

Storage for tasks may be allocated either when the task declaration is elaborated (static creation) or when the task is initiated (dynamic creation). The choice between static allocation and dynamic allocation is determined at compile time by the use of a **pragma** or translator command, e.g.:

```
pragma CREATION (STATIC);
pragma CREATION (DYNAMIC);
```

Dynamic creation is particularly important for task families where the index range provides an upper bound on the number of active processes and storage might be wasted if all tasks were allocated at the same time.

3.2 Entry declarations and the ACCEPT statement

Communication between tasks is provided by **entry** calls and **accept** statements. When one task needs to communicate with another task, it executes an **entry call**. **entry** calls specify the information to be exchanged between the tasks and have exactly the same form as procedure calls. Thus in the bounded buffer example from the last section, a producer task places data in the buffer by executing the **entry** call:

```
BUFFER.WRITE (PRODUCER_DATA);
```

and a consumer task executes the call:

```
BUFFER.READ (CONSUMER_DATA);
```

to retrieve data from the buffer.

In order for an **entry** call to be syntactically correct, the called task must contain an *entry declaration* with a corresponding name and formal part. **entry** declarations resemble procedure declarations and contain information about the type and mode of the formal parameters of the **entry**. An **entry** declaration can also specify an array or family of entries all of which have the same name and parameters. In this case, subscripts must be used to distinguish a particular **entry** in the family. Thus, in a disk head scheduler it may be convenient to associate a distinct **entry** with each track on the disk:

> **entry** TRANSFER (1..200) (D : DATA)

When another task wishes to write on track I, it issues an **entry** call of the form:

> TRANSFER (I) (DATA_REQUEST);

The **accept** statement is analogous to the body of a procedure and indicates to the called task which statements should be executed when a particular **entry** call occurs. The formal part of the **entry** declaration is repeated at the beginning of the **accept** statement in order to emphasize the scope of the **entry** parameters. Following the formal part are the statements to be executed when the entry call is accepted. The **accept** statements for the entries READ and WRITE in the bounded buffer example are shown below:

```
accept WRITE (E ; in PACKET) do
   BUF (INX) := E;
end WRITE;

accept READ (V : out PACKET) do
   V := BUF (OUTX);
end READ;
```

The variables INX and OUTX are integers which point, respectively, to the rear and the front of the buffer and are declared in the body of the task (the complete example is presented later in this section). It is important to note that these variables need not be incremented within the **accept** statements. Since **accept** statements are executed in mutual exclusion, it is important for them to be as short as possible and not contain unnecessary statements. **accept** statements for **entry** families must be subscripted to distinguish different entries in the same family. Thus, **accept** statements for the disk head scheduler example will typically have the form:

> **accept** TRANSFER (D : **in** DATA) **do** ... **end** TRANSFER;

The synchronization between the calling task and the called task in an **entry** call is similar to the **rendezvous** that occurs with Hoare's CSP language [3]. As in Hoare's language there are two possibilities for a rendezvous, depending on whether the calling task issues the **entry** call before or after the corresponding **accept** statement is reached by the called task. In either case the process which reaches the rendezvous first is delayed until the other process has an opportunity to catch up. When the rendezvous is achieved, the **in** parameters of the **entry** call are passed to the called task. The calling task is then suspended while the called task executes the body of the **accept** statement. After execution of the **accept** statement, the values of **out** parameters are passed back to the calling task, and the two tasks are allowed to proceed independently again. A queue of waiting tasks is associated with each **entry** to handle those situations in which several different tasks simultaneously access the same **entry**. Tasks are removed from the queues in a FIFO manner each time that a rendezvous occurs. Note that the naming problem which occurs in Hoare's language is avoided by Ada since it is unnecessary for a called process to know the name of the calling process.

3.3 The select statement

Many of the disadvantages of semaphores stem from lack of control over what happens when a semaphore is found to be busy. Thus, it is not possible to program an alternative action to be executed when a semaphore is busy nor is it possible to wait for one of several semaphores to be free. The **select** statement in Ada provides a mechanism for avoiding this type of problem. Syntactically, the **select** statement resembles a case statement in which each alternative is a conditional statement:

```
select
    when B1 => A1;
    or when B2 => A2;
    ...
    or when BN => AN;
    else S;
end select;
```

Each **when** condition may contain an arbitrary boolean expression involving variables which are visible to the task and may be omitted if the condition is known to be true. The **select** alternatives A1, ..., AN are sequences of statements in which the first statement is always an **accept** statement or a **delay** statement. The **else** clause is simply a sequence of statements and can also be omitted if the guarding conditions B1, ..., BN are mutually exhaustive. A **select** alternative is said to be **open** if there is no preceding **when** clause or if the corresponding condition is true; otherwise it is said to be **closed**.

The execution of a **select** statement is described by the following five rules:

(1) All of the conditions are evaluated to determine which alternatives are open.

(2) An open alternative starting with an **accept** statement may be executed if the corresponding rendezvous is possible.

(3) An open alternative starting with a delay statement may be executed if no other alternative has been selected before the specified time interval has elapsed.

(4) If no alternative statement can be immediately selected and there is an **else** clause, then the **else** clause is executed next. If there is no **else** clause, the task waits until an open alternative can be selected by rule 2 or rule 3.

(5) If all alternatives are closed and there is an **else** clause, the **else** part is executed. If there is no **else** clause, the exception SELECT_ERROR is raised.

With the **select** statement we can now complete the task body in the bounded buffer example:

```
task body BUFFER is
    SIZE          : constant INTEGER := 10;
    BUF           : array (1..SIZE) of PACKET;
    INT, OUTX     : INTEGER range 1..SIZE := 1;
    COUNT         : INTEGER range 0..SIZE := 0;

begin
  loop
    select
      when COUNT < SIZE =>
        accept WRITE (E : in PACKET) do
          BUF (INX) := E;
        end WRITE;
        INX := INX mod SIZE + 1;
        COUNT := COUNT + 1;
      or when COUNT > 0 =>
        accept READ (V : out PACKET) do
          V := BUF (OUTX);
        end READ;
        OUTX := OUTX mod SIZE + 1;
        COUNT := COUNT − 1;
    end select;
  end loop;
end BUFFER;
```

The buffer is represented by a circular array with the variables INX and OUTX indicating the portion of the array which contains data. The guard COUNT < SIZE in the first alternative of the **select** statement protects the buffer from overflow during the execution of a write operation. Similarly, the guard COUNT > 0 in the second alternative protects the buffer from underflow during a read operation. Note that if 0 < COUNT < SIZE and both a read call and a write call occur, the **accept** statement that is selected will be chosen in a completely random manner. The programmer, therefore, must be careful that this non-determinism in the selection of alternatives does not affect the correctness of the program.

3.4   The delay statement, interrupts and generic tasks

In this section we describe three additional process control features provided by Ada. These features do not affect the expressive power of the language as significantly as the features discussed previously and are therefore not described in as great detail.

The first feature is the **delay** statement which can be used to postpone execution of a task for a specified interval of time. The delay statement has the form:

> **delay** <simple expression>

The expression following the delay statement represents the length of time (in units of the real time clock) that the process is to be delayed. A delay statement can be used in place of an **accept** statement in an alternative of a **select** statement. In this case if no rendezvous occurs during the specified time interval, the statement list following the delay statement will be executed. Thus, an additional alternative of the form:

> **or delay** 10.0*MINUTES; **initiate** SYSTEM_TEST;

may be added to the **select** statement in the task body for the bounded buffer example. This modification will cause the diagnostic task SYSTEM_TEST to be run if a ten minute time interval passes in which there are no READ or WRITE **entry** calls.

The second feature is the **interrupt entry**: in Ada, hardware interrupts are simply interpreted as external **entry** calls. An Ada *representation specification* is used to link the **entry** to the physical storage address which records the interrupt. The interrupt is processed exactly the same way that any other **entry** call is processed; thus, the queuing mechanism for **entry** calls can be used to handle multiple interrupts. Likewise, the mechanism for masking interrupts can be hidden from users by incorporating it in the software which connects the interrupts to the **entry** call. To illustrate how interrupts are handled in Ada, we show how a *stop* button can be added to the bounded buffer example. We assume the existence of a console button which can be pressed to cause a hardware interrupt. A representation specification of the form:

for STOP **use at** 8#7777;

can be used to associate the **entry** STOP with the physical address of the interrupt. If the **select** statement in the task body is modified to include the alternative:

or accept STOP; **exit**;

then loop will be terminated when the stop button is pressed.

The final process control feature that we discuss is the **generic task**. The bounded buffer example described earlier in this chapter does not provide users with a general mechanism for declaring buffer tasks. By making the tasks generic, i.e., by changing the specification part of the task to:

```
generic task BUFFER is
    PACKET_SIZE : constant INTEGER := 256;
    type PACKET is array (1..PACKET_SIZE) of CHARACTER;
    entry READ (V : out PACKET);
    entry WRITE (E : in PACKET);
end
```

this difficulty can be overcome. When a user needs to declare a new instance of a bounded buffer, the construction:

task BB **is new** BUFFER:

may be used. READ and WRITE calls on the new instance of the bounded buffer have the syntax:

BB.WRITE (PRODUCER_DATA);
BB.READ (CONSUMER_DATA);

Signals and *semaphores* are provided by Ada as predefined generic tasks. If Ada is implemented on a machine on which these primitives are provided by hardware, then the compiler can directly translate **entry** calls into the corresponding hardware primitives. In doing so, however, it is critical that the semantics of the language remain entirely unchanged. As noted in sub-section 4.2.3, the FIFO semantics of the Ada rendezvous can make this particularly difficult to achieve.

4   Evaluation of process control in Ada

As discussed in Section 2, we believe that the use of multiprocessor systems tends to be most valuable in those applications in which run-time efficiency is a critical concern. For this reason, we feel that the parallel control features provided by an implementation language intended for use with multiprocessors must be designed to allow highly efficient interprocess communication and control. After reviewing the Ada language in detail, we are concerned that the primitives provided by Ada do not allow the programmer to achieve this desired level of efficiency. Furthermore, in order to avoid the efficiency cost associated with the Ada task structure, programmers will be forced to adopt an unnatural coding discipline that will make programs more difficult to read and understand.

4.1   Scheduling and the rendezvous

The most severe problem with the process control features in Ada from the point of view of efficiency is that the transmission of data from a sender process to a receiving process requires excessive scheduler interactions. Our experience is that message passing of this type occurs frequently in real-time applications, and that in such applications it is necessary to reduce the number of interactions with the scheduler to a minimum to meet the relevant time constraints.

4.1.1   An example of scheduling delay

To illustrate the problem, we examine the problem of passing messages from a sender process to a receiving process where no response or acknowledgment is required. Conceptually, we imagine that there is a queue linking the sender and receiver which can hold some finite number of messages in transit. When the sender process generates a message, it enters the associated data at the end of the queue. The receiver process, whenever it is free to accept a new message, simply takes the first message from the queue. In a parallel environment, it is desirable that the sending operation (i.e., entering the data on the queue) be performed without incurring any significant delay so that the sending process can continue its operation as quickly as possible. In particular, when the queue is not full, there should be no required scheduler interactions.

Consider the bounded buffer example presented in sub-section 3.1. This example has been used to demonstrate that buffered message passing with non-blocking senders can be implemented in Ada. If **entry** calls are implemented as described in the *Ada Rationale* [Reference 1, page 11–40], however, the delay arising from scheduler actions seems extremely severe and impossible to avoid. Consider, for example, the scheduler interactions involved when a producer task sends a packet of data to a consumer task. Assume that the producer task executes the **entry** call:

BUFFER.WRITE (PRODUCER_DATA);

to initiate the transfer. Given the semantics of the **entry** call, the producer is now blocked until the buffer task is scheduled and completes the rendezvous. During this time, the producer process is suspended and must wait to be rescheduled when the buffer task completes. Thus, before the producer is allowed to continue, two scheduling operations must occur. Furthermore, the implementation discussion in the *Ada Rationale* indicates that the buffer task should dismiss after completing the rendezvous in order to allow tasks of higher priority to run at that point, so that it will not immediately be able to perform a rendezvous with a consumer process.

Essentially the same sequence of operations is performed when the consumer task executes the corresponding **entry** call:

BUFFER.READ (CONSUMER_DATA);

to receive a message. This implies that a total of four scheduling interactions is required to transmit a single message. Since each scheduler interaction may involve a complete context swap, this implementation of message passing would be prohibitively expensive for many applications.

Note that this problem does not arise if the message passing mechanism is implemented through the use of a message queue or directly by the hardware of the target machine. The queue operations themselves must be protected against concurrent updates through some mutual exclusion mechanism, but in this case it is reasonable to use interlocks or some similar mechanism based on busy waiting without incurring the overhead of a scheduler interaction. From the statistics on lock contention given in Reference 4, we see that neither the producer task nor the consumer task will be delayed for an inordinate period of time.

From our experience with real-time communications systems, it is evident that the scheduling delay above presents a serious problem that must be solved for Ada to be recognized as an acceptable implementation language for multiprocessor systems. In the search for a solution, one has two potential choices:

(1) Without changing the Ada language, develop some mechanism which would permit the translator to produce more efficient code in those cases where it can be determined that the rendezvous is not necessary.

(2)   Add new features to Ada to support a more efficient mechanism for message passing without sender delays.

4.1.2   The Habermann/Nassi implementation of rendezvous

In this section, we describe a solution to the problem of scheduling delay which was developed by Habermann and Nassi and described briefly by Habermann in his commentary on the RED and GREEN candidates for the Ada language [5]. The Habermann/Nassi solution consists of replacing the **entry/accept** interface with an alternative implementation resembling a procedure call. The interesting feature of this change in implementation is that the statements in the range of the **accept** statement are evaluated, not by the called task, but by the caller. If this is done correctly, the calling task need never dismiss its processor and therefore is not forced to wait for the scheduler.

In his evaluation of the Ada tasking facility, Habermann observes that many of the tasks that arise in practical applications are of the 'server' type and consist of one or more **select** statements enclosed in a loop (the BUFFER task above is of this type). Habermann argues that tasks of this type often permit the compiler to eliminate the rendezvous by replacing the **accept** statement linkage with a subroutine which implements the required mutual exclusion and synchronization with some internal primitive such as a semaphore. He briefly outlines a scheme for performing this transformation by analysing a variety of cases. In the paragraphs below, we have attempted to reconstruct this argument in a simpler form and then apply it to the BUFFER example.

In the course of this discussion, we will need to introduce internal semaphore objects to control the program flow. Although semaphores may be implemented in Ada using task entities, we feel that it is clearer to think of these semaphores as data objects of type SEMAPHORE which have two values (LOCKED and UNLOCKED) and two primitive operations (P and V). We will therefore write semaphore operations in the more conventional functional notation (i.e., P(SEM1) instead of SEM1.P).

Later in this section, we will also make use of a special P operation, which we will call JOINTP, which takes two semaphores and waits until *both* semaphores are in an UNLOCKED state. Note that this is not the same as a wait for one semaphore, followed by a wait for the other, since neither semaphore is actually locked until both are available.

As a simple case, consider a task whose body consists entirely of a sequence of **accept** statements in a loop such as:

```
task body EXAMPLE1 is
begin
  loop
    accept ENTRY1 do
```

```
    -- <body of ENTRY1> --
  end ENTRY1;
  accept ENTRY2 do
    -- <body of ENTRY2> --
  end ENTRY2;
  -- more accept statements --
  accept ENTRYn do
    -- <body of ENTRYn> --
  end ENTRYn;
end loop;
end EXAMPLE1;
```

To translate this example into its procedural equivalent, we associate each of the entries (ENTRYi) with an internal semaphore (SEMi) and translate each **accept** statement into a procedure declaration which begins by performing a P operation on its associated semaphore and ends by performing a V operation on the semaphore associated with its successor **entry**. The 'entry procedures' then have the form:

```
procedure ENTRY1 is
begin
  P(SEM1);
  -- <body of ENTRY1> --
  V(SEM2);
end ENTRY1;
```

and so on up to:

```
procedure ENTRYn is
begin
  P(SEMn);
  -- <body of ENTRYn> --
  V(SEM1);
end ENTRYn;
```

In this case, since no code exists in EXAMPLE1 that is not enclosed in **accept** statements, no actual thread of control need exist for EXAMPLE1 and the initiation of EXAMPLE1 consists simply of declaring the semaphores SEM1 to SEMn, with SEM1 initialized to UNLOCKED and the remaining ones in the LOCKED state. After considering the actions of the semaphores in the example above, it should be clear that the control semantics of the procedural version is identical to that of the rendezvous provided that semaphores are implemented so as to ensure the first-in/first-out discipline. Initially, the 'task' will only accept **entry** calls to ENTRY1, since any other call will block on the P operation at entry. The first call to ENTRY1, on the other hand, will succeed, and the V operation at the end of the procedure body will allow the system to accept a call on ENTRY2 or to process an existing call pending on the associated semaphore.

A simple version of the **select** statement may be handled through the use of semaphores in a similar fashion. Consider, for example, the task specification below:

```
task body EXAMPLE2 is
begin
  loop
    select
      accept CASE1 do
        -- <body of CASE1> --
      end CASE1;
    or
      accept CASE2 do
        -- <body of CASE2> --
      end CASE2;
    end select;
  end loop;
end EXAMPLE2;
```

In this example, we will need to declare a semaphore with the **select** statement (SELECT_SEM) to ensure mutual exclusion of the independent entries. This task may be coded in procedure form as follows:

```
procedure CASE1 is
begin
  P(SELECT_SEM);
  -- <body of CASE1> --
  V(SELECT_SEM);
end CASE1;

procedure CASE2 is
begin
  P(SELECT_SEM);
  -- <body of CASE2> --
  V(SELECT_SEM);
end CASE2;
```

Initiation of the task EXAMPLE2 corresponds to setting the state of SELECT_SEM to UNLOCKED thus allowing the first **entry** call to succeed. In this example, the first call on either of the entries CASE1 or CASE2 will succeed and will perform the actions in the body of the associated **accept** statement in mutual exclusion because of the protection provided by the semaphore. Upon completion of the **entry** body, the semaphore will once again become free and the system may service any further calls on either of the entries. It is interesting to note that this program transformation provides for 'random' ordering in the **select** statement by implicitly implementing the 'order of arrival' method discussed in the *Ada Rationale*.

The examples presented above, however, are overly simplified in that they do not provide for code within the body of the task which is not enclosed in an **accept** statement. This case requires a slightly more complex treatment that forces the server task to maintain an independent thread of control. To illustrate the basic notion involved in this generalization, consider the simple task skeleton below:

```
task body EXAMPLE3 is
begin
  loop
    -- <statement body 1> --
    accept ENTRY1 do
      -- <body of ENTRY1> --
    end ENTRY1;
    -- <statement body 2> --
    accept ENTRY2 do
      -- <body of ENTRY2> --
    end ENTRY2;
  end loop;
end EXAMPLE3;
```

With the exception of the intervening <statement body> code, this task is identical in form to that given in task EXAMPLE1, and we would like to identify some similar procedural form for the bodies of the **entry** calls. This can be done by associating each of the <statement body i> segments with a semaphore (STATEMENT_SEMi) in much the same way as the entry semaphore association (here ENTRYi is associated with the semaphore ENTRY_SEMi). Originally, only STATEMENT_SEM1 is UNLOCKED; the remaining semaphores are initialized to the LOCKED state. The task is then divided into a component which represents the 'real' task (i.e., the code outside of the **accept** statements) and the **entry** procedures, giving rise to the code segments below:

```
task body TRANSFORMED_EXAMPLE3 is
begin
  loop
    P(STATEMENT_SEM1);
    -- <statement body 1> --
    V(ENTRY_SEM1);
    P(STATEMENT_SEM2);
    -- <statement body 2> --
    V(ENTRY_SEM2);
  end loop;
end TRANSFORMED_EXAMPLE3;
```

```
procedure ENTRY1 is
begin
  P(ENTRY_SEM1);
  -- <body of ENTRY1> --
  V(STATEMENT_SEM2);
end ENTRY1;
```

and:

```
procedure ENTRY2 is
begin
  P(ENTRY_SEM2);
  -- <body of ENTRY2> --
  V(STATEMENT_SEM1);
end ENTRY2;
```

In this example, each of the statement sequences enables the succeeding **entry** and vice versa, which insures the correct semantics with respect to synchronization and mutual exclusion.

Finally, we need a mechanism for managing the effect of **when** clauses appearing in the **select** statement body. In effect, the **when** clauses, taken together, can be viewed as a single code body outside of the **select** statement which evaluates each of the predicates and determines which of the entries should even be considered. Since the evaluation of these predicates takes place outside the range of **accept** statements, the use of **when** clauses implies that the server task must have a separate thread of control to execute the predicate-evaluation code. For example, suppose that we were to modify the code for EXAMPLE2 to include **when** clauses as in the following example:

```
task body EXAMPLE4 is
begin
  loop
    select
      when PREDFN1(...) =>
        accept CASE1 do
          -- <body of CASE1> --
        end CASE1;
    or
      when PREDFN2(...) =>
        accept CASE2 do
          -- <body of CASE2> --
        end CASE2;
    end select;
  end loop;
end EXAMPLE4;
```

where PREDFN1 and PREDFN2 are some form of predicate (either a function call, as here, or a logical expression) that is used to control which of the **select** clauses should be accepted. As in the previous case, we wish to transform the task body of EXAMPLE4 so that the code required to compute the predicates lies in the body of the 'real' task. We will make use of four semaphores in this example: one for each **when** clause (WHEN1 and WHEN2), one to ensure mutual exclusion for the **select** alternatives (SELECT_SEM), and one to control sequencing (STATEMENT_SEM). Of these, STATEMENT_SEM and SELECT_SEM are initialized to UNLOCKED and the two WHEN semaphores are set to a LOCKED state. The code for computing the predicate expressions is given below:

```
task body TRANSFORMED_EXAMPLE4 is
  P1, P2 : BOOLEAN;
begin
  loop
    P(STATEMENT_SEM);
    P1 := PREDFN1(...);
    P2 := PREDFN2(...);
    if not (P1 or P2) then
       raise SELECT_ERROR;
    end if;
    if P1 then V(WHEN1) end if;
    if P2 then V(WHEN2) end if;
  end loop;
end TRANSFORMED_EXAMPLE4;
```

The code for the two CASE entries, however, is somewhat tricky. We are tempted to write procedure-type entries of the form:

```
procedure CASE1 is
begin
  P(WHEN1);
  P(SELECT_SEM);
  - - <body of CASE1> - -
  V(SELECT_SEM);
  V(STATEMENT_SEM)
end CASE1;
```

Unfortunately, this approach is overly simplified and does not correctly ensure that only one of the **select** alternatives is evaluated. We must take two additional precautions to ensure the correct semantics of the **select** mechanism. First of all, whenever a particular entry is evaluated, we must make it impossible for the system to accept other entry calls by locking the corresponding semaphores controlling the remaining **select** alternatives. This can be accomplished by including a statement of the form:

WHEN*x* := LOCKED;

for each of the remaining alternatives for this **select** statement. Unfortunately, even this does not fully insure semantically correct evaluation because of the ordering constraint on the semaphore operations. Since we test the WHEN semaphores prior to testing SELECT_SEM, it is possible for both CASE1 and CASE2 to have passed the first P operation, even though one will be prohibited from continuing until the other has completed the interior region. When this process completes the body of code and performs the V(SELECT_SEM) operation, there is nothing to prohibit the other branch from executing as well, since the effect of the:

WHEN*x* := LOCKED;

has been negated by the fact that the other thread of control has already passed the point at which this test is relevant. Changing the order of the P operations will not work, since this leaves the system susceptible to deadlock states. Moreover, it is insufficient to introduce internal flags to mark the operation, because it will be impossible to tell, in general, whether any other processes have passed the first P operation unless some other action is performed indivisibly with that call to P.

The simplest correction conceptually is to replace the individual P operations with a JOINTP operation which waits for the two semaphores to become UNLOCKED together. In this case, the code for the **entry** procedures becomes:

```
procedure CASE1 is
begin
   JOINTP(WHEN1, SELECT_SEM);
   -- <body of CASE1> --
   WHEN2 := LOCKED;
   V(SELECT_SEM);
   V(STATEMENT_SEM)
end CASE1;
```

and:

```
procedure CASE2 is
begin
   JOINTP(WHEN2, SELECT_SEM);
   -- <body of CASE2> --
   WHEN1 := LOCKED;
   V(SELECT_SEM);
   V(STATEMENT_SEM);
end CASE2;
```

This technique is adequate to solve the problem, but illustrates some of the complexity that arises in more complicated applications of the Habermann/Nassi technique.

To illustrate the power of the complete mechanism, consider the following transformation of the BUFFER task which combines the individual techniques described above. For simplicity, all statements within the range of a **select** alternative have been moved inside the corresponding **accept** statement, although the technique used in EXAMPLE3 illustrates the general method for restoring the potential concurrency.

```
package NEWBUFFER is
    PACKET_SIZE : constant INTEGER := 256;
    type PACKET is array (1..PACKET_SIZE) of CHARACTER;
    task NEWBUF;
    procedure READ (W : out PACKET);
    procedure WRITE (E : in PACKET);
end NEWBUFFER;

package body NEWBUFFER is
    SIZE              : constant INTEGER := 10;
    BUF               : array (1..SIZE) of PACKET;
    INX, OUTX         : INTEGER range 1..SIZE := 1;
    COUNT             : INTEGER range 0..SIZE := 0;
    STATEMENT_SEM     : SEMAPHORE := UNLOCKED;
    SELECT_SEM        : SEMAPHORE := UNLOCKED;
    WHEN1, WHEN2      : SEMAPHORE := LOCKED;

    task body NEWBUF is
    begin
      loop
        P(STATEMENT_SEM);
        -- given the range of COUNT at least --
        -- one of the following is true so no --
        -- SELECT_ERROR exception can occur. --
        if COUNT < SIZE then V(WHEN1); end if;
        if COUNT > 0     then V(WHEN2); end if;
      end loop;
    end NEWBUF;

    procedure WRITE (E : in PACKET) is
    begin
      JOINTP(WHEN1, SELECT_SEM);
      BUF (INX) := E;
      INX := INX mod SIZE + 1;
      COUNT := COUNT + 1;
      WHEN2 := LOCKED;
      V(SELECT_SEM);
      V(STATEMENT_SEM);
    end WRITE;
```

```
    procedure READ (W : out PACKET) is
    begin
      JOINTP(WHEN2, SELECT_SEM);
      W := BUF (OUTX);
      OUTX := OUTX mod SIZE + 1;
      COUNT := COUNT - 1;
      WHEN1 := LOCKED;
      V(SELECT_SEM);
      V(STATEMENT_SEM);
    end READ;
  end NEWBUFFER;
```

From the point of view of efficiency, it is evident that the above implementation strategy is preferable to the cooperating process model of rendezvous suggested in the *Ada Rationale*, but there are some costs associated with this approach, largely in terms of the complexity this structure imposes on an otherwise simple model. In particular, the Ada semantics cannot be maintained if the body of the **accept** statement is viewed as a subroutine of the caller which communicates with the called task solely through the internal semaphore structure. The generated code must take account of the fact that two separate tasks are involved.

The complexity arises because of the 'identity crisis' which occurs for the task executing the statements within an **accept** body. In many ways, it is convenient to think of the calling and called tasks as completely distinct entities. This view is made explicit in the *Ada Rationale* (page 11–40) which emphasizes that 'the caller executes a procedure himself whereas an **accept** statement is executed by the callee on the caller's behalf'. Under the Habermann/Nassi implementation, this distinction is no longer clear since the savings in efficiency result from allowing the calling task to execute the **accept** body as a procedure call.

In some cases, the identity of the task executing the code may be of some importance. For example, to allow metering of an application program, it is important that the run-time consumed during the **accept** body be charged to the CLOCK attribute of the called task rather than its caller. It is also important to remember that exception conditions which occur during the execution of the **accept** statement must be raised in both the caller and called task. Considerations such as these indicate that some form of context switching to identify the called task must be performed as part of the **entry/accept** linkage.

We also gave several examples earlier that show that the order in which semaphores are locked is extremely important and that there are cases in which the only convenient solution is to use a joint P operation which is capable of waiting for two semaphores to become UNLOCKED simultaneously. There are other issues that complicate this structure, such as the use of the same **entry** name in two or more **when** clauses. These problems are not unsolvable by a compiler; our principal assertion is that they are conceptually more difficult to implement than the basic queuing model of task communication, which is at least as efficient in its implementation. Thus we argue that while the Habermann/Nassi solution is not hopelessly complex, it is at least unnecessarily complex.

4.1.3 Automatic data queuing

An alternative approach to the problem would be to devise a queue implementation which retains the linguistic structure of the **entry/accept** linkage. Presumably, this sort of structure is meaningful only in those cases in which the flow of information is unidirectional and where the synchronization provided by the rendezvous is known to be irrelevant. When these conditions apply, it is possible to achieve a significant increase in message passing efficiency by building a data queue into the task communication structure and allowing the sender to proceed.

It is immediately evident that this type of approach changes the nature of the implementation strategy. In the implementation of the rendezvous proposed in the *Ada Rationale* or the Habermann/Nassi alternative described above, no form of data queuing is ever supported by the implementation. The only entities which are entered in queues are tasks, and each task, because of the structure of the rendezvous, may be entered on at most one queue. This is extremely convenient since it allows arbitrary queuing of tasks without encountering a memory allocation problem; it is sufficient to reserve a queue pointer cell in the activation record of each task. Data queuing, on the other hand, requires that space be available to hold each of the data items on the queue. Assuming that dynamic allocation of this queue space is unmanageable, one is required to impose an upper bound on the queue size which is fixed at translation time.

In order to illustrate the general mechanism, consider the task specification below which performs the inverse of the LINE_TO_CHAR function illustrated in the *Ada Rationale* (page 11–6):

```
task CHAR_TO_LINE is
   type LINE is array (1..80) of CHARACTER;
   entry PUT_CHAR <80> (C : in CHARACTER);
   entry GET_LINE (E : in LINE);
end CHAR_TO_LINE;

task body CHAR_TO_LINE is
   BUFFER : LINE;
begin
   loop
      for I in 1..80 loop
         accept PUT_CHAR (C : in CHARACTER) do
            BUFFER (I) := C;
         end PUT_CHAR;
```

```
      end loop;
      accept GET_LINE (L : out LINE) do
        L := BUFFER;
      end GET_LINE;
    end loop;
  end CHAR_TO_LINE;
```

Note that the syntax of the **entry** declaration has been extended to allow a queue size indicator as in:

entry PUT_CHAR <80> (C : **in** CHARACTER);

The <80> parameter specifies a queue size for communication between the callers of PUT_CHAR and the CHAR_TO_LINE task itself. In this case, the first eighty calls to PUT_CHAR will simply copy their data into the character queue established by the **entry** declaration and proceed, even if the CHAR_TO_LINE task is unable to complete the rendezvous for the PUT_CHAR **entry** (presumably because it is waiting for a call to GET_LINE). Thereafter, additional calls to PUT_CHAR will block and be suspended until characters are taken from the queue by the CHAR_TO_LINE task.

For the most part, the implementation of this extension to the rendezvous mechanism is completely straightforward. For the case of an **entry** which has only **in** parameters, the calling task performs one of two actions when making an **entry** call. If the queue is not full, the input parameters are copied into the pre-allocated data area and added to the end of the queue; if the queue is full, the task activation record is queued for that **entry** in exactly the same manner as that used in the complete rendezvous approach. The server task, upon reaching an **accept** statement, looks to see if the queue is empty. If so, the server task is dismissed and waits for an **entry** call; if there are entries in the queue, the data items from the first **entry** are copied into the server task. As part of the same operation, the parameters from the first task (if any) in the associated queue of sending tasks must be appended to the end of the data queue, at which point the sending task is free to proceed.

A similar mechanism can be used to handle the case of entries which operate in the opposite direction and have only **out** parameters. In this case, receiving tasks are suspended when the data queue is empty and the server must wait when the data queue is full.

This approach makes considerable sense if one argues that many applications require efficient message passing structures and that those structures should be incorporated into the language in a manner consistent with the existing mechanism for synchronization. One important observation about this approach is that the queue size information may be interpreted in the same fashion as a **pragma** statement which the translator is free to ignore. If some translator chooses to implement all

entry calls using the complete rendezvous scheme, this will only affect the efficiency of the resultant program rather than the semantics.

4.1.4   Communication through low-level facilities

One further alternative to be considered is to provide low-level facilities for mutual exclusion which would allow programmers to implement other message passing disciplines. While we do not feel that low-level facilities are required for an efficient solution to interprocess communication, we believe that there are other independent reasons which argue for the introduction of such facilities. If these are provided, it may be unnecessary for the language to supply any additional mechanisms for communication since it will be possible for the users to create additional structures to achieve the necessary level of efficiency.

4.2   Low-level synchronization facilities in Ada

A related problem which limits the potential efficiency of Ada arises from the lack of low-level facilities for protecting shared data against concurrent access. In Ada, the only mechanism available for providing mutual exclusion is the **entry** call. Although it is certainly true that this model is appropriate to a variety of task structures which arise in practical applications, there are limitations in the structure which will make it difficult to use Ada in those environments in which efficiency is of considerable importance.

4.2.1   Synchronization and efficiency

As noted in the previous section, the rendezvous mechanism requires two scheduling events for each execution of a critical region. While this cost may be reduced considerably through the use of alternative implementation strategies, even in the best of circumstances, there will be some overhead cost involved in context switching between the two tasks.

The actual impact of the rendezvous overhead depends on the frequency of access of shared data and on the size of the critical regions. If access to shared data structures is relatively infrequent, the scheduling overhead required to make these accesses will have a minor overall effect. Similarly, if the size of the critical regions is large (in terms of the amount of computation required) in comparison to the rendezvous cost, overall system performance is relatively insensitive to this delay.

On the other hand, consider the extreme case of an application in which access to shared data is frequent (such as of the order of 10% of the instructions executed not counting those required for parallel control) and the size of a typical critical region is very short (perhaps as little as one or two instructions). In this case, system throughput is largely determined by the efficiency of the mutual exclusion mechanism. On most systems, it is possible to design interlock mechanisms based on busy waiting (often referred to as 'spin locks') which require very few instructions to implement. If such a mechanism is used, it is reasonable to expect that a typical cycle from one critical region to the next might require no more than twenty or thirty instructions, assuming that lock contention does not have a significant effect. If scheduling interactions are required to ensure mutual exclusion, the path through a critical region would be significantly more costly and would typically require more than 200 instructions, thereby reducing the overall efficiency by an order of magnitude.

While the severity of the problem is exaggerated by the example above, the ratio of synchronization time to time spent in critical regions is an important factor in many applications. Furthermore, the choice between spin locks and scheduler-based synchronization mechanisms does have a significant impact on synchronization time. In the Hydra system, for example, spin locks are two orders of magnitude faster than the fastest synchronization primitive involving the scheduler (Reference 4). Since spin locks can be implemented using between three and ten instructions on most machines, this factor of 100 is likely to be representative of the relative cost for a wide range of systems.

The effect of this differential on the efficiency of the various synchronization primitives is that different applications may require different mechanisms according to the size of the critical regions involved. After studying the performance of a parallel root-finding application on C.mmp, Oleinick and Fuller [4] conclude that each of the scheduling mechanisms supported by C.mmp or the Hydra operating system has an associated operating range. If the time between synchronization events is relatively short (in this case, less than about 15 milliseconds), spin locks are the only synchronization mechanism available which incurs a synchronization cost of less than 50%. If the interval between synchronization events is longer, the more powerful primitives provided by the scheduler become less costly.

The existence of different operating ranges suggests that some flexibility must be available in the choice of scheduling primitives in order to allow the system to meet the requirements of a particular application. The lack of this flexibility in Ada implies that the language may not be appropriate to applications in which the expected time between synchronization events is small. In our experience, this is frequently the case in real-time applications and we feel strongly that the introduction of low-level synchronization primitives into the Ada language is necessary to handle such applications with the required level of efficiency.

4.2.2   Control-based vs data-based synchronization

In addition to the efficiency concerns discussed in the previous section, the rendezvous mechanism in Ada differs from many conventional primitives for synchronization in that mutual exclusion is a function solely of the task (or control structure) and is independent of the data structures in the application program. This property appears to have an effect on memory utilization if conventional program structuring is used.

Consider an application in which some relatively large number of entities may be manipulated by some moderately large number of actions (for concreteness in this example, assume that there are 100 entities and 10 actions) in such a way that mutual exclusion is required to prevent two actions from occurring simultaneously for the same entity. This type of situation occurs, for example, in the case of a terminal concentrator whose function is to connect some large number of terminals to a network of host computers. In designing software for such a system, it is convenient to represent each terminal as a distinct entity and to define a set of commands which trigger control functions when entered on that terminal.

In Ada, this situation would ordinarily be modelled through the use of a *task family* whose members corresponded to the individual terminal entities. The user commands correspond to entries in the body of the task, which would give rise to the following general structure:

```
task ENTITY (1..100) is
   entry ACTION1;
   entry ACTION2;
   -- entry declarations for remaining actions --
   entry ACTION10;
end ENTITY;

task body ENTITY is
begin
   loop
      select
         accept ACTION1 do
            -- body of action 1 --
         end ACTION1;
      or accept ACTION2 do
            -- body of action 2 --
         end ACTION2;
      -- accept statements for remaining actions --
      or accept ACTION10 do
            -- body of action 10 --
         end ACTION10;
      end select;
   end loop;
end ENTITY;
```

In a more conventional approach in which low-level primitives are available for locking within data structures, the same structure would be implemented by including an interlock with each entity to prevent concurrent access to that entity by more than one action. The individual actions would be coded as procedures, for example:

```
-- INTERLOCK operations defined in Section 3 --

type ENTITY is access
  record
    ACCESS_LOCK : INTERLOCK := UNLOCKED;
    -- local state fields --
  end record;

procedure ACTION1 (ENT : in ENTITY)
begin
  LOCK (ENT.ACCESS_LOCK);
  -- body of action 1 --
  UNLOCK (ENT.ACCESS_LOCK);
end ACTION1;

-- ACTION2 through ACTION10 are similarly defined --
```

The flavour of the two models above is very similar, particularly from the external point of view. In order to perform ACTION3 on some entity k in the task-based Ada approach, one issues the call:

```
ENTITY(k).ACTION3;
```

while in the interlock model, one performs:

```
ACTION3 (pointer to entity k);
```

The semantic properties are also similar since each call is protected against the concurrent execution of other actions for that entity and independent entities may be acted upon in parallel.

In the implementation of the two mechanisms, however, there is a considerable disparity in the storage requirements which arises from the fact that the interlock model views the entities (data) and the actions (procedures) as distinct units. In the task model, each entity in the task family has, as part of its structure, each of the associated entries, which has a multiplicative effect on the storage requirements for each entity. For example, in the interlock model, there are 100 data locks used to manage concurrency; in the task model, this function is managed by 1000 (i.e. 100×10) entries. Since each **entry** must include at least a queue pointer, this approach is clearly inefficient in terms of storage.

It is possible to design the task structure for a particular application so that this cost is eliminated. For example, in the code sequence below there are only 100 entries to perform the necessary actions:

```
type ACTION is (ACTION1, ACTION2, ..., ACTION10);

task ENTITY (1..100) is
  entry PERFORM_ACTION (ACT : in ACTION);
end ENTITY;

task body ENTITY is
begin
  loop
    accept PERFORM_ACTION (ACT : in ACTION) do
      case ACT of
        when ACTION1 =>
          begin
            -- body of action 1 --
          end;
        when ACTION2 =>
          begin
            -- body of action 2 --
          end;
        -- when clauses for remaining actions --
        when ACTION10 =>
          begin
            -- body of action 10 --
          end;
      end case;
    end PERFORM_ACTION;
  end loop;
end ENTITY;
```

While the above solution has the desired effect of reducing the storage requirements, the overall structure has been sacrificed and the resultant program is considerably less natural than the earlier one. It may be possible for the translator to perform optimizations of this kind, but this seems like an exceptionally complex problem.

4.2.3   Implementation of interlocks in Ada

Although the rendezvous can provide the same functionality as programmer-accessible interlocks within the data structure, we feel that such interlocks are necessary in order to allow multiprocessor systems to be implemented with the required level of efficiency. The two preceding sections demonstrate that the interlock model is more efficient than a straightforward implementation of the rendezvous scheme. Because efficiency is of critical importance in most multiprocessor environments, we are concerned that the failure of Ada to provide adequate facilities for low-level interlocks will considerably reduce the overall applicability of the language.

We also believe that low-level facilities for managing interlocks can be added to the language without any significant change in the underlying structure of Ada. One possibility is simply to incorporate the data type INTERLOCK and the procedures LOCK and UNLOCK as part of the Ada language. This solution is sufficiently general to satisfy the efficiency considerations and does so with a very minimal impact on the Ada language. A second alternative would be to define a new statement form, such as the *region* statement from Brinch Hansen [6], which has the effect of ensuring mutual exclusion on a particular interlock throughout a sequence of statements. This alternative offers greater protection against improper use of interlocks at the cost of introducing new syntactic forms into the Ada language.

It is important to note that the implementation of semaphore operations through the use of a generic task (as suggested in the *Ada Reference Manual*) is not a sufficient solution to the mutual exclusion problem, even if these primitives are implemented using special hardware support. There are two problems associated with the P and V operations as defined in Ada. First, tasks (including these generic tasks) are not part of the data environment. One of the principal uses of an interlock in conventional systems is to protect some structure from concurrent access. In Ada, there is no convenient way to associate a semaphore with a specific data object. The best achievable solution is to use integer indices within the object to select the appropriate member of a semaphore family in a relatively cumbersome and obscure way.

The second problem stems from the FIFO semantics of the rendezvous mechanism in Ada. Although the *Ada Reference Manual* (page 9–11) notes that the fact that semaphores are 'predefined authorizes an implementation to recognize them and implement them making optimal use of the facilities provided by the machine or the underlying system', it is still impossible to achieve the efficiency of spin locks in this way without violating the FIFO semantics of the Ada rendezvous.

4.3   Entries and the name problem

Another major problem in Ada stems from the manner in which processes are named. In Ada, tasks which perform some particular set of operations for separate internal data structures or devices are grouped together to form array-structured task families. In order to refer to a specific incarnation of a task, we must specify both the name of the task and the index of the specific process. Furthermore, since tasks in Ada are not data objects, we must supply the name field explicitly in the source code. This treatment of processes has several deficiencies when compared to other structures which allow a more flexible naming scheme.

4.3.1   Limitations of array functionality

One concern that arises from the naming convention is that the array structure imposes a relatively arbitrary task structure which may not fit the nature of the application. Array structured task families are appropriate only when the process structure which they represent has a topology which behaves like an array. Other structures (particularly those which involve linked lists or other pointer-based structures) are cumbersome to implement in terms of a pre-supplied array structure. This problem is similar to the problem of defining linked structures in Fortran or a similar language in which arrays are the primary compound structure.

As an example, let us again consider the case of the terminal concentrator example presented above. In this application, there are a large number of terminals of which only a relatively small fraction are likely to be connected at any given time. The activity for each terminal is monitored by a member of a task family which is assigned to that terminal as long as it is connected to the system. We assume that the total number of terminal tasks is constant (which allows them to be statically allocated) and that the association of terminals and tasks will change as terminals are connected and disconnected from the system. Ordinarily, there will be more terminal tasks than connected terminals at any particular time; these tasks remain idle until they are associated with a newly connected terminal.

The natural structure in which to store the idle terminal tasks is a linked free list. When a terminal is connected to the system, it is assigned to the first free task which is currently at the head of the list. When a terminal is disconnected, its associated process becomes idle and is linked onto the free list. These operations are natural in a structure which permits pointer operations; when faced with an array structure, one is faced with the choice of:

(1)   searching for free entries;

(2)   dynamically compactifying the task table so that the active tasks are contiguous; or

(3)   simulating the free list mechanism through the use of auxiliary arrays.

These alternatives represent possible implementation strategies, but it is our contention that Ada prevents the most natural solution.

4.3.2   The return address problem

A potentially more serious problem posed by the naming convention is the 'return address problem' which is briefly considered in the *Ada Rationale* (page 11–40). The concern here is that a server task has no way to reply to the calling task which requests service unless the identity of the calling task is known at translation time. The problem is not one of authenticating a particular caller but rather one of identifying the calling task in some subsequent **entry** call.

Consider the case of a task whose function is to encrypt a message supplied by a caller and to return the encrypted message. In Ada, the canonical description for this type of server is illustrated below:

```
task ENCRYPTION_SERVER is
  PACKET_SIZE : constant INTEGER := 256;
  type PACKET is array (1..PACKET_SIZE) of CHARACTER;
  entry SEND_NORMAL_MESSAGE (MSG : in PACKET);
  entry GET_ENCRYPTED_MESSAGE (MSG : out PACKET);
end ENCRYPTION_SERVER;

task body ENCRYPTION_SERVER is
  BUF : PACKET;
begin
  loop
    accept SEND_NORMAL_MESSAGE (MSG : in PACKET) do
      BUF := MSG;
    end SEND_NORMAL_MESSAGE;
    -- code to encrypt data in BUF --
    accept GET_ENCRYPTED_MESSAGE (MSG : out PACKET) do
      MSG := BUF;
    end GET_ENCRYPTED_MESSAGE;
  end loop;
end ENCRYPTION_SERVER;
```

While the code above performs the encryption function in a straightforward way and allows arbitrary tasks to call the two entries, it is not optimal in all cases. One potential problem arises in **entry** definitions which make use of a **select** statement to allow the server task to wait for a number of possible events. Because the **select** statement can appear only within the body of the called task, there is an inherent asymmetry in the tasking structure. Suppose that the programmer using ENCRYPTION_SERVER wanted a task within the following logical structure:

```
task body CALLING_TASK is
  -- code which generates PLAINTEXT for encryption --
  SEND_NORMAL_MESSAGE (PLAINTEXT);
  loop
    exit when ENCRYPTION_DONE;
    -- do some other work --
  end loop;
  GET_ENCRYPTED_MESSAGE (CODED_MESSAGE);
  -- code to make use of CODED_MESSAGE --
end CALLING_TASK;
```

While it is not possible to code the calling task in this way directly (because there is no way to transmit the ENCRYPTION_DONE), this type of operation can be achieved if the roles of **entry** call and **accept** statement are reversed for the GET_ENCRYPTED_MESSAGE **entry**.

```
task ENCRYPTION_SERVER is
  PACKET_SIZE : constant INTEGER := 256;
  type PACKET is array (1..PACKET_SIZE) of CHARACTER;
  entry SEND_NORMAL_MESSAGE (MSG : in PACKET);
end ENCRYPTION_SERVER;

task body ENCRYPTION_SERVER is
  BUF : PACKET;
begin
  loop
    accept SEND_NORMAL_MESSAGE (MSG : in PACKET) do
      BUF := MSG;
    end SEND_NORMAL_MESSAGE;
    -- code to encrypt data in BUF --
    GOT_ENCRYPTED_MESSAGE(BUF);
  end loop;
end ENCRYPTION_SERVER;

task body CALLING_TASK is
  -- code which generates PLAINTEXT for encryption --
  SEND_NORMAL_MESSAGE (PLAINTEXT);
  loop
    select
      accept GOT_ENCRYPTED_MESSAGE (MSG : in PACKET) do
        CODED_MESSAGE := MSG;
      end GOT_ENCRYPTED_MESSAGE;
    else
      -- do some other work --
    end select;
  end loop;
  -- code to make use of CODED_MESSAGE --
end CALLING_TASK;
```

Unfortunately, this organization is only effective if there is a single calling task or a single family of callers. In the case that the calling task is a member of a task family, the caller can pass the index of a member as an additional argument to SEND_NORMAL_MESSAGE and then use this index in the subsequent GOT_ENCRYPTED_MESSAGE call, as in:

```
CALLING_TASK(TASK_INDEX).GOT_ENCRYPTED_MESSAGE(BUF);
```

It is impossible to write ENCRYPTION_SERVER as a general utility package which is available for use with any task that calls SEND_

NORMAL_MESSAGE and defines an entry GOT_ENCRYPTED_
MESSAGE for the reply. Because it is impossible to pass the identity of
the calling task to ENCRYPTION_SERVER, there is no way for the
server task to return the message to the appropriate caller. This
restriction seems to preclude the development of task libraries comparable to subroutine libraries in a well-organized environment for software
development.

4.3.3   Tasks as data objects

The obvious solution to both the array topology problem and the return
address problem is to consider individual activations of tasks to be data
objects which can be incorporated into arbitrary structures or passed as
parameters to server tasks. This issue is briefly discussed in the *Ada
Rationale* (page 11–39) and the notion of anonymous activation variables from the language Tartan is introduced. Such a mechanism could
be incorporated into Ada if it were possible to overcome the additional
problems associated with task variables. For example, assume that all
activations of tasks are data objects of the type ACTIVATION_NAME
and that each task implicitly defines the variable MY_NAME to be an
identification of that activation.

The discussion of activation variables in the *Ada Rationale* correctly
observes that the introduction of untyped task variables raises questions
of strong typing similar to those found with procedure parameters in
languages such as ALGOL-60. For example, even though the task
definition:

```
task body GENERAL_SERVER is
   DATA                : PACKET;
   RETURN_ADDRESS   : ACTIVATION_NAME;
begin
   accept SERVER_REQUEST (T : in ACTIVATION_NAME,
                            INPUT : in PACKET) do
      DATA := INPUT;
      RETURN_ADDRESS := T;
   end SERVER_REQUEST;
   - - perform appropriate manipulation on DATA - -
   RETURN_ADDRESS'REPLY(DATA);
end GENERAL_SERVER;
```

solves the return address problem, the use of an untyped process variable
T is dangerous because there is no guarantee that the process referred to
by T has a REPLY **entry** or that its parameter structure is compatible.

This problem, however, may be solved by eliminating the untyped
activation variables in favour of a strongly typed system of specific **entry**
variables. For example, assume that the reserved word **entry** is usable as a

type generating function in a similar fashion as **array**. It is then possible
to declare a return address with no type ambiguity as illustrated below:

```
task body GENERAL_SERVER is
   DATA               : PACKET;
   RETURN_ADDRESS   : entry (in PACKET);
begin
   accept SERVER_REQUEST (T : in entry (in PACKET),
                             INPUT : in PACKET) do
      DATA := INPUT;
      RETURN_ADDRESS := T;
   end SERVER_REQUEST;
   -- perform appropriate manipulation on DATA --
   RETURN_ADDRESS(DATA);
end GENERAL_SERVER;
```

In this case, the caller would issue the **entry** call:

```
SERVER_REQUEST (MY_NAME'REPLY, INPUT_DATA);
```

thereby giving the complete (and unambiguous) address of the return
entry.

There are other possible approaches to this problem; we have
suggested the above scheme in order to demonstrate that strong typing
considerations alone are not a sufficient justification for disallowing
references to process activations within the data structure. We believe
that the ability to code a general server with the ability to correctly
address a reply is of major importance to the design of a rationally
structured parallel control facility and that some mechanism for performing this function should be determined and incorporated into the
Ada language.

4.4   Flexibility in the scheduling discipline

One additional area of concern that has developed during our study of
Ada is the question of whether the scheduling discipline provided by the
language is sufficiently general to support applications with important
timing constraints. In particular, we are concerned that Ada does not
provide adequate control over the scheduling strategy and that the
scheduling algorithm is likely to encounter a number of problems
associated with 'cooperative scheduling'.

To illustrate this problem, imagine that Ada is chosen as the
implementation language for the design and development of a timesharing system for a multiprocessor. It is convenient in such a system to
represent the individual user processes as independent tasks in the

timesharing structure. In order to achieve fairness, timesharing systems typically limit the run-time allowed to a process to some maximum unit of time. If this time period (or quantum) is exceeded, the process is forcibly descheduled to allow other processes to run. The performance of the typical timesharing system is quite sensitive to the size and dynamic behaviour of this quantum limit and it is important to be able to adjust this mechanism to conform to the loading demands.

In Ada, there is no apparent way to specify a run-time limit for a task nor is it possible for one task to control the scheduling or descheduling of another. Without this flexibility, it appears that there are only two possible schemes to provide fairness in a timesharing scheduler:

(1)   Depend on the Ada scheduling discipline for all scheduling and descheduling operations and ensure that the built-in mechanism provides all of the desired flexibility, presumably expressed in the form of pragma declarations to the compiler.

(2)   Design a scheduler which operates 'cooperatively' in the sense that the tasks themselves participate in the scheduling decisions. In this case, each task would be required to periodically check its accumulated run-time and dismiss itself through the use of a delay statement.

Obviously, each of the approaches outlined above is totally unacceptable for a timesharing application. The first either requires the system designer to change the structure of the implementation language or forces the system to make use of a built-in scheduling discipline which may be hopelessly inadequate to perform the more complex scheduling operations required of a timesharing system.

The second approach is equally unworkable in that it requires the compiler to perform complex path analysis and assemble code to poll the scheduler at acceptably frequent intervals. The problems that arise in this type of scheduling are so severe that this alternative tends to be rejected out of hand. In his assessment of the process scheduling facility in Ada [5], Paul Hilfinger writes:

"It seems that the tasks being scheduled must be written to be aware of the fact that they are being scheduled, and to do appropriate sends or procedure calls at intervals. This is a violation of abstraction; no reasonable operating system in existence requires that its processes cooperate to be scheduled."

There are several potential approaches to this problem which affect the structure of the language to varying degrees. Perhaps the most straightforward mechanism is to allow one task to forcibly deschedule another task. This would provide a monitoring task with at least some primitive ability to control the scheduling discipline. This could be implemented through the addition of a new primitive such as:

deschedule T;

or as an extension of the priority mechanism. If one task were allowed to alter the priority of another and changes in priority were implemented so as to force a scheduler transition, one might begin to have an acceptable facility for scheduling control.

5   Conclusions

In this paper, we have argued that multiprocessor systems are frequently used for real-time applications in which run-time efficiency requirements are of critical importance. For this reason, we believe that the design of a high-level language system which is intended for use in real-time, multiprocessor-based applications must be sensitive to these requirements and must allow the programmer to write code which satisfies the efficiency constraints imposed by the application.

We believe that the Ada language, as currently designed, does not meet these needs for several reasons:

(1)   The use of a complete rendezvous system results in unnecessary scheduling delays. This problem is particularly severe in the relatively important case of message passing in that Ada requires the sender of a message to wait for the scheduler before it is allowed to proceed. This structure is considerably less efficient than message passing systems implemented with queues and imposes a relatively high cost on the use of an important communication discipline.

(2)   Ada does not provide sufficient flexibility in its process control structure to allow the programmer to choose the mechanism most closely suited to the requirements of the application. In particular, the fact that the mutual exclusion mechanism is associated with the control structure rather than the data structure leads to convoluted program structures or serious inefficiencies in the use of space.

(3)   The naming conventions used to indicate specific processes in Ada are not sufficiently general to allow the programmer to represent process structures which accurately reflect the underlying structure of the algorithm. Moreover, the fact that no general mechanism exists to allow one process to communicate its identity to other processes in the system severely limits the modularity of the task structure.

(4)   The language does not provide the user with sufficient control over the scheduling discipline.

We contend that the parallel processing facilities currently provided by Ada do not satisfy the requirements of real-time systems such as those typically chosen for implementation on a multiprocessor. On the other hand, we feel that good solutions do exist for most of the problems that we have identified here and that those solutions can be incorporated into Ada with relatively little change to the overall structure of the code. Based on our experience with multiprocessors and real-time systems, we feel that the efficiency cost implied by the current Ada design severely limits the extent to which Ada is acceptable for real-time applications. We strongly urge that modifications such as those suggested in this paper be incorporated into Ada to increase its utility in this important area of application.

Acknowledgments

The research reported in this document was sponsored in part by the Defense Communications Engineering Center under Contract No. DCA100-78-C-0028 and by the National Science Foundation under Grant No. MCS-7908365.

References

[1]   J. D. Ichbiah *et al.* 'Rationale for the design of the Ada programming language', *SIGPLAN Notices*, **14** (6), Part B, entire issue (1979).
[2]   U.S. Department of Defense, *STEELMAN – Requirements for High Order Computer Programming Languages*, Defense Advanced Research Projects Agency, Arlington, Va., June 1978.
[3]   C. A. R. Hoare, 'Communicating sequential processes', *Communications of ACM*, **21**, 666–677 (1978).
[4]   P. N. Oleinick and S. H. Fuller, 'The implementation and evaluation of a parallel algorithm on C.mmp', *Computer Science Department Report CMU-CS-78-125*, Carnegie–Mellon University, June 1978.
[5]   D. A. Lamb (ed), *Commentary on the RED and GREEN Candidates for the Ada Language*, Computer Science Department, Carnegie–Mellon University, April 1979.
[6]   P. Brinch Hansen, *Operating System Principles*, Prentice-Hall, Englewood Cliffs, N.J., 1973.

20

Processes, Tasks and Monitors: A Comparative Study of Concurrent Programming Primitives

Peter Wegner
Brown University

Scott A. Smolka
Brown University and State University of New York
at Stony Brook

Three notations for concurrent programming are compared, namely CSP, Ada, and monitors. CSP is an experimental language for exploring structuring concepts in concurrent programming. Ada is a general-purpose language with concurrent programming facilities. Monitors are a construct for managing access by concurrent processes to shared resources. We start by comparing 'lower-level' communication, synchronization, and nondeterminism in CSP and Ada and then examine 'higher-level' module interface properties of Ada tasks and monitors.

Similarities between CSP and Ada include use of the 'cobegin' construct for nested process initiation and the 'rendezvous' mechanism for synchronization. Differences include the mechanisms for task naming and nondeterminism. One-way (procedure-style) naming of called tasks by calling tasks in Ada is more flexible than the two-way naming in CSP. The general-purpose nondeterminism of guarded commands in CSP is cleaner than the special-purpose nondeterminism of the select statement in Ada.

Monitors and tasks are two different mechanisms for achieving serial

This work was supported in part by the Office of Naval Research under Contract N00014-78-C-0656 and in part by the NASA Graduate Student Researchers Fellowship under Grant NGT-40-002-800.

access to shared resources by concurrently callable procedures. Both rely on queues to achieve serialization, but calls on monitor procedures are scheduled on a single monitor queue while task entry calls are scheduled on separate queues associated with each entry name. Monitors are passive modules which are activated by being called, while tasks are active modules that execute independently of their callers. Monitor procedures represent multiple threads of control each of which may be suspended and later resumed, while tasks have just a single thread of control. The attempt to map a monitor version of a shortest job scheduler into Ada yields interesting insights into the limitations of Ada mechanisms for synchronization, and suggests that Ada packages may be more appropriate than tasks as a user interface for concurrent computation.

Index terms: Ada, concurrent programming, CSP, distributed processes, monitors, processes, tasks.

I Initiation and termination of concurrent processes

The unit of concurrency is called a *process* in CSP [11] and a *task* in Ada [5]. The CSP command below declares and initiates two processes p1, p2 with associated command lists that may contain declarations and statements.

Example 1 – Concurrent Execution Command in CSP

[p1 :: *command-list* ‖ p2 :: *command-list*]

This command imposes a nested (one-in, one-out) structure on task initiation and termination. Execution causes p1 and p2 to be concurrently initiated and requires both to terminate before the next command can be executed.

The Ada procedure WOMAN_WINE_AND_SONG below declares two tasks WOMAN and WINE with separately specified bodies and has a call to a procedure SONG in its statement part.[†] Execution of the procedure WOMAN_WINE_AND_SONG causes the tasks WOMAN and WINE to be initiated on entry to the statement part of the procedure and executed concurrently with the procedure SONG. Exit from WOMAN_WINE_AND_SONG requires execution of the two tasks as well as execution of procedure SONG to be completed.

[†] The phrase 'woman, wine, and song' is attributed to Martin Luther in the *Oxford Book of Quotations*, 1972 edition, p. 321: "Who knows not woman, wine and song, remains a fool his whole life long."

Example 2 – Declaration and Initiation of Tasks in Ada

procedure WOMAN_WINE_AND_SONG **is**
  task WOMAN;
  task WINE;
  task body WOMAN **is separate**;
  task body WINE **is separate**;

begin   -- initiate WOMAN and WINE
  SONG; -- call the parameterless procedure SONG
  -- WOMAN, WINE, and SONG are concurrently executed
  -- all three activities must terminate before exit from the
  -- procedure
end;

The keyword **begin** causes the single thread of control in the declarative part of WOMAN_WINE_AND_SONG to branch into three threads associated with the tasks WOMAN, WINE, and the parent procedure. The keyword **end** requires the three threads to rejoin into a single thread before it can be executed. Associating initiation and termination of tasks with **begin** and **end** keywords ties the lifetimes of task execution to the nested block structure of the program.

Execution of the two tasks WOMAN and WINE concurrently with SONG may be expressed in CSP notation as:

[WOMAN :: task body ‖ WINE :: task body ‖ SONG :: procedure]

Nested task initiation and termination may be syntactically indicated by **cobegin** commands. We can write **cobegin** (T1, T2) to represent nested initiation and termination of two tasks T1 and T2. The statement **cobegin** (T1, **cobegin** (T2, T3), T4) illustrates use of the **cobegin** statement for concurrent execution of three tasks, the second of which in turn involves nested concurrent execution of two tasks. The keyword **cobegin** is not part of CSP or Ada but is introduced here to bring out the common structure of nested task initiation adopted in both languages.

Early concurrent programming languages modeled task initiation by a **fork** (T) command to initiate a new thread of control for a task T, and modeled task termination by a **join** command to rejoin the thread of control of the executing task to its parent. **fork** commands in concurrent programming are like **go to** statements in sequential programming. Their undisciplined use may give rise to an unstructured tangle of threads of control just as the **go to** statement may give rise to an unstructured tangle of paths of control. A tangle of threads of control is potentially worse than a tangle of paths of control since threads of control eat up time and memory resources while paths of control in a sequential process can be exercised only one at a time.

Cobegin-style task initiation and termination are appropriate for applications whose patterns of concurrent execution are known at compile time, such as concurrent operations on non-overlapping components of a predefined array or database. However, dynamically evolving systems such as airline reservation systems and command and control applications have patterns of concurrency that cannot be predicted at compile time. When the number of tasks and their time of creation cannot be predicted, dynamic task-creation mechanisms not tied to the program structure are required.

Both CSP and Ada support nested task initiation and termination, but Ada also permits dynamic task initiation through **access** types (pointers). The procedure AIRPLANES below declares a task type AIRPLANE and an array SQUADRON of task pointers to tasks of the type AIRPLANE. SQUADRON is uninitialized and no tasks are therefore created on entry to the statement part of the AIRPLANES procedure. However, **new** AIRPLANE creates and initiates a new task every time it is executed in the **for** loop. It behaves like a **fork** command in the sense that it launches a new thread of control for each AIRPLANE while continuing execution of the AIRPLANES procedure. But all AIRPLANE tasks must terminate before exit from the AIRPLANES procedure, thus preserving a one-in, one-out flow of control.

Example 3 – Dynamic Task Initiation

```
procedure AIRPLANES is
   task type AIRPLANE;
   type AIRPLANE_PTR is access AIRPLANE;
   SQUADRON : array (1..100) of AIRPLANE_PTR;
   task body AIRPLANE is separate;
begin
   for 1 in 1..100 loop
      SQUADRON(1) := new AIRPLANE;
   end loop;
   -- exit when all tasks are terminated
end AIRPLANES;
```

In the previous example the maximum number of tasks that can be dynamically accessed is fixed by the size of the array SQUADRON. Even greater flexibility can be obtained by associating dynamically created tasks with a list structure. Thus if each airplane in an airline reservation system (or air traffic control simulation) is associated with a task, the set of airplanes can be represented by an array which imposes a maximum on the number of permitted airplanes, or by a list of records with task components whose elements can be dynamically created and deleted during execution. The list-structure approach to dynamic task creation is illustrated in the next example for a fleet of ships.

Example 4 – List Structures of Tasks

```
procedure SHIPS is
   task type SHIP;
   type SHIP_PTR is access SHIP;

   type ELEMENT;   -- incomplete type declaration
   type FLEET is access ELEMENT;

   type ELEMENT is
      record
         INDEX : INTEGER; -- name of ship
         S : SHIP_PTR;        -- pointer to ship task
         NEXT : FLEET;        -- next ship in the list
      end record;
   HEAD, C : FLEET := null;
   task body SHIP is separate;

begin
   for K in 1..100 loop
      -- insert new ship at head of list
      C := new ELEMENT (K, new SHIP, C);
      HEAD := C;
   end loop;
   -- exit when all tasks are terminated

end SHIPS;
```

Examples 2, 3, and 4 represent three successively more dynamic mechanisms for task initiation. The **cobegin** mechanism is the most structured but its use is restricted to the case when patterns of concurrent execution can be specified in the source program. The array and list mechanisms provide greater power but must be used carefully if undisciplined proliferation of tasks is to be avoided.

Use of **begin ... end** for task initiation and termination imposes a one-in-one-out structure on task execution comparable to that imposed by **while ... end** on control paths of a sequential program. **begin** and **end** are specialized forms of **fork** and **join** commands in much the same sense that **while** is a specialized form of the **go to** command. The **begin ... end** (**cobegin**) construct may be referred to as a 'closed' language construct in contrast to **fork** and **join** which may be referred to as 'open' constructs. Dynamic initiation using **access** types may be referred to as semi-open (semi-closed) since it allows dynamic (open) task initiation, but imposes static (closed) termination at the end of the unit in which the task is initiated.

Ada permits task bodies to be defined and compiled separately from the task specification. The separation of specifications and bodies of program units facilitates the modular construction of large systems from their components. Task bodies, like procedure bodies, may contain a sequence of declarations followed by a sequence of statements.

Example 5 – Task Bodies

task body T **is**
   sequence of declarations
begin
   sequence of statements
end;

    Initiation of a task causes the task body to begin execution, starting with its sequence of declarations. Normal termination occurs when control reaches the end of the task body.

    Both CSP and Ada view a task as a sequentially executable sequence of statements. Ada differs from CSP in defining the specification, body description, and initiation of a task by independent language constructs occurring at textually separate points of the program. CSP requires the name, body, and point of initiation of a task to be specified as a single textual unit.

    Concurrent programming widens the gap between static and dynamic (execution-time) program structure. It introduces a new dimension of complexity into program structure which requires a new set of language primitives to manage this complexity. In the present section we have indicated some of the tradeoffs between static structuring and execution-time flexibility for task initiation and termination. In the sections that follow, structuring mechanisms for synchronization and communication among interacting tasks will be considered.

II Communication, synchronization, and rendezvous

Tasks may communicate with each other by message passing or by access to shared data. Both require synchronization to ensure orderly communication. Task initiation increases the logical concurrency in a computation while synchronized communication reduces concurrency by imposing temporal constraints on task execution.

    The communication primitives of both CSP and Ada are message-based in the sense that communication among processes is by synchronization followed by message passing. Communication in CSP is accomplished by input and output commands. Passing of a value x by an output command q!x in a process p to an input command p?y in a process q is illustrated in the next example.

Example 6 – Message Passing by Input and Output Commands

[p :: [...q!x...] ‖ q :: [...p?y...]]

-- The output command q!x in the process p outputs the value of x
-- to process q that is waiting to execute an input command from p.
-- The input command p?y in the process q inputs a value from a
-- process p and stores the result in y.

Communication must be preceded by synchronization between the input and output commands of the processes p and q. If p reaches its output command first it must wait until q reaches its input command and conversely. Synchronization occurs when both p and q have reached their matching communication commands. The two processes can then communicate. When communication has been completed then separate concurrent execution may be continued. The process of synchronization followed by communication is called 'rendezvous,' reflecting the fact that input and output commands must 'meet' at a common point in time for communication to take place. See Figure 1.

CSP requires the sending process p to identify the process q to which the message is being sent, and requires q to identify the process p from which it is receiving the message. There is no distinction in CSP between calling and called processes. The sending process p and receiving process q are equally active in establishing the communication link. As noted in [1], such two-way naming between communicating processes is well-suited for programming 'pipelines': a sequence of concurrent processes in which the output of one process is the input of another.

Ada tasks require a 'specification' that contains the information used by other tasks to communicate with it. Communication is accomplished through task entries whose role in task communication is similar to that of input and output commands in CSP. The following task

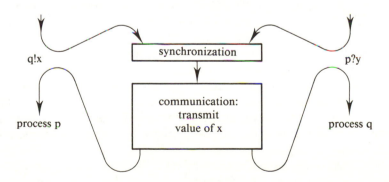

Figure 1   Rendezvous: Synchronization followed by communication.

specification for a queueing task Q has two entries named APPEND and REMOVE with parameters that specify the mode of communication.

Example 7 – A Task Specification

```
task Q is
    entry APPEND (M : in MESSAGE);
    entry REMOVE (M : out MESSAGE);
end Q;
```

Entries are indicated in the task body by **accept** statements that repeat the entry specification and have an **accept** body that specifies the communication to be performed when synchronization has occurred. Calling of a task entry is accomplished by entry calls that are syntactically indistinguishable from procedure calls, and is realized by a rendezvous similar to that of CSP. The example below illustrates calling of an APPEND entry in a queueing task Q from a producer task P.

Example 8 – Rendezvous with One-Way Naming

```
task body P is                  task body Q is
    ...                             ...
    ...                             accept APPEND(M : in
                                    MESSAGE) do
    Q.APPEND(X);                        BUFFER := M;
    ...                             end;
                                    ...
end P;                          end Q;
-- Calling Task P               -- Called Task Q
-- must name the called task    -- does not know the
                                -- names of its callers
```

Execution of Q. APPEND(X) requires rendezvous-style synchronization between the call and the **accept** statement. Synchronization is followed by communication (determined by task entry parameters) and execution of the body of the **accept** statement (between the **do** and **end** keywords). When this has been completed, the calling and called tasks may resume concurrent execution. The body of the **accept** statement could in principle specify an arbitrary computation but should in practice include only computations involving data that are shared between the calling and called tasks, in order to maximize potential concurrency.

Each task entry has an associated entry queue for waiting calls that have not yet been serviced. Tasks impose a serial order of execution on concurrent entry calls that wish to use the computational services it provides. Calls for each entry name are executed in order of arrival, but can be handled only when control in the called task reaches an **accept** statement for the entry name. We shall see later that scheduling of entry calls may involve nondeterministic choice among alternative entries specified in a **select** statement, and that the scheduling rules are quite complex. Scheduling of entry calls for a given task cannot be modified by the programmer.

CSP specifies messages by identifiers in input and output commands while Ada specifies messages as parameters of entry calls. The direction of message passing is specified in CSP by the ! and ? symbols occurring in pairs of sending and receiving processes. It is specified in Ada by the binding modes **in**, **out**, and **in out**. The notion of sending and receiving is separated in Ada from the notion of calling and accepting. Thus, in the following example the calling task is a receiving task.

Example 9 – A Calling Task which Receives a Message

```
                    accept REMOVE (M : out MESSAGE) do
Q.REMOVE(X);           M := BUFFER;
                    end;
```

-- Calling task: Does not specify whether message is to be sent or received.
-- Called task: Specifies message M is to be sent to the calling task upon
-- completion of the body of the accept statement.

Rendezvous in Ada includes synchronization, communication, and execution of the **accept** body. **in** parameters are transmitted before execution of the body, while **out** parameters are transmitted after execution of the body. Thus the semantics of rendezvous is as shown in Figure 2.

The calling and called tasks may reside on remote computers with

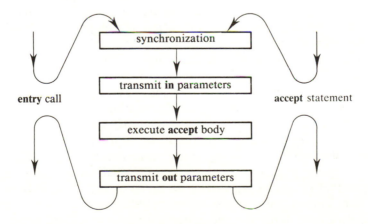

Figure 2   Ada rendezvous: Remote procedure calls.

no shared memory that communicate only by message passing. An Ada rendezvous may be viewed as a remote procedure call which is invoked by a message that transmits values of **in** parameters from the calling to the called task and is terminated by a message that returns values of **out** parameters to the caller. When there are no **in** or **out** parameters the messages become signals that perform synchronization without communication.

In an Ada rendezvous the caller is constrained to wait until execution of the called **accept** statement has been completed. This constraint is stronger than necessary since the caller could resume execution after synchronization and communication of the input parameters to the called procedure. However, delaying the resumption of the caller has the advantage that the caller can rely on the service promised by the **accept** statement as having been performed. Another advantage is that synchronization for the purpose of returning a result becomes unnecessary because it is part of the original rendezvous.

Server tasks for managing access by concurrent processes to shared resources represent an important use of concurrency. The role of **accept** statements in a server task is to allow sharing of the procedures that manage the shared resource by its concurrently executing users. For example, a queueing task allows sharing of the APPEND and REMOVE procedures among producers and consumers of queue elements.

An alternative to the sharing of APPEND and REMOVE procedures is to allow each producing and consuming task to directly append and remove queue elements instead of calling the entry in the server task. This would eliminate the overhead of synchronizing with a server task, which may involve a complete context switch, but would still require mutual exclusion when appending or removing elements to the shared queue data structure. There is thus a tradeoff between the convenience and simplicity of centralized resource management and the potentially greater efficiency of distributed resource management. The circumstances under which this optimization can be performed automatically by distributing the responsibility for executing server tasks to their users have been investigated by Habermann and Nassi and are further examined in [15].

Entry calls such as Q.APPEND(X) and Q.REMOVE(X) must specify the task name Q of the called task. The **accept** statement in the called task need not and cannot name the calling task. This asymmetry of naming between calling and called tasks is similar to that for subprograms. It enables the called module to be written as a library module (server task) without knowledge of the names of its callers. This enables the binding between called modules and their callers to be delayed from the time that programs are written to the time that programs are used. CSP determines a static one-to-one correspondence between calling and called programs that may be modelled by a fixed physical 'wiring diagram'. Ada permits a dynamic many-to-one relationship that may be realized by providing a 'return link' which allows return to the point of call when the rendezvous has been completed.

Ada allows more than one named message to be passed during a single act of communication by entry calls with multiple parameters. CSP also permits more than one named message to be passed in a single input or output command, as in p?(x,y,z). But all messages in CSP must be either input messages or output messages, since the ? or ! symbol is associated with the complete parameter list rather than with individual parameters.

Both Ada and CSP can perform 'pure' synchronization without message passing. Pure synchronization is accomplished in Ada by parameterless entry calls and in CSP by signals such as **request** ( ), which are syntactically written as nullary functions. Pure synchronization in CSP requires matching signal names in input and output commands. For example, p? **request** ( ) in process q can synchronize with q! **request** ( ) in process p.

Ada, unlike CSP, also permits communication through shared nonlocal variables. When shared variables are used in Ada it is the programmer's responsibility to ensure that two tasks do not modify the same shared variable simultaneously. Shared variables allow concurrent processes to communicate efficiently provided the architecture supports shared memory, and accessing conflicts are properly handled.

Access variables provide a mechanism in Ada for implicit sharing between a calling task and a called task. If an access variable is passed as a parameter, the calling and called task share the associated value. As in the case of nonlocal variables, it is the programmer's responsibility to ensure that there are no accessing conflicts. Passing of access variables between tasks can cause serious efficiency and security problems, especially in distributed systems, and could be forbidden by language-level restrictions that prevent access from a given process to the address space of another process.

Message passing may be viewed as a restricted form of sharing where only the communication channel is shared. Sharing of channels by processes raises issues relating to communication protocols that parallel those relating to sharing of variables and are beyond the scope of this paper.

While there are a number of important differences between the communication primitives of CSP and Ada, the underlying synchronization mechanisms are similar. In both languages control must reach synchronization points in both tasks before communication can take place. The first of the two tasks to reach its point of synchronization must wait for the second. When both tasks are ready to communicate we say that a *rendezvous* occurs. During the rendezvous the two threads of control temporarily merge while information between the tasks is communicated. Then both tasks resume independent execution.

III Coroutines, concurrency, and interrupts

It is instructive to examine the similarities and differences between coroutines and concurrent processes. Coroutines, like concurrent processes, have a thread of control that can be suspended and later resumed. Transfer of control between coroutines is realized by **resume** commands which save the current state of the coroutine in a 'stateword' so that it can later be resumed at its current point of execution. The use of **resume** commands in coroutine communication is illustrated in the next example.

Example 10 – Coroutine Resume Calls

```
coroutine P is            coroutine Q is
  -- body of coroutine P     -- body of coroutine Q
  ...                        ...

  resume Q;                  resume P;
  ...                        ...
end;                      end;
```

Coroutine control structures in sequential programming permit multiple threads of control but allow only one thread to execute at a time. Coroutines are sometimes referred to as 'quasi-parallel processes.' Concurrent programs that are constrained to execute on a single processor are like coroutines in that resumption of a given process requires suspension of the currently active process. There are also important differences.

(1) Coroutines explicitly name the process to be resumed, while resumption of concurrent processes constrained to run on a single processor is generally determined by a scheduler.

(2) Processes may be asynchronously interrupted while coroutines are generally assumed to operate in a synchronous environment.

In the absence of asynchronous events, switching among processes could be accomplished entirely by **resume** calls between user processes and the scheduler, and optimizations such as the elimination of critical regions for shared variables could be performed. But the possibility of asynchronous interrupts appears to preclude such optimization. Interrupt messages from remote computers can be just as disruptive as interference from processes that share memory on a given computer.

Concurrent programs are likely to be executed primarily on uni-processing computers for the near future. Logical concurrency may be realized on such computers in an interleaved serial fashion. The degree to which logical concurrency can be realized by coroutines on a uni-processor depends on the extent to which serial computations can be shielded from asynchronous interrupts. Further work is required to understand the circumstances under which logical concurrency can be modeled by coroutines.

A rendezvous may be modeled by **fork, join,** and **resume** commands between calling and called tasks and an operating system. Calling of a task entry as well as arrival at an **accept** statement may be modelled by **resume** commands to the operating system. Rendezvous may be viewed as a concurrent form of coroutine control that requires the operating system to receive **resume** calls from both a calling and a called task, results in temporary merging (**join**) of the calling and called tasks for purposes of executing the body of the **accept** statement, and requires a **fork** with a **resume** call in each branch to resume separate concurrent execution of the calling and the called task when the rendezvous has been completed.

The above discussion indicates that rendezvous is a high-level control structure whose modeling in terms of lower-level primitives such as **fork, join,** and **resume** is quite complex. Since rendezvous is the basic communication mechanism of both Ada and CSP, we must think of both languages as 'high-level' with regard to their communication primitives.

Concurrent programs permit far more complex control structures than sequential programs and require strong structuring mechanisms to manage this complexity. The **cobegin** construct for task initiation and termination and the rendezvous construct for synchronization and communication are examples of such mechanisms. In the next section control structures for nondeterministic selection among alternative courses of action will be considered.

IV   Nondeterminism in CSP and Ada

Nondeterministic control primitives are useful in sequential programming when we do not care about the order in which certain subcomputations are performed. They are useful in concurrent programming when the programmer does not know the order in which concurrent processes will be ready to execute. The examples below introduce the nondeterministic control primitives of both CSP and Ada, and illustrate their differences.

CSP adopts Dijkstra's guarded (nondeterministic) commands as the basic control structure. The two basic commands are alternative commands and repetitive commands.

Example 11 – Alternative Command

[G1 → A1 □ G2 → A2 □ ... □ GN → AN]

```
-- G1, G2, ..., GN are called guards.
-- A guard may contain a Boolean condition followed by an
-- input command, and is said to be true if the Boolean
-- condition is true and the input command is ready.
-- The set of true guards Gi determines the set of actions Ai
-- eligible for execution.
```

-- This alternative command nondeterministically selects
-- one of the eligible actions Ai corresponding to a true
-- guard Gi for execution.
-- If none of the guards Gi is true then an error occurs and
-- the computation is aborted.

The alternative command does not itself introduce concurrency into a computation. But it may be used to map a conceptually concurrent computation onto a single processor by nondeterministic sequential scheduling of its concurrent processes. The conceptually concurrent command [V1 : INTEGER; X?V1 ‖ V2 : INTEGER; Y?V2], which concurrently inputs the values V1 and V2 from the process X and the process Y, can be simulated by a nondeterministic sequential process Z containing an alternative command.

Example 12 – Sequential Simulation of Concurrent Execution

Z :: [V1,V2 : INTEGER; X?V1 $\rightarrow$ Y?V2 □ Y?V2 $\rightarrow$ X?V1]

-- If both X and Y are ready to communicate, choose
-- either alternative arbitrarily.
-- If one is ready to communicate choose that alternative.
-- If neither X nor Y is ready wait for one to become ready.
-- If one or both processes are terminated abort the computation.

As pointed out by Hoare, the semantics of the above command differs from that of the following command.

Example 13 – Simulation that may Result in Deadlock

Z :: [V1,V2 : INTEGER; true $\rightarrow$ X?V1; Y?V2 □ true $\rightarrow$
    Y?V2; X?V1]

-- Z commits itself to an alternative before testing whether
-- processes are ready.
-- If it commits itself to the first alternative and the processes Y and X
-- are synchronized with each other so that Y must communicate with Z
-- before X does, then a deadlock will occur.

CSP does not permit output commands to appear in guards in order to avoid two-way nondeterminism during rendezvous. Thus, sequential simulation of the process Z :: [X!2 ‖ Y!3], which outputs the values 2 and 3 to X and Y, cannot be accomplished using the method of Example 12.

The nondeterministic repetitive command is introduced by the symbol *.

Example 14 – Repetitive Command

*[G1 $\longrightarrow$ A1 $\square$ G2 $\longrightarrow$ A2 $\square$ ... $\square$ GN $\longrightarrow$ AN]

-- The * symbol specifies repetitive execution of this statement
-- until none of the guards Gi are true.
-- Behaves like an alternative command at each iteration in
-- that an action Ai corresponding to one of the true guards
-- is nondeterministically selected for execution.
-- When there are no true guards, the repetitive command is
-- a no-op, whereas the alternative command causes the
-- computation to be aborted.

Repetitive commands in CSP can be illustrated by the following process X which copies characters from a process PRODUCE into a local buffer C and then copies the characters out to the process CONSUME.

Example 15 – Copying Characters via One-Element Buffer

X :: *[C : CHARACTER; PRODUCE ? C $\longrightarrow$ CONSUME ! C]

-- PRODUCE ? C inputs a character from PRODUCE into
-- the buffer C.
-- CONSUME ! C outputs a character from the buffer C to
-- CONSUME.

In order to execute this program, PRODUCE and CONSUME must already have been initiated. Input to X and output from X are handled asymmetrically. The input command PRODUCE ? C is a guard which is triggered when PRODUCE executes a command of the form X ! MESSAGE. The output command CONSUME ! C is executed only when the buffer C has been filled by a PRODUCE command and CONSUME is waiting to execute a command of the form X ? MESSAGE. The input guard PRODUCE ? C causes a delay when the process PRODUCE is executing but has not reached the command X ! MESSAGE, and induces termination of the repetitive command when PRODUCE has terminated.

Note that the program *[C : CHARACTER; PRODUCE ? C; CONSUME ! C] is not equivalent to that of Example 15 because termination of PRODUCE causes this program to abort but causes the program of Example 15 to terminate normally.

Ada has conventional control structures for conditional branching and looping, with a special-purpose construct (the select statement) for nondeterministic scheduling of concurrent processes. The statement *[G1 $\longrightarrow$ A1 $\square$ G2 $\longrightarrow$ A2 $\square$ ...$\square$ GN $\longrightarrow$ AN] of CSP is simulated in Ada by a **select** statement with N guarded **accept** statements and a **terminate** alternative.

Example 16 – Select Statement with Guarded Accept Statements

```
loop
  select
    when guard 1 =>
      accept entry 1 do
        critical section 1
      end;
      concurrently executable code for entry 1

  or
    when guard 2 =>
      accept entry 2 do
        critical section 2
      end;
      concurrently executable code for entry 2

  or
  ...

  or
    when guard N
      accept entry N do
        critical section N
      end;
      concurrently executable code for entry N

  or
    terminate;
  end select;
end loop;
```

-- First evaluate the N guards determining the true (open)
-- alternatives.
-- Then evaluate the subset which are both open and ready
-- to accept.
-- If there are more than one, select among them arbitrarily.
-- If there is exactly one open and ready alternative execute it.
-- Otherwise wait for the first open alternative that becomes
-- ready.
-- A select statement must have at least one branch that is
-- an accept statement; complete syntax is given in Example 19.

The CSP repetitive command does not require an explicit termination statement since it terminates automatically when all guards are false. Ada requires an explicit **terminate** alternative with a complex semantics. It is taken only if all tasks dependent on the program unit on which the task containing the **terminate** alternative depends have either terminated or are waiting at **terminate** alternatives. The set of dependent tasks of a program unit, which effectively corresponds to the set of potential callers of the given task, is not known at the time the task body is written. But it must be known to the system at execution time. Thus callers of a given task are anonymous only at the user level and not at the system level. However, the set of potential callers is determined at runtime and is known only to the system and not to the user, while the callers of a CSP process must be specified at the time the program is written.

Guards in Ada may contain only Boolean conditions, while CSP guards may also contain input commands. The Ada semantics for a guard followed by an **accept** statement is similar to the CSP semantics for a Boolean condition followed by an input command, in the sense that both the truth of the Boolean condition and readiness of the **accept** statement are needed as a precondition for choosing and executing the alternative. However, in CSP an attempt by an input guard to communicate with a terminated process X causes failure of the input guard, while in Ada an **accept** statement cannot know who will communicate with it and waits hopefully, forever. A wait on an **accept** can be avoided by embedding the **accept** in a **select** having an **else** clause. In this case, the **else** clause is chosen for execution whenever rendezvous is not immediately possible.

When more than one alternative is executable then both CSP and Ada may select among these alternatives in an arbitrary manner about which the user cannot make any assumptions. There is no requirement for fairness (a guarantee that each waiting alternative will be selected within a finite time). For example, if the first alternative is always open and ready the selection algorithm could always select it without looking any further, thereby perpetually excluding later alternatives. Issues relating to fairness in Ada are treated formally in [14].

CSP conceptually requires continuous evaluation of both Boolean conditions and input commands appearing in guards until both are ready. However, since the variables in Boolean guards must be local and cannot be changed except by execution of the process itself, Boolean guards need be evaluated just once and input guards corresponding to true Boolean conditions can be polled as in Ada. Ada permits nonlocal variables as well as sharing of local variables by other processes, so that Boolean guards could change their value while a task is waiting for a **select** alternative. Ada therefore provides a precise specification of when in the execution of a **select** statement Boolean guards are to be evaluated.

The CSP program of Example 15 may be realized in Ada by the following program unit.

Example 17 – Replacing Input Guards By Accept Statements

```
task body X is
  C : CHARACTER;

begin
  loop
    select
      accept (M : in CHARACTER);
        C := M;
      end;
    or
      terminate;
    end select;
    accept REMOVE (M : out CHARACTER) do
      M := C;
    end;
  end loop;
end X;
```

The CSP program Z :: [V1,V2 : INTEGER; X?V1 $\longrightarrow$ Y?V2 $\square$ Y?V2 $\longrightarrow$ X?V1] of Example 12 may likewise be written in Ada without guards. In the task body below, the first **accept** statement of each alternative acts like a CSP input guard, while the second acts like a CSP input command in a nonguard position.

Example 18 – Sequential Simulation of Concurrent Execution

```
task body Z is
  V1,V2 : INTEGER;

begin
  select
    accept GETX(X : in INTEGER) do
      V1 := X;
    end;
    accept GETY(Y : in INTEGER) do
      V2 := Y;
    end;
  or
    accept GETY(Y : in INTEGER) do
      V2 := Y;
    end;
    accept GETX(X : in INTEGER) do
      V1 := X;
    end;
  end select;
end Z;
```

The communicating processes X and Y of the CSP example cannot be directly named in Ada. However, local entry names GETX and GETY are used to distinguish between tasks whose value is to be stored in V1 and tasks whose value is to be stored in V2. The **select** statement will make an arbitrary choice if both GETX and GETY are ready to execute, and will choose the first entry that is ready otherwise. Unlike process Z in Example 13, it does not commit itself to an alternative prematurely.

The concurrent programming primitives of Ada include real-time primitives not available in CSP. The **select** statement may include a **delay** alternative which is taken if none of the other alternatives is executed within the specified delay.

Ada has conditional entry calls executed only if the entry can be immediately handled. It has timed entry calls executed only if the entry can be handled within a specified delay. Entry calls are stored in an entry queue associated with each entry name of the called process and are handled by **accept** statements in the order of their occurrence in the entry queue. Tasks which have a priority are handled so that all tasks with a higher priority are scheduled before any task of a lower priority.

The **select** statement is a specialized notation in Ada permitting nondeterminism in the called task. There is no provision in Ada for nondeterminism at the point of call. Another restriction is that Boolean guards (when conditions) can precede only concurrent **select** alternatives (**accept**, **delay** or **terminate** statements). Guards are not permitted for alternatives consisting of just sequential code. Alternatives consisting only of sequential code can be introduced only in an **else** clause, as illustrated by the following syntax for **select** statements:

Example 19 – Syntax for Select Statements

```
selective_wait ::=
    select
      [when condition =>]
         select_alternative
    {or[when condition =>]
      select_alternative}
    [else
      sequence_of_statements]
    end select;

select_alternative ::=
      accept_statement [sequence_of_statements]
    | delay_statement [sequence_of_statements]
    | terminate;
```

The selective wait statement (**select** statement) has a complex syntax and an even more complex semantics, with special rules governing the evaluation and selection of open alternatives, and the execution of **delay**, **terminate**, and **else** alternatives.

In contrast, the CSP mechanism for nondeterminism is orthogonal to its mechanism for concurrency. The statements which follow guards can be either sequential or concurrent. The primary exception to orthogonality is that output guards are not permitted, thereby ruling out rendezvous between two nondeterministic commands. Since output guards are not permitted, every rendezvous is guaranteed to be between a process that is blocked on an output command and a second process that may have several nondeterministic input command alternatives. Such a rendezvous can be realized by a mechanism similar to that used by the Ada **select** statement. Two-way nondeterminism would require a more complex mechanism to guarantee rendezvous.

Nondeterminism at the point of call is useful when a set of tasks must be called and it is not known which of these tasks is ready for execution. Ada can model nondeterminism at the point of call by conditional entry calls, which have the following syntax.

Example 20 – Syntax of Conditional Entry Calls

```
conditional_entry_call ::=
  select
    entry_call [sequence_of_statements]
  else
    sequence_of_statements
  end select;
```

-- Select entry call if it is ready to execute.
-- Otherwise execute sequence of statements following the else.

Conditional entry calls do not directly allow nondeterministic selection among entry calls for alternative tasks. But the effect of nondeterministic selection among alternative tasks may be realized by embedding a conditional entry call in a **for** statement. For example, notification of all tasks in a task array T that an exception has occurred may be accomplished as follows.

Example 21 – Modeling Nondeterministic Entry Calls

```
while not_all_tasks_notified loop
  for 1 in 1..N loop
    if not_notified (I) then
      select
        T(I).ENTRY_NAME;
      else
        null;
      end select;
    end if;
  end loop;
  -- delay a while
end loop;
```

Nondeterminism is achieved by a **for** loop which selects between an entry call and **null** while not all tasks are notified. The conditional entry call allows us to skip tasks which have not been notified and are not ready to rendezvous in favor of those which are ready. In this way, blocking on entry calls to tasks which are not ready to rendezvous can be avoided. However, this solution does suffer from busy waiting; the **for** loop may be traversed an indefinite number of times before a task which is ready to rendezvous may be found. Thus Ada allows two-way nondeterminism to be achieved by two different notations in the calling program and the called program.

As pointed out by Francez and Yemini [7], the asymmetry of the nondeterminism between the calling and called tasks is as important an issue as the asymmetry of naming. Situations where nondeterminism of the caller would be useful include the case when a task wishes to broadcast information to a number of other tasks and there is no information about their readiness to receive the information (conjunctive transmission), such as in Example 21; and the case when a task wishes to call just one of a set of service tasks (say printing tasks) depending on which is first available (disjunctive transmission). In some applications it is natural to include both task calls and **accept** alternatives in a single **select** statement. These include pipeline applications where a given task may wish to choose between sending information to its successor or receiving information from its predecessor, depending on which of these tasks is ready.

Francez and Yemini propose a generalized 'symmetric' **select** statement in which both entry calls and accept statements can appear as alternatives.

Example 22 – Symmetric Select Statement

```
select
    entry calls
        or
    accept statements
        or
    other alternatives
end select;
```

The Ada **select** statement is modeled on server tasks. It does not directly support other 'tasking idioms' such as broadcasting and pipelining which require the more flexible form of nondeterminism provided by the above generalized **select** statement. However, rendezvous between generalized **select** statements may involve many-to-many matching of alternatives. Rendezvous can no longer be handled by considering the unique called task associated with an entry call. A rule for breaking ties is needed when there is more than one pair of matching statements in a given pair of **select** statements, or more than one pair of **select** statements in which there is a match. In the latter case the 'transitive closure' of all potentially matching **select** statements must be considered. These issues are similar to those which arise when output guards are added to CSP and have been addressed, for instance, by Bernstein [2].

V Bounded buffer in CSP and Ada

The nondeterminism of guarded commands in CSP and **select** statements in Ada will be compared using the familiar bounded buffer program as an example. The CSP program includes a declaration of a BUFFER array with a capacity of ten items and of variables IN, OUT. The main loop is a repetitive guarded command to model nondeterministic input of items from an APPEND task and output of items to a REMOVE task.

Example 23 – Bounded Buffer Example in CSP

```
X ::
BUFFER : (0..9) CHARACTER;
IN, OUT : INTEGER; IN := 0; OUT := 0;
*[IN < OUT + 10; APPEND?BUFFER(IN mod 10) → IN := IN + 1;
□ OUT < IN; REMOVE ? MORE( ) → REMOVE !
   BUFFER(OUT mod 10); OUT := OUT + 1]
```

OUT = IN corresponds to an empty buffer and inhibits the consuming process. IN = OUT + 10 corresponds to a full buffer and inhibits the producing process. When OUT < IN < OUT + 10 the buffer is neither empty nor full and selection of the alternative in the repetitive command will depend on whether the producer produces before the consumer is ready to consume.

Note that MORE( ) is a signal sent to the buffer process by the consumer to indicate that it is ready to receive further output from the buffer; it is needed due to the absence of output guards in CSP.

The CSP bounded buffer example may be implemented in Ada by a **select** statement to realize nondeterministic selection of producer or consumer processes, and a loop control structure to implement repetitive execution.

Example 24 – Bounded Buffer Example in Ada

```
task body X is
  BUFFER : array(0..9) of CHARACTER;
  I,O : INTEGER := 0;
begin
  loop
    select
      when I < O + 10 =>
```

```
      accept APPEND (E : in CHARACTER) do
        BUFFER(IN mod 10) := E;
      end;
      I := I + 1;

  or
    when O < I =>
      accept REMOVE(E : out CHARACTER) do
        E := BUFFER(OUT mod 10);
      end;
      O := O + 1;

  or
    terminate;
  end select;
 end loop;
end X;
```

This **select** statement contains two **accept** alternatives whose guards correspond to the Boolean conditions in the CSP repetitive command. Input and output guards with explicit references to external APPEND and REMOVE processes are replaced in Ada by **accept** statements for APPEND and REMOVE entries defined as part of the specification of the called task. The APPEND and REMOVE entries of the Ada task are declared in the task specification so that they are known both to the callers of the task and inside the task body.

VI   Task identification and serial bottlenecks

CSP permits the definition of indexed families of processes, while Ada permits the definition of indexed families of entries. Scheduling of a resource among the family of n processes **user**(1), ..., **user**(n) can be accomplished by the following CSP program.

Example 25 – Mutual Exclusion with Task Identification

resource :: *[(i : 1..n) **user**(i) ? **request**( ) ⟶ **user**(i) ? **release**( )]

This process schedules mutually exclusive execution of code segments between **request** and **release** commands of user processes. It accepts a **release** signal only from the user who executed the immediately preceding **request** signal.

Since called tasks in Ada cannot name their users, this program cannot easily be simulated in Ada. The following Ada program accepts alternate calls of **request** and **release** entries without naming the tasks that request and release the resource.

Example 26 – Anonymous Request and Release

```
task RESOURCE is
  entry REQUEST;
  entry RELEASE;
end;

task body RESOURCE is
begin
  loop
    accept REQUEST;
    accept RELEASE;
  end loop;
end RESOURCE;
```

This task has the same effect as the previous CSP process provided all its callers always perform **request** commands before **release** commands. However, a task that has a release before a request (either inadvertently or maliciously) could completely disrupt mutually exclusive access to the shared resource.

As pointed out by Welsh and Lister [17], user identities can be reintroduced by the use of families of entries.

Example 27 – Identification by Families of Entries

```
type ID is new INTEGER range 1..n;

task RESOURCE is
  entry REQUEST(I : in ID);
  entry RELEASE(ID'FIRST..ID'LAST);
    -- declaration of family of entries
end;

task body RESOURCE is
  USER : ID;
begin
  loop
    accept REQUEST(I : in ID) do
      USER := I;
    end;
    accept RELEASE(USER);   -- USER indexes
      -- RELEASE family of entries
  end loop;
end RESOURCE;
```

A user task must supply a task identification when requesting the resource and can release the resource only by calling the RELEASE entry with the same task identifier. This mechanism will detect inadvertent misuse of the resource but not deliberate misuse such as one user usurping the identity of the other. The use of unforgeable identity keys to make malicious disruption of the scheduler harder is further discussed in Welsh and Lister [17].

Yemini [19] has identified another problem with task identification in Ada. Suppose an application requires an array of ten thousand concurrently executing tasks each of which requires independent initializing information. In CSP, a constituent process of an array of processes can access its index into the array, allowing the process to distinguish itself from the other processes in the array and to access initializing information through its array index. This is not possible for an array of Ada tasks. The only way to pass initializing information to individual tasks of a task array is by initializing entry calls to each task, as illustrated by the following example:

Example 28 – Serial Bottleneck in Task Initialization

```
procedure TEN_THOUSAND_TASKS is
   task type PROTOTYPE is
      entry INITIALIZE (I : in INTEGER range 1..10000);
   end;

   task body PROTOTYPE is
      PARAMETER : INTEGER;
   begin
      accept INITIALIZE (I : in INTEGER range 1..10000) do
         PARAMETER := I;
      end;
      -- concurrent computation using PARAMETER
   end PROTOTYPE;

   T : array (1..10000) of PROTOTYPE;
begin    -- main procedure, create 10000 tasks
   for I in 1..10000 loop
      T(I).INITIALIZE (I);   -- serially initialize each task
   end loop;

   -- concurrent computation by 10000 initialized tasks
   -- exit when all have completed their computation

end TEN_THOUSAND_TASKS;
```

The ten thousand tasks are concurrently created on entry to the main procedure and are immediately suspended at their initialization **accept** statements. The initializing **for** loop is a serial bottleneck to concurrent computation that could easily dominate computation time if the context-switching time for rendezvous is large compared with the time to execute the task body. Yemini has shown that there is no way around this serial bottleneck in current Ada and suggests that this makes Ada unsuitable for expressing certain classes of parallel algorithms.

In highly parallel computer architectures with thousands of processors the elimination of serial bottlenecks such as the above may be a critical factor in making computations economic. Yemini proposes an extension of Ada that allows tasks to have parameters and introduces a **parloop** construct for parallel creation of multiple instances of a task with different parameter values [19]. More research needs to be done on language constructs for highly parallel computer architectures.

VII   Modules and interfaces

CSP processes and Ada tasks are modules that export information to their users and are in turn dependent on imported information from other modules for their execution. A CSP process exports its name to processes desiring to communicate with it and must import the names of all processes with which it desires to communicate. Processes are global to the 'cobegin' command in which they occur. Input and output commands use these names for interprocess communication. CSP variables have types that could be used by a CSP compiler for purposes of type checking. Type declarations for input and output variables could be regarded as part of the process interface.

Processes in CSP cannot share variables and must communicate with each other strictly by message passing. This facilitates the implementation of CSP in a distributed processing environment. However, processes must 'share' the names of processes with which they communicate.

Ada has scope rules to determine the textual scope in which a variable is accessed. A given task may export its name, its entry points, and the types of its formal parameters to any task within the scope of its declaration. It need not be aware of the tasks that wish to use it but must be aware of the entry points of other tasks that it wishes to use. The mode and type of formal and actual parameters involved in task communication may be checked at compile time.

Task modules of Ada have the following interface properties:

(1)   Ada tasks may reference nonlocal variables and thus may communicate both through a shared memory and through message passing. However, the mechanisms for shared variables are orthogonal to those for message passing. By forbidding shared variables we get a set of concurrent processing primitives suitable for distributed processing that is comparable to CSP.

(2)   The rendezvous mechanism, which is a central feature of the communication interface in both CSP and Ada, has a complex semantics. Its complexity in Ada is further compounded by the many special-purpose features of the Ada **select** statement.

(3)   The direction of message passing is determined by the mode of the formal parameter in the entry declaration. It must be compatible

with the type of the actual parameter, but need not be explicitly specified at the point of call.

(4) Entries have queues associated with them. Requests for rendezvous with the entry are serviced one element at a time in a first-come-first-served order.

(5) Ada permits task specifications and task bodies to be separately declared and compiled.

The separation between specifications and bodies of program units is one of the fundamental innovations of Ada. It allows interfaces to be viewed as separate tangible entities that can be separately compiled and manipulated. In order to realize this separation, language designers have carefully partitioned the information in a module into that required by users and that required to implement the resources promised to the user. Study of the partitioning process for tasks provides insight into mechanisms for task communication. For example, the fact that task interfaces consist of entry points with typed parameters indicates that communication by rendezvous is the only mechanism for task communication (global variables aside), and that compatibility of the type and mode of parameters is required during task communication.

The Ada designers used CSP as an important source of ideas in developing the multitasking primitives of Ada, and it is not therefore surprising that Ada has so many features that are similar to CSP. It *is* surprising that there are so many differences. One-way naming is more flexible than two-way naming, as it more readily permits the realization of server and library tasks. The existence of a well-defined task specification separate from the task body encourages an abstract view of tasks whose behavior may be specified separately from its implementation. Replacing the general nondeterministic control primitives of CSP by a special-purpose **select** statement seems to be a step backwards but was dictated by the fact that general nondeterministic primitives were considered to be beyond the state of the art when Ada was designed.

VIII   Ports and entries

The term 'port' is derived from the Latin word 'porta' which means 'door.' It is used in words such as 'airport' to designate points at which goods and people can enter a country or a region. Ports in a concurrent processing module are points at which messages can enter and exit the module. Typically ports are typed – only messages of a specified type may be received from or sent to a given port – and they generally provide temporary storage for messages of communicating input and output processes, and queueing facilities for processes which must wait because port facilities become overloaded. Furthermore, since ports can be accessed by more than one process, they provide an extra level of indirection in the naming scheme for communicating processes. Thus, ports allow communication in which processes do not know each other's names.

We show how ports may be used to model concurrent communication in both CSP and Ada. Communication by two-way naming in CSP corresponds to ports which are associated with precisely one sending and one receiving process. Task entries in Ada can be modeled by ports which are owned by the task in which the entry is declared, can be accessed by anonymous calling processes, and require potentially unbounded queues since the number of waiting calling processes in the environment of use cannot be predicted when the task module is specified.

Silberschatz [16] has suggested a modification of CSP that allows port declarations accessible from other processes (like entries of an Ada task). The modified CSP buffer example below has a port B that is used both for input into the buffer and for output from the buffer. (In order to simplify the presentation, we allow output guards in the following examples.)

Example 29 – Bounded Buffer Example with Ports

```
X ::
B : PORT;
BUFFER : (0..9) CHARACTER;
IN, OUT : INTEGER; IN := 0; OUT := 0;
*[IN < OUT + 10; B ? BUFFER(IN mod 10) → IN := IN + 1;
□ OUT < IN; B ! BUFFER(OUT mod 10) → OUT := OUT + 1]
```

This example differs from Example 23 in that input and output commands of X refer to the internally declared port B rather than externally declared processes. The port B, like Ada entries, is accessible from other processes.

The example below introduces two port names APPEND and REMOVE for appending and removing items from the buffer.

Example 30 – Bounded Buffer Example with APPEND and REMOVE Ports

```
X ::
APPEND,REMOVE : PORT;
BUFFER : (0..9) CHARACTER;
IN, OUT : INTEGER; IN := 0; OUT := 0;
*[IN < OUT + 10; APPEND ? BUFFER(IN mod 10) → IN := IN + 1;
□ OUT < IN; REMOVE ! BUFFER(OUT mod 10) →
   OUT := OUT + 1]
```

This example has a user interface that is more like Ada than like

CSP, but retains CSP guarded commands as its internal control structure. It differs from the Ada bounded buffer task in the following respects.

(1) Its interface does not specify the parameter types explicitly in the PORT declaration, but only implicitly in input and output commands in the body of X.

(2) It has a repetitive command, while the Ada example has a **select** statement enclosed in a **loop** statement.

(3) Ada needs an explicit **terminate** command, while CSP handles termination automatically as part of the nondeterministic control structure.

As a further step in the transition from a CSP-like interface to an Ada-like interface, we can explicitly specify the mode of message passing and the message type in PORT declarations.

Example 31 – Explicit Mode and Parameter Type Declarations

APPEND **in** CHARACTER : PORT;
REMOVE **out** CHARACTER : PORT;

These PORT specifications differ from Ada entry specifications in not specifying a formal parameter name. In Ada one must redundantly specify formal parameter names in both entry specifications and **accept** statements. In designing a PORT interface for CSP we can choose the level of required specification redundancy. There are advantages to the Ada decision to have PORT interfaces that are syntactically indistinguishable from procedure interfaces, but it should be recognized that this introduces specification redundancy.

This section has illustrated the relation between CSP and Ada interface specification by showing how they can both be modeled in terms of ports. The step-by-step modification of CSP-like ports into Ada-like ports provides some insights into design alternatives for ports in concurrent programming languages. Ada believes in explicit specification of the mode and type of parameters for all ports (entries) of its concurrent processing modules, and in handling such specifications as entities which can be separately compiled. CSP does not separate the interface specification from the body of a concurrent processing module, which is clearly less modular.

IX   Monitors, tasks, and packages

Monitors were conceived by Brinch Hansen [8] and further developed by Hoare [10] as modules for managing mutually exclusive access to shared concurrently accessible resources. A monitor has a user interface that provides a set of procedures callable by users, a mechanism for sequential scheduling of calls by concurrently executing users, and an internal mechanism for suspending and subsequently reawakening processes initiated by user calls. Our notation is close to that of Brinch Hansen's Distributed Processes (DP) [9], but contains syntactic sugaring designed to increase readability and bring out analogies with Ada. We assume that a monitor is a distributed process with no direct access to nonlocal variables, and that it can communicate with other monitors only by calling procedures declared in those monitors.

A monitor contains declarations of local data, a set of procedures callable by users of the monitor, and some initializing statements.

Example 32 – Structure of Monitors

```
monitor NAME is
    declarations of local data shared by monitor procedures
    declarations of monitor procedures callable by users
    code that implements monitor procedures
begin
    initializing statements
end monitor;
```

At most one procedure of the monitor may be executing at any given time. When a user calls a procedure of the monitor, and there is no other currently executing procedure, the call can be executed immediately. If the monitor is already executing, the calling procedure is placed on a monitor queue from which called procedures are executed in the order of call.

Both monitors and Ada tasks provide the user with a set of callable resources (monitor procedures, task entries) that are serially reusable in the sense that only one procedure or task entry may be executing at a given time. However, the control mechanisms for scheduling monitor calls and task entries are very different. Completion of the monitor call returns the monitor to an 'initial state' in which it may execute the next monitor procedure on its input queue. In contrast, completion of an **accept** statement in a called task is followed by execution of the statements following the **accept** statement until the task terminates or until another **accept** statement is encountered. Thus, an entry call can execute only if the task reaches a control point where the entry call is expected. One consequence of this difference is that waiting entry calls for a task are placed on different queues for each entry name while waiting procedure calls on a monitor are all placed on the same queue. Other consequences of this difference will become clear later.

Following Brinch Hansen [9], we permit guarded regions with nondeterministic commands within monitor procedures. Guarded regions are introduced by the keyword **when** and have a body consisting of a set of guarded statements. They cause a process to be suspended when all guards are false and to be resumed when a guard within the guarded region becomes true.

Example 33 – Syntax of Guarded Regions

when B1 : S1 □ B2 : S2 □ ... □ Bn : Sn **end**;

-- Execute an arbitrary statement Si corresponding to a true Bi.
-- If no Bi is true suspend and wait until one becomes true.
-- Suspended process is placed in a queue associated with the guarded
-- region.

Monitors containing procedures with guarded regions may be illustrated by a resource scheduler with REQUEST and RELEASE procedures.

Example 34 – Monitor for Scheduling Resources

```
monitor RESOURCE is
  FREE : BOOL;
  procedure REQUEST : when FREE : FREE := FALSE;
    end; end;
  procedure RELEASE: if not FREE : FREE := TRUE;
    end;
begin
  FREE := TRUE;
end;
```

If a REQUEST call occurs while FREE is false then the REQUEST procedure will be suspended until FREE becomes true. Further RE-QUEST calls (along with the original call) will be placed in a queue associated with the guarded region. Internal queues associated with guarded regions receive priority over the monitor queue containing calls by users. Thus when FREE becomes true following execution of a RELEASE call, suspended REQUEST calls have priority over execution of waiting calls from external procedures on the monitor queue.

The **if** statement in the RELEASE procedure is a guarded (alternative) command which aborts when RELEASE is executed with FREE = TRUE. Thus an attempt to release a resource before it has been requested leads to a program error.

This monitor, like the Ada task of Example 26, executes REQUEST and RELEASE calls in alternate order and can be used to schedule mutually exclusive access to a shared resource by a group of distributed processes provided that they always execute REQUEST calls before RELEASE calls.The difference in program structure reflects the fact that Ada tasks consist of sequentially executable statements while monitor procedures have no inherent sequential order. Sequential execution of monitor procedures must be realized by explicit scheduling using a nonlocal variable or semaphore, while sequential execution in Ada is inherent in the control structure.

Sequential execution of entry calls is specified more naturally by Ada tasks than within monitors. However, choice among a set of procedures on the basis of which is called first is specified more naturally by monitors. The monitor call mechanism is effectively a **select** statement with a common queue for all procedures.

It is instructive to compare the effect of nondeterminism in a **when** statement within a monitor procedure and in a **select** statement within an Ada task. Both use a similar mechanism for selecting among viable alternatives when they are immediately executable. Both suspend themselves when no alternative can be executed. But monitors can activate a waiting procedure on an external or internal monitor queue when the current thread of control is suspended, while tasks must wait until an external event allows an alternative to be executed.

The ability to suspend and subsequently reactivate monitor procedures cannot be easily simulated in Ada. Tasks have no internal mechanism for initiating a secondary activity when a primary activity has been interrupted. We shall see below that this causes difficulty in implementing a job scheduler which places jobs on a queue when they arrive and reawakens them when it is their turn to execute.

Monitors have no mechanism for associating guards with callable procedures (like the guarded **accept** statements of Ada). But guarded regions occurring as the first statement of a callable procedure achieve the same effect, as illustrated by the following monitor version of the bounded buffer problem.

Example 35 – Monitor Version of Bounded Buffer

```
monitor X is
   BUFFER : array(0..9) of CHAR;
   IN, OUT : INTEGER;
   procedure APPEND(E : in CHAR);
      when IN < OUT + 10 : BUFFER(IN mod 10) := E;
      IN := IN + 1; end;
   end APPEND;
   procedure REMOVE(E : out CHAR);
      when OUT < IN : E := BUFFER(OUT mod 10);
      OUT := OUT + 1; end;
   end REMOVE;

begin
   IN := 0; OUT := 0;
end X;
```

This monitor differs from the Ada bounded buffer program in that the queues for APPEND and REMOVE are associated with internal guarded regions of the monitor rather than with external entry points. If the buffer becomes full (IN = OUT + 10) then calls of APPEND will wait to enter the guarded region of APPEND and will be placed on an internal queue. An incoming REMOVE call frees a place in the buffer and will cause the next APPEND call on the internal APPEND queue to be executed with higher priority than calls on the external queue. Thus entry queues of Ada tasks may be modeled by internal monitor queues associated with guarded regions.

A monitor may be viewed as a concurrently executable Ada package. Whereas tasks consist of a sequence of instructions whose execution determines a thread of control and which terminate when execution is completed, monitors consist of a set of operations (procedures) on a private data structure. Operations of a monitor, like operations of a package, cause the monitor to 'wake up,' to perform the required operation, and to go back to sleep. Monitor calls must be initiated by a synchronization mechanism such as a rendezvous, and are placed on a queue if the monitor is busy at the time of call. There is a single queue for all operations of the monitor rather than a separate queue for each entry. If an executing operation is suspended because it must synchronize with another process, it is returned to the monitor queue when it is ready to resume execution.

Ada has chosen the procedure model for tasks both in not requiring a called tasks to know the names of its callers and in requiring a task to consist of a sequence of statements rather than a set of callable operations. Neither the coroutine model nor the package model were chosen although there were concurrent programming languages in which these models were being used. Modeling tasks as a concurrent extension of procedures provides a pleasing consistency. However, there is not enough experience with concurrent programming languages to evaluate the tradeoffs between the procedure model, coroutine model and package model as a starting point for the design of concurrent processes. It is generally acknowledged that the concurrent programming primitives of Ada are the least well understood and highest risk parts of the language.

Monitors, like Ada packages, may have initializing statements that perform arbitrarily long computations. The shortest-job-next scheduler of Brinch Hansen [9] has initializing statements that form an infinite loop. This loop is executed as a coroutine with REQUEST and RELEASE procedures called by the processes being scheduled.

Example 36 – Shortest-Job-Next Scheduler

```
monitor SCHEDULER is
    -- local declarations for scheduler
    procedure REQUEST(WHO,TIME : INTEGER);
        -- place process in queue noting value of WHO and TIME
```

```
      -- suspend and call initializing statements as a coroutine
      -- to recompute job with shortest time
      -- wake up when job has been scheduled by initializing code
   end REQUEST;
   procedure RELEASE;
      -- RELEASE resource
      -- so that it can be reallocated by initializing code
   end RELEASE;

   begin   -- initializing statements
      -- Infinite loop activated by REQUEST and RELEASE calls
      -- when REQUEST occurs recompute job with shortest TIME
      -- when RELEASE occurs schedule job with shortest TIME
   end SCHEDULER;
```

The initializing statements are effectively an internal anonymous procedure that is executed as a coroutine with other monitor procedures. However, the mechanism used for transfer of control and synchronization between coroutines within a monitor are guarded regions rather than **resume** calls. Whereas **resume** calls name the coroutine to which control is to be transferred, guarded regions rely on system-defined scheduling rather than explicit naming to determine the next executable coroutine when a given coroutine gives up control, and the processes are executed in quasi-parallel mode.

Now that we have seen a monitor with an active initializing computation, let's return to the analogy between packages and monitors. Ada packages are structured like monitors with a local data structure, a set of callable procedures, and initializing statements. Initializing statements in packages may call procedures of the package and may determine an infinite computation. But it would not make sense in a sequential context to perform an infinite computation at the time of package initialization because this would forever prevent execution of other program units.

Concurrency fundamentally alters strategies for specifying flow of control in sequential components of a concurrent computation. Because monitors are executed concurrently with other components, they may have control structures fundamentally different from those appropriate for a sequential package. In particular, the role of initializing statements within a monitor may be much greater than in packages. In our example the initializing statements consist of an infinite loop and provide the glue for cooperative execution of monitor procedures. They provide a common local program unit that may be thought of as dual to the common local data.

The monitor implementation of the shortest job scheduler cannot be directly mapped into Ada because Ada tasks do not support coroutine-like scheduling within a concurrent programming module. The Ada rendezvous provides no way of suspending a task and subsequently resuming it except by synchronization with another task.

Let us try to implement a shortest job scheduler in Ada by a task with the following specification.

Example 37 – Task Interface with Request and Release Entries

```
task SCHEDULER is
   entry REQUEST(WHO,TIME : INTEGER);
   entry RELEASE;
end;
```

The task body corresponding to this specification must contain **accept** statements for accepting REQUEST and RELEASE calls. A REQUEST call should record its name and time of execution in the REQUEST queue, put itself to sleep, and return control to the calling task when it is reawakened by the scheduler.

Example 38 – Desired Body for REQUEST Entry

```
accept REQUEST(WHO,TIME : INTEGER) do
   -- record identity and time of requesting process
   -- suspend request call until scheduled
   -- return control to calling task when scheduled
end;
```

In deciding when to exit from the **accept** statement we must choose between two unsatisfactory alternatives:

(1) Exit from the **accept** statement after recording the time and identity of the user. This causes premature resumption of the requesting task before it is scheduled.

(2) Remain in the critical section until the request is scheduled. This does not permit RELEASE entry calls or additional REQUEST entry calls to be properly handled.

It appears that there is no way to define a shortest job scheduler in Ada with the above task interface. The task mechanism cannot properly handle entry calls which require synchronization after some initial computation.

The scheduler may be realized by an alternative task specification which replaces the REQUEST entry by the two entries SAVE and ACQUIRE.

Example 39 – Alternative Task Specification

```
type TASK_ID is new INTEGER range 1..n;

task MODIFIED_SCHEDULER is
    entry SAVE(WHO,TIME : INTEGER);   -- record identity and time
    entry ACQUIRE(TASK_ID'FIRST..TASK_ID'LAST);
                            -- family of entries
    entry RELEASE;
end;
```

It is unreasonable to require a user to call both a SAVE and an ACQUIRE entry. However, we can hide the task in a package with the following specification.

Example 40 – Package Specification for Scheduler

```
package SCHEDULER is
    procedure REQUEST(WHO,TIME : INTEGER);
                            -- obtain access to resource
    procedure RELEASE;         -- free resource
end;
```

where the procedure REQUEST, hidden in the package body, contains calls to SAVE and ACQUIRE entries of a local scheduler task, say T:

```
procedure REQUEST(WHO,TIME : INTEGER) is
    T.SAVE(WHO,TIME);   -- call task entry local to package
    T.ACQUIRE(WHO);      -- call entry in entry family
end;
```

The package specification allows users to call REQUEST and RELEASE procedures in a manner that is indistinguishable from that required by task entry calls. A call of the REQUEST procedure gives rise to a SAVE entry call followed by an ACQUIRE entry call of a task local to the package body. Control is returned to the caller of REQUEST only after the resource has been acquired. But these details of implementation of REQUEST calls are hidden from the user.

The structure of the body of the task local to the SCHEDULER package is now given.

Example 41 – Body of Shortest-Job-Next Scheduler

```
task body MODIFIED_SCHEDULER is
    FREE : BOOLEAN := TRUE;   -- initially resource is free
    NEXT : INTEGER;   -- id of task next in line to use resource
    -- declarations for a priority queue and
    -- other local declarations
```

```
begin
  loop
    select
      accept SAVE(WHO,TIME : INTEGER) do
        -- save WHO on priority queue ordered by TIME
        -- let NEXT be the id at the head of the queue
      end;
    or
      when FREE =>     -- grant resource to user NEXT
        accept ACQUIRE(NEXT) do
          FREE := FALSE;
        end;
    or
      when not FREE =>
        accept RELEASE do
          FREE := TRUE;   -- free resource
        end;
    end select;
  end loop;
end;
```

This example illustrates that direct simulation of monitors by tasks is not always possible because tasks cannot simulate the coroutine-like protocols of monitors. However, monitor-like behavior can be realized by providing a package interface for monitor procedures and implementing synchronization within procedures by entry calls of a task local to the package body. It is no accident that simulation of package-like behavior of monitors is facilitated by the use of packages. However, the task synchronization mechanism of Ada is not, without the use of package interfaces, flexible enough to allow **accept** statements to simulate calls of procedures which may suspend themselves during execution.

The package SCHEDULER provides a monitor-like user interface. The package body contains a task that may be executed by package procedures either as a coroutine or concurrently. The mechanisms for synchronization within a package differ from those within a monitor but the user need never know about them.

The synchronization mechanisms for tasks in Ada are at a higher level than semaphores but at a lower level than guarded regions. Task interfaces may be too low-level to be appropriate as user interfaces for server tasks. The present example suggests that packages may be an appropriate user interface for server tasks, and that language mechanisms such as entry calls and **accept** statements should be hidden from users and encapsulated in the package body.

X   Discussion

The paper by Andrews and Schneider [1] is a worthwhile recent review of concepts and notations for concurrent programming. Our comparative study of concurrent programming primitives is most closely related to the study of Welsch and Lister [17]. They have performed a qualitative and quantitative comparison of CSP, DP, and Ada, concentrating on the issues of task identification, synchronization, and nondeterminism. Roberts *et al.* [15] evaluate Ada in the context of real-time multiprocessor systems and conclude that Ada is somewhat lacking in this regard. Van den Bos [4] provides a critical review of the concurrent programming facilities of Ada. Williamson and Horowitz [18] evaluate several concurrent programming primitives from the perspective of their implementability.

Our review of concurrent programming primitives suggests the following conclusions:

(1)   The one-way naming mechanism of Ada is more flexible than the two-way naming requirement of CSP because of its support of server tasks with anonymous callers, in spite of the fact that one-way naming complicates task identification and termination.

(2)   The simplicity and uniformity of CSP guarded commands appears to be preferable to the special-purpose nondeterministic facilities of Ada, but the tradeoffs between the generality of guarded commands and the potentially greater efficiency of **select** statements are not well understood. An alternative which stops short of general-purpose nondeterminism is the symmetric **select** statement that accommodates both task calls and **accept** statements and allows tasking idioms such as broadcasting and pipelining to be realized.

(3)   The entry call interface of Ada tasks cannot support coroutine-like suspension and resumption of subprocesses within a task. However, packages provide a monitor-like interface to procedures which can simulate suspension and resumption of multiple subprocesses by internal concurrency.

As we gain experience in the development of hardware and software for concurrent programming a number of broad application areas are emerging, each with their own tasking idioms. These include numerical applications, embedded applications, distributed processing applications, and computer networks. Ada was designed primarily for numerical applications and embedded applications for tasks that share memory. Numerical applications generally have static patterns of processes whose initiation and termination may be modeled by **cobegin** statements, and are concerned with concurrency primarily to achieve faster computation in repetitive structures. Embedded computations model the evolution of systems and organizations, and must allow dynamic task creation and termination.

Distributed and network applications have special requirements that are sufficiently common to be included in general-purpose languages. Primitives for distributed programming languages such as Argus [12] and Plits [6] and for network languages such as Nil [13] have not been considered in this paper. However, a successor to Ada should probably include constructs such as Argus guardians that model nodes of a distributed system and restrict communication to message passing. It should also include more finely grained access control such as selective access to some but not all entries of a task, and dynamic control of access rights by capabilities that may be passed from one module to another, independently of the block structure mechanism for static inheritance of access rights. The development of a comprehensive set of concurrent programming primitives based on a better understanding of tasking idioms is an important topic for further research.

Another class of concurrent applications not mentioned in this paper are those associated with distributed databases. The reader is referred to [3] for a discussion of issues in this area. Message passing with no shared memory and applications involving multiple activities on a shared database should both be supported in concurrent programming languages of the future. Ada allows both message passing and sharing among concurrent processes but does not provide language-level support for database concurrency control.

We hope that this paper will help readers gain a better appreciation of design issues for concurrent programming languages, offer perspectives concerning design decisions in Ada, and provide input to future designs of concurrent programming languages.

Acknowledgments

The authors would like to express their appreciation to D. Taffs and S. Yemini for critical reading of the manuscript.

References

[1]   G. R. Andrews and F. B. Schneider, 'Concepts and notations for concurrent programming,' *ACM Comput. Surveys*, June 1983.

[2]   A. J. Bernstein, 'Output guards and nondeterminism in "communicating sequential processes,"' *ACM Trans. Programming Languages Syst.*, **2**, pp. 234–238, Apr. 1980.

[3]   P. A. Bernstein and N. Goodman, 'Concurrency control in distributed database systems,' *ACM Comput. Surveys*, **13**, pp. 185–221, June 1981.

[4]   J. van den Bos, 'Comments on Ada process communication,' *SIGPLAN Notices*, **15**, pp. 77–81, June 1980.

[5]   U.S. Dep. Defense, 'Reference manual for the Ada programming language,' MIL-STD 1815A, Feb. 1983.

[6]   J. A. Feldman, 'High level programming for distributed computing,' *Commun. Ass. Comput. Mach.*, **22**, pp. 353–368, 1979.

[7]   N. Francez and S. Yemini, 'A fully abstract and composable inter-task communication construct,' IBM T. J. Watson Research Center, Yorktown Heights, NY, Nov. 1982.

[8]   P. Brinch Hansen, *Operating System Principles*. Englewood Cliffs, NJ: Prentice-Hall, 1973.

[9]   ——, 'Distributed processes: A concurrent programming concept,' *Commun. Ass. Comput. Mach.*, **21**, pp. 934–941, 1978.

[10]   C. A. R. Hoare, 'Monitors: An operating system structuring concept,' *Commun. Ass. Comput. Mach.*, **17**, pp. 549–557, Oct. 1974.

[11]   ——, 'Communicating sequential processes,' *Commun. Ass. Comput. Mach.*, **21**, pp. 666–677, Aug. 1978.

[12]   B. Liskov, 'Guardians and actions: Linguistic support for robust, distributed programs,' in *Proc. 9th Ann. ACM Symp. on Principles of Programming Languages*, Albuquerque, NM, Jan. 1982, pp. 7–19.

[13]   F. N. Parr and R. E. Strom, 'Nil: A high level language for distributed systems programming,' IBM T. J. Watson Research Center, Yorktown Heights, NY, Dec. 1982; to be published in the *IBM Syst. J.*

[14]   A. Pnueli and W. P. DeRoever, 'Rendezvous with Ada – A proof theoretical view,' in *Proc. AdaTEC Conf. on Ada*, Arlington, VA, Oct. 1982, pp. 129–137.

[15]   E. S. Roberts, A. Evans, R. Morgan, and E. M. Clarke, 'Task management in Ada – A critical evaluation for real-time multiprocessors,' *Software–Practice and Experience*, **11**, pp. 1019–1051, 1981.

[16]   A. Silberschatz, 'Port directed communication,' *Comput. J.*, **24**, pp. 78–82, 1981.

[17]   J. Welsh and A. Lister, 'A comparative study of task communication in Ada,' *Software – Practice and Experience*, **11**, pp. 257–290, 1981.

[18]   R. Williamson and E. Horowitz, 'Concurrent communication and synchronization mechanisms,' Dep. Comput. Sci., Univ. Southern California, Los Angeles, CA, Tech. Rep., 1982.

[19]   S. Yemini, 'On the suitability of Ada multitasking for expressing parallel algorithms,' in *Proc. AdaTEC Conf. on Ada*, Arlington, VA, Oct. 1982, pp. 91–97.

21

Schemes for Multiprogramming and Their Implementation in Modula-2

N. Wirth
E T H

Two sets of primitive operators for communication among concurrent processes are presented. They characterize the schemes of communication via *shared variables* and signals for synchronization and by *message passing* through channels. Their use is demonstrated by simple and typical examples, and their implementation is described in terms of Modula-2. Both implementations are based on coroutines for a single-processor computer (Lilith). The primitives for coroutine handling are also presented as a Modula-2 module, demonstrating the language's low-level facilities. A variant of the module for signals is adapted to the needs of discrete event simulation,

   These modules, whose implementation is brief and efficient, demonstrate that, although Modula-2 lacks a specific construct for multiprogramming, such facilities are easily expressible and that a programmer can choose a suitable scheme by selecting the appropriate low-level (library) module. The conclusion is that, if a language offers low-level facilities and an encapsulation construct, it need not offer specific features for multiprogramming. To the contrary, this might hamper the programmer in his search for an appropriate and effective solution.

Key words: multiprogramming, coroutines, simulation, Modula-2.

Introduction

A multiprogram is a program specifying several (perhaps many) sequential processes which are executed concurrently. The objective of multiprogramming is to achieve and guarantee a harmonious cooperation among the processes. This requires principles, paradigms, and primitives

515

for communication among and synchronization of concurrent activities. Numerous concepts have been postulated in the literature, several have been incorporated in programming languages, and thorough comparisons and evaluations have recently been published [6, 9, 10].

Common to these proposals is the notion that individual processes are sequences of actions performed at arbitrary speed. Hence the notion of time is absent, with the exception that synchronization primitives allow a given process to be delayed until a certain condition has been established by other processes. Typically, such synchronizations occur infrequently; hence, we speak of *loosely coupled* processes in contrast to arrays of processes which 'march in locked step'.

Processes have to be synchronized when a cooperation is planned. In computing processes, cooperation is synonymous with communication. Communication implies the exchange of information, i.e., of data. Here we distinguish between two views, namely communication by *sharing variables* and by *passing messages*. They reflect an implied assumption of an underlying mechanism to execute the processes, which, if all details are ignored, distinguishes between individual processors sharing a common store (i.e., being connected by a common bus with high bandwidth), or being truly distributed and communicating via 'thin' wires. Although it is possible to realize each view with a system representing the other, it is appropriate not to carry the idea of abstraction too far, because the price of inefficiency can become unreasonably high. The message passing paradigm has only recently become relevant, because modern technology has made systems with larger numbers of distributed processors economically attractive. It is therefore not surprising that programming languages are mainly oriented towards facilities for communication via shared variables (e.g., Concurrent Pascal, Modula, Ada). The shift of interest to message based communication is evident in Occam [11].

Although we shall see that implementations of the two schemes on a single-processor system are very similar, we must keep in mind that the essence of message passing is that the information is transmitted *by value*, and that no shared variables exist. A system in which so-called messages are pointers (e.g., pointing to sections of a shared buffer), cannot honestly be classified as a message passing system. It is the very fact of transmission by value which makes this scheme conceptually simple and therefore attractive.

A particular instance of synchronization that stems from the paradigm of communication via shared variables is *mutual exclusion*. It embodies a facility to grant exclusive access to certain variables, i.e., to exclude other processes from access until the one process relinquishes its privilege. Mutual exclusion is a practical necessity. Although it can be programmed using synchronization primitives, it is advantageous to offer a specific language construct to express mutual exclusion over specific procedures. Such a construct is the so-called monitor [2]. Message passing systems require no mutual exclusion.

Another important, basic notion is that processes are truly concurrent, that each is executed by an individual processor. In practice, thanks to our postulate that no assumption about speed is made, a processor may be utilized to execute several processes in pieces. We therefore must distinguish between logical processes and physical processors, keeping in mind that this distinction is a matter of implementation technique. If individual computer users represent the processes, we speak about time-sharing systems; if the processes represent distinct concurrent activities of the same user, we rather speak about multiprocessing, but both represent the same idea of utilizing the same processor for several processes. Instead of genuine concurrency we speak about *quasi-concurrency*. The important point is that the processes are conceived such that it does not matter whether several processors are employed or a single one is used in time-shared fashion. This gives the implementor the desirable freedom to utilize his resources optimally, and makes the program independent of the configuration of actual systems. This kind of abstraction from actual processor configurations is at the heart of multiprogramming.

It follows that actual resource management functions must be evoked only when a process specifies synchronization or communication which – as we have seen – are tightly coupled concepts. As a consequence, resource allocation, i.e., processor switching activities, can be hidden behind synchronization and communication statements. The former are implemented in lower-level modules, the latter are calls of procedures of these modules. It is crucial to keep these levels conceptually separated, for this is an indispensable precondition for being able to adapt the resource managing procedures to individual processor configurations.

Subsequently, several schemes of multiprogramming will be presented. Each provides a set of primitives for synchronization or communication in the form of a set of procedures. They are specified in terms of a Modula-2 definition module [8]. Brief examples of applications will be shown which are clients of these definition modules. Then, we discuss their corresponding implementation modules representing the lower-level resource management. The implementations are based on a single processor configuration. The implementation is such that specifics of the used computer occur only rarely.

Coroutines

The basic facility of all systems that allow the switching of a processor from one logical process to another is the *coroutine*. A process is implemented as a coroutine. It is evident to the programmer that processes are executed in alternation, and his program explicitly states the places when a switch must occur. We denote the primitive statement of switching from a coroutine p to a coroutine q by *Transfer* (p, q). The receiving coroutine q is resumed after the Transfer statement it last executed, and finds the computation in exactly the same state as the sender p put it before executing that transfer statement. Hence, this statement is nothing more than an explicit processor scheduling operator.

A coroutine consists of a piece of program specifying the activities and (in general) a set of variables that are local to it. In Modula-2, it is expressed in terms of a procedure and a so-called workspace within which local data are allocated upon procedure calls. A coroutine is established by the primitive procedure *InitCoroutine*. Its parameters are the procedure P which constitutes the program, the address *wsp* of its workspace, and the size of that workspace. A call of InitCoroutine does not activate the coroutine, i.e., does not divert the processor. Instead, it merely initializes a descriptor placed within the workspace such that a later Transfer statement starts the new coroutine with the first statement of P. The workspace address is used as parameter in the Transfer statement. The use of the type ADDRESS manifests that the coroutine is a low-level concept. The two primitives Transfer and InitCoroutine are defined in terms of the following definition module:

```
DEFINITION MODULE Coroutines;   (*NW 16.3.84*)
   FROM SYSTEM IMPORT ADDRESS, ADR;
   PROCEDURE Transfer(VAR from, to : ADDRESS);
   PROCEDURE InitCoroutine(P : PROC; wsp : ADDRESS;
                              size : CARDINAL);
END Coroutines.
```

The following implementation of the module is specific for the Lilith computer. For other machines, it would typically be programmed in assembler code, as the actual procedure bodies consist of a few instructions only. The type Coroutine defines the structure of the coroutine descriptor which is placed at the head of the workspace and represents the coroutine's state while it is suspended (G, L, PC, M, S, H denote actual processor registers).

```
IMPLEMENTATION MODULE Coroutines;   (*NW 18.3.84*)
   (*implementation for Lilith system*)
   FROM SYSTEM IMPORT ADDRESS, ADR;

   TYPE CorPtr = POINTER TO Coroutine;

      Coroutine =
        RECORD
           G :   ADDRESS;
           L :   ADDRESS;
           PC :  ADDRESS;
```

```
    M :    BITSET;
    S :    ADDRESS;
    H :    ADDRESS;
    err :  CARDINAL;
    trapMask : BITSET;
    start : PROC;   (*start of workspace*)
    scnt :   CARDINAL
  END;

PROCEDURE GlobalBase( ) : ADDRESS;
  CODE 25B; 0   (*LGA 0*)
END GlobalBase;

PROCEDURE CALL;
  CODE 357B   (*call procedure variable*)
END CALL;

PROCEDURE TRA(VAR from, to : ADDRESS);
  CODE 256B; 0   (*transfer*)
END TRA;

PROCEDURE Transfer(VAR from, to : ADDRESS);
BEGIN TRA(from, to)
END Transfer;

PROCEDURE InitCoroutine(P : PROC; wspa : ADDRESS;
                               size : CARDINAL);

  VAR cor : CorPtr;

  PROCEDURE SetPC;
    PROCEDURE pc( ) : CARDINAL;
      CODE 40B; 2   (*LLW 2*)
    END pc;
    BEGIN cor↑.PC := pc( ) + 1
  END SetPC;

BEGIN cor := wspa;
  WITH cor↑ DO
    G := GlobalBase( ); L := 0;
    M := { };              S := ADR(scnt) + 1;
    H := wspa + size;  err := 0;
    trapMask := { };
    start := P;              scnt := 0
  END;
  SetPC;
  RETURN;
  CALL; HALT
END InitCoroutine;
END Coroutines.
```

In general, we do not recommend the use of coroutines in this direct
form. It leaves a system no free room for its own resource management

and burdens the program with details of processor allocation that obscure the actual task. However, in cases where the management strategy is simple and obvious, and where efficiency is of prime importance, the use of this lowest-level facility is justified. Such a case is the handling of coprocessors (devices) which communicate by interrupts.

We regard a device (such as a printer) as a processor. Since we usually wish to include in the printer process certain activities, such as buffer handling and status checking, which are beyond the device's capabilities, the process is split up into two parts. One part consists of the (non-programmable) activities of the device (such as the actual printing), the other of the programmed activities requiring the capabilities of a general processor. This obviously requires processor switching. When the programmed part is completed (which involves the activation of the device), the programmable processor is switched by an *explicit* transfer statement to any other resumable activity. When the device has completed its part, it indicates this fact by an interrupt signal. This causes an *implicit* transfer statement to be executed, switching the general processor back to the point of resumption determined by the explicit transfer. The following application example shows this scheme in connection with a laser printer. The programmed part is usually called *interrupt routine*, the part executed by the printer is represented by the explicit Transfer statement. We consider it as crucial to view the interrupt routine as part of the whole, cyclic process, and the interrupt as a non-scheduled coroutine transfer. This view clarifies otherwise rather obscure matters considerably. It raises the machine-level facility of interrupt to that of a structured language and permits implementation without sacrifice of efficiency, which in this case is essential.

```
MODULE PrinterDriver;
  IMPORT ADDRESS, WORD, ADR, InitCoroutine, Transfer;
  EXPORT out;

  CONST size = 100;
  VAR printer, main : ADDRESS;   (*coroutine pointers*)
      buffer : ...
      wsp : ARRAY [0..size − 1] OF WORD;

  PROCEDURE P;
  BEGIN
    LOOP
      (*if buffer not empty, fetch data from buffer and feed them to
          printer interface register, then activate printer*)
      Transfer(printer, main)
    END
  END P;

  PROCEDURE out(data : Type);
  BEGIN (*deposit data in buffer*)
```

```
    IF "printer idle" THEN Transfer(main, printer) END
  END out;

BEGIN (*initialize buffer*)
  InitCoroutine(P, wsp, size); printer := ADR(wsp)
END PrinterDriver.
```

Signals

If we wish to genuinely abstract from the handling of physical processors and wish to assume that an individual agent executes each process, the coroutine concept fails. The key to a better abstraction lies in making processes anonymous in the sense that they do not explicitly specify suspension and resumption of a named partner. Their synchronization is achieved by a new primitive. Such primitives are for example the *semaphore* [1] and the *condition* [2]. Here we present *signals* which effectively are identical to conditions [4].

A signal is declared like a variable, although it has no value and therefore must not be copied or assigned. It can be sent and received. The sending of a signal s signifies that a certain condition P_s (among variables) has been established. After receiving s the receiving process can therefore proceed under the assumption of this condition. P_s is a precondition of send(s) and a postcondition of receive(s). The signal s is the message that P_s holds. These operations are defined in the definition module *Signals*, which also contains a procedure *StartProcess* (P) and a Boolean function *Expected* (s). P is a parameterless procedure that constitutes the program of the started process, and *Expected* (s) means 'at least one process is waiting to receive s.'

```
    DEFINITION MODULE Signals;   (*NW 23.3.84*)
      TYPE Signal;

      PROCEDURE StartProcess(P : PROC);
        (*start a concurrent process with program P*)
      PROCEDURE Send(VAR s : Signal);
        (*one process waiting to receive s is resumed*)
      PROCEDURE Receive(VAR s : Signal);
        (*wait until you receive s*)
      PROCEDURE Expected(s : Signal) : BOOLEAN;
      PROCEDURE InitSignal(VAR s : Signal);
    END Signals.
```

The use of signals is demonstrated by the well-known example of a pair of processes cooperating as producer and consumer of data that are fed through a buffer. The buffer and its associated variables – a count n of the number of items in the buffer and indices denoting the next empty slot and the next item to be fetched – together form the interface between the two processes. This interface is appropriately formulated as a (local) module and constitutes a monitor over the buffer. It contains the signals *nonempty* with associated condition $n > 0$ and *nonfull* with condition $n < N$.

An interface (monitor) typically contains those local variables which are shared among processes. Since signals are inherently shared, signals should only occur within interfaces. The rule that shared objects always be declared within the interface constitutes an important discipline in multiprogramming and was postulated by Hoare and Brinch Hansen.

Shared variables should be protected by mutual exclusion. This means that within the interface the ordinary rules of sequential programming apply, because no two processes can be performing interface actions at the same time. In our example, we have omitted a mutual exclusion specification. We have the right to do so under the assumptions that the program is executed on a system with a single (shared) processor, and that processor switching cannot occur except through sending or receiving a signal.

It should be noted that in this example it is evident which process receives a signal when it is sent, because there are only two participants. But this is not the case in general; the receiver may be any of a number of processes waiting for the specified signal. However, a single send operation will cause (at most) one receive operation (no broadcast).

```
MODULE ProdCons;   (*NW 17.3.84*)
  FROM Terminal IMPORT Read, Write;
  FROM Signals IMPORT
    Signal, StartProcess, Send, Receive, InitSignal;

  MODULE Interface;
    IMPORT Signal, StartProcess, Send, Receive, InitSignal;
    EXPORT get, put;
    CONST N = 8;

    VAR n, in, out : CARDINAL;
      nonfull, nonempty : Signal;
      buf : ARRAY [0..N − 1] OF CHAR;

    PROCEDURE put(ch : CHAR);
    BEGIN
      IF n = N THEN Receive(nonfull) END;
      n := n + 1; buf[in] := ch; in := (in + 1) MOD N;
      Send(nonempty)
    END put;

    PROCEDURE get(VAR ch : CHAR);
    BEGIN
      IF n = 0 THEN Receive(nonempty) END;
      n := n − 1; ch := buf[out]; out := (out + 1) MOD N;
```

```
    Send(nonfull)
  END get;

BEGIN n := 0; in := 0; out := 0;
  InitSignal(nonfull); InitSignal(nonempty)
END Interface;

PROCEDURE Producer;
  VAR 1 : CARDINAL; ch : CHAR;
    text : ARRAY [0..99] OF CHAR;
BEGIN Write("(");
  i := 0; text := "ABCDEFGHIJKLMNOPQRSTUVWXYZ";
  WHILE text[i] > OC DO
    Write("!"); Write(text[i]); put(text[i]); i := i + 1
  END;
  Write("!"); Write(")"); put(OC)
END Producer;

PROCEDURE Consumer;
  VAR ch : CHAR;
  BEGIN Write("[");
    Write("?"); get(ch);
    WHILE ch > OC DO
      Write(ch); Write("?"); get(ch)
    END;
    Write("]")
  END Consumer;

BEGIN
  StartProcess(Producer); Consumer; Write("$"); Write(36C)
END ProdCons.
```

Verification of correctness is now possible without considering possible sequences of process interactions. It begins with establishing an interface invariant, which in this case specifies that the buffer cannot be emptier than empty and not fuller than full: $0 \leq n \leq N$. Together with the postcondition of *Receive*(*nonfull*), $n < N$, and of *Receive*(*nonempty*), $n > 0$, it follows that an item is fetched only if $0 < n \leq N$, and deposited if $0 \leq n < N$. Note that all verification deliberations can be carried out with the interface, because they involve local objects only.

As Dijkstra noted long ago, this classical solution has one drawback: signals are sent more often than needed. For example, *nonempty* is sent whenever the producer has deposited an item, whereas it has an effect only if the consumer had actually been waiting for it. This could be overcome by subjecting *send*(*nonempty*) to the condition (guard) *Expected*(*s*). Dijkstra thereupon proposed the inclusion of this information in the counter variable n and called his solution the 'sleeping barber'. Values $n > 0$ denote the number of items (clients) in the buffer (ante room), values $n < 0$ denote the number of waiting consumers (idle barbers). Once again, we note that the scheme smoothly extends to the case of several consumers and producers without affecting the reasoning necessary to establish correctness. We subsequently present the interface modified to reflect the 'sleeping barber' metaphor.

```
MODULE Interface;
  IMPORT Signal, StartProcess, Send, Receive, InitSignal;
  EXPORT get, put;
  CONST N = 8;

  VAR n : INTEGER; in, out : CARDINAL;
    nonfull, nonempty : Signal;
    buf : ARRAY [0..N - 1] OF CHAR;

  PROCEDURE put(ch : CHAR);
  BEGIN n := n + 1;
    IF n > N THEN Receive(nonfull) END;
    buf[in] := ch; in := (in + 1) MOD N;
    If n <= 0 THEN Send(nonempty) END
  END put;

  PROCEDURE get(VAR ch: CHAR);
  BEGIN n := n - 1;
    IF n < 0 THEN Receive(nonempty) END;
    ch := buf[out]; out := (out + 1) MOD N;
    IF n >= N THEN Send(nonfull) END
  END get;

  BEGIN n := 0; in := 0; out := 0;
    InitSignal(nonfull); InitSignal(nonempty)
  END Interface
```

Implementation of signals

One might suspect that the implementation of the signalling mechanism with its implied processor management might be fairly complex and thereby introduce detrimental inefficiencies. In fact, most available multi-tasking operating systems lend ample justification for such suspicion. Fortunately, an implementation can be straightforward and efficient, as the following solution demonstrates.

It is based on the premise that each generated process is represented by a descriptor. All descriptors are linked in a ring structure. The one process currently under execution is designated by the pointer variable cp. (In the case of a system with several processors, each processor has its private cp.) StartProcess(P) allocates a new descriptor (RingNode) and inserts it in the ring. It also allocates a workspace for the process and initializes the descriptor. The details of initializing the workspace are the same as in the module Coroutines, witnessing the fact that the scheme using signals is built on the basis of coroutines.

Particularly noteworthy is the representation of signals. Instead of letting processes specify the signal for which they are waiting, a signal specifies the processes which are waiting for another process to send it. Hence, a signal is a pointer variable heading the list (queue) of waiting processes. The procedure Send(s) merely implies a coroutine transfer to a process in the list s and the removal of the respective descriptor from the list. Even fairness of scheduling can easily be guaranteed; processes are always appended at the list's tail, and removed from its head. The procedure Receive(s) is only slightly more complicated: After traversing the list down to its tail to append the descriptor of the current process, a search proceeds along the ring to find any resumable (ready) process. If none exists, the system of processes is in deadlock.

A more sophisticated solution would remove waiting processes from the ring, i.e., actually move them from the ring to the signal's list. This would require that they be moved back to the ring when receiving the sent signal. The gain in efficiency (when searching through the ring) does not seem to warrant the additional complexity in pointer manipulation, unless the waiting processes far outnumber the ready ones.

```
IMPLEMENTATION MODULE Signals;   (*NW 23.3.84*)
FROM SYSTEM IMPORT ADDRESS, WORD, ADR, TSIZE;
FROM Heap IMPORT Allocate;

CONST WorkspaceSize = 200B;

TYPE Signal = POINTER TO RingNode;
     CorPtr = POINTER TO Coroutine;

RingNode =
  RECORD
    next, prev : Signal;   (*ring*)
    queue :    Signal;     (*queue of waiting processes*)
    cor :      CorPtr;
    ready :    BOOLEAN
  END;

Coroutine =
  RECORD
    G :       ADDRESS;
    L :       ADDRESS;
    PC :      ADDRESS;
    M :       BITSET;
    S :       ADDRESS;
    H :       ADDRESS;
    err :     CARDINAL;
    trapMask : BITSET;
    start :   PROC;   (*start of workspace*)
    scnt :    CARDINAL;
    wsp :     ARRAY [0..WorkspaceSize - 1] OF WORD
  END;
```

```
    VAR cp : Signal;   (*current process*)
        aux : Signal;
        free : Signal;   (*chain of free process descriptors*)

PROCEDURE TRANSFER(VAR from, to : CorPtr);
    CODE 256B; 0
END TRANSFER;

PROCEDURE StartProcess(P : PROC);

    PROCEDURE GlobalBase( ) : ADDRESS;
        CODE 25B ; 0   (*LGA 0*)
    END GlobalBase;

    PROCEDURE CALL;
        CODE 357B   (*CF*)
    END CALL;

    PROCEDURE SetPCandTransfer;
        PROCEDURE pc( ) : CARDINAL;
            CODE 40B; 2   (*LLW 2*)
        END pc;
    BEGIN cp↑.cor↑.PC := pc( ) + 1; TRANSFER(aux↑.cor, cp↑.cor)
    END SetPCandTransfer;

BEGIN aux := cp;
    (*allocate a RingNode and a workspace contiguously*)
    IF free = NIL THEN
        Allocate(cp, TSIZE(RingNode)); Allocate(cp↑.cor,
                                                TSIZE(Coroutine))
    ELSE cp := free; free := free↑.next
    END;
    WITH cp↑ DO
        next := aux↑.next; prev := aux; queue := NIL; ready := TRUE
    END;
    aux↑.next := cp; cp↑.next↑.prev := cp;
    WITH cp↑.cor↑ DO
        G := GlobalBase( );   L := 0;
        M := { };               S := ADR(wsp);
        H := ADR(wsp) + WorkspaceSize;
        err := 0;       trapMask := { };
        start := P;     scnt := 0
    END;
    SetPCandTransfer;
    RETURN;

    CALL;   (*activate process body P*)
    aux := cp; cp := aux↑.next;
    cp↑.prev := aux↑.prev; aux↑.prev↑.next := cp;
    aux↑.next := free; free := aux; aux := cp;
    WHILE NOT cp↑.ready & (cp # aux) DO cp := cp↑.next END;
    IF cp↑.ready THEN TRANSFER(free↑.cor, cp↑.cor) END;
    HALT (*deadlock*)
END StartProcess;
```

```
PROCEDURE Send(VAR s : Signal);
  VAR this : Signal;
BEGIN this := cp;
  IF s # NIL THEN cp := s;
    s := cp↑.queue; cp↑.ready := TRUE
  ELSE (*release*)
    REPEAT cp := cp↑.next UNTIL cp↑.ready
  END;
  IF cp # this THEN TRANSFER(this↑.cor, cp↑.cor) END
END Send;

PROCEDURE Receive(VAR s : Signal);
  VAR this : Signal;
BEGIN (*insert cp at end of queue s*)
  IF s = NIL THEN s := cp
  ELSE this := s;
    WHILE this↑.queue # NIL DO this := this↑.queue END;
    this↑.queue := cp
  END;
  this := cp; this↑.queue := NIL;
  REPEAT cp := cp↑.next UNTIL cp↑.ready;
  this↑.ready := FALSE;
  IF cp = this THEN (*deadlock*) HALT END;
  TRANSFER(this↑.cor, cp↑.cor)
END Receive;

PROCEDURE Expected(s : Signal) : BOOLEAN;
BEGIN RETURN s # NIL
END Expected;

PROCEDURE InitSignal(VAR s : Signal);
BEGIN s := NIL
END InitSignal;

BEGIN free := NIL; Allocate(cp, TSIZE(RingNode));
  WITH cp↑ DO
    next := cp; prev := cp; ready := TRUE
  END
END Signals.
```

If a process reaches the end of the procedure which constitutes its body, the process supposedly terminates. Control then returns to the point after the statement CALL which initiated the process. The subsequent statements transfer the processor to any ready process in the ring, and they reclaim the terminating process's workspace by inserting it into the list headed by the pointer variable *free*. Hence, the presented implementation also incorporates a primitive management of workspace allocation and recycling. Normally, process creation and termination occurs far less frequently than the sending of a signal, i.e. the switching of the processor. As far as efficiency is concerned, only the procedures Send and Receive need to be planned carefully.

Closely related to signals are also the semaphores as originally postulated by Dijkstra. A semaphore consists of a counter and an associated signal. The P-operation decrements the counter and, if the result is negative, waits until the signal is received. The V-operation increments the counter and, if the result is not positive, sends the signal. A negative value of the counter indicates how many processes are waiting in the signal's queue.

Channels

If a multiprocess system consists of truly distributed processors connected with data channels rather than of processors accessing a common store, communication cannot be expressed using shared variables. One will then prefer the scheme proposed by Hoare in CSP [5] and embodied by the language Occam [11]. Basically it consists of the following facilities:

(1) The statement PAR S_0, S_1 ... S_{n-1} specifies that the statements S_0, S_1, ..., S_{n-1} are executable concurrently.

(2) The declaration CHAN ch introduces a communication channel.

(3) The statement 'ch?x' specifies the reception of a value from channel ch and the value's assignment to variable x.

(4) The statement 'ch!x' specifies the evaluation of expression x and the sending of the resulting value over channel ch.

We first propose a translation of the terse Occam notation into an equivalent form in Modula-2, and then present an implementation. Evidently, the mentioned Occam facilities are defined in terms of a definition module.

```
DEFINITION MODULE Channels; (*NW 21.3.84*)
  TYPE Message = INTEGER;
       Process;
       Channel = RECORD prod, cons : Process END;

  PROCEDURE Parallel(P,Q : PROC);
  PROCEDURE Send(VAR ch : Channel; msg : Message);
  PROCEDURE Receive(VAR ch : Channel; VAR msg : Message);
  PROCEDURE SenderWaiting(VAR ch : Channel) : BOOLEAN;
  PROCEDURE ReceiverWaiting(VAR ch : Channel) : BOOLEAN;
  PROCEDURE InitChannel(VAR ch : Channel);
END Channels.
```

In order to emphasize their relation to the scheme using signals, the output operator ! is translated into Send, the input operator ? into Receive. The signal, which may be regarded as an empty message, is replaced by a message having a value. The Occam statement PAR P Q is translated into the statement Parallel(P′, Q′), where P′ and Q′ are (parameterless) procedures representing the Occam statements P and Q. PAR P Q R is expressed as Parallel(P, QR), where QR is a procedure with body Parallel(Q, R). The additional function procedures SenderWaiting and ReceiverWaiting are analogous to Expected(s).

The properties of channels are the following:

(1) If a sender outputs a message to a channel, it is delayed until a receiver picks up the message (at the other end of the channel). This may be instantaneous, if a receiver was already waiting on the channel.

(2) A receiver expecting input from a channel gets delayed until a sender outputs a message on the channel. This may be instantaneous, if a sender was already waiting for his message to be picked up.

It follows that a channel automatically also acts as a synchronizing agent; synchronization and communication have become the same. Also, the channel is truly a 'wire' and has no implied buffering capability. It therefore forces sender and receiver to a rendezvous; the channel is not a mailbox, just a meeting point.

The paradigm of Occam is that a program represents a system of processes connected by channels, and that the connections are fixed. We may therefore assume that each channel connects one sender with one receiver.

The following application demonstrates a simple but typical system using a channel. Process P reads a sequence of numbers from the input medium and feeds them into the channel. Every 4th number is a checksum and is not passed on. Process Q receives the numbers from the channel, computes a checksum after every 7th number, and feeds them to the output medium.

```
MODULE Sequences;
  FROM Channels IMPORT Channel, InitChannel, Parallel, Send, Receive;
  FROM InOut IMPORT ReadInt, WriteInt;

  VAR ch : Channel;

  PROCEDURE P;
    VAR i : CARDINAL; x, sum : INTEGER;
  BEGIN ReadInt(x);
    WHILE x # 0 DO i := 3;
      WHILE i > 0 DO
        Send(ch, x); sum := sum + x; i := i − 1; ReadInt(x)
      END;
      sum := sum + x; (*check sum = 0*) ReadInt(x)
    END;
    Send(ch, 0)
  END P;
```

```
    PROCEDURE Q;
      VAR i : CARDINAL; x, sum : INTEGER;
    BEGIN Receive(ch, x);
      WHILE x # 0 DO
        i := 6; sum := 0;
        WHILE i > 0 DO
          WriteInt(x, 6); sum := sum − x; i := i − 1; Receive(ch, x)
        END;
        WriteInt(sum, 6)
      END

    END Q;

    BEGIN InitChannel(ch); Parallel(P, Q)
    END Sequences.
```

Implementation of channels

The implementation of channels resembles that of signals to a high
degree. Processes are again linked in a ring, each element (node) containing (a pointer to) a coroutine workspace. A further field stores the
address of the message to be passed. It is necessary to store an address
instead of the message itself, because then upon arrival of the sender it
can store the message in the variable designated by the waiting receiver's
VAR parameter.

The data type *Channel* assumes the role of the type Signal. It
contains two record fields, one for a waiting receiver, the other for a waiting sender. The alternative solution with a single process field and a
discriminator between senders and receivers was rejected, because it
requires a more cumbersome program.

Because of the chosen scheme of process creation, processes always
occur in pairs. Each process descriptor therefore contains a field
designating the partner. Whereas in the case of signals the termination of
a process had no other effect, in this case termination implies an implicit
synchronization. The creating process proceeds only after both offsprings
have terminated. This requires knowledge about the identity of the partner.
In fact, in the presented implementation the statement Parallel(P, Q)
does not create two new processes, but rather only one. The other is
identical to the generating process. This is practically mandatory,
because otherwise half of the requested workspace would be wasted for
ancestors awaiting termination of both of their offsprings.

```
    IMPLEMENTATION MODULE Channels;   (*NW 25.3.84*)
      FROM SYSTEM IMPORT ADDRESS, WORD, ADR, TSIZE;
      FROM Heap IMPORT Allocate;

      CONST WorkspaceSize = 200B;
```

```
TYPE
  Process = POINTER TO RingNode;
  ProcessState = (ready, waiting, terminated);
  CorPtr = POINTER TO Coroutine;

  RingNode =
    Record
      next, prev : Process;   (*ring*)
      partner :    Process;
      cor :        CorPtr;
      state :      ProcessState;
      msgAdr :     POINTER TO Message
    END;

  Coroutine =
    RECORD
      G :  ADDRESS;
      L :  ADDRESS;
      PC : ADDRESS;
      M :  BITSET;
      S :  ADDRESS;
      H :  ADDRESS;
      err : CARDINAL;
      trapMask : BITSET;
      start : PROC;  (*start of workspace*)
      scnt : CARDINAL;
      wsp : ARRAY [0..WorkspaceSize − 1] OF WORD
    END;

VAR cp  : Process;   (*current process*)
    free : Process;   (*chain of free process descriptors*)
    aux : Process;

PROCEDURE TRANSFER(VAR from, to : CorPtr);
  CODE 256B; 0
END TRANSFER;

PROCEDURE Parallel(P,Q : PROC);
  VAR new : Process; (*process to be created*)

  PROCEDURE GlobalBase( ) : ADDRESS;
    CODE 25B; 0   (*LGA 0*)
  END GlobalBase;

  PROCEDURE CALL;
    CODE 357B   (*CF*)
  END CALL;

  PROCEDURE SetPCandCall;

    PROCEDURE pc( ) : CARDINAL;
      CODE 40B; 2   (*LLW 2*)
    END pc;
```

```
    BEGIN new↑.cor↑.PC := pc( ) + 1;
      P;
      WHILE new↑.state # terminated DO
        (*release*) aux := cp;
        REPEAT cp := cp↑.next UNTIL cp↑.state = ready;
        IF cp = aux THEN HALT (*deadlock*) END;
        aux↑.state := terminated; TRANSFER (aux↑.cor, cp↑.cor)
      END;
      aux := new↑.prev; new↑.prev↑.next := new↑.next;
      new↑.next↑.prev := aux; new↑.next := free; free := new
    END SetPCandCall;

BEGIN
  (*allocate a RingNode and a workspace contiguously*)
  IF free = NIL THEN
    Allocate (new, TSIZE (RingNode));
    Allocate (new↑.cor, TSIZE (Coroutine))
  ELSE new := free; free := free↑.next
  END;
  WITH new↑ DO
    next := cp↑.next; prev := cp; partner := cp; state := ready
  END;
  cp↑.next := new; new↑.next↑.prev := new;
  WITH new↑.cor↑ DO
    G := GlobalBase( );   L := 0;
    M := { };             S := ADR (wsp);
    H := ADR (wsp) + WorkspaceSize;
    err := 0;             trapMask := { };
    start := Q;           scnt := 0
  END;
  SetPCandCall;
  RETURN;

  CALL(*Q*);
  aux := cp;
  IF cp↑.partner↑.state = terminated THEN
    cp := cp↑.partner; cp↑.state := ready
  ELSE
    REPEAT cp := cp↑.next UNTIL cp↑.state = ready;
    IF cp = new THEN HALT (*deadlock*) END
  END;
  aux↑.state := terminated; TRANSFER (aux↑.cor, cp↑.cor)
END Parallel;

PROCEDURE Send(VAR ch : Channel; msg : Message);
  VAR this : Process;
BEGIN this := cp;
  IF ch.cons # NIL THEN (*wake up consumer*)
    cp := ch.cons; ch.cons := NIL;
    cp↑.state := ready; cp↑.msgAdr↑ := msg
```

```
    ELSE (*wait for consumer*)
      IF ch.prod # NIL THEN HALT END;
      ch.prod := cp; cp↑.msgAdr := ADR(msg);
      REPEAT cp := cp↑.next UNTIL cp↑.state = ready;
      this↑.state := waiting;
      IF cp = this THEN HALT (*deadlock*) END
    END;
    TRANSFER(this↑.cor, cp↑.cor)
  END Send;

  PROCEDURE Receive(VAR ch : Channel; VAR msg : Message);
    VAR this : Process;
  BEGIN this := cp;
    IF ch.prod # NIL THEN (*wake up consumer*)
      cp := ch.prod; ch.prod := NIL;
      cp↑.state := ready; msg := cp↑.msgAdr↑
    ELSE (*wait for producer*)
      IF ch.prod # NIL THEN HALT END;
      ch.cons := cp; cp↑.msgAdr := ADR(msg);
      REPEAT cp := cp↑.next UNTIL cp↑.state = ready;
      this↑.state := waiting;
      IF cp = this THEN HALT (*deadlock*) END
    END;
    TRANSFER(this↑.cor, cp↑.cor)
  END Receive;

  PROCEDURE SenderWaiting(VAR ch : Channel) : BOOLEAN;
  BEGIN RETURN ch.prod # NIL
  END SenderWaiting;

  PROCEDURE ReceiverWaiting(VAR ch : Channel) : BOOLEAN;
  BEGIN RETURN ch.cons # NIL
  END ReceiverWaiting;

  PROCEDURE InitChannel(VAR ch : Channel);
  BEGIN ch.prod := NIL; ch.cons := NIL
  END InitChannel;

BEGIN free := NIL; Allocate(cp, TSIZE(RingNode));
  WITH cp↑ DO
    next := cp; prev := cp; state := ready
  END
END Channels.
```

The complexity of the implementation of Channels is somewhat greater than that of Signals. This is mainly due to the synchronization upon termination. Also, the scheme is less flexible, because each channel can be associated (at a time) with only one sender and one receiver, whereas a signal may (at the same time) be expected by many processes. But this reflects the natural situation in many cases, and a superchannel to which many senders and receivers can be connected simultaneously would certainly be a bad choice for a communications primitive, because its characteristics would already be nontrivial to describe, let alone to implement. Nevertheless, it is probably fair to say that the solution with signals is to be preferred over channels, if the underlying system consists of shared processors and a common, shared store.

Simulation

A language with a facility to express concurrent processes and an implementation with low overhead in process switching are particularly well suited for the simulation of discrete event systems. The previously presented implementation requires only a minimal extension to cater to the needs of discrete event simulation. We subsequently present a possible solution which in its concepts goes back to Simula and proposals by Hoare [3].

The only addition needed, in fact, is the concept of time. In a discrete event simulation, each agent belongs to a category (class, type) of processes (such as customers, tellers, service men in a supermarket), and its behaviour is therefore characterized by a fixed, sequential program. Each identifiable action, taking time t in reality, is in the simulation program expressed by an appropriate statement followed by $hold(t)$. The latter statement suspends the process, until system time has increased by t.

```
DEFINITION MODULE Simulation;   (*NW 3.4.84*)
  TYPE Signal;
    Process = PROCEDURE (CARDINAL);

  VAR Time : CARDINAL;   (*read only*)

  PROCEDURE StartProcess(P : Process; n : CARDINAL);
    (*start a concurrent process with program P(n)*)
  PROCEDURE Send(VAR s : Signal);
    (*one process waiting to receive s is resumed*)
  PROCEDURE Receive(VAR s : Signal);
    (*wait until you receive s*)
  PROCEDURE Hold(t : CARDINAL);
    (*hold process for t seconds*)
  PROCEDURE InitSignal(VAR s : Signal);
    (*compulsory initialization*)
END Simulation.
```

An example of an application demonstrating the ease with which discrete event systems can be expressed in terms of these simple facilities is the following problem:

One day, the Chinese Emperor issued the order that the minimal distance to each of his empire's villages from the capital was to be determined. The method to be followed was the following: Large groups of scouts were to march out into the country, notably at constant speed, in each direction, i.e. on each emanating path. Once they would encounter the next village, the group would split up, each subgroup proceeding on an outgoing path. One man would march back to report the time it took to reach the village, another would remain to report to groups arriving later that he had been first.

Our solution is based on each village being represented by a record specifying the village's name (number), the number of outgoing paths, and for each path its destination and distance. The record is also used to record whether the village had been visited already.

```
MODULE Army;   (*NW 4.5.84*)
  FROM InOut IMPORT Done,
          OpenInput, ReadCard, Write, WriteLn, WriteCard, CloseInput;
  FROM Simulation IMPORT Time, StartProcess, Hold;
  CONST MaxNofVil = 32; MaxNofPaths = 8;
  TYPE Village =
    RECORD nofp : CARDINAL;
      visited : BOOLEAN;
      path : ARRAY [0..MaxNofPaths − 1] OF RECORD destination,
              distance : CARDINAL END
    END;

  VAR i : CARDINAL;
      vil : ARRAY [0..MaxNofVil − 1] OF Village;

  PROCEDURE Scout(x : CARDINAL);
  (*x = currentVillage * MaxNofPath + direction*)
    VAR here, dir : CARDINAL;
    BEGIN Write(" +"); here := x DIV MaxNofPaths; dir := x MOD
            MaxNofPaths;
      LOOP Hold(vil[here].path[dir].distance);
        here := vil[here].path[dir].destination;
        IF vil[here].visited THEN EXIT END;
        WriteCard(here, 6); WriteCard(Time, 6); WriteLn;
        vil[here].visited := TRUE; dir := vil[here].nofp − 1;
        WHILE dir > 0 DO
          StartProcess(Scout, here * MaxNofPaths + dir); dir := dir − 1
        END
      END;
      Write(" −")
    END Scout;

  PROCEDURE ReadData;
    VAR A, B, d, i : CARDINAL;
    BEGIN OpenInput("NUM"); ReadCard(A);
      FOR i := 0 TO MaxNofVil − 1 DO
        vil[i].nofp := 0; vil[i].visited := FALSE
      END;
```

```
      WHILE Done DO
        ReadCard(B); ReadCard(d);
        WITH vil[A] DO
          path[nofp].destination := B; path[nofp].distance := d;
          nofp := nofp + 1
        END;
        WITH vil[B] DO
          path[nofp].destination := A; path[nofp].distance := d;
          nofp := nofp + 1
        END;
        ReadCard(A)
      END;
      CloseInput
    END ReadData;

  BEGIN ReadData; vil[0].visited := TRUE;
    FOR i := 0 TO vil[0].nofp − 1 DO StartProcess(Scout, i) END;
    Hold(9999); Write("!"); WriteLn
  END Army.
```

Implementation of simulation

Implementation is straightforward: delayed processes are queued in a list corresponding to an internal signal called TQ, which is sent whenever no process remains ready at the current time. In contrast to the scheme used in module Signals, however, this list is not a first-in first-out queue, but the processes are ordered according to their wake-up time. When no ready process is found (either after a Receive or a hold statement), instead of detecting deadlock, the first process in the queue TQ is resumed after increasing system time (Time) to the value specified as wake-up time. This scheme requires an additional field in the process descriptor, and insertion after hold must include a search for the proper insertion point. Actually, the signal TQ represents a level of lower priority: delayed processes are resumed, i.e., the system time is stepped up only after no processes are found ready at the current time.

```
    IMPLEMENTATION MODULE Simulation;   (*NW 3.4.84*)
      FROM SYSTEM IMPORT ADDRESS, WORD, ADR, TSIZE;
      FROM Heap IMPORT Allocate;

      CONST WorkspaceSize = 200B;

      TYPE Signal = POINTER TO RingNode;
           CorPtr = POINTER TO Coroutine;

        RingNode =
        RECORD
          next, prev : Signal;   (*ring*)
          queue :      Signal;   (*queue of waiting processes*)
```

```
    cor :        CorPtr;
    ready :      BOOLEAN;
    waketime :   CARDINAL
  END;

Coroutine =
  RECORD
    G :          ADDRESS;
    L :          ADDRESS;
    PC :         ADDRESS;
    M :          BITSET;
    S :          ADDRESS;
    H :          ADDRESS;
    err :        CARDINAL;
    trapMask :   BITSET;
    start :      Process;   (*start of workspace*)
    param :      CARDINAL;
    scnt :       CARDINAL;
    wsp :        ARRAY [0..WorkspaceSize − 1] OF WORD
  END;

VAR cp : Signal;   (*current process*)
    aux : Signal;
    free : Signal;   (*chain of free process descriptors*)
    TQ : Signal;   (*chain of delayed processes; time queue*)

PROCEDURE TRANSFER(VAR from, to : CorPtr);
  CODE 256B; 0
END TRANSFER;

PROCEDURE StartProcess(P : Process; n : CARDINAL);

  PROCEDURE GlobalBase( ) : ADDRESS;
    CODE 25B; 0   (*LGA 0*)
  END GlobalBase;

  PROCEDURE CALL;
    CODE 357B   (*CF*)
  END CALL;

  PROCEDURE SetPCandTransfer;
    PROCEDURE pc( ) : CARDINAL;
      CODE 40B; 2 (*LLW 2*)
    END pc;
  BEGIN cp↑.cor↑.PC := pc( ) + 1; TRANSFER(aux↑.cor, cp↑.cor)
  END SetPCandTransfer;

BEGIN aux := cp;
  (*allocate a RingNode and a coroutine workspace*)
  IF free = NIL THEN
    Allocate(cp, TSIZE(RingNode)); Allocate(cp↑.cor,
      TSIZE(Coroutine))
```

```
    ELSE cp := free; free := free↑.next
  END;
  WITH cp↑ DO
      next := aux↑.next; prev := aux; queue := NIL; ready := TRUE
  END;
  aux↑.next := cp; cp↑.next↑.prev := cp;
  WITH cp↑.cor↑ DO
    G := GlobalBase( ); L := 0;
    M := { };              S := ADR(WSP);
    H := ADR(wsp) + WorkspaceSize;
    err := 0;        trapMask := { };
    start := P;
    param := n;    scnt := 1
  END;
  SetPCandTransfer;
  RETURN;

  CALL;   (*activate process body P*)
  aux := cp; cp := aux↑.next;
  cp↑.prev := aux↑.prev; aux↑.prev↑.next := cp;
  aux↑.next := free; free := aux; aux := cp;
  WHILE NOT cp↑.ready & (cp # aux) DO cp := cp↑.next END;
  IF cp↑.ready THEN TRANSFER(free↑.cor, cp↑.cor)
  ELSIF TQ # NIL THEN
    cp := TQ; TQ := TQ↑.queue; cp↑.ready := TRUE;
    Time := cp↑.waketime; TRANSFER(free↑.cor, cp↑.cor)
  ELSE (*deadlock*) HALT
  END
END StartProcess;

PROCEDURE Send(VAR s : Signal);
  VAR this : Signal;
BEGIN
  IF s # NIL THEN
    this := cp; cp := s;
    WITH cp↑ DO
     ·s := queue; ready := TRUE
    END;
    TRANSFER(this↑.cor, cp↑.cor)
  END
END Send;

PROCEDURE release;
  VAR this : Signal;
BEGIN
  this := cp;
  REPEAT cp := cp↑.next UNTIL cp↑.ready;
  this↑.ready := FALSE;
  IF cp = this THEN (*advance time*)
```

```
      IF TQ # NIL THEN
        cp := TQ; TQ := TQ↑.queue; cp↑.ready := TRUE;
        TIME := cp↑.waketime
      ELSE (*deadlock*) HALT
      END
    END;
    TRANSFER(this↑.cor, cp↑.cor)
  END release;

  PROCEDURE Receive(VAR s : Signal);
    VAR this : Signal;
  BEGIN (*insert cp at end of queue s*)
    IF s = NIL THEN s := cp
    ELSE this := s;
      WHILE this↑.queue # NIL DO this := this↑.queue END;
      this↑.queue := cp
    END;
    cp↑.queue := NIL; release
  END Receive;

  PROCEDURE Hold(t : CARDINAL);
    VAR T : CARDINAL; this, q0, q1 : Signal;
  BEGIN T := Time + t;
    IF TQ = NIL THEN
      TQ := cp; cp↑.queue := NIL
    ELSIF TQ↑.waketime > T THEN
      cp↑.queue := TQ; TQ := cp
    ELSE q0 := TQ;
      LOOP (*q0 # NIL*) q1 := q0↑.queue;
        IF q1 = NIL THEN
          q0↑.queue := cp; cp↑.queue := NIL; EXIT
        ELSIF q1↑.waketime > T THEN
          cp↑.queue := q1; q0↑.queue := cp; EXIT
        ELSE q0 := q1
        END
      END
    END;
    cp↑.waketime := T; release
  END Hold;

  PROCEDURE InitSignal(Var s : Signal);
  BEGIN s := NIL
  END InitSignal;

BEGIN free := NIL; Time := 0; TQ := NIL; Allocate(cp, TSIZE
                                              (Ring Node));

  WITH cp↑ DO
    next := cp; prev := cp; ready := TRUE
  END
END Simulation.
```

Evaluation

The three schemes of process cooperation by coroutine transfer, by signalling, and by message passing have been compared by three test programs CorTest, SigTest, and ChanTest listed subsequently. Each of them contains two processes, among which the processor is switched repeatedly. The times measured for 30 000 switches back and forth are:

CorTest	1.8 s
SigTest	5.0 s
ChanTest	5.5 s

```
MODULE CorTest;   (*NW 25.6.84*)
  FROM Coroutines IMPORT InitCoroutine;
  FROM Terminal IMPORT Read, Write;
  FROM SYSTEM IMPORT ADR, WORD, ADDRESS;

  CONST WspSize = 200;

  VAR n : CARDINAL; ch : CHAR;
    main, proc : ADDRESS;
    wsp : ARRAY [0..WspSize − 1] OF WORD;

  PROCEDURE Transfer(VAR from, to : ADDRESS);
    CODE 256B; 0
  END Transfer;

  PROCEDURE P;
  BEGIN
    LOOP n := n − 1; Transfer(proc, main) END
  END P;

BEGIN n := 60000; proc := ADR(wsp); InitCoroutine(P, proc, WspSize);
  Write("["); Read(ch);
  REPEAT Transfer(main, proc) UNTIL n = 0;
  Write("]")
END CorTest.

MODULE SigTest;   (*NW 24.6.84*)
  FROM Signals IMPORT Signal, StartProcess, Send, Receive, InitSignal;
  FROM Terminal IMPORT Read, Write;

  VAR n : CARDINAL; ch : CHAR; tested : Signal;

  PROCEDURE P;
  BEGIN
    LOOP n := n − 1; Receive(tested) END
  END P;

BEGIN n := 60000; InitSignal(tested);
  Write("["); Read(ch); StartProcess(P);
  REPEAT (* n > 0 *) Send(tested) UNTIL n = 0;
```

```
    Write("]")
END SigTest.

MODULE ChanTest;   (*NW 24.6.84*)
  FROM Channels IMPORT Channel, Parallel, Send, Receive,
    InitChannel;
  FROM Terminal IMPORT Read, Write;

  VAR n : INTEGER; ch : CHAR; chan : Channel;

  PROCEDURE P;
    VAR k : INTEGER;
  BEGIN
    REPEAT Receive(chan, k) UNTIL k = 0
  END P;

  PROCEDURE Q;
  BEGIN
    REPEAT n := n - 1; Send(chan, n) UNTIL n = 0
  END Q;

BEGIN n := 30000; InitChannel(chan);
    Write("["); Read(ch); Parallel(Q,P); Write("]")
END ChanTest.
```

Conclusions

Several schemes of multiprogramming have been presented. They are based on different sets of primitives for synchronization and communication. Implementation reveals that despite seeming conceptual differences they are closely related. The presented programs provide an estimate for the required complexity and overhead in the primitive operations.

All implementations have been expressed exclusively in Modula-2 which displays the adequacy of this language as a system programming tool. Even details which pertain to the particular computer used (Lilith) are fully expressible with the language's low-level facilities, and their extent is very small (see definition module Coroutines).

The moral of the story is that it may be wise to refrain from including multiprogramming facilities in a language, unless concurrency plays a dominant role and syntactic conveniences may become sufficiently important. In most cases, a general-purpose language can be used, provided it offers adequate low-level facilities whose use can be properly encapsulated by an appropriate structuring concept.

References

[1] E. W. Dijkstra. Cooperating sequential processes. In *Programming Languages,* F. Genuys (ed), Academic Press, 1968.

[2]   C. A. R. Hoare. Monitors: An operating system structuring concept. *Communications of the ACM*, **17** (8), 549–557 (1974).

[3]   W. H. Kaubisch, R. H. Perrott, C. A. R. Hoare, Quasiparallel programming. *Software – Practice and Experience*, **6**, 341–356 (1976).

[4]   N. Wirth. Modula: A programming language for modular multiprogramming. *Software – Practice and Experience*, **7** (1), 37–52 (1977).

[5]   C. A. R. Hoare. Communicating sequential processes. *Communications of the ACM*, **21** (8), 666–677 (1978).

[6]   J. Welsh, A. Lister, E. Salzman. A comparison of two notations for process communications. *Language Design and Programming Methodology*, **1**, 225–254 (1980).

[7]   J. Welsh, A. Lister. A comparative study of task communication in Ada. *Software – Practice and Experience*, **11**, 257–290 (1981).

[8]   N. Wirth. *Programming in Modula-2.* Springer-Verlag, 1982.

[9]   M. Ben-Ari. *Principles of Concurrent Programming.* Prentice-Hall International, 1982.

[10]   R. Williamson, E. Horowitz. Concurrent communication and synchronization mechanisms. *Software-Practice and Experience*, **14** (2), 135–151 (1984).

[11]   Inmos Ltd. *Occam Programming Manual.* Prentice-Hall International, 1984.

Appendix: Revisions and amendments to Modula-2

On November 21, 1983, a meeting was held with participants from several firms who had implemented Modula-2. Numerous features and facilities were proposed for addition or correction. The following subset was agreed upon. These rules should be regarded as revisions of Modula-2. Future implementors are encouraged to comply with these revisions, and existing compilers should be adapted. Although any change in a language is subject to resentment, the number of changes adopted here is very small and, I believe, each one is a genuine improvement.

1   Restrictions and clarifications

1.1   The types of a formal VAR-parameter and that of its corresponding actual parameter must be *identical* (i.e., not merely compatible). This rule is relaxed in the case of a formal parameter of type ADDRESS, which is also compatible with all pointer types, and in the case of the type WORD, where the compatible types are specified for each implementation.

1.2   The types of the expressions specifying the starting and limiting values of the control variable in a for statement must be *compatible* (i.e., not merely assignment compatible) with the type of the control variable.

1.3 A process initiated in a module at priority level n must not call a procedure declared in a module at priority level m < n. Calls of procedures declared without priority are allowed.

1.4 Pointer types can be exported from definition modules as opaque types. Opaque export of other types may be subject to implementation restrictions. Assignment and test for (in)equality are applicable to opaque types.

1.5 All modules imported to the main module are initialized *before* the importing module is initialized. If there exist circular references, the order of initialization is not defined.

1.6 If a module identifier is imported, this does *not* imply that the identifiers of objects of this module become visible. However, those which are exported in qualified mode can be accessed by prefixing them with the module identifier.

2 Changes

2.1 *All* objects declared in a definition module are exported. The explicit export list is discarded. The definition module may be regarded as the implementation module's separated and extended export list.

> DefinitionModule = DEFINITION MODULE ident ";" {import}
>   {definition }
> END ident ".".

2.2 The syntax of a variant record type declaration with missing tag field is changed from

> FieldList = | CASE [ident ":"] qualident OF ...

to

> FieldList = | CASE [ident] ":" qualident OF ...

The fact that the colon is always present makes it evident which part was omitted, if any.

2.3 The type PROCESS in module SYSTEM is deleted. Its place is taken by the type ADDRESS.

3 Extensions

3.1 The syntax of the case statement and the variant record declaration is changed from

```
case = CaseLabelList ":" StatementSequence.
variant = CaseLabelList ":" FieldListSequence.
```

to

```
case = [CaseLabelList ":" StatementSequence].
variant = [CaseLabelList ":" FieldListSequence].
```

The inclusion of the empty case and the empty variant allows the insertion of superfluous bars similar to the empty statement allowing the insertion of superfluous semicolons.

3.2   A string consisting of n characters is said to have *length* n. A string of length 1 is compatible with the type CHAR.

3.3   The syntax of the subrange type is changed from

```
SubrangeType = "[" ConstExpression ".." ConstExpression "]".
```

to

```
SubrangeType = [ident] "[" ConstExpression ".." ConstExpression "]".
```

The optional identifier allows to specify the base type of the subrange. Example: INTEGER [0..99].

3.4   Elements of sets had been restricted to be constants. This restriction is now relaxed. The syntax of sets and factors changes to

```
ConstFactor = ...| ConstSet |... .
ConstSet = [qualident] "{" [ConstElement {"," ConstElement}] "}".
ConstElement = ConstExpression [".." ConstExpression].

factor = ...| set |... .
set = [qualident] "{" [element {"," element }] "}".
element = expression [".." expression].
```

3.5   The character "~" is a synonym for the symbol NOT.

3.6   The identifiers LONGCARD, LONGINT, and LONGREAL denote standard types (which may not be available on some implementations).

3.7   The type ADDRESS is compatible with all pointer types and with either CARDINAL, or LONGCARD, or LONGINT. The interpretation of addresses as numbers depends on the implementation.

3.8   The new standard functions MIN and MAX take as argument any scalar type (including REAL). They stand for the type's minimal resp. maximal value.

22

Limitations of Synchronous Communication with Static Process Structure in Languages for Distributed Computing

Barbara Liskov
Massachusetts Institute of Technology

Maurice Herlihy
Carnegie–Mellon University

Lucy Gilbert
Autographix, Inc.

Modules in a distributed program are active, communicating entities. A language for distributed programs must choose a set of communication primitives and a structure for processes. This paper examines one possible choice: synchronous communication primitives (such as rendezvous or remote procedure call) in combination with modules that encompass a fixed number of processes (such as Ada tasks or UNIX processes). An analysis of the concurrency requirements of distributed programs suggests that this combination imposes complex and indirect solutions to common problems and thus is poorly suited for applications such as distributed programs in which concurrency is important. To provide adequate expressive power, a language for distributed programs should abandon either synchronous communication primitives or the static process structure.

This research was sponsored by the Defense Advanced Research Projects Agency (DOD), ARPA Order No. 3597, monitored by the Air Force Avionics Laboratory under Contract F33615-81-K-1539.

The views and conclusions contained in this document are those of the authors and should not be interpreted as representing the official policies, either expressed or implied, of the Defense Advanced Research Projects Agency or the US Government.

545

1   Introduction

A distributed system consists of multiple computers (called nodes) that communicate through a network. A programming language for distributed computing must choose a set of communication primitives and a structure for processes. In this paper, we examine one possible choice: synchronous communication primitives (such as rendezvous or remote procedure call) in combination with modules that encompass a fixed number of processes (such as Ada tasks or UNIX processes). We describe and evaluate the program structures needed to manage certain common concurrency control problems. We are concerned here not with computational power, but with expressive power: the degree to which common problems may be solved in a straightforward and efficient manner. We conclude that the combination of synchronous communication with static process structure imposes complex and indirect solutions, and therefore that it is poorly suited for applications such as distributed programs in which concurrency is important. To provide adequate expressive power, a language for distributed programming should abandon either synchronous communication primitives or the static process structure.

Our analysis is based on the *client/server model*, in which a distributed program is organized as a collection of modules, each of which resides at a single node in the network, Modules do not share data directly; instead they communicate through messages. Modules act as clients and as servers. A *client* module makes use of services provided by other modules, while a *server* module provides services to others by encapsulating a resource, providing synchronization, protection, and crash recovery. The client/server model is hierarchical: a particular module may be both a client and a server.

Although other models for concurrent computation have been proposed, the hierarchical client/server model has come to be the standard model for structuring distributed programs. Lauer and Needham [16] argued that the client/server model is equivalent (with respect to expressive power) to a model of computation in which modules communicate through shared data. Nevertheless, the client/server model is more appropriate for distributed systems because speed and bandwidth are typically more critical in the connection between a module and its local data than between distinct modules. Although certain specialized applications may fit naturally into alternative structures such as pipelines or distributed coroutines, the hierarchical client/server model encompasses a large class of distributed programs.

This paper is organized as follows. In Section 2, we propose a taxonomy for concurrent systems, focusing on primitives for intermodule communication and the process structure of modules. In Section 3, we formulate the basic concurrency requirement for modules: if one activity within a module becomes blocked, other activities should be able to make progress. In Section 4, we describe and evaluate the program structures needed to satisfy the concurrency requirement using synchronous communication primitives with a static process structure. We conclude that the only reasonable solution to certain problems requires using the available primitives to simulate asynchronous communication primitives and/or a dynamic process structure. In Section 5, we summarize our results and make suggestions about linguistic support for distributed computing.

2   Choices for communication and process structure

In this section we review the range of choices for communication and process structure and identify the choices made in various languages.

2.1   Communication

There are two main alternatives for communication primitives: synchronous and asynchronous. *Synchronous* mechanisms provide a single primitive for sending a request and receiving the associated response. The client's process is blocked until the server's response is received. Examples of synchronous mechanisms include procedure call, remote procedure call [21], and rendezvous [7]. Languages that use synchronous mechanisms for communication include Mesa [20], DP [5], Ada [7], SR [1],[†] MP [24], and Argus [18].

   Asynchronous communication mechanisms typically take the form of distinct *send* and *receive* primitives for originating requests and acquiring responses. A client process executing a send is blocked either until the request is constructed, or until the message is delivered (as in CSP [13]). The client acquires the response by executing the *receive* primitive. After executing a send and before executing the receive, the client may undertake other activity, perhaps executing other sends and receives. Languages that use send/receive include CSP and PLITS [8].

2.2   Process structure

There are two choices for process structure within a module. Module having a *static* structure encompass a fixed number of threads of control (usually one). The programmer is responsible for multiplexing these threads among a varying number of activities. Examples of modules having a static process structure include Ada tasks, DP monitors, and

---

[†] In addition to remote call, SR provides the ability to send a request without waiting for the response.

CSP processes, where there is just one process per module, and SR, where there may be multiple processes per module. The multiplexing mechanisms available to the programmer include guarded commands and condition variables.

An alternative to the static structure is the *dynamic* structure, in which a variable number of processes may execute within a module. (Note that a module's process structure is independent of the encompassing system's process structure; the number of processes executing within a module may vary dynamically even if the overall number of processes in the system is fixed.) The system is responsible for scheduling, but the programmer must synchronize the use of shared data. Ada, MP, Argus, and Mesa are examples of languages in which the basic modular unit encompasses a dynamic process structure.

2.3 Combinations

All four combinations of communication and process structure are possible. Figure 1 shows the combinations provided by several languages. In Argus, the basic modular unit is the *guardian*, which has a dynamic process structure. In MP, a language for programming highly parallel machines, shared data are encapsulated by *frames*, which encompass a dynamic process structure. In CSP, the process itself is the basic modular unit. A *monitor* in DP contains a single thread of control that is implicitly multiplexed among multiple activities. A *resource* in SR can contain a fixed number of processes. In Mesa monitors, the processes executing in *external* procedures have a dynamic structure. Access to shared data is synchronized through *entry* procedures that acquire the monitor lock. In Starmod [6], a dynamic process model with synchronous communication can be obtained through the use of *processes*; a static process model with asynchronous primitives can be obtained through the use of *ports*.

In Ada, a *task* is a module with a static process structure. A server task exports a collection of entries, which are called directly by clients. A server task's process structure is static because a task encompasses a single thread of control. (Although a task can create subsidiary tasks dynamically, these subsidiary tasks cannot be addressed as a group.) The

	Static	Dynamic
Synchronous	Ada Tasks, DP, SR	Argus, Mesa, Starmod, MP
Asynchronous	CSP, PLITS, Starmod	

Figure 1 Communication and process structure in some languages.

programmer of the server task uses select statements to multiplex the task among various clients. Note that a *task family* (an array of tasks) does not qualify as a module, because the entire family cannot be the target of a call; instead a call must be made to a particular member of a family.

Alternatively, a distributed Ada program might be organized as a collection of *packages* that communicate through interface procedures. This alternative, however, can be rejected as violating the intent of the Ada designers. The Ada Rationale [14] explicitly states that internode communication is by entry calls to tasks, not by procedure calls to packages.[†] This alternative can also be rejected on technical grounds; we argue in Section 4.3 that certain extensions to Ada are necessary before packages can be used effectively as modules in distributed programs.

We are not aware of any languages that provide asynchronous communication with dynamic processes. Although such languages may exist, this combination appears to provide an embarrassment of riches not needed for expressive power.

3 Concurrency requirements

In this section we discuss the concurrency requirements of the modules that make up a distributed program. Our discussion centers on the concurrency needs of modules that act as both clients and servers; any linguistic mechanism that provides adequate concurrency for such a module will also provide adequate concurrency for a module that acts only as a client or only as a server.

The principal concurrency requirement is the following: if one activity within a module becomes blocked, other activities should be able to make progress. A system in which modules are unable to set aside blocked activities may suffer from unnecessary deadlocks and low throughput. For example, suppose a server cannot carry out one client's request because another client has locked a needed resource. If the server then becomes blocked, rendering it unable to accept a request to release the resource, then a deadlock will occur that was otherwise avoidable. Even when there is no prospect of deadlock, a module that remains idle when there is work to be done is a performance bottleneck.

We can distinguish two common situations in which an activity within a module might be blocked:

(1) *Local Delay* A local resource needed by the current activity is found to be unavailable. For example, a file server may discover that the request on which it is working must read a file that is

---

[†] 'Note ... that on distributed systems (where tasks do not share a common store) communication by procedure calls may be disallowed, all communication being achieved by entry calls.' (Page 11–40).

currently open for writing by another client. In this situation, the file server should temporarily set aside the blocked activity, turning its attention to requests from other clients.

(2) *Remote Delay*   The module makes a call to another module, where a delay is encountered. The delay may simply be the communication delay, which can be large in some networks. Alternatively, the delay may occur because the called module is busy with another request or must perform considerable computing in response to the request. While the calling module is waiting for a response, it should be able to work on other activities.

We do not discuss the use of I/O devices in our analysis below, but it is worth noting that remote delays are really I/O delays, and remarks about one are equally applicable to the other.

4   Program structures

We now discuss several program structures that might be used to meet the concurrency requirement stated above. First, we review several techniques used to make progress in the presence of local delays. We conclude that the synchronous communication/static process combination provides adequate expressive power for coping with local delays (although the particular mechanisms provided by Ada are awkward for this purpose). In the second part, however, we argue that this combination provides inadequate expressive power for coping with remote delays.

In the following discussion, examples are shown as Ada tasks. We chose Ada because we assume it will be familiar to many readers. Although we call attention to some problems with Ada, this paper is not intended to be an exhaustive analysis of the suitability of Ada for distributed computing (see, however, [23, 9, 15]). Instead, the examples are intended to illustrate language-independent problems with the sychronous communication/static process combination.

4.1   Local delay

Our evaluation of techniques for coping with local delays is based on work of Bloom [4], who argued that a synchronization mechanism provides adequate expressive power to cope with local delays only if it permits scheduling decisions to be made on the basis of the following information:

- the name of the called operation,
- the order in which requests are received,

- the arguments to the call, and
- the state of the resource.

We use these criteria to evaluate techniques for avoiding local and remote delays.

Languages combining static process structure with synchronous communication provide two distinct mechanisms for making progress in the presence of local delay:

(1) *Conditional Wait* The conditional wait is the method used in monitors. An activity that encounters a local delay relinquishes the monitor lock and waits on a queue. While that activity is suspended, other activities can make progress after acquiring the monitor lock. Conditional wait is quite adequate for coping with local delays because scheduling decisions can employ information from all the categories listed above.

(2) *Avoidance* Avoidance is used in languages such as Ada and SR. Boolean expressions called *guards* are used to choose the next request. A server will accept a call only after it has ascertained that the local resources needed by the new request are currently available. Avoidance is adequate for coping with local delay as long as the guard mechanism is sufficiently powerful. In SR, for example, guards may employ information from all of Bloom's categories. In Ada, however, guards for **accept** statements cannot depend on the values of arguments to the call, and therefore the Ada guarded command mechanism lacks the expressive power needed to provide a general solution to the problem of local delays.

The shortcomings of the Ada guarded command mechanism can be illustrated by the following simple example. which will be used throughout the paper. A *Disk Scheduler* module synchronizes access to a disk through REQUEST and RELEASE operations (c.f. [12, 4]). Before reading or writing to the disk, a client calls REQUEST to identify the desired track. When REQUEST returns, the client accesses the disk and calls RELEASE when the access is complete. The scheduler attempts to minimize changes in the direction the disk head is moving. A request for a track is postponed if the track does not lie in the head's current direction of motion. The direction is reversed when there are no more pending requests in that direction.

Perhaps the most natural implementation of the disk scheduler server in Ada would provide two entries:

```
task DISK_SCHEDULER is
    entry REQUEST(ID : in TRACK);
    entry RELEASE;
end DISK_SCHEDULER;
```

Internally, the server keeps track of the current direction of motion, and the current head position:

```
task body DISK_SCHEDULER is
  type STATUS = (UP,DOWN,NEUTRAL);
  -- current head position.
  POSITION : TRACK;
  -- current direction of motion.
  DIRECTION : STATUS;
  ...
end DISK_SCHEDULER
```

A naive attempt at scheduling is:

```
select -- Warning : not legal Ada!
  when (DIRECTION = UP and POSITION <= ID) =>
    -- Move up.
    accept REQUEST(ID : in TRACK) do ...
or  when (DIRECTION = DOWN and POSITION >=ID) =>
    -- Move down.
    accept REQUEST(ID : in TRACK) do ...
or  when (DIRECTION = NEUTRAL) =>
    -- Move either way.
    accept REQUEST(ID : in TRACK) do ...
```

This program fragment is illegal, however, because Ada does not permit an argument value (i.e., ID) to be used in a **when** clause. As a consequence of this restriction, modules whose scheduling policies depend on argument values must be implemented in a more roundabout manner.

In the remainder of this section, we use the disk scheduler example to illustrate five alternative techniques for avoiding local delay. We argue that although some of these techniques will help in special cases, only one of them, the Early Reply structure, is powerful enough to provide a fully general solution to the local delay problem.

(1)   *Entry Families*   It is possible to treat an argument specially by using an indexed *family* of entries. If the index is viewed as an argument to the call, entry families provide a limited ability to accept requests based on arguments.

For example, REQUEST could be implemented as a family containing an entry for each track. The index provides an indirect way to incorporate the track number into the entry name, and so, for example, the task can delay accepting a request to write to a track that lies in the wrong direction from the disk head.

```
case DIRECTION is
  when UP =>
    for I in POSITION..TRACK'LAST
    loop
      accept REQUEST(I) do ...
    end loop;
  when DOWN =>
    for I in reverse POSITION..TRACK'FIRST
    loop
      accept REQUEST(I) do ...
    end loop;
  when NEUTRAL =>
    for I in TRACK'RANGE
    loop
      accept REQUEST(I) do ...
    end loop;
end case
```

A source of awkwardness here is that the accept statement can refer only to values of local variables (l in this case). The first two arms of the **case** statement must poll each of the entries in turn, and in the third arm, the entire family must either be polled sequentially as shown, or each track must have its own **accept** statement. Neither choice is attractive, particularly if the number of tracks is large. Similar problems have been noted by [27].

Perhaps a more important limitation of entry families is that they are effective only when the subsumed argument's type is a discrete range. For example, entry families could not be used if the range of disk tracks were to vary dynamically, or if requests were granted on the basis of a numeric priority, as in the 'shortest job first' scheduler of [26].

(2) *Refusal* A server that accepts a request it is unable to service might return an exception to the client to indicate that the client should try again later.

Refusal can eliminate local delays, but it is an awkward and potentially inefficient technique. When a client receives such an exception, it must decide whether to try again or to pass the exception to a higher level. If it tries again, it must decide when to do so, and how many times to retry before giving up. Note that such decisions present a modularity problem, because they are likely to change as the underlying system changes. For example, if a server's load increases over time, it will refuse more requests, and its clients will be forced to adjust their timeout and retry strategies. The server might also have to roll back work already done on the client's behalf, work that may have to be redone later, perhaps several times.

(3) *Nested Accept*   A server that encounters a local delay might **accept** another request in a nested **accept** statement.

The following code fragment shows an unlikely way of programming a disk scheduler. The server indiscriminately accepts calls to REQUEST. When it discovers that it has accepted a request for a track that lies in the wrong direction, it uses a nested **accept** statement to **accept** a different request. When the disk head direction changes, the server resumes processing the original request.

```
accept REQUEST(ID : in TRACK) do
   -- If the direction is wrong,
   -- then accept something else.
   while DIRECTION = UP and ID < POSITION
   loop
      select
         accept REQUEST(ANOTHER_ID : in TRACK) do
         ...
      or
         terminate;
      end select;
   end loop;
   ...
end REQUEST;
```

At first glance the nested **accept** technique might appear similar to the conditional wait technique supported by monitors, in which an activity that is unable to make progress is temporarily set aside in favor of another activity. The critical difference between the two techniques is that the use of nested **accept** statements requires that the new call be completed before the old call can be completed, an ordering that may not correspond to the needs of applications. Monitors do not impose the same last-in-first-out ordering on activities. A second difficulty with nested **accept** statements is deciding which request to accept. For example, the disk scheduler will be no better off if it accepts another request for a track that lies in the wrong direction. Note that if it were possible to decide which requests to accept after getting into trouble, then it should have been possible to accept only non-troublesome requests in the first place, thus avoiding the use of the nested **accept**. This observation suggests that the nested **accept** provides no expressive power that is not otherwise available.

(4) *Task Families*   Instead of using a single task to implement a server, one might use a *family* (i.e., an array) of identical tasks.[†]

[†] DP and SR provide analogous mechanisms.

These tasks would together constitute the server, and would synchronize with one another in their use of the server's data. If one task encounters a local or remote delay, the server need not remain idle if another task is still able to service requests.

The principal difficulty with task families lies in allocating tasks among clients. As mentioned above, a client cannot make a call to a task family as a whole; instead it is necessary to allocate family members to the clients in advance of the call. If the server's clients can be identified in advance, then it is possible to have a task family member for each client, and each client can be permanently assigned its own private task. This structure can avoid local delays, but such static assignments are not feasible for many applications.

If static allocation is not possible, then two alternative methods might be used. A client could choose a task on its own, perhaps at random, and then use a timed or conditional entry call to determine if it is free. If the task is not free, the client could try again. Such a method is cheap if contention for tasks in the family is low, but it can result in arbitrary delays when contention is high.

Alternatively, the server could provide a manager task that assigns tasks to clients. Although the manager can avoid conflicts in the use of family members, extra messages are needed when a task is allocated or freed. A manager is expensive if a task is used just once for each allocation; the cost decreases as the number of uses per allocation increases.

In either the static or dynamic case, task families require enough family members to make the probability of contention acceptably low. Since most tasks in the family are likely to be idle at any time, the expense of the technique depends on how cheaply idle tasks can be implemented.

If the number of clients is static, task families do provide a solution to local delay. Nevertheless, they do not provide a general solution because often the number of clients is dynamic (or unknown). In this case, task families can at best provide a probabilistic guarantee against delay.

(5) *Early Reply* A fully general solution to the concurrency problem can be constructed if synchronous primitives are used to simulate asynchronous primitives.

A server that accepts a request from a client simply records the request and returns an immediate acknowledgment. The server carries out the request at some later time, and conveys the result to the client through a distinct exchange of messages. Numerous examples employing Early Reply appear in the literature (e.g., see [10, 26, 25]).

A disk scheduler task employing Early Reply would export three entries: a REGISTER entry, a REQUEST entry family, and a RELEASE entry. The client calls REGISTER to indicate the disk track desired. The

```
task DISK_SCHEDULER is
   ...
   entry REGISTER (ID : in TRACK; CLIENT_ID : out INDEX);
   entry RESPONSE (INDEX);
   entry RELEASE;
   ...
end SERVER;
task body SERVER is
   ...
begin
  loop
    BUSY := false;
    NEXT_CLIENT := UNKNOWN;
    -- Accept and enqueue new requests.
    select
      accept REGISTER (ID : in TRACK;
                       CLIENT_ID : out INDEX) do
        -- Allocate and return index.
        CLIENT_ID := ... ;
      end REGISTER;
      ...
      -- Enqueue request and client id.
      -- compute next client and next track.
      NEXT_CLIENT := ...
      NEXT_TRACK := ...
    or
      when not BUSY and NEXT_CLIENT /= UNKNOWN =>
        accept REQUEST (NEXT_CLIENT);
        POSITION := NEXT_TRACK;
        BUSY := true;
    or
      when BUSY =>
        accept RELEASE;
        BUSY := false;
        ...
        -- Change direction if necessary.
        NEXT_CLIENT := ...
        NEXT_TRACK := ...
    end select;
  end loop.
end SERVER;
```

Figure 2   Using Early Reply to avoid local delays.

server records the request and responds with an index into the
REQUEST entry family.

> **entry** REGISTER (ID : **in** TRACK, CLIENT_ID : **out** INDEX);

An outline of disk scheduler server employing early reply to avoid local
delays appears in Figure 2. Although early reply provides a general
technique for avoiding local delays, it is potentially inefficient and
awkward. Efficiency may suffer because an additional remote call is
needed whenever a delay is possible (e.g., when requesting a disk track).
Program clarity may suffer because the server must perform its own
scheduling, explicitly multiplexing its thread of control among multiple
clients.

When the server is ready to grant a client's request, it accepts a call
to that client's member of the REQUEST entry family. For this structure
to work, the client must follow a protocol in which it first registers its
request, and then makes a second call to receive its response. To avoid
delaying the server, the client should follow the REGISTER call with an
immediate call to REQUEST:

> SERVER.REGISTER (TRACK_ID, MY_ID);
> SERVER.REQUEST (MY_ID);

Most of the techniques discussed in this paper, including Early Reply,
work best if clients access server tasks indirectly through procedures
exported by a package local to the client's site. The package enhances
safety by enforcing protocols and by ensuring that identifiers issued to
clients are not misused.

4.2 Remote delay

We now go on to discuss the problem of remote delays. We do not claim
that it is impossible to avoid remote delay under the synchronous
communication/static process structure combination. We argue instead
that this combination imposes complex and indirect solutions to common problems that arise in distributed programs. To illustrate this point,
we review the techniques discussed above for coping with local delay.
The only technique that provides a general solution to the remote delay
problem is Early Reply. We focus on two servers: the *higher-level* server
called by a client, and a *lower-level* server called by the higher-level
server. Most of the techniques previously considered for coping with
local delay are clearly inadequate for coping with remote delay:

- *Conditional Wait* The inability of monitors to cope with remote
  delay is known as the *nested monitor call* problem [19, 11]. When a
  monitor makes a call to another monitor, the calling activity retains

the monitor lock, and the monitor must remain idle while the call is in progress.

- *Avoidance*   Remote delay cannot be eliminated by avoidance. A server cannot choose to avoid a client's request just because it may lead to a remote delay. The lower-level server could avoid accepting the higher-level server's call if it would otherwise encounter a local delay, but the higher-level server is delayed in the meantime. Avoidance can thus lead to both deadlock and performance problems.

- *Refusal*   Refusal is no more effective for dealing with remote delays than it is for dealing with local delays.

- *Nested Accept*   One might attempt to avoid remote delays through the use of nested **accept** statements in the following way: a task creates a subsidiary task to carry out the remote call while the creating task executes a nested **accept**. However, the necessity of finishing the nested call before responding to the outer call renders this technique of dubious value.

- *Task Families*   The remarks made about task families when discussing local delays apply to remote delays as well. Task families work well when the number of clients is static and predetermined. Otherwise, task families provide only a probabilistic guarantee against delay. Probabilistic guarantees concerning performance might well suffice for some applications, but probabilistic guarantees concerning deadlock seem less useful.

Only Early Reply provides a general solution to the problem of remote delay, but the efficiency and program complexity problems noted above become more acute. If the lower-level server employs early reply, then the higher-level server will be subject to remote delay if it requests its response prematurely. To avoid waiting, the higher-level server might use periodic timed or conditional entry calls to check for the response. This structure is potentially inefficient, since the higher-level server is making multiple remote calls, and it may also yield complex programs because the higher-level server must explicitly multiplex these calls with other activities. An alternative structure in which the lower-level server returns its response by calling an entry provided by the higher-level server is no better. To avoid delaying the lower-level server, the higher-level server must **accept** the call in a timely fashion, and the need for explicit multiplexing is unchanged.

These shortcomings of Early Reply can be alleviated by the introduction of dynamic task creation in the higher-level server. In this structure, the higher-level server uses Early Reply to communicate with clients. When the higher-level server receives a request, it creates a subsidiary task (or allocates an existing task) and returns the name of that task to the client. The structure is illustrated in Figure 3. The client later

```
task SERVER is
  ...
  entry REQUEST (... , HELPER : out access HELPER_TASK);
  task type HELPER_TASK is
    -- From server :
    entry FORWARD_REQUEST (...);
    -- From client :
    entry RESPONSE(...);
  end HELPER_TASK;
end SERVER;

task body SERVER is
  ...
  task body HELPER_TASK is
    ...
  begin
    accept FORWARD_REQUEST (...) do
    ... -- Put arguments in local variables.
    end FORWARD_REQUEST;
    ... -- Do work for client,
    ... -- including lower-level calls.
    accept RESPONSE(...) do
    ... -- Return response to client;
    end RESPONSE
  end HELPER_TASK;

begin
  loop
    select
      accept REQUEST(... , HELPER : out access HELPER_TASK)
      do
        HELPER := new HELPER_TASK;
        HELPER.FORWARD_REQUEST(...);
      end REQUEST;
    ...
    or
      terminate;
    end select;
  end loop;
end SERVER;
```

Figure 3   Early Reply and dynamic task creation.

calls the subsidiary task to receive the results of its request:

> SERVER.REQUEST(..., TASK_ID);
>
> ...
>
> TASK_ID.RESPONSE(...);

The subsidiary task carries out the client's request, making calls to lower-level servers, and using shared data to synchronize with other subsidiary tasks within the higher-level server. When work on the request is finished, the subsidiary task accepts the client's second call to pick up the response.

This structure avoids the program complexity problems associated with Early Reply. The higher-level server need not perform explicit multiplexing among clients because the tasking mechanism itself multiplexes the processor(s) among the various activities, although, as mentioned above, subsidiary tasks must synchronize through shared data. This structure also alleviates the need to synchronize with lower-level servers. The server as a whole is not affected if one subsidiary task is delayed, because other subsidiary tasks can still work for other clients.

One disadvantage of this structure is that creating and destroying the server tasks may be expensive, although this cost can be avoided by reusing the subsidiary tasks.[†] This structure also requires two message exchanges for each client/server interaction. The most striking fact about this mechanism, however, is that we are using synchronous rendezvous to simulate asynchronous send and receive primitives, and dynamic task creation to simulate a dynamic process structure. The need to use one set of primitives to simulate another suggests that the combination of the static process structure with synchronous communication does not provide adequate expressive power to satisfy the concurrency requirements of distributed programs.

4.3   Remarks about Ada

Although this paper is not intended to be a systematic critique of Ada itself, it does raise some questions about the suitability of Ada for distributed computing. One way to circumvent the limitations of Ada tasks is to use packages instead of tasks as the basic modular unit for constructing servers. A server package would export a collection of interface procedures, which would be called directly by clients. These procedures could synchronize with one another by explicit calls to entries of tasks private to the package. (This structure is similar to a Mesa monitor [20].)

[†] In the microVAX-II implementation of Argus, it takes only 160 microseconds to create, run, and destroy a null process.

A server package would solve the concurrency problem by providing a dynamic process structure; an arbitrary number of client processes can be executing within the package's interface procedures. The programmer is responsible for synchronizing access to shared data, but not for scheduling the processes.

Nevertheless, Ada packages suffer from critical limitations unrelated to the main focus of this paper. In applications such as distributed computing, it is often necessary to store module names in variables, and to pass them as parameters. For example, the Cedar remote procedure call facility [2] uses Grapevine [3] as a registry for server instances and types. Similarly, dynamic reconfiguration, replacing one module with another [15], may be necessary to enhance functionality, to accommodate growth, and to support fault-tolerance. Ada permits names of tasks (i.e., their **access** values) to be stored in variables and used as parameters, but not names of packages or procedures. Consequently, a distributed program in which the package is the basic modular unit could not support Grapevine-like registries of services or dynamic reconfiguration. These observations suggest that Ada would provide better support for distributed programs if it were extended to treat packages as first-class objects.

5 Discussion

We have argued that languages that combine synchronous communication primitives with a static process structure do not provide adequate expressive power for constructing distributed programs. Although our discussion has focused on distributed programs, our conclusions are valid for any concurrent program organized as clients and servers (e.g., interprocess communication in UNIX [22] or programming for highly parallel machines [24]).

Languages that combine synchronous communication with a static process structure can provide adequate expressive power for avoiding *local delays*, in which an activity is blocked because a local resource is unavailable, as illustrated by monitors and by languages with a fully general guarded command mechanism. (Ada's guarded **accept** mechanism, however, lacks expressive power because it does not allow the call's arguments to be used in guards.) The languages under consideration do not, however, provide adequate expressive power for avoiding *remote delays*, in which an activity is blocked pending the completion of a remote call. For monitors, this problem has come to be known as the *nested monitor call* problem [11, 19]. The thesis of this paper is that languages in which modules combine synchronous communication with a static process structure suffer from an analogous problem.

We examined a number of techniques to avoid such delays using

Ada tasks. Although certain techniques are adequate for particular applications, e.g., entry families, the only fully general solution requires using synchronous primitives to simulate asynchronous primitives, and dynamic task creation to simulate a dynamic process structure. The need to use one set of primitives to simulate another is evidence that the original set lacks expressive power.

We believe that it is necessary to abandon either synchronous communication or static process structure, but a well-designed language need not abandon both. If the language provides asynchronous communication primitives, in which the sender need not wait for the receiver to accept the message, then the time spent waiting for the early reply in our examples would be saved. In addition, the lower-level server need not be delayed waiting for the higher-level server to pick up the response, and only two messages would be needed. The need to perform explicit multiplexing remains a disadvantage of this choice of primitives.

Alternatively, if a language provides dynamic process creation within a single module, as in Argus and Mesa, then the advantages of synchronous communication can be retained. When a call message arrives at a module, a new process is created automatically (or allocated from a pool of processes) to carry out the request. When the process has completed the call, a reply message is sent back to the caller and the process is destroyed or returned to the process pool. Only two messages are needed to carry out the call. The new process has much the same function as the subsidiary tasks created by the server in Figure 3. It ensures that the module is not blocked even if the request encounters a delay. The process must synchronize with other processes in the module but all the processes are defined within a single module, which facilitates reasoning about correctness. Finally, a dynamic process structure can mask delays that result from the use of local input/output devices, and may permit multiprocessor nodes to be used to advantage. We think synchronous communication with dynamic processes is a better choice than asynchronous communication with static processes; a detailed justification for this opinion is given in [17].

A language mechanism cannot be considered to have adequate expressive power if common problems require complex and indirect solutions. Although synchronous communication with static process structure is computationally complete, it is not sufficiently expressive. Synchronous communication is not compatible with the static process structure, and languages for distributed programs must abandon one or the other.

Acknowledgments

The authors would like to thank Beth Bottos, Larry Rudolph, and the members of the Argus design group, especially Paul R. Johnson, Robert

Scheifler, and William Weihl for their comments on earlier drafts of this paper.

References

[1] Andrews, G. R. 'Synchronizing Resources'. *ACM Trans. on Programming Lang. and Systems* **3**, 4 (October 1981), 405–430.

[2] Birrel, A. D., and Nelson, B. J. 'Implementing Remote Procedure Calls'. *ACM Transactions on Computer Systems* **2**, 1 (Feb. 1984), 39–59.

[3] Birrel, A. D., Levin, R., Needham, R., and Schroeder, M. 'Grapevine: an Exercise in Distributed Computing'. *Comm. ACM* **25**, 14 (April 1982), 260–274.

[4] Bloom, T. Evaluating Synchronization Mechanisms. Proceedings of the Seventh Symposium on Operating Systems Principles, ACM-SIGOPS, December, 1979.

[5] Brinch Hansen, P. 'Distributed processes: A concurrent programming concept'. *Comm. ACM* **21**, 11 (November 1978), 934–941.

[6] Cook, R. P. 'Starmod – a language for distributed programming'. *IEEE Transactions on Software Engineering* **6**, 6 (November 1980), 563–571.

[7] Dept. of Defense. Reference manual for the ADA programming language. ANSI/MIL-STD-1815A-1983.

[8] Feldman, J. A. 'High Level Programming for Distributed Computing'. *Comm. ACM* **22**, 6 (June 1979), 353–368.

[9] Gehani, N. 'Concurrency in Ada and Multicomputers'. *Computer Languages* **7**, 2 (1982).

[10] Gehani, Narain. *Ada: an advanced introduction.* Prentice-Hall, Englewood Cliffs, New Jersey, 1984.

[11] Haddon, B. K. 'Nested monitor calls'. *ACM Operating Systems Review* **11**, 4 (October 1977), 18–23.

[12] Hoare, C. A. R. 'Monitors: an operating system structuring concept'. *Comm. ACM* **17**, 10 (October 1974), 549–557.

[13] Hoare, C. A. R. 'Communicating sequential processes'. *Comm. ACM* **21**, 8 (August 1978), 666–677.

[14] Ichbiah, J., *et al.* 'Rationale for the design of the Ada programming language'. *SIGPLAN Notices* **14**, 6 (June 1979).

[15] Knight, J. C., and Urquhart, J. I. A. 'On the implementation and use of Ada on fault-tolerant distributed systems'. *Ada Letters* **4**, 3 (Nov. 1984).

[16] Lauer, P. E., and Needham, R. M. On the duality of operating systems structures. Proc. Second International Symposium on Operating Systems Structures, October, 1978. Reprinted in Operatings Systems Review, **13** (2) April 1979, pp. 3–19.

[17] Liskov, B., and Herlihy, M. Issues in Process and Communication Structure for Distributed Programs. Proceedings of the Third IEEE Symposium on Reliability in Distributed Software and Database Systems, October 1983.

[18] Liskov, B., and Scheifler, R. 'Guardians and actions: linguistic support for robust, distributed programs'. *ACM Trans. on Programming Lang. and Systems* **5**, 3 (July 1983), 381–404.

[19] Lister, A. 'The problem of nested monitor calls'. *ACM Operating Systems Review* **11**, 2 (July 1977), 5–7.

[20] Mitchell, J. G., Maybury, W., and Sweet, R. Mesa language manual, version 5.0. CSL-79-3, Xerox Palo Alto Research Center, April, 1979.

[21] Nelson, B. Remote Procedure Call. CMU-CS-81-119. Carnegie–Mellon University, 1981. Ph.D. Thesis.

[22] Rashid, R. An inter-process communication facility for Unix. CMU-CS-81-124, Carnegie–Mellon University, 1980.

[23] Schuman, S. A., Clarke, E. M., and Nikolaou, C. N. Programming Distributed Applications in Ada: a First Approach. Proceedings of the 1981 Conference on Parallel Processing, Aug., 1981.

[24] Segall, Z., and Rudolph, L. PIE – a programming and instrumentation environment for parallel processing. CMU-CS-85-128, Carnegie–Mellon University, 1985.

[25] Wegner, P., and Smolka, S. 'Processes, tasks, and monitors: a comparative study of concurrent programming primitives'. *IEEE Transactions on Software Engineeering* **9**, 4 (July 1983), 39–59.

[26] Welsh, J., and Lister, A. 'A comparative study of task communication in Ada'. *Software – Practice and Experience* **11** (1981), 257–290.

[27] Yemini, S. On the suitability of Ada multitasking for expressing parallel algorithms. Proceedings of AdaTEC Conference on Ada, Oct., 1982.

PART FIVE
Concurrent Programming Issues

As mentioned earlier, concurrent programming introduces yet another dimension of complexity to the already difficult task of writing correct sequential programs. Concurrent programs are susceptible to a whole new range of potential errors that are not encountered in sequential programs, for example, a concurrent program can 'deadlock' – that is, although the program has not terminated, it is not making progress. There is also the possibility of timing errors. Such errors are very hard to locate because they are, in general, extremely difficult to reproduce.

The papers in this section discuss algorithms and tools developed to help detect concurrent programming errors and warn of potential problems.

23

Anomaly Detection in Concurrent Programs

G. Bristow, C. Drey, B. Edwards and W. Riddle
University of Colorado at Boulder

An approach to the analysis of concurrent software is discussed. The approach, called *anomaly detection*, involves the algorithmic derivation of information concerning potential errors and the subsequent, possibly non-algorithmic determination of whether or not the reported anomalies are actual errors. We give overviews of algorithms for detecting data-usage and synchronization anomalies and discuss how this technique may be integrated within a general software development support system.

I   Introduction

In developing software systems, especially large, complex ones, practitioners require analytic techniques to help them assess the validity of the system. In this paper, we explore an approach to providing these analytic techniques which we call *anomaly detection*.

In the anomaly detection approach, assessment is a two-step procedure. First, algorithms are employed to discover potential errors (anomalies) as evidenced by deviations from the developers' expectations. Second, non-algorithmic analysis, relying upon the experience, knowledge, and expertise of the developers themselves, is employed to determine whether or not a reported anomaly represents an actual error.

To focus our work, we have established the following criteria. First, our techniques must be applicable to programming language representations of the software system. Thus, they will not have to await the acceptance of some modeling representation by the system developers. Second, our techniques should be oriented toward expectations that arise

This work was supported by grant NSG 1476 from NASA Langley Research Center.

from general problem-domain considerations, the semantics of programming languages, or general rules of good practice. Thus, we do not have to develop techniques for specifying problem-specific expectations in order to have our techniques be applicable to a wide range of systems. Third, our techniques should not be restricted to sequential systems, but should apply also to systems with concurrency. This makes them applicable to those complex systems which involve either actual or apparent parallelism. Finally, our techniques should be of 'reasonable' quality. We desire techniques that are considerably more effective than the trivial one which always, for all programs, announces 'There's possibly an error somewhere in the program;' but we want techniques in which the algorithms have pleasing computational properties.

It should be stressed that we view anomaly detection as only one of the types of analytic techniques which should be made available to development practitioners. We feel that by not attempting to do complete analysis, we can find useful techniques which have reasonable computational requirements and are generally applicable over a broad range of software systems. We also feel that our current work gives rise to immediately usable techniques, but that it is preliminary in nature and many questions remain concerning its effectiveness and the degree to which anomaly detection techniques may be integrated into a full set of analytic techniques.

In the next two sections, we give a brief overview of the anomaly detection system we envision and present a small example to convey an intuitive understanding of the purpose and functioning of its various modules. The following sections address the modules in turn, covering the capabilities of the anomaly detection algorithms we have developed. In the concluding section, we discuss the implications of some of the constraints we have imposed and indicate future directions we plan to pursue.

II Anomaly detection system overview

We envision that anomaly detection facilities would be provided as part of a variety of development support tools within some software development environment. Guided by some overall methodology, development practitioners would use the various tools to gradually evolve a detailed description of the system under development. The tools based upon our anomaly detection algorithms would be among those by which developers could periodically assess the validity of the evolving system.

The anomaly detection tool for which we strive is depicted in Figure 1. We have been working with a particular language, HAL/S [7]; but for the purpose of this paper we consider a generic language, which we call X, having facilities for concurrent programming. It will be apparent from the examples that our techniques can be particularized to most all current-day, concurrent programming languages.

The anomaly detection task may be decomposed into two major subtasks. The first is to derive a representation of the program under analysis which retains the information pertinent to the anomalies under examination and presents this information in a form which may be conveniently used by the anomaly detection algorithms. The second task is the anomaly detection itself. In Figures 2–5, we indicate the major modules which perform these tasks.

So that the anomaly detection subsystem may easily be generalized to other languages, the initial processing module performs a program-to-parse-tree transformation (Figure 2). Identifying this as a separate module leads to two subsidiary benefits. First, it allows the use of existing scanner and parser generation systems in the preparation of the X Language Processor module. Second, the overall system may be easily modified to use representations of X programs other than the program text. In particular, the system may use the intermediate representation produced by the X language's compiler.

The next module which we identify has the task of building a flow graph representation of a program (see Figure 3). In a flow graph, nodes represent program statements (or perhaps fragments of statements) and arcs represent the flow of control within sequentially executed segments of the program (i.e., within programs and tasks). Identifying this as a separate module again eases our task since it is possible for us to consider using existing techniques in the design of the Flow Graph Builder module.

We decompose the Flow Graph Analyzer as indicated in Figure 4. In approaching the processing in this way, we separate out the task of constructing the Inter-Process Precedence Graph in which attention is focused upon synchronization interactions and arcs are introduced to indicate the precedence of operations enforced by these interactions. This Inter-Process Precedence Graph may be used directly for the detection of synchronization anomalies, or the information contained in this graph may be injected into the flow graph to produce a combined Flow And Precedence Graph which may be used in the detection of data-usage anomalies.

Finally, we identify the modules depicted in Figure 5. These divide the task of constructing an Inter-Process Precedence Graph into three steps. First, the Flow Graph is processed to eliminate those nodes and arcs which do not pertain to the use of synchronization constructs or directly affect the flow of execution of synchronization operations. Then arcs reflecting the order of execution imposed by the synchronization operations are inserted into the graph. Finally, most (or ideally all) of the arcs which reflect impossible execution sequences are removed from the graph. The identification of these last two modules allows separate focus upon the simple task of obtaining a representation of the effect of the synchronization operations and the much more difficult task of

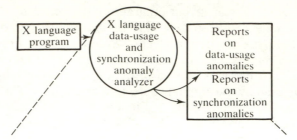

Figure 1   Target anomaly detection system.

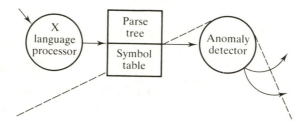

Figure 2   Organization of X-language data-usage and synchronization anomaly detector.

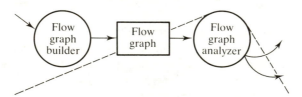

Figure 3   Organization of anomaly detector.

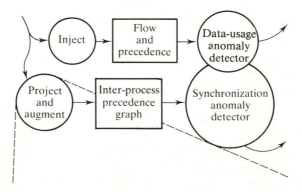

Figure 4   Organization of flow graph analyzer.

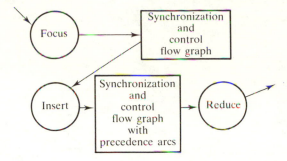

Figure 5 Organization of project and augment.

obtaining a representation which reflects the actual runtime behavior of the program under analysis.

III An example

In Figure 6 we present a hypothetical program in the X language and show the various information structures produced during processing. The example is self-explanatory, except perhaps for the origins of node 24 – it represents the collection of nodes (1–5) at the beginning of the main process, none of which individually affects the synchronization interactions among the processes.

IV Related work

Closely related to our own work is that of Taylor and Osterweil [21]. They share an interest in producing a general software development support system, and Osterweil has been actively involved in the DAVE data-usage anomaly detection system [9]. Although our paths of development differ, we have arrived at essentially the same point.

Reif's recent work [13] on the analysis of interacting processes deals with formal models of concurrent systems and decidability. It relates most directly to the formal foundational work which is a basis for the work reported here ([5], [8], [10], [11], [12], [14], [15], [16], [17], [20], [22]).

The Inter-Process Precedence Graph is an intermediate representation for describing the partial ordering of synchronization events within concurrent systems. Thus, it is closely related to other techniques that have recently been developed for this purpose ([2], [5], [6], [18], [20]). Its representational power is equivalent to that of event expressions, defined in [18].

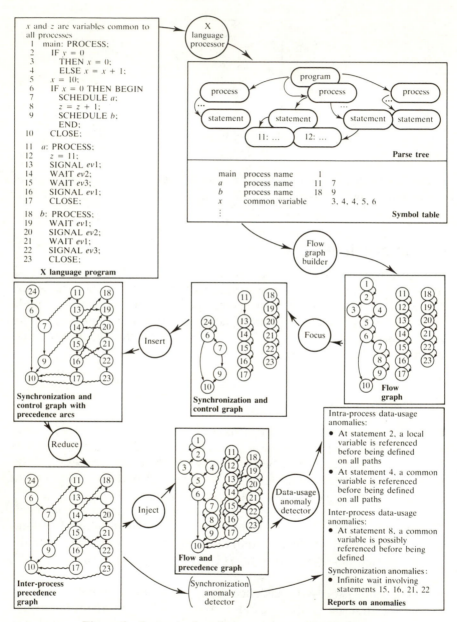

Figure 6   Example showing program representations.

Our synchronization anomaly detection algorithms were developed after initially attempting to employ the static deadlock detection algorithms developed by Saxena [19]. However, we found the requirements for use of those algorithms to be too strict for our purposes.

The data-usage anomaly detection phase of our system is derived from the DAVE system for analyzing FORTRAN programs [9]. Faster, more efficient algorithms [4] evolved from the original system and the elements of the analysis performed by them are essentially language independent. These algorithms have been applied to the HAL/S language for single-process programs to design a DAVE-HAL/S system [3]. This work has been extended to include analysis of multi-process HAL/S programs as well and will be described here in relation to the X language.

V   Graph building

The first major task is to derive an abstraction of the program being analyzed. This abstraction must contain all information which is pertinent to the anomalies under detection and must be in a form which is conveniently used by the anomaly detection algorithms.

(We have not included the details of our processing algorithms in this paper, choosing for the sake of brevity to give intuition-based discussions of them. Detailed, pseudo-code specifications of the algorithms are available in a companion report [1].)

V.1   Flow graph

The flow graph is derived from the parse tree and symbol table for a program specified in the X language. The flow graph is an abstraction of the control structure of the program and is used to detect anomalous data flow patterns.

The flow graph is composed of a subgraph for each subprogram unit in the program under analysis. Each subgraph contains:

(1) N, a set of nodes $\{n_1, n_2, n_3, ..., n_k\}$.
(2) E, a set of ordered pairs of nodes (edges), $\{(n_{j_1}, n_{j_2}), (n_{j_3}, n_{j_4}), (n_{j_5}, n_{j_6}), ..., (n_{j_{m-1}}, n_{j_m})\}$, where the n_{j_i}s are not necessarily distinct.
(3) n_e, the unique entry node, $n_e \in N$.
(4) n_x, the unique exit node, $n_x \in N$.

The nodes in the graph roughly correspond to statements in the program. The edges in the graph indicate the (sequential) flow of control from one node to the next. Each node $n_j \in N$, has the following information associated with it:

(1) P, the set of predecessor nodes. $n_i \in P$ if the edge $(n_i, n_j) \in E$.

(2) S, the set of successor nodes. $n_i \in S$ if edge $(n_j, n_i) \in E$.

(3) t, the type of the node, indicating the type of statement in the language X which the node represents.

(4) r, a representation of the actual statement or statement fragment which the node represents.

(5) m, the sequential number of the statement which the node represents.

V.2   Inter-process precedence graph

The Inter-Process Precedence Graph, derived from the Flow Graph, is an abstraction of the synchronization constructs and the control structures which directly affect the flow of execution of the synchronization operations. The Inter-Process Precedence Graph is used to detect anomalous patterns of synchronization operations.

The graph is composed of subgraphs for each process in the program. Each subgraph is a flow graph which reflects the synchronization operations and the pertinent control structures in the process.

The synchronization constructs are modeled by combinations of SET, RESET, and WAIT operations applied to event variables. Event variables are binary valued variables. They may be set to true (SET), set to false (RESET), or a process may be suspended until a logical expression over event variables is true (WAIT). For the languages we have considered, SET, RESET, and WAIT appear to be sufficient to model all synchronization constructs.

The subgraphs are linked together by inter-process precedence edges (IPPEs) as shown in Figures 7. An IPPE is an edge:

$$(n_{i_k}, n_j) \in \{(n_{i_1}, n_j), (n_{i_2}, n_j), ..., (n_{i_m}, n_j)\}$$

such that at least one of the n_{i_k}s must execute before n_j can execute. Thus the IPPEs indicate inter-process orderings.

Since a WAIT on an event variable cannot be satisfied until a SET for that event variable has been executed, the IPPEs may be viewed as

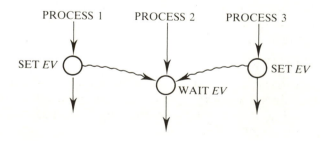

Figure 7

linking all SETs for a particular event variable to all of the WAITs for that same event variable.

The WAIT condition can be a logical expression over event variables, and many SETs can occur for any particular event variable. This results in multiple IPPEs which lead to the same WAIT node. These IPPEs are grouped in conjunctive normal form.

In the X language, the synchronization constructs can be modeled as follows:

(1) SCHEDULE   a schedule is treated as a SET on an event variable representing permission for a process to execute.

(2) PROCESS   a process is treated as having a WAIT on the event variable representing permission to execute.

(3) CLOSE   a close is treated as a RESET on the event variable representing permission for the process to execute.

(4) SIGNAL   a signal is treated as a SET, followed immediately by a RESET.

V.3   Spurious IPPE elimination

The last step in the construction of the Inter-Process Precedence Graph is to remove arcs which reflect impossible execution sequences.

The presence of each IPPE in this graph should indicate that three conditions have been satisfied:

(1) The predecessor node causes a term in the wait condition of the successor node to become true.

(2) The predecessor node will execute before the successor node in at least one legal execution sequence.

(3) In at least one of the execution sequences in (2) the term will not become false again before the wait has completed.

During the initial building of the graph, however, the IPPEs which are inserted satisfy only condition (1) above, and it is possible for some of these to violate condition (2) or (3) above. Those that do are spurious, and for more accurate results should be removed prior to performing any analysis.

For example, Figure 8 contains a section of an Inter-Process Precedence Graph, as it would appear immediately following IPPE insertion. The section corresponds to parts of two parallel processes, synchronizing themselves using one event variable, *ev*. Originally, *ev* has the value false, and no other processes are using it. The node numbering is chosen arbitrarily. The presence of an IPPE from node 3 to node 4 should indicate that in some sequences it is the execution of node 3 that allows for the completion of the wait at node 4. However, inspection of

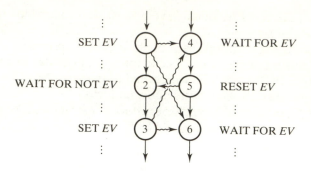

Figure 8

the code reveals that node 5 must execute before the wait at node 2 can complete, preventing node 3 from being reached until after the wait at node 4 is completed. The IPPE therefore violates condition 2, and should be removed. In addition, the IPPE from node 1 to node 6 should indicate that the wait at node 6 can complete at any time after node 1 has executed. However, node 1 must always execute before the wait at node 4 can complete, and hence its effect will be negated by node 5 before node 6 can be reached. This IPPE should also be removed, as it violates condition 3.

Spurious IPPEs can be removed by using two algorithms, BEFORE and AFTER. These recursive algorithms determine the sets of nodes whose execution will occur before or after each node n in the graph. The BEFORE(n) set is calculated so that it contains all those nodes which, if they are executed at all, are executed before node n. To do this, the BEFORE set of the strongly connected component containing n is first determined and added to BEFORE(n). Then, nodes in the intersection of the BEFORE sets of those nodes with edges into n and lying on elementary paths from an entry node to n's component are added. Finally, members of the intersection of the BEFORE sets of nodes which are tails of IPPEs into n are included also. The AFTER(n) set likewise contains all nodes which, if executed at all, are executed after node n; it is computed in a manner similar to BEFORE.

If, for any IPPE, the predecessor node is in the AFTER set of the successor node, or the successor node is in the BEFORE set of the predecessor node, condition (2) above is violated, and the IPPE is removed. If, for any IPPE, a node negating the effect of the predecessor node occurs in the AFTER set of the predecessor node and the BEFORE set of the successor node, the IPPE violates condition (3) above and is removed. The removal of an IPPE may alter the generated BEFORE and AFTER sets, so these must be regenerated after an IPPE is removed. The process iterates until no more spurious IPPEs can be found. Note that the presence of spurious IPPEs acts to increase potential concurrency so that the generated BEFORE and AFTER sets will be subsets of the actual BEFORE and AFTER sets. This implies that the relative orderings we use are genuine, and only spurious IPPEs can be removed.

If, at any time during the IPPE elimination a node is found to be in its own BEFORE or AFTER set, this indicates the presence of a guaranteed deadlock in the code. The effect of the deadlock may permeate throughout the entire graph in an unpredictable manner, so the analysis will terminate at this point.

VI   Data-usage anomaly detection

The data-usage anomaly detection system will first be described in relation to the detection of intra-procedural and inter-procedural anomalies in programs containing no synchronization constructs. This will be followed by a discussion of the modifications necessary to incorporate concurrency into the analysis to enable detection of inter-process data-usage anomalies.

The single-process analysis system is designed to detect anomalous data flow patterns, symptomatic of programming errors, not only along paths within subprogram units but also along paths which cross unit boundaries. The algorithms used to detect these patterns of variable usage employ two types of graphs to represent execution sequences of a program. The first, a flow graph, is used to represent the flow of control from statement to statement within a subprogram unit. Note that while a statement containing a subprogram invocation is represented as a single node, that node actually represents all the data actions which occur inside the called unit. Because of the order in which subprogram units are processed, the data flow information in the called unit can be passed across the boundary without placing its control structure at the point of invocation in the calling unit.

The other type of graph used is the call graph, which has the same form as a flow graph, but its nodes represent subprogram units and its edges indicate invocation of one unit by another. The call graph is used to guide the analysis of the units comprising a program in an order referred to as 'leafs-up.' The leaf subprograms, which invoke no others, are processed first; then those units which invoke only processed units are analyzed in a backward order with the main program being processed last. In order to use this approach, the call graph must be acyclic. If the call graph contains cycles, indicating recursion, analysis is terminated.

At the core of the data flow analysis is the idea of sets of variables called 'path sets,' which are associated with nodes in the flow graph. Membership of a variable in a path set for a node indicates that a particular sequence of data actions on that variable occurs at the node. The three possible actions are reference, define, and undefine. For statements containing no procedure or function invocations, determination of path set membership is straightforward. For instance, for the assignment statement, $\alpha = \alpha + \beta$, associated with a node n, α and β will be placed in those path sets which represent a reference as the first data action at n. α will also be placed in those path sets representing an arbitrary sequence of actions followed by a definition. A variable γ appearing in the same subprogram, would be placed in the path set representing no action upon the variable at node n.

Let us consider a leaf subprogram. Once the path sets have been determined for the nodes in its flow graph, the path sets for the unit as a whole can be constructed using the algorithms described in [4]. The same procedures are followed whether analyzing variables declared in the unit or global to it. For formal parameters and global variables, the path sets are used for passing variable usage information across subprogram boundaries and are saved in a master table as each unit is analyzed. At the same time as these path sets for the unit as a whole are created, additional path sets are formed for each node reflecting what sequences of data actions occur entering and leaving that node. By intersecting path sets representing sequences of actions entering (or leaving) the node and occurring at the node, anomalous data flow patterns are detected. The three types of anomalies found in this manner are:

(1) a reference to an uninitialized variable;

(2) two definitions of a variable with no intervening reference;

(3) failure to subsequently reference a variable after defining it.

When a non-leaf subprogram is analyzed, path set membership is determined as for a leaf with this exception: when a subprogram invocation is encountered at a node, path set information must be passed from the invoked unit to this node. First the path sets for the invoked routine as a whole are retrieved from the master table. Then the actual arguments are placed in the same path sets as their corresponding formal parameters. This is also done for any global variables which are members of the path sets for the invoked unit. Thus, the data actions which occur in the invoked subprogram are reflected in the path sets for the node containing the invocation. Other than this, the analysis follows the same steps as outlined for a leaf unit.

In addition to the aforementioned anomalous path detection, the analysis provides information which may be used for program documentation. This includes the order in which subprograms may be invoked, which variables must be assigned values before entry to a unit and which variables are actually assigned values there, as well as the side-effect data flow of global variables as a result of the subprogram's invocation.

Now let us consider the effect of the inclusion of synchronization constructs upon the analysis. To analyze the usage of variables global to more than one process, we must consider the entire Flow and Precedence Graph at once. We cannot use the leafs-up ordering technique as we did for subprogram units in single-process programs since now the subgraphs for the units may contain IPPEs connecting them to other processes' subgraphs. Although that technique could still be used for those variables not participating in the concurrency, it would be preferable to be able to process all variables in parallel. This can be done by performing the analysis for all variables over the entire Flow and Precedence Graph, in which case the call graph would not be needed. However, it appears advantageous to integrate the leafs-up technique where possible to enable variable usage information gathered about subprograms to be compressed and inserted at each invocation point.

When performing data flow analysis on concurrent processes, paths through the flow graph give information on sequential patterns of references and definitions, but it is also necessary to know what other nodes in the graph could be executing concurrently with a given node. Therefore preliminary analysis must be performed upon the graph itself to find these sets of concurrent nodes. We first determine the sets of nodes whose execution will occur before or after each node n using the BEFORE and AFTER algorithms described in Section V.3. Then, for node n in process p, CONCURRENT (n) contains those nodes m, not in p, such that $m \notin$ BEFORE(n) and $m \notin$ AFTER(n).

By using the knowledge of the dominators of a node, these sets can be further subdivided into BEFORE, ALWAYS_BEFORE, AFTER, ALWAYS_AFTER, CONCURRENT, and ALWAYS_CONCURRENT, hereafter collectively referred to as the execution sequence sets. ALWAYS_BEFORE(n) is the subset of BEFORE(n) which contains those nodes m' such that all paths from the start of the process to n include node m'; whereas $m \in$ BEFORE(n) indicates the m lies on at least one path from the start of the process to n. Similarly for AFTER(n) and ALWAYS_AFTER(n). The execution of a member of ALWAYS_CONCURRENT(n) may occur either before, after, or in parallel with n. This possibility exists for all execution sequences which include n. However, for a member of CONCURRENT(n), the potential for concurrency of execution exists for at least one sequence which includes n, but not necessarily for all sequences.

The form of the path sets and the anomaly detection techniques for multi-process programs are similar to those for single-process programs, but the data flow algorithms must be modified to work on the expanded process flow graph containing precedence edges. Now, predecessors and successors of a node may be in different processes.

Consider the graph segment in Figure 9. Assume that no usage of alpha has appeared prior to this segment. Node 1 must execute before node 2 and is the head of an IPPE originating in process q. Since a definition of alpha occurs on all paths into node 4, it will occur before the execution of node 1, and thus node 2. Therefore, the data flow along the IPPE (4, 1) is treated differently from that along a regular flow graph edge. Similarly, in Figure 10, although it appears that beta is defined twice within q on the path through nodes 4, 5, 6, 7, 8 with no intervening reference, because of the IPPEs (5, 1) and (3, 7), the analysis will indicate that beta will always be referenced between the definitions.

The three types of anomalies detected in single-process programs are also applicable to multi-process programs. In addition, the concurrent node sets enable the detection of the possibility of references and definitions of variables at these nodes occurring in an unspecified order.

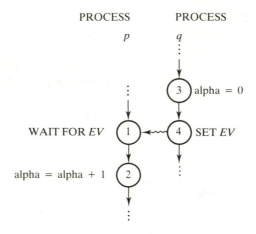

Figure 9

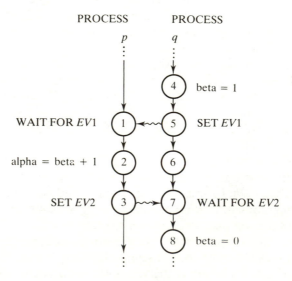

Figure 10

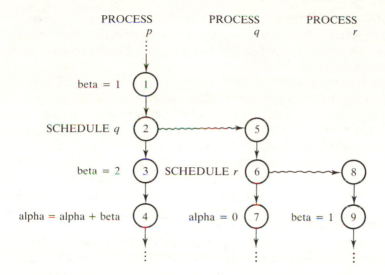

Figure 11

Consider, for example, the situation in Figure 11. Here, alpha may or may not be defined when node 4 is executed since node 7 ∈ CONCUR-RENT(4). This is a possible case of anomaly type (1), a reference to an uninitialized variable. An example of anomaly type (2), two definitions of a variable with no intervening reference, occurs on the path 1, 2, 3 involving the variable beta. Another case of double definition, this time involving concurrency and representing a race condition, concerns beta at the concurrent nodes 3 and 9: the value of beta used in the computation at node 4 depends upon the order of execution of these nodes. Finally, anomaly type (3), the failure to subsequently reference a variable after defining it, is exemplified in Figure 10 by beta, last assigned a value at node 8. (Algorithms for the detection of these anomalies are presented in [1].)

VII   Synchronization anomaly detection

In addition to aiding in the search for data-usage anomalies, the execution sequence sets as each node can be used in the detection of potential synchronization anomalies. These are anomalies arising directly from potential concurrencies in the programs. It was encouraging to discover that these sets are sufficient for the detection of the three types of synchronization anomalies upon which we focused.

The first such anomaly is the potential for infinite waits, which includes deadlock as a subset. A process will wait indefinitely at a WAIT statement if the wait condition is false when the WAIT is reached during execution, and either no combination of statements will be executed in other processes that would set the wait condition to true, or all such combinations will be prevented from executing while waiting on this process (a deadlock).

The detection method involves considering each WAIT node in turn for legal execution sequences resulting in an infinite wait. Note that in order to produce reasonable time and space bounds for the algorithm, all possible combinations of loops and branches in a process are treated as legal execution sequences, even though some of these may constitute unexecutable paths due to the particular branch and loop conditions. This implies that all potential anomalies of this type will be discovered, but in addition some potential anomalies may be flagged where they do not exist.

The wait condition will have already been converted to conjunctive normal form during the insertion of IPPEs. For a potentially infinite wait, there must be at least one conjunct which can remain indefinitely false from the time the wait is started. This would require all the terms in that conjunct to remain indefinitely false. Therefore, each conjunct, and each term in the conjunct, is checked for the potential to remain indefinitely false. If it cannot be proved that the wait is always finite, an anomaly is assumed.

The worst possible case is assumed while checking a term. It is assumed that a legal execution sequence exists in which the only nodes that occur setting the term to true must always execute; i.e., those nodes setting the term to true from the ALWAYS_BEFORE, ALWAYS_CONCURRENT and ALWAYS_AFTER sets for the WAIT node. Further, it is assumed that all nodes from the concurrent sets will, in fact, execute before the WAIT is reached. Given these assumptions, and considering only those nodes which now will execute before the WAIT is reached, the term will be indefinitely false if each node setting it to true can be followed by another setting it back to false. Thus the wait at WAIT node w can be infinite if there exists a conjunct c in the wait condition such that:

for each term t in c and
for each node n_T setting t to true,

$$n_T \in \{\text{ALWAYS\_BEFORE}(w) \cup \text{ALWAYS\_CONCURRENT}(w)\}$$

there exists a node n_F setting t to false,

$$n_F \in \{\text{CONCURRENT}(n_T) \cup \text{AFTER}(n_T)\}$$
$$\cap \{\text{BEFORE}(w) \cup \text{CONCURRENT}(w)\}$$

The algorithm itself is a direct implementation of the above set expression.

Two other types of anomalies proved readily detectable from the execution sequence sets. The first of these is the possibility that a process can be rescheduled while it is still running. Checking for this requires examining the execution sequence sets at each schedule or close node. If at either of these nodes, a different schedule or close on the same process appears in the CONCURRENT set, then there is a potential anomaly. Further, if a different schedule on the same process appears in the BEFORE set at a schedule node, and the corresponding close is not also in the BEFORE set, this also signifies a potential anomaly.

The last type of anomaly is the possibility of the premature termination of a process. Although this is generally not a language definition violation, it may be indicative of a programming error. For instance, if a process which updates a database is terminated prematurely, it may leave the database in an inconsistent state. Checking for premature termination requires looking at the execution sequence sets at each terminate node. If the close node of any process that could be terminated by a particular terminate statement is in either the CONCURRENT set or the AFTER set of the terminate node, that process could be terminated prematurely.

We anticipate that anomalies specific to other concurrent languages will also prove to be readily detectable from the execution sequence sets, although this work still remains to be done.

An additional area that we are exploring is the checking of assertions. It is likely that, in certain circumstances, the system developer will wish to obtain information about the system that is unrelated to any specific anomaly, e.g., whether a particular execution ordering is forced, possible, or impossible. The execution sequence sets may be used to test assertions about the time orderings of individual nodes. By examining the sets at the open and close nodes we can readily test assertions about whole processes. Other time-ordering assertions must be ultimately reducible to combinations of assertions about individual nodes.

We are currently investigating the needs of system developers to determine additional assertions that would be useful.

VIII   Conclusion

The anomaly detection technique appears to provide an approach to software system analysis that does not suffer from many of the traditional problems of decidability and computational complexity. Its value is highly dependent on the ability to derive high-quality information concerning anomalies. However, the dual aims of obtaining high-quality information and using algorithms with pleasant computational complexity characteristics are sometimes in conflict. We have been successful so far in obtaining polynomial-time algorithms; but more formal work is needed to determine the limits of this approach with respect to specific problems.

We plan to expand the scope of our results by considering other languages within the class we have roughly delineated here. We expect this will bring us to considering the question of how best, with respect to specific language constructs and specific behavioral properties, to determine an abstract representation (akin to our present Flow and Precedence Graphs) which contains the information required for analysis.

We also plan to broaden the scope of the anomalies we can detect and enhance our system by the addition of anomaly definition capabilities.

References

[1]   Bristow, G., Drey, C., Edwards, B., and Riddle, W. Design of a system for anomaly detection in HAL/S programs. CU-CS-151-79, Dept. of Computer Sci., Univ. of Colorado at Boulder, March 1979.

[2]   Campbell, R. A., and Habermann, A. N. The specification of process synchronization by path expressions. In *Lecture Notes in Computer Science*, **16**, Springer-Verlag, Heidelberg, 1974.

[3]   Drey, C. 'DAVE-HAL/S: A system for the static data flow analysis of single-process HAL/S programs,' University of Colorado Technical Report CU-CS-141-78, November 1978.

[4]   Fosdick, L. D., and Osterweil, L. J. Data flow analysis in software reliability. *Computing Surveys*, **8**, 3 (September 1976), 305–330.

[5]   Greif, I. A language for formal problem specification. *Comm. ACM*, **20**, 12 (December 1977), 931–935.

[6]   Habermann, A. N. Path expressions. Computer Sci. Dept., Carnegie–Mellon Univ., Pittsburgh, June 1975.

[7]   *HAL/S Language Specification*. Intermetrics, Inc., Cambridge, Massachusetts, June 1976.

[8]   Ogden, W. F., Riddle, W. E., and Rounds, W. C. Complexity of expressions allowing concurrency. *Proc. Fifth ACM Symp. on Prin. of Programming Languages,* Tucson, January 1978, pp. 185–194.

[9]   Osterweil, L. J., and Fosdick, L. D. 'DAVE – A validation, error detection and documentation system for Fortran programs,' *Software – Practice and Experience*, **6**, (1976), 473–486.

[10] Peterson, J. L., and Bredt, T. H. A comparison of parallel computation. *Proc. IFIP Congress 74*, Stockholm, August 1974, pp. 466–470.

[11] Peterson, J. L. Computation sequence sets. *J. of Comp. and Sys. Sci.,* **13**, 1 (August 1976), 1–24.

[12] Peterson, J. L. Petri nets. Dept. of Computer Sci., Univ. of Texas, Austin, August 1978.

[13] Reif, J. H. Analysis of communicating processes. TR 30, Computer Sci. Dept., Univ. of Rochester, New York, May 1978.

[14] Riddle, W. E. The hierarchical modelling of operating system structure and behavior. *Proc. ACM 72 National Conf.*, Boston, August 1972, pp. 1105–1127.

[15] Riddle, W. E. A design methodology for complex software systems. *Proc. Second Texas Conf. on Computing Systems*, Austin, November 1973, pp. 22.1–22.8.

[16] Riddle, W. E. The equivalence of Petri nets and message transmission models. SRM/97, Computing Lab., Univ. of Newcastle upon Tyne, England, August 1974.

[17] Riddle, W. E. An approach to software system modelling and analysis. To appear: *J. of Computer Languages*.

[18] Riddle, W. E. An approach to software system behavior description. To appear: *J. of Computer Languages*.

[19] Saxena, A. The static detection of deadlocks. CU-CS-122-77, Dept. of Computer Sci., Univ. of Colorado at Boulder, November 1977.

[20] Shaw, A. C. Software descriptions with flow expressions. *IEEE Trans. on Software Engineering*, **SE-4**, 3 (May 1978), 242–254.

[21] Taylor, R. N., and Osterweil, L. J. A facility for verification, testing and documentation of concurrent process software. *Proc. Compsac*, **78**, Chicago, November 1978, pp. 36–41.

[22] Wileden, J. C. Modelling parallel systems with dynamic structure. RSSM/71 (Ph.D. Thesis), Dept. of Computer and Comm. Sci., Univ. of Michigan, Ann Arbor, January 1978.

24

A General-Purpose Algorithm for Analyzing Concurrent Programs

Richard N. Taylor
University of Victoria

Developing and verifying concurrent programs presents several problems. A static analysis algorithm is presented here that addresses the following problems: how processes are synchronized, what determines when programs are run in parallel, and how errors are detected in the synchronization structure. Though the research focuses on Ada, the results can be applied to other concurrent programming languages such as CSP.

CR categories and subject descriptors: D.2.2 [**Software Engineering**]: Tools and Techniques; F.3.1 [**Logics and Meanings of Programs**]: Specifying and Verifying and Reasoning about Programs – Ada

General terms: algorithms, verification

Additional key words and phrases: concurrent software, process synchronization errors, static analysis.

I Introduction

Designers of concurrent software systems are faced with a number of difficult verification problems. One problem is ensuring that the system will never enter an infinite wait. Another problem concerns program actions that may occur in parallel: it must be ensured that no undesirable parallelism is present. Fundamental to these problems, at least for programs written in Ada, is knowledge of all the synchronization that may occur during execution. This paper addresses the issue of constructing a tool to aid in these determinations.

Experience in verifying and testing sequential software has indicated the value of a number of different approaches to verification tasks. Different tools allow the system to be studied from various viewpoints: each tool possesses its own strengths and weaknesses and is appropriate at different times during the software life cycle. One capability found useful is static analysis, that is, analysis that is performed on a model of the program without requiring test executions [12].

An earlier paper considered the detection of several concurrency-related anomalies through the application of one static analysis technique, data flow analysis [13]. While there were some encouraging results, they were obtained only for a highly restrictive concurrent programming language (a subset of HAL/S [11]). In particular, no intertask synchronization was allowed; a task could only schedule other tasks or wait for their completion. Efforts to extend these techniques to a larger subset of HAL/S, one that included intertask synchronization, met with substantial difficulty. It was surmised that this was largely due to the undisciplined nature of the HAL/S synchronization primitives, but subsequent investigations, as described below, have shown the need for an entirely different approach.

To provide a specific basis for the following discussion, reference will be made to programs written in Ada, although the results have applicability to any programs that use rendezvous-like synchronization. (Included in this category are programs written in CSP [6] and Distributed Processes [2].)

Briefly described, Ada allows the specification and simultaneous execution of any number of tasks. The means of task synchronization and primary method of intertask communication is a *rendezvous*. (Tasks may also access shared objects.) As the Ada reference manual [8] states:

> *"An entry call is written as a procedure call; it specifies that the task issuing the call is ready for a rendezvous with another task that has this entry. The called task is ready to accept the entry call when its execution reaches a corresponding accept statement, which specifies the action then to be performed. After completion of the rendezvous, both the calling task and the task having the entry may continue their execution in parallel. A select statement allows a selective wait for one of several alternative rendezvous."*

A task reaching an entry call may not proceed until a rendezvous has been made; similarly, a task reaching an accept statement may not proceed until a rendezvous has been made. As several tasks may simultaneously call the same entry, the system supervisor may have to decide the order in which they will be serviced. While waiting for a rendezvous, the entry calls are queued on order of arrival. The reader unfamiliar with Ada is referred for further details to the Ada language Reference Manual [8].

Section 2 describes the analysis tasks in more detail and illustrates the accuracy that may be obtained. The latter is an important issue since static analysis requires assumptions concerning path executability. Several algorithm design principles are also noted. A formalization of the tasks may be found in a companion paper [14]. Sections 3 and 4 proceed to describe the analysis algorithm. It is fully capable of ascertaining all rendezvous which may take place during execution, all actions which may occur in parallel, and all infinite wait situations which may arise. Section 4 also argues that the algorithm may well be efficiently applied in some practical situations, a significant issue since [14] demonstrates that for all but the most trivial programs the decision problems corresponding to the analysis tasks are either NP-complete or inherently exponential. Section 5 presents a number of conclusions.

2   Analysis tasks

The formulation of the analysis tasks, as well as the analysis algorithm, is influenced in substantial measure by the need to provide certain characteristics in an analysis tool. These characteristics, which are not independent or even necessarily compatible, are the factors that determine the tool's utility. The prime characteristic is accuracy of the results. It must be assured that no error phenomenon will be missed, but at the same time the amount of superfluous reports must be kept to a minimum. Some superfluous phenomena are unavoidable, of course, because all intratask program paths are assumed to be executable in the static analysis model. The second characteristic is a consequence of this inaccuracy: the tool user must be able to effectively determine which anomaly reports correspond to real errors in the software and which are spurious. The third characteristic is efficiency.

The first of the analysis tasks and the issue of accuracy of results may best be described via examples. In Ada, determination of all possible synchronization translates to determination of all rendezvous that may occur during execution. The rendezvous that will be detected by the analysis algorithm are indicated in the following two examples.

The first example is shown in Figure 1. The flowgraphs of two tasks, $T1$ and $T2$, are presented. It is assumed that both are activated simultaneously by some other (unshown) program; furthermore, only $T1$ attempts to rendezvous with $T2$'s entry, P. The flow of control within each task is straightline. A naive way of graphically indicating the rendezvous that could occur is by adding edges I, II, III, and IV between the two flowgraphs. Clearly, edges III and IV represent rendezvous that will never occur in any execution of the program. Thus, they are not possible rendezvous and should not be included in the model. If a less strict view of precision is taken and edges III and IV were included in the analysis model, the quality of the analysis would be compromised. For instance, assuming V to be a variable global to $T1$ and $T2$, it could be inferred from edge III that the reference and definition of V could take place in parallel, and hence, in an unpredictable and possibly wrong order. Similarly, if edge IV represents a rendezvous which occurs in some

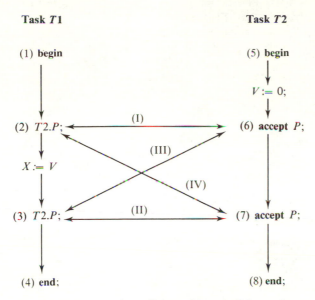

Figure 1 Examples of possible and impossible rendezvous.

execution E of the program, then we must also assert that in E the entry call on P at statement 3 will never be satisfied, and $T1$ will enter an infinite wait.

Figure 2 illustrates that for some programs it is unavoidable that some rendezvous deemed possible in the model as a result of static analysis will not correspond to any rendezvous which may actually occur. Similar assumptions are made for the tasks of Figure 2 as were made for Figure 1: both $T1$ and $T2$ are activated simultaneously by some other program and only $T1$ attempts to rendezvous with $T2$'s entry, P. This figure illustrates that $T1$'s control flow is no longer straightline, but includes two if-then-else statements, both of which test the same Boolean condition B. It is clear that the possible rendezvous indicated by edge I may indeed occur, while that represented by edge II will never occur in any execution. Realizing that fact requires the knowledge that the path in $T1$ indicated by statement sequence (1)(2)(4)(6) is unexecutable. In the general case, such a determination would require use of symbolic execution techniques [7]. (Even then it may not be possible to determine the path executability.) Consequently, the analysis algorithm will allow the rendezvous indicated by both edges I and II. Our analysis, therefore, is accurate up to the point where symbolic execution is required.

Determination of the actions in a program that may occur in parallel results from inferring the (transitive) effects of the rendezvous which are deemed possible. The first example above illustrated such an inference. Assuming rendezvous I to occur, $V := O$; and $X := V$; will not occur in

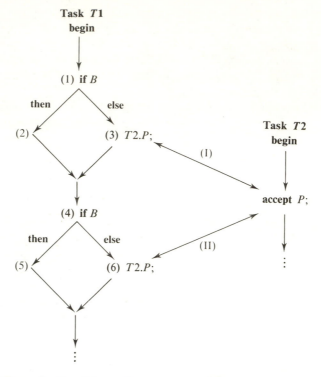

Figure 2   Possible rendezvous according to static analysis.

parallel; assuming III to occur, the two statements may be inferred to possibly execute simultaneously.

Detection of infinite waits that may arise is defined to be detection of situations where a task can become permanently blocked at a given node. Such blockage may occur at an entry call, accept statement, or end node, and may propagate to other tasks, causing their blockage. With this definition the traditional notion of deadlock is subsumed. Referring to Figure 2, if B is true and the only calls on P are those shown in the diagram then task $T2$ will be indefinitely blocked at *accept P*. Additional examples in the subsequent sections in addition to consideration of the analysis algorithm itself will serve to make these informal notions clearer.

3   Analysis preliminaries

3.1   Input

The items of information required by the analysis procedure of Section 4 are described below. Each is available as a by-product of the program compilation process. (Effective integration of an analysis tool with expected constituents of an Ada programming support environment (APSE) [3] is therefore anticipated.) The analysis procedure is described in generic terms in order to communicate the essential notions and permit application to languages other than Ada. Many language specific details which are not essential to the analysis procedure are not considered.

The first two items required are commonly known: the program call graph and program scope information. The call graph indicates the subprogram invocation structure – what each program unit may call and what may call it. The scope information indicates the nesting, or hierarchical structure of a program's constituents.

Let UNIT denote the set of uniquely identified program units for a program S. For our purposes we will consider a block to be a unit, as well as procedures, functions, and tasks. (Consideration of packages would serve only to add distracting detail inessential to the presentation. No loss of generality results from this simplification.) Let the number of elements in UNIT be denoted U.

Denote by $CG(S) = (P, I)$ the call graph of a program S. P is the set of nodes, I the set of arcs. There is a one-to-one correspondence between the nodes p_i of P and the elements of set UNIT. $(p_i, p_j) \in I$ iff the unit that p_i represents may invoke the unit represented by p_j. p_i may invoke p_j if:

(1) p_j is a subprogram and p_i may call it or

(2) p_j is a block within the body of p_i

The scope information of greatest concern is that which indicates the nesting of task declarations. In Ada task types may be declared. Objects of those types (individual tasks) may be declared in inner scopes or anywhere the type declarations can be seen. Our consideration of task types that are components of other types, such as access types, records, or arrays, is subject to the restrictions described further below. Tasks are activated upon entry to the scope in which the task object is declared; they may continue to exist as long as the task in which the declaration appears continues to exist.

Let TASKS denote the set of all tasks t_i declared in program S. Thus TASKS is a subset of UNITS. $|\text{TASKS}| = T$. The main subprogram is implicitly considered and counted as a task. (If the main routine is recursive, a new main routine is created whose sole action is to call the subprogram that was originally the main program. Thus the main routine can safely be considered a task.)

The third item required as input by the analysis procedure is the annotated program flowgraph. The flowgraphs which represent a program are defined to correspond to the elements of set UNIT.

DEF   An Ada program S is a set of rooted, directed flowgraphs $\{G_i, ..., G_U\}$, where $U = |\text{UNIT}|$. Each $G_i = (N_i, A_i, r_i)$ where N_i is the set of nodes in G_i, each node representing a statement of unit i; A_i is the set of arcs of G_i, each arc representing possible flow of control: and $r_i \in N_i$ is the root node of unit i, representing unit i's first executable statement. (Since blocks are considered units in their own right, a single node is used in the unit declaring the block, taking the place of the block and representing a call on the implicit procedure defined by the block.)

Annotated flowgraphs produced by compilation systems typically mark each node fully, indicating the type of statement the node represents, the program objects the statement contains (variables, functions, entries, etc.), the particular use of each object (e.g., referenced or defined), and so on. Such complete, detailed information for every node is not necessary for the synchronization analysis. It only requires a small subset of nodes to be annotated. These nodes include the synchronization statements themselves, some begin and end statements, and, for analysis of parallel actions, nodes which manipulate shared objects. They are listed in detail in Section 4.

Since the analysis described in this paper is only concerned with the synchronization structure of a program, the input flowgraphs need not contain all the structural information they normally do. In fact, if the input flowgraphs are provided by part of a compilation system, synchronization analysis can be speeded up slightly by removing some of the information typically provided. On the other hand, if a special purpose tool generates the required input, streamlined flowgraphs may be produced directly [4]. Specifically, edges (and nodes) that are unnecessary in determining possible sequences of synchronization activities need not appear in the flowgraphs (though no harm is caused if they do). Figure 3 presents an example, showing a flowgraph segment adequate for variable definition and reference analysis and the corresponding flowgraph which is sufficient for synchronization analysis purposes.

If an analysis of actions which may occur in parallel is to be performed, then the statements operating on the global objects cannot be removed from the flowgraph; sequences of such operations can be combined into summary nodes, or blocks, however. Some reduction in flowgraph size may also be obtained through combination of some synchronization nodes. If the order and kind of synchronization activities that are performed on the branches of an if or case statement are identical, then the branches may be combined into straight line code. The annotation of the nodes in the straight segment should then reflect that the nodes represent two or more statements. As a result, error messages, anomaly reports, and the like, which involve the doubly annotated nodes, must be interpreted as applying to both branches of the original control structure.

This combination process can be extended further to branches

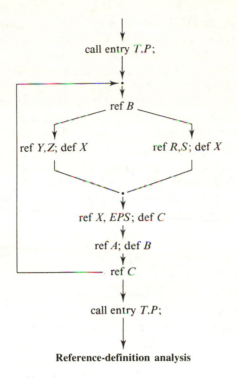

ref X, EPS; def C

ref A; def B

ref C

call entry T.P;

Reference-definition analysis

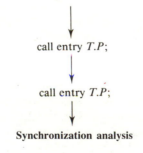

Synchronization analysis

Figure 3 Corresponding flowgraphs sufficient for variable usage analysis and for synchronization analysis.

which are equivalent only on their first activity. This activity can be removed from both branches, suitably annotated, and placed before the branch node. An analogous operation is possible if identical activities are performed as the last operation on all branches entering an end-if or end-case node.

The above description of the flowgraphs dealt only with properties they may enjoy that result in a modest improvement in analysis speed.

One simple flowgraph transformation is possible that has the effect of improving the quality of the analysis: unfolding of definite loops. A definite loop is one where the number of iterations performed is invariant with respect to different input data and the value of the invariant loop parameter can be determined at compile time. Identification and unfolding of such loops prevents analysis of spurious paths which reflect greater or fewer loop executions than are called for. It should be noted that this transformation of the flowgraph is optional, as are the previously mentioned reductions. There are surely many programs where elimination of spurious anomalies after analysis is a more efficient operation than unfolding loops and analyzing the expanded flowgraph. The manner in which this transformation improves analysis will be more clearly seen later.

3.2 Restrictions

Three restrictions on the analysis procedure exist. The first restriction is inherent to all static analysis algorithms that analyze events relative to individual program objects. If the program objects can be subscripted by variable expressions or referenced through a chain of pointers, a static tool is usually incapable of determining the particular identity of an object. In static data flow analysis (of single-process programs), difficulty is encountered in differentiating between elements of an array. In concurrency analysis of Ada programs, this problem manifests itself, for example, as difficulty in differentiating between members of a family of entries. Thus, if entry call $T.P(I)$, is encountered, it may be impossible to determine to which particular entry the reference pertains. Furthermore, difficulty may be encountered with indexed task types, arrays of records that include a task as a member, or tasks that are objects of access types. A static tool is often forced in such situations to consider the family of objects to be a single object, and every individual reference to an element of the family to be a reference to the single object representing the family. A concomitant reduction in the quality of the analysis performed must be expected.

The second restriction deals with real-time operations. In Ada programs , the only facility for controlling program actions relative to a real-time clock is the delay statement. Execution of a delay statement suspends further execution of the task for at least the amount of time specified in the command. The delay statement can be used in conjunction with knowledge of implementation hardware, scheduler algorithm, and other environmental information to aid in controlling program synchronization. This environmental information is not available to an analysis algorithm, so the only reliable procedure to follow is to ignore all such statements and determine what synchronization may occur throughout the range of possible environmental constraints. It then becomes the user's responsibility to determine if, in a particular environment, execution of the delay statement will preclude an anomaly reported by the analyzer. It should be clear, though, that dependence upon environmental factors is an inherently unsafe and certainly nonportable method of synchronization, thus this restriction is not at all unreasonable.

The third restriction arises in analyzing synchronization structures in the presence of certain types of dynamic task creation. For instance, the problem arises when a recursive procedure declares (and thus activates) a task which then calls entries external to the recursive procedure. Alternatively, when parallel action analysis is performed, the problem arises if the dynamically created task accesses global objects. An additional situation is presented if a task type is an object of an access type, and the task type specifies operations similar to those above. The difficulty in analyzing such a situation arises because of the potentially infinite number of entry calls/references to global objects which must be considered. A sufficient restriction is to bound the number of tasks that may exist simultaneously. Further consideration of the modeling of recursive procedures is found in the next section.

4 Analysis techniques

Analysis techniques are now presented for determining possible rendezvous, parallel actions, and detecting infinite waits. The algorithm is exponential in complexity for arbitrary programs (to the order of the number of tasks in the system), but optimizations are described which promote efficient analysis of a class of programs. This complexity is a consequence of the NP-completeness results of [14]. The presentation begins with a number of definitions used throughout the section. The basic technique for possible rendezvous and infinite wait analysis is then described, followed by a consideration of how several language features such as recursion are handled. Optimization of the analysis procedure is then considered as well as extensions to the basic technique which enables analysis of parallel actions. The section concludes with a short description of how analysis reports of possible events can be refined to yield reports of events that always occur.

4.1 Definitions

The following definitions are used in the description of the analysis procedures.

DEF   A tasking activity is the execution of an entry call statement, accept statement, delay statement, abort statement, or declaration of a task type, task object, or data type/object which contains a task type/object.

Note that tasks, subprograms, and blocks may all perform tasking activities.

DEF   A program unit may directly perform a tasking activity if any of the above listed statements or declarations appear within the body or declarative part, respectively, of the unit.

A program unit may also indirectly perform a tasking activity in the following manner. Let p_i and p_j be distinct nodes in the call graph $CG(S)$ of program S.

DEF   If p_j may directly perform a tasking activity and there is a path in $CG(S)$ from p_i to p_j, then p_i is said to indirectly perform a tasking activity.

Determination of the set of program units which may directly or indirectly perform a tasking activity is readily accomplished through use of information propagation techniques. The call graph $CG(S)$ supplied as input is marked to indicate the units which may directly perform a tasking activity (a characteristic easily noted during parsing). This marking is then propagated throughout the call graph such that, at the end of the propagation, if there is a path $p_i \xrightarrow{*} p_j$ in $CG(S)$ where p_j may directly perform a tasking activity, then p_i is marked as possibly indirectly performing such an activity.

This relationship can be computed using a standard transitive closure algorithm [1]. Alternatively, standard intraprocedural data flow analysis [5] is capable of performing this operation, and can do so in time roughly proportional to the number of nodes in the call graph.

State nodes will be used in the following algorithm as the points at which the relative progress of tasks are characterized.

DEF   A state node c_i in a flowgraph $G_b = (N_b, A_b, r_b)$ is a node in N_b that corresponds to any of the following statements: entry call, accept, select, select-else, delay, abort, task begin, task end, and subprogram begin, subprogram end, subprogram call, block begin, and block end, but only where the subprogram or block may directly or indirectly perform a synchronization activity. (To be completely precise, proper modeling of Ada semantics requires entry call statements and accept statements to be represented by more than one flowgraph node and thus more than one state node. Entry calls are represented by a pair of nodes, call-pending and call-engaged. Accept statements are represented by nodes awaiting-call, accept-engaged, and accept-end. Furthermore, when an accept (or entry call) is a select alternative, the select node stands for and replaces every awaiting-call (or call-pending) node. This level of detail will not be retained in the examples that follow, as the reader's sense of Ada's semantics will likely be a reliable guide.) Thus the set of state nodes in G_b is a subset of N_b.

Note   The delay statement is included in the definitions of tasking activity and state node in order to provide diagnostic information, as described later.

The successor of a state node is defined as follows. Let $G_b = (N_b, A_b, r_b)$ be a flowgraph for a unit of program S. Let c_i be a state node in N_b.

DEF   The set of successor nodes of state node c_j, denoted succ (c_i), is the set of all state nodes $c_j \in N_b$ for which there exists a path p from c_i to c_j in G_b such that there is no state node $c' \in N_b$ on p between the first node of the path (c_i) and the last node on the path (c_j).

Note that typically there will be several nonstate nodes on each path from a state node to its successors. These nodes correspond to statements governing flow of control, assignment statements (particularly those that reference global variables), and so forth. Also note that one state node may have several successors. In Figure 4, for example, the accept P node in task $T1$ has as successors the select node and the task end node. As with determining the set of program units that may indirectly perform a tasking activity, information propagation techniques may be used to determine the set of successors of a state node. Specifically, standard intraprocedural data flow analysis techniques are sufficient. In the subsequent discussion, it is assumed that the set of successor nodes is known for all state nodes.

The primary concept utilized by the analysis procedure is now defined: Let T' be the number of distinct tasks in program S. (For purposes of the following definitions we let $T' = T$, the number of tasks declared in S. In fact, T' may be greater than T due to task objects being declared in reentrant and recursive procedures. The number of tasks $T' - T$ introduced by such procedures is defined further below. Program construction that results in a task i being activated, terminated, and later reactivated does not affect the number T'.)

DEF   A concurrency state C is an ordered T'-tuple $(c_1, c_2, ..., c_{T'})$ where each c_i, $1 \leq i \leq T'$, is a state node in some flowgraph G_j, $1 \leq j \leq U$, or c_i is the marker 'inactive.' Each c_i denotes either the next state node to be executed in task i, or that task i is inactive.

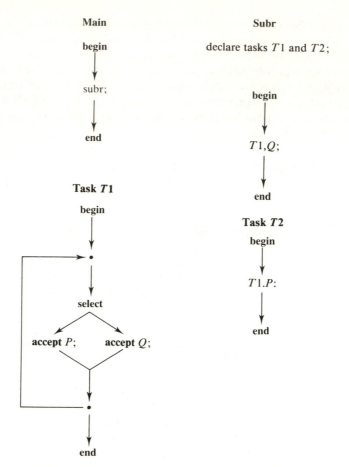

Figure 4   Example program for synchronization analysis.

A successor relationship for concurrency states is now defined. Let $C = (c_1, ..., c_{T'})$ and $\bar{C} = (\bar{c}_1, ..., \bar{c}_{T'})$ be two concurrency states for program S.

DEF $\bar{C}$ is a successor of C, denoted $\bar{C} \in \mathrm{SUCC}\,(C)$ if and only if:

(1)   For all i, $1 \leq i \leq T'$, either:
   (i) $\bar{c}_i \in \mathrm{succ}\,(c_i)$
   (ii) $\bar{c}_i = c_i$
   (iii) $c_i = $ "inactive" and $\bar{c}_i = $ begin task i or
   (iv) $c_i = $ end task i and $\bar{c}_i = $ "inactive";

(2)   There exists at least one $\bar{c}_j$, $1 \leq j \leq T'$, which represents application of case (i), (iii), or (iv) above;

(3)   Adherence to the semantics of Ada is reflected in the application of the four cases above to the definition of each $\bar{c}_i$, including any selection of $\bar{c}_i$ from $\mathrm{succ}\,(c_i)$.

Note that part (2) of this definition does not imply that $C \neq \bar{C}$, because a state node may be in its own successor set, i.e., $c_i \in \mathrm{succ}(c_i)$.

As an example of how the execution rules of Ada must be followed, let $C = (q, \bar{q})$, where q is an entry owned by task 2. The state C denotes that the next state node to be executed in task 1 is an entry call on q, while the next state node in task 2 is an accept statement for entry q. Suppose $s \in \mathrm{succ}\ (q)$ in task 1 and $t \in \mathrm{succ}\ (\bar{q})$ in task 2. Then the state (s, t) $\in \mathrm{SUCC}\ (C)$, while $(s, q) \in \mathrm{SUCC}\ (C)$ and $(q, t) \in \mathrm{SUCC}\ (C)$. State $(s, \bar{q})$ *represents that task 1 executed and completed the entry call while task 2 did not execute the accept statement, which violates the semantics of a rendezvous. A more extensive example is provided below, which illustrates the nondeterminism possible in the formation of SUCC* (C) *and the meaning of 'inactive.'* Concurrency states may be annotated to enable fulfilment of requirement(s), for example, entry queue positions must be marked.

DEF   A terminal concurrency state is a concurrency state that has no successor. A nonterminal state has at least one possible successor.

DEF   A concurrency history of program S, denoted $CH(S)$, is a sequence $C_1, ..., C_k$ of concurrency states such that:

   (i) $C_1 = (begin \ll \mathrm{MAIN\ TASK} \gg, \text{"inactive,"} ..., \text{"inactive"})$
  (ii) For all i, $1 \leq i \leq k - 1$, $C_{i+1} \in \mathrm{SUCC}\ (C_i)$.

DEF   A proper concurrency history of program S, denoted $PH(S)$, is a finite concurrency history of length k, such that for all i, j, $1 \leq i \leq k$, $1 \leq j \leq k$, $i \neq j$ implies $C_i \neq C_j$ and C_k is either a terminal state or C_k has a successor C'_k, such that there exists an m, $1 \leq m \leq k$ for which $C'_k = C_m$. (Thus a proper concurrency history has no loops.)

DEF   A complete concurrency history of a program S, denoted $H(S)$, is the set of all possible $PH(S)$.

An example will help clarify the meaning and illustrate the utility of the definitions above. A program consisting of four program units is presented in Figure 4 by showing the annotated flowgraph representations of each of the units. The main routine calls subprogram Subr, which declares (and activates) two tasks $T1$ and $T2$. Task $T1$ owns entries P and Q; Subr calls Q and task $T2$ calls P. Figure 5 presents a numbered list of all possible concurrency states for the program. Figure 6 presents four representative proper concurrency histories, listing by number and in order the concurrency states in each history. Within Figure 5 the token '_' is used to denote 'inactive.' Some explanatory notes follow.

State 24 (begin Subr, begin, begin) indicates that Subr has been

States (Main task, Task $T1$, Task $T2$)	Successor States
1. (begin, _, _)	2
2. (Subr, _, _)	24
3. ($T1.Q$, begin, begin)	4, 13, 5
4. ($T1.Q$ begin, $T1.P$)	5
5. ($T1.Q$, select, $T1.P$)	6, 16, 17, 18
6. (end Subr, end, $T1.P$)	7, 19
7. (end Subr, end, end)	8, 9, 10
8. (end Subr, _, end)	10
9. (end Subr, end, _)	10
10. (end Subr, _, _)	11
11. (end Main, _, _)	12
12. (_, _, _)	Terminal
13. ($T1.Q$, select, begin)	5, 14, 15, 6, 16
14. (end Subr, select, begin)	6
15. (end Subr, end, begin)	16, 21, 23
16. (end Subr, end, $T1.P$)	23
17. ($T1.Q$, end, end)	34, 35, 36
18. ($T1.Q$, select, end)	7, 19, 22, 9, 20
19. (end Subr, select, end)	20
20. (end Subr, select, _)	Terminal
21. (end Subr, _, begin)	23
22. ($T1.Q$, select, _)	9, 20
23. (end Subr, _, $T1.P$)	Terminal
24. (begin Subr, begin, begin)	3, 25, 26, 4, 5, 13, 27
25. (begin Subr, select, begin)	13, 27, 5
26. (begin Subr, begin, $T1.P$)	4, 27, 5
27. (begin Subr, select, $T1.P$)	5, 28, 29, 17, 18
28. (begin Subr, select, end)	18, 30, 22
29. (begin Subr, end, end)	17, 31, 32, 33, 34, 35, 36
30. (begin Subr, select, _)	22
31. (begin Subr, _, end)	33, 34, 36
32. (begin Subr, end, _)	33, 35, 36
33. (begin Subr, _, _)	36
34. ($T1.Q$, _, end)	36
35. ($T1.Q$, end, _)	36
36. ($T1.Q$, _, _)	Terminal

Figure 5 Concurrency states for program of Figure 4.

Representative Histories

1	1	1	1
2	2	2	2
24	24	24	24
3	3	25	3
4	13	27	13
5	15	29	14
6	16	17	6
7	23	34	19
8		36	20
10			
11			
12			

Figure 6   Four representative concurrency histories.

called and has completed elaboration of its declarations. The subprogram body and the two tasks are shown as poised for execution. State 5 ($T1.Q$, select, $T1.P$) indicates that the main task, which is currently executing in Subr, is waiting for acceptance of its entry call on Q. Task $T2$ is shown as waiting for acceptance of its call on P, while task $T1$ is shown as poised at its select statement, ready to accept either a call on P or on Q (thus the select 'stands for' the choice of awaiting-call on Q or awaiting-call on P). One possible successor of this state is state 6 (end Subr, select, $T1.P$). The transition from 5 to 6 indicates that, of the two rendezvous possible, nondeterministic choice caused the rendezvous involving entry Q to occur. Furthermore, given end Subr $\in$ succ($T1.Q$) in Subr and select $\in$ succ(accept Q) in $T1$, these successors were chosen in the transition. (An intermediate state, showing the rendezvous engaged, is not shown. While required by the formalism this detail is unnecessary for purposes of the example.) The other successors of state 5, namely, states 16, 17, and 18, show all of the other transitions which could legally occur. Finally, note that (end Main, end, end) is not a state in the list of Figure 5. Since $T1$ and $T2$ are declared in Subr, they must become inactive before Subr returns to the main program.

The reader is encouraged to follow through the histories of Figure 6 before proceeding to the next section. The number of concurrency states which exist for a system will be considered later. We only remark here that the relatively large number of states present in this example reflect the many ways the system can begin execution and the orders in which the tasks can terminate. Note that the number of states would be substantially reduced if '_' was used in place of 'end' for tasks $T1$ and $T2$. This would be a reasonable action because, in these cases, task termination is not dependent on the termination of any other tasks.

4.2 Basic analysis algorithm

The function of the algorithm described below is essentially to generate the complete concurrency history for a program. In so doing, all possible rendezvous are determined, all possible infinite waits are detected, and, subject to the modifications described in a subsequent section, parallel action information is obtained. The example of the preceding section should suggest how the history can be generated; the algorithm in essence simulates the synchronizaton aspects of program behavior. (The algorithm does not truly generate the complete history for a program; a few redundant transitions, and thus, histories, are eliminated as described later.)

At first it may seem unnecessary to generate the complete concurrency history just in order to obtain the above information. In fact, presentation of the histories is one of the most useful features of the algorithm. Scanning the history or histories of concurrency activities that result in an infinite wait, for example, enables the user to determine if the error may actually occur or if the error report is spurious. This analysis is possible because the concurrency history presents the sequence of task activations, terminations, rendezvous, delays, and so forth that occur along the execution sequence to the error. Some rendezvous may be ruled out because unexecutable intratask paths were taken. Others may be ruled out because of the semantics of guards attached to accept statements within select statements. Still others may be ruled out in particular operating environments because of timing characteristics (thus the need for indicating delay statements in the histories).

As was discussed in Section 2, this ability to efficiently refine analysis reports is very important. The position taken here is that the analysis algorithm should provide as much information as is possible and reasonable to aid in this subsequent analysis. Furthermore, automated aids should be developed to assist in human manipulation and query of the analysis reports. Intelligent 'browsers' like this would be appropriate components of Ada support environments. No extra work is entailed in providing the concurrency histories to a browser, as the history information is developed during rendezvous, parallel action, and infinite wait analysis. We therefore proceed to describe how this information is produced.

As illustrated in Figure 7, the complete concurrency history for a program can be represented as a graph, thus eliminating the need for full storage of identical states which appear in more than one history. (Note that Figure 7 does not show all the state transitions that are indicated in Figure 5. The omissions are explained and justified below.) A similar style of representation is assumed by the algorithm. Specifically, a table of fixed length records is used to hold the unique concurrency states. The location of a particular state in the table can be determined, for example,

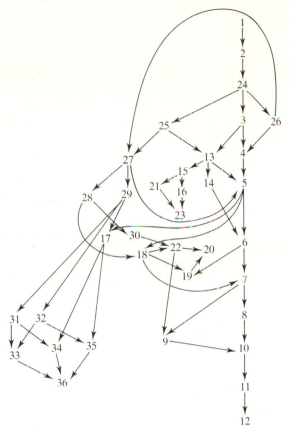

Figure 7 Graphical representation of histories developed by analysis algorithm.

by a hashing scheme [10]. (States are objects like identifiers; a lexicographic order [9] can be established which governs the placement of the objects in the table, as is done with identifiers in a symbol table.) In order to permit usage of a table with fixed length records, each unique state record contains only the fixed length state description, the index of the parent state, and indication of which tasks in the parent 'moved,' resulting in the current state. This latter information is useful in parallel action analysis, as well as by a post-process browser. Duplicate states, when created, are entered in a duplicate state table. Each fixed length record there contains three items useful in the browsing process; a pointer to the duplicated state in the unique state table, a pointer to the parent state (also in the unique state table), and indication of the moving tasks in the parent state.

As a matter of convenience we will also introduce a terminal state table, which consists solely of pointers to the states in the unique state

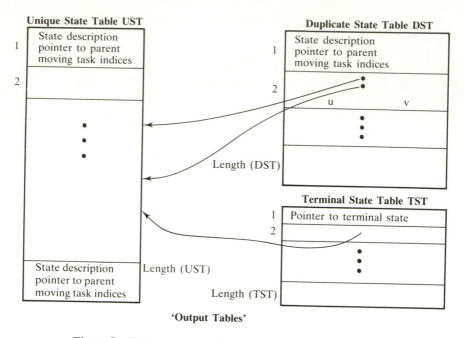

Unique State Table UST

State description
pointer to parent
moving task indices

Figure 8   Tables produced by analysis algorithm.

table which are terminal. A tool that allows the user to browse and prune the information in the tables may find additional fields useful, such as a reference count in the unique table, but such data and operations are auxiliary to this discussion. These three tables are summarized in Figure 8.

Given that the purpose of the algorithm is to determine all possible concurrency states and how they relate to each other, it is important to consider some assumptions the algorithm must *not* make. In particular, the algorithm must not make any assumptions regarding the execution environment of the program that would influence the computation of the concurrency states. Examples of such things are assumptions regarding the number of processors, the relative speeds of the processors, the algorithm used in making 'nondeterministic' choices, and processor time-slicing schemes. An assumption regarding relative processor speed, for example, could preclude a particular rendezvous from ever being possible. If software certified under such an assumption was ever installed in an environment not meeting the assumption, recertification would be required. The particular manner in which these 'nonassumptions' influence the algorithm formulation is discussed below.

The algorithm is sketched in Figure 9, using a worklist paradigm. The algorithm is initialized by placing the initial state (begin << MAIN

TASK >>, _, _, ..., _) on the worklist and entering it as the first entry in the unique state table. During the subsequent execution, a state is taken from the worklist and examined in order to determine all possible successor states. Each successor state is checked against the unique state table. If it is a new state it is entered in the UST and then placed on the worklist itself. If the state duplicates a state already in the UST, it is simply entered in the duplicate state table and is not examined any further. Thus the worklist only contains states whose successors, if any, have never been determined. When a state is pulled off the worklist and examination determines that it has no successors, it is then entered into the terminal state table.

```
procedure Simulate;

    Worklist := null;
    Push initial state on list and enter initial state in UST;

    while Worklist not empty loop

        q := first element on Worklist;

        -- States on the worklist are unexamined elements of the UST

        for i in 1..T' loop

            -- check current node in task i to see if it is possible
            -- to generate a successor state on the basis of task i's
            -- performing a rendezvous, task activation, or the like.

            if moveable (i) then

                New state z is created, reflecting task i's
                movement, as well as other tasks as required (such
                as in the case of a rendezvous occurring);

                -- z is checked against the UST

                if unique (z) then

                    Enter z in UST;
                    Push z onto Worklist;

                else enter z in duplicate state table;

                end if;

            end if;

        end loop;

    end loop;

end Simulate;
```

Figure 9   Analysis algorithm.

The point at which assumptions regarding the execution environment are not to be made is clearly in the determination of a state's successors. For instance, if the state $C_1 = (P$, accept P, Q, accept $Q)$ is being examined, two rendezvous are possible. Suppose each statement has only one successor. Denote that successor 'succ(n).' The state $C_2 = ($succ (P), succ (accept $P)$, succ (Q), succ (accept $(Q))$ is a successor state and may be the only successor state which will ever occur in a multiprocesssor environment. However, $C_3 = ($succ (P), succ (accept $(P))$, Q, accept $Q)$ is also a successor and may occur as well. Thus, C_3 (and the analogous state C_4 involving Q) *must* be generated. Furthermore, since $C_2 \in$ SUCC (C_3) and $C_2 \in$ SUCC (C_4) (and will be created when C_3 and C_4 are examined) nothing is gained by generating $C_2 \in$ SUCC (C_1). The appropriate approach, therefore, to take is to generate all successor states which result from the movement of as few tasks as possible. It can then be assured that no possible states will be overlooked. Thus, the algorithm does not truly generate the complete synchronization history $H(S)$ for a program; rather it generates all possible states and indicates the most useful history information. The history that is created is $H(S)$ minus those transitions that represent several tasks moving, where not all tasks need to move at once. (Therefore Figure 7 does not show, for example, the possible direct transition from state 7 to state 10. Only the sequences state 7 to state 8 to state 10 and state 7 to state 9 to state 10 are shown.)

The examination of a state and the generation of successors takes the form of a single scan of a state. If a begin statement is found in position i, then all the successor states representing the possible movements of task i (alone) are generated. If an entry call is encountered, the node in the task which owns the entry is examined to determine if a rendezvous is possible. If so, the state representing initiation of a rendezvous is generated. If an end statement is found in position i, tasks declared within task i are examined to see if they are all inactive. If so, the successor state representing 'movement' of task i to the inactive state is generated, all other tasks remaining unchanged. It is easy to see how the semantics of all the various statements can be modeled.

4.3   Correctness

On the basis of this discussion, correctness of the algorithm is clearly dependent upon correct generation of the successor states. This involves demonstrating that the semantics of the language are correctly reflected in the generation operation. This demonstration is left to the informal comments above, arguing that the generation operation is an implementation detail.

Proof of termination rests upon the observation that the number of possible, distinct concurrency states for any given system meeting the stated assumptions is finite. The only states examined by the algorithm are those placed on the worklist. Before a state is placed on the worklist it is checked against the unique state table; only those not already appearing in the table are entered onto the worklist and in the table. Thus no state is examined more than once. Termination is assured if indeed the number of possible distinct states is finite.

Recalling the earlier definitions, T' is the number of tasks in the system and thus the dimension of the concurrency states. Let m_1 be the total number of state nodes in the flowgraphs comprising task 1 (i.e., the number of state nodes in task 1's flowgraph plus the state nodes in the subprograms that it directly or indirectly calls), m_2 the total number of state nodes in task 2, and so forth. The worst case, as far as number of concurrency states is concerned, occurs if every state node in each task can appear in a state with every state node from all other tasks. If such were the case, there would be $m_1 \cdot m_2 \cdot m_3 \cdot ... \cdot m_{T'}$ possible states, each unique. This number is clearly well defined, and so termination is assured.

The complexity bound for the algorithm is apparent from the discussion of termination. If we let n = total number of state nodes in program S, each $m_i = O(n)$. If $T' = T$, we then have the bound of $O(n^T)$ for worst case performance of the algorithm. (The cost of checking for duplicates will be a constant factor.) As noted in [14], if severe enough restrictions are imposed on control flow, use of the select statement, and entry usage, algorithm performance will be linear in the number of state nodes. The required length of the tables used by the algorithm varies accordingly.

4.4 Modeling of language features

It is interesting to consider the effects reentrancy and recursion have on the analysis algorithm of the preceding section. The major impact they have is in determining the value T', the dimension of the concurrency state.

Reentrancy may be considered by examining three basic ways a reentrant procedure can perform a tasking activity. The first case is that of procedures which contain entry calls, abort statements, and delay statements. In this case the algorithm will correctly analyze the execution, as it simulates the copying of the procedure body into the calling task.

The second and third cases stem from reentrant procedures that declare tasks. The second case is that of the inner tasks declaring entries, and those entries being called only from the body of the reentrant procedure or other tasks declared by the procedure. In such situations, the rendezvous and infinite waits which may occur can be determined by analyzing the procedure body and its tasks separately from the rest of the system.

If the inner tasks communicate with other tasks outside the procedure, the analysis procedure cannot be broken up so simply, and we obtain the third case. Since each call of the reentrant procedure (by different tasks) creates a unique incarnation of the inner tasks, the load on the system is increased because the number of entry calls on the external entries is a function of the number of task incarnations. This load must be simulated in the algorithm. If r separate tasks (or their subprograms) call the reentrant procedure and the procedure declares s tasks, then the dimension of the concurrency state must be increased by $r \cdot s$ over what the dimension would be without the reentrant procedure. This increase allows each set of task incarnations to be modeled. (Of course, each instance of a set of tasks is uniquely identified.) It is once again apparent that the complexity of analysis is directly related to the actual number of tasks that may be active in the system. (Note however that only if the r calls on the procedure can all occur at the same time will the $r \cdot s$ tasks be simultaneously active.)

The handling of recursive procedures can be considered by examining three cases. The first case is that of procedures that perform entry calls, delays, or aborts, but do not declare any task objects. As with reentrant routines, the algorithm as stated above correctly models the execution.

The second case is procedures that declare tasks that communicate only among themselves, with the procedure that declared them, or with any routines called by the body of the procedure (down to the point where the next recursive call is made). As with the analogous situation involving reentrancy this subsystem is self-contained, thus analysis for possible rendezvous and infinite wait may be done within the subsystem, apart from analysis of the remainder of the program.

The third case is that of recursive procedures that declare task objects that communicate with tasks outside of those declared in the procedure. In this case the situation can arise where an unbounded number of tasks may be active simultaneously (thus the artifice used for reentrant procedures is inapplicable). In view of the highly artificial nature and dubious utility of this case, it appears reasonable to restrict the generality of the analysis. One restriction is to prohibit the case altogether; perhaps a better one is to set a bound on the depth of recursion. The dimension of the concurrency state vector is then increased by the product of the number of tasks declared in the procedure and the recursive depth allowed. A similar situation can arise if a task type is the object of an access variable and the allocation process occurs in an indefinite loop. Again, a bound may be set on the number of tasks which may be active simultaneously.

4.5 Parceling of analysis

The basic analysis algorithm is exponential in the number of tasks in the system. In view of the results of [14], this exponentiality is inescapable for some programs, but many practical applications need not entail such expensive analysis. A trivial example illustrates this. Suppose disjoint sets of tasks A and B begin execution in program S. Further suppose the tasks in A do not communicate with those in B (either by rendezvous or abort), nor does any task in A effect the activation or termination of any task in B. The same is true in the other direction. Lastly, S does not communicate with A or B, but only activates both sets. Clearly the analysis for possible rendezvous and infinite wait can be done independently for sets A and B. Since they may be done independently, the number of tasks considered by the analysis algorithm is reduced, resulting in an overall increase in the analysis speed for the whole system.

This subsection explores, therefore, techniques for speeding up the analysis of some programs through reduction in the number of tasks that must be considered at a time. This class of programs and the reduction process will be described in two stages. First, it will be assumed that *all* tasks are simultaneously activated – thus, only the relationship of communication to parceling will be considered. Second, the impact of task activation and termination relationships will be considered.

It should be noted at the outset that the practical utility of the techniques presented here remains to be shown. Their applicability is dependent on the style of concurrent programming that emerges for Ada. The aspects of style that will be determinative are apparent in the following discussion.

In order to simplify the presentation, instead of referring to 'statements that a task or one of its subprograms may execute,' the discussion will simply refer to 'statements a task may execute.' Also for simplicity, recursive procedures that declare tasks that communicate with tasks external to the procedure will not be considered, nor will reentrant procedures that declare tasks.

A key notion is that of a task graph.

DEF A task graph is a graph $TG = (V, E)$, where the vertex set V represents the elements of the set TASKS, and $(v_i, v_j) \in E$ iff v_i and v_j both reference the same entry (by either an entry call or an accept statement) or if v_i can abort v_j.

Recall that a graph is connected if there is a path between any two of its vertices and that a connected component of a graph is a maximal connected subgraph. Note that a task graph for a program need not be connected and, in fact, the edge set E may be empty.

THEOREM 1   *The connected components of a task graph may be analyzed separately for possible rendezvous and infinite wait.*

> **PROOF**   Possible rendezvous and infinite wait both involve entry interaction. Abort actions may also be an influence. If there is no such communication with another set of tasks, those tasks cannot influence the analysis of the component in question.
>
> With respect to the analysis algorithm, suppose that a complete program, composed of connected components A, B, ..., Z is presented for analysis. Upon reaching a state where a task in A, for example, is waiting at an entry call, from the definition of connected component it is evident that only another task in A has the possibility of making the required rendezvous. Furthermore, no task in any component B, ..., Z has the ability to affect the possible sequences of state nodes in any of the tasks of component A (since the sets of entries referenced by the tasks are disjoint and no task in any component is aborted by a task in a different component). Thus, it is evident that if the elements of the concurrency states corresponding to tasks in components B, ..., Z are held fixed by the analysis algorithm, say, at their begin nodes, and all other states generated (corresponding to execution in component A alone), then all rendezvous and infinite wait which may occur as a result of activity within A will be reported. Similarly, tasks in components A, C, D, ..., Z can be fixed and all the rendezvous and infinite wait resulting from activity in component B generated. Thus, each connected component may be analyzed separately.

Note that if analysis is done in this manner, the definition of 'terminal state' given early in this section must be changed slightly. That definition provides that, even though two tasks may be locked with respect to each other, as long as some other task represented in the state may proceed, the state is not terminal. In the analysis just described, if the locked tasks represent a connected component, then a 'terminal state' would be indicated for that component, independent of the actions of the remainder of the system.

In some cases it is possible to break up the analysis of a connected component. First, some definitions are required. The biconnected components of a connected graph G are determined by an equivalence relation on the edges of G. Two distinct edges of G are in the same equivalence class if and only if they both occur on a cycle in G. A biconnected component of G is the graph given by the set of edges in one of the equivalence classes and the set of vertices of those edges. The articulation points of a biconnected component are those vertices that are also in at least one other biconnected component of G.

The procedure is to identify the biconnected components of

a connected component, and examine the tasks represented by the articulation points to determine if they possess the properties required for parceling analysis. (An algorithm for identifying biconnected components of a graph in $O(n)$ time is found in [1].) We proceed with some further definitions.

Let B be a biconnected component of the task graph of a program S. Let TB be the set of tasks $\{t_1, ..., t_x\}$ that are represented by the vertices of B. Let $ART = \{a_1, ..., a_y\} \subseteq TB$ be the tasks that are represented by the articulation points of B. Assume $y \geq 1$. Let $EXT = TASKS - TB$, the set of tasks that are not represented in B. Without loss of generality we can number the elements of EXT $\{t_{x+1}, ..., t_T\}$, where $T = |TASKS|$. Finally, let $E_i = \{e_{i1}, ..., e_{ib}\}$ be the state nodes in task $t_i \in ART$ that are entry call or accept statements that communicate with any task in EXT. (Thus $E_i \subseteq N_i$ the nodes of the flowgraph of task t_i.)

DEF   A node $e_{ij} \in E_i$ is unconstrained if there is no path p from the root node of t_i to e_{ij} such that a node of E_i is on path p.

Note that this restrictive definition precludes cycles in t_i that include e_{ij}. (Relaxation of this restriction is considered below.) Whether or not a node e_{ij} is unconstrained can be determined using data flow analysis techniques. In contrast to the earlier definitions which could be checked with intraprocedural data flow analysis, interprocedural analysis must be done since subprograms can be part of the 'body' of the task. For this definition LIVE analysis is suitable.

THEOREM 2   If all e_{ij}, $1 \leq i \leq y$, are unconstrained, then the tasks in TB may be analyzed separately from the tasks in EXT.

PROOF   The procedure involved considers the external communication points e_{ij} always executable. That is, during the analysis of TB using the simulation algorithm, whenever an e_{ij} occurs in a concurrency state, it is assumed that the necessary rendezvous with the external task will occur. On completion of analysis of TB, another biconnected component of the system will be selected for analysis. In such subsequent steps it can be checked that all rendezvous which were assumed to occur during analysis of TB do in fact occur as required. Similarly, if a rendezvous involving e_{ij} is assumed to occur during analysis of TB, and that rendezvous must be assumed to occur during all possible executions of the tasks in TB, then the subsequent analysis steps must likewise reveal that the rendezvous will always occur on all possible executions.

Therefore, given this procedure and the definition of unconstrained node the validity of the theorem becomes apparent. Since a biconnected component is being analyzed, the occurrence of an external rendezvous can only affect the timing of actions within the biconnected component, and not the set of possible rendezvous or any infinite wait (assuming that the external rendezvous *will* occur sometime). Since each external node is unconstrained, the occurrence of a rendezvous involving it is not dependent upon previous rendezvous with the external task. The case is simply, 'Will the rendezvous always occur, or will it only occur sometimes?' This latter condition is checked in a final analysis of the entire system, comparing the assumptions made during analysis of each biconnected component with the discovered characteristics of the other components.

Several remarks are in order concerning this procedure. First, simply because a biconnected component meets all the requirements for parceled analysis, one cannot infer that the other biconnected compo-

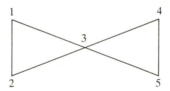

Task graph

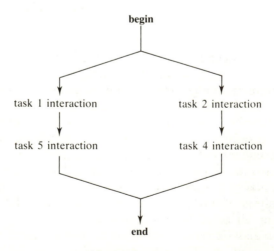

Flowgraph of task 3

Figure 10   Articulation task which permits parceling.

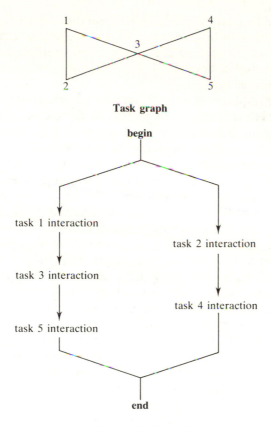

Task graph

Flowgraph of task 3

Figure 11   Articulation task not permitting parceling.

nents with which it communicates do also. Thus, to avoid possible duplication of effort, deciding if analysis can be split at an articulation point demands examination of the synchronization activities in the articulation task 'from both sides.' Figures 10 and 11 serve to illustrate this. In Figure 10 tasks 1, 2, and 3 constitute a biconnected component; so do tasks 3, 4, and 5. Task 3 is the articulation point for both components. Viewed as a member of component {1, 2, 3}, the flowgraph of task 3 reveals that all points of communication with tasks 4 and 5 are unconstrained. Likewise, when viewed as a member of component {3, 4, 5} all points of communication with tasks 1 and 2 are unconstrained. Thus, {1, 2, 3} and {3, 4, 5} may be analyzed separately.

Changing the flowgraph of task 3 to that shown in Figure 11 changes matters. Though the task graph remains the same, biconnected component {1, 2, 3} can no longer be analyzed as a parcel. This is seen by examining task 3 as a part of {1, 2, 3}. Its flowgraph shows that all points of communication with tasks 4 and 5 are not unconstrained: the task 5 interaction on the left side of the graph is constrained by the task 4 interaction preceding it. Though {3, 4, 5} remains a parcel, all five tasks must be analyzed together.

Second, the implied restriction that nodes e_{ij} cannot occur in a loop seems quite severe. It may be appropriate, therefore, to weaken the definition of unconstrained nodes to allow paths from node e_{ij} to itself, without, of course, allowing any other e_{ik} on such paths. This would require a more sophisticated post-process, however. For example, if analysis of the biconnected component containing e_{ij} necessarily assumed that a rendezvous involving it either occurred one, five, or an unlimited number of times, the subsequent analysis of the biconnected component that actually contains that rendezvous must reveal corresponding results. Of course there is no guarantee that when the tasks in the first component require five rendezvous that the remaining tasks would 'provide' exactly five, as opposed to only one or an unlimited number. The potential infinite waits which would result from such a mismatch would have to be reported in a final summary of the results.

Studies of the properties and structure of actual Ada programs are needed to determine if this avenue of research should be pursued. The obvious methodological implication is that articulation tasks should possess the simplest synchronization structure possible, so as to promote efficient analysis. This appears consistent with the goal of specifying conceptually simple interfaces between modules.

We now turn to parceling analysis in the presence of varying task activation times. The example presented in Figure 12 indicates why the foregoing procedure is inadequate. Task $T0$ is declared and activated in

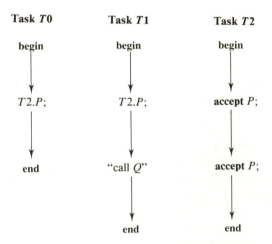

Figure 12 Illustration of need to account for task activation times.

procedure Q. It is evident that the possible rendezvous are between the entry call in $T1$ and the first acccept in $T2$, and between the call in $T0$ and the second accept in $T2$. If, however, all tasks had been assumed to start simultaneously, four possible rendezvous would be indicated.

With regard to the analysis of a connected component, the activation considerations may be taken into account by determining the program unit which dominates the activation of all tasks in the connected component. The simulation algorithm begins with that task active and proceeds from there. Other tasks which would normally be simulated as a result of starting at this dominating task need not be simulated as long as their activations cannot affect the activation or termination of any task in the connected component. Whether or not a given program unit (task or subprogram call) is necessary to the simulation can be determined through use of the call graph and task nesting information. Analysis of biconnected components in the presence of varying activation times would be handled in a similar manner: by determining the dominating task and by not simulating activities that cannot influence tasks in the component under analysis.

4.6   Analysis to determine parallel actions

The determination of actions that may occur in parallel can be accomplished through a slight modification to the above procedure coupled with a post-process. The modification required is that necessary to ensure the concurrency states produced by the simulation reflect all possible pairs of sections of code, that is, code immediately following a state node. These concurrency states may then be examined in a post-process and the parallel sections reported. If desired this report may be examined and various verification results inferred.

As the simulation algorithm and its input are described above, the concurrency states reported will not indicate all the sections of code that may occur in parallel. Consider the manner in which rendezvous are modeled. Certainly the occurrence of an entry call node in a state is not justification for inferring that the code which immediately follows it can occur in parallel with the code following the other nodes in the state; this would only be true on rendezvous completion. Yet once a rendezvous is made, both tasks are moved by the simulation algorithm to their successors. A new node, call-completed, must therefore be inserted to function as the successor of the call-engaged. No modification is required to the modeling of the accept statements as the acccept-end already adequately serves the 'rendezvous completed' function. (It was included originally to allow handling of accept bodies.) With this addition the entry calls and accept statements are sufficiently broken down so that each state node may be deemed to stand for the code which follows it (down to the next state node). A similar argument leads to the establishment of the after-block-end and subprogram-call-end nodes. The modifications, therefore, are the inclusion of the call-completed, after-block-end, and subprogram-call-end nodes in the input flowgraphs and their being correctly handled by the generate new state function.

Once the simulation algorithm has produced the list of concurrency states that may occur, a post-process may be invoked to report the parallel actions. Clearly if there are n state nodes in the entire system, a maximum of n^2 distinct parallel actions are possible. (As noted above, a state node stands for or summarizes the nonsynchronization activities of the statements which follow it, 'down to' its successors. Details of this summarization can be posted at the state node for subsequent reference.) An $n \times n$ binary valued symmetric matrix PAR is therefore postulated. A single pass over the unique concurrency states is made. At the end of the pass PAR $(i, j) = 1$ if and only if n_i can execute in parallel with n_j. The pass over the states, which establishes the values of the matrix, examines each state once, determining the parallel actions represented in the state. For each state this theoretically involves inserting the $T'(T' - 1)/2$ possible unordered pairs of nodes into the table, where T' is the dimension of the concurrency vector. This is an $O(T'^2)$ process. However, since each state is accompanied by an indication of how the state differs from its predecessor, by means of marking the states which moved, duplication of effort can be avoided. Only the combinations which include a changed (moved) state node need be inserted. In general this reduces the number of PAR table insertions (or checks for duplicates) to $O(T')$ for each state.

Using the completed PAR table, verification results can be inferred by comparing the activities summarized for each pair of nodes n_i and n_j such that PAR $(i, j) = 1$. For instance, assuming the summary information indicates references and definitions of global variables, if n_i indicates variable V is referenced following n_i and n_j indicates V is defined following execution of n_j, then if PAR $(i, j) = 1$ it follows that a reference and definition of V can occur in parallel, in an unpredictable order.

Finally, it should be noted that the use of globals may significantly degrade the performance of the simulation algorithm. For analysis purposes global variables can be thought of as an undisciplined synchronization technique whose elements can appear virtually anywhere. If the sets of tasks in which the globals appear do not correspond to the parcels identified for rendezvous analysis, the number of tasks necessarily considered at a time will be increased.

4.7 Development of MUST results

For verification purposes it is profitable to consider the set of rendezvous, parallel actions, and terminal states that *must* occur regardless of execution path taken. This is because, of course, no post-processing is required to determine if in fact the 'must' situations can occur during some executions. The problem of refining the 'may' results, as reported by the algorithm described above, to must results is therefore considered.

Refining possible infinite waits to infinite waits that must always occur is the easiest operation. If a given terminal state must always occur, regardless of execution path, then it will be the only terminal state reported by the analysis technique. This may be trivially established by examination of the terminal state table. The other possibility that exists, however, is that the system may enter an infinite (synchronous) loop. For such a condition, no additional terminal state will be entered in the terminal state table; rather the concurrency history will indicate a cycle, a repeating set of concurrency states. Therefore, verifying that the terminal state will always occur requires showing that the concurrency history contains no such cycles.

This demonstration may be done by transforming the concurrency history, as embodied in the unique state table (UST) and duplicated state table (DST), into a directed graph and then examining the graph for cycles. (As will be seen shortly, this transformation is key to efforts to refine rendezvous and parallel action results as well.) As it stands the unique state table is already a directed graph (which happens to be a tree). The representation employed above is that of having a son node point to its parent. For the discussion that follows we will assume that this representation is transformed to the more customary one of having a parent point to its sons. Since each entry in the duplicate state table contains a pair (parent, son), this information can easily be incorporated into the UST such that a given node has pointers to all its possible sons. (An edge–list representation may be used, for example.) This representation can then be examined for cycles using a depth first search, in time linearly proportional to the size of the graph [1].

Determination of rendezvous that always occur can be done in time linearly proportional to the size of this graph as well. To do so the nodes of the graph are annotated to indicate the rendezvous (if any) which occur in the state represented by the node. Intraprocedural data flow analysis techniques may then be used to propagate this information such that, at termination, the set of rendezvous which will always occur will be posted at the root node.

Two remarks are in order here. First, annotating the nodes as to the rendezvous which occur is a trivial step, as the concurrency states themselves may be interpreted as the annotation. Second, efficient data flow analysis algorithms employ so-called parallel bit vector operations [5]. Each entry in the bit vector represents a particular rendezvous. The length of the vector, and thus the amount of information that will be propagated is given by $\sum_{i=1}^{n} e_i a_i$, where e_i is the number of entry calls on entry i, a_i is the number of accept statements for entry i, and n is the number of entries in the program. Most likely this sum will be less than the number of variables declared in the program; it at least seems reasonable that they will be of the same magnitude. A standard data flow analysis package such as would be useful for program optimization could then be expected to adequately handle this task.

This latter remark is particularly significant when one considers refining parallel action results. Since there is such a close analogy between parallel actions and rendezvous it is easy to see how the above technique could be applied to this task. Yet the number of parallel actions which may occur in a program is clearly much greater than the number of possible rendezvous which may occur. Bit vectors of the size of the 'parallel-action table' described in the preceding section would therefore be required. Propagating such a large amount of information through the graph could be prohibitively slow. It seems most appropriate, therefore, to recommend that particular possible parallel actions be singled out for subsequent refinement. The technique used for rendezvous analysis could then be employed.

5   Conclusions

5.1   Summary of results

The crucial need for verification techniques applicable to software systems composed of concurrent communicating tasks has motivated the research presented in this paper. The central goal has been the development of analytic tools capable of statically detecting concurrency-related errors and facilitating understanding of the synchronization structure of a system. Three major problems were addressed in this context: determining the rendezvous which may occur during execution, determining the actions which may occur in parallel, and detecting errors in the synchronization structure which result in permanent blockage of a task. Accuracy of the analytic results was held as a primary concern, while provision for effective human interface and efficiency was also made.

The algorithm described fully answers the analysis problems listed. The answers provided are as accurate as can be obtained from static tools without resorting to symbolic execution techniques. Furthermore, the answers are provided in such a way as to promote effective post-analysis of the results. All information necessary for determining whether or not an error report describes a condition that may indeed arise during execution is available from the analysis.

Because of the related complexity results the algorithm is necessarily exponential. Fortunately the degree of exponentiality is bounded by the number of tasks present in the system undergoing analysis, and is affected by the communication pattern exhibited by the tasks. If systems are constructed so as to allow parceling of analysis and the number of tasks in a parcel is small, then acceptably efficient analysis may be expected. If, however, certain applications are naturally programmed with a large number of tasks and parceling is ruled out, then analysis may be unacceptably slow. We must wait until a number of applications have been coded in Ada before stating which, if either, is more likely to occur. It is important to note, however, that program characteristics that result in small parcels appear to correspond to application of guidelines that promote one type of 'well-structured' programs. The full impact of this entire issue is clearly an area for future investigation.

5.2 Implications of results for other languages

The analytic procedures described are essentially dependent only on the high level characteristics of the Ada synchronization mechanisms. As such, the results apply to a variety of other languages that utilize similar constructs. Clearly the results described here apply to design notations that employ the rendezvous synchronization construct. Since the rendezvous concept is a high level mechanism for controlling concurrency, it is only to be expected that design languages will use it, especially those used on systems to be coded in Ada. Since it is only on this notion that the results depend, it is also evident that CSP [6], with its version of the rendezvous, falls under the purview of this algorithm.

A language design issue is at stake here, however, and that is the use of shared objects. Even with all possible synchronization known, verifying that objects shared between tasks are used 'safely' is a difficult job. Section 4 indicated that even if the tasking structure and use of rendezvous allowed parceling of analysis, indiscriminate use of shared objects could preclude the efficiency gains otherwise made possible through parceling. Many applications may be expected to share objects between tasks until suitable mechanisms are found for ensuring efficient intertask communication.

5.3 Implications for programming methodology

The discussions with regard to parceling of the analysis indicate a programming methodology for concurrent systems. Application of the methodology will result in development of systems that may be efficiently analyzed. A reasonable supposition is that application of the methodology will also promote the creation of understandable, modular programs. (It seems plausible to assert that, in most cases, if analysis is difficult (intractable), then human comprehension will be difficult as well).

The methodology which may be inferred from the parceling

discussion may be summarized by stating that communication should be 'localized,' and that use of shared variables should correspond to the task parcels established by the communication pattern. The task graph defined is the main vehicle for describing the localization of communication. This means that a small set of tasks may communicate in any way among themselves, but communication with another set of tasks (if necessary) should be done only through a single task, and therefore by means of a single synchronization statement. The tasks in the communicating set should also be closely related with respect to their point of declaration, of course. If it is necessary to share objects between tasks, then this should be done such that only tasks in a communicating set access the objects.

5.4 Future research directions

Several areas for future research are suggested by this work. Most important is a study of the properties of actual Ada application programs in concert with the construction and evaluation of an analyzer. Resulting from such a study would be indication of the practical benefits of analysis, cost, and a determination of the effectiveness of attempts to parcel the analysis. This construction should take place in the context of an APSE to determine the proper interfaces to other tools. The author is currently engaged in such a study.

Acknowledgments

Lee Osterweil provided tremendous encouragement and direction during the course of this work, for which I am thankful. The referees gave many insightful and helpful comments, which are also appreciated.

References

[1] Aho, A. V., Hopcroft, J. E., and Ullman, J. D. *The Design and Analysis of Computer Algorithms.* Addison-Wesley, Reading, Massachusetts, 1974.
[2] Brinch Hansen, P. Distributed processes: a concurrent programming concept. *Comm. ACM,* **21**, 11 (Nov. 1978) 934–941.
[3] Buxton, J. N., and Stenning, V. Requirements for Ada programming support environments: 'Stoneman.' Department of Defense, Feb. 1980.
[4] Gallucci, Michael A. SAM/SAL User Manual and Report. University of Colorado Technical Report #CU-CS-198-81, Department of Computer Science, Feb. 1981.
[5] Hecht, Matthew S. *Flow Analysis of Computer Programs.* North-Holland, New York, 1977.

[6] Hoare, C. A. R. Communicating sequential processes. *Comm. ACM*, **21**, 8 (August 1978), 666–677.

[7] Howden, W. E. Symbolic Testing and the DISSECT symbolic evaluation system. *IEEE Trans. Software Engineering*, **SE-3**, 4 (July 1977), 266–278.

[8] Ichbiah, J. D., Krieg-Brueckner, B., Wichmann, B. A., Ledgard, H. F., and Heliard, J. Reference manual for the Ada programming language: Proposed standard document. Report AD-A090 709/7, Department of Defense, July 1980.

[9] Knuth, D. E. *The Art of Computer Programming, Volume 1/Fundamental Algorithms*. 2nd Ed., Addison-Wesley, Reading, Massachusetts, 1973.

[10] Knuth, D. E. *The Art of Computer Programming, Volume 3/Sorting and Searching*. Addison-Wesley, Reading, Massachusetts, 1973.

[11] Martin, F. HAL/S – The avionics programming system for shuttle. *Proc. AIAA Conference on Computers in Aerospace*. Los Angeles, CA (Nov. 1977), 308–318.

[12] Osterweil, L. J., and Fosdick, L. D. DAVE – A validation, error detection, and documentation system for Fortran programs. *Software – Practice and Experience*, **6** (1976) 473–486.

[13] Taylor, R. N., and Osterweil, L. J. Anomaly detection in concurrent software by static data flow analysis. *IEEE Trans. Software Engineering*, **SE-6**, 3 (May 1980), 265–278.

[14] Taylor, R. N. Complexity of Analyzing Concurrent Programs. Department of Computer Science Technical Report #DCS-9-IR, University of Victoria (May 1981).